WORD
BIBLICAL
COMMENTARY

WORD
BIBLICAL
COMMENTARY

VOLUME 16

Ezra, Nehemiah

H.G.M. WILLIAMSON

WORD BOOKS, PUBLISHER • WACO, TEXAS

Word Biblical Commentary
EZRA-NEHEMIAH
Copyright © 1985 by Word, Incorporated

Library of Congress Cataloging in Publication Data
Main entry under title:

Word biblical commentary.

   Includes bibliographies.
   1. Bible—Commentaries—Collected works.
BS491.2.W67   220.7'7   81–71768
ISBN 0–8499–0215–0 (vol. 16)   AACR2

Printed in the United States of America

The map reproduced on p. 203 is used with permission of Macmillan Publishing Company
and George Allen & Unwin Publishers, Ltd., from *Macmillan Bible Atlas*, revised edition, by Yo-
hanan Aharoni and Michael Avi-Yonah. Copyright © 1964, 1966, 1968, 1977 by Carta Ltd.
(Map #171: "The Land of Judah in the Days of the Return," p. 109.)

Scripture quotations in the body of the commentary marked RSV are from the Revised Standard
Version of the Bible, copyright 1946 (renewed 1973), 1956, and © 1971 by the Division of
Christian Education of the National Council of Churches of Christ in the USA and are used
by permission. Those marked NIV are from the New International Version of the Bible, copyright
© 1973 by New York Bible Society International. The author's own translation of the text
appears in italic type under the heading "Translation."

67898 FG 98765432

To
J. A. Emerton

Contents

Author's Preface

After having spent a number of years studying the books of Chronicles, I was naturally delighted when an invitation from the editors of the *Word Biblical Commentary* gave me the opportunity to give more attention than had previously been possible to the books of Ezra and Nehemiah. Although I have been confirmed in my opinion that they are separate from Chronicles, they are nevertheless the products of the same community, so that a detailed knowledge of both is essential for the student of the post-exilic period of biblical history and thought.

In spite of having devoted to this commentary all the time available to me for research and writing during the past three and a half years (including spells of sabbatical leave during the Michaelmas terms of 1980 and 1983), I am conscious that there are still many areas which require further work. It is to be hoped that readers will find that fresh ground has been broken in various directions, not least concerning the literary history and composition of these books. Those who, like the author, believe that such matters are of special interest and importance will find that careful attention has been paid to them in the sections on *Form/Structure/Setting*.

While I have made every effort to take full account of the secondary literature on these books, it is inevitable these days that some contributions will have been overlooked, and for this I must apologize. In particular, I am aware of two or three German monographs from the earlier part of this century which I have been unable to consult. Furthermore, it has not been possible to include references to work appearing after the end of 1983. Mention here must be made, however, of D. J. A. Clines, *Ezra, Nehemiah, Esther* (NCBC; Grand Rapids: Eerdmans/London: Marshall, Morgan & Scott, 1984; by courtesy of Mr. Clines, however, I was able to make use of his typescript on Ezra) and the first volume of *The Cambridge History of Judaism*, edited by W. D. Davies and L. Finkelstein (Cambridge: Cambridge University Press, 1984). The latter covers the same historical period as the present commentary, and will naturally be indispensable for all future research.

I am indebted to many friends and colleagues for help and support in numerous ways. In particular, I should like to thank Professor J. A. Emerton and Mr. J. G. Snaith for twice shouldering additional teaching responsibilities while I was on leave. I am grateful to the Carta Publishing House for their permission to use map no. 171 from the *Macmillan Bible Atlas* (p. 109). Not least, my thanks are again due to Mrs. Judith Hackett for her marvelously quick and efficient preparation of the final typescript.

It gives me great pleasure to dedicate this book to my former teacher and present colleague, Professor J. A. Emerton. His support and encouragement over more than ten years have meant more than words can express. I cannot pretend that he will agree with all the positions which I have adopted in the commentary. I hope, however, that he may find within it that faithfulness to the evidence of the text, fair and courteous attention to the views of others and clarity of expression which he has always taught and exemplified.

Cambridge   H. G. M. WILLIAMSON
March 1984

Editorial Preface

The launching of the *Word Biblical Commentary* brings to fulfillment an enterprise of several years' planning. The publishers and the members of the editorial board met in 1977 to explore the possibility of a new commentary on the books of the Bible that would incorporate several distinctive features. Prospective readers of these volumes are entitled to know what such features were intended to be; whether the aims of the commentary have been fully achieved time alone will tell.

First, we have tried to cast a wide net to include as contributors a number of scholars from around the world who not only share our aims, but are in the main engaged in the ministry of teaching in university, college and seminary. They represent a rich diversity of denominational allegiance. The broad stance of our contributors can rightly be called evangelical, and this term is to be understood in its positive, historic sense of a commitment to scripture as divine revelation, and to the truth and power of the Christian gospel.

Then, the commentaries in our series are all commissioned and written for the purpose of inclusion in the *Word Biblical Commentary*. Unlike several of our distinguished counterparts in the field of commentary writing, there are no translated works, originally written in a non-English language. Also, our commentators were asked to prepare their own rendering of the original biblical text and to use those languages as the basis of their own comments and exegesis. What may be claimed as distinctive with this series is that it is based on the biblical languages, yet it seeks to make the technical and scholarly approach to a theological understanding of scripture understandable by—and useful to—the fledgling student, the working minister as well as to colleagues in the guild of professional scholars and teachers.

Finally, a word must be said about the format of the series. The layout in clearly defined sections has been consciously devised to assist readers at different levels. Those wishing to learn about the textual witnesses on which the translation is offered are invited to consult the section headed "Notes." If the readers' concern is with the state of modern scholarship on any given portion of scripture, then they should turn to the sections on "Bibliography" and "Form/Structure/Setting." For a clear exposition of the passage's meaning and its relevance to the ongoing biblical revelation, the "Comment" and concluding "Explanation" are designed expressly to meet that need. There is therefore something for everyone who may pick up and use these volumes.

If these aims come anywhere near realization, the intention of the editors will have been met, and the labor of our team of contributors rewarded.

General Editors: *David A. Hubbard*
Glenn W. Barker †
Old Testament: *John D. W. Watts*
New Testament: *Ralph P. Martin*

Abbreviations

BOOKS, PERIODICALS, AND SERIALS

AASOR	*Annual of the American Schools of Oriental Research*
AD	Driver, *Aramaic Documents*
AHW	W. von Soden, *Akkadisches Handwörterbuch*
AJBA	*Australian Journal of Biblical Archaeology*
AJSL	*American Journal of Semitic Languages and Literature*
AnBib	Analecta biblica
ANET	*Ancient Near Eastern Texts*, ed. J. B. Pritchard (3rd ed.; Princeton: University Press, 1969)
AnOr	Analecta orientalia
AOAT	Alter Orient und Altes Testament
AOS	American Oriental Series
APEF	*Annual of the Palestine Exploration Fund*
AramP	Cowley, *Aramaic Papyri*
ArOr	*Archiv orientální*
ASTI	*Annual of the Swedish Theological Institute*
ATANT	Abhandlungen zur Theologie des Alten und Neuen Testaments
ATD	Das Alte Testament Deutsch
AusBR	*Australian Biblical Review*
AUSS	*Andrews University Seminary Studies*
BA	*Biblical Archaeologist*
BASOR	*Bulletin of the American Schools of Oriental Research*
BDB	F. Brown, S. R. Driver, and C. A. Briggs, *Hebrew and English Lexicon of the Old Testament* (Oxford: Clarendon Press, 1907)
BeO	*Bibbia e oriente*
BET	Beiträge zur biblischen Exegese und Theologie
BEvT	Beiträge zur evangelischen Theologie
BHS	*Biblia hebraica stuttgartensia*
Bib	*Biblica*
BibS	Biblische Studien
BL	H. Bauer and P. Leander, *Grammatik des Biblisch-Aramäischen* (Halle: Max Niemeyer, 1927)
BMAP	E. G. Kraeling, *The Brooklyn Museum Aramaic Papyri* (New Haven: Yale University Press, 1953)
BMik	*Beth Mikra*
BO	*Bibliotheca orientalis*
BSac	*Bibliotheca sacra*
BTB	*Biblical Theology Bulletin*
BWANT	Beiträge zur Wissenschaft vom Alten und Neuen Testament

BZ	*Biblische Zeitschrift*
BZAW	Beihefte zur *ZAW*
CAD	*The Assyrian Dictionary of the Oriental Institute of the University of Chicago*
CAH	*Cambridge Ancient History*
CAT	Commentaire de l'Ancien Testament
CB	Century Bible
CBQ	*Catholic Biblical Quarterly*
CRAIBL	*Comptes rendus de l'Académie des inscriptions et belles-lettres*
CV	*Communio Viatorum*
DBSup	*Dictionnaire de la Bible, Supplément*
EI	*Eretz-Israel*
EncJud	*Encyclopaedia Judaica* (1971)
EstBib	*Estudios bíblicos*
EvQ	*Evangelical Quarterly*
ExpTim	*Expository Times*
FRLANT	Forschungen zur Religion und Literatur des Alten und Neuen Testaments
GKC	*Gesenius' Hebrew Grammar*, ed. E. Kautzsch, tr. A. E. Cowley (2nd ed.; Oxford: Clarendon Press, 1910)
GTT	*Gereformeerd Theologisch Tijdschrift*
HAT	Handbuch zum Alten Testament
Hist. Eccl.	Eusebius, *Historia Ecclesiastica*
HKAT	Handkommentar zum Alten Testament
HSAT	Die heilige Schrift des Alten Testaments
HSM	Harvard Semitic Monographs
HTR	*Harvard Theological Review*
HUCA	*Hebrew Union College Annual*
IB	*Interpreter's Bible*
ICC	International Critical Commentary
IDB	G. A. Buttrick (ed.), *Interpreter's Dictionary of the Bible*
IDBSup	Supplementary volume to *IDB*
IEJ	*Israel Exploration Journal*
ISBE	G. W. Bromiley (ed.), *The International Standard Bible Encyclopedia* (rev. ed.; Grand Rapids: Eerdmans, 1982)
JAOS	*Journal of the American Oriental Society*
JBL	*Journal of Biblical Literature*
JBLMS	*JBL monograph series*
JNES	*Journal of Near Eastern Studies*
JNSL	*Journal of North-West Semitic Languages*
JPOS	*Journal of the Palestine Oriental Society*
JQR	*Jewish Quarterly Review*
JSJ	*Journal for the Study of Judaism in the Persian, Hellenistic and Roman Period*
JSOR	*Journal of the Society for Oriental Research*
JSOT	*Journal for the Study of the Old Testament*
JSS	*Journal of Semitic Studies*
JTS	*Journal of Theological Studies*

KHAT	Kurzer Hand-Kommentar zum Alten Testament
KS	A. Alt, *Kleine Schriften* (3 vols.; Munich: Beck, 1953–59)
NCB	New Century Bible Commentary
NICOT	New International Commentary on the Old Testament
OBO	Orbis Biblicus et Orientalis
OLZ	*Orientalische Literaturzeitung*
OTS	*Oudtestamentische Studiën*
PEQ	*Palestine Exploration Quarterly*
PJ	*Palästina-Jahrbuch*
PTR	*Princeton Theological Review*
RB	*Revue biblique*
RVV	Religionsgeschichtliche Versuche und Vorarbeiten
SBB	Stuttgarter biblische Monographien
SBLDS	SBL Dissertation Series
SBLSBS	SBL Sources for Biblical Study
SBT	Studies in Biblical Theology
SJLA	Studies in Judaism in Late Antiquity
SNTSMS	Society for New Testament Studies Monograph Series
SSI	J. C. L. Gibson, *Syrian Semitic Inscriptions* (3 vols.; Oxford: Clarendon Press, 1971–82)
ST	*Studia theologica*
SUNT	Studien zur Umwelt des Neuen Testaments
SUNVAO	Skrifter utgitt av Det Norske Videnskaps-Akademi i Oslo
TDOT	G. J. Botterweck and H. Ringgren (ed.), *Theological Dictionary of the Old Testament* (tr. J. T. Willis *et al.*; Grand Rapids: Eerdmans, 1977–)
TGUOS	*Transactions of the Glasgow University Oriental Society*
THAT	*Theologisches Handwörterbuch zum Alten Testament*, ed. E. Jenni and C. Westermann (2 vols.; Zurich/Munich: Chr. Kaiser-Verlag, Theologischer Verlag, 1971–6)
TOTC	Tyndale Old Testament Commentaries
TWAT	G. Botterweck and H. Ringgren (eds.), *Theologisches Wörterbuch zum Alten Testament* (Stuttgart: Kohlhammer, 1970–)
TynB	*Tyndale Bulletin*
TZ	*Theologische Zeitschrift*
UF	*Ugaritische Forschungen*
VT	*Vetus Testamentum*
VTSup	VT Supplements
WMANT	Wissenschaftliche Monographien zum Alten und Neuen Testament
WO	*Die Welt des Orients*
WUNT	Wissenschaftliche Untersuchungen zum Neuen Testament
ZA	*Zeitschrift für Assyriologie*
ZAW	*Zeitschrift für die alttestamentliche Wissenschaft*
ZDPV	*Zeitschrift des deutschen Palästina-Vereins*
ZNW	*Zeitschrift für die neutestamentliche Wissenschaft*

Texts, Versions, and Ancient Works

A	The Alexandrian Codex of the LXX
B	The Vatican Codex of the LXX
B. Bat.	*Baba Batra*
G	Greek
K	Kethibh
L	The Lucianic recension of the LXX
LXX	The Septuagint
MT	Masoretic Text
Q	Qere
Syr. (Pesh.)	The Syriac (Peshiṭta)
Vg	The Vulgate
Vrs	Ancient versions

Modern Translations

AB	Anchor Bible
AV	Authorized Version
JB	Jerusalem Bible
KJV	King James Version
NAB	New American Bible
NEB	New English Bible
NIV	New International Version
RSV	Revised Standard Version
RV	Revised Version
TEV	Today's English Version

The commentary is based on the printed Hebrew text of the *Biblia Hebraica Stuttgartensia* (Stuttgart: Deutsche Bibelstiftung, 1967–77). Chapter and verse enumeration throughout are those of the Hebrew Bible. Where these differ from the standard English versions, references to the latter have been noted in parentheses or brackets following. When not the author's own, the English translations are drawn from a variety of versions, depending on what makes most clear the topic under discussion. As often as not, this will be found to be the Revised Version of 1884, when not otherwise identified. The LXX text cited is that of A. Rahlfs, *Septuaginta* (Stuttgart: Württembergische Bibelanstalt, 1935) and (for 1 Esdras) R. Hanhart, *Esdrae liber I* (Göttingen: Vandenhoeck & Ruprecht, 1976).

Biblical and Apocryphal Books

Old Testament

Gen	Genesis	Deut	Deuteronomy
Exod	Exodus	Josh	Joshua
Lev	Leviticus	Judg	Judges
Num	Numbers	Ruth	Ruth

1 Sam	1 Samuel	Jer	Jeremiah
2 Sam	2 Samuel	Lam	Lamentations
1 Kgs	1 Kings	Ezek	Ezekiel
2 Kgs	2 Kings	Dan	Daniel
1 Chr	1 Chronicles	Hos	Hosea
2 Chr	2 Chronicles	Joel	Joel
Ezra	Ezra	Amos	Amos
Neh	Nehemiah	Obad	Obadiah
Esth	Esther	Jonah	Jonah
Job	Job	Mic	Micah
Ps(s)	Psalm(s)	Nah	Nahum
Prov	Proverbs	Hab	Habakkuk
Eccl	Ecclesiastes	Zeph	Zephaniah
Cant	Song of Solomon	Hag	Haggai
Isa	Isaiah	Zech	Zechariah

New Testament

Matt	Matthew	1 Tim	1 Timothy
Mark	Mark	2 Tim	2 Timothy
Luke	Luke	Titus	Titus
John	John	Phlm	Philemon
Acts	Acts	Heb	Hebrews
Rom	Romans	Jas	James
1 Cor	1 Corinthians	1 Pet	1 Peter
2 Cor	2 Corinthians	2 Pet	2 Peter
Gal	Galatians	1 John	1 John
Eph	Ephesians	2 John	2 John
Phil	Philippians	3 John	3 John
Col	Colossians	Jude	Jude
1 Thess	1 Thessalonians	Rev	Revelation
2 Thess	2 Thessalonians		

Apocrypha

Add Esth	Additions to Esther	2 Macc	2 Maccabees
Bar	Baruch	3 Macc	3 Maccabees
Bel	Bel and the Dragon	4 Macc	4 Maccabees
1 Esdr	1 Esdras	Pr Azar	Prayer of Azariah
2 Esdr	2 Esdras	Pr Man	Prayer of Manasseh
4 Ezra	4 Ezra	Sir	Sirach
Jdt	Judith	Sus	Susanna
Ep Jer	Epistle of Jeremy	Tob	Tobit
1 Macc	1 Maccabees	Wis	Wisdom of Solomon

OTHER ABBREVIATIONS

abs	absolute	adj	adjective
act	active	Akk.	Akkadian
accus	accusative	Arab.	Arabic

Aram.	Aramaic	inf	infinitive
art	article	Iran.	Iranian
conj	conjunction	juss	jussive
const	construct, construct state	lit.	literally
		mg	margin
corr	corrupt, corruption	MS(S)	manuscript(s)
def	definite	N.F.	neue Folge
den	denominative	niph	niphal verb stem
det	determinate, determinative	NM	Nehemiah Memoir
		nomin	nominative
dir	direct	ns	new series
dittogr	dittograph, dittography	NT	New Testament
		O.A.	Old Aramaic
EM	Ezra Memoir	O.P.	Old Persian
Eng.	English	obj	object, objective
Ev(v)	English verse (verses)	OT	Old Testament
fem	feminine	P	Priestly Source
gen	genitive	pass	passive
gl	gloss	pers	person
Gr.	Greek	pf	perfect
h.l.	*hapax legomenon*	prep	preposition
haplogr	haplography	pres	present
Heb.	Hebrew	ptcp	participle
hiph	hiphil verb stem	sc.	*scilicet* (namely)
homoiotel	homoioteleuton	sg	singular
hoph	hophal verb stem	st	state
impers	impersonal	subj	subject
impf	imperfect	suff	suffix
impv	imperative	v(v)	verse(s)
indic	indicative	*	the original hand in a MS or word cited
indir	indirect		

Main Bibliography

Commentaries (referred to in the text by authors' names alone)

Ackroyd, P. R. *I & II Chronicles, Ezra, Nehemiah.* Torch Bible. London: SCM Press, 1973. **Batten, L. W.** *A Critical and Exegetical Commentary on the Books of Ezra and Nehemiah.* ICC. Edinburgh: T. & T. Clark, 1913. **Bertheau, E.** *Die Bücher Esra, Nehemia und Ester.* Kurzgefasster exegetisches Handbuch zum Alten Testament. Leipzig: Hirzel, 1862. **Bertholet, A.** *Die Bücher Esra und Nehemia.* KHAT. Tübingen: Mohr, 1902. **Bewer, J. A.** *Der Text des Buches Ezra.* Göttingen: Vandenhoeck & Ruprecht, 1922. **Bowman, R. A.** "Introduction and Exegesis to the Book of Ezra and the Book of Nehemiah." *IB* III, 551–819. **Brockington, L. H.** *Ezra, Nehemiah and Esther.* NCB. London: Nelson, 1969. **Browne, L. E.** "Ezra and Nehemiah." *Peake's Commentary of the Bible,* ed. M. Black and H. H. Rowley. London: Nelson, 1962, 370–80. **Clines, D. J. A.** *Ezra, Nehemiah and Esther.* NCB. Grand Rapids: Wm. B. Eerdmans, 1984. **Coggins, R. J.** *The Books of Ezra and Nehemiah.* The Cambridge Bible Commentary. Cambridge: Cambridge University Press, 1976. **Fensham, F. C.** *The Books of Ezra and Nehemiah.* NICOT. Grand Rapids: Eerdmans, 1982. **Galling, K.** *Die Bücher der Chronik, Esra, Nehemia.* ATD. Göttingen: Vandenhoeck & Ruprecht, 1954. **Gelin, A.** *Le livre de Esdras et Néhémie.* La Sainte Bible. Paris: Les Éditions du Cerf, 1953. **Gotthard, H.** *Der Text des Buches Nehemia.* 2nd ed. Wiesbaden: Otto Harrassowitz, 1958. **Hölscher, G.** "Die Bücher Esra und Nehemia." *Die heilige Schrift des Alten Testaments,* ed. E. Kautzsch and A. Bertholet. 4th ed. Tübingen: Mohr, 1923. **Keil, C. F.** *The Books of Ezra, Nehemiah, and Esther.* Tr. S. Taylor. Edinburgh: T. & T. Clark, 1873. **Kidner, F. D.** *Ezra and Nehemiah.* TOTC. Leicester: IVP, 1979. **Michaeli, F.** *Les livres des Chroniques, d'Esdras et de Néhémie.* CAT 16. Neuchâtel: Delachaux & Niestlé, 1967. **Myers, J. M.** *Ezra. Nehemiah.* AB. Garden City: Doubleday, 1965. **Noordtzij, A.** *Ezra-Nehemia.* Kampen: Kok, 1951. **North, R.** "The Chronicler: 1–2 Chronicles, Ezra, Nehemiah." *The Jerome Biblical Commentary,* ed. R. E. Browne et al. London, Dublin, Melbourne: Chapman, 1968, 402–38. **Rudolph, W.** *Esra und Nehemia.* HAT 20. Tübingen: Mohr, 1949. **Ryle, H. E.** *The Books of Ezra and Nehemiah.* The Cambridge Bible for Schools and Colleges. Cambridge: Cambridge University Press, 1897. **Schneider, H.** *Die Bücher Esra und Nehemia.* HSAT IV/2. Bonn: Peter Hanstein, 1959. **Siegfried, D. C.** *Esra, Nehemia und Esther.* HKAT. Göttingen: Vandenhoeck & Ruprecht, 1901. **Witton Davies, T.** *Ezra, Nehemiah and Esther.* CB. London: Caxton, 1909.

General (referred to in the text by short titles)

Ackroyd, P. R. *The Age of the Chronicler.* Auckland: Colloquium, 1970. ———. "God and People in the Chronicler's Presentation of Ezra." *La Notion biblique de Dieu,* ed. J. Coppens. Leuven: University Press, 1976, 145–62. **Ahlemann, F.** "Zur Esra-Quelle." *ZAW* 59 (1942–43) 77–98. **Bayer, E.** *Das dritte Buch Esdras.* BibS. Freiburg im Breisgau: Herdersche Verlagshandlung, 1911. **Boyce, M.** *A History of Zoroastrianism,* vol. 2. Leiden: E. J. Brill, 1982. **Braun, R. L.** "Chronicles, Ezra, and Nehemiah: Theology and Literary History." VTSup 30 (1979) 52–64. **Bright, J.** *A History of Israel.* 3rd ed. London: SCM Press, 1981. **Cazelles, H.** "La Mission d'Esdras." *VT* 4 (1954) 113–40. **Childs, B. S.** *Introduction to the Old Testament as Scripture.* London: SCM Press, 1979. **Cook, J. M.** *The Persian Empire.* London, Melbourne and Toronto: Dent, 1983. **Cowley, A.** *Aramaic Papyri of the Fifth Century B.C.* Oxford: Clarendon Press, 1923. **Cross, F. M.**

"A Reconstruction of the Judean Restoration." *JBL* 94 (1975) 4–18. **Driver, G. R.** *Aramaic Documents of the Fifth Century B.C.* Oxford: Clarendon Press, 1957. **Driver, S. R.** *A Treatise on the Use of the Tenses in Hebrew.* 3rd ed. Oxford: Clarendon Press, 1892. **Ehrlich, A. B.** *Randglossen zur hebräischen Bibel,* VII. Leipzig: J. C. Hinrichs'sche Buchhandlung, 1914. **Ellenbogen, M.** *Foreign Words in the Old Testament.* London: Luzac, 1962. **Ellison, H. L.** *From Babylon to Bethlehem.* Exeter: Paternoster, 1976. ———. "The Importance of Ezra." *EvQ* 53 (1981) 48–53. **Emerton, J. A.** "Did Ezra go to Jerusalem in 428 B.C.?" *JTS* ns 17 (1966) 1–19. **Fischer, J.** *Die chronologische Fragen in den Büchern Esra-Nehemia.* BibS. Freiburg im Breisgau: Herdersche Verlagshandlung, 1903. **Frye, R. N.** *The Heritage of Persia.* London: Weidenfeld and Nicolson, 1962. **Galling, K.** *Studien zur Geschichte Israels im persischen Zeitalter.* Tübingen: Mohr, 1964. **Gunneweg, A. H. J.** "Zur Interpretation der Bücher Esra-Nehemia." VTSup 32 (1981) 146–61. ———. "Die aramäische und die hebräische Erzählung über die nachexilische Restauration—ein Vergleich." *ZAW* 94 (1982) 299–302. **Hensley, L. V.** *The Official Persian Documents in the Book of Ezra.* University of Liverpool: unpublished dissertation, 1977. **Houtman, C.** "Ezra and the Law." *OTS* 21 (1981) 91–115. **In der Smitten, W. Th.** *Esra: Quellen, Überlieferung und Geschichte.* Studia Semitica Neerlandica 15. Assen: Van Gorcum, 1973. ———. "Die Gründe für die Aufnahme der Nehemiaschrift in das chronistische Geschichtswerk." *BZ* N.F. 16 (1972) 207–21. **Japhet, S.** "The Supposed Common Authorship of Chronicles and Ezra-Nehemiah Investigated Anew." *VT* 18 (1968) 330–71. ———. "Sheshbazzar and Zerubbabel." *ZAW* 94 (1982) 66–98 and 95 (1983) 218–29. **Joüon, P.** *Grammaire de l'Hébreu Biblique.* Rome: Pontifical Biblical Institute, 1923. ———. "Notes philologiques sur le texte hébreu d'Esdras et de Néhémie." *Biblica* 12 (1931) 85–89. **Kapelrud, A. S.** *The Question of Authorship in the Ezra-Narrative: a Lexical Investigation.* SUNVAO. Oslo: Dywbad, 1944. **Kaufmann, Y.** *History of the Religion of Israel. Volume IV: From the Babylonian Captivity to the End of Prophecy.* Tr. C. W. Efroymson. New York: KTAV, 1977. **Kellermann, U.** *Nehemia: Quellen, Überlieferung und Geschichte.* BZAW 102. Berlin: Töpelmann, 1967. ———. "Erwägungen zum Problem der Esradatierung." *ZAW* 80 (1968) 55–87. ———. "Erwägungen zum Esragesetz." *ZAW* 80 (1968) 373–85. **Kent, R. G.** *Old Persian: Grammar; Texts; Lexicon.* 2nd ed. AOS 33. New Haven: American Oriental Society, 1953. **Klein, R. W.** "Ezra and Nehemiah in Recent Studies." In *The Mighty Acts of God: In Memoriam G. Ernest Wright,* ed. F. M. Cross, W. E. Lemke and P. D. Miller. Garden City: Doubleday, 1976, 361–76. **Koch, K.** "Ezra and the Origins of Judaism." *JSS* 19 (1974) 173–97. **König, E.** *Historisch-kritisches Lehrgebäude der Hebräischen Sprache: zweite Hälfte, 3. Theil: Syntax.* Leipzig: J. C. Hinrichs'sche Buchhandlung, 1897. **Kutscher, E. Y.** *Hebrew and Aramaic Studies.* Jerusalem: Magnes Press, 1977. **Lefèvre, A.** "Néhémie et Esdras." *DBSup* 6, 393–424. **Mendels, D.** "Hecataeus of Abdera and a Jewish 'patrios politeia' of the Persian Period (Diodorus Siculus XL, 3)." *ZAW* 95 (1983) 96–110. **Meyer, E.** *Die Entstehung des Judenthums.* Halle: Max Niemeyer, 1896. **Mosis, R.** *Untersuchungen zur Theologie des chronistischen Geschichtswerkes.* Freiburger theologische Studien 92. Freiburg: Herder, 1973. **Mowinckel, S.** "Die vorderasiatischen Königs- und Fürsteninschriften." *Eucharisterion. H. Gunkel zum 60. Geburtstage.* FRLANT 36. Göttingen: Vandenhoeck & Ruprecht, 1923, 278–322. ———. "'Ich' und 'Er' in der Ezrageschichte." In *Verbannung und Heimkehr: Beiträge zur Geschichte und Theologie Israels im 6. und 5. Jahrhundert v. Chr.,* ed. A. Kuschke. Tübingen, Mohr, 1961, 211–33. ———. *Studien zu dem Buche Ezra-Nehemia I: Die nachchronistische Redaktion des Buches. Die Listen.* SUNVAO. Oslo: Universitetsforlaget, 1964. ———. *Studien zu dem Buche Ezra-Nehemia II: Die Nehemia-Denkschrift.* SUNVAO. Oslo: Universitetsforlaget, 1964. ———. *Studien zu dem Buche Ezra-Nehemia III: Die Ezrageschichte und das Gesetz Moses.* SUNVAO. Oslo: Universitetsforlaget, 1965. **Nikel, J.** *Die Wiederherstellung des jüdischen Gemeinwesens nach dem babylonischen Exil.* BibS V/2 and 3. Freiburg im Breisgau: Herder, 1900. **North, R.** "Civil Authority in Ezra." In *Studi in Onore di Edoardo Volterra,* vol. 6. Milan: Giuffré,

1971, 377–404. **Noth, M.** *Überlieferungsgeschichtliche Studien.* Halle: Max Niemeyer, 1943. **Olmstead, A. T.** *History of the Persian Empire.* Chicago: University Press, 1948. **Pavlovský, V.** "Die Chronologie der Tätigkeit Esdras. Versuch einer neuen Lösung." *Bib* 38 (1957) 275–305 and 428–56. **Plöger, O.** "Reden und Gebete im deuteronomistischen und chronistischen Geschichtswerk." In *Festschrift für Günther Dehn,* ed. W. Schneemelcher. Neukirchen: Kreis Moers, 1957, 35–49. **Pohlmann, K.-F.** *Studien zum dritten Esra. Ein Beitrag zur Frage nach dem ursprünglichen Schluss des chronistischen Geschichtswerkes.* FRLANT 104. Göttingen: Vandenhoeck & Ruprecht, 1970. **Polzin, R.** *Late Biblical Hebrew. Toward an Historical Typology of Biblical Hebrew Prose.* HSM 12. Missoula: Scholars Press, 1976. **Porten, B.** *Archives from Elephantine. The Life of an Ancient Jewish Military Colony.* Berkeley and Los Angeles: University of California Press, 1968. ———. "The Documents in the Book of Ezra and the Mission of Ezra" (Hebrew). *Shnaton* 3 (1978–79) 174–96. **von Rad, G.** *Das Geschichtsbild des chronistischen Werkes.* BWANT 54. Stuttgart: W. Kohlhammer, 1930. ———. "Die Nehemia-Denkschrift." *ZAW* 76 (1964) 176–87. **Rosenthal, F.** *A Grammar of Biblical Aramaic.* Porta Linguarum Orientalium ns 5. Wiesbaden: Harrassowitz, 1961. **Rowley, H. H.** "Nehemiah's Mission and Its Background." In *Men of God: Studies in Old Testament History and Prophecy.* London: Nelson, 1963, 211–45. ———. "Sanballat and the Samaritan Temple." In *Men of God,* 246–76. ———. "The Chronological Order of Ezra and Nehemiah." In *The Servant of the Lord and Other Essays on the Old Testament.* 2nd ed. Oxford: Blackwell, 1965, 137–68. **Schaeder, H. H.** *Esra der Schreiber.* Tübingen: Mohr, 1930. **Scott, W. M. F.** "Nehemiah—Ezra?" *ExpTim* 58 (1946–47) 263–67. **Smend, R.** *Die Listen der Bücher Esra und Nehemia.* Basel: Schultze, 1881. **Smith, M.** *Palestinian Parties and Politics that Shaped the Old Testament.* New York and London: Columbia University Press, 1971. **Snaith, N. H.** "The Date of Ezra's Arrival in Jerusalem." *ZAW* 63 (1951) 53–66. **von Soden, W.** *Akkadisches Handwörterbuch.* Wiesbaden: Harrassowitz, 1965–81. **Stern, E.** *The Material Culture of the Land of the Bible in the Persian Period 538–332 B.C.,* tr. E. Cindorf. Warminster: Aris & Phillips, and Jerusalem: Israel Exploration Society, 1982. **Talmon, S.** "Ezra and Nehemiah." *IDBSup* 317–28. **Theis, J.** *Geschichtliche und literarkritische Fragen in Esra 1–6.* Münster: Verlag der Aschendorffschen Buchhandlung, 1896. **Torrey, C. C.** *The Composition and Historical Value of Ezra-Nehemiah.* BZAW 2. Giessen: J. Ricker'sche Buchhandlung, 1896. ———. *Ezra Studies.* Chicago: University Press, 1910. **Tuland, C. G.** "Ezra-Nehemiah or Nehemiah-Ezra?" *AUSS* 12 (1974) 47–62. **de Vaux, R.** *Ancient Israel. Its Life and Institutions,* tr. J. McHugh. London: Darton, Longman & Todd, 1961. ———. "The Decrees of Cyrus and Darius on the Rebuilding of the Temple." *The Bible and the Ancient Near East,* tr. D. McHugh. London: Darton, Longman & Todd, 1972, 63–96. ———. "Israel (Histoire de)." *DBSup* 4, 729–77. **Vogt, E.** *Lexicon Linguae Aramaicae Veteris Testamenti.* Rome: Pontifical Biblical Institute, 1971. **Vogt, H. C. M.** *Studie zur nachexilische Gemeinde in Esra-Nehemia.* Werl: Dietrich Coelde-Verlag, 1966. **Welch, A. C.** *Post-exilic Judaism.* Edinburgh and London: Blackwood, 1935. **Widengren, G.** "The Persian Period." In *Israelite and Judaean History,* ed. J. H. Hayes and J. M. Miller. London: SCM Press, 1977, 489–538. **Williamson, H. G. M.** *Israel in the Books of Chronicles.* Cambridge: University Press, 1977. ———. *1 and 2 Chronicles.* NCB. Grand Rapids: Eerdmans and London: Marshall, Morgan & Scott, 1982. ———. "The Origins of the Twenty-Four Priestly Courses." VTSup 30 (1979) 251–68. ———. "The Composition of Ezra i-vi." *JTS* ns 34 (1983) 1–30. ———. "Nehemiah's Wall Revisited." *PEQ* 116 (1984) 81–88. **Wright, J. S.** *The Date of Ezra's Coming to Jerusalem,* 2nd ed. London: Tyndale Press, 1958. ———. *The Building of the Second Temple.* London: Tyndale Press, 1958. **Yamauchi, E. M.** "The Reverse Order of Ezra/Nehemiah Reconsidered." *Themelios* 5 (1980) 7–13. ———. "The Archaeological Background of Ezra." *BSac* 137 (1980) 195–211. ———. "The Archaeological Background of Nehemiah." *BSac* 137 (1980) 291–309.

Introduction

UNITY AND EXTENT

In approaching any piece of literature, it is important to know whether the work being studied is a complete text, an extract or a collection. Naturally, allowances will have to be made in interpretation according to the answers given to this preliminary question.

In the case of the books of Ezra and Nehemiah, these issues are not easily resolved. Many scholars believe that they are only the conclusion of an originally much longer work which started with the books of Chronicles. Others maintain, on the basis of the apocryphal Greek book of 1 Esdras, that the work of the Chronicler originally concluded with Ezra 1–10 and Neh 8; the narrative concerning Nehemiah is thought to have been added only later.

While the evidence on which these opinions are based will naturally occupy our attention later, it is worth observing at the outset that none of them has tradition on its side. Jewish tradition is clear in its opinion that these two works were originally one, and that they were to be regarded as separate from other books. Ryle helpfully collects six strands of evidence that favor the unity of the two books in antiquity: (1) in order to make sense of Josephus' enumeration of the biblical books (*Contra Apionem* §40), it must be assumed that he counted Ezra and Nehemiah as one. (2) Melito, Bishop of Sardis, quotes Jewish sources in Palestine which speak of the whole work as "Ezra"; cf. Eusebius *Hist. Eccl.* 4.26.14. (3) The Talmud includes the activities of Nehemiah in the book of Ezra and even asks, "Why, then, was the book not called by his name?" (*Bab. Sanh.* 93b; cf. *B. Bat.* 14b, where only Ezra is listed). (4) The Masoretes clearly regard the books as one because they count Neh 3:22 as the middle verse and add their annotations for the whole only at the end of Nehemiah. (5) The medieval Jewish commentators move directly from Ezra to Nehemiah without interruption; cf. the commentaries of Ibn Ezra and Rashi *ad loc.* in any Rabbinic Bible, e.g. *Biblia Rabbinica* (Jerusalem: Makor, 1972). (6) In the earliest Hebrew manuscripts the books are not divided. To this list we should add that (7) in the earliest manuscripts of the LXX the two books are treated as one.

The separation between Ezra and Nehemiah, first attested by Origen (cf. Eusebius *Hist. Eccl.* 6.25.2, though with acknowledgment that in Hebrew tradition they are reckoned as one) and then by Jerome in the Vulgate (but as two books of Ezra rather than as Ezra and Nehemiah, although in his *Prologus galeatus* he too acknowledges their unity in Hebrew tradition), was probably effected in the Christian Church; it was adopted into Jewish tradition only in the Middle Ages, being attested first in the early printed editions of the Hebrew Bible. While the heading in Neh 1:1 makes this understandable, it is clear that it is a completely secondary division. The books themselves show that the work of the reformers is meant to be regarded as a unity and not in isolation; cf. Neh 12:26 and 47 and the interweaving of the narratives about Ezra and Nehemiah.

If this evidence for the unity of Ezra and Nehemiah is strong, the case for taking them as an integral part of the work of the Chronicler receives no external support in the textual history of the Hebrew Bible. In the ordering of the books of the third division of the canon, the Writings, they are generally listed toward the end but before Chronicles; in some traditions, Chronicles stands at the head of the Writings, with Ezra and Nehemiah last. We do not, however, find Chronicles placed immediately before Ezra and Nehemiah, as one might expect if they were to be regarded as one.

In the tradition of the Greek Bible, the LXX, the books were arranged according to a different principle, and this has affected the order adopted for most English translations. Here, the historical books are grouped together, and a chronological order is followed. Thus Ruth is placed between Judges and Samuel, Chronicles follows Kings, and then come Ezra-Nehemiah and Esther. Again, however, Ezra-Nehemiah is always treated separately, and this is underlined by the fact that frequently 1 Esdr stands between Chronicles and Ezra-Nehemiah; cf. H. B. Swete, *An Introduction to the Old Testament in Greek* (Cambridge: University Press, 1902) 201–10.

This external attestation of the treatment of Ezra and Nehemiah in antiquity should not, of course, be accepted uncritically. Nevertheless, I have argued in some detail elsewhere (cf. *Israel*, 5–70; *1 and 2 Chronicles*, 4–11) that in this case it is also fully justified on critical grounds, and with this a number of other scholars agree. Certainly if this position is accepted as a working hypothesis, then, as it is hoped this commentary as a whole will show, Ezra-Nehemiah can be understood without particular reference to Chronicles. Indeed, for some of its most important historical presuppositions, such as the centrality of the Exodus or the history of the northern kingdom of Israel, Ezra-Nehemiah is dependent upon aspects of the Deuteronomic history at points where Chronicles differs from it. Only in one or two parts of Ezra 1–6 can a particular affinity with Chronicles be detected, but this can be explained without recourse to the theory that these chapters, let alone the whole work, were once part of Chronicles; cf. *JTS* ns 34 (1983) 1–30. It may therefore be claimed that the present commentary reinforces the case already made elsewhere for the separate treatment of Ezra-Nehemiah.

There is only one piece of external evidence that has been held to offer support for the contrary view, and that is the Greek work known in English as 1 Esdras (3. Esra in German). This work is largely a Greek translation of 2 Chr 35–36; Ezra; and Neh 8:1–13. It includes some other material not found in the Hebrew Bible (most notably at 1 Esdr 3:1—5:6), and also rearranges the order of Ezra 1–4. Despite this, it has been claimed by some that this book is an important witness to the "original ending" of the work of the Chronicler.

Naturally, this case has been carefully examined in the course of the discussions referred to above, and so need not be dealt with again here. This commentary does, however, add two significant arguments whose force I had not previously appreciated. First, it will be maintained in *Form* at Ezra 2 below that the list of those returning from Babylon is borrowed directly from Neh 7, and that (as Ezra 3:1 shows) Neh 7 and 8 were already joined together. If this is correct, then 1 Esdr, which includes a translation of Ezra 2, must have already known a version of the Hebrew text which included Neh 7; it cannot, therefore, be used as evidence that Neh 8 once followed Ezra 10. Second, it will be argued at Neh 8 that that chapter is far more likely to have stood once between Ezra 8 and 9, not after Ezra 10. Indeed, it is questionable whether the latter option would ever have been entertained were it not for 1 Esdr. Again, if this argument is sound, it follows that 1 Esdr must be a secondary compilation. While we shall not, therefore, use 1 Esdr as an important witness in literary-critical issues, its value for the history of the text itself remains important and will be cited where appropriate in the *Notes*.

We may therefore conclude by affirming that there is good reason to approach Ezra and Nehemiah as two parts of a single work and that this work is to be regarded as complete as it stands.

SOURCES

The aim of this discussion is to summarize the results of the commentary's detailed analysis as regards the sources in Ezra and Nehemiah, and in the next section to indicate the stages by which they were combined into the present book.

EZRA 1–6

Under the prevailing scholarly consensus that Chronicles, Ezra, and Nehemiah were all part of a single work (with or without the NM in its "first edition"), Ezra 1–6 has not received the attention it deserves in scholarly research. This is because it has not been thought to display any distinctive editorial methods. It has been supposed that we could learn more of the Chronicler's methods by studying his synoptic account of the Israelite monarchy than by speculating on this otherwise unparalleled narrative. Of the sources on which he here drew, there has been general agreement that the Aramaic section (4:6—6:22) was one (see most recently Gunneweg, *ZAW* 94 [1982] 299–302), the list in chap. 2 another, and the inventory of temple vessels in 1:9–11 a third. More controversial was the question whether the decree of Cyrus in 1:2–4 was also based on an earlier source, or whether the Chronicler himself composed it on the basis of 6:3–5.

As already noted, the present commentary does not share the view that these books are part of the same work as Chronicles. Working in detail through Ezra 1–6 without this presupposition has led to the formulation of a fresh hypothesis about the composition of these chapters. For a full discussion, the reader is referred to my article in *JTS* ns 34 (1983) 1–30.

This commentary will contend that various sources lay in front of the writer in their original, unedited form; we find no evidence to favor the opinion that parts (such as the Aramaic source) had already been joined together by a narrative framework before they reached his hand. Indeed, there are some hints that he was working directly from the original documents.

The sources isolated are as follows: (1) the decree of Cyrus (1:2–4); (2) the inventory of temple vessels (1:9–11); (3) the list of those returning (chap. 2, a compilation of those who returned during the first twenty years or so of Achaemenid rule); (4) two letters which the editor summarizes at 4:6 and 7. He may have used part of the information contained in these letters in his writing of 4:1–3; (5) a letter in Aramaic from Rehum and others to Artaxerxes (4:8–16) and (6) Artaxerxes' reply (4:17–22); (7) a letter from Tattenai to Darius (5:6–17) and (8) Darius' reply (6:3–12), which included a transcript of a separate decree of Cyrus (vv 3–5). In addition to these sources, the editor will, of course, have been familiar with such relevant biblical material as is found, for instance, in Haggai and Zech 1–8. It is suggested that nearly all the narrative framework that links these sources together was derived by common sense from the information that the documents will themselves have included in their original form. Naturally, they were read in the light of the editor's prevailing ideology and purpose, such as his desire to present the return from exile as a second Exodus.

THE NEHEMIAH MEMOIR

It has long been recognized—and is today universally agreed—that substantial parts of the Book of Nehemiah go back to a first-person account by Nehemiah himself (or someone writing under his immediate direction). Broadly speaking, this material is to be found in Neh 1–7; parts of 12:27–43, and 13:4–31. There is dispute about whether or not the lists in chaps. 3 and 7 (both of which have an independent origin) were included by Nehemiah; whether 11:1–2 is based on his account; about the relationship between chap. 13 and the remainder; and about the degree to which later additions may be detected elsewhere. All these matters are discussed at appropriate points in the Commentary and need not affect our present general assessment. Rather, our concern here must be the purpose and circumstances of Nehemiah's literary activity.

The conventional term "Nehemiah Memoir" (NM) is retained here for convenience. It is, however, obviously inappropriate as a literary classification of this source, as Mowinckel, *Studien II*, 50–92, has patently shown. This conclusion is not affected by the fact that parts may not have been preserved for us (see *Form* on Neh 11).

As to how to classify this source, scholars have advanced various suggestions. Mowinckel himself must receive the credit for broaching the topic in the first place, initially in a Norwegian publication of 1916 and then in a more easily accessible essay in German in the Gunkel *Festschrift*, "Die vorderasiatischen Königs- und Fürsteninschriften" (see also his more recent *Studien II*, 92–104). Since there is no parallel for such a composition within the OT, Mowinckel drew attention to several points of comparison with a number of Ancient Near Eastern royal inscriptions which commemorate the achievements of the king in question.

As a refinement of Mowinckel's thesis, von Rad, *ZAW* 76 (1964) 176–87, compared the NM to some tomb and temple inscriptions from Egypt, available in German translation in E. Otto, *Die biographischen Inschriften der ägyptischen*

Spätzeit (Leiden: Brill, 1954). These inscriptions date roughly from the period of Nehemiah; they recall in first-person narrative the duties of senior officials faithfully performed, often in spheres of public life that closely resemble those in the NM. On occasion, one even finds an equivalent of the "remember" formula so characteristic of the NM. As a result of this comparison, von Rad was able to conclude that, despite some significant points of difference, this group of texts furnished the nearest parallel known to us for the NM.

A third approach takes the distinctive "remember" formula as its starting point, and hence finds the closest parallels to the NM in the common votive or dedicatory inscriptions best known in several Aramaic dialects from later times. This view, too, may be regarded as in some senses an attempt to refine Mowinckel's original hypothesis. It is widely mentioned in introductory textbooks, but has not been worked out as fully as it might be. However, see W. Schottroff, *"Gedenken" im alten Orient und im Alten Testament* (WMANT 15, 2nd ed.; Neukirchen-Vluyn: Neukirchener Verlag, 1967), 218–22 and 392–93. Characteristic of these inscriptions is the prayer that God will "remember" the author "for good" because of some particular act of piety that is commemorated.

Next, we may briefly note a view that has always attracted a number of adherents, namely, the suggestion that Nehemiah needed to write in order to justify himself in some way or another to the Persian king. Working more on the basis of the contents of the text than on formal analogies with other sources, this view suggests that suspicions had been raised, if not accusations leveled, against Nehemiah by some of his opponents. This theory has, then, to explain why the document appears to be addressed to God, not the king, and herein lies one of its principal weaknesses.

Finally, the most recent major study of the NM (Kellermann, *Nehemia*) starts from a position similar to the view just noted, but then compares the NM with the type of psalm often known as the "Prayer of the Accused." The obvious differences between these two bodies of literature are supposedly to be explained by the particular circumstances in which Nehemiah found himself.

Of these five principal views (not to speak of variations and alternatives), none has commended itself sufficiently to enable us to speak even of a consensus. Kellermann, *Nehemia*, 76–84, has raised a number of telling criticisms against the first four proposals, principally that none of them does justice to all the evidence; they each fit one part well while ignoring or contradicting another. Meanwhile, his own suggestion has been even more severely criticized (cf. Emerton, *JTS* ns 23 [1972] 171–85; Schottroff, *"Gedenken,"* 392–93). While there is not space here to discuss these criticisms fully, it should be apparent that a satisfactory solution to the problem has not yet been found; what Emerton, 185, has said of Kellermann could equally well be applied to the others: "Even when his solutions of problems may be rejected, it is not always easy to suggest alternatives." What follows is therefore said in full recognition of the difficulties that confront any new suggestion.

In my opinion, it has been a fundamental mistake to tackle the form-critical issue before first establishing the unity of the material. Certainly, hints of disquiet have been expressed (e.g., Galling, 249; Schneider, 35; Ackroyd,

The Age of the Chronicler, 28–29), but they have never been fully or systematically worked out. Without going into great detail, the following points should not be overlooked.

There is a long and unexplained chronological gap between the account of the wall-building, with related events, and the incidents recounted in chap. 13. This commentary defends the view that Neh 13:6 is historically accurate in saying that Nehemiah was governor of Jerusalem for twelve years, then had a break in Babylon, and later returned to Jerusalem. The NM thus appears to describe approximately one year's activity in considerable detail and then to include several isolated topics from perhaps as many as fifteen years later. This fact can hardly be ignored, while suggestions that nothing of significance happened in the meantime are highly implausible.

Few will disagree that a solution to the problem of the NM will have to account adequately for the "remember" formula. This formula occurs in positive form at 5:19; 13:14, 22, 31; and in negative form (i.e., against Nehemiah's enemies) at 6:14 and 13:29. Perusal of these passages reveals something of which no one seems to have taken account, namely, that not one of them refers to the building of the wall! Indeed, only one—and that a negative use of the formula (6:14)—relates at all to the early period of Nehemiah's work. None of the rest, including 5:19 (cf. 5:14), can have been written until twelve years later, at the earliest. It would be strange, to say the least, that if Nehemiah composed the whole memoir as some kind of votive inscription, however defined, he should not have specifically offered his most outstanding achievement as a major reason for God to remember him.

Concentrating for the moment upon the deeds that Nehemiah asks God to keep in remembrance, we find that they are as follows:

5:19   Nehemiah has desisted from eating "the bread of the governor" throughout his first term of office, because of the people's economic burdens. The earlier part of the chapter showed that much of this resulted from debt slavery.

13:14   Two points are included here, namely, Nehemiah's care for "the house of God," which may refer to the expulsion of Tobiah, and for "its services," which refers to the restoration of tithes necessary to support the cultic personnel.

13:22   Sanctification of the Sabbath day.

13:31   Although no specific deed is mentioned, and while this expression may round off the chapter generally, the foregoing paragraph has treated mixed marriages, the duties of the priests and Levites, the wood-offering, and the first-fruits.

Perusal of this list at once reveals that every item here mentioned can be directly associated with one or another of the clauses of the pledge in Neh 10. Yet the commentary will show that Neh 10 cannot have been part of the NM. It is part of an independent account of how the people collectively undertook certain obligations, probably shortly after the events mentioned in Neh 13.

The three observations just made about the NM seem to me to go beyond the possible bounds of coincidence and to demand some sort of explanation. Though such a solution may appear old-fashioned, a division of the material provides far and away the easiest way out. No difficulty confronts the relegation of 5:14–19; 13:4–14, 15–22, 23–31 to a subsequent phase of composition. These few paragraphs have much in common: each concludes with a positive "remember" formula; each offers a brief description without particular chronological setting; each takes place long after the building of the wall, and each can be linked in some way with chap. 10. On the other hand, the rest of the NM now also takes on a degree of coherence: all is related to the task of building the wall, together with its immediate sequel; nothing need come later than a year after Nehemiah's arrival in Jerusalem, if that. Further, the removal of the "remember" formulae (on 6:14 see immediately below) leaves this narrative much more a description or report than a votive or dedication text.

Only two details might appear to disturb this simple division. The first is that within 5:14–19 there is reference to the continuing work on the wall. This causes no real problem, however. It is beyond question (cf. v 14) that the paragraph reflects on the whole of Nehemiah's term as governor and cannot have been written before its conclusion. 5:16 is therefore out of place according to a strict chronological view in any case. However, if it be allowed that the whole paragraph has been added later (and 5:1–13 provides an obvious setting for Nehemiah to make his point), then to include such a general reference to the work on the wall as well as other aspects of Nehemiah's governorship is understandable enough. In other words, 5:16 could easily have been included as part of a later addition, but 5:14–19 cannot have been included in a document contemporary with the overall context.

More problematic, I concede, is 6:14. It introduces a "remember" formula into what we are postulating is the earlier account. Here there are two suggestions that may be made: (1) Unlike any of the other comparable verses, 6:14 refers to something for which there is no warrant in the preceding narrative, namely "Noadiah, the prophetess, and the rest of the prophets. . . ." Could it be that when Nehemiah was reworking his earlier account he inserted this verse, using his later style, with reference to some more recent events, otherwise unknown to us? (2) At one point in the earlier narrative, Nehemiah seems to be reliving the events in so vivid a fashion that he includes the words of a prayer without introduction; see 3:36–37 (4:4–5). On that occasion it is clear that the passage is to be understood as a prayer that was uttered in the historical context; it is not a comment of the author as he later describes the events. It is thus possible that 6:14, which is also a prayer against the enemy rather than a positive request that Nehemiah's good deeds be remembered, is to be understood in the same way.

Either of these two possibilities would remove the difficulty of 6:14 for the general view we are advocating. Either seems to me easier to accept than the fact that the clear division between the two types of material in the NM is purely accidental.

We are now in a position to offer a speculation concerning the development of the NM that will account for these various points. (1) It may be deduced from 2:6 that Nehemiah's original commission was for a comparatively short time and for the specific task of rebuilding the walls. Certainly a twelve-year term as governor was not envisaged. There is then no good reason to doubt that the substance of the NM was written up as a report on how the commission was fulfilled. It would thus perhaps have been composed a year, or at the most two, after Nehemiah's journey to Jerusalem (cf. the duration of Ezra's commission). This theory accounts for many of the points that Mowinckel made about the style of the NM, and naturally is closest to those theories that see a report as the basis for the NM. It avoids, however, the difficulties these theories encounter, namely, their inability to explain precisely those features that we have excluded as being later additions. (2) Even without these additions, our present text cannot exactly represent the wording of this report. No doubt it would have been written in Aramaic, and the prayers (1:4–11, 3:36–37 [4:4–5] and 6:14) would probably not have been included. However, a positive view of Nehemiah's achievements and defense against any possible criticisms, especially from neighboring provincial leaders, would both be matters of course. (3) Very much later, after the pledge of chap. 10 had been sealed, Nehemiah may have felt that justice was not being done to him within his own community. We shall find that there are alternative accounts of a number of his measures, in which the people act without reference to him. We suggest that he was thus moved to rework his old report, adding to it a number of short paragraphs dealing specifically with those points for which he felt he was not being given due credit. The style of these sections comes closest to that of the texts noted by von Rad and the later votive and dedicatory inscriptions (Schottroff). This would be an appropriate style if our reconstruction of his motivation is correct. It also explains why the parallels so adduced suit only a small part of the material as a whole.

Our conclusion, then, is that the NM developed in two stages, and, in consequence, represents a mixture of literary genres. It is thus not surprising that no comparison with any other single text has ever proved convincing.

THE EZRA MEMOIR

As in the case of the NM, so here the conventional term "Ezra Memoir" (EM) is retained for convenience only, without prejudice to the issue of literary genre.

Material in which Ezra plays a dominant role is to be found in Ezra 7–10 and Neh 8. (Some would further add Neh 9–10.) Assessment of these chapters has called forth the widest possible diversity of scholarly opinion, and that at a much more fundamental level than in the case of the NM. Moreover, the situation is complicated by the fact that it is difficult to speak of a general development of consensus; rather, ever since critical attention was first focused on the issue, it has been possible to find equally prominent representatives of most of the major viewpoints at all stages of the debate.

Almost until the end of the nineteenth century, the EM was generally taken at face value. The first major radical examination came with the publication in 1896 of Torrey's *Composition and Historical Value*. Torrey followed this brief monograph with a number of important essays, collected in 1910 under the title *Ezra Studies*. Largely on the basis of an analysis of style, Torrey concluded that the EM could not be distinguished from the editorial work of "the Chronicler" elsewhere in Ezra-Nehemiah, as well as in Chronicles. He therefore concluded that there was no separate Ezra source. From this, Torrey went on to cast doubts upon the historical existence of Ezra.

This final step went too far for most scholars, and probably resulted in Torrey's literary arguments being given less serious attention than they deserved. Among the few who appreciated the weight of his evidence was Hölscher, whose commentary should be mentioned in particular. Torrey's rearrangement of the order of the chapters (Ezra 7–8; Neh 8; Ezra 9–10; Neh 9–10), by contrast, attracted much more wide-ranging attention and support. However, in 1944, in *The Question of Authorship,* 95, Kapelrud subjected the whole issue to fresh examination and came to a more palatable conclusion, namely that "the Ezra-narrative, as we now have it, comes from Chronicle circles," but that it was based on some antecedent, though irrecoverable, tradition. At the same time, similar conclusions were reached on the slightly different grounds of literary and historical criticism by Noth, *Studien,* 145–48. As a result of these further studies it is possible to find a number of scholars who have been able to discount the possibility of an Ezra source while nevertheless holding on to the historicity of Ezra himself.

In recent years, two scholars have offered something of a refinement of the view just outlined. They are Kellermann, *Nehemia,* 56–69, and in *ZAW* 80 (1968) 55–87; and in In der Smitten, *Esra,* 6–66 and in *BZ* N.F. 16 (1972) 207–21. Both accept the authenticity of most, though not the whole, of the Artaxerxes edict in Ezra 7:12–26; Kellermann also toys with the possibility that Ezra 8:26–27 derives from an earlier source, while In der Smitten accepts the list in 8:1–14 as earlier. Both also believe that the author of the EM knew the NM. They therefore maintain that the EM is a midrash on the Artaxerxes edict, composed by the Chronicler with little, if any, other antecedent source material. Much of the account is thus a "writing up" of the edict with the particular purpose of extolling Ezra at the expense of Nehemiah. Whether or not the introduction of the label *midrash* is a help in this discussion is questionable. To all practical intents and purposes, this view is similar to that of Noth already mentioned.

Spanning the entire period under review are the contributions of Mowinckel. His early work (1916) did not achieve great influence because it was written in Norwegian. However, his contribution to the Rudolph *Festschrift,* " 'Ich' und 'Er' " (1961), followed in 1965 by his detailed *Studien III,* makes further neglect inexcusable. Mowinckel's treatment is far more conservative than the view just noted, but, paradoxically, it is far from traditional. On the one hand, Mowinckel detects in these chapters an editorial hand "touching up" an earlier account of Ezra's activity. Unlike Kellermann and In der Smitten, who find several redactional layers, some of which are later than the Chronicler, Mowinckel identifies this editor with the Chronicler. Therefore, he argues, the Chronicler must have been working with an earlier Ezra source. On the other hand, Mowinckel does not regard this source as composed by Ezra; he is unable to find any reason why Ezra should have written it. Rather, it is the work of someone who had been a young man during Ezra's activity and who, years later (370 B.C.), wrote up his idealized version of the events, not as an historical account, but as an edifying narrative (*"erbauliche Geschichtser-zählung"*). Though based on historical recollection, its main purpose was to challenge and inspire a later generation. One must, therefore, make allowances for all manner of "legendary" embellishments. To the objection that this was not an obvious understanding of a first-person narrative, Mowinckel had no difficulty in adducing a considerable number of texts, both biblical and extrabiblical, that used precisely this device, and for comparable purposes. A broadly similar understanding of the EM was advanced by Ahlemann in *ZAW* 59 (1942–43) 77–98.

Finally, we should not forget that there have never been lacking those who have taken a more traditional approach to the EM, although since Torrey's time only the most extremely conservative (e.g., in recent years Kidner and Fensham) have rejected the view that Neh 8 (and perhaps 9–10) originally stood with Ezra 7–10. Schaeder, *Esra der Schreiber;* Rudolph; and Koch, *JSS* 19 (1974) 173–97, may be cited as representative examples, though many others seem to adopt a comparable stance, without, however, offering full justification for their assertions. According to this view, the EM was originally composed in the first person by Ezra himself in order to give an account of his work to his Persian overlord, who had commissioned him. It was later reworked by the Chronicler who, among other things, cast parts of it into the third person. Opinions are divided over whether he also rearranged the order of the material or whether that is the result of accidental textual transposition.

Brief as this survey of opinions has been, it is hoped that enough has been said to make it clear that these problems cannot be resolved by a few general remarks. Nothing less than a thorough analysis of the text in all its dimensions, together with other evidence, will suffice, and even then certainty or full agreement will remain unattainable.

Throughout the relevant chapters of the commentary, we have borne in mind the issues raised and have discussed them as far as is practical. We can here only summarize the conclusions that emerge and refer the reader to the commentary for their justification.

First, however, we should note that the argument from style, which, as we have seen, was Torrey's starting point, cannot today be held to provide decisive evidence either way. A preliminary response to Torrey was provided by Rudolph, 163–65; Mowinckel too, *Studien III*, 74, accepts that progress cannot be made from this angle. More recent studies, working from different points of view, have reinforced this conclusion; cf. Williamson, *Israel*, 37–59; Polzin, *Late Biblical Hebrew;* M. A. Throntveit, "Linguistic Analysis and the Question of Authorship in Chronicles, Ezra and Nehemiah," *VT* 32 (1982) 201–16. Without going into detail again here, it is now clear that most of the stylistic traits that Torrey identified are common to the Hebrew of the late Biblical period, while other features can be shown to favor a separation between the style in Ezra and in Chronicles. At the same time, the text is too short to enable us to say whether the style of the EM differs significantly from other editorial parts of Ezra-Nehemiah in such a way as to demonstrate its separate literary origin. In addition, we have in any case to reckon with more editorial intervention here than in the NM (see below).

It is therefore best to leave aside the question of style at this stage of our knowledge. With that conclusion, we may note in passing, we also lay to rest the opinion of W. F. Albright, "The Date and Personality of the Chronicler," *JBL* 40 (1921) 104–24 (and cf. Myers, lxviii–lxx), that Ezra was himself the Chronicler.

In the commentary, several indications are noted which suggest that an antecedent source underlies the Ezra material. Among these we here mention the following in particular: (1) In Ezra 7:1–10 there are points of literary tension with the later narrative, which, we have argued, are best explained by the theory that an editor is here rewriting an earlier, first-person account. (2) While there is often a close conformity between the terms of the Artaxerxes edict (7:12–26) and the subsequent narrative, there are also some differences, most markedly the lack of any reference to the appointment of "magistrates and judges" (v 25). These discrepancies are difficult to explain if the narrative is deliberately composed as a piece of fiction on the basis of the edict. It is much easier to suppose that there is a measure of historical constraint at work here, and this is most naturally understood as pointing to a contemporary or nearly contemporary account. (3) It is argued that Neh 8 originally stood between Ezra 8 and 9, and that its move was a deliberate editorial act. This is strong evidence that the editor of these books was working with antecedent source material at this point. (4) There are one or two suggestions that material known to the editor may have been omitted (e.g., at 10:16, on which see also *Form* on Neh 9), or rearranged (e.g., the list in 10:18–44a). This too points to literary activity on an antecedent source. (5) The switches from first to third person are discussed in full in *Form* on chap. 10. It is there maintained that editorial activity on an original first-person narrative remains the most plausible explanation. (6) Certain small points of detail (e.g., at Ezra 8:15, 17, 26–27; 10:9,13) have always been recognized as an embarrassment to the view that these chapters have been composed *de novo* by a much later writer.

If, then, we conclude that a first-person account underlies the narrative in Ezra 7–8, Neh 8, and Ezra 9–10, who was its author, and what was his purpose in writing? In answer to the first question, we must clearly think of Ezra himself (or somebody working at his behest) unless strong arguments can be brought to the contrary. Examination quickly shows that those who deny this conclusion do so most often because they have already decided that there is no such document as the EM. This is clearly unacceptable in the light of the preceding discussion. Only Mowinckel (followed briefly by Ahlemann) has argued seriously that there was an Ezra source but that the EM was not written by Ezra. He in turn fails, however, to allow for the considerable editorial activity on the text that has already been noted above; yet it is just here that the features of idealization that lead Mowinckel to his conclusion are most likely to have entered the text.

If, then, Ezra was responsible for the original narrative, it can hardly be doubted that his aim in writing was to show as nearly as possible how his activity conformed to his commission. And here it may be significant that he records the events of exactly one year. With sensitive issues, like the delivery of treasures for the temple, his account is painstakingly exact. The main terms of his commission—inquiry on the basis of the law—are shown to have been fulfilled (see *Comment* for detail), albeit on occasions in slightly unexpected ways. This looks much more like the writing of someone trying to justify his record than it does like the work of a later pious and idealizing biographer. Finally, there are some gaps in the account, as already noted, that have given rise to historical speculation. Even without this, it would be possible to uphold our view, for it could be that after one year's frustratingly slow progress Ezra had simply not advanced far enough to make these appointments. Yet, as the parallel with the NM suggests, it was at this point that, as a matter of regular protocol, he was obliged to submit his report. Though we cannot now reconstruct his account, there is nothing in what we know of it to enable us to say on grounds stronger than subjective guesswork that it is inappropriate; even the prayer in Ezra 9:6–15 includes sentiments that he would not have been ashamed to have a Persian superior read (cf. v 9).

There is, of course, a speculative element in this view. It may be suggested, however, that this is true of all the views that were outlined at the start of this section. The case here advanced is close to that of the scholars noted above who take a more traditional approach; the speculations derive straight from the evidence of the text rather than being an opening hypothesis in the light of which the text must then be read. Only a theory which shares this method but produces a more satisfactory explanation for the EM should be preferred.

OTHER

In the later chapters of Nehemiah, there is a collection of different types of material whose origins have been variously explained. Several recent studies have suggested that parts of this material may represent additions to the text at dates even as late as the second century B.C. Since each paragraph requires individual study, a full discussion here would only repeat what may already be found in the commentary itself, especially in the section on *Form* at each passage. A summary of conclusions must therefore suffice at this point.

Nehemiah 9 and 10 are not to be regarded as part of the EM, though they have been thoughtfully combined with Neh 8 into a new unity of their own. Only a fragment that underlies Neh 9:1–5 may, we have suggested, originally have stood between Ezra 10:15 and 16. The prayer that makes up the bulk of Neh 9 will have been known separately to the editor from contemporary liturgical usage. The list in Neh 10:2–28 we have tentatively assigned to his own compilation in order to show the full participation of the community in the pledge that is transcribed in the remainder of Neh 10.

Consideration of the terms of this pledge shows that it has a number of points of close contact with reforms that Nehemiah also claims to have initiated. The implications of this observation have not previously been appreciated, for we should not fail to observe that it is true also of some of the other material in these chapters. For instance, 11:1–2 with its attendant list (vv 3–20) cannot come from the NM, although it may be deduced from 7:4–5 that something comparable must also have stood in Nehemiah's account.

Rather, there are one or two small indications in 11:1–2 which suggest that its origin is closely associated with the pledge in chap. 10; it too, therefore, attributes to the community a measure for which Nehemiah also claimed credit. The same point is suggested for the source that has been combined with the NM to create the description of the dedication of the wall in 12:27–43, and 13:1–3 may originate from the same circles. (12:44–47 is probably the editor's own composition.) Finally, it should not be forgotten that Neh 3, though included in the NM, was originally an independent record of the building of the wall, which emphasized again the full involvement of the community with the high priest at its head. (See, from a different perspective, Japhet, *ZAW* 94 [1982] 86–89.)

When these passages are thus considered together, it will be seen that they share a number of features in common, principally their stress on the wholehearted participation in various activities and reforms by all the people under priestly leadership. Moreover, these activities are all paralleled in the NM, but Nehemiah himself does not feature in any of them. We therefore propose that they were drawn by the editor from the temple archives, where they had been compiled by circles that were favorable to the reforms themselves but less wholehearted, for whatever reason, in their allegiance to Nehemiah. They thus form an important corrective to Nehemiah's one-sided account of his own achievements, and indeed we have suggested above that they may even have prompted him to revise his original account of the wall-building into the NM as we now know it.

Finally, it is argued in the commentary that the lists in 11:21–36 and 12:1–26 represent later supplements to the work of the main editor, supplements that amplify various aspects of what precedes them on the basis of contemporary knowledge and other archival material.

COMPOSITION

Discussion of the composition of the books of Ezra and Nehemiah from their constituent sources has been immeasurably complicated, in my view, by the presupposition that they are a continuation of Chronicles. Some circles (see especially Mowinckel and Pohlmann) have refined this view and see in 1 Esdras the shape of the "original ending" of the Chronicler's work. Although it need not necessarily do so, this approach has in practice resulted in the suggestion by some German-speaking scholars of various levels of "post-chronistic" redactions, as well as the suggestion by the American school of Cross and those who follow him, of several editions of the Chronicler's work itself; cf. *JBL* 94 (1975) 4–18.

It would serve little purpose to review and evaluate these theories here, since they are so fundamentally at variance with the conclusions that have emerged from the preparation of this commentary. It will aid clarity simply to summarize these conclusions here; some of the other approaches are examined at relevant points of the commentary, but for a critical discussion from the point of view of Chronicles see also my *Israel; 1 and 2 Chronicles*, 3–17; and *TynB* 28 (1977) 120–30.

The most important single clue towards resolving this question lies in the observation that Ezra 2:1—3:1 is dependent upon the parallel passage in Neh 7. This has been recognized by the majority of commentators for excellent reasons. Only those who wish to uphold the priority of 1 Esdras over MT are obliged to oppose it, but their arguments have been found unconvincing; cf. *JTS* ns 34 (1983) 2–8. The significance of this observation will be apparent once it is realized that the passage borrowed in Ezra 2:1—3:1 demonstrates that Neh 8 must already have been in its present position; in other words, Ezra 1–6 must have been composed *after* the combination of the Ezra and Nehemiah materials. Rudolph's tortuous attempt (15) to avoid this conclusion shows that he was only too well aware of the damage it would cause to the general view of these books' composition, a view which he shared.

A history of composition must, therefore, start with the combination of the Ezra and Nehemiah memoirs. The same process demands, however, the inclusion of most of the rest of the material in Neh 9–12: chaps. 8–10 are a carefully constructed compilation around the theme of covenant renewal; 11:1–2 and its dependent list are clearly intended as a narrative continuation of 7:4–5; the splicing of other material into Nehemiah's account of the dedication of the wall (12:27–43) is most reasonably to be taken as part of this same editorial activity, and 12:44—13:3 is consciously placed to introduce the remainder of the NM. In fact, only 11:21—12:26 cannot be regarded as part of this major phase in the book's composition.

Motivation for, and method in, this activity are not hard to find. We know from other sources that many of the problems that Ezra and Nehemiah tackled were not quickly solved, but continued to plague the community for many decades to come. The desire to make the work of the reformers more widely known was thus intelligible enough. In doing so, however, the editor was careful to arrange his material in a panel fashion (Ezra 7–10; Neh 1–7; Neh 8–10; Neh 11–13) in order to suggest that the work of reform was a unity theologically, even if it was separated and carried through by two men historically. Furthermore, in giving new direction to his contemporaries, he showed that physical restoration and even separation from foreigners were but the prerequisite for the reception of the Law and response to it. There can be little doubt that Neh 8–10 is to be seen as the climax of the work in this form and that these chapters were intended by the editor to function paradigmatically within his own later community as it struggled to maintain its identity and sense of religious purpose. At the same time, the working in of a number of accounts of reform undertaken by the people as a whole in the final section of the work may have been intended to prevent too great a feeling of dependence upon the need for the initiative of individual leaders.

Only after the composition of Ezra 7—Neh 13 was complete was Ezra 1–6 added. The editorial method in these chapters has already been noted above, namely the incorporation of a variety of original sources using certain theological preconceptions. The author's purpose here is both positive and polemical. On the one hand, he is concerned to trace lines of continuity between the restored community and the Israel of pre-exilic times, between the second and first temples, and so on. Legitimacy is clearly a fundamental issue. On the other hand, he goes to considerable lengths to justify the rejection of the offer of northern participation in the restoration itself.

These predominant themes should be combined with a consideration that this editor should probably be linked with the circle of those who had previously subjected the books of Chronicles to a pro-priestly redaction; cf. VTSup 30 (1979) 251–68; *JTS* ns 34 (1983) 26–29, and the comments on Ezra 3:8; 6:18 and 19–22 below. It is then attractive to suppose that part of his purpose in writing was to counter the claims of the newly built Samaritan temple on Mount Gerizim. This he achieved by supplying an introduction to the work of his distant predecessors, Ezra and Nehemiah, and by demonstrating the broken but now-restored lines of continuity between their community and that of the first temple period, especially as presented in Chronicles. It is, of course, no coincidence that Chronicles is also to some extent a back-projection of these later ideals.

To summarize, three basic stages are to be identified in the composition of Ezra and Nehemiah: (1) the writing of the various primary sources, all more or less contemporary with the events they relate; (2) the combination of the EM, NM, and other sources to form Ezra 7:1—Neh 11:20; 12:27—13:31 (11:21—12:26 were added separately); (3) the later addition of the introduction in Ezra 1–6. It may be suggested that a further point in favor of this whole approach is its simplicity as compared to most other reconstructions.

DATE

Under this heading, discussion concerns the date of the books' composition, not, of course, of their constituent sources. Two main criteria are available: not dating a historical book earlier than the last person or event to which it refers; ascertaining if its purpose is directed toward an identifiable situation, then using that basis to establish an approximate date for the work.

Neither criterion is without its difficulties for the books under discussion; consequently widely varying dates have been proposed. Moreover, the issue is further complicated for those who include Chronicles as part of the same work, while, as we have noted, others see important earlier stages in the development of the books which all require separate dating. Rudolph, for instance, sees no need to set the date later than about 400 B.C. This, of course, is impossibly early for those who date Ezra's journey to Jerusalem in 398 B.C. Others believe that the Jaddua of Neh 12:11 and 22 was the high priest in the time of Alexander the Great, while others see phases in the later redaction of these books stretching at least as late as the Maccabean period in the second century B.C.

It needs to be recognized that these dates are often assigned on a very narrow basis of evidence—a single name, for instance, or the possibility of a late interpolation of doubtful textual validity (e.g., see on Neh 11:10). Not surprisingly, no consensus has been reached from this angle. Similarly, the dating which we here propose can be read straight out of our earlier discussion of composition, and therefore runs the risk of rejection by those who adopt an alternative approach to that issue.

Our understanding of the purpose and provenance of Ezra 1–6 leads us to a date reasonably early in the Hellenistic period (say around 300 B.C.); cf. Williamson, *JTS* ns 34 (1983) 1–30 and the literature cited at Neh 13:28 on the date of the building of the Samaritan temple. We have argued that this was the final stage in the books' composition, and we are not aware of any evidence that demands a later date. The books were therefore brought to completion in their present form at that time. Those who seek a later date generally do so on the basis of Josephus and 1 Esdras, a line of evidence which we believe to be unjustified.

Before that date, an earlier editor had already combined the material concerning Ezra and Nehemiah. Since we do not accept a late date for Ezra, a *terminus post quem* for this activity must be the end of Nehemiah's activity; on the basis of Neh 13:6 this cannot have been earlier than about 430 B.C. nor later than the death of Artaxerxes in 424 B.C.

Greater precision is not easy to obtain, though it seems reasonable to assume the passage of a certain amount of time in order to allow the memories of Ezra and Nehemiah to merge to some extent. Our best evidence is likely to come from the lists of high priests in 12:1–26. Here we can only summarize our detailed discussion in *Form* on that passage: Since the paragraph as a whole is a later addition to its prevailing context, its date must therefore furnish a *terminus ad quem* for the work of our editor. The name Jaddua is a later addition, and his date is therefore not that of the passage's compilation as a whole. The perspective of the author of these lists is no earlier than Johanan the high priest, known from *AramP* 30 to have been in office at the very end of the fifth century B.C. He therefore probably worked shortly after that time, i.e., early fourth century B.C. His perspective fits well with what we know of the development of the families of cultic officials at that time. The Ezra and Nehemiah material must have been combined before that, say around 400 B.C.

We thus conclude that the two major stages in the books' composition are to be dated at about 400 B.C. and 300 B.C.

HISTORICAL TOPICS

The books of Ezra and Nehemiah naturally raise a great many questions of a historical nature. Most of these relate primarily to the interpretation of a single text, and in all such cases discussion will be found at the appropriate point in the commentary. The identity of individuals is usually discussed at their first appearance in the text (e.g., Sheshbazzar at Ezra 1:8; Zerubbabel at 2:1–2, and so on). Because a decision about a historical problem often depends upon the results of literary analysis, readers are advised that they should consult *Form* on the relevant passage as well as the verse-by-verse exposition. For instance, over the much-debated topic of the course of rebuilding of the second temple, the whole issue turns on the nature of the narrative in Ezra 3; once this is resolved in *Form,* the historical reconstruction proposed follows as a matter of course.

There are one or two important topics which have been much debated, but which cannot be hung on so convenient a peg. The evidence needs to be pieced together from a number of texts. In surveying these here, the fuller discussion of the commentary on each individual verse or passage is naturally presupposed.

THE IDENTIFICATION OF THE BOOK OF THE LAW

Strictly speaking, two separate issues should be distinguished here; first, can the law that Ezra brought to Jerusalem (Ezra 7:12, 25–26) be identified, and, second, what law does the author/compiler of Ezra and Nehemiah as a whole recognize as authoritative? Because of its relevance to the development of the Pentateuch, the first question has received a great deal of attention; for surveys of scholarship with extensive bibliographies, cf. U. Kellermann, "Erwägungen zum Esragesetz," *ZAW* 80 (1968) 373–85, and C. Houtman, "Ezra and the Law," *OTS* 21 (1981) 91–115; more briefly, Klein, "Ezra and Nehemiah in Recent Studies," 366–68, and Widengren, "Persian Period," 514–15.

Since the rise of the documentary hypothesis of Pentateuchal origins, most scholars have believed that Ezra's law book was either P or the Pentateuch as a whole, though some have always felt that it was necessary to adopt a more nuanced position, preferring not to support so explicit an identification; see, for instance, von Rad, *Geschichtsbild,* 38–41, who believes that parts, at least, of the major law codes must have been included in the book, but that it cannot yet be identified with the Pentateuch in its entirety. A similar opinion is expressed by M. Noth, *The Laws in the Pentateuch and other Essays* (tr. D. R. Ap-Thomas [Edinburgh and London: Oliver & Boyd, 1966]), 76, and by Rudolph, 169. Following their surveys of research, however, both Kellermann and Houtman adopt radical, minority opinions.

Kellermann's approach is governed by his literary-critical conclusion that only in Ezra 7:12–26 do we find historically reliable information about Ezra, the remainder of the Ezra material being a midrash on this passage added by the Chronicler (cf. "The Ezra Memoir" above). He believes that 7:25–26 rules out a law book that includes any narrative material (such as the Pentateuch or P), and that the only law code that seems to have exerted any influence on the nearly contemporary NM and Malachi was Deuteronomy. He therefore identifies Ezra's law book as a form of the Deuteronomic code. To this we would reply that we do not accept Kellermann's minimalist position with regard to what material is available for a reconstruction of the history of Ezra; that Kellermann has given no sound reason for his assertion that Ezra 7:25–26 rules out the inclusion of narrative in the law; and that it is not certain that Neh 13 shows no knowledge of P: the relation of Neh 13 to Neh 10 is noted in the commentary. It will be seen there that in some cases the problems involved in keeping the law and the solutions proposed involve the juxtaposition of priestly and other legal codes.

Houtman's approach to our problem goes beyond an identification of Ezra's law book to that presupposed in these books as a whole. He works through passages that make explicit reference to the law (Ezra 6:18; Neh 8:14–15; 10; 13:1–3) and comes to the conclusion that some cannot be explained on the basis of the existing Pentateuch. He therefore revives a rather neglected opinion of B. D. Eerdmans that the references are to "a law-book with a character of its own which is not transmitted to us." He uses the recently published Temple Scroll from Qumran as evidence for such alternative collections of laws beside the Pentateuch.

Naturally, Houtman's thesis is of such a kind that it cannot be disproved beyond all doubt. Nevertheless, it cannot be regarded as very probable, and it is certainly unnecessary.

First, the analogy with the Temple Scroll is not exact; the Scroll represents a first-person address by God and is not evidence for the view that "there were circles of men who held themselves entitled to promulgate existing laws anew in the name of Moses." Second, that "the Book of the Law of Moses which the Lord had commanded for Israel" (Neh 8:1) should have been a document quite separate from the Pentateuch seems most unlikely in view of the significance of this book in the formation of Judaism. That it should have been lost without trace or other mention while the Pentateuch, unmentioned here according to this view, should have silently risen to its place of supreme authority seems an extraordinary hypothesis; after all, we are not dealing with a breakaway group, like the people of Qumran, nor is there any evidence that these latter had any doubts about the supreme authority of the Pentateuch, despite the existence of the Temple Scroll. Third, it is noteworthy that in Neh 13:1 the title "the Book of Moses" is used for a law book, but the quotation from it in vv 1–2 shows that it must have included our Deuteronomy. The text is followed closely even at the expense of smoothness of style. It seems unlikely that the harsh change of person in Deut 23:5 (4), followed by Nehemiah, would have been preserved also in some alternative code. At the same time, however, it is difficult to drive a wedge between "the Book of Moses" here and "the Book of the Law of Moses" in Neh 8:1.

Finally, we must ask if Houtman's theory is necessary; the answer to this question will lead us toward a positive statement on the matter. The evidence on which the theory is based consists of the presence of discrepancies between citations from the law and the text of the Pentateuch, and the inclusion of laws which are not directly commanded in the Pentateuch (e.g., the wood offering of Neh 10:35 [34] and 13:31). To this it may be replied that we should not expect such exactitude from an author in antiquity; the citations of the OT in the NT show similar variation, though no one doubts that it is our OT to which they refer. What matters is that, on the basis of the kind of methods of biblical interpretation current at that time, it should be possible to explain how the present formulations arose out of the laws as we know them. And this we have sought to do at the relevant passages, particularly Neh 8 and 10.

Once it is accepted on grounds of general probability that Ezra's law book stood in at least some sort of relation to the Mosaic law as we know it, and once it is accepted, further, that Ezra 9:1–2 and Neh 8:13–18 may both be admitted as evidence for what the book contained, then it must be accepted that it included parts, at least, of both D and P, in which case it was similar to, if not yet fully identical with, our Pentateuch. This conclusion, of course, is shared by many scholars who have studied the matter from different points of view. What has not, however, received sufficient attention hitherto is appreciation of the need for, extent of, and nature of the interpretation which is already being applied to this text. It is not a new law that Ezra presents, but one whose demands frequently cannot be simply applied to the contemporary setting. It is a sobering reflection that his hermeneutic can even lead some to fail to recognize the text which lies behind his application.

Finally, if this conclusion is true for the law of Ezra, then it is likely to hold also for the rest of the books, since they are mostly to be dated after him. Nehemiah himself, it is true, has the strongest affinity with Deuteronomy, but that is probably because of his lay status and the sphere of his activity. The documents included in Ezra 1–6 are to be dated before Ezra, but they shed no light on our problem. The editor of these documents represents, in our view, the latest strand of all; ironically, it is he who has penned one of the most difficult verses in this whole area (see *Comment* on Ezra 6:18). The fact that so late an author could still write with this degree of freedom strengthens our case that the same could have happened in the earlier period.

THE CHRONOLOGICAL ORDER OF EZRA AND NEHEMIAH

No critical issue raised by the books of Ezra and Nehemiah has evoked more discussion than this question. Since Nehemiah's date is generally agreed (see on Neh 1), the controversy centers on the date at which Ezra came to Jerusalem. The literature on this topic is enormous, and a comprehensive listing is out of the question. Because the literary and historical issues are intertwined, discussion of them is found in all the standard histories of Israel, introductions to the literature of the OT, commentaries on these books, and dictionary/encyclopedia articles. In addition, there have been many special studies (mostly articles) devoted to this question. Extensive surveys of research may be found in Rowley, "Chronological Order"; Kellermann, *ZAW* 80 (1968) 55–87; In der Smitten, *Esra,* 91–105; Yamauchi, *Themelios* ns 5 (1980) 7–13; and, more briefly, Klein, "Ezra and Nehemiah," 370–72, and Widengren, "Persian Period," 503–9. Some other major contributions will be noted below.

It is important to start with a reminder of the results of our literary analysis of the Ezra material. We argue that only Ezra 7–10 and Neh 8 give us information about Ezra's activity, and that in the original EM the substance of Neh 8 stood between Ezra 8 and 9. (It has, of course, been extensively worked over by the editor responsible for its new setting.) We conclude from these two points that the whole of Ezra's recorded ministry lasted just one year, and that there is no historical evidence for an overlap between the work of Ezra and Nehemiah. This conclusion at once makes irrelevant a number of the points that have been raised on all sides of the debate.

Next we should observe that there are three main options for Ezra's date. The seventh year of Artaxerxes I, i.e., 458 B.C. (cf. Ezra 7:7–8), is the date that the biblical text suggests at first glance, and it was unquestioned until

1889. It has never lacked support, and in recent years many who have written on the subject have defended it in preference to the alternatives noted below. Among the more significant contributions, we should note de Vaux, *DBSup* 4, 764–69; Scott, *ExpTim* 58 (1946–47) 263–67; Wright, *Date;* Koch, *JSS* 19 (1974) 173–97; Tuland, *AUSS* 12 (1974) 47–62; In der Smitten, *Esra,* 91–105; Cross, *JBL* 94 (1975) 4–18. Kellermann, *ZAW* 80 (1968) 55–87, discounts the precise date in Ezra 7:7–8 as part of the Chronicler's midrash, but nevertheless argues for a similar date (shortly before 448 B.C.) on other grounds.

The major alternative is to date Ezra in the seventh year of Artaxerxes II, i.e., 398 B.C., well after Nehemiah. Since, as we have seen, the EM was not originally intertwined with the NM, this is not so radical a proposal as it might first appear. It involves no textual emendation of Ezra 7 and is believed to remove a number of difficulties which confront the traditional view. It was originally worked out in a series of publications by A. Van Hoonacker between 1890 and 1924. Among significant discussions that uphold this view we may mention Snaith, *ZAW* 63 (1951) 53–66; Cazelles, *VT* 4 (1954) 113–40; Bowman; Galling, *Studien,* 149–84; Rowley, "Chronological Order"; Mowinckel, *Studien III,* 99–106; Emerton, *JTS* ns 17 (1966) 1–19; and Widengren, "Persian Period," 503–9.

A minority view proposes that Ezra came to Jerusalem not in the seventh, but in the thirty-seventh year of Artaxerxes I, i.e., 428 B.C. This view recognizes the difficulties which confront the traditional date, but seeks also to avoid the problems raised by dating Ezra in 398 B.C. Further, it is able to do justice to the closer correspondence between the reforms of Ezra and those of Nehemiah's second term (Neh 13) than those of his first term. Not all who uphold this view agree on the details of the consequential historical reconstruction. Nevertheless, they may be grouped together here for convenience. They include Rudolph, in what may be considered the finest available commentary on these books, as well as the enormously influential *History of Israel* by J. Bright, 3rd ed. (Philadelphia: Westminster Press, 1981), 391–402; see also Lefèvre, *DBSup* 6, 414–21, and Pavlovský, *Bib* 38 (1957) 275–305, 428–56.

Although this third view has led to some attractive attempts to reconstruct the sequence of historical events, we should hesitate long before following them, in my opinion. The theory demands a totally unsupported textual emendation of Ezra 7:7–8 and therefore faces from the outset the drawback of special pleading. From the point of view of method, it should not even be considered unless both other alternatives are shown to be impossible. The view depends in considerable part on a rejection of the traditional date for the same reasons as are advanced by those who favor the 398 B.C. date. As noted above, these have been seriously questioned in recent years; see especially Kellermann. It is thus unfortunate that Bright has not reacted to these studies in the more recent editions of his *History.* The article of Emerton, *JTS* ns 17 (1966) 1–19, is devoted to a thorough examination of this view to see in particular whether it is to be preferred to the later date of 398 B.C. Again, it is disappointing that Bright has only rejected, not refuted, Emerton's arguments in the later editions of his *History.* It may be significant that there have been no recent advocates of this position. In view of the objections that have been leveled against this theory, together with the question of method noted above, and because the hypothesis is so speculative, resting largely on circumstantial evidence, we shall not pursue it further here.

In turning, then, to the major topic of whether Ezra came to Jerusalem before or after Nehemiah, we find that the points at issue fall into several categories. First, and most frequently cited, there are a number of individual points which, it is maintained, make better sense if Nehemiah preceded Ezra. For instance, did Ezra find a wall already built (Ezra 9:9)? Was the Jehohanan to whose room Ezra withdrew (Ezra 10:6) the high priest of the same name whom we know from *AramP* 30:18 to have been in office in 408 B.C., long after the traditional date for Ezra? Was "Meremoth, son of Uriah the priest" a young and active wall builder under Nehemiah (Neh 3:4, 21) but a senior figure in the community when Ezra came to Jerusalem (Ezra 8:33–34)? Indeed, was he part of a committee which Nehemiah had earlier established (Neh 13:13)? All these, and some other similar points of particular detail, are dealt with in the comments on the verses indicated. It is found that none of them carries convincing weight in the discussion. *If* Ezra came after Nehemiah, these verses might be explained in the manner indicated, but for each one alternative explanations are just as possible, and in some cases, we argue, they are in fact more probable.

A second group of arguments relates to extrabiblical data, both sides claiming that their view fits best with the prevailing historical circumstances in the Persian Empire at the time. As is outlined at Ezra 4:11–16, the period 459–448 B.C. was a turbulent one in the west, with first a revolt in Egypt and then the Megabyzus' rebellion, which won extensive support in the satrapy Beyond the River. Egypt rebelled and regained her independence in 401 B.C., and Artaxerxes II was then immediately faced with his brother Cyrus' rebellion, which lasted for several years. None of our sources, biblical or otherwise, makes a direct connection between any of these affairs and the situation in Jerusalem. It is thus possible to make out a case both for 458 and for 398 B.C. on the ground that the Persians would have welcomed a regime in Jerusalem that was loyally favorable toward them. In other words, knowledge of Ezra's date might enable us to relate his appointment to Persian policy, but knowledge of Persian policy cannot conversely help us to determine the date of Ezra's journey.

A further argument under this general heading relates to the so-called "Passover Papyrus" (*AramP* 21), a letter written by one Hananiah to the Jewish colony at Elephantine in 419 B.C. Although the papyrus is damaged, it is generally believed to refer to an attempt by the Persian authorities to enforce the Jewish law relating to the Feast of Unleavened Bread and Passover on the colony. Bright, *History*, 399, in particular has argued that Ezra's journey to Jerusalem cannot be dated later than this because of the unlikelihood that "Jewish practice was being regulated in a far corner of Egypt—and perhaps via Jerusalem—before this had been done in Jerusalem itself." Emerton, *JTS* ns 17 (1966) 8–9, responded to this argument by underlining the uncertainties upon which it is based: the papyrus is damaged and of dubious interpretation; it does not refer to the whole law; Ezra's mission itself need not have been a total innovation but rather a reaffirmation of existing policy, and so on. Bright has replied that he still regards his interpretation as the most probable. However, even if we accept the usual reconstruction of the papyrus (and Emerton is perhaps unnecessarily cautious here), Bright's conclusion does not necessarily follow. The most detailed recent study of the papyrus, that of B. Porten, *BA* 42 (1979) 74–104 (88–92), proposes a restoration in line with that presupposed by Bright, but it includes among possible interpretations the suggestion that the letter is a "reaffirmation of the Jews' right to observe the Passover in the face of Egyptian antagonism." Since clearly only one aspect of the law is referred to, this seems as plausible an approach as any. To conclude: the Passover Papyrus cannot support a late date for Ezra; one interpretation of it might favor an early date, but this is very far from certain. It is thus best not adduced as evidence either way.

Finally under this general heading, Kellermann, *ZAW* 80 (1968) 55–87, in trying to appeal to broader considerations than the kind noted under our first category of arguments, has turned the evidence relating to the religious policy of the Achaemenids in a different direction. (In der Smitten, *Esra*, 110–23, uses some of the same evidence as background to his interpretation of Ezra's mission; however, he does not appear to use it as an argument for the early date in quite the way that Kellermann does.) Kellermann maintains that encouragement to promote local law was a mark of the first as opposed to the second half of the period of Achaemenid rule and that Ezra's mission is thus better dated early rather than late. He sees the start of the reign of Artaxerxes II as the crucial turning point in this regard. In addition to citing such familiar evidence as the Demotic Chronicle (see *Comment* on Ezra 7:25), Kellermann also adduces the fact that the early Achaemenids knew of no law code that would serve for the whole of their empire; each community enjoyed the freedom to enforce its own indigenous code. This began to change as early as the time of Darius I, and the mission of Ezra in 458 B.C. may be seen as a late example of the early Achaemenid policy.

While this line of argument may be said slightly to favor the early date for Ezra, it cannot be judged in any way to be decisive, nor can it carry the weight that Kellermann seeks to put upon it. He has not been able to establish a firm date for the change in policy, for he cites the reign of Darius I in one connection and the start of the reign of Artaxerxes II, over a century later, in another. Nor has he demonstrated the impossibility of Ezra's mission at the later date; if the Jews had been granted religious freedom by Cyrus and Darius, there is no reason why their successors should not have continued this policy if it was in their interests to do so. It seems that Kellermann's approach is spread across too broad a background to determine so specific an issue as the date of Ezra.

Thus far, we have suggested that neither matters of detail nor arguments based on Achaemenid policy are adequate to determine the date of Ezra's journey to Jerusalem. We must turn, therefore, to a final area of evidence, namely, a broader approach to the biblical material itself. While we shall argue from this for the early date for Ezra, it hardly need be said that proof is unattainable; we can only set out what we regard as the most probable case.

First, the history of the composition of these books presented in this commentary requires that far more weight than usual should be placed upon the testimony of the present biblical order of events. Cazelles, *VT* 4 (1954) 119, for instance, uses evidence from Ezra 4 to suggest that "the Chronicler" did not feel himself bound by strict chronological considerations; many other scholars have appealed to what they regard as the poor level of historicity in the books of Chronicles to make the same point. All this is irrelevant, however; the material relating to Ezra and Nehemiah was not put into its present order by the Chronicler, nor even by the editor of Ezra 1-6. The dependence of Ezra 2/3 on Neh 7/8, supported by the overwhelming majority of scholars, demonstrates (as, ironically, very few have then been prepared to spell out) that the combining of the Ezra and Nehemiah material must have been one of the earliest phases in the books' composition. Indeed, we have suggested above that it came little more than a generation after the end of Nehemiah's work. If that is so, then in a case such as the present one where other evidence is so ambiguous, we believe that this clear statement of the text as it stands should be given the greatest possible weight.

Second, neither reformer refers to the work of the other (though see *Comment* below on Neh 12:36). This in itself is not surprising, since we have argued that they worked independently and had very personal motives and purposes in writing their accounts. Besides, even such contemporaries as Haggai and Zechariah do not refer to each other. Despite this, however, we may reasonably ask whether the work of one of them more probably presupposes the work of the other than *vice versa*. Some details where Ezra is thought to presuppose the work of Nehemiah have already been dismissed as unsatisfactory; but what of the reverse? It is often said that Nehemiah's handling of mixed marriages (Neh 13:23-28) must have preceded Ezra's more drastic and systematic treatment (Ezra 10). Our exegesis shows that this is not so: Nehemiah was dealing with a very local manifestation of the problem. Once the incident is seen in this light, the whole argument may be turned on its head, so as to favor Ezra's priority. If the abuse was as widespread as it seems to have been before Ezra's time, what was Nehemiah doing in attacking such a local and particular manifestation? It looks much more as though the general problem had been solved and he was merely dealing with a specific instance of contravention. Again, it is argued in some detail at Ezra 9:1-2 that although Ezra did not introduce a new law, he did introduce a new method of interpretation whereby what had come to be regarded as outmoded laws were given a new application. It is significant that in Neh 13:25 Nehemiah bases himself on the same approach. This suggests that Ezra's interpretation of the law, which is not attested in the earlier period, has now become generally accepted in Judah. For two separate reasons, therefore, Neh 13:23-28 is more easily understood if preceded by the work of Ezra.

A third point is related to that just made. In the comments on Neh 10 and 13, a close relationship is noted between the two sets of reforms involved, and it is suggested that this can best be explained historically if Neh 10 follows soon after Neh 13. However, the pledges made in Neh 10 are based on both a reflection on a wide sweep of Pentateuchal law, embracing P and D, and on a hermeneutic which, once again, we note at Ezra 9 and Neh 8 is peculiarly characteristic of Ezra. This again suggests the influence of his earlier ministry.

Fourth, the degree of support that Ezra received in his handling of mixed marriages leads us to wonder whether it should be placed after Nehemiah. Unlike Ezra, Nehemiah seems to have polarized opinion in Jerusalem to a considerable extent, and we may deduce from his treatment of Tobiah (13:4–8) and Sanballat's son-in-law (13:28) that he would not have endeared the whole population to a policy of rigorous separation. In particular, we may suppose that many of the priests were antagonized by his policy. Were this already the case before Ezra's time, we might have expected opposition to his policy to be more vigorous and widespread. As it was, the general agreement he found suggests that attitudes towards this issue had not yet hardened.

Fifth, because the work of the two reformers overlaps in some particulars, it is frequently assumed that one or the other of them must have failed in their mission. It is possible to exaggerate this assumption (see below), but it is nevertheless worth asking whether this is more likely to be true of one than the other. When put in these terms, the evidence points firmly towards the priority of Ezra: there are several aspects of the decree of Artaxerxes of whose fulfillment we have no record. On the other hand, Nehemiah achieved all that he was originally sent to do (cf. Neh 2:1–9) and a good deal more besides. Similarly, that Nehemiah, if he was not initially appointed, at least was later appointed governor, implies that greater civil authority was needed to see his reforms through than Ezra enjoyed; it would then be strange if Ezra came later without such authority in order to complete what Nehemiah had failed to achieve.

Finally, we would include here two points of detail which it was not possible to fit in earlier. (1) Despite the assertions of many scholars, it is argued at Neh 12:36 that the reference to Ezra the scribe in the account of the dedication of the walls is very probably original, being necessary to maintain the symmetry of the two processions. This does not imply any major change in our assessment of his role and mission (see below), but it does indicate that he had come to Jerusalem before Nehemiah and continued to live there as a private, though in some ways prominent, individual after he had completed what he could of his mission. (2) Ezra 4:12, it is argued, is best understood as referring to a group known to Artaxerxes, who had only recently returned to Jerusalem. In view of the probable date of the letter in question this would fit well with a journey by Ezra in 458 B.C. Of course, it might refer to some other group, but we have no evidence whatever for its existence. The completely independent testimony of this letter should, we believe, be taken as important historical evidence. (Neh 1:3, by contrast, does not furnish certain evidence of a return shortly before, as some have argued.)

We therefore conclude this lengthy discussion by expressing the view that Ezra probably came to Jerusalem in 458 B.C.; this raises, however, the question of just what he, and to a lesser extent Nehemiah, managed to achieve, and to this issue we may now turn.

THE ACHIEVEMENTS OF EZRA AND NEHEMIAH

It is not our purpose in this section merely to recapitulate the biblical account; such summaries are to be found in many standard textbooks, besides which the commentary itself provides ample material on an assessment of what is to be learned from the text. Our intention here, rather, is to attempt a more formal historical placing and assessment of these two men. Such an exercise is inevitably speculative because of the frequent necessity to fill in precisely the gaps of what the text does not say.

Nehemiah presents the more straightforward case of the two, so we shall begin with him. As one who enjoyed peculiarly privileged access to the king (Neh 1:11—references in the following are usually to passages where the commentary supplies fuller details), Nehemiah was able to turn this position to his advantage in having Artaxerxes I retract an earlier command (Ezra 4:21) and give authorization for the refortification of Jerusalem.

It was probably not many years prior to this that an attempt to rebuild the city walls had been construed as rebellion (Ezra 4:9–23). At that time, in consequence, the previously separate province of Judah had come under direct rule from Samaria. Tobiah, a high-ranking official under Sanballat, the Samarian governor, had been sent to Jerusalem to assume control for the time being (see on Neh 2:10 and 5:14–15). Since Nehemiah was apparently appointed governor from the start or very soon after (5:14), it is not surprising that his arrival was bitterly resented by those who had just begun to get used to their extended sphere of influence.

By the end of his first year in office, Nehemiah was able to report that the initial task to which he had been commissioned, the wall-building, had been successfully completed. We have argued above that this report, fully to be expected on the basis of 2:6, formed the substance of what we now call the NM. Had it not been the case that much later Nehemiah was stung into reworking his report and added a few paragraphs in votive or dedicatory style, we should never have known either that he continued as governor for twelve years, or that he later returned for a second visit (whether or not as governor) for an undefined period. This is a salutary reminder that our knowledge of these men is very much at the mercy of the specific purposes for which they wrote.

We thus know virtually nothing of the bulk of Nehemiah's work as governor. As a man of some private means (see on 2:1–10 and chap. 5) but not, as Kellermann, *Nehemia*, maintains, of royal descent (see on 2:3), Nehemiah was apparently able to govern in a spirit of some liberality towards those of his own province while remaining more than a little wary of any outside intervention. In accordance with the custom of the time, as well as his own personal convictions, he evidently sought to uphold the cult of his God and the people's obedience to God's law (chap. 13). Beyond such a general assessment, however, our sources are silent; since we have no choice but to respect this, we have to confess that we know nothing about at least nine-tenths of Nehemiah's work as governor, nor of what happened to him eventually. All that we know for certain is that by 408 B.C. he was no longer in office, for *AramP* 30 speaks of one Bagohi as governor of Judah. It is thus ironic, from a purely historical point of view, that Nehemiah came, in time, to be remembered for wall-building, the one accomplishment for which he did not specifically pray to be remembered:

> The memory (זכר) of Nehemiah also is lasting;
> He raised for us the walls that had fallen,
> And set up gates and bars
> And rebuilt our ruined houses (Sir 49:13).

Unlike Nehemiah, Ezra is not mentioned in Sirach's "praise of famous men" (for a possible explanation with reference to alternative views, cf. P. Höffken, "Warum schwieg Jesus Sirach über Esra?" *ZAW* 87 [1975] 184–202; see also Emerton, *JTS* ns 23 [1972] 184–85), nor is he referred to in the NT. Nevertheless, he came to hold a place of outstanding significance in later Judaism, as may be seen from the number of pseudepigraphical works that are named after him and by the number and nature of the references to him in the Talmud and other texts (cf. Myers, lxxii–lxxiv; In der Smitten, *Esra*, 81–85). This already suggests a somewhat ambivalent attitude toward Ezra's achievements, an ambivalence which more recent scholars also frequently find in a dichotomy between a historical appraisal of his achievements and the biblical presentation of his ministry. The possibility must therefore be investigated that Ezra's later reputation owes as much to the present literary presentation of his role as to his actual historical success.

His position in government circles under the Achaemenids in Babylon is uncertain. That Ezra must have been a Jewish leader of some prominence is self-evident; but it is seen at Ezra 7:12 that Schaeder's suggestion that he was the "Secretary of State for Jewish affairs" remains conjectural. Nevertheless, the royal edict in 7:12–26 clearly invested considerable authority in him, even if he remained dependent on the civil authorities for the execution of sanctions against those who would not obey the law which he brought (see *Comment* on 7:26).

Our analysis of the edict suggests that Ezra was sent to fulfill four main tasks. Of these, two were carried out to the letter, and the meticulous way in which this is spelled out in the subsequent report suggests a conscious aim to demonstrate this fact. These were the leading to Jerusalem of any Jews who wished to go and the transportation and delivery of certain gifts and grants for the temple cult. If, as has frequently been surmised, Ezra was prematurely called to account for his actions, we can understand that he would have been particularly anxious to justify himself in the second of these two points.

Regarding a third stipulation of the edict, the requirement to conduct an inquiry in Judah and Jerusalem, our exegesis at Ezra 7:14 and 10:16–17 suggests that this too was carried out, though not in quite so obvious a manner. The emphasis in the present text is clearly upon the definition of the community, whereas in the edict it lies rather on the conformity of the temple cult with the stipulations of the law. Whether or not the original EM included more detail about this latter point it is impossible to tell. Even without this, however, there is hardly enough here to justify our speaking of a failure on Ezra's part.

The final stipulation of the edict, the command to appoint magistrates and judges and to teach the law (7:25), receives only partial attention in the following narrative. No doubt Neh 8, in its original wording and position (following Ezra 8), was intended to show that a preliminary move, at least, had been made in this direction. However, of the institutions for the continuance of this work and for its introduction to Jews living beyond the province of Judah we hear nothing.

This may be variously explained. For instance, we may conclude that the ending of Ezra 10 is sufficiently abrupt to suggest that the original end of the EM was omitted by the editor for reasons of his own. It is difficult to believe, however, that this is an adequate explanation. What we know of the subsequent history lends it no support whatever, but rather the reverse. The debacle of the second half of Ezra 4, together with the likely consequences of the dissolution of the mixed marriages, suggests that fairly soon after the recorded period of Ezra's ministry things began to go seriously wrong. We have no evidence whatever that Ezra himself was personally involved in the abortive attempt to rebuild the walls, but even if he was still active at that time (which is uncertain), it can have done his standing no good in the Achaemenid court, and we can scarcely believe that he would have been allowed to continue in office thereafter. By that time at the latest he must have been called to account for his stewardship, and there can be no probability that Jerusalem would have been vouchsafed any kind of responsibility for the Jewish communities outside Judah for the period immediately following.

In view of the time-span covered by the EM, however, perhaps the most likely explanation is that Ezra's commission was for a more limited period from the start and that, because of the difficulties which he encountered, he was not able to see the whole of his task successfully completed. Given the circumstances of the time, this is hardly surprising, and if he was indeed present at the later dedication of the wall under Nehemiah (Neh 12:36), then he is unlikely to have failed to the point of complete disgrace. Moreover, his inability to provide adequate institutions to maintain the reforms that he had initiated would help explain why they were later allowed to lapse, as attested in the closing chapters of Nehemiah.

Are we then justified in saying that Ezra failed? Our answer will depend much on the basis for our assessment. From an external and political point of view he clearly did not succeed in fulfilling all the terms of Artaxerxes' edict—and this, it should be noted, would have to be our conclusion even if Ezra were dated after Nehemiah. The present text suggests, however, that Ezra did not consider such matters to be his most important task (even if our analysis in the commentary does not allow us to go as far as the wideranging claims of Koch, *JSS* 19 [1974] 173–97). Ezra's concern, rather, was to establish the law of God as the basis for the life of all the people (see *Comment* on Neh 8 and Ellison, *EvQ* 53 [1981] 48–53) and to introduce an approach to its interpretation that would rescue it from the danger of falling into neglect because of historical and political changes. Judged by this criterion, Ezra was brilliantly successful. In the short term, the reforms of Nehemiah suggest that the approach introduced by Ezra quickly permeated into the fabric of the life of the community; the "alternative account" of parts of Nehemiah's work that we have detected as running parallel to much of the NM shows that his achievements were not only a personal triumph but met with a ready response in a far wider circle. In the longer term, the history of Judaism testifies to the abiding influence of Ezra's work. Finally, we are bound to conclude that in his arrangement of the material, and especially in his repositioning of Neh 8, the editor showed an appreciation of where Ezra's true importance lay. Appropriately enough, it was ultimately in this Scripture, rather than in any political institution, that Ezra's role was preserved, and through it he continued to exercise an influence long after both he and, indeed, the Achaemenid empire itself had passed into the realms of distant history.

A THEOLOGICAL READING

It is not easy to know how best to approach a theological summary of Ezra and Nehemiah. One possibility is to analyze what they say under the headings of a traditional systematic theology; see, for instance, the excellent sketch along these lines in Kidner, 19–27, which proves the value of such an approach. The difficulty here, however, is to maintain a correct balance between what the author takes for granted (because he stands fairly late in the development of the OT) and what it is his intention positively to contribute. Another legitimate approach is thematic: a commentator may pick out those points that receive most frequent attention in the narrative and group them in a more orderly fashion. It is to be hoped that justice will be done to such matters at the appropriate points of the commentary.

In recent years, however, greater attempts have been made to do justice to the medium of narrative through which the books address us. If we are attracted to this approach in the following, it is because it takes more seriously than any other the character of the books themselves. It gives exegesis a greater prominence and draws back from imposing foreign, a priori categories of interpretation on the material; and it enables us to avoid some of the more obvious objections that might be raised as a result of our literary analysis. No one will doubt that substantial parts of Ezra and Nehemiah are based on sources. In addition, we have argued for the growth of the books in two stages—the combining of Ezra 7–Neh 13 and the later prefacing of Ezra 1–6. It then becomes difficult to say whose theology should be described—Ezra's? Nehemiah's? the redactor's?—and difficult, too, to know to what extent one is in full agreement with another. Given the circumstances of the way these books developed, the safest starting point seems, therefore, to be to attend to their overall shape, since it is in the arrangement of their sources that the editors have had most effect and where their intention is thus most clearly discernible; cf. Childs, *Introduction*, 630–37; Gunneweg, VTSup 32 (1981) 146–61.

We must start by noting that although the books have an initial appearance of straightforward historical narrative, they do not regard chronology in the same rigid manner as we do. The events recorded are selected for their contribution to the total presentation of the restoration and then welded together without particular concern for the intervening passage of time. Noteworthy examples of this are the introduction to Ezra 7, "After these things," which covers a gap of more than fifty years in the history, but which is intended to indicate that the account of Ezra's mission is the next formative step in the constitution of the post-exilic community; the interlocking of the ministries of Ezra and Nehemiah in order to emphasize the united effect of their reforms; the bracketing of Zerubbabel and Nehemiah in Neh 12:47; and the bracketing of Joiakim, Nehemiah, and Ezra in the later 12:26. In all these instances, the events referred to are loosened from their strictly historical moorings and regarded more in their relation to each other than to their original settings. This provides an instructive example of the development of a history of salvation. Events are now judged by their theological significance; it is at this level, the level of divine causality, that continuity is to be perceived. The normal laws of cause and effect are totally subordinated to this perspective.

Next, we may observe that, as a result, a certain pattern becomes evident in the major chapters of this history. The first "chapter," Ezra 1–6, is clear enough. Through his agent, the Persian king, God secures the opening for the return of his people from exile to Judah with permission to rebuild the temple (Ezra 1:1–4). When they arrive, however, the people's initial move in this direction is frustrated by external opposition (3:3; 4:1–5, further illustrated in the remainder of the chapter). Under prophetic influence, however, this opposition is overcome and the temple rebuilt. It is dedicated in a joyful ceremony (6:16–18) followed by the Passover. The chapter concludes with a further acknowledgment of God's hand in the restoration being exercised through the secular authorities.

The next two "chapters" begin in a very similar manner, but their conclusion is held over in order to be presented at the end as a united celebration. Thus, Ezra first is sent to Jerusalem with full authority from the Persian king, not only to continue support for the temple, but also to teach and implement the law of the God of heaven. This, too, is seen as resulting from God's overriding influence on the king (7:27). While the parallel continues with a return of exiles to Jerusalem, the nature of the problem encountered there differs to some extent. Instead of frontal opposition from external enemies, the danger now comes from within, from those of the community who have married outsiders. While this is, from the writer's point of view, successfully overcome (Ezra 10), the section ends abruptly and without celebration. We cannot accept that the precise pattern of the earlier section should be restored by a physical rearrangement of the chapters (e.g., Rudolph, xxii–xxiii). It must be our first endeavor to interpret the text as it stands.

The third section (Neh 1–7) follows precisely the pattern of the first. The emphasis on prayer in Neh 1 and 2:1–10 shows that the royal authorization is once more to be seen as the instrument of divine initiative. Journey, opposition, and successful completion of the task follow in a manner well enough known. Here too, however, the closing celebration is delayed, and in this case the rearrangement of the NM, of which nothing is found between Neh 7 and 12:27–43, shows clearly that this is the result of purposeful redactional design.

Thus far, we are presented with the restoration of the temple, the community, and the city of Jerusalem. Now, in Neh 8–12, the suspended climax is reached in a way that gathers together the concerns of all three preceding sections. At the opening, in place of a royal command we find the proclamation of the law of God. As Childs has stressed, "Ezra does not read the law in order to reform Israel into becoming the people of God. Rather, the reverse move obtains. It is the reformed people to whom the law is read" (*Introduction*, 636). In such a situation there can be no opposition, but rather confession (Neh 9) and recommitment, not least to the service of the temple. "We will not neglect the house of our God" is the summarizing conclusion of the pledge in Neh 10. Neh 11:1–20 then returns to record the successful realization of another of Nehemiah's concerns, the repopulation of the city, before the dedication of the walls (11:21—12:26 are added later) and its conclusion in the temple brings the work of Ezra and of Nehemiah to its united celebration. The parallels between this and the end of Ezra 6 are evident and striking.

Neh 12:43 seems so satisfactory a conclusion to this reading of Ezra and Nehemiah in four great "chapters" that chap. 13 might appear to come as something of an embarrassment. Are we then justified in treating it as a later appendix, and so not relevant to our overall interpretation (Gunneweg, 158)? Far from it! But before returning to this point, it may be helpful to summarize the major concerns that emerge from the stylized narrative just examined.

First, the books make a clear statement about the role of the Persian kings in the divine purposes; cf. Japhet, *ZAW* 94 (1982) 66–98. From God's "stirring up" of the spirit of Cyrus in order that he might fulfill older prophecies as recorded in the first verse through to Artaxerxes' permission to Nehemiah to return a second time to Jerusalem in Neh 13:6, the attitude of sources and redactors is consistent, with scarcely a dissenting voice (see below). Even where a royal decision went against the community's interests, it was caused by hostile misrepresentation rather than fixed policy (Ezra 4). This univocal statement was a major contribution to the attempts of Judaism to come to terms with the loss of political autonomy at the hands of the Babylonians. Developing a trend in the prophets to see foreign potentates as instruments, often unwitting, in God's hands (cf. Isa 10:5; Jer 25:9; Isa 45:1, etc.), the books take a positive stance toward the possibility of faithful life under foreign rule. Of necessity, this must have grown up more positively among the exiles than among those who were left in the land, where nationalism died harder. Moreover, it was made easier by the peculiarly liberal policy of the Achaemenids towards the religious sensibilities of their subjects; experience under the later Seleucids was to take a very different turn. Providentially, the initial process of adaptation was concluded in favorable conditions so that the books have no difficulty demonstrating the advantages of a politically quietist position.

Second, being defined more by race and religion than by nationality, the Jewish community is urged to observe a strict program of separation in order to maintain its identity. An attempt to explain this, together with critical evaluation of some of the means used to carry it out, is offered in *Explanation* following Ezra 9 and 10. It is found in each of the four great sections of these books, and is the source of much of the opposition which the people faced. See the rejection of a northern offer of help in Ezra 4:1–5 with consequences, according to the present arrangement, in the remainder of the chapter; the policy toward mixed marriages in Ezra 9–10; Nehemiah's rejection of the "share, right, or traditional claim" of Judah's neighbors in Jerusalem (Neh 2:20) with their consequent harassment of his every move, and the several affirmations of separation in Neh 8–13. While there are occasional concessions toward a slightly less rigid approach (e.g., Ezra 6:21), the general impression is of an embattled community which nevertheless has both religious and political right on its side.

It is not surprising to find that a third concern to emerge from the narrative is a striving for legitimacy. The people will constantly have needed reassurance that they and their institutions indeed stood in direct line with those of pre-exilic Israel. Especially in the latest portions of the books to be written, therefore, we find a frequent drawing of typological patterns with the earlier history. In Ezra 1–6, the return of the people is presented as a second Exodus, the temple vessels are brought back, the building of the second temple is described in terms reminiscent of the building under Solomon, the people themselves are genealogically linked with those who had gone into exile, and so on. Some similar concerns are present also in the editorial handling of the Ezra material.

The greatest source of continuity, however, is the Book of the Law of Moses. Its frequent mention is reinforced by its prominence in the structure of the books (cf. Neh 8). Through Ezra's "new hermeneutic" the possibility was opened up that these older laws could again become a formative influence on all aspects of the people's life. In this way they could stand in direct succession to the earlier heroes of the faith (e.g., Neh 8:17).

There has been a great deal of discussion in recent studies of these books, and of the post-exilic period in general, concerning the existence of two major "parties" within the community. One, often labeled "theocratic," is said to have accepted the status quo and to have urged faithfulness to God, the law, and its institutions within a generally subservient attitude to the Persian rulers. From what has been said above, it is not surprising that these books are generally regarded as chief exponents of this position. The other party is thought to have been "eschatological" in orientation, dissatisfied with the present situation and looking for, if not actively working for, the overthrow of foreign rule and the establishment of an independent, even messianic, kingdom.

While we may readily accept that this tension is likely to have been experienced by the people of Judah during the period of Persian rule, it is less certain that we should speak of "parties" in the manner that this theory suggests. It is more likely that shifting historical circumstances caused general opinion to tilt now this way and now that, though with representatives of either extreme balancing such shifts at all times. More important for our present purpose is the further consideration that the two viewpoints are not wholly exclusive: it is possible for one to accept, even to embrace, the present situation, while at the same time reserving the view that it is not perfect and looking for change in the longer term. This, at any rate, seems to be the stance adopted in Ezra and Nehemiah. We have already said enough about attitudes concerning the present. But what of the future? Two passages clamor for attention.

The first is Neh 9. Both the structure of the prayer as analyzed below and the words of its concluding lines make a clear statement: there is an almost unbearable contradiction between God's promise of freedom in the land and the present subservience of the people to foreign kings. Of course, one may reply that this passage is of independent origin and not typical of the books as a whole. Nevertheless, the compiler of the Ezra and Nehemiah material deliberately selected it for inclusion and revealed his true feelings by continuing, "In spite of all this, we are making a firm agreement . . ." (Neh 10:1 [9:38]). Nothing could show more clearly the holding-in-tension of present faithful acceptance with future aspiration.

The second passage is Neh 13, held over from our earlier analysis. It is significant that the editor did not so arrange things that the narrative concluded with 12:43. Although, as the commentary will show, the chronological notes are intended to avoid the impression that the people quickly broke all the terms of the pledge so recently made in chap. 10, it remains significant that examples of failure in each area of the book's major concerns are incorporated into this closing chapter. The temple and its services (e.g., v 11), the separation from foreigners (vv 23–28), and the use of the wall (vv 15–22) remind us of the first three major sections of the work. The fact that, at the end, there are still abuses which require rectification affords us a clear sense as we leave them of "Now, and not yet. . . ." Although there is very little in the way of direct divine intervention in these books after the manner found in Chronicles, this does not mean that the future is closed. Rather, the narrative structure itself points to past achievement as a model for future aspiration.

Ezra

Permission to Return (Ezra 1:1–11)

Bibliography

Ackroyd, P. R. "The Temple Vessels—A Continuity Theme." VTSup 23 (1972) 166–81. **Bartel, A.** "Once Again—Who Was Sheshbazzar?" (Heb.). *BMik* 79 (1979) 357–69. **Ben-Yashar, M.** "On the Problem of Sheshbazzar and Zerubbabel" (Heb.). *BMik* 88 (1981) 46–56. **Berger, P.-R.** "Zu den Namen ששבצר und שנאצר." *ZAW* 83 (1971) 98–100. ———. "Der Kyros-Zylinder mit dem Zusatzfragment BIN II Nr. 32 und die akkadischen Personennamen im Danielbuch." *ZA* 64 (1975) 192–234. **Bickerman, E. J.** "The Edict of Cyrus in Ezra 1." *Studies in Jewish and Christian History*. Part One. Leiden: Brill, 1976, 72–108. **Dion, P. E.** "ששבצר and סנורי." *ZAW* 95 (1983) 111–12. **Galling, K.** "Die Proklamation des Kyros in Esra 1." *Studien*, 61–77. ———. "Das Protokoll über die Rückgabe der Tempelgeräte." *Studien*, 78–88. **Ginsberg, H. L.** "Ezra 1:4." *JBL* 79 (1960) 167–69. **Goldman, M. D.** "The True Meaning of Ezra 1, 4." *AusBR* 1 (1951) 58. **Gray, G. B.** "The Title 'King of Persia,' " *ExpTim* 25 (1913–14) 245–51. **Grossheide, H. H.** "Twee Edicten van Cyrus ten gunsten van de Joden." *GTT* 54 (1954) 1–12. **Halevi, A. A.** "Investigations in the Books of Ezra and Nehemiah in the Light of Greek Sources" (Heb.). *Yaacov Gil Jubilee Volume*, ed. Y. Hocherman, M. Lahav, and Z. Zemarion. Jerusalem: Rubin Mass, 1979. 109–17 (109–10). **In der Smitten, W. Th.** "Historische Probleme zum Kyrosedikt und zum Jerusalemer Tempelbau von 515." *Persica* 6 (1972–74) 167–78. **Japhet, S.** "Sheshbazzar and Zerubbabel." *ZAW* 94 (1982) 66–98. **Kuhrt, A.** "The Cyrus Cylinder and Achaemenid Imperial Policy." *JSOT* 25 (1983) 83–97. **Levine, B. A.** "Comparative Perspectives on Jewish and Christian History." *JAOS* 99 (1979) 81–86. **Liver, J.** "The Beginning of the Restoration of Zion" (Hebrew). *Studies in Bible and Judean Desert Scrolls*. Jerusalem: Bialik Institute, 1971. 249–62. **Mayer, R.** "Das achämenidische Weltreich und seine Bedeutung in der politischen und religiösen Geschichte des antiken Orients." *BZ* N.F. 12 (1968) 1–16. **Rost, L.** "Erwägungen zum Kyroserlass." *Verbannung und Heimkehr. Wilhelm Rudolph zum 70. Geburtstage*, ed. A. Kuschke. Tübingen: Mohr, 1961. 301–7. **Tadmor, H.** "The Historical Background to the Decree of Cyrus" (Heb.). *Sepher Ben Gurion*. Jerusalem: Kiryat Sepher, 1964. 450–73. **Torrey, C. C.** "The First Chapter of Ezra in Its Original Form and Setting." *Ezra Studies*, 115–39. **Vaux, R. de.** "Decrees." **Welch, A. C.** *Post-Exilic Judaism*, 87–107. **Williamson, H. G. M.** "The Composition of Ezra i–vi." *JTS* ns 34 (1983) 1–30. **Wilson, R. D.** "The Title 'King of Persia' in the Scriptures." *PTR* 15 (1917) 90–145.

Translation

[1] In [a] the first year [b] of Cyrus, king of Persia, in order that the word of the Lord spoken by [c] Jeremiah might be fulfilled, the Lord stirred up the spirit of Cyrus, king of Persia. He issued a proclamation throughout his kingdom (it was also written down) [d] as follows:

[2] "This is what Cyrus, king of Persia, says: 'The Lord, the God of heaven, has given me all the kingdoms of the earth, and he has commanded me [a] to build him a temple in Jerusalem, which is in Judah. [3] Who is there among you of all his people? [a] May his god [b] be with him! And let him go up [c] to Jerusalem, which is in Judah, and build the temple of the Lord, the God of Israel—that is to say, the god [b] who is in Jerusalem. [4] And those who remain behind [a] who belong to

any of the places [b] *where he is living shall help* [c] *him . . .* [d] *with silver and gold, with goods and livestock, together with any freewill offerings for the house of God which is in Jerusalem.' "*

[5] *Then the heads of the families of Judah and Benjamin, and the priests and the Levites arose, even all* [a] *whose spirit God had stirred up to go up to rebuild the house of the Lord in Jerusalem.* [6] *All their neighbors assisted them* [a] *with silver vessels,* [b] *with gold, goods, and livestock, and with choice gifts in abundance* [c] *in addition to any freewill offering.* [d]

[7] *Furthermore, King Cyrus brought out the vessels of the temple of the Lord which Nebuchadnezzar had removed* [a] *from Jerusalem and which he had put in the temple of his god.* [8] *Cyrus, king of Persia, handed them over to Mithredath* [a] *the treasurer,* [b] *who then delivered them with an inventory* [c] *to Sheshbazzar,* [d] *the prince of Judah.*

[9] *And this was the inventory:*

golden dishes [a]	*30*
silver dishes	*1,000*
(of which) duplicates [b]	*29*
[10] *golden bowls*	*30*
silver bowls	*. . .* [a]
(of which) duplicates [b]	*410*
other vessels	*1,000*
[11] *total of silver and golden vessels*	*5,400.*

Sheshbazzar brought them all up at the time when the exiles were brought up from Babylon to Jerusalem.

Notes

1.a. MT starts with the conj *and.* This is common for narrative books of the OT, though, except in the case of ויהי, there is generally the suggestion of a close association with what precedes.

1.b. For the construction, cf. GKC § 134o–p and Dan 9:1, 2; 11:1.

1.c. מפי "from the mouth of"; 2 Chr 36:22 has בפי "in the mouth of." Both are common, with no appreciable difference in meaning. The text in Chr is probably secondary, the בפי of v 21 having influenced the textual transmission.

1.d. וגם במכתב "and also in writing" is loosely attached. The emphasis falls on the oral proclamation, with this as a parenthetical afterthought.

2.a. The use of עלי favors this translation rather than "appointed me" (NIV, Myers, etc.); see also In der Smitten, *Persica* 6 (1972–74) 170.

3.a. Or "Whoever is among you . . ." (RSV, etc.). However, a direct question suits better the heraldic form of address (LXX; Bowman).

3.b. Probably intended in a pagan sense (see below). For this reason, 2 Chr 36:23 substituted יהוה "Yahweh" for יהי "may he be."

3.c. The jussives יעל and יבן may express permission rather than a strict command; cf. Driver, *Tenses,* 54–55, and Bewer, 11.

4.a. Collective sg. See further under *Comment.* Several emendations have been proposed, e.g., by Bewer, 12 (השב "who returns"), and Ginsberg, *JBL* 79 (1960) 167–69 (וכל הנושא, a mistaken translation into Hebrew of a conjectured Aram. original: וכל די יטל "And anyone who sets out"). However, since neither proposal enjoys textual support (on Bewer, see Rudolph), and since good sense can be made of MT, it is preferable to avoid emendation.

4.b. מכל המקמות "from all the places": legal terminology; cf. Bickerman, "Edict," 86, and Ezra 8:17.

4.c. For the piel of נשא with this meaning, cf. 1 Kgs 9:11; Esth 9:3; Ezra 8:36. Goldman's conjecture (*AusBR* 1 [1951] 58) that it means "to impose a levy" is without parallel and rests on a probable misunderstanding of the earlier part of the verse.

4.d. MT here has אַנְשֵׁי מְקֹמוֹ, "the men of his place." This is usually taken as the subj of the verb, with וְכֹל הַנִּשְׁאָר "and all who remained" as a *casus pendens* linked to the resumptive verbal suff in יְנַשְּׂאוּהוּ: "And whosoever is left, in any place where he sojourneth, let the men of his place help him" (rv). This leads to difficulties in interpretation, however; cf. *Comment.* While the sense advocated by Bickerman, "Edict," 83–87 (and supported by 1 Esdr and Vg), is preferable, his grammatical analysis, though correct as an explanation of MT, is too cumbersome to carry conviction. I suggest that אַנְשֵׁי מְקֹמוֹ "men of his place" be regarded as either an explanatory gl or as a "double reading" for the whole of the earlier phrase; for the phenomenon in general, cf. S. Talmon, "Double Readings in the Massoretic Text," *Textus* 1 (1960) 144–84. As often with legal jargon, the opening phrase of the verse is cumbersome and not readily intelligible. אַנְשֵׁי מְקֹמוֹ may therefore have originally served as a layman's equivalent for וְכֹל־הַנִּשְׁאָר מִכָּל הַמְּקֹמוֹת אֲשֶׁר הוּא גָר שָׁם the preceding part of the verse. Alternatively, the similarity between the consonants of נִשְׁאָר "were left" and אַנְשֵׁי "men of" with מְקוֹם "place" following in each case suggests the possibility of the one arising as a misreading of the other. Either way, it is clear that for reasons of scribal caution both synonymous readings came to be preserved within a single text. For a fuller defense of this rendering, cf. *JTS* ns 34 (1983) 9–11.

5.a. לְכֹל "even all" is used regularly in late biblical Heb. with this resumptive force; cf. BDB, 514b and GKC § 143e. For an alternative explanation (לְ = Arabic *la*, "verily"), cf. P. Haupt, "A New Hebrew Particle," *Johns Hopkins University Circulars* 13 (1894) 107–8.

6.a. This is the only occurrence of the piel of חֹזֵק + בְּ with this sense. Normally the piel governs an accus while the hiph may be followed by בְּ = "sustain." This may, therefore, represent a mixed form, or else it is the result of scribal error (delete בְּ); cf. Torrey, *Ezra Studies*, 122.

6.b. Despite 1 Esdr which suggests reading בַּכֹּל בַּכֶּסֶף "with gifts of every kind, silver" etc. (neb and many moderns), and despite the fact that this emendation would bring the text closer to the list in v 4, MT should be retained as one of several intentional allusions in this passage to the Exodus; see *Comment.*

6.c. לְבַד, meaning "besides," is always followed by מִן, never עַל as here. Read לָרֹב "in abundance" with 1 Esdr.

6.d. Inf constr used as a noun; cf. König, *Syntax* § 233a.

7.a. LXX, 1 Esdr and Vg all translate the two occurrences of הוֹצִיא "brought out" with different words. While the meaning is not affected, this is stylistically preferable. Perhaps read הֵבִיא "brought out."

8.a. A very common Persian name; cf. F. Justi, *Iranisches Namenbuch* (Marburg: Elwert, 1895), 209–13.

8.b. A loan-word. Though not yet attested in Old Persian, its existence is conjectured with certainty on the basis of derived languages; cf. *AD*, 77, n. 2; M. Ellenbogen, *Foreign Words*, 55.

8.c. Lit., "counted them out to." In view of the semitechnical use of מִסְפָּר in the next verse, "send" is less probable, *contra* L. Kopf, "Arabische Etymologien und Parallelen zum Bibel-wörterbuch," *VT* 9 (1959) 268.

8.d. A Babylonian name, *šaššu-aba-uṣur* (= may *šaššu* [*šamaš*, the sun-god] protect the father); cf. Berger, *ZAW* 83 (1971) 98–100, and Dion, *ZAW* 95 (1983) 111–12. Despite the many ways in which this is transmitted in the Greek versions (cf. Torrey, *Ezra Studies*, 136–38), there can be no question of an identification with the Shenazzar of 1 Chr 3:18, as suggested by Meyer, *Entstehung*, 76–77, and many others since.

9.a. The word occurs only in this passage. Its form (five root consonants) points strongly to its being a loan-word, though no certain etymology has been proposed. Earlier, unsatisfactory suggestions were discussed by Ellenbogen, *Foreign Words*, 9–11, and Galling, *Studien*, 82. That it should derive directly from Gr. κάρταλλος, "basket," seems improbable in view of the sense required by the context. More likely, both Heb. and Gr. words, together with equivalents in later Aram. dialects, derived independently from a common original. The Vrs render variously, suggesting that no common tradition of its meaning survived. While many modern translations render "dishes," this is no more than a guess: the shape of the vessels remains unknown.

9.b. מַחֲלָפִים: again uncertain. It has traditionally been translated "knives" (חֲלָף = "pierce"), following Vg, *cultri*, but this is etymologically improbable and inappropriate to the context. The most influential alternative proposals out of many are by (1) Bewer, 15–16, who joins the initial מ to the previous word to read אֲלָפִים "2,000," and deletes the remaining חֲלָפִים as a dittogr; (2) Rudolph, who repoints as a hoph ptcp. מָחֳלָפִים. He regards this as a marginal gloss, meaning "to be changed." It was originally a comment on the number by a scribe who had observed that the total in v 11 did not agree with the individual figures. Rudolph similarly reads מְשֻׁנִּים (pual ptcp "to be changed") for משנים in v 10. The difficulty with his view is the improbability of two different words being used for the same kind of comment in the same passage; (3) Galling, *Studien*, 83–85. He adopts the same pointing as Rudolph, but understands the first as "to which repairs had been undertaken" (by replacing damaged sections) and the second as "damaged." It would be extremely odd, however, if only the silver dishes had been repaired (Galling refers the repair to their condition before their capture by the Babylonians) and if only the silver bowls had been damaged during storage. Thus no proposal carries conviction. It therefore seems most prudent to stay close to MT, with the full recognition of its possible corr nature. NEB attempts to do this with its "vessels of various kinds," but this too is anomalous since we would then expect them to be included with the "other vessels" at the end of the list. For further considerations based on the structure of the list, see *Form/Structure/Setting*.

10.a. The structure of the list suggests that a numeral has dropped out, probably אלף "1,000" by homoiotel after כסף "silver."

10.b. See 9.b. above.

Form/Structure/Setting

For this introductory chapter to his work the author had available two items of earlier material, the decree of Cyrus (vv 2–4) and the inventory of temple vessels (vv 9–11a). These provided him with sufficient information to construct the rest of his narrative. In doing so, he also made plain his theological interpretation of his sources.

At first sight it appears that another version of the decree of Cyrus has been preserved at 6:3–5. In fact, however, they are quite distinct both in form and content. Whereas the latter is an official, written memorandum (see the commentary *ad loc.*), the present decree is presented as a message in oral form; cf. C. Westermann, *Basic Forms of Prophetic Speech*, tr. H. C. White (London: Lutterworth, 1967), 100–115. As is usual with this form, it is introduced by the messenger formula, "Thus says . . . ," continues with a report in the perfect tense describing the present, new situation (v 2), and concludes with an imperative section which offers the choice of decision to the one addressed (vv 3–4). There are many examples of this form both in the OT and elsewhere, e.g., Gen 45:9; Num 22:4b–6; 2 Kgs 19:3–4. It is worth observing that hardly ever do they include within the message a note of the person addressed; it is thus not surprising to find this element lacking here too, *contra* Galling, *Studien*, 66.

Needless to say, a message is normally intended for an individual or single group of people. Here, however, the narrator has introduced it (v 1) as a royal proclamation announced, presumably by heralds, over a wide area. That this was a common practice in the ancient world is certain; cf. Bickerman, "Edict," 74–76. We have much less knowledge, however, of the nature of such proclamations (Bickerman's attempt, p. 108, to relate the form of the decree of Cyrus to the Roman *edictum* being unconvincing), since they are usually reported only indirectly, e.g., 2 Chr 24:9; Ezra 10:7. Where the content is recorded, however, it includes imperative material alone; cf. Exod 36:6; Neh 8:15; Dan 3:4–6. (2 Chr 30:5–9 is not comparable, since here the Chronicler has merely put a Levitical sermon into the mouths of the king's messengers.) Lack of sufficient comparative data forbids dogmatism at this point, but it looks on this basis as though what was originally intended as a moderately localized announcement, probably to the leaders of the Jewish community, has been expanded into a more universal proclamation by the new setting in which the narrator has placed it with his composition of v 1.

Next, it must be emphasized as a further and certain conclusion of the analysis of the decree as a "message" that it ties together inseparably the authorizations both to return to Jerusalem and to rebuild the temple. It is because God has commanded Cyrus to rebuild the temple (v 2; see *Comment* for the nature of this language) that he authorizes the exiles' return (juss). This further sets the decree apart from the memorandum of 6:3–5, for not only is there no reference to the return in the memorandum, but the authorization to rebuild is tied to the specifications of the structure and the provision of the costs from public funds. Finally, we should note that whereas in 6:3–5 there is mention of the temple vessels, in the present chapter they are not referred to in the decree at all, but are the subject of a quite separate paragraph.

It is thus difficult to see, on the basis of form and content, how the decree of 1:2–4 could have been written up by the narrator solely on the basis of 6:3–5. Moreover, we have already begun to observe a tension between the decree itself and its narrative setting, and this point will be further emphasized below. On these grounds, to which more will be added in the *Comment*, it begins to look as though the decree was part of the material that the narrator inherited.

There is much greater agreement among the commentators (cf. especially Rudolph and Galling) that the inventory of temple vessels is based on an authentic source. Clear indications of this come from the use of the Aram. כפור, "bowl," in v 10, and the uncertain loan-word and *h.l.* אגרטל "dish," in v 9, to say nothing of the confused condition of the list itself (see *Notes*). In addition, the use of the Persian loan-word גזבר, "treasurer," again a *h.l.*, suggests that v 8 contains the rewritten form of an introduction to the inventory, stating who handed over the vessels to whom, and probably when, while the unique absence of the definite article in כל־כלים, "all (the) vessels," v 11, points to the final sum having been also included. It is thus reasonable to conjecture that the list has been translated from Aramaic, the diplomatic language of the Persian empire, and that, as in similar instances known to us (e.g., the Arsames correspondence; cf. J. D. Whitehead, "Some Distinctive Features of the Language of the Aramaic Arsames Correspondence," *JNES* 37 [1978] 119–40), it included a fair sprinkling of words of Persian origin.

As to the form which this list took, there need be little doubt since we have a close parallel in *AramP* 61 and 63, even though both are badly damaged. It probably began, "Memorandum (זכרן)," followed by a summary statement that Mithredath the treasurer handed over certain vessels to Sheshbazzar, and then the date (cf. *AramP* 61:12). Thus *AramP* 61 starts: "Memorandum: cups of bronze . . . Ḥanan son of Haggai into the hand of (ליד) . . ." With the further help of Ezra 5:14, the narrator could without difficulty have composed vv 7–8 from such a heading (Galling, *Studien*, 80–81). The list itself would be set out with the items in a column on the right hand side and the figures, using numerical notations rather than words, on the left; cf. the illustration in E. Sachau, *Aramäische Papyrus und Ostraka aus einer jüdischen Militär-*

Kolonie zu Elephantine: Tafeln (Leipzig: Heinrich, 1911), plate 55, col. 2, and plate 53 (reverse). This may account for some of the confusion in the numbers of our present text. We may guess that the document concluded with the final summary, and that it was probably signed in the presence of witnesses.

The structure of the list also appears to be orderly, though Rudolph has conjectured, not unreasonably, that some items may have dropped out and that this explains the discrepancy in the numbers. (Alternatively, if the list is badly damaged, one might conjecture that some of the figures originally referred to weight rather than number, as in the comparable Num 7:84–86.) The main part of the list falls into two parallel halves: each starts with thirty gold items ("dishes" or "bowls") and continues then with their silver equivalent. This orderly progression leads to the conjecture that the missing number in v 10 should be 1,000, to balance that in v 9b. These round numbers therefore suggest that Cyrus may not have returned all the vessels at this time, *contra* Ackroyd, VTSup 23 (1972) 178, and Coggins. Then there follows in each half of the list the most puzzling element (see *Notes*), in which a word of uncertain meaning (but different in each case) is followed by a number (again different in each case) for which there is no obvious explanation, since they are not round numbers. Because the list continues again with a round number (1,000 "other vessels"), we are forced to conclude that the two anomalous items must refer in each case to some characteristic of a number of the vessels in the preceding item. The translation above gives "duplicates" only because it stays close to MT: it is unable to explain why different words are used. So, while our appreciation of the structure of the list is considerably advanced, its exact translation remains uncertain.

The remainder of the chapter (i.e., vv 1, 5–6, parts of 7–8 and 11b) may all be ascribed directly to our author. Using the information of his sources, he has composed not just a narrative framework for them, but also a highly charged theological interpretation of them. While the details must be reserved for the *Comment* below, it is appropriate to point out here that this brings the decree of vv 2–4 into some tension with its present context: note the observations on *Form* above regarding v 1, and the shift from v 4 to v 6 in the interests of presenting the return as a second Exodus. This provides a further indication of the independent origin of vv 2–4.

Comment

1 Because of the captivity of the Jews in Babylon, the biblical writer reckons "the first year of Cyrus" from the time when he entered that city in triumph, October of 539 B.C. His "proclamation" would then probably have been issued in 538 B.C. In fact, however, this event marked the climax, not the start, of the astonishingly rapid rise to dominance over the Near East by Cyrus, who only twenty years previously had begun to reign as a vassal king to the Mede Astyages. The course of his conquests and their immediate aftereffects have been frequently chronicled. Primary sources include the Histories of Herodotus, the Nabonidus Chronicle (*ANET*, 305–7), the "Verse Account of Nabonidus" (*ANET*, 312–15), and the "Cyrus Cylinder" (*ANET*, 315–16); the last-named must now be supplemented by Berger, *ZA* 64 (1975)

192–234, which includes a newly discovered fragment of the text (lines 36–45) as well as a fresh edition of the remainder. For secondary accounts, cf. G. Widengren, "Persian Period," 515–20, and *Peoples of Old Testament Times,* ed. D. J. Wiseman (Oxford: Clarendon Press, 1973), 315–20; fuller treatments include Olmstead, *History,* 34–85; M. E. L. Mallowan, "Cyrus the Great," *Iran* 10 (1972) 1–17; D. Stronach, *Pasargadae* (Oxford: Clarendon Press, 1978), 283–95; Cook, *Persian Empire,* 25–43; and various articles in *Acta Iranica,* 1ère Série, 1–3 (1974).

Thus "king of Persia" must be understood simply as a title for identification, as regularly given with the Achaemenid kings in these books, and not as indicating that his proclamation is to be dated to the start of his reign in general. It may be noted that he is already referred to under this title in the Nabonidus Chronicle (2:15) and that he and some of his successors are so styled by various Greek authors writing still within the Persian period (Wilson, *PTR* 15 [1917] 90–145); see further on v 2.

The biblical writer, however, is concerned not merely with the external facts of history, which he may have derived from the heading or other note of identification on the copy of the decree itself, or, indeed, from the decree of 6:3; rather he is concerned with their divine ordering and purpose. Thus he notes that to the eye of faith Cyrus's move took place "in order that the word of the Lord spoken by Jeremiah might be fulfilled." "The word" has been generally misunderstood by commentators as a reference to such passages as Jer 25:11–12 and 29:10 that look forward in a general way to the fall of Babylon and the end of the exile. This interpretation is far too generalized, however, and probably owes its origin to the comparable 2 Chr 36:21. (Note that there the reference to "seventy years" makes the link with the Jeremiah passages explicit.) What the present context clearly demands is a passage predicting that the Lord would stir up the spirit of Cyrus (העיר את־רוח כרש) in such a way that he would order the rebuilding of the temple and the return of the exiles.

This has understandably led a few commentators (e.g., Siegfried and Batten) to cite a number of passages from Deutero-Isaiah in this connection; striking parallels are found in the following:

Isa 41:2   "Who stirred up (העיר) one from the east
      whom victory meets at every step? . . ."
      (This is commonly understood as an allusion to Cyrus.)
Isa 41:25 "I stirred up (העירותי) one from the north,
      and he has come. . . ."
Isa 44:28 ". . . who says of Cyrus, 'He is my shepherd,
      and he shall fulfill all my purpose';
      saying of Jerusalem, 'She shall be built,'
      and of the temple, 'Your foundation shall be laid.' "
Isa 45:1 "Thus says the Lord to his anointed, to Cyrus, . . ."

Perhaps most striking of all in this regard is Isa 45:13:

"I have aroused him (העירתהו) in righteousness,
    and I will make straight all his ways;

> he shall build my city
> and set my exiles free. . . ."

It is difficult not to suppose that the writer of Ezra indeed had such passages in the forefront of his mind, so close is their language and content to that which he is describing as the fulfillment of prophecy.

The usual explanations of why this is attributed to Jeremiah are, however, unconvincing. The suggestion that the problem is purely textual (read "Isaiah" for "Jeremiah") lacks any external evidence whatever. Equally, the idea that Isa 40–55, being an exilic composition, originally circulated independently and was in some circles attributed to Jeremiah (cf. B. Duhm, *Das Buch Jeremia* [Tübingen and Leipzig: Mohr, 1901] ix) must be judged improbable: the links between Isa 40–55 and 1–39 are being increasingly appreciated, and make it quite certain that the later chapters were always intended to accompany the earlier. We have no evidence that they were ever transmitted in isolation.

At this point, a different passage from Jeremiah should also be drawn into the discussion. Jer 51 is a highly poetical prediction of the fall of Babylon which has a number of close links with the Isaianic tradition. Note, for instance, the characteristic title, "The Holy One of Israel," in v 5, and cf. S. Erlandsson, *The Burden of Babylon* (Lund: CWK Gleerup, 1970) 154–59. Its opening verse (and cf. 50:9), possibly echoing Isa 13:17, states "Behold, I will stir up (מעיר) the spirit of a destroyer against Babylon," and this is further explained by a later prose addition which interrupts its present context in v 11: "The Lord has stirred up the spirit of (העיר יהוה את־רוח) the kings [LXX: king] of the Medes, because his purpose concerning Babylon is to destroy it, for that is the vengeance of the Lord, the vengeance for his temple." It is this prediction, we may suggest, that our author sees as being fulfilled in the events he is describing, and from it he drew the language with which he phrased his conviction. However, because of the catchword העיר ("stir up") and the explicit reference to Cyrus, he would have expected his readers to interpret the negative prophecy of Jer 51 in the light of the positive statements of Isa 41, 44, and 45: God's whole purpose in raising up Cyrus to destroy Babylon was to assure that the temple in Jerusalem might be rebuilt and the exiles returned to their homeland. In this way our writer, no less than the prophet of Isa 40–55, brings the whole of Cyrus's rise into subservience to God's will for his exiled people.

"He issued a proclamation throughout his kingdom": cf. *Form* above for OT parallels and the view that by this phrase the writer has, as part of his theological interpretation of his primary sources, universalized an originally local announcement.

"(It was also written down)": in itself, this statement is not at all surprising. It was quite usual in the ancient world for oral messages to be backed up by written documents, as the OT itself makes clear; cf. 2 Kgs 19:9–14; 2 Chr 17:9; 30:1. (The question of the historicity of the passages in Chronicles is irrelevant here; it is sufficient to observe that the Chronicler expected matters to be conducted in this way.) Moreover, the word מכתב "writing" is generally used elsewhere for the authoritative written form of something that the context shows was also orally proclaimed; cf. Exod 32:16; Deut 10:4; Isa 38:9; 2 Chr 35:4 with reference back to 8:14; and possibly 2 Chr 21:12

(note the introductory "Thus saith the Lord"). The only exception, then, is Exod 29:30. This appears also to have been the rule outside Israel; cf. Bickerman, "Edict," 105–8, and K. A. Kitchen, *Ancient Orient and Old Testament* (London: Tyndale Press, 1966), 135–38. *AramP* 32 provides a particularly striking parallel.

Less likely is the suggestion of Bickerman (and cf. Myers) that the reference is to the decree being publicly placarded for all to read, for, as noted above, it was originally addressed to a more restricted audience. By this word the author has, rather, left a syntactically loosely related (and hence parenthetical) allusion to the written source he was following.

2 כה אמר כרש (literally, "Thus has Cyrus said") is the standard formula for introducing a message in both secular and religious contexts. While its equivalent is frequent too in the Old Persian edicts of the Achaemenid kings (cf. R. G. Kent, *Old Persian,* 107–63), these are all rather historical reports, lacking the imperative section of the message.

The title "king of Persia" is surprising in the present context. While it was noted above that this is attested (occasionally) in a narrative context, there is no evidence that Cyrus ever used this title of himself. Nor do I know of anything beyond wishful thinking to support Tadmor's surmise ("Background," 468) that it continued to be used as a popular, oral title for Cyrus after the capture of Babylon. Of the other Achaemenid kings, it is used by Darius in the Behistun inscription for particular reasons (but even there not on its own, as here), and once by Xerxes. (The apparent use of the title by Cambyses in his message to the Ethiopians, Herodotus III:21, cannot be admitted here, both because it is not firsthand evidence, and because it is included in a third-person, not a first-person, message.) It is noteworthy in this connection that in the remainder of Ezra the title is used only by the narrator, never in the documents from which he cites. In respect to this particular verse, therefore, Gray's conclusions (*ExpTim* 25 [1913–14] 245–51) have not been overthrown by Wilson's reply (*PTR* 15 [1917] 90–145). The word פרס "of Persia" must therefore be attributed to a (probably unconscious) addition by the narrator.

Difficulty has also been felt with the titles for God in this decree: "The Lord (Yahweh)," "the God of heaven," and "the God of Israel." How could Cyrus have known these titles, and is it likely in any case that he would have attributed his victories to this God? In answer to the first question, it may be suggested that the decree is a response to a petition by the Jews, and that it follows the language of the petition quite closely in these particulars. At any rate, this is certainly the case in other similar circumstances; cf. *AramP* 32, which authorizes the Jews to rebuild their temple and maintain its cult following its destruction by the Egyptians, all in reply to *AramP* 30, as analyzed by B. Porten, *H. L. Ginsberg Volume, EI* 14 (1978) 165–77, and the Xanthos trilingual inscription, on which a petition in Greek and Lycian for permission to establish and maintain a new cult is answered by the Satrap's favorable reply in Aramaic; cf. A. Dupont-Sommer, *CRAIBL* (1974) 132–49, and J. Teixidor, "The Aramaic Text in the Trilingual Stele from Xanthus," *JNES* 37 (1978) 181–85. Thus it seems that part of the language of the decree is itself of Jewish origin.

As to the second question posed above, it need only be noted that it was consistent Achaemenid policy (in contrast with that of the preceding empires) to use the title of the god or gods recognized by the local population, but that this does not in any way imply that they themselves were "converted" to these religions from their own worship of Ahura Mazda; cf. Bickerman, "Edict," 79–80 and 91–98, Boyce, *History*, 62–66, and de Vaux, "Decrees," 64–79. The best-known example of this is the Cyrus Cylinder, in which Cyrus elaborately attributes his victories to Marduk, the Babylonian god: e.g., he "declared him to be(come) the ruler of all the world" . . . "whose rule Bel and Nebo love, whom they want as king to please their hearts." Indeed, Cyrus here goes so far as to call himself a worshiper of "Marduk, the great Lord." Yet at Ur Cyrus can equally say that "The great gods have delivered all the lands into my hand"; cf. C. J. Gadd and L. Legrain, No. 194 *Ur Excavation Texts 1: Royal Inscriptions* (London: British Museum, 1928) 58, while from the temple of Sin in the very same city comes a broken foundation cylinder with an inscription probably by Cyrus, reading "Sin, the Nannar [illuminator?] of heaven and earth, with his favourable omen delivered into my hands the four quarters of the world. I returned the gods to their shrines" (ibid. no. 307, p. 96; for further examples, cf. de Vaux, "Decrees"). So close is the outlook and even the wording of these texts to our present verse that the latter takes its place quite naturally among them.

The title "The God of heaven" makes its first appearance here as a description for the God of the Bible. Quite common among Israel's neighbors in the pre-exilic period, it now evidently became acceptable in Jewish circles too (cf. the Elephantine Papyri; Ezra 5:12; 6:9–10; Neh 1:4–5; 2:4, 20, etc.). Bowman speculates that "since Ormazd, the Persian god, was a celestial god, portrayed with a winged sun-disk in the heavens and acknowledged as creator of heaven and earth, the epithet may have been adopted by the Persians for their god and then popularized as one that was inoffensive and acceptable to most of the subject peoples." This theory is developed further by D. K. Andrews, "Yahweh the God of the Heavens," in W. S. McCullough, ed., *The Seed of Wisdom* (Toronto: University of Toronto Press, 1964), 45–57. He sees the use of the title here both as a claim by the Jewish petitioners that the cult of their God should be recognized by the Persians, and so qualify for support, and as an acceptance of this claim by the Persian authorities. The title is thus to be seen as a product of administrative terminology by which the deities of subject peoples might be tested for their relation to Ahura Mazda. It is certainly noteworthy that its use in the OT is largely confined to points of official contact between Jews and Persians.

"Jerusalem, which is in Judah": this is typical bureaucratic pendantry; cf. Hensley, *Documents*, 213–14. The objection that no such province as Judah existed before the time of Darius, or even Artaxerxes I (Galling, *Studien*, 71, following A. Alt, "Die Rolle Samarias bei der Entstehung des Judentums," *KS* II, 316–37), is misplaced. "Judah" need not necessarily be identified with the later province "Yehud"; it could be purely geographical, or a continuation of the earlier political name. Equally, however, there is no positive evidence available to deny that Judah was constituted a province from the earliest days of Persian rule; see on Neh 5:14.

3 "Who is there among you of all his people?": this phrase has frequently been said to reflect the election tradition of the OT to the point where it would be impossible in a genuine decree of Cyrus (cf. Galling, *Studien,* 72–73). This may perhaps be true of the word "all," which is unnecessary in the present context, and yet which imparts an allusion to such heavily ideological phrases elsewhere in the OT as "all Israel." (Note that its equivalent is lacking in 1 Esdr.) Even this, however, could be explicable if the decree is citing a petition drafted by the Jews themselves. Either way, it is highly unlikely, either historically or on the basis of the ideological outlook of the writer, that any reference is intended to the lost tribes of the old Northern Kingdom of Israel (*contra* Rudolph and Myers). For the remainder, however, there is no problem at all (cf. Bickerman, "Edict," 82). Such language was common throughout the Ancient Near East (cf. M. Smith, *JBL* 71 [1952] 141; e.g., in the Cyrus Cylinder Marduk is described as "a protector of his people"), and it is difficult to see what else might stand in its place here. Only on the prior assumption that the decree is to be attributed to the narrator does the argument carry any weight.

"May his god be with him!'": as Bickerman, "Edict," 81–82, and Bowman have seen, the roots of this phrase are pagan, the deity being understood as the attendant spirit of the individual. Note how it has been changed into the harmless, regular greeting formula in 2 Chr 36:23. In fact, of course, the Jews had no "gods" (in the form of images) to take back with them to their restored sanctuary, unlike the other peoples whom Cyrus reinstated. See further below. This too favors the originality of the decree.

"Let him go up to Jerusalem": the permission (rather than command; cf. *Notes*) to return is necessary in the present context but irrelevant in the decree of 6:3–5. Nothing points up better the completely different purpose each served. The extreme historical scepticism that formerly attended the whole idea of a return at all (cf. especially Torrey) is now almost entirely set aside; cf. Mayer, *BZ* N.F. 12 (1968) 1–16. It is known not to be unique, for Cyrus tells us with regard to certain towns in or near Babylonia that "I (also) gathered all their (former) inhabitants and returned (to them) their habitations" (Cyrus Cylinder; cf. *ANET,* 316. For other, more remote parallels, cf. Halevi, "Investigations").

It is important not to overpress the evidence of this text. In a significant study, Kuhrt, *JSOT* 25 (1983) 83–97, has shown that it is composed in accordance with traditional Mesopotamian royal building texts, that it relates exclusively to the fortunes of Babylon and, by extension, to the Babylonian pantheon, and that it does not speak of the restoration of destroyed cult centers. This latter point needs emphasis in view of the English translation in *ANET,* "the sanctuaries of which have been ruins for a long time." However, in a personal communication of 7 November 1983, J. N. Postgate has commented as follows on the contentious phrase *ša ištu panā-ma nadû šubatsun:* "I see two possible translations: (a) 'whose settlements had been established of old' and (b) 'whose settlements had previously been abandoned.' Two things seem certain: 1) that he does *not* say the cities had been destroyed (or the temples), and 2) that the events meant by *nadû* took place some while ago, not immediately before Cyrus' accession." From this we must conclude that the Cyrus Cylinder makes no reference to a general return of displaced people, among whom the Jews could have been included, and that even the parallel with the biblical text, though valuable as far as it goes (cf. Berger, *ZA* 64 [1975] 219), is not as close as has frequently been claimed. Furthermore, Kuhrt has also shown that Cyrus's acts were not as unprecedented as is often thought, and that his policy was sometimes reversed when necessary.

These reservations suggest that we must rely primarily on the biblical evidence for any historical reconstruction and admit only that the Cyrus Cylinder is compatible with a positive evaluation of this evidence. Fortunately, the suggestion that there was a repatriation of the Jews receives substantial support both from the tensions it evoked within the post-exilic community and which are attested in a wide variety of texts, and from archaeological indications (cf. Vogt, *Studie*, 13–18). Moreover, it fits well with what can be reconstructed of early Achaemenid policy in terms of defensive building in the Levant generally; cf. M. Dunand, "La défense du front mediterranéen de l'empire achéménide," in W. A. Ward (ed.), *The Role of the Phoenicians in the Interaction of Mediterranean Civilizations* (Beirut: American University, 1968) 43–51. Such a return would naturally have required permission, and this is recorded here and nowhere else. A single, united return need not have been envisaged, and it is likely that it extended over a number of years (cf. *Form*, Ezra 2:1–70). As with the authorization to "build the temple of the Lord" (cf. Ezra 5–6), so with the permission to return; the force of the decree can have extended over a number of years without needing to be repeated.

"Which is in Judah . . . that is to say, the god who is in Jerusalem." See on "Jerusalem, which is in Judah" in v 2. Precise parallels occur once more in the Elephantine Papyri.

4 "Those who remain behind." While it is true that נשאר can carry the technical sense of "remnant," not least in the books of Ezra and Nehemiah, this is by no means its only or inevitable meaning. It never has this meaning when it stands alone, as here (contrast, for instance, Neh 1:3), and if it did, the progression of thought from v 3 to v 4 would be harsh. It more frequently bears the quite neutral meaning of "the rest, remainder; that which remains after a part has been removed"; cf. H. Wildberger, *THAT* II, 844–55. This most naturally suggests that those referred to should be closely related to those who are going, that is to say, Jews. (This seems more probable in the context than "survivor," RSV, i.e., "those who had escaped from the sword" in 2 Chr 36:20.) Moreover, once it is realized that אנשי מקמו "the men of his place" is either a gloss or a double reading (see *Notes*), it immediately becomes clear that those referred to are the subject of the sentence; the widespread view that some of the Jews were too poor to go, but that after receiving aid from their neighbors they too joined the return, is thus ruled out. The meaning of the passage is clear: not all Jews by any means wanted to return. They were therefore encouraged to assist those who did. At no point is a reference to their Gentile neighbors either necessary or historically credible (though see on v 6 below). That view has been incorporated into several translations of the passage and many commentaries on it, either by a misunderstanding of the text or by a desire to justify the prior assumption that this cannot be an essentially accurate copy of a genuine decree.

"Who belong to any of the places where he is living." Not only in the case of the Jews in exile in Babylon, but throughout the Ancient Near East there are examples of displaced peoples preserving their original identity in groups for considerable periods of time (Bickerman, "Edict," 86–91). This phrase does no more than make explicit (albeit by means of a rather involved construction, not unparalleled in legal documents) that each "colony" of Jews should support any from their own group who might be undertaking the return. גר "sojourn" need not carry theological overtones any more than נשא in the previous phrase.

"Goods." This word (רכוש) can also refer to animals. If that were so here, they would have to be pack-animals for the journey (cf. NEB mg), since בהמה, "livestock," always means "domesticated animals," namely flocks and herds. Where רכוש refers to animals, however, this latter is usually also its meaning. It thus seems best to retain the more general, but equally well attested, translation "goods" in the present context.

"Freewill offerings for the house of God." Cyrus's permission for Jews to return no doubt implied a measure of guaranteed safe conduct for the journey (cf. Neh 2:7–9 and the implication of Ezra 8:22). Those remaining need therefore feel no qualms about sending gifts toward the restoration of the temple, and Cyrus, whose treasury was also bearing part of the expense (6:3–5), would have been anxious to encourage such support. The exact phrasing, however, will again have originated with the Jews themselves, נדבה "freewill offering" being a somewhat technical priestly term when used in such a context as this.

5 The language of this and the following verse is so close to that of vv 2–4 that there can be no doubt that the narrator, knowing from his source in chap. 2 that a number of Jews did return, simply wrote up their response on the basis of the decree itself. The verses, the only ones that suggest an immediate and united return, do not therefore have the value of an independent historical account. Their importance lies in their interpretation of the events rather than in the narrative detail. That events stretching over a number of years should be compressed into a single account is not unusual in biblical historical writing. What mattered to the author was that, in response to God's prompting, a number did return. In the divine economy this may be regarded as a single event, even if the secular historian suggests that it was spread over a number of years (cf. Ezra 2:1–70, *Form/Structure/Setting*).

The returning group, as often in Ezra-Nehemiah, is divided into the three classes of priests, Levites, and laity. For the latter stand "the heads of families" (ראשי האבות), a shortened form of "the heads of the fathers' houses" (ראשי בית האבות). This is the regular sociological division of the people in the Persian period, the "father's house" being an extended family standing between the larger tribe and the smaller family grouping, equivalent to the משפחה ("family") of the pre-exilic period; cf. J. P. Weinberg, "Das *beit ʾābōt* im 6.-4. v.u.Z.," *VT* 23 (1973) 400–14; H. G. Kippenberg, *Religion und Klassenbildung im antiken Judäa* (Göttingen: Vandenhoeck & Ruprecht, 1978) 23–41. Three tribes, Judah, Benjamin and Levi, are thus represented. This, again, is typical of the outlook of Ezra-Nehemiah, in which these three, being the continuation of the former southern kingdom of Judah, are regarded as the only true community. (Cf. Vogt, *Studie*. Chronicles offers a rather different picture. Contrast von Rad, *Geschichtsbild*, 18–37, with Williamson, *Israel*.)

"Even all whose spirit God had stirred up": the response, as much as the issuing of the decree itself (cf. the use of the same phrase in v 1), resulted from God's prompting rather than human opportunism. At the same time the narrator quietly introduces a theological explanation of why not all those in exile returned to Jerusalem.

6 "All their neighbors." This refers to Gentile neighbors. Had the writer intended fellow-Jews, he would have used a word like אחיהם "their brethren" (Rudolph, 220). That being the case, there is a clear shift between the text of the decree itself (cf. v 4) and the narrator's account of the response to it (a shift that provides strong evidence that the decree existed as an antecedent source). This is to be explained by his evident concern to present the return as a second Exodus. The motif of the "despoiling of the Egyptians" is quite prominent in the Exodus accounts (Exod 3:21–22; 11:2; 12:35–36; Ps 105:37); cf. G. W. Coats, *VT* 18 (1968) 450–57. While many other Exodus motifs are taken up in relation to the return, especially by Deutero-Isaiah (cf. B. W. Anderson, "Exodus Typology in Second Isaiah," in B. W. Anderson and W. Harrelson [eds.], *Israel's Prophetic Heritage* [London: SCM Press, 1962], 177–95), it appears that our author is the only one to reapply this particular element in typological terms. That he did so is confirmed by another slight change between the wording of the decree and its fulfillment, namely the addition of the word כלי "vessels." "Vessels of silver and vessels of gold" are referred to specifically in each of the three Exodus passages listed above. See further the paragraph immediately following, and vv 8 and 11.

7 While a source evidently underlies the description of the return of the temple vessels (see above), we need not doubt that this too has been included by the narrator in part because it furthered his Exodus typology. Already in his prophecy of the departure from Babylon, which includes several very striking allusions to the first Exodus (Isa 52:11–12), Deutero-Isaiah had introduced an additional reference to those who would be carrying with them "the vessels of the Lord." While not an overt part of the descriptions of the Exodus itself, it seems likely that this element had nevertheless come to be associated with it in the hopes for restoration, and that our author is pleased to be able to tell of its fulfillment.

Second, however, we should note another theme of importance that is introduced here, namely that of the continuity of religious life which these vessels symbolized; cf. Ackroyd, VTSup 23 (1972) 166–81, in particular. There is some confusion in the sources as to the precise fate of the temple vessels in the successive Babylonian invasions leading to the eventual destruction of the temple; cf. 2 Kgs 24:13; 25:13–15; 2 Chr 36:7, 10, and 18. Nonetheless, it need not be doubted that some were indeed carried away from Jerusalem by Nebuchadnezzar and "put in the temple of his god," for they would thus have taken the place in symbolic fashion of the images of the gods of other defeated peoples. Their deposit in the temple of the victor's god was intended to underline to their devotees the inability of their god to save. Moreover, the source underlying this very passage is important historical evidence to the same end.

In the case of some of his other subjects, Cyrus could state that with regard to a number of places "I returned to (these) sacred cities on the other side of the Tigris . . . the images which (used) to live therein. . . . Furthermore,

I resettled . . . all the gods of Sumer and Akkad whom Nabonidus has brought into Babylon" (*ANET*, 316). Again, this option was not possible in the case of the Jews, but we may assume that the returned vessels played much the same role. The continuity of the religious practice of the writer's day with that of earlier generations, whose deeds were regularly recited in the cult as exemplary, is being underlined.

8 For the development of the narrative from the written source in this verse, see above *Form*.

"Sheshbazzar, the prince of Judah": this title occurs nowhere else, and Sheshbazzar is himself at best a shadowy figure. He is referred to later in this paragraph (v 11) without further qualification, and at 5:14 and 16, where it is said that Cyrus had appointed him governor (פחה) and that he laid the foundations of the temple. With this may be compared the data relating to Zerubbabel, who is also called פחה (Hag 1:1), who also seems to have been involved in early work on the temple (Ezra 3), and who has also been held by many to have led the return under Cyrus (cf. 2:2).

These similarities have led a number of writers, both ancient and modern, to identify the two men. Josephus, who mainly follows 1 Esdr for his account of this period, apparently does so (cf. *Ant.* xi:13–14), and for a recent statement of the same view, cf. Bartel, *BMik* 79 (1979) 357–69; contrast Ben-Yashar, *BMik* 88 (1981) 46–56. This is an improbable hypothesis, however, for two reasons. First, the names tell strongly against it. This is not to deny the possibility, established with certainty in quite a number of other cases, that one individual was known by two names (e.g., Daniel–Belteshazzar), but rather to observe that in this case both names are Babylonian while at the same time the man is, *ex hypothesi*, a Jew. We could well understand a member of the royal line having both a Jewish and a Babylonian name, but it seems highly unlikely that he would have had two Babylonian names only.

Second, Ezra 5:14–16 seems clearly to distinguish the two, for Zerubbabel is present on that occasion, whereas Sheshbazzar is referred to as one unknown to Tattenai and not present at the incident. While it is true that in Aramaic (the language of that passage) people do sometimes speak of themselves in the third person for particular effect, that is not sufficient to explain the artificiality of the exchange in this particular case if the two are, in fact, the same.

Next, it must also be observed that there is no direct evidence for regarding Sheshbazzar as a member of the Judean royal family. The suggestion that he should be identified with the Shenazzar of 1 Chr 3:18 must now be abandoned (see *Notes*), while the designation "prince" by no means necessarily indicates royalty (cf. Gen 23:6; Exod 22:27 [28]; Lev 4:22; Num 1:16; Josh 9:15, etc.). He is not mentioned in the royal genealogy of 1 Chr 3, which appears to aim at comprehensiveness for the exilic and post-exilic periods. Finally, while it would not contradict Achaemenid policy to appoint as governor a member of the old ruling classes, there is no evidence that they necessarily did so in every case.

The title "prince of Judah" has never been satisfactorily explained, no suggestion having ever been able to account for its unique occurrence in this passage where a more regular term, such as "governor" (cf. 5:14), would

appear to serve equally well. (See most recently Japhet, *ZAW* 94 [1982] 66–
98. Our suggestion which follows is fully compatible with the main observations of her article.) Our earlier observations concerning the nature of the
author's composition in this chapter enable us to resolve the difficulty. With
his aim of presenting the return as a "second Exodus," his thoughts at this
point will have turned naturally to the account of the journey through the
wilderness, as recorded particularly in Numbers. There we find as a well-
known characteristic of the narrative that on several occasions there are lists
of those who were "princes" of the various tribes; cf. Num 2:3–31; 7:1–83;
34:18–28. Moreover, at Num 7:84–86 they are associated with a number of
gold and silver vessels given for the dedication of the altar, which may well
have attracted our author's attention in the context of his own comparable
source. We may suggest, therefore, that Sheshbazzar was quite simply the
first governor of Judah under the Persians, as is stated explicitly in chap. 5.
(The suggestion of Welch, *Post-Exilic Judaism,* 98–101, that he was governor
of the whole province "Beyond the River" is highly unlikely in view of the
fact that Ezra 5:14 presupposes that he was unknown to Tattenai who, according to this view, would have been his successor.) He never bore the title
"Prince of Judah," which would otherwise be quite without parallel. That
was simply a description of him supplied by our author, who wrote long
after the event, as part of his intention in this chapter of presenting various
aspects of the return as a second Exodus. He, therefore, regarded Sheshbazzar
as a prominent member of the tribe of Judah, and to this surmise there can
be no objection. It is well known that a number of Jews had Babylonian
names, and it would be in line with Achaemenid policy to appoint someone
who would command the respect of his people.

For several reasons, this explanation is to be preferred to that which links
the title "prince" with the prince of Ezek 40–48 (e.g., Rost, "Erwägungen,"
302). First, it is probable that the prince there is regarded as a Davidic figure,
as he certainly is in the earlier chapters of Ezek (7:27; 12:10, 12; 19:1; 21:30
[25]; 34:24; 37:25 and cf. 43:7, 9); cf. the full discussion in J. D. Levenson,
Theology of the Program of Restoration of Ezekiel 40–48 (Missoula, MT: Scholars
Press, 1976) 57–73. This rules out an identification with Sheshbazzar; contra
H. Gese, who goes so far as to argue that such an identification proves the
equation (which we now know to be impossible) of Sheshbazzar with Shenazzar; cf. *Der Verfassungsentwurf des Ezechiel* (Tübingen: Mohr, 1957), 118. Those
who drive the thickest wedge in this regard between Ezek 1–39 and 40–48
in fact attempt to relate the latter very closely to the P material in Numbers
and to date both rather later than the time of Sheshbazzar himself. Were
their position justified, it would still rule out the historical attribution of
this title to Sheshbazzar on the one hand, while on the other hand we must
assume that our author would, by his later date, have read the book of Ezekiel
as a unity. In that case he would not have appreciated this finer distinction
and, regarding the prince as Davidic in the light of chaps. 1–39, would then
probably not have used it as a title for Sheshbazzar.

Second, in Ezekiel the title "the prince" tends to be used in an absolute
sense, and so to be a pan-Israelite figure. In our passage, however, the title
is restricted by the addition "of Judah," which v 5 suggests should be inter-

preted as a tribe in the narrow sense. This too is far closer to the situation in Numbers, where each tribe has its own prince, than to Ezekiel.

Finally, whereas the influence of Ezek 40–48 would be completely isolated to this single expression, our suggestion makes it possible to integrate the title into a wider scheme of interpretation that runs throughout this chapter.

It only remains to add that the mysterious way in which Sheshbazzar disappears from the subsequent narrative need cause no surprise whatever; it is simply the result of the chronological distribution of the sources that were at our author's disposal. The fact is that no firsthand account of either the return or its immediate sequel was preserved. That Sheshbazzar led some kind of a return was deduced from the document underlying 5:14 and 16 and from the assumption that advantage was taken of the permission of 1:2–4 and the more particular details of 1:8*–11a. Beyond that, however, no account survived, since the remainder of the material all relates to Zerubbabel and his later activity. Thus we have absolutely no source on which to base a decision between the various guesses that have been advanced as to Sheshbazzar's fate: perhaps he died in Palestine between 538 and 520 B.C. (Bright, *History*, 366); perhaps he was removed from office either when Cambyses wished to strengthen this part of his empire for his offensive against Egypt or because he became caught up in the rash of rebellions that marked the accession of Darius to the throne (E. Sellin, *Geschichte des Israelitisch-Jüdischen Volkes*, II [Leipzig: Quelle und Meyer, 1932] 97); perhaps his initial commission was restricted to the moving and safe housing of the temple vessels in Jerusalem, and thereafter he returned home (Rudolph, 62). There is simply no evidence to tip the balance of probability one way or the other.

9–10 See the discussion above under *Notes* and *Form.*

11 The final sentence will again be a free composition by our author, who had no means of knowing that the return was not a single undertaking; see the discussion of chap. 2. The passive verb "were brought up" is deliberately chosen in order to imply divine activity. It thus echoes the descriptions of the Exodus in which, it may be noted, it is העלה ("bring up," as here) rather than הוציא ("bring out") which is followed by the "from . . . to" formula; cf. Gen 50:24; Exod 3:8, 17; 33:1 and J. Wijngaards, "הוציא and העלה, A Twofold Approach to the Exodus," *VT* 15 (1965) 91–102. The statement "brought up from Babylon to Jerusalem" thus becomes the counterpart of "brought up out of the land of Egypt, unto the land . . ." (Exod 33:1).

Explanation

The destruction of the Jerusalem temple in 587/6 B.C., the end of Davidic rule, and the exile of a large part of the population to Babylon were events of unprecedented significance in the development of the faith and the literature of the OT. Many and varying responses to them are recorded, and in their wake is to be traced the transition from the religion of Israel to that of Judaism. Initially, it is clear that the experience of judgment led to the sensation of disorientation and discontinuity, a radical break with the past.

By the time the books of Ezra and Nehemiah were composed, however, a measure of restoration had already been achieved. In contributing his narrative of this process to the task of theological reconstruction, our author evidently felt the need to emphasize the lines of continuity between the community of his own day and the history of the nation which had preceded it. The effects of judgment and discontinuity had been sufficiently assimilated; the need now was to encourage the faith of his readers by reminding them of the riches of their heritage and the legitimacy of their present institutions as vehicles through which that heritage could be mediated to them. This first chapter contributes to his purpose in three main ways.

Continuity is recognized first in the interpretation of the historical facts of the return as an act of the same Lord who had both permitted the exile as an instrument of judgment and prophesied that it would be of limited duration (cf. v 1). Both the decree of Cyrus and the obedience of some of the people (v 5) are alike presented as a response to the gracious promptings of the Lord in answer to his own promises through Jeremiah and Deutero-Isaiah.

This receives support, second, from the presentation of the return as a second Exodus. The evidence for this has been noted in the comments on vv 5, 6, 7, 8, and 11. The purpose of this typological pattern is to encourage the readers to interpret the return as an act of God's grace that can be compared in its significance with the very birth of the nation of Israel itself. There may have been a temptation to play down what had happened, and from a historical point of view it was probably a slow, drawn-out process. Yet typology opens the eye of faith to the hand of God behind the historical process, inviting an appreciation of his action in bringing his people to a point of rebirth no less wonderful than that which had been accomplished in the deliverance of Israel from the slavery of Egypt.

Third, within this overall patterning, the continuity of the instruments of the cult receives a particular emphasis. At the simplest level this was a means of demonstrating, in the absence of any image for God after the manner of most other nations, that the new temple at Jerusalem and its paraphernalia were indeed a restoration in direct, physical line with what had gone before, and not an innovation without historical roots. More significantly, as the people of that time made their response to God in worship at the temple, they were reminded in a direct manner that that very act was a testimony to the oneness of God and the unity of his people.

For the Christian faith, continuity rests less on the externals of religion and more on the "endless life" of our risen high priest (cf. Heb 7:16). Yet it is noteworthy that it is in the context of worship that the call comes to "remember me," and that the New Testament, too, repeatedly models our salvation on the pattern of the Exodus, demonstrating in a fuller way that the continuity of Israel and the Church is to be found in the God who has acted consistently in deliverance for both.

The List of the Exiles Who Returned
(Ezra 2:1-70)

Bibliography

Allrik, H. L. "1 Esdras According to Codex B and Codex A as Appearing in Zerubbabel's List in 1 Esdras 5:8–23." *ZAW* 66 (1954) 272–92. ———. "The Lists of Zerubbabel (Nehemiah 7 and Ezra 2) and the Hebrew Numeral Notation." *BASOR* 136 (1954) 21–27. **Cogan, M.** "The Men of Nebo—Repatriated Reubenites." *IEJ* 29 (1979) 37–39. **Galling, K.** "Die Liste der aus dem Exil Heimgekehrten." *Studien,* 89–108. (This is a revision of "The 'Gōlā-List' According to Ezra 2//Nehemiah 7." *JBL* 70 [1951] 149–58.) **Haran, M.** "The Gibeonites, the Nethinim and the Sons of Solomon's Servants." *VT* 11 (1961) 159–69. **Hervey, A. C.** "The Chronology of Ezra II. and IV. 6–23." *The Expositor* iv/7 (1893) 431–43. **In der Smitten, W. Th.** "Der Tirschātāʾ in Esra-Nehemia." *VT* 21 (1971) 618–20. **Japhet, S.** "Sheshbazzar and Zerubbabel." *ZAW* 94 (1982) 66–98; 95 (1983) 218–29. **Klein, R. W.** "Old Readings in 1 Esdras: The List of Returnees from Babylon (Ezra 2//Nehemiah 7)." *HTR* 62 (1969) 99–107. **Levine, B. A.** "The Netînîm." *JBL* 82 (1963) 207–12. **Meyer, E.** *Entstehung,* 94–102; 190–98. **Mowinckel, S.** *Studien I,* 29–45; 62–109. **Pohlmann, K.-F.** *Studien,* 57–64. **Schaeder, H. H.** *Esra,* 15–23; 29–30. **Schultz, C.** "The Political Tensions Reflected in Ezra-Nehemiah." In *Scripture in Context. Essays on the Comparative Method,* ed. C. D. Evans, W. W. Hallo, and J. B. White. Pittsburgh: The Pickwick Press, 1980. 221–44. **Sellin, E.** *Geschichte des israelitisch-jüdischen Volkes. Vol. 2. Vom babylonischen Exil bis zu Alexander dem Grossen.* Leipzig: Quelle & Meyer, 1932. 84–91. **Smend, R.** *Listen,* 15–23. **Theis, J.** *Geschichtliche und literarkritische Fragen in Esra 1–6.* Münster: Verlag der Aschendorffschen Buchhandlung, 1910. 60–67. **Thomson, A.** "An Inquiry Concerning the Books of Ezra and Nehemiah." *AJSL* 48 (1931–32) 99–132. **Torrey, C. C.** *Composition,* 39–42. **Weinberg, J. P.** "Demographische Notizen zur Geschichte der nachexilischen Gemeinde in Juda." *Klio* 54 (1972) 45–59. ———. "Nᵉtînîm und 'Söhne der Sklaven Salomos' in 6.-4. Jh. v. u. Z." *ZAW* 87 (1975) 355–71. **Welch, A. C.** *Post-Exilic Judaism,* 126–41. **Williamson, H. G. M.** "The Composition of Ezra i–vi." *JTS* ns 34 (1983) 1–30. **Zadok, R.** "Notes on the Biblical and Extra-Biblical Onomasticon." *JQR* 71 (1980) 107–17.

Translation

¹ These are the people of the province ᵃ who came up from the captivity of the exiles whom Nebuchadnezzar ᵇ king of Babylon had taken into exile to Babylon ᶜ and who returned to Jerusalem and Judah, each to his own town. ² They came with Zerubbabel, Jeshua, ᵃ Nehemiah, Seraiah, ᵇ Reelaiah, ᶜ [Nahamani],ᵈ Mordecai, Bilshan, Mispar, ᵉ Bigvai, Rehum (and) Baanah.
The list ᶠ of the men of the people of Israel:

³ The family ᵃ of Parosh	2,172
⁴ The family of Shephatiah	372
⁵ The family of Arah	775 ᵃ
⁶ The family of Pahath-Moab, ᵃ namely ᵇ the families of Jeshua and ᶜ Joab	2,812 ᵈ
⁷ The family of Elam	1,254
⁸ The family of Zattu	945 ᵃ

[9] The family of Zaccai	760
[10] The family of Bani [a]	642 [b]
[11] The family of Bebai	623 [a]
[12] The family of Azgad	1,222 [a]
[13] The family of Adonikam	666 [a]
[14] The family of Bigvai	2,056 [a]
[15] The family of Adin	454 [a]
[16] The family of Ater, that is, [a] of Hezekiah	98
[The family of Azzur	432
The family of Hodiah	101][b]
[17] The family of Bezai	323 [a]
[18] The family of Jorah [a]	112
[19] The family of Hashum	223 [a]
[20] The family of Gibbar [a]	95
[21] The men [a] of Bethlehem	123
[22] The men of Netophah	56 [a]
[23] The men of Anathoth	128
[24] The men [a] of (Beth-)Azmaveth [b]	42
[25] The men [a] of Kiriath-jearim, [b] Kephirah and Beeroth	743
[26] The men [a] of Ramah and Geba	621
[27] The men of Michmas	122
[28] The men of Bethel and Ai	223 [a]
[29] The inhabitants [a] of Nebo [b]	52
[30] The inhabitants of Magbish	156
[31] The inhabitants of the other Elam	1,254 [a]
[32] The inhabitants of Harim	320
[33] The inhabitants of Lod, Hadid and Ono	725 [a]
[34] The inhabitants of Jericho	345
[35] The inhabitants of Senaah	3,630 [a]

[36] The priests:

The family of Jedaiah, namely the house of Jeshua	973
[37] The family of Immer	1,052
[38] The family of Pashhur	1,247
[39] The family of Harim	1,017

[40] The Levites:

The families of Jeshua and Kadmiel, namely the family of Hodaviah [a]	74

[41] The singers:

The family of Asaph	128 [a]

[42] The gatekeepers: [a]

The family of Shallum, the family of Ater,
the family of Talmon, the family of Akkub,
the family of Hatita, the family of Shobai

	total:	139 [b]

[43] The temple servants:
The family of Ziha
The family of Hasupha
The family of Tabbaoth

44 *The family of Keros*
   The family of Sia [a]
   The family of Padon
45 *The family of Lebanah*
   The family of Hagabah
   The family of Akkub [a]
46 *The family of Hagab*
   The family of Salmai [a]
   The family of Hanan
47 *The family of Giddel* [a]
   The family of Gahar
   The family of Reaiah
48 *The family of Rezin*
   The family of Nekoda
   The family of Gazzam
49 *The family of Uzza*
   The family of Paseah
   The family of Besai
50 *The family of Asnah* [a]
   The family of the Meunim [b]
   The family of the Naphishim [c]
51 *The family of Bakbuk*
   The family of Hakupha
   The family of Harhur
52 *The family of Bazluth* [a]
   The family of Mehira [b]
   The family of Harsha
53 *The family of Barkos*
   The family of Sisera
   The family of Temah
54 *The family of Neziah*
   The family of Hatipha
55 *The sons of Solomon's servants:*
   The family of Sotai
   The family of Hassophereth [a]
   The family of Perudah [b]
56 *The family of Jaalah*
   The family of Darkon
   The family of Giddel [a]
57 *The family of Shephatiah*
   The family of Hattil
   The family of Pochereth-Hazzebaim [a]
   The family of Amon [b]
58 *Total of the temple servants and the sons of Solomon's servants:* 392
59 *The following came up from Tel-Melah, Tel-Harsha, Kerub, Addan, (and)* [a] *Immer, but they were unable to demonstrate that their family* [b] *or their descent were* [c] *of Israel:*
   60 *The family of Delaiah*

The family of Tobiah
The family of Nekoda   652 ª
61 And of ª the priests:
    The family of Hobaiah
    The family of Hakkoz
    The family of Barzillai. (The latter had married one of the daugh-
    ters of Barzillai the Gileadite and was called by his ᵇ name.)
  62 These searched for their registration (amongst) ª those who had been enrolled
by genealogy but they could not be found, so they were debarred from the priesthood
as unclean. ᵇ 63 And the governor ª ordered them not to eat of the most holy food ᵇ
until a priest should arise who could ᶜ consult Urim and Thummim.
  64 The whole assembly together   42,360
    65 (apart from their 7,337 menservants and maidservants; and they
    also had 200 ª men and women singers).
  66 Their horses   736
    Their mules   245
  67 Their camels   435
    Donkeys ª   6,720
  68 When ª they arrived at the temple of the Lord in Jerusalem, some of the heads
of families gave freewill offerings towards the rebuilding of the temple of God on its
original site. 69 According to their means they gave to the fund for this work 61,000
drachmas ª of gold, 5,000 minas of silver, and 100 priestly vestments. 70 The priests,
the Levites, some of the people, the singers, the gatekeepers, and the temple servants
settled in their own towns, and all (the rest of) Israel in their own towns. ª

Notes

    A parallel version of this list appears in Neh 7, though with a considerable number of differ-
ences, particularly with regard to the numbers. This is because of a random process of corruption
during the course of the later transmission of the text, perhaps largely in the use of numerical
notations; cf. Allrik, BASOR 136 (1954) 21-27. In many cases it is thus no longer possible to
determine which, if either, form of the text is original. In the translation presented here, therefore,
the MT is retained in such cases, with no attempt to reintroduce their original identity. In
view of such uncertainties, it has not seemed worthwhile generally to integrate into the discussion
an analysis of the Gr. Vrs, where considerable variations are also to be observed; for these, cf.
Bewer and Batten.

    1.a. For some etymological speculations, cf. M. Fraenkel, ZAW 70 (1958) 253-54 and 77
(1965) 215.
    1.b. So Q, which thus conforms the text to convention. As at Jer 49:28, K has נבוכדנצור
which, like the G Ναβουχοδονοσορ, is closer to the Babylonian ending -uṣur.
    1.c. Accidentally omitted at Neh 7:6 by parablepsis.
    2.a. The form ישוע "Jeshua" continues the contraction from יהושוע "Jehoshua" to ישוע
"Joshua." It is reflected also in the familiar G form Ἰησοῦς "Jesus."
    2.b. Neh 7:7 has עזריה "Azariah." Either is possible.
    2.c. Nehemiah has רעמיה "Raamiah." Neither name is attested elsewhere. Rudolph prefers
the form in Nehemiah since it can be construed ("The Lord has thundered"), though this is
not decisive.
    2.d. Lacking in MT, but supplied on the basis of Nehemiah. This brings the number of
leaders to twelve, a number supported by 1 Esdr.
    2.e. "Number," improbable as a personal name. Nehemiah has מספרת, a fem form "Misper-
eth." Possibilities include repointing as מְסַפֵּר "Mesapper" (Rudolph) or regarding it as a corr

of אספדת, "Aspadat," a Persian name, on the basis of 1 Esdr 5:8 Ασφαρασου "Aspharasou." Perhaps there has been some influence on MT from the מספר "list" four words later.

2.f. Lit., = "number," but this broader sense is supported by 1 Chr 11:11 and 25:1.

3.a. Lit. "sons of."

5.a. Neh 7:10 has 652. A peculiarity of MT is that only here does the units' figure precede that of the tens ("five and seventy"). If, therefore, the number was once 757, the difference is less difficult to explain, for it involves confusion over only one stroke in the notation for the hundreds and one for "five," both attested elsewhere in the list (cf. Allrik, *BASOR* 136 [1954] 21–27).

6.a. = "The governor of Moab," a family name which may derive from the united monarchy when Moab was under Judean control. It was perhaps originally בעל־מואב "Lord of Moab" (cf. 1 Chr 4:22, though the name itself is not attested) and this was later changed to the present form (and cf. 8:4; 10:30; Neh 3:11; 10:15 [14]) to avoid the offensive overtones of "Baal."

6.b. Cf. 1:5.

6.c. Read וְיָאָב for MT יואב; cf. Neh 7:11.

6.d. Nehemiah has 2,818. This may reflect confusion of the similar words שמנה "eight" (7:11) and שנים "two" (as also at v 10), and thus derive from a later stage in the text's transmission rather than reflecting errors based on a misreading of numerical notations.

8.a. Neh 7:13 has 845, the difference again being only one stroke for the hundreds (cf. v 5).

10.a. Neh 7:15 has בנוי "Binnui." Bayer, *Das dritte Buch Esdras*, 43, concludes on the basis of 10:29, 34 and Neh 10:15–16 that these are separate families, and that both perhaps stood here originally.

10.b. Neh 7:15 has 648; cf. v 6[d].

11.a. Neh 7:16 has 628; has there been vertical influence one way or the other between this and the 648 of the previous verse?

12.a. Neh 7:17 has 2,322, a difference of one unit only in the case of the thousands and the hundreds. Haplogr of a final *mēm* on אלף "thousand" in the Ezra text might also account for the drop of a thousand.

13.a.–15.a. Compare the following:

	Ezra	Nehemiah
	666	667
	2,056	2,067
	454	655

In each case, the final unit in Nehemiah is one higher than in Ezra, while for vv 13 and 14 the final two figures in Nehemiah are the same (–67). This situation well illustrates the impossibility in such lists of deciding between errors caused by the notation system, in which a unit of one could easily be lost, and regular scribal errors such as assimilation and parablepsis.

16.a. Cf. 1:5.

16.b. 1 Esdr 5:15 has an addition at this point whose textual worth has been analyzed by Bewer. He shows that part of it is no more than a marginal correction of v 31, where 1 Esdr is corr, but establishes that the remainder rests on an authentic *Vorlage*, as the list in Neh 10:18–19 (17–18) shows. Thus read (with *BHS*) בני עזור ארבע מאות שלשים ושנים בני הודיה מאה ואחד "the family of Azzur 432. The family of Hodiah 101." Note that in 1 Esdr 5:15 this is followed immediately by the family of Hashum, as in Nehemiah, whereas in the present list they have been moved down two places to v 19.

17.a. Neh 7:23 has 324, again a difference of one.

18.a. Neh 7:24 has Hariph, and this is probably correct on account of Neh 10:20 (19). It is difficult to see how the error could have arisen on purely mechanical grounds, since the words are quite distinct. The suggestion that the change came through association of meaning, though not fully convincing, is thus more probable: יורה "Autumn rain"; חריף "sharp, fresh" may be related to חרף "harvest time."

19.a. See n. 16.b. for the order. The difference of 105 in the figure (Neh 7:22 has 328) is the same as at v 5*above.

20.a. Neh 7:25 has the place-name Gibeon. Either reading is reasonable, since in any case the list switches in the next verse to grouping by locality rather than family. However, the presence of בני "family" in both forms of the list at this point slightly favors the text in Ezra. Others (e.g., Batten, Bowman) favor it on the ground that the list moves from south to north, so that a reference to Gibeon would be out of place, but this pattern is not so neat as to be without exceptions.

21.a. MT here again has בני "family," but this is clearly an error caused by the influence of the preceding verses. Sense, the context as determined by the following verses, and Neh 7:26, all demand the reading אנשי "men of."

22.a. Neh 7:26 combines Ezra 2:21 and 22 ("The men of Bethlehem and Netophah: 188"), though its total is nine larger than the combination of Ezra (123 + 56 = 179).

24.a. Cf. v 21.a. Here and in vv 25 and 26 the emendation enjoys the additional support of 1 Esdr.

24.b. MT: "Azmaveth" alone, but cf. 1 Esdr and Neh 7:28.

25.a. Cf. 24.a.

25.b. MT ערים "cities"; read יערים "Jearim" with Neh 7:29, LXX, 1 Esdr and many MSS.

26.a. Cf. n. 24.a.

28.a. Neh 7:32 has 123, again a difference of exactly 100.

29.a. The list now reverts consistently (to v 35) to the בני "family" form. However, as the groupings are still by geographical locality (though cf. Comment), "inhabitants of" is preferable in translation to "sons, family of." Neh 7:33 here retains אנשי, but runs parallel with Ezra thereafter, and so should be emended; contrast v 21.a.

29.b. Nehemiah here inserts אחר "other." However, since there has not been any previous reference to Nebo, this seems to have come in erroneously from v 31 (note that v 30 is omitted in Nehemiah). There it is quite acceptable, in view of v 7. For the identification of Nebo, see Cogan, IEJ 29 (1979) 37–39.

31.a. It is more than a little strange that this number is identical with that of the Elam of v 7. If the whole verse has not arisen as an erroneous duplicate, it is at least likely that the numbers have been assimilated to each other in the course of transmission. The Gr. Vrs suggest that the number in the present verse could have originally been larger.

33.a. Neh 7:36–37, which reverses the order of vv 33 and 34, has 721, a discrepancy for which no particularly obvious solution is apparent.

35.a. Contrast Neh 7:38, which has 3,930.

40.a. So MT. Neh 7:43, however, suggests "The family of Jeshua, namely of Kadmiel, of the family of Hodaviah" (omitting the ל "to" before הודוה "Hodaviah"). While it is not possible to force all the lists of Levites in the post-exilic period into a completely tidy scheme, Neh 9:4–5 suggests the further possibility, favored by Batten, Rudolph, etc., of reading בני ישוע לקדמיאל בָּנִי הודיה, "The family of Jeshua, namely Kadmiel, Bani, Hodaviah."

41.a. Neh 7:44 has 148.

42.a. MT has בני, "the families, sons of." This is out of place in the heading of a section of the list: contrast vv 36, 40, 41, and 43 (the situation is, of course, quite different at v 53). NEB's attempt to circumvent the difficulty by translating "The guild of," though possible in itself, also seems out of place. Since the word is lacking in Neh 7:45 and 1 Esdr 5:28, it may be deleted as an accidental addition under the influence of the repetitive nature of the list which follows.

42.b. Neh 7:45 has 138, again a difference of one.

44.a. So Neh 7:47. MT has סיעהא, a forma mixta of סיעא (as in Nehemiah) and סיעה (Bewer).

45.a. 1 Esdr 5:30 has two additional names here: "The family of Outa; the family of Ketab." It is probable that they were originally a part of the list (cf. Torrey, Ezra Studies, 89–90, and Rudolph, contra Bewer). The difficulty that scribes experienced in copying the list was heightened at this point by the similarity between Hagabah (v 45) and Hagab (v 46). In Neh 7:48, the eye of a scribe evidently jumped from one to the other, so that all in between is omitted.

46.a. K has "Shamlai," but Q, Neh 7:48, and some G witnesses all favor שלמי "Salmai."

47.a. It is possible that rather than being an abbreviated Yahwistic name (גדליה "The Lord has made great") this should be revocalized as גָּדֹל "big" (cf. 1 Esdr 5:33), a name found frequently in the Elephantine Papyri. It would then fit better the characteristics of a number of the other names in this list of temple servants; cf. Comment.

50.a. Accidentally omitted by Neh 7:52.

50.b. K: "Meinim," but Q, Nehemiah, and the Vrs favor מעונים "Meunim." Since no such personal name is known (and confusion over this may have given rise to the K/Q variant), it should probably be taken as a gentilic with reference to the people mentioned in 1 Chr 4:41; 2 Chr 20:1; 26:7; see further under Comment.

50.c. The case here is similar. K is this time closest to the form to be preferred on the basis of Gen 25:15; 1 Chr 1:31; 5:19, viz. נפישים (K נפיסים; Q נפוסים; Neh 7:52 has a *forma mixta*, K נפושסים, Q נפישסים, which gives partial support to our reconstructed form).

52.a. Or Bazlith, as in Neh 7:54.

52.b. MT here and in Neh 7:54 has the unexplained "Mehida," but many MSS and Syr. have מחירא "bought" which gives an attractive nickname in this context.

55.a. "The scribe" (fem), a profession which, as frequently happens, has become a proper name; cf. n. 2.e. Neh 7:57 omits the def art.

55.b. Neh 7:57 and 1 Esdr 5:33 פרידא "Perida."

56.a. Cf. n. 47.a.

57.a. "The gazelle hunter," again a feminine formation (cf. n. 55.a.).

57.b. MT: אמי "Ami" probably a corr of אמון "Amon," Neh 7:59.

59.a. Neh 7:61 includes the copula. Since none of these places is otherwise known, it is impossible to be sure whether they are to be taken as single or double names.

59.b. Cf. 1:5.

59.c. For the syntax of הם "they" in this position, cf. König, *Syntax*, § 414b-d.

60.a. Neh 7:62 has 642, a difference of ten, which can be accounted for by the loss of just one stroke in numerical notation.

61.a. Read ומן with Neh 7:63 and 1 Esdr 5:38.

61.b. MT: שמם "their name," which presupposes the whole clan of Barzillai as antecedent; cf. König, *Syntax*, § 346h. More probably, however, we should read שמו "his name"; cf. 1 Esdr 5:38.

62.a. MT can hardly be construed as it stands (cf. GKC § 131r), though the sense is clear enough. Any slight emendation to ease the syntax (e.g., Rudolph's proposal to add a ב before כתבם) can be no more than guesswork.

62.b. גאל II is a byform of געל I; cf. *TDOT* II, 351, and III, 45–48; there is consequently no need to emend the א to ע, *contra* Joüon, *Bib* 12 (1931) 85.

63.a. התרשתא; cf. Neh 7:65, 69 (70); 8:9; 10:2 (1). In the latter two passages it refers to Nehemiah (though see *Notes ad loc.* for textual problems), while the person referred to in the present context (Ezra 2:63 = Neh 7:65) is not identified. Literary considerations suggest that its use gained entry into the biblical text through its presence in this list and spread thence to the narrative passages in Nehemiah. Hence there is a possibility that its original meaning was misunderstood by the biblical writers. It is, of course, the meaning that *they* attached to the word that is determinative for exegesis. It seems clear from the use of the word in its present biblical context that it is given some such meaning as "governor," and is little more than a variation for פחה, a title ascribed to Sheshbazzar, to Zerubbabel, and to Nehemiah, one of whom must be intended by the writer in this present context. Several suggestions have been made as to its etymology, though it may be questioned whether any of these would (and some of them cannot) have been known at the level of the present text. (i) A Persian name, Atarečithra (cf. Mowinckel, *Studien I*, 106–8). A problem for this view at any level is that whereas, as noted above, it seems most probable that its original usage was in the list of Ezra 2/Neh 7, no official of this name who could have been involved with Judah is known to us from any source. (ii) "Eunuch," with reference to New Persian *tarash*, "to cut"; cf. E. Meyer, *Geschichte des Altertums*, IV (3rd ed.; Stuttgart: J. G. Cotta'sche Buchhandlung, 1939), 33 (cf. below for an alternative view of Meyer's); Theis, *Fragen*, 64–67. This view has been virtually abandoned by modern scholars, however, who think that the present passage most probably refers to Zerubbabel, not Nehemiah. (iii) "The circumcised one," In der Smitten, *VT* 21 (1971) 618–20. This is a refinement of (ii), using the same etymology. It is thought to have been a nickname used by the Persians for Zerubbabel and Nehemiah (both Jews), but its meaning was later forgotten. The difficulty for this suggestion, however, is the improbability of such a nickname being used in an official document. (iv) "Excellency," from Old Persian *tarsa-* "to fear," hence "the one to be feared, respected"; cf. Meyer, *Entstehung*, 194; I. Scheftelowitz, *Arisches im Alten Testament* I (Berlin: S. Calvary & Co., 1901), 93–94; Rudolph; Galling, *Studien*, 57, 81; E. M. Yamauchi, *ZAW* 92 (1980) 136–37, etc. This meaning fits the context best, though it is not entirely free of linguistic difficulties (cf. In der Smitten), both because it would most naturally be construed as "one who is made to tremble," and because there are other words known from Old Persian with the meaning "Excellency." In sum, therefore, the derivation of the word remains uncertain, but it is clearly used in the biblical text with some such meaning as "governor."

63.b. The context of v 62 shows that this is not to be understood in distinction to "the holy food." The two terms were not always carefully differentiated (cf. Num 18:9 and 10), so that emendation (Rudolph) is unnecessary.

63.c. Lit. "with" or "for."

65.a. Neh 7:67 has 245 singers, but this is deceptive: a scribe has accidentally jumped from the 200 of this verse to the 200 of v 66 and omitted all the material in between. Unfortunately, the major Eng. versions of Neh 7:67 follow the inferior, harmonizing MSS and Vrs which reintroduce the omitted material but which fail to correct the erroneous 245. That 1 Esdr 5:42 does the same may be a further pointer to its knowledge of Neh 7, and so to its secondary nature as a compilation (cf. *Introduction*, "Unity and Extent").

67.a. Or "Their donkeys," with some MSS and Vrs, and the shape of the list as a whole. It involves the loss of only one letter (חמריהם for חמרים). Perhaps, however, MT should be retained as the more difficult, though fully intelligible, reading.

68.a. From this point on there are substantial differences between Ezra 2 and Neh 7; cf. *Form/Structure/Setting* below.

69.a. I defend this translation (rather than "darics") in "Eschatology in Chronicles," *TynB* 28 (1977) 123–26; see also S. Segert, *ArOr* 24 (1956) 396, and contrast Ezra 8:27.

70.a. For a full discussion of the text of this verse, see discussion on Neh 7:72a (73a).

Form/Structure/Setting

In its present form, the list has the appearance of being well ordered, and it may be simply analyzed: heading (1–2), lists of lay people (3–35), of priests (36–39), Levites (40), singers (41), gatekeepers (42) and other temple servants (43–58), and of those whose genealogies could not be proved (59–63); totals (64–67); summary of gifts for the temple building (68–69), and conclusion (70).

Closer inspection reveals, however, that this order has probably been imposed upon originally diverse material. The long list of lay people, for instance, switches without warning from those enrolled by family association (3–20) to those enrolled by place of domicile (21–35), though no reason is apparent for this different principle of arrangement. Second, vv 21–35 are further subdivided into a list introduced by אנשי, "the men of," and one introduced by בני, "the inhabitants (lit.: sons) of." In such a passage, these terms are synonymous, so that again the change cannot be explained within the context of an originally unified list. Third, while the chapter retains its archival character throughout, its concluding paragraphs go considerably further than the heading of v 1, while the introduction of narrative material within these paragraphs also distinguishes them from the preceding.

It would, of course, be foolish to demand modern standards of precision from a writer in antiquity; yet these points, when coupled with the historical considerations to be adduced below, are strongly indicative of the composite nature of this list.

This conclusion enables us to bypass in part the old debate concerning the original extent of the list based on formal considerations (e.g., Hölscher; Mowinckel, *Studien I;* Rudolph), for if the list was not conceived *ab initio* as a unity then the point of its conclusion cannot be determined on grounds of internal consistency. The only outstanding question concerns the point at which the narrator's own composition resumes after chap. 1. This, however, is closely bound up with the issue of the relationship of this chapter with the parallel Neh 7, and this has, in the nature of the case, to be decided on literary-critical grounds (see below). If the list is composite, it cannot be resolved in advance on the basis of a prior decision as to where the "original" list must have concluded.

Discussion of Ezra 2 is further complicated by the fact that it has a close parallel in Neh 7:6–72 (73). Most of the differences between the two passages are to be explained simply as later, textual corruption (cf. *Notes*). Toward the end of the list, however, some more substantial differences emerge.

The first point to observe is that the two texts in fact run parallel beyond the conclusion of the list itself; compare the narrative in Ezra 3:1 and Neh 7:72b (73b)—8:1. Since in both cases these verses introduce the next section rather than serving as a summary or conclusion of the preceding list, it is quite clear that one passage must have been dependent directly upon the other. The facts cannot be explained on the hypothesis that both drew independently from the common original source.

This being so, it should be possible to determine which passage borrowed from which. Most who have studied the issue since the rise of critical scholarship have concluded that Ezra 2 is dependent on Neh 7 (cf. out of very many Galling; Hervey, *The Expositor* IV/7 [1893] 431–43; Keil; Meyer, *Entstehung;* Michaeli; Nikel, *Wiederherstellung,* 71–80; Rudolph; Schaeder, *Esra;* Siegfried; Smend, *Die Listen;* Theis, *Geschichtliche . . . Fragen;* Weinberg, *Klio* 54 [1972] 45–59; etc.), and this for two main reasons. (i) In the continuation of the narratives, "the seventh month" of Neh 7:72 (73) shows itself to be an integral part of its context by the reference to the same month in 8:2, whereas in Ezra 3 it is left completely in the air. In agreeing with this judgment we may add the further consideration that such a form of dating would be out of place within Ezra 1–6, where the narrator is usually concerned to relate events to a given year of the king (e.g., 1:1; 4:24; 6:15) and to specify his dates elsewhere by other means (e.g., 3:8) or by the context (6:19). On the other hand, it fits very well within the dating scheme of the material concerning Ezra, where months on their own can be referred to in this way (cf. Ezra 8:31; 10:9, 16–17; Neh 8:2). (ii) It is generally argued that Ezra 2:68–69 represents a summarizing of Neh 7:69–71 rather than Nehemiah an expansion of Ezra (see most recently Japhet, *ZAW* 94 [1982] 84), and the figures involved seem to bear this out. For instance, in the matter of priestly garments Neh 7:69–70 (70–71) has 67 + 30 items, which Ezra 2:69 has rounded up to 100. Again, for silver minas the sum in Nehemiah is 500 + 2,200 + 2,000 which Ezra 2 has rounded up to 5,000. The suggestion that the process was the other way round (Mowinckel, *Studien I,* 31; Pohlmann, *Studien*) fails to explain why the redactor did not divide the totals accurately, whereas according to the usual view one need only suppose that he brought the totals up to the nearest round number, an eminently more sensible suggestion. (On the reason why Ezra 2 summarizes at this point, see *Comment.* It is, incidentally, no argument to say that no motive for such an abbreviation can be found; cf. Mowinckel, *Studien I,* 30; Pohlmann, *Studien,* 60–61. It may simply be retorted that neither do these scholars suggest why there should be an expansion in Neh 7!)

To these two arguments, we may add two more. (iii) Within the usually shorter account of Ezra 2:68–69, v 68 in fact constitutes a plus over against

Neh 7:70. This plus, however, exactly fits the narrative context, the outlook, and even the specific vocabulary of the narrator of Ezra 1–6, so that the suspicion is hard to resist that he has added it to his *Vorlage* rather than that precisely this particular verse has been omitted by Nehemiah. Noteworthy are the expressions "the temple of the Lord (which is) in Jerusalem," which is identical with the expression in 1:5, which we attributed to the narrator's own hand, and "gave freewill offerings" (התנדבו), which again was a prominent concept in Ezra 1; note also "when they arrived at the temple . . . ," which compares closely with 3:8, where it creates a slightly unusual impression. Finally, it goes without saying that "the rebuilding of the temple of God on its original site" will be the theme of the following chapters. (iv) It will be argued at Neh 7:72a (73a) that we have the trace of an original sentence from the NM and that this too has been expanded in the interests of its new context by the narrator in Ezra.

In the face of these arguments, the counterproposals of those who ascribe priority to Ezra 2 seem weak indeed, all the more so when it is realized that in nearly every instance (e.g. Hölscher; Mowinckel, *Studien I;* Pohlmann, *Studien;* Noth, *Studien,* 128–29; etc.) the case is being defended in the interests of the wider view that 1 Esdr represents the original shape of the ending of the Chronicler's work, a case which could not stand if Neh 7 were prior, in literary terms, to Ezra 2. I have examined these arguments in detail at *JTS* ns 34 (1983) 4–7 and have endeavored to expose their weaknesses. It is unnecessary to repeat that discussion here. (The question of the *textual* superiority of 1 Esdr 5 in some cases is, of course, a quite separate issue; on this, see Klein, *HTR* 62 [1969] 99–107, though his arguments are weakened by his failure to deal with Allrik's strong case to the contrary.)

It may therefore be concluded that Ezra 2 with 3:1 is dependent upon Neh 7 in its present form. The implications of this for the composition of these books as a whole must not be overlooked. Since Neh 7–8 is the point at which the originally independent Ezra and Nehemiah material have been most clearly interwoven, it is evident that the narrator of our chapter found that material already heavily worked over. The composition of Ezra 1–6 may thus be regarded as a quite separate, and later, undertaking, a conclusion that goes a long way toward explaining what has already been noted of the narrator's method in these chapters.

With the exception of Torrey, *Composition,* all scholars agree that this list is much earlier in origin than its first incorporation into the books of Ezra and Nehemiah. Its original purpose, however, has been widely debated.

The view that it is simply a list of all who returned in a single caravan in immediate response to the decree of Cyrus is difficult to maintain for a number of reasons. (i) Apart from its position, the list has no connection with chap. 1. Sheshbazzar is not mentioned, nor are the temple vessels included with the gifts of 2:68–69. Moreover, the introduction of the "Tirshatha" (governor) in v 63 is abrupt and argues against an original integration with chap. 1. There is thus no internal evidence to limit the contents of the list to a single return or to a specific date. (ii) Certain aspects of the list seem to be composed from within the context of the people having already returned. As already seen, some of those listed are grouped according to the place of their residence, and the expression "each to his own town" in v 1 is decisive in this regard. Again, the "Tirshatha," who is evidently a leader of some sort, is presupposed to be already active in his work (v 63). (iii) There is at least one Persian name in the list (Bigvai, v 2), and possibly more (see *Notes*). This is not a problem in itself, for we know that some Jews certainly did take such names. However, it would be surprising to find a leader so named as early as the first year of Persian rule; a somewhat later date would be more readily intelligible. (iv) The composite nature of the list has already been noted, and it rules out any "single event" explanation of the list.

In the face of such evidence, a number of alternative suggestions as to the list's origin have been made (cf. the partial survey in Schultz, "Tensions"). Some of these too take no account of the composite nature of the list, and so may be discounted (e.g., Hölscher, who thought it was drawn up for purposes of taxation; or A. Alt, *KS* 2, 334–35, who thought it was drawn up by Zerubbabel in order to determine land rights). Also to be borne in mind are the indications from the list which point towards a comparatively early dating within the Persian period (cf. Meyer, *Entstehung;* Sellin, *Geschichte;* Rudolph). (i) In v 61 the family of Hakkoz is excluded from the priesthood, but by 8:33 (cf. Neh 3:4, 21) and the later 1 Chr 24:10 it seems already to have been reinstated. (ii) The registration of those without genealogical record according to the (obscure) Babylonian places from which they came (v 59) only makes sense within a period shortly after their return. (iii) The setting of the list presupposes a time when there is no "priest with Urim and Thummim." In the post-exilic period this is without doubt a reference to the high priest (cf. Exod 28:30; Lev 8:8; Num 27:21), in which role Jeshua was certainly active from 520 B.C. onwards. (iv) The presentation of the minor cultic officials (vv 40–58) reflects an earlier situation in the development of their position by comparison with other lists in these books and in Chronicles. (v) The use of the gold drachma (v 69) probably antedates the introduction of the daric by Darius. (vi) The distribution of the population is not what we would have expected if the list had been drawn up in, say, Nehemiah's time (cf. Sellin, *Geschichte,* 89).

It must, therefore, be concluded that most of the component parts of the list were already fixed by the time that work began in earnest on the rebuilding of the temple. (Does this perhaps explain why in the more primitive form of the list of gifts in Neh 7:69–71 [70–72] no reference is made to the temple?) And if the list is indeed composite, the most reasonable explanation will be that it reflects a number of more modest journeys of return at various times throughout the reigns of Cyrus and Cambyses.

We cannot now be sure what prompted the drawing together of the various elements into the one list which was eventually incorporated into Ezra-Nehemiah. An attractive suggestion is that of Galling, who points to the need posed by Tattenai's inquiry (5:3–4, 10) for a list of all who were covered by Cyrus's permission to return from exile and to rebuild the temple. (Note also Schultz's appeal, "Tensions," in support of this theory to the parallel situation in the rebuilding of the Eanna sanctuary, from which a text survives that guarantees the rights of the workers there too; cf. D. B. Weisberg, *Guild Structure and Political Allegiance in Early Achaemenid Mesopotamia* [New Haven

and London: Yale University Press, 1967].) While such a possibility may readily
be entertained, it remains speculative and should not be allowed to overshadow the important historical testimony of this chapter to a gradual return
by various groups in the first twenty years or so of Achaemenid rule, a period
quite reasonably defined by a much later writer as "at the first" (Neh 7:6[5]).

Comment

1–2   Since "the men of the people of Israel" introduces only the laity
of vv 3–35 and is thus parallel to the later subheadings "The priests" (v
36), "The Levites" (v 40) etc., it cannot be taken as a duplicate heading to
the whole of the following list (*contra* Mowinckel, *Studien I*, 63). The list
has only one heading (vv 1–2a); it introduces what follows and gives the
names of the leaders. Since these number exactly twelve and since Sheshbazzar
is not included, it is likely that the whole of this heading is a slightly artificial
construction, listing a selection of those who were prominent in the various
returns between 537 and 520 B.C. The aim is to show that those returning
were representative of Israel in its full extent (twelve tribes) and thus perhaps
to provide an echo of the first Exodus.
   In the light of our analysis, it becomes improbable (though it must be
admitted, not quite impossible) that this is in some way a list of the leaders
of Judah down to a much later time. There certainly were governors called
Zerubbabel, Nehemiah, and Bigvai (cf. *AramP*), but the names of others who
are also now thought to have held office are lacking; cf. N. Avigad, *Bullae
and Seals from a Post-Exilic Judean Archive* (Jerusalem: The Hebrew University,
1976). Moreover, it can hardly be seriously supposed that the well-known
Ezra would ever be differently named (Seraiah; Neh 7:7, Azariah).
   We thus have extra information about only the first two mentioned in
the list, for they emerge as the real leaders of the community in the reign
of Darius. Zerubbabel was a descendant of the Davidic family. Generally referred to as "the son of Shealtiel" (e.g., 3:2, 8; Hag 1:1), he nevertheless
occurs in the genealogy of 1 Chr 3 as a son of Pedaiah (v 19), one of Shealtiel's
younger brothers. It is likely that both ascriptions should be taken seriously,
for the former occurs in sources contemporary with Zerubbabel, while the
latter, which is later in date, is the one which gives him a less exalted position
and thus is unlikely to be pure fabrication. Various harmonizations are possible, but all have in common that Zerubbabel was the physical son of Pedaiah
and that he was linked to Shealtiel as the result of some legal fiction such
as adoption or levirate marriage (Deut 25:5–10). The Jehoiachin Tablets
(*ANET*, 308) suggest that Zerubbabel's father may have been born early in
Jehoiachin's captivity. Zerubbabel himself could then have been born any
time after about 575 B.C. and so have been old enough to lead a return at
any time after 538 B.C. Most of the rest of our knowledge about him is drawn
from the following chapters of Ezra; see especially on 3:1—4:5 and 5:1–2,
and also K.-M. Beyse, *Serubbabel und die Königserwartungen der Propheten Haggai
und Sacharja* (Stuttgart: Calwer Verlag, 1972). A valuable recent discussion
is Japhet, *ZAW* 94 (1982) 66–98; 95 (1983) 218–29. She demonstrates the
possibility that Zerubbabel was the governor of Judah after Sheshbazzar and

plausibly explains the lack of reference to this in Ezra-Nehemiah (contrast Haggai) as resulting from the editor's religio-historical outlook. His conviction that Judah's status within the Persian empire was the result of divine grace (cf. 1:1 etc.) led him to play down Zerubbabel's Davidic connections and his political position.

Jeshua, called elsewhere "the son of Jozadak" (3:2; Hag 1:1, etc.), was the grandson of the last officiating high priest before the exile (cf. 2 Kgs 25:18 and 1 Chr 5:40 [6:15]). Jeshua himself soon assumed that office. It became much more prominent during the post-exilic period, as foreshadowed already in Zech 1–8.

"The people of the province": it is generally supposed that this refers to Judah, and so reflects the post-return outlook of the remainder. It has been observed, however, by F. C. Fensham, "Mĕdînâ in Ezra and Nehemiah," *VT* 25 (1975) 795–97, that it can refer to other provinces (e.g., at 7:16), and he suggests that it refers in the present context to Babylonia from which the exiles returned. In this, Fensham is dependent upon the questionable assumption that a separate province of Judah did not exist before Nehemiah's time, though in any case מדינה might mean no more than "administrative district." Moreover, as a summary heading supplied to the list somewhat later than the events it describes, it can be most naturally understood to mean "of all those who live in the province, these are the ones who returned from the exile."

3–35 The listing of lay people first may be contrasted with later practice. As already noted, it is probable that the list is made up of three sections: those identified by family (vv 2–20) and two sets of those identified by place of residence (vv 21–28, 29–35).

2b–20 Many of the names listed here recur in later passages too (Ezra 8; Neh 10), but not, generally speaking, in pre-exilic texts. It is thus evident that they represent clan or family names, and that often only a part (as numbered) of each clan returned at this stage. No further genealogical connection is supplied; presumably they were well known and their identity as Israelites not in question. Unfortunately, it is not possible, for reasons of space, to deal with each name individually; cf. the standard textbooks on Hebrew personal names together with the commentaries of Bowman, Brockington, and Myers.

21–35 Not all the questions raised by this section of the list can be confidently answered. Are the names geographical, or are there also some personal names? Commentators are divided concerning this issue. The view adopted in the translation above is that, since a number certainly are geographical and since this applies to names introduced both by בני "sons/inhabitants of" and by אנשי "men of," it is probable that they should all be so understood; cf. the identifications in Bowman. It must be recognized, however, that not all are certainly identified; that the last named has, in addition, a very large number associated with it; and that this may, therefore, be too tidy an approach for a document of antiquity. If we are correct in regarding the list as a compilation, it might be even more disjointed than we suppose.

How is the geographical distribution of names to be accounted for? Most come from the Jerusalem area, mainly from originally Benjaminite territory.

None occurs from more than a few miles south of Jerusalem in Judah proper, while the trio of Lod, Hadid, and Ono (v 33) are somewhat isolated as being much further to the west. While it is difficult to link these facts with the precise circumstances of the post-exilic community, it is possible that they are related to three earlier events, namely (i) the expansion of the southern kingdom under Josiah, which led to the inclusion of such places as Bethel and Ai (v 28) and the western trio (v 33; cf. Alt, *KS* 2, 276–88), (ii) the fact which has been well established by archeological investigation that the cities of Benjamin escaped relatively lightly in the Babylonian invasions of 597 and 587 B.C. (cf. Stern, *Material Culture*, 51; S. S. Weinberg, *Post-exilic Palestine— An Archaeological Report* [The Israel Academy of Sciences and Humanities Proceedings, vol. 4, no. 5. Jerusalem: Ahva (Hebrew), 1969]), and (iii) the fact that the south of Judah was already completely cut off in the first Babylonian invasion (Jer 13:19), so that there might have been none from this district to return from the exile in any case (Rudolph). Are we, then, to infer that this is in fact a list of those who were not taken into exile, but who were only gradually integrated with the community of those who returned (cf. J. P. Weinberg, *ArOr* 42 [1974] 341–53, and *JSJ* 6 [1975] 242)? This suggestion would seem to be contradicted by the context of the list and runs into difficulty over the nonappearance of such places as Jerusalem and Mizpah, which certainly continued to be inhabited. The evidence thus points rather strongly to the view that these are towns from which the people had been exiled, and not necessarily in every case those to which they returned. For instance, settlement in the western group of Lod, Hadid, and Ono (v 33) is most unlikely. It is clear that even in the time of Nehemiah they were still regarded as remote from the center of the Judean community (cf. Neh 6:2).

What remains most uncertain of all is why some families were listed by locality in the first place. Clearly, in the light of vv 59–63 it cannot be that their genealogy was uncertain or unknown. Nor is it likely, on the basis of the numbers involved, that all those in vv 3–20 were residents of Jerusalem (*contra* Keil). More likely is the suggestion of Meyer, *Entstehung*, 152–54, that these represent "the poor of the land" (2 Kgs 25:12) who, in contrast with those in vv 3–20, had no land or property in their own name. Even then, however, the separate halves of the list are left unexplained. Perhaps, therefore, we must simply reckon with different systems of registration by the different groups of those who returned, which the compiler of the list has not been concerned to reduce to a fully coherent order.

35 Senaah: while it is possible to suggest geographical identifications (cf. Bowman), the numbers are unusually large. This led some earlier commentators to read the word as שנואה/ה "the hated one," whose "inhabitants" would be a derogatory term for either the lower-class citizens of Jerusalem or for members of the northern tribes who returned (cf. 1 Chr 9:3). This is improbable in an official list, however. The problem is not solved by regarding this as a personal name on the basis of Neh 3:3 either, for none of those listed in vv 3–20 has such a large number. The problem thus remains; the possibility of textual error should not be overlooked.

36–39 Only four priestly families are listed (others returned later; cf. Ezra 8:2–3), but their numbers make up a full tenth of the total, no doubt reflecting the fact that they had most to gain from a return. In the post-exilic period there was a steady development of the priestly hierarchy, a development attested in various lists in the OT which culminated in the emergence of the system of twenty-four priestly courses. This unsophisticated list clearly stands near the start of that process, though the names remain in the later expanded lists; cf. 10:18–22; Neh 12:1–7; 1 Chr 24:7–18. Note that there is no reference to the priests as "the sons of Aaron," as regularly used later.

36 "The house of Jeshua": if this refers to the Jeshua of v 2, this explanation must have been added later.

40 Evidently not many Levites were willing to return, as Ezra later on also discovered; cf. 8:15. This may have been because of the decrease in their significance at this period (cf. Ezek 44:10–14), together with the possibility that, because of their lower status, not so many were exiled in the first place.

41 Neither the singers nor the gatekeepers are apparently yet classified as Levites, again a contrast with what developed later (cf. 1 Chr 6:23–26, etc., and *Comment* on 3:10 below). By that time, furthermore, they were divided into three classes, the sons of Asaph, of Heman, and of Jeduthun. It has been argued by H. Gese, *Vom Sinai zum Zion* (Munich: Chr. Kaiser Verlag, 1974), 147–58, that this is to be explained as reflecting a primitive point in the development of the guilds rather than being merely a question of members of the other families not returning.

42 Similar remarks may be made about the gatekeepers, a development in whose status and ordering can also be traced through the post-exilic lists, starting from this point; cf. Neh 11:19; 12:25; 1 Chr 9:17–32; 26:1–19 and VTSup 30 (1979) 251–68.

43–58 The temple servants and the sons of Solomon's servants are bracketed together, as is shown by the combining of their totals in v 58. Apart from a single reference in 1 Chr 9:2, which is in any case in a context close to the present one, these two groups are attested in the OT only in Ezra and Nehemiah, though it is widely agreed that their origins must be sought in the pre-exilic period.

It is evident from 7:24 that at least the temple servants (נתינים *nethinim*), and so by implication the sons of Solomon's servants too, are cultic officials (*contra* Weinberg, *ZAW* 87 [1975] 355–71). This is confirmed by 8:20, which describes them as a group "whom David and the princes had given for the service of the Levites." Even if this statement has to be read in the light of the tendency anachronistically to ascribe all the ordering of the cultic officials to David, it nevertheless stands as an incontrovertible witness to their status in the writer's own day. (Ezek 44:6–9 may, therefore, refer to the same group.) It is thus probable that just as the Levites were "given" (נתן) to serve the priests (Num 3:9; 8:19, etc.) so the *nethinim* were "given" to serve the Levites, implying at best they were responsible for the very menial tasks that must have needed to be done around the temple. We have no means of distinguishing the nature of their tasks from those of the sons of Solomon's servants; Haran's suggestion, *VT* 11 (1961) 159–69, that the former served inside, and the latter outside, the temple is a pure guess with no basis in the text.

Apart from their names, there is no reason to suppose that they were slaves in the strict sense; indeed, there is much evidence to the contrary; cf. Levine, *JBL* 82 (1963) 207–12. They are included in these lists as part

of the "assembly" (v 64) from which servants are treated separately as property
(vv 65–67). They were exempted from paying taxes (7:24), had their own
quarters in Jerusalem (Neh 3:26, 31), and were signatories to the new covenant
of Neh 10. Thus *nethinim* need mean no more than "devoted" (see above),
while the word עבד (as in "servant" of Solomon) has a wide usage, covering
even those high up in the royal service.

As to their origins, it is clear from their status in the post-exilic period
that any association with the Gibeonites (Josh 9:27) or with the servants of
Solomon in 1 Kgs 9 can at best be speculative and that their situation would
have had to have changed dramatically over the years. A more secure indication comes from their names, a very high percentage of which are foreign;
cf. Zadok, *JQR* 71 (1980) 107–17. Moreover, Bowman observes that "many
names are such informal nicknames as might be given to servants." Noteworthy in particular are the families of the Meunim and the Nephishim (v 50;
cf. *Notes*), which suggest that many of these families may have come to Israel
initially as prisoners of war, since these are the names of tribes whom we
know were defeated during the period of the monarchy. This suggestion
would fit the presumed humble nature of their duties. On the hostile attitude
towards them in Talmudic times, cf. B. A. Levine, "Later Sources on the
Netînîm," in H. A. Hoffner (ed.), *Orient and Occident* (AOAT 22. Neukirchen-
Vluyn, Neukirchener Verlag, 1973), 101–7.

44 Keros occurs in a text on an ostracon from Arad which shows him
active in a cultic setting. It is very tempting to identify the two names and
to see in this one of the rare references to this class in a definitely pre-
exilic setting; cf. B. A. Levine, "Notes on a Hebrew Ostracon From Arad,"
IEJ 19 (1969) 49–51.

46 Hagab occurs in ostracon I from Lachish, which A. Lemaire sees as
another possible pre-exilic reference to the Nethinim; cf. *Inscriptions Hébraïques*
I (Paris: Les éditions du Cerf, 1977), 96 and 182–83. This is a much less
certain case, however, in view of the lack of any cultic allusion in the ostracon.

58 It is noteworthy that for these minor officials the figures suggest an
average of only eight or nine to a clan.

59–63 Although we know from elsewhere (e.g., 6:21) that there were
different avenues into the community at this time, the concern for racial
purity was dominant (cf. 9:1–2). Evidently great care was taken of family
records, perhaps especially during the exile when the other great guarantee
of continuity, the land itself, was lost. This explains both the origin and
the abundance of such lists at this period. In Ezra and Nehemiah, as the
present passage shows, they serve primarily as a means of excluding alien
elements from the community. (Contrast 1 Chr 1–9 which presents them as
an expression of inclusion; cf. my *1 and 2 Chronicles*, 38–39, 46–47.) "But
underneath the notion of legitimacy and racial purity is the desire to express
the continuity of the people of God, that is to say, the identity of the new
Israel of the restoration with the old Israel of the monarchy," M. D. Johnson,
The Purpose of the Biblical Genealogies (Cambridge and New York: Cambridge
University Press, 1969), 43–44.

59–60 Three lay groups were unable to establish their Israelite connection. However, while we have no knowledge of what happened to them eventually, the fact that they are listed here with their number indicates that while

they awaited clarification of their status, they were treated in the same way as the earlier families. It has been suggested that the uncertainty resulted from their proselyte origins, but neither the text nor their Yahwistic names supports this conjecture. The names of the towns from which they came are likewise unknown. The context, however, shows that they must have been places of exile in Babylon (*contra* Brockington); presumably they are mentioned here as a substitute for the lacking genealogical points of reference.

61–63 The situation with priests was more serious because of the danger that they might desecrate the cult. They, therefore, were suspended from duty, which also meant the loss of their means of livelihood in the form of the sacred contributions.

61 Hakkoz, at least, appears later to have been reinstated (cf. *Form*, p. 31). The fate of the other two is unknown. The difficulty in Barzillai's case was presumably that he had taken the name of his wife, who was not of a priestly family. He may have done this in order to become the family's heir. Kidner suggests that this could have been regarded as a renunciation of his priesthood since priests were forbidden an inheritance in the land (Num 18:20). In any event, it casts an interesting light on the care with which genealogies were preserved to see that the family link is considered certain as far back as the time of David (cf. 2 Sam 17:27; 19:32; 1 Kgs 2:7).

63 "The governor": cf. *Notes*. The use of this Persian title may lend some support to Galling's view that the list was put together in its final form as a response to some official inquiry. He is not more closely identified here, but the fuller version of the list of gifts in Neh 7:70 suggests that he was a Jew, and so presumably either Sheshbazzar or Zerubbabel. The former is more likely if the assumption is correct that Zerubbabel's return was rather later than 538 B.C. and that this passage presents the governor as already active at the time of the returns summarized in this chapter.

"Urim and Thummim" were sacred lots from which answers to direct questions could be received. They could have been two small objects, such as pebbles or sticks, which were marked in some way and which were drawn out of the Ephod to give, according to the combinations, a "yes," "no," or "no answer" response; cf. 1 Sam 14:36–37; 23:9–12; 30:7–8, etc. The meaning of the words themselves is quite uncertain; is it significant that they begin with the first and last letters of the Hebrew alphabet respectively? They are not said to have been in use later than the period of the united monarchy, so that their sudden appearance here is difficult to evaluate. Since there can be no doubt that the governor did not expect to wait indefinitely for the difficulty to be resolved, we must assume that in this context the expression is intended to refer to the time of the proper reconstitution of the cultic life of the community with its high priest who, according to the Pentateuchal texts noted on p. 31 above, was thought to carry the Urim and Thummim. Whether he actually did or not is less important than that he would be the one who would have the authority to decide in such a dispute as this one. In the meantime, the governor "played for safety."

64 The total given is some 11,000 higher than the sum of the preceding numbers, the exact figure of which varies between the different recensions; the situation is thus comparable with 1:9–11. Unless there has been even more extensive corruption in the figures during the course of transmission than we already know about, this is probably to be explained by the inclusion of women in the total. They certainly could be included in the קהל "assembly," a technical term for the religious community (cf. 10:1; Neh 8:2, etc.). Weinberg, *Klio* 54 (1972) 45–59, explains the smaller number of women than men by the suggestion that a majority of those returning would have been young men, not yet married.

65 Care is taken to make plain that slaves were not included in the assembly; they come more into the category of property, like the animals in the next verse. The inclusion of both men and women argues for their inclusion in the total of the previous verse too. The singers here are not, of course, cultic functionaries (contrast v 41), but rather musicians retained by the wealthy for their entertainment (cf. 2 Sam 19:35; Eccl 2:8). The picture of the community's economic status contrasts sharply with Hag 1. We may conjecture that the wealth of those returning early rapidly evaporated because of a succession of bad harvests (cf. Hag 1:6, 10–11) while that of those who had only just arrived in 520 B.C. may have helped stimulate fresh hopes and determination in those who had grown despondent.

66–67 Appropriately, it is beasts of burden and travel that are listed here. The numbers are far too high to be restricted to those required for the rebuilding of the temple (Galling, *Studien,* 101).

68–69 It was seen on pp. 29–30 above, that v 68 is the narrator's own addition to his *Vorlage,* whereby he integrated the list more closely into its present literary context. In fact, the gift of "priestly vestments" might be thought better to have suited a time when the temple was already rebuilt. In v 69, by contrast, he was seen to have abbreviated Neh 7:69–71 (70–72). This may have been simply to avoid the repetitive nature of the material in Nehemiah, but more probable is Galling's suggestion (*Studien,* 104–5) that he found the reference to the governor's (Tirshatha's) gifts (Neh 7:70) awkward in the new context he has provided for the list. It is probable that he identified the Tirshatha with Sheshbazzar (cf. v 63). He has already provided a detailed list of the vessels which Sheshbazzar brought (1:9–11); he therefore felt that it would avoid confusion or misunderstanding if he amalgamated the detailed list of contributions in his *Vorlage.* On "drachmas," cf. *Notes.* The Persian daric had not yet been minted. A mina was of Babylonian origin and quite familiar to the exiles as a unit for silver coins; cf. Ezek 45:12.

70 For a discussion of the textual development of this verse, see discussion on Neh 7:72a (73a). The present author has incorporated it in order to indicate somewhat schematically the settlement of all the groups of the preceding list as a means of easing the transition to his later narrative. Certainly, if our analysis of the list has been correct, the suggestion of the once-for-all dispersal of a huge returning caravan would be historically a gross over-simplification. But to treat the text in this manner would be to misunderstand its literary purpose in the present context.

Explanation

Chapters like Ezra 2 are among the most uninviting portions of the Bible to the modern reader both because of their tedious nature and because of their overtones of racial exclusivism and pride. However fascinating the chapter may be to the antiquarian, it is unlikely that his enthusiasm will ever be shared by more than a few. It is more prudent to admit the difficulties from the start and to suggest instead one or two points of value that emerge from a consideration of the list as a whole.

In chap. 1, there were observed several lines of continuity between pre-exilic Israel and the community of the restoration. Chap. 2 develops this theme both by emphasizing the twelvefold leadership of the nation (cf. vv 1–2) and more importantly by underlining the identity of pre- and post-destruction Israel in terms of its constituent membership. Vv 59–63, which deal with those unable at the time to trace their descent with exactitude, serve only to indicate the lengths to which all participants in the return were prepared to go to ensure that this continuity was beyond question. Finally, a further contribution to this theme is suggested by the geographical interest of the chapter. It both opens and closes with a reference to the dispersal of the people "each to his own town" (vv 1, 70), and contains a substantial section (vv 21–35) concerning those identified by their cities of origin. This may then be compared with the accounts of the first settlement in the second half of the book of Joshua.

People and land were the two most precious elements in God's promises to Israel, for they had lain at the heart of God's first call to Abraham (Gen 12:1–3) and his later dealings with the patriarchs and the nation which developed from them. It is true, of course, that it was never intended that these blessings should be enjoyed with an exclusive or superior attitude; that too was an element of the initial call (Gen 12:2–3) and Israel's role as God's servant was in part that she might act as "a light to the nations" (Isa 42:6; 49:6). Indeed, this list itself almost certainly bears witness to this fact in terms of the past, for it includes many whose origin must have been non-Israelite (cf. especially vv 43–58), and in the future this very community was again to demonstrate (albeit in a restricted manner) the self-same awareness; cf. 6:21. But at this crucial moment of transition the emphasis was understandably placed on maintaining an identifiable continuity.

The dangers of this situation are, however, all too obvious. A concern for pedigree and purity can easily turn to pride and superiority. This trend was tragically exemplified by many of the community's later descendants, despite prophetic voices of protest, some even within the OT itself. It is a danger to which every second generation is prone, and the NT not infrequently points out that "he is not a Jew, which is one outwardly" (Rom 9:6) and that "God is able of these stones to raise up children unto Abraham" (Matt 3:9). It is a danger, furthermore, to which the Church has all too frequently shown itself to be prone, even though the gospel in fact eliminates *every* cause of pride in the basis of our relationship with God; cf. Eph 2:8–9. If even our negative feelings toward this chapter can help eliminate this prideful attitude from the Church and the individual believer, it will have played a valuable role within the total context of Scripture.

The Restoration of Worship   (Ezra 3:1—4:5)

Bibliography

Ackroyd, P. R. *Exile and Restoration. A Study of Hebrew Thought of the Sixth Century BC.* OTL. London: SCM Press, 1968, 138–52. **Alt, A.** "Die Rolle Samarias bei der Entstehung des Judentums." *KS* 2, 316–37. **Andersen, F. I.** "Who Built the Second Temple?" *AusBR* 6 (1958) 3–35. **Baynes, N. H.** "Zerubbabel's Rebuilding of the Temple." *JTS* 25 (1924) 154–60. **Coggins, R. J.** "The Interpretation of Ezra iv.4." *JTS* ns 16 (1965) 124–27. **Gelston, A.** "The Foundations of the Second Temple." *VT* 16 (1966) 232–35. **Goettsberger, J.** "Über das III. Kapitel des Ezrabuches." *JSOR* 10 (1926) 270–80. **Heltzer, M.** "A propos des banquets des rois achéménides et du retour d'exil sous Zorobabel." *RB* 86 (1979) 102–6. **Hogg, W. E.** "The Founding of the Second Temple." *PTR* 25 (1927) 457–61. **Petersen, D. L.** "Zerubbabel and Jerusalem Temple Construction." *CBQ* 36 (1974) 366–72. **Rothstein, J. W.** *Juden und Samaritaner.* BWANT 3. Leipzig: J. C. Hinrichs'sche Buchhandlung, 1908. **Smith, M.** *Palestinian Parties and Politics that Shaped the Old Testament.* New York and London: Columbia University Press, 1971. 193–201. **Theis, J.** *Geschichtliche und literarkritischen Fragen in Esra 1–6,* 68–82. **Würthwein, E.** *Der 'amm ha' arez im Alten Testament.* Stuttgart: W. Kohlhammer Verlag, 1936. 57–64.

Translation

[1] *When the seventh month came, the Israelites being [a] settled in their towns,[b] the people all [c] gathered together as one man to Jerusalem.* [2] *Then Jeshua the son of Jozadak and his fellow-priests and Zerubbabel the son of Shealtiel with his kinsmen started to rebuild the altar of the God of Israel so that they might be able to sacrifice burnt offerings upon it as prescribed in the law of Moses, the man of God.* [3] *They set up the altar on its original site,[a] for they were in a state of fear [b] because of the peoples of the land,[c] and they sacrificed [d] burnt offerings to the Lord upon it, both the morning and the evening offerings.* [4] *They kept the Feast of Tabernacles as prescribed,[a] offering each day the number of burnt offerings required by ordinance for that day,[a]* [5] *and afterwards (they sacrificed)[a] the regular burnt offerings,[b] the offerings for new moons and for all the sacred appointed feasts of the Lord as well as sacrificing on behalf of [c] any who brought a freewill offering to the Lord.* [6] *From the first day of the seventh month they began to sacrifice burnt offerings to the Lord, though the foundation of the temple of the Lord itself had not yet been laid.*

[7] *Then they gave money to the quarrymen and the stone-masons,[a] and food, drink, and oil to the Sidonians and the Tyrians to bring cedar-wood by sea [b] from Lebanon to Joppa according to the permission granted them by Cyrus, king of Persia.*

[8] *In the second year after their arrival at the house of God in Jerusalem, in the second month, Zerubbabel the son of Shealtiel and Jeshua the son of Jozadak and the rest of their kinsmen (namely the priests and the Levites and all who had come from the captivity to Jerusalem) started by appointing the Levites of twenty years old and more to supervise the work on the house of the Lord.* [9] *Jeshua, with his sons and brothers, Kadmiel, Binnui, and Hodaviah,[a] joined together to supervise those en-*

gaged ^b in the work on the house of God [the sons of Henadad, their sons and their brothers, the Levites].^c ¹⁰ When the builders laid the foundation ^a of the temple of the Lord, then the priests in their vestments with trumpets, and the Levites, the sons of Asaph, with cymbals, took their places ^b to praise the Lord in the manner prescribed by David, king of Israel. ¹¹ They sang antiphonally as they gave praise and thanks to the Lord, chanting

"For he is good;
his steadfast love for Israel endures for ever."

And all the people raised a great festal shout of praise to the Lord, because the foundation of the house of the Lord had been laid. ¹² But many of the older priests, Levites, and heads of families, who had seen the first temple, wept out loud when they saw the foundation ^a of this house, while many others shouted for joy at the tops of their voices. ¹³ Consequently, no one ^a could distinguish the sound of the shout of joy from that of the weeping because the people were shouting so very loudly; the noise could be heard from far away.

^{4:1} When the enemies of Judah and Benjamin heard that the returned exiles were building a temple for the Lord, the God of Israel, ² they approached Zerubbabel ^a and the heads of families and said to them, "Let us build with you, for like you we seek your God, and we have been sacrificing to him ^b ever since the time of Esarhaddon, king of Assyria, who brought us here." ³ But Zerubbabel, Jeshua, and the rest of the heads of families of Israel replied, "You have nothing in common with us to enable you to build ^a a house for our God; rather, we alone ^b will build (it) for the Lord, the God of Israel, as King Cyrus, king of Persia, has commanded us."

⁴ Thus ^a the people of the land discouraged ^b the people of Judah and made them afraid ^c to build ^d ⁵ and bribed counselors to work against them so as to frustrate their purpose all the days of Cyrus, king of Persia, and until the reign ^a of Darius, king of Persia.

Notes

3:1.a. Circumstantial clause; cf. GKC § 156.

1.b. Read בְּעָרֵיהֶם; cf. Neh 7:72(73) and *BHS.*

1.c. Perhaps insert כֹּל־ "all" before הָעָם "the people" with Neh 8:1 as providing the necessary balance to the following כְּאִישׁ אֶחָד "as one man."

3.a. This must be the equivalent of עַל־מְכוֹנוֹ "on its original site," 2:68. If the pl of MT is to be taken seriously (though it is not particularly well attested), it will mean "on its (previous) foundations."

3.b. MT is not so impossible as has generally been supposed; it has an *exact* syntactical equivalent in 2 Chr 16:10, כִּי־בְזַעַף עִמּוֹ עַל־זֹאת "because of rage against him for this." If both passages are considered corrupt, the phrase can be most simply emended (to give the same meaning) to בָּא אֵימָה "dread had come," postulating a haplogr of the א in a position where it is known to drop out quite often; cf. F. Delitzsch, *Die Lese- und Schreibfehler im alten Testament* (Berlin/Leipzig; de Gruyter, 1920) § 14c, and Williamson, "Sources and Redaction in the Chronicler's Genealogy of Judah," *JBL* 98 (1979) 354. Although אימה "dread" is fem, a preceding masc predicate would be by no means unparalleled; cf. GKC § 145o. In that case, it might have been the very fact of a slight anomaly that influenced a scribe to copy as in MT. 1 Esdr 5:50 does not support more adventurous emendations, once it is correctly understood (cf. Bewer). Nor is it necessary to dismiss the clause as a gl (Rudolph), which in any case would not solve the syntactical problem; it is needed to explain why they acted with such precision (cf. n.3.a.). Moreover, the "summary notation" in 4:4–5 (cf. *Form* below) further confirms the general correctness of MT.

3.c. This is simply a stylistic variant, quite common in late biblical Heb., for עמי הארץ "peoples of the land."

3.d. Read וַיַּעֲלוּ "and they offered up" with Q.

4.a-a. Lit. "The burnt offering of each day by number, according to the ordinance (or custom) of the matter of (each) day in its day."

5.a. Not present in MT, this has to be understood to complete the sense (cf. Keil).

5.b. 1 Esdr 5:51 suggests inserting here לשבתות "for the Sabbaths," and this is preferred by many, including NEB. Its loss is difficult to account for, however, whereas its addition in 1 Esdr can be explained as having been made by someone who felt that the recommencement of the regular daily offerings was already covered by v 3b. In fact, however, the latter refers only to the sacrifices offered on the occasion of the consecration of the restored altar.

5.c. Naturally, the narrator will have thought that only the priests actually sacrificed, and this explains his seemingly harsh transition here. There is no suggestion of the need to offer sacrifices *for* those who brought freewill offerings, so that the difficulty which many emendations have made their starting point is nonexistent.

7.a. חרש has a wide range of meaning, which can certainly cover skill in the working of stone (cf. 2 Sam 5:11), and the context favors this rather than the usual translation, "carpenters."

7.b. Lit. "to the sea, Joppa."

9.a. It is widely conjectured on the basis of 2:40 that MT's ובניו בני־יהודה "and his sons, the sons of Judah" is a corr of the not dissimilar ובנוי והודיה. Certainly the lack of the copula before קדמיאל "Kadmiel" raises suspicion.

9.b. For עשה "makers" as a pl form, cf. Keil on 1 Chr 23:24.

9.c. The bracketed section cannot have stood here originally since it lacks any connection with the foregoing. Either it is misplaced from earlier in the verse or, more probably, it represents a later expansion on the basis of Neh 3:18, 24; 10:10 (9).

10.a. ו + perf becomes increasingly common in late biblical Heb. as a narrative tense; cf. Driver, *Tenses* §§ 130–34.

10.b. The indefinite 3 pers pl may be construed by a passive, "the priests were set forward." The absence of את before הכהנים "the priests" and הלוים "the Levites" is unexpected, however, in view of its use after the same verb in v 8. There is some MS and Vrs support for reading the qal, וַיַּעַמְדוּ "and they took their places," and this is preferable.

12.a. The Masoretic punctuation links the reference to the foundation with the first temple, but historically that would be impossible while grammatically it leaves the following words unattached. ביסדו "when it was founded" should therefore be construed with what follows. It is not necessary to regard זה הבית "this (is) the house" as an explanatory gl to the suff (Rudolph); the somewhat awkward word order is designed to stress the contrast between "the first house" and "this house."

13.a. It is a moot point whether or not it is necessary to delete העם "the people" here and later in the verse (cf. BHS, following Ehrlich, *Randglossen*), but the meaning is in any event clear enough.

4:2.a. 1 Esdr suggests the addition here of "and Jeshua," and this is favored by many because of v 3. In view of later priestly rivalries, however, it is equally possible that the narrator may have wished to represent the approach as being deliberately directed towards the lay leadership alone, since they might have expected a more sympathetic response from that quarter.

2.b. Read ולו, with Q and a number of the Vrs. K, "and not," is less appropriate to the context, though cf. D. Kellermann, "Korrektur, Variante, Wahllesart?" *BZ* 24 (1980) 66–67; it is a polemical correction introduced after the time when these "enemies" were identified with the much later Samaritans.

3.a. Lit., "It is not for you and for us to build . . ."

3.b. This would now seem to be established as an acceptable rendering of יחד "together or alone"; cf. J. C. de Moor, "Lexical Remarks Concerning YAHAD and YAHDĀU," VT 7 (1957) 350–55, and note the earlier articles of J. Mauchline, "The Uses of YAHAD and YAHDĀU in the Old Testament," TGUOS 13 (1947–49) 51–53, and M. D. Goldman, AusBR 1 (1951) 61–63. It derives from the idea of "we together," i.e., "without your help." Against the attempt by S. Talmon, "The Sectarian יחד—A Biblical Noun," VT 3 (1953) 133–40, to see here the biblical noun "community," note the absence of the article.

4.a. Cf. *Form* below.

4.b. Lit., "weakening the hands of."

4.c. Although Q has the more common מבהלים "terrified," K, with מְבַלְהִים "caused them to be troubled" (from בלה), is quite acceptable. The meaning is not seriously affected.

4.d. Note that there is no grammatical justification for such historically harmonistic renderings as "made them afraid to continue building" (NEB; cf. NIV).

5.a. For the switch in form of chronological notation, cf. G. Brin, *ZAW* 93 (1981) 190.

Form/Structure/Setting

Apart from a few extremely radical proposals (e.g. Goettsberger, *JSOR* 10 [1926] 270–80), most treatments of this chapter have fallen under one of two headings. First, there are those who, by implication, have understood its form as that of straightforward historical narrative and who have also regarded its historical setting as being identical with its present literary setting. They then read the historical account as follows: very soon after the united return in the first, or perhaps second, year of Cyrus, the exiles gathered at Jerusalem to rededicate the altar (vv 1–6). A year or two later, a start was made on the temple building under the direction of Zerubbabel and Jeshua (vv 7–13), but this was soon stopped by outside interference (4:1–5). Work only resumed in the second year of Darius under the influence of Haggai and Zechariah (chaps. 5–6).

Apparent difficulties to this view are explained simply enough. (i) How can it be reconciled with the statement of 5:16 that Sheshbazzar, not Zerubbabel, laid the foundations for the new temple? Apart from scholars who identify Sheshbazzar with Zerubbabel, it is suggested that while Zerubbabel was actually responsible for the foundation-laying, the Jews in chap. 5 attributed the work to Sheshbazzar because Zerubbabel was working under his authority and it would have been his name (cf. 1:8) that was recorded in the Persian archives. (ii) How does this picture square with the impression gained from Haggai that the work begun in 520 B.C. was a fresh undertaking rather than the continuation of an interrupted work? Here it is explained that after a gap of some twenty years little evidence would remain of the first abortive undertaking. Moreover, יסד "to found" in Hag 2:18 need not imply a completely fresh start; it can also have the meaning "to restore," etc.; cf. 2 Chr 24:27. Similarly, חרב "be desolate" (Hag 1:4, 9) need not mean that there was nothing there, but that it was "deserted" or the like; cf. Hogg, Andersen, and Gelston, *inter alia.*

The second main approach to this chapter takes more seriously the apparent links with the material in Haggai and Zechariah, particularly in the matter of leadership. Acknowledging that the narrator was not as clear about the precise chronology of the period as he might have been, and perhaps that he was led astray by his mistaken identification of Zerubbabel and Sheshbazzar, they ascribe the whole account to 520 B.C., parallel with chaps. 5–6. Whatever measures Sheshbazzar may have taken earlier are irrelevant. This chapter describes a fresh undertaking by Zerubbabel, who may not have returned from Babylon until shortly before, or even during the first year of, the reign of Darius.

It is a serious flaw with regard to both these approaches that they do not on the whole discuss the nature of the writer's composition in this section or his handling of possible sources. A decisive advance in this regard is marked by a brief, but significant, contribution from S. Talmon, who in *IDBSup* 322 identifies 4:4–5 as a "summary notation," a literary device which, he explains, "recapitulate(s) the contents, and thus also delineate(s) the extent of a preceding textual unit." According to this view, the reference in 4:4 to the people of the land making the Jews afraid to build does not mark a new step in the historical development, but rather recapitulates the earlier statement of 3:3. If this is correct, then the statement of 4:5b will imply that no work at all was done on the temple until the second year of Darius. In other words, 4:4–5 will be the narrator's way of explaining that 3:1–6 refers to an altar dedication in the reign of Cyrus, that for fear of the peoples of the land no building was undertaken at that time, and that 3:7—4:3 describes the start of the work in the time of Darius. It is the failure to appreciate the important distinction between the two halves of the section that has led to so much difficulty in its interpretation.

These observations naturally raise in a sharper form the question of the nature of the composition in this section as a whole, for it begins to become apparent that it is not quite so straightforward as has generally been supposed. Closer examination shows it to be extremely stylized, for at almost every turn parallels are drawn, either by phraseology or by content, with the account of the building of the first temple under Solomon. For the details, see *Comment* below. It may be observed here that some of the parallels are more remote than others, but the interpretation may, it is claimed, be legitimate provided enough certain examples are adduced to establish that this was the author's concern in this account as a whole. Since this was seen to be a characteristic of our author's method in his own contributions to chap. 1, we are thus left with the strong impression that he himself was responsible for the present narrative as well.

This conclusion receives further support from the fact that there is virtually nothing here that demands the use of sources other than those which we already know lay at his disposal. It will be possible in the *Comment* to account for very nearly every verse on the basis of (i) deduction from the other sources contained in Ezra-Nehemiah, (ii) the prophecies of Haggai and Zechariah, (iii) the inclusion of language and ideas intended to draw attention to parallels with the building of the first temple, and (iv) the cultic practices of the writer's own day.

There are only two exceptions to this. First, the apparently surprising reference to Esarhaddon in 4:2 makes it probable that the incident recounted in 4:1–3 is based on earlier, independent material (see *Comment* below). It may be suggested that this was one of the two letters that the author only summarizes in 4:6–7. The self-designation of another group in 4:10 favors the view that the comparable information in 4:2b could have been similarly preserved. Furthermore, the whole incident might have been recounted in the body of the letter as part of a historical retrospect on Judean-Samarian relations (cf. 4:15). It is not difficult to see how the substance of 4:1–3 could have contributed to such an accusation, as well as why the admitted foreign origins of the group in question led our author, writing much later under the impact of the more exclusive attitudes that then prevailed, to rewrite the account as we have it and to justify its tone so elaborately in the rest of chap. 4.

Second, since by making Zerubbabel and Jeshua responsible for the first moves towards temple restoration in 3:1–6 our author has established a certain tension with 5:16, it may be that here too he is acting under the constraint of a source. An additional pointer in the same direction may be seen in the fact that only in this verse does he cite the leaders in the order Jeshua-Zerubbabel. This is not quite so secure as the first example, however, since he may simply have been attracted by their prominence in the later rebuilding, and he may have been anxious to have a member of the Davidic family involved from the start, with Jeshua listed first in this purely religious ceremony. Uncertainty here is particularly unfortunate because of the consequent effects for historical reconstruction: if Zerubbabel was present at the dedication of the altar, then he must have been among the first to return to Judah after the exile; if not, his return could be dated any time before the second year of Darius. On the basis of a "flat" reading of chap. 2, our author probably thought in terms of the former. If the more nuanced approach to the sources advocated here is correct, then the possibility remains that he came only later, perhaps as a replacement for Sheshbazzar. Both Cambyses, who went on to conquer Egypt to the west, and Darius, who faced many revolts at the start of his reign, would have had good reason to want in Jerusalem a loyal governor who could also command his own people's support. There is no reason to doubt that, as a Davidide, Zerubbabel could have fulfilled this role. (In this connection, we may note the implication of 1 Esdr 3:1—5:6 that Zerubbabel came to Jerusalem only at the start of the reign of Darius. It is generally agreed, however, that this account is of no historical value; cf. Pohlmann, *Studien*, 35–52. Heltzer, *RB* 86 [1979] 102–6, succeeds only in showing the possibility of one aspect of the story, not its probability.) Nevertheless, the evidence seems on balance to point to the use of some earlier tradition in these opening verses, and so to favor the early date for Zerubbabel's return.

To summarize: the author's aim in this passage is to write a typological account of the founding of the second temple, for which purpose he has juxtaposed events from the reigns of both Cyrus and Darius. Much of his account here is thus parallel with chaps. 5–6 and the Book of Haggai, and it offers a theological interpretation of the events that he is later to record in a more matter-of-fact manner on the basis of his sources. Since, with one, or perhaps two, exceptions the narrative is constructed out of other biblical material, it is both a mistake of method, and a misunderstanding of the writer's intention, to use this section primarily for the purpose of historical reconstruction.

Comment

1–6 The dedication of the altar and the restoration of the regular sacrifices.

1 It has already been seen in the discussion of chap. 2 that this verse was taken over, together with the preceding list, from Neh 7 and 8:1. The only need was to change "the open space in front of the Water Gate" to the less specific "Jerusalem" in order to conform the verse to its new historical setting. It is thus evidently inappropriate to seek to identify "the seventh month" more closely, whether of the first or second year of Cyrus. As its use in Nehemiah reminds us, it was the sacred month *par excellence* for the Jews, and it included several of their most important festivals; cf. Lev 23:23– 36. The writer would thus have been happy to take it over from his source as the month most suitable for such an occasion.

2 For the historical issues raised by this verse, see *Form* above. The "kins- men" (literally, "brothers") of Zerubbabel would have been fellow lay-people as distinct from the priests, and not simply members of the royal family. According to Japhet, *ZAW* 94 (1982) 84, they are mentioned here because of the editor's concern to transfer the emphasis in the restoration from the leaders to the people at large; see also vv 1, 7–8, 13 and 4:2–3. The first concern of the returning community is presented as having been to restore the cult as it used to be: "as prescribed in the law of Moses" (and cf. v 4). The theme of the continuity of the cult noted in the second half of chap. 1 here extends to its associated activities.

"So that they might be able to sacrifice." It is by no means improbable that sacrifices continued to be offered here throughout the exile; cf. Jer 41:5, but contrast D. R. Jones, "The Cessation of Sacrifice after the Destruction of the Temple in 586 B.C.,"*JTS* ns 14 (1963) 12–31. For the purposes of our writer, however, it will become increasingly evident that the continuity of religious tradition ran through the community in exile alone, so that a fresh dedication of the altar would have been regarded as indispensable.

3 The theme of continuity leads also to the emphasis on the siting of the new altar. It has been repeatedly demonstrated by archeological discover- ies that the veneration of sacred sites persisted long after their physical de- struction. In the present instance, the exiles, to say nothing of the later community of the writer's own day, would have been most anxious to ensure that they centered their cult on the precise spot where God had revealed that "the altar of burnt offering for Israel" should be situated (1 Chr 22:1). The literary patterning of the one building on the other in the second half of this chapter undoubtedly arose out of such convictions about the impor- tance of the physical continuity between the two.

The expression "peoples of the land" is not one to which the same meaning can be ascribed at every occurrence in the OT; cf. E. W. Nicholson, "The Meaning of the Expression עם הארץ in the Old Testament,"*JSS* 10 (1965) 59–66. Though the present context does not enable us to be very specific, it clearly refers in a general way to those who were not part of the returned community, both those within the province of Judah and their near neighbors (cf. Vogt, *Studie*, 152–54). The possibility of true Jews being among them is simply not envisaged in these books. Not surprisingly, the small band of exiles stood in some fear of them; their response, therefore, was twofold. First, they exercised every care to follow correct cultic procedure in order to maintain the benefit of divine protection. Second, though, they refrained from inciting opposition by not rebuilding the temple at this early stage (v 6; 4:4). Only much later did they find the confidence to take this further step.

4–6 The Feast of Tabernacles falls within the seventh month (as does the Day of Atonement, but that could hardly be observed before the temple was rebuilt), and so was celebrated according to the detailed prescriptions of Num 29:12–38. This was only one aspect, however, of the recommencement of the whole round of daily and monthly sacrifices. According to v 6, these began "on the first day of the seventh month," whereas it appears from v 5 that they began only later in the month, following the Feast of Tabernacles. Probably we should not press this apparent discrepancy. Verse 6 may refer only to the sacrifices at the rededication of the altar (v 3), but in fact its purpose is probably quite other: if the community only assembled "when the seventh month came" (v 1; note the unparalleled use of וַיִּגַּע with time), it is difficult to see how they could have started the sacrifices so soon. The intention of v 6 rather is to emphasize that they wasted no time, but restored the worship of the cult as soon as they could. Compare the description of Hezekiah's temple reform in 2 Chr 29:3 with 17.

"Though the foundation of the temple of the Lord had not yet been laid." This concludes the first section of the chapter, after which, according to 4:4–5, we jump to the reign of Darius when the foundation was laid (3:10 with Hag 2:18). It did not serve the purpose of the author's narrative to emphasize the time gap between the two parts of his description at this point, for his focus is entirely positive—on the community's eager service and on the continuity with the worship of the first temple which they were restoring. Elsewhere, however, he makes it clear that he was indeed fully aware of the historical realities.

7–13 Preparations are made for the rebuilding of the temple and the foundations are laid. In this section, parallels are repeatedly drawn with the building of the first temple.

7 The gathering of the necessary materials reminds us at once of 1 Chr 22:2–4; 2 Chr 2:7–15 (8–16). While it is undoubtedly true that the general similarities would have been dictated by historical necessity, the verbal parallels (the shipment by sea to Joppa; the payment of food, drink, and oil; the bracketing of the Sidonians and the Tyrians) are sufficiently striking to demonstrate that this is a conscious allusion to the earlier description.

8 The date for the start of the work furthers the typological comparison, for Solomon too began to build "in the second month"; cf. 2 Chr 3:2. It has generally been assumed that "the second year" relates to the exiles' return from captivity, so that this section would then still be within the reign of Cyrus. In fact, however, the writer makes clear that this is not his meaning by adding the striking qualification, "of their coming to the house of God." In the context of the previous verse and of 2:68, this obviously refers to the time when they turned their attention in earnest to the work of rebuilding by starting to collect the materials. (Our author speaks directly of coming "from Babylon to Jerusalem" [1:11] when he intends the return from exile.) It would have taken a considerable amount of time to ship the timber from Lebanon, so they wisely did not begin the construction work until the preparations were sufficiently advanced. In that case, "the second year" is part of the typological comparison: the first temple took seven years to build (1 Kgs 6:38). Now, according to 6:15, the second temple was completed in the twelfth month (Adar) of the sixth year of Darius, construction having been begun in his second year (4:24 with 5:1). Thus by dating the start to "the second year" of "their coming to the house of God" our writer could suggest that the total operation also lasted for some seven years.

The appointment of Levites "to supervise the work on the house of the

Lord" (לנצח על־מלאכת בית־יהוה) may be compared with the identical phraseology of 1 Chr 23:4, where David is making arrangements for the building of the first temple. Their entering into service at the age of twenty compares with 1 Chr 23:24 and 27 but contrasts with 23:3 (and Num 4:3, etc.). 1 Chr 23 gives evidence of much later revision (cf. VTSup 30 [1979] 251–68), and our writer agrees with the latest stages in its development. His statement may thus be a small pointer towards the circle from which he came (cf. *Introduction*, "Composition").

9 With the Levites supervising the work, it was appropriate that overall responsibility should be in the hands of their leading families. Consequently, they are introduced here from 2:40.

10–11 In this account interest centers less on the process of foundation-laying and more on the accompanying religious celebration (cf. Petersen, *CBQ* 36 [1974] 366–72). Similar descriptions are to be found in other post-exilic historical works, such as 1 Chr 15–16; 2 Chr 5; 7, etc. This is due not to the suggestion that they were necessarily written by the same man but to the fact that this was the nature of religious ceremonial occasions at the time of the writers. Not surprisingly, therefore, the practice conforms to such legal prescriptions as Num 10:8 and 10.

The description, once again, echoes the dedication of Solomon's temple. Some of the verbal parallels with 2 Chr 5:11 and 7:6 are particularly striking. The awareness of continuity between the worship of pre- and post-exilic times is further heightened by the insistence on all being conducted "in the manner prescribed by David." Just as Moses was believed to have established the patterns of sacrifice (see on vv 2–6), so David was believed to have introduced certain necessary changes into the regulations concerning levitical service when, with the building of the temple, they were no longer required to carry the ark; cf. 1 Chr 15–16; 23–26; 2 Chr 7:6; 29:25–26; and von Rad, *Geschichts-bild*, 98–115. It is as though our writer wishes to emphasize that, despite the exile, and despite the fact that physically the second temple was not the same as the first, yet from the point of view of forms of worship nothing has changed.

The reference to "the Levites, the sons of Asaph" reflects instructively the varying influences on the writer in his composition. On the one hand, by his day all the temple singers were classed as Levites but were divided into three families. On the other hand, the list of the singers in Ezra 2:41 mentions only the sons of Asaph among those who returned (though it does not appear to regard them as Levites). It was not difficult for our writer then to construct his account out of this material, both elements of which he would have regarded as historically determinative.

The psalm fragment quoted here occurs several times in the Psalter; cf. Pss 100:4–5; 106:1; 107:1; 118:1; 136:1. It is thus probable that, as with its use by the Chronicler, so here it is intended to be illustrative of the type of psalms of praise that would have been used on such an occasion.

12–13 A final specific point of continuity between the first and second temples is provided by a reference to the older members of the congregation whose long lives further helped to bridge the interrupted worship on this site. Based, no doubt, on Hag 2:3, some clearly found the comparison bitterly disappointing. Others, however, refused to consider this as merely a "day of small things" (Zech 4:10), but rather in faith rejoiced aloud that ever such a day of restoration should have dawned at all.

4:1–3 This little paragraph, in which an offer of help by an ill-defined group is rebuffed by Zerubbabel and his colleagues, has caused the commentators much difficulty. A few general introductory remarks may therefore help avoid misunderstandings. (i) The interpretation of vv 4–5 presented here shows that it is not to be read as the direct continuation of 1–3. This means, among other things, that it is not necessary to date 1–3 to the reign of Cyrus, nor to identify "the enemies of Judah and Benjamin" (v 1) with the "people of the land" (v 4). (ii) We have presented reasons for dating this incident, in fact, to the reign of Darius. Here it both fits well and, indeed, is almost required by 5:3. Tattenai's inquiry into who authorized the Jews to rebuild the temple can best be understood as an investigation prompted as an act of reprisal by those whose help is here refused (Rudolph). This, of course, would rule out a date as early as the time of Cyrus. It is less likely, however, that we should also follow Rothstein's proposal (*Juden und Samaritaner*) of seeing in this incident the background to Hag 2:10–14; cf. K. Koch, "Haggais unreines Volk," *ZAW* 79 (1967) 52–66; H. G. May, " 'This People' and 'This Nation' in Haggai," *VT* 18 (1968) 190–97. (iii) It is unhelpful to attempt an evaluation of this incident on the basis of much later Jewish-Samaritan polemic; cf. M. Cogan, *Imperialism and Religion: Assyria, Judah and Israel in the Eighth and Seventh Centuries B.C.E.* (Missoula, MT: Scholars Press, 1974), 103–10. It is now widely agreed that that controversy arose very much later; cf. R. J. Coggins, *Samaritans and Jews. The Origins of Samaritanism Reconsidered* (Oxford: Blackwell, 1975). Despite later Jewish polemic, there is no biblical evidence whatever that justifies identifying the Samaritan sect of later times with the settlers imported into northern Israel after the fall of the kingdom.

1 "The enemies of Judah and Benjamin" is our writer's own description of this group, based upon a long period of confrontation during which attitudes had hardened considerably. Part of the reason for his inclusion of the remainder of chap. 4 is his desire to justify this description. At the time, they did not necessarily appear to be so.

2 We have no reason to doubt their self-description. They were those (or perhaps just some of those) who had been imported by the Assyrians into the territory of the old Northern Kingdom and who had adopted the local religion (cf. 2 Kgs 17:24–41). That some from the north had indeed continued to sacrifice on their visits to Jerusalem during the period of the exile is confirmed by Jer 41:5. Their offer of help may therefore have arisen as a disguise for their feeling of offended proprietary rights, and may have hidden motives not apparent from their recorded statement.

Nowhere else in the OT are we told that Esarhaddon, king of Assyria, was responsible for settling foreigners in Israel. The major tradition, as found in 2 Kgs 17, suggests a much earlier settlement by Sargon II. This evidence of an additional later settlement (and cf. v 10) is thus unlikely to be pure fabrication, though we cannot be sure to what extent each new wave of colonists maintained their separate identities. Support for its historicity comes first from Isa 7:8, whose reference to sixty-five years may well bring us to the reign of Esarhaddon, and second from the historical texts of Esarhaddon's reign (*ANET*, 289–94), which testify to his successful campaigns in the west and which thus suggest a plausible setting for a policy of resettlement.

3 Whether or not Zerubbabel and his colleagues considered the possibility that there was more to the request than met the eye, they were firm in declining the offer. The reason they gave was, strictly speaking, quite correct: it was they, and they alone, whom Cyrus had authorized to build the temple; cf. 1:2–4. The self-confessed foreign origin of those asking to help was sufficient, on political grounds, to bar them from participation. As the form of Tattenai's subsequent inquiry shows, they might have jeopardized the whole undertaking if they had not kept to the letter of the authorization granted them. (This was why they insisted, somewhat misleadingly, that their work was a direct and uninterrupted continuation of what had been started in Sheshbazzar's time; cf. 5:16.) We cannot tell at this distance whether an inherently religious exclusivism also lay behind this politically understandable response. It may have, though we should note that at least they were willing to absorb individuals into their community as opposed to groups who maintained a distinct identity; cf. 6:21. But the inquirers can hardly be expected to have appreciated so fine a distinction, and by their subsequent actions, no doubt goaded by this rebuff, they showed themselves ultimately to be "the enemies of Judah and Benjamin."

4–5 For the purpose and primary significance of this "summary notation," see *Form* above. "The people of the land" will have the same meaning as at 3:3. It may include the "adversaries" of vv 1–3, but cannot be restricted to them. This interpretation excludes the rather far-reaching theories of Alt *KS* 2, 316–37, and Würthwein, *Der 'amm ha'arez*, 57–64, who find here a reference to the ruling classes of Samaria and who go on to draw consequences for the political history of the area from these verses (cf. Smith, *Parties*, 193–201).

"And bribed counselors." It is clear that our author has no further information on what exactly happened. He may have in mind the following paragraph, surmising that similar tactics are likely to have been employed in the earlier period too.

Explanation

"Seek first God's kingdom and his righteousness, and all these things shall be added unto you" (Matt 6:33). To this abiding theme of Scripture the present passage adds its voice in its own particular manner. In writing of a period partly covered by the events recorded here, Haggai could castigate his contemporaries for devoting all their attention to material prosperity while neglecting the ruined temple in their midst—a tell-tale indication of their failure to appreciate the necessity for divinely ordered priorities. Such an approach was not open to our author, who was obliged to seek to influence his readers by way of historical narrative. Instead he presents the community of the return in an exemplary light, as demonstrating some of the very virtues that Haggai seems to have found lacking. That this is only part of the story he makes clear by 4:4–5 and the subsequent narrative. But, in his view, the community faced problems enough to make this understandable. Also they had shown by their early move to renew the altar and restore the regular round of sacrifices that at the start, their priorities were right. It is on this positive portrayal that he chooses to dwell.

Second, we cannot fail to note the element of joy and willingness which throughout accompanies the sacrifices and the worship, even though these are unashamedly cultic in expression. Indeed, the disappointment of some of the older men (3:12) only highlights the uninhibited exultation of the remainder. This is something that is rarely understood by those outside the community of faith, for whom such exercises appear as dry, or even legalistic, formalism. However, where worship is an expression of the heart's affections, experience brings understanding, so that the participants in these events doubtless felt at one with the Psalmist, whose "soul yearns, even faints for the courts of the Lord," and for whom "one day in your courts is better than a thousand elsewhere" (Ps 84:2, 10). Similarly, the Christian, for whom indeed the OT expressions of worship have been largely superseded, also knows the otherwise inexplicable joy of worship, regarding it less as a duty than as a delight.

Third, the increasingly familiar theme of continuity reappears in this section. In chap. 1, it dealt primarily with the continuity of saving experience; in chap. 2, of the community and their land; now in chap. 3 these two move toward their goal in the restoration of worship on the site of the first temple, reintroducing the very same forms and expressions that had been previously ordained by Moses and David.

Finally, at this point, when the community seems to be making progress in restoration, the first ominous note of opposition is struck, and it is one that will dominate much of the rest of these books. The message is made clear from the outset: however attractive the offer of help might seem, the work can only proceed on the basis of God's revealed will, expressed in this case through the decree of Cyrus. Individuals might certainly join the community by their complete identification with it, but the community cannot conversely jeopardize its identity by merging with other groups as such. Time and again, the sequel is to show that this seemingly unattractive stance was nevertheless the correct one. For the Church, the circumstances have been radically changed so that it is not possible simply to take attitudes and agendas from such OT situations without considerable further qualification, not least from within the OT itself. Nevertheless it remains clear that the Church will never retain its effectiveness as "salt" and "light" through compromise and lack of a positive identity. Rather, it must seek new ways in which these necessary properties can be applied in a spirit of love and reconciliation to a world whose need of them is everywhere apparent.

Opposition (Ezra 4:6-24)

Bibliography

Alexander, P. S. "Remarks on Aramaic Epistolography in the Persian Period." *JSS* 23 (1978) 155–70. **Altheim, F.** and **Stiehl, R.** *Die aramäische Sprache unter den Achaimeniden.* Frankfurt am Main: Klostermann, 1963. **Cameron, G. G.** *History of Early Iran.* Chicago: University of Chicago Press, 1936, 185–211. **Dion, P.-E.** "Les types épistolaires hébréo-araméens jusqu'au temps de Bar-Kokhbah." *RB* 96 (1979) 544–79. **Driver, G. R.** "Studies in the Vocabulary of the Old Testament. III." *JTS* 32 (1931) 361–66. **Eilers, W.** *Iranische Beamtennamen in der Keilschriftlichen Überlieferung.* Leipzig: Brockhaus, 1940. **Fitzmyer, J. A.** "Some Notes on Aramaic Epistolography." *JBL* 93 (1974) 201–25. A slightly revised form of this article appears in *A Wandering Aramean: Collected Aramaic Essays.* Missoula, MT: Scholars Press, 1979, 183–204, and in *Semeia* 22 (1981) 25–57. **Galling, K.** "Kronzeugen des Artaxerxes? Eine Interpretation von Esra 4, 9f." *ZAW* 63 (1951) 66–74. **Hensley, L. V.** *Documents.* **Hervey, A. C.** "The Chronology of Ezra iv.6–23." *The Expositor* iv/8 (1893) 50–63. **Hoffmann, G.** "Namen und Sachen." *ZA* 2 (1887) 54–55. **Jensen, P.** "Alttestamentlich—Keilinschriftliches." *ZAW* 52 (1934) 121–23. **Kutscher, E. Y.** "Aramaic." *Current Trends in Linguistics.* Vol. 6. *Linguistics in South West Asia and North Africa,* ed. T. A. Seboek. The Hague: Mouton, 1970, 347–412. **Leuze, O.** *Die Satrapieneinteilung in Syrien und im Zweistromlande von 520–320.* Halle: Max Niemeyer, 1935. **Liagre Böhl, F. M. Th. de.** "Die babylonischen Prätendenten zur Zeit des Xerxes." *BO* 19 (1962) 110–14. **Liver, J.** "The Problem of the Order of the Kings of Persia in the Books of Ezra and Nehemiah" (Heb.). *Studies in Bible and Judean Desert Scrolls.* Jerusalem: Bialik Institute, 1971. 263–76. **Luria, B. Z.** "There have been Mighty Kings also over Jerusalem (Ezra 4:20)" (Hebrew). *BMik* 53/2 (1973) 176–82. **Malamat, A.** "The Historical Background of the Assassination of Amon, King of Judah." *IEJ* 3 (1953) 26–29. **Meyer, E.** *Entstehung.* **Morgenstern, J.** "Jerusalem—485 B.C." *HUCA* 27 (1956) 101–79; 28 (1957) 15–47; 31 (1960) 1–29. ———. "Isaiah 49–55." *HUCA* 36 (1965) 1–35. ———. "Further Light from the Book of Isaiah upon the Catastrope of 485 B.C." *HUCA* 37 (1966) 1–28. ———. "The Dates of Ezra and Nehemiah." *JSS* 7 (1962) 1–11. **Polotsky, H. J.** "Aramäisch *prš* und das 'Huzvaresch'." *Le Muséon* 45 (1932) 273–83. **Rainey, A. F.** "The Satrapy 'Beyond the River'." *AJBA* 1 (1969) 51–78. **Rowley, H. H.** "Nehemiah's Mission." **Schaeder, H. H.** *Iranische Beiträge* 1. Halle: Max Niemeyer, 1930. **Smith, S.** "Foundations: Ezra iv, 12; v, 16; vi, 3." *Essays in Honour of the Very Rev. Dr. J. H. Hertz,* ed. I. Epstein, E. Levine, and C. Roth. London: Edward Golston, 1945, 385–96. **Snell, D. C.** "Why Is There Aramaic in the Bible?" *JSOT* 18 (1980) 32–51. **Torrey, C. C.** "Old Testament Notes: 1. The Meaning of וּבְעֶנֶת." *JBL* 16 (1897) 166–68. ———. *Ezra Studies,* 140–207. **Tuland, C. G.** " 'uššayyā' and 'uššarnâ: a Clarification of Terms, Date, and Text." *JNES* 17 (1958) 269–75. **White, J. L.** (ed.). *Studies in Ancient Letter Writing. Semeia* 22 (1982). **Whitehead, J. D.** "Some Distinctive Features of the Language of the Aramaic Arsames Correspondence." *JNES* 37 (1978) 119–40. **Williamson, H. G. M.** "The Composition of Ezra i–vi." *JTS* ns 34 (1983) 1–30.

Translation

[6] *In the reign of Xerxes,* [a] *at the beginning of his reign, they wrote an accusation against the residents of Judah and Jerusalem.*

[7] *And in the days of Artaxerxes,* [a] *Bishlam,* [b] *Mithredath, Tabeel, and the rest of his colleagues wrote to Artaxerxes, king of Persia, and the document* [c] *was written in the Aramaic script but translated. (Aramaic:)* [d]

[8] *Then* [a] *Rehum the chancellor* [b] *and Shimshai the secretary wrote a letter about* [c] *Jerusalem to Artaxerxes the king as follows:*

[9] *Rehum* [a] *the chancellor and Shimshai the secretary and the rest of their colleagues—the judges* [b] *and the envoys,* [c] *the men of Tarpel,* [d] *Sippar,* [e] *Erech, Babylon, Susa* [f] *(that is,* [g] *Elam)* [10] *and the rest of the peoples whom the great and illustrious Osnappar* [a] *deported and resettled in the city* [b] *of Samaria and in the rest of the province Beyond the River.* [c]

[11] *(This is a copy of the letter which they sent to him:)*

To King Artaxerxes (from) your servants, the men of Beyond the River.
[12] *And now: Be it known to the king that the Jews who came up from you to us (and who) have arrived at Jerusalem are rebuilding the rebellious and wicked city; they are moving towards the completion of the walls* [a] *and have (already) laid* [b] *the foundations.* [c] [13] *Now be it known to the king that if this city is rebuilt and its walls* [a] *completed, then they will no longer pay tribute, tax, or dues,* [b] *and in the end* [c] *it* [d] *will prove damaging to the royal interests.* [e] [14] *Now, since we are under obligation to* [a] *the court, and it is not fitting for us to witness the king's dishonor,* [b] *therefore we are sending herewith to inform* [c] *the king,* [15] *so that a search may be made* [a] *in your fathers' record-books.* [b] *In the record-books you will discover and learn that this city is a rebellious city, damaging to kings and provinces, and that sedition has been fomented within it in times past. That is why this city was laid waste.* [16] *We submit to your majesty* [a] *that if this city is rebuilt and its walls* [b] *completed, then you will have no more stake in the province Beyond the River.*

[17] *The king sent this reply:*

To Rehum the chancellor and Shimshai the secretary and the rest of their colleagues resident in Samaria and elsewhere in Beyond the River, greetings. [18] *And now: the letter which you sent us has been read verbatim* [a] *in my presence.* [19] *I ordered a search to be made and it was discovered* [a] *that in times past this city has risen in revolt against kings and that rebellion and sedition have been fomented there.* [20] *However,* [a] *there have been powerful kings over Jerusalem who also ruled over the whole of Beyond the River, and tribute, tax, and dues were paid to them.* [21] *Now, therefore, issue orders to stop these men; that city is not to be rebuilt except by my express command.* [a] [22] *Be warned against acting negligently in this matter, lest the threat grow to the point of damaging the royal interests.*

[23] *Then as soon as a copy of the letter from King Artaxerxes had been read to Rehum* [a] *and Shimshai the secretary and their colleagues, they hurried to Jerusalem to oppose the Jews and forcibly compelled them to stop.*
[24] *Then the work on the house of God in Jerusalem stopped and it remained at a standstill until the second year of the reign of Darius, king of Persia.*

Notes

6.a. אֲחַשְׁוֵרוֹשׁ, generally transcribed as Ahasuerus. From Old Persian *Khshayârshâ*, it occurs in *AramP* as חשירש (2:1) and חשיארש (5:1), thus making identity with Xerxes certain. Schaeder, *Beiträge*, 71–72, suggests that the OT form is a corrupt representation of the Akk. spelling *ḫi-ši-ar-ši* (u).

7.a. There is considerable variation as to detail in the spelling of this name both within the OT (and even within this verse) and elsewhere. The first form in this verse is closest to the Old Persian; Schaeder, *Beiträge*, 70.

7.b. Not otherwise known as a personal name, though understood so by 1 Esdr and Vg. With support of other Vrs, some understand it as the Aram. equivalent of בשלום "with the agreement, consent of"; cf. NEB, ". . . with the agreement of Mithredath, Tabeel and all his colleagues wrote . . ." This has the advantage of explaining the singular verb and the singular suffix on כנותו "his colleagues." It is nevertheless difficult to accept, because an intrusive Aram. form of so common a word is inexplicable and because the word order is unusual: in Heb., we should expect such a phrase to follow the word it qualifies. An alternative proposal (cf. *BHS*) is to read בירושלם "in Jerusalem" (Rudolph) or בשם ירושלם (Galling; parablepsis from one ש to the other), "concerning/in the matter of Jerusalem." This makes excellent sense, but is pure conjecture. It does not, of course, remove the slight difficulty of the sg verb and suff. It thus seems best to retain MT; a sg verb before a multiple subject is common in these books. The sg suff probably refers back to Bishlam, with Mithredath and Tabeel mentioned as being his most prominent colleagues.

7.c. Despite Dion, *Semeia* 22 (1981) 80–81, it would appear from *AramP* 17:3 (נשתונא כתיב) that a נשתון was not necessarily a written document (for the etymology, cf. Ellenbogen, *Foreign Words*, 116). The slightly awkward use of כתב before it here (lit., "the writing of the document was written . . .") betrays awareness of this fact and ensures that no misunderstanding should arise. It is therefore unnecessary to follow Meyer, *Entstehung*, 18, *et al.* in regarding כתב as a later explanatory gl.

7.d. It seems likely, by analogy with Dan 2:4, that the second occurrence of ארמית "Aramaic" is a scribal note to warn the reader that what follows (4:8—6:18) is in Aram. See further under *Comment*.

8.a. Cf. 9.a.

8.b. See also *AramP* 26:23. In neither case is any military association apparent, so that "commanding officer" is an inappropriate rendering. The word is probably borrowed from Akk. and appears to refer to a bureaucratic intermediary; cf. Porten, *Archives from Elephantine*, 56, and Hensley, *Documents*, 54–56, both with further literature.

8.c. Or "against."

9.a. The verse starts אדין "then," after which we expect a verb; RV and RSV supply "wrote," but this makes the passage into a doublet of v 8 for no apparent reason. Others tacitly omit the word (e.g., NEB, NIV), while Bertholet regards it as a confused doublet of דיניא "judges," and Rudolph emends it to די אנון "they (the senders) were." If it is right to regard this fuller list of names as originating from some part of the document separate from the main text, such as the address or summary (see *Form* below), then we do not expect אדין here or any amended form either. It may tentatively be suggested that, owing to the identical openings of the two verses, it came to be misplaced in the course of transmission from the start of v 8, where it fits naturally and where its loss has created a certain abruptness.

9.b. Vocalize דָּיָנַיָּא "the judges" (Hoffmann, *ZA* 2 [1887] 54–55), with 1 Esdr^L 2:16. Though considerable uncertainty still attends this verse, the widespread view is adopted here that the unfamiliar titles at the head of this list came in the course of time to be misunderstood as gentilics in view of the continuation; cf. Rosenthal, *Grammar* § 58. For a radically different approach, cf. Galling, *ZAW* 63 (1951) 66–74.

9.c. For this translation, cf. Eilers, *Beamtennamen*, 30–40. He suggests that it represents O.P. *fraištaka-* or *fraistaka-*. It is thus to be distinguished from אפרסכיא in 5:6 and 6:6, since this derives from *frasaka*, "investigator, inspector."

9.d. It is not certain where the change from officials to peoples comes. It is placed at this point because only the first two words in the list are linked with the copula; cf. Vogt's Lexicon, *sub* אפרסי. "Tarpel" would appear from the context to be an otherwise unknown place or region in Babylon, though Galling thinks rather of "Tripolis" (cf. NIV and *VT* 4 [1954] 418–

22); Bowman, however, argues that the next two names are also officials (cf. NEB: "the judges, the commissioners, the overseers, and chief officers"), while Rudolph links the third and fourth words, reading טַרְפְּלָיֵא פָּרְסָיֵא (deletion of א that arose from dittogr; cf. Bewer) to yield "the Persian tarpelites"—an as yet unidentified class of official. (Rudolph rightly rejects Jensen's [*ZAW* 52 (1934) 121–23] appeal to Latin *tabellarius*, "courier.") No solution to the problems of this verse is fully satisfactory.

9.e. Reading סִפְרָיֵא "(men of) Sippar" with Vogt, *Lexicon*, following Ginsberg; see n. 9.d. above. Since so much must have been well-nigh unintelligible to later copyists, it is not difficult to suppose that the word was corrupted into its present form during the course of transmission under the influence of the start of the word אֲפַרְסַתְכָיֵא "envoys" just before. As an alternative suggestion, one might note the similarity between this word and אֲפַרְסַתְכָיֵא, while at 5:6 and 6:6 we have, in comparable contexts, אֲפַרְסְכָיֵא. Meyer, *Entstehung*, 35–41, endeavored to explain the latter as "the Persians," namely, פָרַס, with the well-attested preformative א for Iran. names and the Iran. adjectival suffix *-ka* (see n. 9.f.). Were he right, אֲפַרְסַתְכָיֵא would stand out as anomalous, and we could postulate that אֲפַרְסְיֵא was originally an explanatory gl upon it. This part of the list might then be rendered, "The judges and the Persians (i.e., Persian officials), the men of Tarpel, . . . Erech, etc." The first two mentioned would still be differentiated from the rest of the list (resettled colonists) by the conj; there would be no suggestion that they had been resettled by Ashurbanipal. Against this, however, cf. n. 9.c.

9.f. שׁוּשַׁנְכָיֵא "men of Shushan (Susa)." The כ is a Persian element, as in סוֹנכן, "man of Syene" at *AramP* 67:3 etc.

9.g. Read דִי הוּא, or דְהוּא (Rosenthal, *Grammar* § 35) with K.

10.a. I.e., Ashurbanipal. The confusion of *l* and *r* at the end of the word may reflect Persian influence, but the loss of medial רב cannot be explained on such philological grounds; cf. Rudolph and A. R. Millard, "Assyrian Royal Names in Biblical Hebrew," *JSS* 21 (1976) 11–12.

10.b. A number of the Vrs have a pl, while we should have in any case expected the det form here (קִרְיְתָא). Many have therefore followed Torrey, *Studies*, 186, in vocalizing קָרְיְתָה (pl with anticipatory suff), while Rosenthal, *Grammar* § 62, simply declares קִרְיָה itself to be an irregular pl det. In view of the following phrase, however, a pl is not required. We could as well suggest קִרְיָה, an irregular form of the sg noun with anticipatory suff, misunderstood by a later scribe.

10.c. וּכְעֶנֶת, "and now," stands here in MT, but it always introduces a new section of a letter, and so is out of place. It may have been accidentally copied from the end of v 11. Torrey's conjectures, *JBL* 16 (1897) 166–68, as to the meaning and use of the word, later misunderstood by the Masoretes, have been strikingly confirmed by the papyri.

12.a. K is clearly impossible, but Q (וְשׁוּרַיָּא שַׁכְלִילוּ "and they have completed the walls") is no better since vv 13 and 16 use the same vocabulary to show that the walls were not yet completed. NEB follows Vg in reading an impf (יְשַׁכְלְלוּן), while Torrey, *Studies*, 186–87, even defends K as a form of the impf with initial א. More speculatively, Rudolph proposes corr by haplogr of an original וְשָׁרִיו שׁוּרַיָּא לְשַׁכְלָלָה "and they are beginning to complete the walls." Some form of the impf, which stays close to MT, conveys the required sense.

12.b. This has generally been taken as an unusual form of the impf haph of חוט/חיט, but, being without final *nūn*, the form is strictly juss, and in any case fits uneasily with the implication of the previous clause that work is already progressing on the walls themselves. Similar objections tell against the attempts to link with חטט (cf. Syr.) "to dig out," and with Akk. *ḫāṭu* "to examine" (Driver, *JTS* 32 [1931] 364; there is no justification for NEB's attempt to get round this problem by reversing the order of clauses as well as emending). It is preferable by far to follow Rosenthal, *Grammar* § 178, in postulating *יחט as a by-form of חוט (Vogt in his Lexicon compares טיב and יטב), of which this would be a 3 masc pl pael pf. This gives the required sense without the need to emend conjecturally to יהיבו "have been laid" (Seybold, *OLZ* 8 [1905] 353; Bewer; Rudolph, etc.).

12.c. Though disputed in earlier times, the derivation from Akk. *uššu* (ultimately Sumerian) and the meaning are now fully assured; cf. Smith, "Foundations," and Tuland, *JNES* 17 (1958) 269–75.

13.a. The final *hē* and the Vrs strongly favor pointing with the suff: וְשׁוּרַיָּה "and its walls."

13.b. It is impossible to be certain of the exact equivalents for these three sorts of tax. The first and third, and so probably the second also, are loan-words from Akk.: *maddattu*, *biltu*, and *ilku*. For further details, cf. the Akk. dictionaries, which indicate the ranges of meaning and usage. It may be noted that, because of its association with *alāku*, הלך "to go," the third has often been rendered "toll," but it is now known to be related to payments in cash or kind to a feudal landlord; cf. *AD*, 70 (on 8:5).

13.c. A loan-word of uncertain meaning. The attempt to find a noun, "revenue, treasury," as in many Evv, has not proved successful, since Avestan *pathma* means only "storehouse." More satisfactory is either O.P. **apatam-am*, "eventually" (Schaeder, *Beiträge*, 74), but this is a conjectured form, or Akk. *appitti(-ma)*, meaning either "accordingly" (*CAD*) or "eventually" (von Soden), but not "suddenly" (Driver, *JTS* 32 [1931] 364–65), which in any case would not fit the context. For further discussion of the many other (less likely) suggestions, cf. Rudolph; Ellenbogen, *Foreign Words*, 36–37; Hensley, *Documents*, 46–49.

13.d. Fem sg, used either in an abstract sense or referring back to "the city."

13.e. Lit., "kings," with Hebraizing pl ending. These last two points are certainly both disturbing. However, where so much of the context is uncertain, it has been deemed wisest to retain MT if at all possible. Otherwise the proposal to emend to מלכי מהנזק, "my king will suffer loss," is enticing.

14.a. This is Myers' rendering. MT has literally "since we have salted the salt of the palace" or, with repointing to מְלַחֲנָא, "since our salt is the salt of the palace." The reference is to some solemn pledge, which was often linked with salt in ancient times; cf. Lev 2:13; Num 18:19; 2 Chr 13:5. Less probably it might mean "in the pay of the court."

14.b. Lit., "nakedness."

14.c. Lit., "we have sent and we have informed," the so-called epistolary pf; for its Heb. equivalent, cf. GKC § 106i; Driver, *Tenses* § 10; and 2 Chr 2:12(13).

15.a. Impers 3 masc sg.

15.b. Cf. Torrey, *Studies*, 188.

16.a. NEB. Lit., "We inform the king."

16.b. Cf. n. 13.a.

18.a. The traditional rendering, "clearly, distinctly," makes little sense in this context: how else would we expect it to be read to the king? Attractive, but unfortunately completely speculative and without any philological justification, is Schaeder's suggestion, *Beiträge*, 6–8, that this is a technical term for *extempore* translation by the reader into a language the king could more easily understand. Moreover, such a rendering would not fit the only other contemporary passage where this word is attested in Aram., *AramP* 17:3. (Schaeder's view has been rejected on other grounds by Altheim-Stiehl, *Die aramäische Sprache*, 5–9, who favor the rendering "distinctly." Polotsky, *Le Muséon* 45 [1932] 273–83, and Kutscher, "Aramaic," 393–99, are critical of certain aspects of his theory, though they remain favorably disposed to its main conclusion with regard to the present passage.) From the root "to separate, divide," the pael ptcp appears to have some such meaning as "piece by piece," and hence in the present context "word by word," i.e., "in full," not just in summary.

19.a. Two impers pls.

20.a. Adversative *wāw*. For this interpretation of the verse, see *Comment*. It is usually translated in such a way as to imply that the reference is to Judean, not Persian, kings; e.g., NIV: "Jerusalem has had powerful kings ruling over the whole of Trans-Euphrates."

21.a. Lit., "until a decree shall be issued by me." For this idiom, cf. Kutscher, *Studies*, 87.

23.a. We would certainly expect Rehum's title "the chancellor" to be included here, despite its very poor versional attestation.

Form/Structure/Setting

It is important in this passage to make a careful distinction between the historical and the literary setting of the events recorded.

Historically, the exchanges of letters are securely dated to the reigns of Xerxes (v 6) and Artaxerxes (vv 7, 8–23), that is, the two kings who follow the Darius of v 5. This is supported by the fact that the substance of the section deals with the rebuilding of the city walls, not the temple. This was certainly a contentious issue later (cf. Neh 1), whereas we have no evidence for its significance in the earlier period. Although some earlier scholars sought to avoid this conclusion by suggesting the identity of Xerxes and Artaxerxes with the earlier Cambyses and Pseudo-Smerdis (or in one case, even, Cyrus), their position is no longer defended by anyone; for a full summary of these views with judicious discussion, cf. Rowley, "Nehemiah's Mission." In addition, it is evident that such identifications in ancient texts like Josephus arose directly out of the difficulties of this passage, and cannot be used as independent sources of information for its elucidation. For further historical remarks, see *Comment.*

By contrast, the closing verse of the chapter takes us back in time to the reign of Darius, and this continues as the historical setting throughout chaps. 5 and 6. It is thus clear that the literary setting is not to be identified with the historical. How is this curious situation to be explained?

In my opinion, the difficulty can be satisfactorily resolved once v 24 is correctly identified as a device known as "repetitive resumption" (cf. C. Kuhl, "Die 'Wiederaufnahme'—eine literarisches Prinzip," *ZAW* 64 [1952] 1–11; B. Lang, "A Neglected Method in Ezekiel Research," *VT* 29 [1979] 42–44. That the device may indeed be used to bracket sections longer than Kuhl or Lang discuss is shown by I. L. Seeligmann, "Hebräische Erzählung und biblische Geschichtsschreibung," *TZ* 18 [1962] 314–24; S. Talmon and M. Fishbane, *ASTI* 10 [1975–76] 129–53; Williamson, VTSup 30 [1979] 265; and H. Van Dyke Parunak, *Bib* 62 [1981] 160–62). It will be noted that it repeats the substance (and in part the wording) of vv 4–5. A considerable number of examples of this kind of repetition has now been recognized, and in each case their purpose is to mark the resumption of a narrative flow that has been broken by the insertion of some digressionary material. We could almost say that it may be understood as the ancient writer's equivalent of brackets or footnotes. If v 24 is taken in this way, its purpose will not be to add a new development to the narrative, still less to suggest that Darius followed Artaxerxes; it will simply be a device for marking out vv 6–23 as a digression from the development of the narrative. See further the *Comment* on v 24.

It is not difficult to explain why the writer should have wanted to include this digression here. He had just recorded an apparently harsh rejection of an offer of help with the rebuilding of the temple. Here he has sought to justify this by showing how, in the light of history, his earlier designation of this group as "the enemies of Judah and Benjamin" (4:1) was entirely justified. (Note how the similarity of v 10 with v 2 links together the groups referred to.) The digression which this section represents from a narrative point of view is thus fully intelligible in terms of the writer's overall purpose.

As a second, and lesser, consideration, it may be suggested that another factor also influenced him at this point. If we are correct in arguing that the author of Ezra 1–6 wrote after the remainder of Ezra and Nehemiah had already been worked together, but that he wished to include some reference to this material which was available to him from his collection of official documents, then it was inevitable that his inclusion of them should be chronologically disturbing, since the events recorded come down to a point later than the start of the Ezra material. Faced with this dilemma, he chose to insert the material where it could contribute positively to the development of his theme, but made clear what he was doing by using literary markers at both 4:4–5 and 4:24.

Not all scholars, of course, would accept this interpretation of the author's method. Of the many alternative proposals, only the two most widely held can be mentioned here. First, there has always been a minority which boldly asserts that the writer was simply mistaken in his views on chronology or, which comes to much the same thing, that he regarded Xerxes and Artaxerxes as "typical" Achaemenid names and so wrongly attributed these events to the reigns of earlier kings. On this view, בֵּאדַיִן "then" (v 24) has sequential significance: "the next thing that happened." The particular merit of this view is that בְּטֵלַת "stopped" and הֲוָת בָּטְלָא "it remained at a standstill" can then be readily taken as the direct continuation and consequence of וּבַטִּלוּ "and compelled (them) to stop" in the preceding verse.

While this possibility should not be dismissed out of hand, yet along with its advantages, it has also difficulties to face. Chief among these is the very clear statement that v 24 refers to the temple, while the preceding exchange of letters deals explicitly with the walls of Jerusalem. It is unlikely that our editor would have been confused about so obvious a distinction as this. Second, 6:14 suggests that the editor knew that Artaxerxes came after, not before, the Darius who issued a decree concerning the temple. Third, we know from Josephus that a knowledge of the correct order of the early Achaemenid kings was preserved in Jerusalem until much later times. Fourth, and more generally, we may note that this view is frequently associated with the presupposition that our editor should be identified with the Chronicler, and that the Chronicler was an inaccurate or muddle-headed historian. This identification is not accepted in this commentary, however, and by contrast we have already noted that the compiler of Ezra 1–6 shows considerable care and skill in the use of the sources available to him. Fifth, therefore, if an explanation of this passage can be provided that exonerates him from gross chronological error by identifying both his purpose in composition and the use of the kind of literary devices we know he uses elsewhere, this is to be preferred from the point of view of method. Only if we fail in this are we justified in attributing such a blunder to an otherwise careful writer. Sixth, it should be noted that already in v 5 the narrative has explicitly been brought down to the reign of Darius. This evidence for the writer's knowledge of chronology should not be overlooked in our haste to find fault with v 24. Rather, this latter verse should be understood in the light of the former, and this we have sought to do above. We thus conclude that this understanding of 4:24 incurs more difficulties than the one that we favored above.

A second, and superficially much more attractive, alternative approach was advanced by Schaeder, *Beiträge*, 14–27, in amplification of an earlier suggestion by Klostermann. Schaeder argued that v 7 was the introduction to a memoir by Tabeel. Tabeel was a Jew, and, with the agreement of Mithredath, he wrote to Artaxerxes urging the Jewish case that permission be granted for rebuilding the walls. He thus included first the accusations of the community's opponents, and then countered this by showing how earlier Persian kings had been favorably disposed toward the Jews and had encouraged them with the rebuilding of the temple. When the Chronicler (as Schaeder thinks) incorporated this memoir into its present setting, he omitted material not relevant to his narrative, which actually contained the clues to the memoir's original purpose, and also added one or two sections, such as 5:1–2.

Rudolph, Rowley ("Nehemiah's Mission"), Liver ("Problem"), and others have argued strongly against Schaeder, so that his suggestion is no longer so popular as it once was. However, Rudolph's principal objection, that "the Chronicler" did not write in Aramaic, is itself unacceptable, as will be argued in chaps. 5 and 6 below. Rather, we would urge against Schaeder's hypothesis that it inserts a stage of composition between the source documents themselves and the final compiler of Ezra 1–6, for which we find no evidence at all. The methods of composition here show no divergence from those of the earlier chapters, as the style and use of such "link verses" as 4:24 and 5:1–2 clearly show; see further *JTS* ns 34 (1983) 1–30. Moreover, we have shown that it is possible satisfactorily to explain the chronology of chap 4. This explanation removes the difficulty from which Schaeder started in the first place. Third, "Tabeel's argument was not a very convincing one, since the edicts of Cyrus and Darius had concerned the rebuilding of the *Temple*, whereas he was invoking them to obtain permission to rebuilt the *walls* of the city" (de Vaux, "Decrees," 82). There is no reason to suppose that the Persians would have overlooked this fundamental disparity between the two enterprises. Finally, Schaeder's need to postulate omissions and additions by the final narrator, thereby fortuitously obliterating every scrap of evidence that might betray the memoir's original purpose, is a more difficult supposition than the view of composition defended in this commentary of a straightforward compilation from source documents. While further points could be made against Schaeder's suggestion, these are enough for our present purpose. Interested readers may compare the presentation of individual verses with those of Schaeder, e.g., at 4:7.b. above.

We may thus conclude that our author has consciously given this section a literary setting at variance with its strict historical setting, but that this was much to his purpose and that he has left clear literary markers to indicate what he was doing. He drew the material from the unedited collection of official documents that underlies so much of Ezra 1–6. We have no evidence of any intermediate stage of composition. It is thus incorrect to argue that he "moved" this passage from some earlier literary setting following chap. 6 (e.g., Galling; Myers) or that it "has strayed from its proper place in Nehemiah" (Witton Davies).

The section takes the form of a simple juxtapositioning of either reports about or the actual text of correspondence between local officials hostile to the Jews and the kings Xerxes and Artaxerxes. Only a minimal amount of narrative framework is supplied, principally in v 23. No source beyond the text of the letters themselves and what can be deduced from them is necessary to account for this section.

A strict form-critical analysis of the two letters which have been at least partially transcribed (vv 8–16, 17–22) is hampered by the fact that we cannot now be sure to what extent the author may have introduced slight changes in order to work the letters into a more satisfactory narrative style. For instance, it is known from numerous contemporary examples that Aramaic letters could include subscripts, summaries of contents and addresses, all separate from the main text of the letter. It seems probable that our author may have used this material too in his compilation (e.g., in vv 9–10), but clearly there can be no certainty about the extent to which such material may have influenced his composition.

Despite these uncertainties, it may be confidently asserted that, even as we have them, the text of the letters can be satisfactorily placed only against the background of official Aramaic correspondence of the Achaemenid period; this conclusion speaks strongly in favor of their substantial authenticity. (Older arguments against their authenticity were answered as early as Meyer, *Entstehung*, 54–59, and cf. Schaeder, *Beiträge*, 27–56, while in the light of our vastly increased knowledge of Aramaic epistolography they are seldom voiced today.) The study of Aramaic epistolography has advanced rapidly in recent years (Fitzmyer, *JBL* 93 [1974] 201–25; Hensley, *Documents;* Alexander, *JSS* 23 [1978] 155–70; Whitehead, *JNES* 37 [1978] 119–40; Dion, *RB* 96 [1979] 544–79; cf. *Bibliography;* and from this a reasonable agreement has emerged concerning conventions of letter-writing and the degree of variety within it, based, for example, on the relative standing of addressor and addressee.

Several of these features emerge in the present passage: subordinates writing to superiors use a more elaborate form of personal address than the more curt address of the reply; cf. vv 9–11 and v 17; the use of a greetings formula following the address, v 17; the communication of information followed by instructions or request in the body of the letter, vv 12–16, 18–22; the use of stereotyped formulae both for transitions from one part of the letter to the next (וכען and equivalents, "and now," vv 11, 13, 14, 17, 21) and as introductory terms (e.g., ידיע להוא ל, lit., "let it be known to . . . ," vv 12, 13), and so on. All these features can be exactly paralleled in contemporary documents, a fact that becomes all the more striking when they are compared with the quite different practices of Greek letter-writing later on (Hensley, *Documents*). We may thus conclude that the documents on which our author drew took the form of official Aramaic correspondence as commonly practiced in Achaemenid times.

Comment

6 Xerxes ascended the throne in November 486 B.C., but his first full regnal year would have been dated from 485 B.C. The expression "the entry of his reign" is probably a technical term referring to the intervening five months; cf. *AramP* 6:1–2 for a comparable situation, though there the period is called ראש מלוכתא "Beginning of his reign" rather than תחלת מלכותו "entry of his reign" as here.

It is known that just prior to Xerxes' accession Egypt rebelled against her Persian overlord, obliging Xerxes to pass through Palestine during 485 B.C. (cf. Olmstead, *History*, 227–28 and 234–36). Perhaps this explains the archeological evidence for disturbances at a number of sites at this time; cf. G. E. Wright, *Shechem* (London: Duckworth, 1965) 167–69. It is tempting, though ultimately conjectural, to link this accusation against the Jews with these events, though their specific cause remains unknown. It is clearly implied that the same basic group of "enemies" was involved as in vv 1–3. Although our author doubtless had a copy of the letter before him (cf. v 7), he chose not to include its contents in detail—possibly because it showed up the Jews in a genuinely bad light, unlike the patently absurd accusations of vv 12–16. In no way, however, can these possibilities justify the sweeping theory of Morgenstern (cf. *Bibliography*), and de Liagre Böhl, "Die babylonischen Prätendenten zur Zeit des Xerxes," *BO* 19 (1962) 110–14, that a catastrophe of major proportions befell the Jewish community at this time; cf. Rowley, "Nehemiah's Mission," and Widengren, "Persian Period," 525–26.

7 Since this second accusation (as the context implies it must be) is not dated more specifically than "in the days of Artaxerxes" (465–424 B.C.), there is even less basis on which to hazard a suggestion as to its occasion. Rainey, *AJBA* 1 (1969) 62, conjectures "with great reservations" that Bishlam might be identified with Belshunu, mentioned as governor of Beyond the River in a text of 462 B.C. and replaced as such at some time before 456 B.C. by Megabyzus. However, even if this were correct, it would still not enable us to identify the incident more exactly.

Again, the letter presumably came from Samaria. Mithredath, to judge by his name, would have been a Persian official while Tabeel, an Aramaic name, is suggestive of a local resident.

However it might be understood in detail, the second half of the verse clearly shows that a copy of the letter lay before our author as he wrote, but that again he chose not to reveal its full contents. Analogy with other such letters strongly supports the view that it would have been drafted originally in Aramaic. It is thus most unlikely that we should render the concluding words of the verse by "and translated into Aramaic." Rather, "Aramaic" is a scribal note referring forward to the following verses (see *Notes*) and "translated" must imply that the copy of the letter to which our author had access had already been translated from Aramaic into some other language for which, in the context, Hebrew presents itself as the only possible candidate. This might explain the verse's Aramaisms (e.g. על for "to") and would account for our author's use of Hebrew up to this point in his narrative. He makes particular reference to these matters because he apparently considered it noteworthy that a letter now in Hebrew should be written "in the Aramaic script." (That this is the significance of כתוב "written" in such a context is assured by Esth 1:22; contrast there the use of לשון for "language.") This verse then stands as an early testimony to the transition from the old Hebrew script to the Aramaic square script for the writing of Hebrew, evidenced, but still apparently somewhat unusual, at the time of our author, *ca.* 300 B.C. (cf. *Introduction*, "Date").

8 As the third accusation which our author records was written in Aramaic, and since he is going to cite it extensively, he switches appropriately to the Aramaic language for this brief introduction. (For a different explanation of this change, cf. Snell, *JSOT* 18 [1980] 32–51.) The names of the senders clearly distinguish this accusation from that of v 7.

Rehum would appear to have been a high-ranking administrative official (not military: see *Notes*), though it is unlikely that we should think of him as the governor, since the latter is invariably styled פחה. It is well known, however, that as a check on the powers of local leaders the Achaemenids ensured that some of the posts within a satrapy were answerable directly to the king, while annual independent inspections of each province were undertaken by royal agents (cf. Olmstead, *History*, 59). Thus there are several roles into which Rehum could be fitted and whereby he could have been used as a mouthpiece to the king for local complaints.

After "as follows," we should expect the opening of the letter itself, but this does not come until v 11b. Unless vv 9–10 have been displaced from a position following v 11, which seems unlikely, we must suppose that our author has been uncharacteristically awkward in copying the full list of senders from some other part of the letter. He himself perhaps appreciated that the result was not as smooth as could be wished, and so added v 11a as a recapitulation to avoid any ambiguity.

9–10 Although the interpretation of these verses is uncertain (see *Notes*), it seems most likely that the "colleagues" of the two principal addressors were a combination of provincial officials and other (presumably leading) members of the population of Samaria whose ancestors had been deported from various regions of Babylonia. It is difficult to be certain that this was literally true in every case; it could well have served their purpose thus to present themselves, for it would have given the impression of a distancing from the indigenous population and so of greater loyalty to the crown.

This is not, however, to deny their self-description *in toto*. It is difficult to see why a later writer should fasten on Ashurbanipal, who is not otherwise linked with such a deportation. On the other hand, we now know of his conquest of Elam in 642 B.C. and that in the following year he became the only Assyrian king ever to capture Susa, while in the years after that (640–639 B.C.) he was campaigning again in the west to subdue an extensive rebellion that had broken out there (cf. Malamat, *IEJ* 3 [1953] 26–29; Cameron, *History*). A movement of population from these areas of Babylon to the west at that time is extremely plausible.

"Beyond the River" (עבר־נהרה), or "Trans-Euphrates," as it is sometimes translated, was originally a purely geographical designation for the whole wide area from the river Euphrates westwards to the Mediterranean, thus including Judah and Samaria. Already by Assyrian times, however, it had been adopted as an administrative title for the same region, and so continued thoughout the period of Babylonian and Persian rule. Under the Persians it was initially linked with Babylon under one governor, but later it became a province in its own right, perhaps during the reign of Darius (cf. Leuze, *Satrapieneinteilung*; Rainey, *AJBA* 1 [1969] 51–78). It is regularly mentioned without further qualification in these books.

11–16 The letter is not dated. Clearly it cannot have been written later than the time of Nehemiah (445 B.C.), who finally succeeded in building the walls, but beyond that there can be no certainty. (Against the minority view that it is Nehemiah's wall that is here referred to, cf. Rowley, "Nehemiah's Mission," 238.) If v 12 indeed refers to Ezra's caravan, then it cannot have been written earlier than the seventh year of the reign, 458 B.C. The most widespread view has therefore been to link the accusations with the revolt of Megabyzus, the satrap of Beyond the River, in 448 B.C. (e.g., Olmstead, *History*, 313; Rudolph; Galling, etc.). Rainey, *AJBA* 1 (1969) 63, however, objects to this suggestion on the grounds that in these verses "the officials of the province appear as supporters of the Persian monarchy" and that this therefore "militates against any connection with Megabyzus' rebellion." Rainey thus favors an earlier date, linking the accusations with an Egyptian revolt that broke out, indeed, before Ezra's time in 459 B.C., but which was not finally put down until 454 B.C. Since it was precisely in 456 B.C. that the Persians (through Megabyzus) began their effective moves against Egypt (Olmstead, *History*, 308), Rainey's earlier date would not be impossible chronologically. His objection to the more usual view is not, however, fatal to it, since it could be argued that the fact that the letter was written by a chancellor, not the governor, and by the resettled population only, is significant in terms of those whom it does not mention. There is thus little substantial evidence on which to base a choice between these two options. Note, however, that in order to account for the vividness of Neh 1, Rainey has to postulate that after the work had been stopped in v 23, more severe steps still were taken to destroy the walls in the aftermath of Megabyzus' rebellion.

12 Despite Rudolph's assertion that "from you to us" is a purely geographical description, and that this verse therefore refers to the initial return under Cyrus, it reads much more naturally if it alludes to a recent movement of which Artaxerxes was aware. If, therefore, we tentatively link it with Ezra's mission, then it should be noted that this would by no means necessarily imply, as Rudolph seems to think, that Ezra himself was therefore caught up in any act of sedition. Note that we have no other source of knowledge for the details of the restoration of the walls referred to here. "The foundations" refers in fact to "lower foundations," which, in Mesopotamian architecture, were double the thickness of the actual walls that were laid into them (Smith, "Foundations").

13–16 The accusation that the Jewish community would have been in a position first to withhold taxes (v 13) and then to spread a rebellion that would result in the loss to the Persians of the whole of Beyond the River (v 16) was, of course, absurd. But in the troubled years through which the empire was passing (see above), such rumors about a distant part of the empire would no doubt have been sufficient to cause alarm, and the authors of the letter play on their awareness of this likely reaction.

They further invite credibility, first by a somewhat obsequious affirmation of loyalty (v 14) and, second, by inviting the king to refer to Jerusalem's past as recorded in the state annals. By "your fathers' record books" they do not refer simply to Artaxerxes' immediate forbears; rather, the reference is to his predecessors, among whom he would certainly have included the Babylonian and perhaps even the Assyrian kings. The Persians regarded themselves as the legitimate successors of the Babylonians, whose empire they took over. In these records there would, of course, be found the successive captures of Jerusalem by Nebuchadnezzar in 597 and 587 B.C., and its eventual destruction (v 15). The writers naturally overlook the long passage of time in between and the completely changed circumstances of the Jewish community now living there.

17–22 The king's reply, which exactly follows the epistolary conventions of the time, repeats much of the substance of the original letter and confirms that a search has revealed the truth of its allegations. Whether the king really thought that Jerusalem's history justified his present suspicions (v 19), or whether we are still at this later date to detect the work of "bribed counselors" (v 5) who advised the king against the Jewish community, it is hard to say.

20   It is generally assumed that this verse refers to powerful Judean kings who controlled an empire in the area from which they received taxes. Decisions then vary over which kings are involved, e.g., David, Solomon, Jeroboam II of Israel, Uzziah, Hezekiah, etc. (cf. Luria, *B Mik* 53/2 [1973] 176–82). This interpretation, however, is inappropriate to the context, since (i) it has nothing to do with the charge of sedition and (ii) it is unlikely that this would be the kind of information appropriate to the annals: David and Solomon were much earlier than the periods of Assyrian or Babylonian rule while the later kings suggested do not fit the description given here. In the annals they would doubtless have been referred to merely as those who withheld their tribute from the empire.

The translation offered above is therefore preferable; see also Galling. The argument is that many of Artaxerxes' predecessors, who indeed "ruled over the whole of Beyond the River," received tribute even from the seditious Jerusalem. Why, then, should not Artaxerxes take steps to ensure that he was in no less powerful a position than they?

21   On this basis, the king orders his subordinates to take whatever steps are necessary. It has been suggested that "except by my express command" may be a later addition to explain how the same king could later authorize Nehemiah to rebuild the wall. This is possible, though *AD* 1 and 8 show that Achaemenid administration was not totally inflexible in its operation. The possibility of a provisional ruling here should not, therefore, be ruled out.

22   The letter ends with a thinly veiled threat against negligence; cf. *AD* 4 and 7.

23   The king's order was only that the work be stopped, not that it be destroyed, and in his account the narrator does not indicate that Rehum and his colleagues overstepped this commission, though he paints as negative a picture as he can by introducing the strong element of force. With no other source of information than the copy of the letter itself, it is possible that he was unaware of the fact that the walls were destroyed at this time (cf. Neh 1:3). Alternatively, Rainey, *AJBA* 1 (1969) 51–78, (see *Comment* on vv 11–16 above) could equally be right in arguing that the destruction referred to there came later. Since this verse is based on the text of the letter, it is clearly a precarious undertaking to use it as independent evidence for the letter's date.

24   The literary function of this verse has been outlined under *Form* above. It is the narrator's own device for returning the reader to the point where he had introduced the digressionary matter of vv 6–23.

This conclusion is of considerable historical importance. We have sought to maintain in 3:1—4:5 above that the building of the temple (as opposed to the rededication of the altar) was in its entirety confined to the reign of Darius. This, however, is the one and only verse that seems to state the alternative that the work began earlier but was then interrupted. For yet a third alternative, which equally cannot be reconciled with this verse at face value, compare 5:16. There is thus considerable variation in our sources over this issue, and before we conclude that they are contradictory to the point where two out of the three must simply be declared wrong, it is preferable to see whether they are not themselves to be differently understood. Thus in connection with the present verse, its identification as a literary marker alone means that it should not be pressed historically, and with it the case for an interrupted work on the temple collapses.

It may, further, be in support of this conclusion that the first word of the verse, באדין "then," though it can have sequential significance and so might be held to indicate that the author thought of Darius as following Artaxerxes, nevertheless is not quite the same as the word used for temporal "then" in the foregoing context (אדין, vv 9 and 23). Perhaps by the use in v 24 of a different form the author was seeking to draw attention to the different nuance of the word. However, the use of באדין in 5:2 and 6:1 does not support this suggestion. Nevertheless, the interpretation favored here is equally not ruled out by the mere presence in the verse of the word באדין; cf. Keil.

Finally, the more radical suggestion of Rudolph that (i) the verse was originally written in Hebrew and was only later translated into Aramaic because of the context, and (ii) that באדין is a corruption of כדנה "thus, in similar manner," is quite unjustified. It derives from his prior assumption that our author wrote only Hebrew, not Aramaic, and that this verse is his only contribution to 4:6—6:18. However, the reason for the use of Hebrew in vv 6–7 has already been explained above, while it will be seen later that there is no reason to deny our narrator's hand in the connecting portions in chaps. 5–6 below any more than there was in the previous chapters. Similarly, Rudolph's emendation is pure conjecture. It is necessitated only by his failure to recognize in this verse the literary device of repetitive resumption.

Explanation

Although from a narrative point of view this section has to be regarded as parenthetical, it nevertheless serves the important function of providing an apt comment both on that which immediately precedes it and, by way of anticipation, on that which is to follow.

The writer has just recorded (4:1–3) a seemingly harsh rejection of what appears on the surface to be a genuine offer to help in the rebuilding of the temple. While the response was couched in "correct" political terms (see *Comment* on 4:1–3), that was clearly not satisfying from a religious point of view. From this derived the need to include this section just here, in order to show the true colors of those who had made the initial approach. Although considerable time has elapsed, the indefinite subject in v 6 ("they") indicates the essential identity of those involved.

Continuity of a different sort from that seen in earlier chapters is thus introduced here. Previously, it has been presented positively, but here, negatively. It sets the tone for much of the remainder of these two books, in which opposition dogs the feet of the restorers and frequently threatens the very existence of the community. On this occasion, the attack is frontal; elsewhere, though from the same or a similar source, it will work more insidiously from within. If continuity is a many-sided theme from which the readers were expected to take comfort, then this countertheme of the continuity of opposition would serve as a warning to them, to encourage them to face it while it was still "outside," rather than allowing it, as could so easily have happened on this occasion, to gain a foothold that would enable it to be even more destructive when operating from within.

The work of God in all ages has known the pressures and persecutions of those who would seek to frustrate its advance. The gross distortions in the charges brought against the Jews in this passage and the apparently unnecessary display of force at its conclusion are no more strangers to the Church than to Israel. Indeed, the misinterpretation of a spiritual stance as being political was never more clearly seen than in the trial of Jesus himself. He, therefore, must provide the pattern of response for the Christian: an implacable hatred for sin and a willingness to fight its manifestations in organized or subhuman guises, coupled at the same time with an unqualified love for the individual sinner who may be in the grip of forces quite beyond his understanding. These two can only be held together when it is recognized that the weapons of our warfare are spiritual and that the victory of the cross was won by loving and sacrificial self-giving rather than by confrontation. Thus while history and fuller revelation may refine our understanding of the nature of the opposition and our appropriate response, the people of God dare not ignore this section's testimony to the threat that so persistently confronts them.

The Rebuilding of the Temple   (Ezra 5–6)

Bibliography

Beyse, K. M. *Serubbabel und die Königserwartungen der Propheten Haggai und Sacharja.* Stuttgart: Calwer Verlag, 1972. **Bickerman, E. J.** "The Edict of Cyrus in Ezra 1." *Studies in Jewish and Christian History.* Part One. Leiden: Brill, 1976, 72–108. **Bowman, R. A.** "An Aramaic Journal Page." *AJSL* 58 (1941) 302–13. ———. "גְּלָל אֶבֶן—*aban galâlu* (Ezra 5:8; 6:4)." *Doron: Hebraic Studies,* ed. I. T. Naamani and D. Rudavsky. New York: National Association of Professors of Hebrew, 1965. 64–74. **Fitzmyer, J. A.** "The Syntax of כל, כלא, 'All' in Aramaic." In *A Wandering Aramean: Collected Aramaic Essays.* Missoula: Scholars Press, 1979. 205–17. **Galling, K.** "Kyrusedikt und Tempelbau." *OLZ* 40 (1937) 473–78. **Gershevitch, I.** "Iranian Nouns and Names in Elamite Garb." *Transactions of the Philological Society* (1969) 165–200. **Gunneweg, A. H. J.** "Die aramäische und die hebräische Erzählung über die nachexilische Restauration—ein Vergleich." *ZAW* 94 (1982) 299–302. **Hensley, L. V.** *Documents.* **Joüon, P.** "Le mot אֲשַׁרְנָא dans Esdras 5, 3 (9)." *Bib* 22 (1941) 38–40. **Leuze, O.** *Die Satrapieneinteilung in Syrien und im Zweistromlande von 520–320.* Halle: Max Niemeyer, 1935. 36–42. **Liagre-Böhl, F. M. Th. de.** "Die babylonischen Prätendenten zur Anfangszeit des Darius (Dareios) I." *BO* 25 (1968) 150–53. **Mowinckel, S.** "אֲשַׁרְנָא Ezr. 5:3, 9." *ST* 19 (1965) 130–35. **Olmstead, A. T.** "Tattenai, Governor of 'Across the River.'" *JNES* 3 (1944) 46. **Parente, F.** "Ezra, 6.11. La pena comminata a chi altera l'editto di Dario." *Henoch* 1 (1979) 189–200. **Porten, B.** "Aramaic Papyri and Parchments: A New Look." *BA* 49 (1979) 74–104. ———. "Structure and Chiasm in Aramaic Contracts and Letters." In *Chiasmus in Antiquity,* ed. J. W. Welch. Hildesheim: Gerstenberg Verlag, 1981. 169–82. **Rundgren, F.** "Über einen juristischen Terminus bei Esra 6:6." *ZAW* 70 (1958) 209–15. **Segal, J. B.** *The Hebrew Passover from the Earliest Times to A.D. 70.* London: Oxford University Press, 1963. **Thomson, H. C.** "A Row of Cedar Beams." *PEQ* 92 (1960) 57–63. **Tuland, C. G.** "ʾuššayyāʾ and ʾuššarnâʾ. A Clarification of Terms, Date, and Text." *JNES* 17 (1958) 269–75. **Ungnad, A.** "Keilinschriftliche Beiträge zum Buch Esra und Ester." *ZAW* 58 (1940–41) 240–44. **Vaux, R. de.** "Decrees." **Wright, J. S.** *Building.*

Translation

[1] Now the prophets Haggai the prophet [a] and Zechariah the son of Iddo prophesied to the Jews in Judah and Jerusalem in the name of the God of Israel which was over them. [b] [2] Then Zerubbabel the son of Shealtiel and Jeshua the son of Jozadak set about beginning to build the house of God in Jerusalem. The prophets of God were with them and supported them. [a]

[3] At that time there came to them Tattenai, the governor of Beyond the River, and Shethar-bozenai [a] and their associates, and they spoke to them in this manner: "Who authorized you to build [b] this house and to complete (the preparation of) this material?" [c] [4] Then they [a] also asked them, "What are the names of the men who are erecting this building?" [5] But the eye of their God was upon the elders of the Jews and they did not stop them before a report should reach Darius [a] and a written order about this be returned.

⁶ *A copy of the letter which Tattenai the governor of Beyond the River and Shethar-bozenai and his colleagues, the inspectors* ᵃ *of Beyond the River, sent to Darius the king;* ⁷ *they sent him a report, and in it there was written as follows:*

To King Darius, all peace. ᵃ

⁸ *Be it known to the king that we went to the province of Judah* ᵃ *and found the elders of the Jews in the city of Jerusalem building* ᵃ *the house of the great God. It is being built with dressed stone* ᵇ *with timber set in the walls. This work is being done thoroughly* ᶜ *and is making good progress in their hands.* ⁹ *Then we questioned these elders, asking them: "Who authorized you to build* ᵃ *this house and to complete (the preparation of) this material?"* ¹⁰ *Moreover, we asked them their names so that we could inform you;* ᵃ *what we are recording in writing* ᵃ *is the names* ᵇ *of their leaders.*

¹¹ *They gave us the following reply: "We are the servants of the God of heaven and earth, and we are rebuilding the house which was originally built many years ago; a great king of Israel built and completed it.* ¹² *But because our fathers angered the God of heaven, he gave them over into the power of Nebuchadnezzar the Chaldean, king of Babylon; he both destroyed this house and exiled the people to Babylon.* ¹³ *However, in the first year* ᵃ *of Cyrus, king of Babylon, King Cyrus issued a decree* ᵇ *to rebuild* ᶜ *this house of God.* ¹⁴ *Furthermore King Cyrus brought out of the temple in Babylon the gold and silver vessels of the house of God which Nebuchadnezzar had removed from the temple in Jerusalem and had brought to the temple in Babylon, and he gave them to a man named* ᵃ *Sheshbazzar, whom he had appointed governor.* ¹⁵ *He said to him, 'Take these* ᵃ *vessels and go and put them in the temple which is in Jerusalem, and let the house of God be rebuilt on its original site.'* ¹⁶ *Then this Sheshbazzar came (and) laid the foundations of the house of God in Jerusalem. From that day to this it has been under construction but it has not yet been finished."*

¹⁷ *And now, if it please your majesty, let a search be made in the royal archives* ᵃ *there* ᵇ *in Babylon to see if it is really so that King Cyrus issued a decree to rebuild that house of God in Jerusalem. Then let the king send us his good pleasure about this.*

⁶:¹ *Then King Darius issued an order, and a search was made in the archives where the treasures were deposited in Babylon.* ² *But it was in the fortress* ᵃ *of Ecbatana, in the province of Media, that a scroll was found* ᵇ *in which was written as follows:*

Memorandum
³ *In the first year of King Cyrus, King Cyrus issued a decree:*

THE HOUSE OF GOD IN JERUSALEM

Let the house be rebuilt on the place where they used to offer sacrifices ᵃ *and let its foundations be retained.* ᵇ *Its height shall be* ᶜ *thirty cubits, its length* ᶜ *sixty cubits and its width twenty* ᵈ *cubits,* ⁴ *with three courses of dressed stone and one* ᵃ *course of timber. The cost will be paid from the royal treasury.* ⁵ *Furthermore, the gold and silver vessels belonging to the house of God which Nebuchadnezzar removed from the temple in Jerusalem and brought to Babylon are to be restored;* ᵃ *each one is to be put* ᵇ *in its own place in the temple in Jerusalem, and you* ᶜ *shall deposit them in the house of God.* ᵈ

⁶ *Now, Tattenai, governor of Beyond the River, Shethar-bozenai* ᵃ *and you, their* ᵃ *colleagues, the inspectors of Beyond the River, keep away from there!* ⁷ *Leave the work on this house of God alone; let the governor of the Jews and the elders* ᵃ *of the Jews rebuild this house of God on its original site.*

⁸ *I hereby issue an order detailing what you shall do for these elders of the Jews for the rebuilding of this house of God: the expenditure is to be paid to these men in full from the royal account made up from the taxes of Beyond the River so that the work be not discontinued.* ᵃ ⁹ *And whatever is needed in the way of bullocks, rams, or sheep for the burnt offerings to the God of heaven, or wheat, salt, wine, or oil as requested by the priests in Jerusalem is to be given them daily without fail,* ¹⁰ *so that they may offer pleasing sacrifices to the God of heaven and may pray for the life of the king and his sons.*

¹¹ *I hereby further decree that if anyone violates* ᵃ *this edict, a beam is to be pulled out of his house and, fastened erect to it, he shall be flogged,* ᵇ *and his house is to be made into a dunghill* ᶜ *for this.* ¹² *May the God who has caused his name to dwell there overthrow any king or people who lifts a hand to violate (this edict)* ᵃ *or to destroy* ᵇ *this house of God in Jerusalem. I, Darius, have decreed it; let it be diligently carried out.*

¹³ *Then Tattenai, the governor of Beyond the River, Shethar-bozenai, and their colleagues acted diligently in accordance with the decree which King Darius had sent.* ¹⁴ *The elders of the Jews* ᵃ *went on successfully with the building* ᵃ *under the prophesying of Haggai the prophet and Zechariah the son of Iddo, and they completed the building according to the command* ᵇ *of the God of Israel and the decree* ᵇ *of Cyrus and Darius and Artaxerxes the king of Persia.* ¹⁵ *So this house was completed* ᵃ *on the twenty-third* ᵇ *day of the month of Adar, in the sixth year of the reign of King Darius.*

¹⁶ *Then the people of Israel, the priests and the Levites and the rest of the exiles, celebrated the dedication of this house of God with joy.* ¹⁷ *For the dedication of this house of God they offered a hundred bulls, two hundred rams, and four hundred lambs, and, as a sin offering for all Israel, twelve he-goats, corresponding to the number of the tribes of Israel.* ¹⁸ *They installed the priests in their divisions and the Levites in their courses for the service of the house of* ᵃ *God in Jerusalem, as prescribed in the book of Moses.*

¹⁹ *The exiles kept the Passover on the fourteenth day of the first month,* ²⁰ *for the priests had purified themselves, and the Levites* ᵃ *were all pure to a man, and they slaughtered the Passover for all the exiles, and for their brothers the priests, and for themselves.* ²¹ *The Israelites who had returned from exile ate it, together with all who had joined them by separating themselves* ᵃ *from the uncleanness of the Gentiles of the land to seek the Lord, the God of Israel.* ²² *And for seven days they celebrated the Feast of Unleavened Bread with joy, because the Lord had made them glad by changing the attitude of the king of Assyria toward them so that he supported them in the work of the house of God, the God of Israel.*

Notes

1.a. Omitted by 1 Esdr 6, doubtless because of the repetition. However, in the absence of a patronymic (and perhaps as an indication of status; cf. J. R. Porter, "Son or Grandson (Ezra

X.6)?" *JTS* ns 17 [1966] 57–58) Haggai is also marked out by the addition of this title (cf. 6:14; Hag 1:1 etc.), which should therefore be retained.

1.b. Ambiguous. It could equally refer to the Jews (cf. Deut 28:10 etc.) or the prophets (cf. Jer 15:16).

2.a. Moral, rather than manual, support is suggested by 6:14.

3.a. Earlier suggestions for the radical emendation of this name are obviated by the occurrence of the very similar שתברזן in *AramP* 5:16, while Bowman (*AJSL* 58 [1941] 304–5 and 312) thinks he may even be able to read שתרבוזן (OP, *Xšathrabūjyāna*) in a fragmentary Aram. papyrus. Either form is apparently possible as an Iranian name.

3.b. The absence of the usual preformative *mēm* for the inf is now attested in several earlier passages in Aram.; cf. J. C. L. Gibson, *Textbook of Syrian Semitic Inscriptions*, Vol. II (Oxford: Clarendon Press, 1975), 63.

3.c. Though this word has been much discussed, its range of meaning is now reasonably clear from its frequent occurrence in the papyri; cf. *AramP* 26:5, 9, 21; 27:18; 30:11; *BMAP* 3:23. It refers to material in the building of a boat, house, or temple, and in each case is most probably to be regarded as woodwork (Mowinckel, *ST* 19 [1965] 130–35; Joüon, *Bib* 22 [1941] 38–40). This would be appropriate also to the Jerusalem temple, which certainly used timber in its construction (cf. v 8 and 6:4) and for which the assembling of wood was one of the first requirements (cf. 3:7; Hag 1:8). Older renderings, such as "wall" (following Vg) or "structure," should thus be abandoned, and likewise more recent suggestions such as "specification" (Galling, *OLZ* 40 [1937] 473–78, who seems himself subsequently to have abandoned this idea). The derivation of the word from OP **āčarna-* (whence Elamite *hazarna*, etc.) is likewise assured (Gershevitch, *Transactions of the Philological Society* [1969] 165–200). This obviates the need for an uncertain appeal to Arabic (Joüon; Rudolph). What remains uncertain, however, is the precise nature and use of the timber, and hence the stage of building reached. Tuland, *JNES* 17 (1958) 269–75, argues that it must be prior even to the laying of the foundations, but this completely overlooks the statement of v 8. NEB goes to the other extreme, "and complete its furnishings," suggesting that the work is nearly finished. But would Tattenai have waited so long before making his inquiry, and what would be the purpose of Darius' reply (6:7–8) permitting the building to continue? The context thus suggests a time during the main structural construction, so that the reference would be to the building materials, perhaps particularly the timber for the walls (v 8) and roof.

4.a. MT has "Then we spoke thus to them," but this can scarcely be right: if the "we" refers to Tattenai and his colleagues, such a first-person reference would be out of place in this narrative context. If it refers to the Jews ("Then we told them what the names were . . ."), then כנמא cannot be introducing direct speech, which it always does elsewhere (its use at 6:13 is different, having nothing to do with speech), and their response would not be a reply to the questions posed (Rudolph). There has clearly been contamination from v 9. Correct to אמרין (or אמרו "they said," though this is not quite so close orthographically) with some of the Vrs, or omit the whole clause (Rudolph). The possibility must not be overlooked, however, that since the narrator is here constructing his account out of the letter of vv 7–17, he himself may have simply failed on this occasion to make the necessary alteration from first to third person.

5.a. Alternatively, "until Darius's order came," with the more regular meaning of טעם in biblical Aram., and the use of the prep ל rather than על; cf. Vogt, *Lexicon*, sub ךה, and Rosenthal, *Grammar* §178. However, it then becomes less easy to derive satisfactory sense from the following clause. See further Dion, *Semeia* 22 (1981) 80.

6.a. Cf. n. 4:9.c.

7.a. The syntax of כלא, long disputed, has been settled by Fitzmyer, *Wandering Aramean*, 205–17 (emphatic state of כל used as an appositive following a definite noun).

8.a-a. This clause is lacking in MT, which has to be translated, "to the province of Judah, to the house . . ." 1 Esdr 6:8, however, has an addition here that corresponds to the translation given in the text. Since v 9 presupposes a reference to "the elders" earlier in the letter (obscured in NIV by the omission of "these"), this is to be preferred.

8.b. Most Eng. versions have linked גלל with the root "to roll," and have thought of stones so large that they needed to be rolled; hence "huge stones" (RSV) etc. Others have guessed "square stones" from the context. These unparalleled guesses are now obviated, however, by the occurrence of the root in connection with stone in a large number of Akk. and Aram. texts referring to such diverse objects as stelae, pillars, window frames, and dishes. The manner in which it is qualified shows that it means simply "stone," but the contexts often suggest that, whatever its etymology, the meaning "smoothed (stone) polished (by a specific technique)"

(*CAD* sub *galālu*) is appropriate. Had the writers meant to say "stone" only, אבן would have sufficed; it is thus better to qualify it in the manner suggested (*contra* Bowman, *Doron*, 64–74).

8.c. This meaning is now generally agreed, though cf. P. Nober, "El significado de la palabra aramea *'āsparnā'* en Esdras," *EstBib* 16 (1957) 393–401, and "De nuevo sobre el significado de *āsparnā* en Esdras," *Est Bib* 19 (1960) 111–12.

9.a. The pointing is often emended to לְמִבְנְיָה, but Rosenthal, *Grammar* § 149 suggests that it is "a form [of the infinitive] expanded into the det. st." Such forms are attested elsewhere.

10.a-a. Relative clause used as the subject of a nominal sentence; cf. A. Spitaler, "*al-ḥamdu lillāhi lladī* und Verwandtes," *Oriens* 15 (1962) 112–14.

10.b. Distributive sg; cf. BL § 87k.

13.a. Cf 1:1.b. and Rosenthal, *Grammar* § 74.

13.b. Though translated differently, the idiom is the same as in v 3.

13.c. Cf. 3.b.

14.a. Lit., "Sheshbazzar, his name"; cf. BL §§ 108p-q, with references to the identical idiom in the papyri, and Kutscher, *Studies*, 71.

15.a. K is to be preferred as the form attested in Imperial Aram., whereas Q seems thus far to be attested only in O.A. Its position before the noun is not uncommon; cf. Rosenthal, *Grammar* § 34.

17.a. Lit. "treasures." We might have expected the inclusion of בית ספריא "in the house of archives" as in 6:1, but the meaning is not in doubt.

17.b. Omitted by all the Vrs and slightly awkward before the following די. It may be a secondary intrusion from 6:1, though Hensley, *Documents*, 162–63, maintains that it is an authentic mark of bureaucratic style.

6:2.a. Apposition; omit the initial ב. Rudolph argues convincingly that (i) this is the reading of several Vrs; (ii) the following clause must refer to Ecbatana, not "the fortress," which is therefore in apposition; and (iii) this is the usually attested form. Cf. בירתא יב of the Elephantine Papyri and the use at Neh 1:1 and Dan 8:2.

2.b. A masc form, permissible when its fem subj follows the verb; cf. BL §§ 98g-h.

3.a. It has become common to translate "as a place where sacrifices are offered" (NEB), justified by Rudolph as an accus of effect. However, elsewhere in similar contexts the emphasis is always on the rebuilding of the altar or the temple "on its original site" (2:68; 3:3; 5:15; and 6:7 with the use of the same vocabulary; see also *AramP* 32:5). It is therefore preferable to take אתר here as an accus of place. The ptcp דבחין could have a present reference, but the stress on the continuity with the site of the first temple favors a reference to continuous and habitual past action. That this should not be misunderstood to imply that the new sanctuary should be built on the site of the old altar of burnt offerings is assured by the following clause; cf. Galling, *Studien*, 130–31.

3.b. The root *sbl* (Akk. *zabālu*) means "to carry," from which comes also the idea "to support, to maintain." (Against the proposed derivation from Akk. (*w*)*abālu*, cf. S. A. Kaufman, *The Akkadian Influences on Aramaic* [Chicago and London: University of Chicago Press, 1974], 103.) It is thus difficult to justify the traditional rendering, "let its foundations be laid" (NIV, etc.). Since we expect a transition to the building instructions which follow, and perhaps (following the previous phrase) an indication of the precise setting of the sanctuary, the popular emendation of ואשוהי to וַאֲשׁוֹהִי, "and burnt offerings (are brought)" (RSV; cf. 1 Esdr 6:24), is not satisfying. It also leaves the 3 masc sg suff unexplained. The translation offered above follows Kraeling, *BMAP*, 186, who has been supported by (*inter alia*) Galling; Vogt, *Lexicon;* Myers; and Th. A. Busink, *Der Tempel von Jerusalem*, vol. 2 (Leiden: Brill, 1980), 803–7. In form, the word appears to be a poel ptcp. Others conjecture reading the pael, מסבלין but this is scarcely necessary

3.c-c. תְּלָתִין אַרְכֵּהּ אַמִּין "thirty cubits, its length" is restored conjecturally, following Rudolph. It is clear that the dimension of length has been lost from MT by parablepsis (from one אמין to the next), and comparison with 1 Kgs 6:2 points the way to the restoration.

3.d. MT, "sixty," which is absurd. It has clearly been assimilated to the previous "sixty." Read עשרין, with Syr. and 1 Kgs 6:2.

4.a. MT has "new" (חדת); since the technique of the construction is here being prescribed, this is out of place; cf. 1 Kgs 6:36 and *Comment*. LXX and the parallel with the previous "three" support deletion of the last letter to read חד.

5.a. Impers pl.

5.b. Lit., "and let it go . . . ," a distributive sg, as the sg suff on לאתרה shows. It does not, therefore, seem necessary to restore כלה.

5.c. Bickermann, *Studies*, 74, adduces several parallels for this seemingly abrupt change of person.

5.d. It is often assumed that a line has dropped out here, e.g., "Then King Darius issued this order:" (NEB). However, see *Form* below.

6.a. 3 masc pl suff. This is quite regular for a vocative when those addressed are not present, so that no emendation is necessary; cf. König, *Syntax* § 344l, and Torrey, *Studies*, 193. The rendering of NIV catches this idiom nicely, and is reproduced above.

7.a. It is doubtful whether we should regard ולשבי "and the elders" as an example of the so-called emphatic *lāmed*, as suggested by F. Nötscher, "Zum emphatischen Lamedh," *VT* 3 (1953) 380, and cf. Keil. It is more probably the *lāmed* of introduction or enumeration; cf. BDB, 514B. Some, however, would prefer to delete the reference to "the governor of the Jews," in which case it would be possible to make "the elders" the object of the first verb of the verse, though the word order would be awkward. The overall meaning is not seriously affected either way.

8.a. Lit., "so as not to stop," with no object expressed. The reference could be to the payment of the money, but a summarizing reference to the building work seems more appropriate before moving on to the sacrifices to be offered.

11.a. Not "changes," as usually translated; cf. Dan 3:28 and Syr. שנא מן = "disobey."

11.b. Lit., "and lifted up he shall be beaten upon it." This has frequently been understood as a reference to impalement (so most recently Parente, *Henoch* 1 [1979] 189–200), which was practiced by the Persians according to Herodotus III:159 and the Behistun Inscription §§ 32, 33, 43, 50. This may be right, but מחא would be an odd verb to use for such an idea. Others favor "crucified," since "lifted up" came to have this more technical meaning later on; but such a form of punishment was not commonly (if ever) practiced under the Persians, and the evidence that this is the meaning of זקף is late.

11.c. The meaning of this word is quite uncertain; cf. Hensley, *Documents*, 56–57. NIV's "pile of rubble" apparently follows earlier commentators in relating the root to a supposed Akk. *nawālu*, but it is doubtful now whether this word exists. It is possible that Syr. *nawwel*, Arab. *nw/yl* should be compared to give the meaning "confiscate"; cf. NEB, "his house shall be forfeit." This certainly explains the rendering in LXX. The translation offered above, which has a very long tradition behind it, is based on later Aram. and Heb. נול, "become offensive/repulsive."

12.a. The object, though not expressed, is clear from the context; cf. the parallel with v 11.

12.b. Alternatively, this might be construed as a gerundial use of the inf constr, "by destroying."

14.a-a. Lit. "built and prospered."

14.b. The word used is טעם in each case, but the vocalization is different, probably to indicate the distinction between a divine and a human command.

15.a. Cf. S. A. Kaufman, *The Akkadian Influences on Aramaic*, 104–5, who disputes the common explanation of this word as the causative of Akk. (*w*)*aṣû*.

15.b. MT has "third," but 1 Esdr 7:5 has "twenty-third." In addition to the fact that textually it is easier to explain the loss of a word than to explain its gain, cf. *Comment*.

18.a. בית "house" must be restored here (cf. LXX^L and Syr.) on account of the following די בירושלם "which is in Jerusalem."

20.a. It is clear from the second half of the verse that MT makes no sense if translated "For the priests and the Levites had purified themselves together; all of them were clean" (RSV). NIV, without justification, bypasses the difficulty by inserting "the Levites" as the subject of "slaughtered" in the second half of the verse. Alternatively, many commentators delete "the priests and" as a later addition. If our understanding of the circle of authorship of Ezra 1–6 is correct (cf. *Introduction*, "Composition"), then a reference to the priests is attractive in the context (cf. *Comment*). The translation offered above is compatible with all these demands and is grammatically possible, even if not the most obvious at first sight.

21.a. Lit. "who had separated themselves to them." For the use of prepositions in such pregnant constructions, cf. GKC §§ 119ee-gg.

Form/Structure/Setting

Although this section is longer than most, it has a transparent unity not only in the fact that it all deals with the rebuilding of the second temple, but also in the fact that, apart from the introduction and conclusion, it centers entirely on Tattenai's inquiry and its outcome. To attempt a division into smaller independent units would thus be a quite arbitrary procedure. Of course, the narrative is made up of a number of easily recognizable paragraphs, but these relate closely to one another and so cannot be treated exegetically in isolation.

The work of building comes to its conclusion by 6:15. The reference in v 14 to the prophesying of Haggai and Zechariah and the command of the God of Israel forms a clear narrative *inclusio* with the start of the section in 5:1, while the allusion to the decrees of the Persian kings acts as a summary recapitulation of the section as a whole. In terms of content, however, this can hardly be separated from the next paragraph, which describes the dedication of the temple (6:16–18), so that appropriately enough the author continues here in Aramaic, the language he has used throughout the account of the rebuilding (see further below).

Only 6:19–22 may thus be recognized as somewhat less closely attached. It describes the first Passover immediately following the dedication of the temple. The reference to the Lord's changing the attitude of the ruling king toward the Jews so that he supported them manifests exactly the same theological outlook as seen already at 1:1, while others have noted the similarities with the end of chap. 3. This little paragraph thus serves as a most appropriate conclusion to the whole of Ezra 1–6. Consciousness of this fact, we may suggest, caused the author to revert to Hebrew. He thereby drew attention to the nature of this paragraph as a conclusion to his whole account and not just that of the events of 520–515 B.C. He may have also considered it more fitting to round off his narrative in Hebrew, it being the traditional language of his people and the language in which he had presented most of his material.

The author's general method in this section is no different from the one he has already used elsewhere. There is therefore no need to postulate an intermediate level of redaction and so to think of the whole Aramaic portion as having been available to the narrator in a single, unified source. He has some primary sources in the form of a letter from Tattenai to Darius (5:7–17) and the reply of Darius, which probably included the copy of the edict of Cyrus (6:3–12). Moderately extensive as it is, his narrative framework which makes up the rest of this section can then all be explained without difficulty.

The narrative framework is made up of 5:1–6; 6:1–2 and 13–22. It will be argued in *Comment* below that it is not necessary to postulate any otherwise unknown source for the material of these verses; it can all be most naturally explained as a writing up of the two major documents in these chapters (5:7–17; 6:3b–12) together with the knowledge culled from other biblical books and the practices of the author's own day.

This position is confirmed by the additional observation that nothing is told us of many aspects of the rebuilding of the temple, which we would have expected to be recounted were further sources available and which would have been of great interest both to the hypothetical first redactor, whose existence most scholars unjustifiably postulate, and to our own author. There is no description of the process and progress of the building itself, nothing about the role of Zerubbabel, Jeshua, or other leaders, and so on. Though this remains an argument from silence, the absence of such information suggests that only the sources of which we now have knowledge from the text were available to our author.

Certain important implications follow from this conclusion. First, the composition of this whole section may be attributed directly to the same author, as seen elsewhere in Ezra 1–6. He uses the same method of writing his connective narrative from the sources that were available to him and that he cites in full. There was, therefore, no intermediate Aramaic source that he took over (*contra*, most recently, Gunneweg, *ZAW* 94 [1982] 299–302). It is arbitrary to assert that he could not have written in Aramaic; Rudolph's desperate suggestion that he wrote 4:24 in Hebrew and that it was later translated into Aramaic is quite unnecessary. He switched to Aramaic at 4:8 in order to cite his source in its original language. Since all his primary sources for the remainder of chaps. 4–6 were also in Aramaic, he continued with that language for the whole of the account of the building, reverting to Hebrew, as already noted, merely to indicate the end of the building account, the commencement of regular worship, and the conclusion of his composition.

Second, the section provides further evidence that this author cannot be identified with the Chronicler; see especially on 6:18 and 20 below. Finally, he is also to be distinguished from the authors and redactor of the remainder of Ezra-Nehemiah; see, for instance, the *Comment* on 5:5 below.

Turning to the correspondence (5:7–17; 6:6–12), the position taken here regarding the form of these two letters is comparable with those in chap. 4; cf. especially de Vaux, "Decrees," and Hensley, *Documents*. Since the address has in part been used to furnish the narrative introduction, the letters are clearly not preserved entirely in their original form, but with this caveat we need not hesitate to conjecture that they lay before our author as copies of genuine letters of the Achaemenid period. Address (as reconstructed), salutation, introductory terms, formulation of request (cf. 5:17), quotations, etc.— all these formal features, together with the heavy influence of Persian on the language of the letters, combine to underscore this conclusion, from which few, if any, would dissent today. The only really new elements by comparison with chap. 4 are the threat of punishment in 6:11 and the warning of 6:12. Parallels for these features, together with discussion of individual points of difficulty on a historical or literary level which have been expressed at various times, will be supplied in the *Comment* below.

A few additional points regarding the form of the memorandum of Cyrus (6:3–5) deserve mention. First, it is called a דכרונה "a memorandum." In *AramP*, this term (strictly, זכרן) is used for two sorts of text—lists or inventories, as noted already at 1:9–11, and for *AramP* 32. This latter text, like the edict of Cyrus here, also grants permission for the rebuilding of a temple, but beyond this important point of similarity a number of differences become apparent; cf. Dion, *Semeia* 22 (1981) 84. *AramP* 32 is an aide-memoir for oral permission to build, somewhat carelessly executed (cf. Porten, *BA* 49 [1979] 74–104), whereas our text is the record of a decision for retention in the royal archives. This will account for its make-up, as correctly analyzed by Hensley, *Documents*, 87; (1) heading—דכרונה; (2) date; (3) summary—

"the house of God in Jerusalem"; (4) text—vv 3b–5. This form makes sense in terms of the document's archival setting (whether independently or as part of a larger text that dealt with a number of such decisions), for its introductory matter (sections 1–3) includes all that would be necessary for identifying it quickly. Thus the date appropriately comes at the beginning rather than at the end, so reversing the practice on other contemporary documents that were designed for dispatch rather than filing (cf. Hensley, *Documents*, 112). These important differences between *AramP* 32 and Ezra 6:3–5 mean that we cannot draw any conclusion from the fact that "in both Cyrus' document and Bagoas' the recipient received the order directly and personally" (Hensley, *Documents*, 88, noting the first person reference of *AramP* 32:1–2 and the second person reference of Ezra 6:5). The settings of the two documents are quite distinct, as indeed are the settings of Ezra 6:3–5 and 1:2–4. Though impossible to verify in detail, some such conclusion as Bickerman's (*Studies*, 73) seems reasonable: "This is an order in the form of an impersonal enactment. Such a minute recorded a single decision, given orally at a cabinet meeting or pursuant to a report presented for consideration." A slightly different conclusion is reached by Myers. He follows R. T. Hallock, "A New Look at the Persepolis Treasury Tablets," *JNES* 19 (1960) 90, in observing that at Persepolis two types of document have been found—"letters directing payments to be made and memoranda indicating that such payments had been made." While Bickerman's suggestion would put the decree into the former category, Myers favors the latter. The text of the decree itself favors Bickerman's position. It is more likely that the source underlying 1:8–11 fits the type of memorandum to which Myers refers.

Finally, we must consider whether or not a copy of this decree was included in the letter of Darius to Tattenai. Since the latter now lacks its formal address, there is disagreement concerning the point at which it starts. Many commentators imply that it began only at v 6, and they even insert a heading there to this effect. This is conjectural, however, and at the same time leaves unanswered the question how a copy of Cyrus's edict could have reached Jerusalem (and so our author) if not in the letter of Darius itself. (It was clearly not available before; cf. 5:17.) It is more reasonable to suppose that it was included in the letter, the transition from its citation to Darius's own command being clearly marked by the stereotyped כְּעַן "now," with repetition of the names of the addressees. We must thus conclude that a fuller introduction once stood at the head of the letter before the copy of Cyrus's decree. It would have included the address and salutation, together with a record of the finding of the decree which is then cited. Once our author had abstracted this material to furnish his narrative in vv 1–2, he did not repeat it, and this accounts for the present slight confusion.

Comment

1–2 This material is based on the books of Haggai and Zechariah themselves, which tell how the prophets stirred the people to action in the second year of Darius; cf. 4:24. The first two years of Darius's reign were ones of universal political upheaval, as his own Behistun Inscription testifies; see also de Liagre-Böhl, *BO* 25 (1968) 150–53. The extent to which this may have influenced the prophets is debated, but it certainly receives no emphasis in the present passage, written so long after the event.

The prophets are introduced in their usual manner, except that Zechariah is called "son of Berechiah, son of Iddo" at Zech 1:1. This is less likely to be a case where "son" equals "grandson" as a reference to status, Iddo having been the head of a priestly family; cf. Neh 12:4 and 16, and J. R. Porter, *JTS* ns 17 (1966) 57–58.

For Zerubbabel and Jeshua, see *Comment* on 2:1–2. In view of the narrator's method in this section, no weight should be put on the fact that they are not mentioned by name again (though cf. 6:7). He composed all his narrative directly out of the available sources, and in these the Jews dealt collectively with Tattenai following the terms of Cyrus's permission to them. Since Zerubbabel would not have been mentioned in the Persian records, it would not have assisted their case to emphasize his leadership. The silence about what happened to Zerubbabel should thus not be interpreted as implying that he was removed from office because of involvement in seditious activity or the like, as has sometimes been supposed. This is in any case most unlikely, since (a) Jeshua is not mentioned again either, though no one doubts that he continued in office. (b) Darius explicitly confirmed Zerubbabel in office and allowed his work to continue after Tattenai's inquiry (6:6–7). This permission would not have been given had there been any suggestion of involvement in sedition. (c) It appears from Ezra 4 that "the enemies of Judah and Benjamin" waited until the walls of Jerusalem were being rebuilt in the reign of Artaxerxes before accusing the city and its inhabitants of being "rebellious and wicked" (4:11–16). Again, this delay would be hard to explain if there had been occasion for such an accusation in the earlier period. Thus we simply do not know (nor, probably, did our author) what happened to Zerubbabel after the events of this chapter, though it seems likely on the basis of Zech 4:9 that he at least lived long enough to see the building completed.

Although it is true that "set about beginning to build" does not have to imply a completely fresh start, yet in this case it probably does, as argued above at chap. 3. This also fits the natural meaning of Haggai's words best. See *Comment* on v 16 below.

3–4 These verses are a narrative summary constructed out of Tattenai's own firsthand account in the letter that follows. The verbal parallels are sufficient to indicate that we should look no further for their source.

3 There is nothing in the text to demand that Tattenai's inquiry be understood as hostile in intent or as something maliciously instigated by the inhabitants of the north. Indeed, "its form suggested that he expected that there was some legal justification for what was happening" (H. L. Ellison, *From Babylon to Bethlehem* [Exeter: Paternoster, 1976], 21). Tattenai himself is now known to have been at this time governor of Beyond the River only, and thus subordinate to Ushtannu, who was governor of Beyond the River and Babylon together; cf. Olmstead, *JNES* 3 (1944) 46, and Ungnad, *ZAW* 58 (1940–41) 240–44. (It is not known for certain when these two provinces eventually came to be administered separately.) The use of the title "governor" (פחה) is thus seen to be quite flexible (cf. Leuze, *Satrapieneinteilung*, 38–39), so that there is no need to deny the evidence of Hag 1:1, 14; 2:2, 21 that Zerubbabel also carried it, though obviously within a much-reduced sphere of authority.

Tattenai was accompanied by an otherwise unknown Shethar-bozenai, whom many have assumed to be his secretary, as in the apparently similar case of Shimshai (4:8). This is not stated, however, whereas at v 6 below his colleagues are probably said to be "inspectors"; for their role within the administration of the Persian empire, see *Comment*, 4:8. Their presence in just such an inspection as this one is highly plausible.

The date of this inspection is not specified. Rudolph thinks it could have been nearer 515 than 520 B.C. because he interprets the last phrase of the verse as referring to the inner wooden paneling of the temple. However, as indicated in *Notes* above, it seems more probable that it refers to a much earlier stage in the construction (see also *Comment* on v 8), though the precise date remains unknown.

4 On the possibility that Tattenai's request may have prompted the collecting of the list of Ezra 2, see that chapter's section on *Form*.

5 While this verse does not arise verbally out of the following letter or its reply (though its reference to "the elders of the Jews" clearly does), it is not an unreasonable inference from their contents. It is thus an exaggeration on Rudolph's part to say that it gives us information not otherwise available to us, as though some alternative source or firsthand knowledge underlay it. The verse is clearly editorial in composition, commenting theologically on the narrative just recorded.

"The eye of God" is certainly a somewhat unusual expression (cf. Ps 33:18; 34:16 [15]; Job 36:7) that speaks of his caring watchfulness over his people. It may be contrasted with the more common "hand of God" which occurs frequently in the narratives of both Ezra and Nehemiah. There may be a hint in this difference of usage that the narrator of Ezra 1–6 is to be distinguished from the one who gave the remainder of the books their present shape.

Perhaps the expression was intended to suggest a contrast with the Persian inspectors. These were known popularly as "the king's eye," and must have been regarded as somewhat threatening and sinister. The biblical author knows, however of One whose care overrides even their potential menace.

6 This narrative heading to the letter would have been written up on the basis of the letter's own address. This would explain why the address in the letter itself (v 7b) is shorter than we would otherwise have expected; material already included here has been omitted there in order to avoid unnecessary repetition.

7–17 Although Tattenai must have been reasonably satisfied with the Jews' response, confirmation of the authority to build could only be had by recourse to the state archives and the final decision of the king (v 17). He therefore writes requesting this in the typical style of the period; cf. *Form* above.

7 בגוה "in it" is used in some Aramaic legal documents as a technical term to refer specifically to what was written in the main text of the letter rather than on its verso; cf. Y. Yaron, *Introduction to the Law of the Aramaic Papyri* (Oxford: Clarendon Press, 1961), 16–17. This fact may have influenced the writer's choice of words at this point.

8 Since it is attested in the Persepolis fortification tablets, "the great God" need no longer be regarded as a strange designation for a Persian official to use; cf. R. T. Hallock, *Persepolis Fortification Tablets*, nos. 353 and 354 (Chicago: University of Chicago Press, 1969).

The use of timber as a structural component is certain for the first as well as the second temple and for one other building (cf. 1 Kgs 6:36; 7:12; Ezra 6:4). Thomson, *PEQ* 92 (1960) 57–63, has demonstrated that this was customary at many places in the Ancient Near East in all periods. It may have been intended to help protect from earthquakes as well as to help bond the building together. Evidently, therefore, the building was well under way by this time.

"The elders of the Jews" is not our author's own term for the leaders; he prefers "heads of families" (1:5; 3:12; 4:3). The use of "elders" at v 5 and at 6:13 therefore derives from this and the following verse, together with Darius's reply, again based on this letter, in 6:7 and 8. It was therefore probably Tattenai's own designation, and should not be used as evidence for detailed conclusions concerning the administrative basis of Judah at this time.

9–10 See *Comment* on vv 3–4 above. It follows from the conclusion of v 10 either that the list of leaders' names was sent separately or that this letter has been abbreviated by our author, possibly to avoid further repetition of the substance of chap. 2 or its near equivalent.

11–16 In their reply to Tattenai's inquiry the Jews were anxious to emphasize the continuity of their project, both with the existence of the first temple and with the authorization of Cyrus to rebuild which had been granted quite a number of years previously. These two considerations were not unnaturally considered to be most likely to secure Tattenai's approval, and they account for most of the features of this paragraph.

11 For "the God of heaven," see *Comment* on 1:2. The addition of "and earth" to the title underlines the importance of this deity, who should therefore be considered worthy of a temple. Solomon is not referred to by name, but as "a great king of Israel," since he would have been unknown to the Persians.

12 If the original temple had been dedicated to this great God, it would have been reasonable to ask why, then, it was destroyed. The Jews anticipate this objection to their case with a candor that shows to what extent the exilic prophets and history writers had succeeded in rescuing the exiles from religious despair and restoring their faith in a God who had demonstrated his sovereignty over even the institutions of the religion of his worshipers.

The reference to the exile of the people to Babylon quietly assumes a later return and suggests the identity of the present community with those who returned.

13 The choice of the title "king of Babylon" for Cyrus was no doubt motivated by a desire to demonstrate the continuity with the events of the previous verse ("exiled . . . to Babylon"). Nevertheless, it should at the same time not be forgotten that Cyrus himself used this title in the Cyrus Cylinder; cf. *ANET*, 316. "The decree" referred to was recorded in quite different forms and contexts in the material lying behind 1:2–4 and 6:3–5. While the former was the one through which Cyrus's decision became known to the Jews, it is not surprising that in the royal archives it was the latter version that was found.

14–15 This adds little to what is known already from 1:7–11 except that only here are we explicitly told that Sheshbazzar was appointed governor. For convenience, however, this fact has already been included in the comments on the earlier passage.

Some have protested that Cyrus would not have commanded Sheshbazzar to deposit the vessels in a temple which was not yet built. On this basis (among others) they deny the authenticity of this letter. It must be remembered, however, that this is only the Jews' account to Tattenai; there is no claim that it records the exact words of Cyrus's order. In 6:3–5, the more logical order of building and restoration of vessels is preserved (and also in chap. 1, by implication). It is pedantic criticism of the worst kind that denies that the Jews could have spoken in this slightly looser fashion when under questioning. The first reference to the temple merely anticipates its rebuilding. The emphasis they wish to make, of course, does not depend on such considerations, and it comes through clearly in the text as it now stands: Cyrus himself ordered the rebuilding of the temple, and by the restoration of the vessels he showed that he recognized this new building to be the successor of the old.

16 In order to underline that, even so much later, the enterprise was still the same as that which Cyrus had authorized, the Jews made a statement here that conflicts with all our other sources, including the firsthand account of Haggai. Whatever may have happened at the time of the first return, it is clear that no building had been done on the temple site for many years prior to 520 B.C.

Since this is agreed by all, it seems arbitrary to insist on the evidence of this same verse alone that Sheshbazzar must have "laid the foundations of the house of God" (though cf. Japhet, *ZAW* 94 [1982] 89–94), when the statement that "from that day to this it has been under construction" is acknowledged to be an untrue statement if taken literally. We have argued at chap. 3 above that the altar was rededicated soon after the return in Cyrus's reign, when we may surmise that Sheshbazzar was still governor. We also argued that the account of the foundation-laying later in that chapter should be referred to the time of Darius. What mattered to the Jews was that enough had been done at the first to show that Cyrus's edict was not simply ignored; they therefore felt able to justify their present activity as being its continuation, which may have been true in spirit, though clearly not in letter (cf. Meyer, *Entstehung*, 44–45). On the testimony of this very verse, therefore, it becomes unnecessary any longer to cling to a foundation-laying by Sheshbazzar.

This being so, it may be asked why the Jews insisted on mentioning him at all at this point; note his absence from the account of 3:1–6. The answer is that he was the one who was mentioned in the official Persian records; cf. 1:8–11 and its evident link with 6:3–5. Knowing this, the Jews wisely used his name to underline the connection of their work with the edict of Cyrus and its associated documents.

17 Tattenai now briefly makes his requests arising out of this report. The formula "if it pleases X" (הן על־X טב) is another standard feature in official Aramaic epistolography, e.g., *AramP* 27:21, 22; 30:23; *AD* 3:5; 10:2, etc.

As a matter of course, he requests that a search for a copy of the decree be made in Babylon. The fact that it turned out to be filed elsewhere "is a small confirmation that we are reading an actual copy of the letter" (Kidner).

6:1–2 As in the case of 5:6, the material for these verses has been drawn from the text of the following letter itself. Consequently, the letter has then been considerably abbreviated, and this helps account for the rather rough juxtapositioning of vv 3–5 and 6–12 (see *Form* above).

Bowman has observed that at Persepolis rooms for housing archives were found to be linked with the treasury. The superficially curious phrasing in v 1 is thus quite acceptable.

Though the search was understandably made first in Babylon, the text was eventually found in Ecbatana, the summer residence of the Achaemenid kings on account of its less oppressive climate. It is known that Cyrus left Babylon in the spring of 538 B.C. and it is reasonable to suppose that Ecbatana was his destination. "A foreigner operating in Palestine without the information which we possess could hardly have been so accurate" (de Vaux, "Decrees," 89).

The use of "a scroll" for the recording of the edict is again no surprise once it is allowed that it was written in Aramaic rather than Old Persian, for which tablets would have been used. In addition to the literary evidence in favor of such usage (de Vaux, "Decrees," 90, and *AD*, 1–3), we now have also the *AD* which support the use of leather as a writing material within the civil service.

3–5 The decree itself has two main parts: permission to rebuild the temple with attendant material provision, and permission to restore the temple vessels. The comments on chap. 1 have already given sufficient indication of the manner in which both these elements dovetail with what is now known of Achaemenid religious policy towards their subject peoples (see also de Vaux, "Decrees," for what remains the most convenient collection of relevant data), while formal considerations have been treated in *Form* above. It is therefore necessary here only to deal with a few outstanding details.

3 For the importance throughout this account of the identity of the site of the second temple with that of the first, see *Notes*.

3b–4 The old objection to the authenticity of the edict—that Cyrus would not have concerned himself with the details of the size of the temple and the materials with which it was to be made—can no longer be sustained. As restored, the text specifies the dimensions of the first temple, and the nature of the construction seems also to be similar (see *Comment* on 5:8). These he would have been able to discover without difficulty, and he would hardly order the restoration of a temple about which he knew nothing at all. There remains also the strong possibility that his edict was in any case drawn up in response to a Jewish petition; see *Comment* on 1:2. It therefore looks as though Cyrus was permitting a restoration of, or a replacement for, the first temple, but no more. And since the expense was to be borne by the royal treasury, this restriction was quite understandable.

Second, it cannot be argued either that such generosity would have been unparalleled. De Vaux, "Decrees," 92–93, adduces numerous instances of just such support for the cults of their subjects during the reigns of Cambyses and Darius, while "the discovery of bricks bearing the stamp of Cyrus in the Persian repairs to the Eanna at Uruk and to the Enunmah at Ur proved beyond any doubt that they were state undertakings supported by public funds."

Third, Hölscher has objected that such funds cannot have been available, since Haggai and Zechariah knew nothing of them, but urged their hearers not to allow economic difficulties to hold them back from building. Here, however, we should note the light that v 8 sheds on our passage. There it is stated that in Darius's time the expenses should be paid out of the taxes due from Beyond the River. It is reasonable to suppose that the same was true earlier in the reign of Cyrus. In that case (a) by the time of Darius it is possible that the availability of these privileges had been forgotten or over-looked; (b) they would in any case have taken the form of an allowance against tax due, which would not have been of any help to a community that was already struggling economically, and (c) it would have been at the discretion of the governor of Beyond the River, who may not have been overanxious to supplement the allowance at such a later date without express command from the court.

5 See *Comment* on 1:8–11 and 5:14–15 above.

6–12 Darius, who in many ways was a much truer successor of Cyrus than was Cambyses (cf. Boyce, *History,* 124–28), endorses the former's decree and adds further details and warnings of his own. For the connection between these verses and vv 3–5, see *Form* above.

6 Tattenai and his associates (see *Comment* on 5:3) are told to "keep away" from the temple. Clearly this cannot be meant literally: the governor of the province must have been allowed access for inspection and so on. The meaning, therefore, must be "do not interfere with or impede the work of building." Rundgren, *ZAW* 70 (1958) 209–15, however, goes much further than this, for he thinks that the expression (lit., "to be far from") carries the same overtones here as it does in the Egyptian Aramaic papyri of "to renounce a claim on" someone or something: e.g., *AramP* 13:6–7; 14:6 and 11; 20:9; 28:11; *BMAP* 3:11, etc. However, unless there is a great deal more background to this incident than our texts enable us to know, such as the possibility that the leaders in Samaria, who are not mentioned here at all, had claimed to have jurisdiction and even property rights over Jerusalem, and that they were in league with Tattenai, for which there is no evidence, then it is difficult to see how the phrase could carry quite the same meaning here as in the papyri. In any case, even in the papyri the phrase has more than one single meaning; cf. Y. Yaron, *Introduction to the Law of the Aramaic Papyri* (Oxford: Clarendon Press, 1961), 81–82. It is therefore sufficient to observe that it is probably legal terminology, but that its precise significance must be determined by the context.

7 The verse simply reinforces what has already been said. "The governor of the Jews" was Zerubbabel. If the text here is sound, it would furnish conclusive evidence that he was recognized as governor by the Persians and hence that Judah enjoyed a measure of autonomy within the province of Beyond the River from the time of the return. Though possible, the text is not as smooth as one could wish, so that some prefer to delete this reference.

8 Darius also upholds Cyrus's command that the expenses for the building are to be met from the taxes of the province; see *Comment* on 6:3b–4 above.

9–10 In addition to this, however, he further orders that provision is to be made for the daily offerings in the temple. This would be because they were to include prayer on behalf of the royal household. For the same reason, only the daily offices, not the annual festivals, are entitled to such support. This element too need not surprise us, either from the Persian or the Jewish side. The Cyrus Cylinder includes a similar concern: "May all the gods whom I have resettled in their sacred cities ask daily Bel and Nebo for a long life for me. . . . To Marduk, my lord, they may say this: 'Cyrus, the king who worships you, and Cambyses, his son. . . ,'" (*ANET*, 316). Meanwhile it is clear that the Jews would not have been averse to complying with such a request; cf. Jer 29:7 and *AramP* 30:25–26. Rudolph lists later examples of the same practice.

Some commentators have found difficulty with the detail of these two verses, and particularly with the fact that some of the terms are notably "Jewish" in character; e.g., for "pleasing sacrifices" (ניחוחין), cf. Exod 29:18; Lev 1:9, etc. All the elements listed functioned in various ways in the daily offerings (note in particular that at Exod 29:40 fine flour [from wheat] and oil are added to the daily sacrifices, and wine is mentioned there for an accompanying drink offering; salt was to be added to every sacrifice; cf. Lev 2:13), and Bowman argues that "since the sacrifices are listed in an order favored by the Chronicler . . . and the expression 'day by day' is such as he favors . . . the verses are best explained as an expansion by the Chronicler."

Such objections, however, are not serious. (a) There are plenty of other examples of the Persians entering into detail in the regulation of the cults of the peoples of their empire. De Vaux, "Decrees," 92, points tellingly to the Passover Papyrus (*AramP* 21), in which it is recorded that word had been sent from the king (Darius II) to Arsames giving detailed regulations about the Feast of Unleavened Bread and probably the celebration of Passover. One finds other examples of a similar nature in the reigns of Cambyses and Darius I (de Vaux, "Decrees," 73–74). (b) Bowman's argument from the order in which the sacrifices are listed is not strong, since it extends to the first three items only, namely "bullocks, rams, or sheep." It does not cover the items listed later. But this order of animals is a rather obvious and stereotyped one, paralleled also, for instance, in the laws of sacrifice in Leviticus; cf. Lev 1:3 and 10 with regard to the burnt offering, etc. This should not, then, be taken as an example of the characteristic style of a single author. (c) The "Jewishness" of the list is no objection either, since we have observed repeatedly that Jews were doubtless involved in one way or another with the drafting of legislation that concerned their religion and its cult; see *Comment* on 1:2 and 6:3b–4 above.

11 The addition of a penalty clause to laws or contracts was common generally in the Ancient Near East. From the inscriptions of Darius himself, see the Behistun Inscription, § 67 (Kent, *Old Persian,* 132) and the tomb inscription from Naqš-i-Rustam, § 9*b* (Kent, 140). Unfortunately, the nature of the punishment is uncertain (see *Notes*). The translation offered above follows NEB, but the possibility of impalement on a sharpened timber from the house cannot be ruled out. This, however, would seem to be an exceedingly drastic measure in the circumstances. On the ruining of the offender's house, cf. Dan 2:5; 3:29.

12 Although some have argued that Darius would never have envisaged the possibilities mentioned in this verse, his inscriptions just referred to at v 11 together with others of a similar nature show that this objection is not valid. The invocation of the relevant god to safeguard what would have been regarded as his own interests is also common. Jewish influence on the drafting of the decree is again to be discerned in the typically Deuteronomic phrase "the God who has caused his name to dwell there"; cf. Deut 12:11, etc.

13–15 It is not necessary to postulate any further source for the remainder of this chapter. The present paragraph mainly records the prompt execution of Darius's orders, a reasonable inference by the author. It is again noteworthy that in vv 13–14a in particular he uses the characteristic vocabulary of the correspondence (e.g., compare "acted diligently" with the end of v 12), while the theological outlook of v 14b can hardly be divorced from that of v 22, which undoubtedly comes from the narrator. It would thus be a mistake to use v 14 as evidence for the length of ministry of Haggai and Zechariah. Their continuing assistance is simply assumed, as in 5:1, and they are included here to form an *inclusio* around the work of temple-building.

The only fresh information this paragraph conveys is the date of the completion of the temple. This, it may be granted, could well have been preserved in an inscription or temple record known to the author. Inscribed bricks are well known from buildings of the Achaemenid period, while we may surmise that some record would have been kept of so momentous a day. Either possibility might help explain the otherwise awkward repetition of דנה "this" in vv 15–17.

At the same time, however, the precise date could have been calculated by the author on other grounds. As Brockington explains, the twenty-third day of Adar "may be due to a desire to have what may be regarded as a liturgically apt date. Adar is the twelfth month, and if the dedication was an eight-day festival then the new year could be celebrated afterwards"; see also J. Morgenstern, "The Calendar of the Book of Jubilees, Its Origin and Its Character," *VT* 5 (1955) 63.

14 The inclusion of Artaxerxes at this point is surprising, since the events of this chapter date from before his reign. (Mention of Cyrus and Darius follows naturally, of course, from vv 3–12 above.) It has occasionally been maintained that this confirms the fact of our author's genuine confusion in his chronology in chap. 4 (e.g., Meyer, *Entstehung,* 14), but this cannot be right since (i) no one could suppose that in chap. 4 Artaxerxes did anything positive towards the Jews in Jerusalem, and (ii) that chapter relates in any case to the building of the walls, not the temple. It is much more probable that we have here an anticipation of Artaxerxes' support for the temple and

its services in 7:15–24, 27 (and perhaps 9:9), but whether by our author himself, or by a later glossator, it is difficult to tell. If the editor of Ezra 1–6 wrote with a knowledge of the remainder of Ezra and Nehemiah, the former possibility need not be hastily dismissed.

15 "The sixth year of the reign of King Darius" was 515 b.c., just seventy-two years after the destruction of the first temple. This is so close to the seventy years of Jer 25:11–12; 29:10, itself probably intended originally as a round figure (cf. R. Borger, "An Additional Remark," *JNES* 18 [1959] 74), that it may have led to the interpretation of the seventy-year period in quite literal terms, with well-known results for the chronological speculations of the apocalyptic writers (e.g., Dan 9:2, 24–27).

16–18 Again, there is no need to postulate the use of a source here, though the possibility of access to some temple archives cannot be entirely ruled out. The style is that of our author, it is clear. The practices of his own day combined with reflection on the dedication of the first temple (1 Kgs 8) and on general probability would provide sufficient material to construct this passage. As already noted in *Form*, the switch from Aramaic to Hebrew after v 18 is not to be taken as an indication of a change of authorship.

16–17 At this solemn moment, the community is understood to be not just men of Judah, but to represent the whole "people of Israel." This accounts too, our author is careful to point out, for the number of he-goats presented as a sin-offering. Vogt, *Studie*, 48–55, observes that the word "Israel" is mentioned exactly twelve times in Ezra 4–6 and argues that this is a further example of the author's emphasis on this important number. However, in view of the literary divisions of the text and the method of composition as analyzed here, it seems more likely to be purely fortuitous. The division of the population into the three categories of priests, Levites and laity is usual for our author, reflecting the regular pattern of his day; see *Comment* on 1:5.

18 The ascription of the priestly and Levitical divisions or courses to "the book of Moses" (though no direct justification for this is to be found in the Pentateuch) could not come from the Chronicler, who consistently makes David responsible for them (1 Chr 23–27, etc.). However, there is to be discerned within the books of Chronicles a somewhat later redaction characterized in particular by a concern for the safeguarding of priestly privileges; cf. VTSup 30 (1979) 251–68. This redaction does not go quite so far as the statement of this verse either, but it comes close to it on occasions (cf. 1 Chr 24:1–2). It is very probable that the author of Ezra 1–6 comes from the same circle as the later pro-priestly reviser of Chronicles; see further below. Against the attempt by Houtman, *OTS* 21 (1981) 91–115, to use this verse as evidence that "the book of Moses" is to be distinguished from the Pentateuch, see the *Introduction*, "The Identification of the Book of the Law."

19–22 Reverting to Hebrew for reasons already noted, the author rounds off his narrative with an account of the first festival which follows the new year (see *Comment* on vv 13–15), namely Passover, and with a concluding summary that reflects on the building process in Ezra 1–6 as a whole.

20–21 It is difficult not to suppose that this account has been written with a sidelong glance at the Chronicler's accounts of the Passovers of Hezekiah and Josiah, which also followed temple restoration of a sort (cf. 2 Chr

30 and 35). However, there is an important difference in that, whereas on the first of those earlier occasions the priests came in for a measure of censure by comparison with the Levites because they "had not sanctified themselves in sufficient number" (2 Chr 30:3), here the preparedness of the priests is emphasized first. This may be taken as another small pointer to the circle to which the author of Ezra 1–6 belonged; see *Comment* on v 18 above.

The slaughter of the Passover lambs by the Levites is not envisaged in the Pentateuch (Exod 12:6; Deut 16:2), but evidently became established practice in the second temple period. Equally prominent is the stress on ritual purity (cf. Segal, *Passover*, 12 and 226), both by the officials and the laity (v 21b). This too was common at this period; cf. the accounts in Chronicles and the Passover papyrus (*AramP* 21), as analyzed by Porten, *BA* 49 (1979) 92. Such a stress may well have begun to emerge only at this time, when Judaism was taking on increasingly the character of a religious community and one which felt the consequent threat of defilement from contacts with those who were "outsiders," even though they might be living close to or among them. In light of this, those who separated "themselves from the uncleanness of the Gentiles of the land to seek the Lord" should be regarded as proselytes: in the outlook of this writer's circle, the recognition of legitimate Jews who nevertheless stood in a different tradition from their own was generally denied. "The Israelites who returned from exile," together with those from any other background without distinction who joined them with whole-hearted allegiance, are the only ones recognized as members of the community.

22 As we should expect, Passover was followed by "the Feast of Unleavened Bread"; cf. Exod 12:15; Lev 23:6. The unaffected note of joy that accompanied the resumption of temple worship (see also 3:10–13) should not be overlooked. The suggestion that the Judaism of the post-exilic period degenerated into a cold and ritualistic formalism is quite the reverse of the evidence presented in any of the texts we have.

The author concludes by reminding his readers that, as he had also indicated at the outset (cf. 1:1), what might have appeared as a catalogue of purely human fortune was in fact within the unseen control of the God of Israel. He thus invites us to interpret his historical account in theological terms, which implies that from it his readers may also learn lessons and draw conclusions of a less time-bound nature.

The reference to one who can only be identified as Darius (Bowman surprisingly thinks of Artaxerxes) as "the king of Assyria" poses a difficulty that has not been resolved to full satisfaction. It is possible that the mistake is purely scribal, though we then have no evidence on which to conjecture an emendation. If it is correct, however, then we must regard the phrase as a stereotyped description of a foreign ruler, since Babylon inherited the Assyrian empire, and Persia the Babylonian. Although it was eventually Babylon that came to have this symbolic value in apocalyptic literature and elsewhere (e.g., 1 Pet 5:13; Rev 14:8; 18:2, etc.), Neh 9:32 would lend some support to the view that in this earlier period that position was held by Assyria; see further Japhet, *ZAW* 94 (1982) 74. This development may have been assisted by the fact that in some respects the Achaemenids regarded themselves as successors to the Assyrians as well as the Babylonians; cf. the newly discovered fragment of the Cyrus Cylinder (see on 1:1 above) with discussion by Kuhrt, *JSOT* 25 (1983) 88–89. It may be significant that in Ktesias' influential *Persika* the Medes are presented as the immediate successors of the Assyrians; cf. A. Kuhrt, "Assyrian and Babylonian Traditions in Classical Authors: a Critical Synthesis," *Mesopotamien und seine Nachbarn* (2 vols.), ed. H. Kühne, H.-J. Nissen, and J. Renger (Berlin: Dietrich Reimer, 1982), 539–53.

Explanation

The fall of Jerusalem to the Babylonians at the beginning of the sixth century B.C. initiated as an inevitability the transition of the religion of Israel into the religion of a community that could no longer be politically defined. The Jews themselves were not now free to order their own affairs, and in any case the population of Judah was quite mixed, with not all adhering to the one religion. At the same time the majority of their co-religionists lived outside the boundaries of the province, whether in the remainder of the earlier land of Israel, or in Babylon and other centers of the diaspora.

This meant that one of the fundamental problems that confronted the community of the post-exilic restoration was that of defining itself in relation to others who lived in the same region and, as a most important extension of this, of determining what should be its relationship with the dominant ruling powers. The evidence we have shows that different attitudes were proposed and adopted, and that no solution could be regarded as definitive at any point within the period of the second temple.

Through his presentation of the account of the building of the temple, our author makes it clear by his editorial comments that one of his primary aims is to urge that Judaism need not suffer because of these changed circumstances. First, by a contrast with the position in chap. 4, he shows the genuine Persian official Tattenai conducting a fair and open-minded inquiry into the renewed building activity. Moreover, reference back to the court not only unearths Cyrus's original permission to build, but also elicits Darius's insistence that this favorable situation should be encouraged in every possible way. At the political level, therefore, our author suggests that in the still-prevailing circumstances of Persian administration his readers have rights and support for the practice of their religion that they need not hesitate to exploit.

Second, however, and perhaps in contrast to those who urged that such a politically "quietist" position was a denial of the rule of God, the writer makes clear at both the start (5:1–5) and the close (6:14, 22) of his account that God himself was active in causing the Persian kings to adopt this favorable attitude and that, through his prophets Haggai and Zechariah, he had deliberately stirred up the people to build the temple without any suggestion that the existing political circumstances needed first to be overthrown.

What the author's attitude might have become in later times is impossible for us now to tell. The problem of a state that forbade or distorted the worship of the God of the Bible was simply not a live issue in his day. Positively, however, it is apparent that at a minimum he would urge the pursuance of religion as far as possible without confronting the ruling powers. There is no necessary and automatic clash here between the interests of Church and state; their spheres of interest and responsibility can generally both be respected, and indeed God is not so small that he may not still "rule in the kingdom of men" and "give it to whomsoever he will" (Dan 4:17). This approach was adopted also by our Lord (cf. Matt 22:15–22) and the later writers of the NT (e.g., Rom 13:1–7; 1 Pet 2:13–17). Where such a distinction was felt to be no longer possible, the attitude became one of passive disobedience with a willingness to accept the legal consequences, rather than any suggestion of seeking to defeat tyranny by the use of tyranny's own methods; cf. the continuation of the passage in 1 Pet 2, citing Jesus' own passion as an example to be emulated.

Beyond these more particular concerns, our author here also draws his account of the first phase of the post-exilic restoration to a triumphant conclusion. Time and again we have noted the emphasis he lays on continuity with pre-exilic times, and here again this theme is present. In earlier chapters he has dealt in some detail with particular aspects of this theme. Here, by contrast, no one aspect may be said to dominate the account. Rather, the theme is recapitulated and summarized through his use of many particular details (e.g., at 5:15; 6:3, 4, and the very fact of a restored temple and cultus) in such a way that the point becomes almost taken for granted: this community with its temple and all the attendant apparatus and personnel of the cult is now to be regarded as the direct continuation of what had preceded, and it is heir as well to all the privileges and responsibilities of the earlier period. In this way the writer can urge his readers not to struggle to achieve that former status, but to recognize who in fact they are and so to pursue their religion in the full assurance of that faith. Small wonder it is that he thus concludes his narrative on a note of joy, "because the Lord had made them glad."

Introduction to Ezra (Ezra 7:1–10)

Bibliography

Bibliography relevant to the particular issue of the date of Ezra's journey to Jerusalem is listed in the *Introduction,* "The Chronological Order."

Ackroyd, P. R. "The Chronicler as Exegete." *JSOT* 2 (1977) 2–32. ———. "God and People." **In der Smitten, W. Th.** *Esra,* 7–11. **Kellermann, U.** *Nehemia,* 57–59. **Koch, K.** "Ezra and the Origins of Judaism." *JSS* 19 (1974) 173–97. **McKane, W.** *Prophets and Wise Men.* SBT 44. London: SCM Press, 1965. **Mowinckel, S.** *Studien III,* 18–20. **Noth, M.** *Studien.* **Schaeder, H. H.** *Esra der Schreiber.*

Translation

¹*After these things, in the reign of Artaxerxes, king of Persia, Ezra the son of Seraiah, son of Azariah, son of Hilkiah,* ²*son of Shallum, son of Zadok, son of Ahitub,* ³*son of Amariah, son of Azariah, son of Meraioth,* ⁴*son of Zerahiah, son of Uzzi, son of Bukki,* ⁵*son of Abishua, son of Phinehas, son of Eleazar, son of Aaron the first*[a] *priest—*⁶*this Ezra*[a] *came up from Babylon. Now he was a scribe who was skilled in the law of Moses which the Lord, the God of Israel, had given; and the king granted him all that he asked for, according to*[b] *the hand of the Lord his God upon him.* ⁷*Some of the Israelites and some of the priests, the Levites, the singers, the gatekeepers, and the temple servants came up*[a] *to Jerusalem in the seventh year of Artaxerxes the king,* ⁸*and they reached*[a] *Jerusalem in the fifth month, in the seventh year of the king;* ⁹*for he had arranged*[a] *the day of departure*[b] *from Babylon on the first day of the first month, and on the first day of the fifth month he reached Jerusalem, according to the good hand of his God upon him.* ¹⁰*For Ezra had committed himself*[a] *to the study of the law of the Lord and its practice and to the teaching of statute and ordinance in Israel.*

Notes

5.a. "Chief priest" would also be possible, but is less likely in the context; cf. S. Japhet, *VT* 18 (1968) 343–44.

6.a. Resumptive, after the lengthy genealogy. For this use of הוא cf. BDB 215b (1.e). The general order of the Hebrew has here been preserved to help make the following discussion clear. NEB renders more idiomatically by moving the verb up to v 1: ". . . there came up from Babylon one Ezra son of Seraiah, . . ."

6.b. Emendation to כי יד "for the hand . . ." is ruled out by the occurrence of the formula elsewhere (e.g., v 9).

7.a. Because Ezra is not mentioned in this verse, it has been proposed to emend ויעלו to ויעל "And he (Ezra) brought up" the various groups mentioned. In the absence of any external support for this suggestion, it is preferable to seek an alternative solution to the problem (cf. *Form*).

8.a. MT "and he reached," but there is strong MS and Vrs support for the plural ויבאו; the *wāw* may have been lost by haplogr before the following *yōd*. There is no need to follow

MT on account of v 9 (Bewer): there, Ezra is clearly acting in his capacity as leader, whereas here the whole caravan is involved.

9.a. MT's "that was the foundation of the going up" is extremely awkward. It is better to take הוא as an emphatic reference to Ezra to mark the change of subject from v 8, and to repoint יְסַד as יָסַד. The proposal to add נסן (הוא) "that is, Nisan," as an explanation for "the first month" should be rejected, because the months are only numbered, never named, in the Ezra material.

9.b. Lit., "going up."

10.a. Lit., "had prepared his heart."

Form/Structure/Setting

It is argued in this commentary that Ezra 1–6 was written later than the editing of the material concerning Ezra and Nehemiah (cf. "Date," *Introduction*). The first phrase of this section ("After these things") will have been added at the same time. Previously, the section will have stood as the introduction to the first combined account of Ezra and Nehemiah. Any apparent connection between it and the end of chap. 6, such as the sixth year of 6:15 and the seventh year of 7:7, or the emphasis on God's direction of the Persian kings in 6:22 and 7:6 and 9 (Rudolph), is thus quite fortuitous.

The principal critical problems here concern the literary unity of the passage, its relationship to the first-person Ezra material, and its historical setting. The latter question is treated separately in the section on "Chronological Order" in the *Introduction*. The conclusion defended there is that Ezra came to Jerusalem in the seventh year of Artaxerxes I (458 B.C.). The first two problems referred to, however, must be examined here.

There are several uneasy transitions within the development of the paragraph. Ezra's genealogy (vv 1–5) is not well integrated into the narrative, as the resumptive "this Ezra" (v 6) shows. The switch from singular to plural subjects between vv 6 and 7 and back to singular again in v 9 is awkward, and the attempt to get around this difficulty by emendation is purely conjectural. Finally, the repetition of the date, the seventh year of the king, in vv 7 and 8, has been found awkward by many.

Scholars have often responded to these difficulties by suggesting that the text has been subjected to later revision; for instance, several think that v 7 is intrusive, while Noth, *Studien*, 125, suggests that vv 8 and 9 are also an addition (albeit earlier) to the original text. Others argue that the genealogy too has been added, or at least expanded, secondarily.

Before deciding about this issue, we should also observe, however, that there are some tensions between this paragraph as a whole and the first-person account of Ezra's commissioning and journey which follows. (i) The statement that "the king granted him all that he asked for" (v 6) contrasts with Ezra's refusal to ask for a bodyguard for the journey in 8:22. Nowhere else in the subsequent narrative are we told that he requested anything of the king. (ii) Whereas in v 9 the departure is said to have been fixed for the first day of the first month, 8:31 gives the actual date of departure as the twelfth day. Again, there is no other reference later to the first day. (iii) In v 7, singers and gatekeepers are said to have formed part of Ezra's caravan, though they are not mentioned in the later list of those who accompanied him (8:1–20). (iv) On a slightly different level, it is probable that the word "scribe" (v 6) is used in a sense different from that intended later (vv 12 and 21); see *Comment*.

None of these points of apparent discrepancy is so serious as to be properly contradictory, as the *Comment* will show. Nevertheless, it is unlikely on the one hand that they would have been introduced without explanation by a writer if he had been responsible for the composition of the whole of Ezra 7–8 (whether as an historical or as a fictional account), while on the other hand it is also hard to see how they could have arisen if an editor had simply fabricated this introductory paragraph on the basis of the later first-person account alone. The most plausible explanation, therefore, is that the editor has rewritten an earlier account, which in all probability was the opening part of the first-person narrative. He would have done this because he felt that it made a more suitable opening to his work as a whole, and he then allowed the incorporation of Artaxerxes' letter following to introduce the change to the first-person account.

This suggestion has the merit of explaining both sets of difficulties that have been observed with regard to this paragraph. The earlier account may well have contained fuller details of Ezra's request, and an indication of the fact that the first day of the first month was only the target date for the departure, while the shift in the use of the word "scribe" and the amplification of the Levites (cf. 8:18–19) to include minor cultic officials may be naturally ascribed to the editor in the light of the practices of his later day.

At the same time, however, we may without difficulty attribute directly to him those elements which some have felt should be regarded as secondary expansions. The changes in subject, for instance, are much less of a problem in a first-person account, where "I" is already well defined. Thus it is preferable to retain the plural form in v 7 and restore it in v 8 (see *Notes*) with the clear reversion to singular in v 9 (as marked by the pronoun הוא "he," reflecting an original first-person singular), rather than conjecturally to restore the singular throughout. If the plurals were originally in the first person, Ezra himself would have been included throughout, though that is no longer apparent in the third-person form of vv 7 and 8. Again, it will be the editor who expanded the brief title in v 1 with most, if not all, of the genealogy and who also, of course, added the adulatory descriptions of Ezra in vv 6 and 10. Third, since *ex hypothesi* he knew the NM, there is no difficulty in holding that he used his knowledge of Neh 2:8b to phrase his compression of Ezra's requests of the king (v 6b). Finally, as Koch, *JSS* 19 (1974) 177, has observed, the only parallel for the split dating of vv 7–8 is in Neh 7:72b (73b) with 8:2, again in a third-person account relating to Ezra. This could have been the style of the original first-person account, but is more likely to be that of the editor as he sought to make the dates of his *Vorlage* more specific.

We conclude, therefore, that, with the exception of the first three words, this paragraph represents a rewriting of Ezra's original account by the editor who first combined the Ezra and Nehemiah material. He expanded some parts and abbreviated others to suit his purpose. The implications of this conclusion should not be overlooked; the tensions found within the narrative have been sufficient to postulate an earlier text underlying it. If this is a correct interpretation of the evidence, it speaks strongly in favor of some form of an original EM (see *Introduction,* "The Ezra Memoir").

Comment

1a Assuming that the king is Artaxerxes I (465–425 B.C.) "after these things" would cover some fifty-seven years (much more, of course, if Artaxerxes II is intended). But the phrase was added only in the final phase of the book's composition (see above), and it is uncertain how detailed a knowledge of chronology the writer had. Its intention is to pick out Ezra's journey as the next formative step in the post-exilic restoration. This is typical of the theological approach to history writing that underlies these books, even though in some respects they are among the most annalistic in the whole OT. The flow of history, with its links of cause and effect, is here traced in relation to religious, not social or political, significance; see further the *Introduction,* "A Theological Reading," and Gunneweg, VTSup 32 (1981) 146–61.

1b–5 Ezra (probably a shortened form of עזריה, "the Lord has helped," though he is never so called in our present texts) is supplied with a full, though by no means complete, genealogy. It is highly unlikely that this all stood in the original EM (contrast Neh 1:1); only enough would have been given to establish his Jewish identity. For the later editor, however, not only was it important to emphasize Ezra's priestly status (accurately enough; cf. 7:12, etc.) in order to justify his subsequent actions, but, in view of the increasingly prominent role that the high priests came to play in the political arena, he wished to underline Ezra's link with the high-priestly family. His actions, particularly with regard to the law, could thus be regarded as fully legitimate from the Jewish as well as the Persian side.

Koch, *JSS* 19 (1974) 190–93, with some support from Ackroyd, *JSOT* 2 (1977) 18–19, uses this material as evidence for his suggestion that "Ezra came to Jerusalem as the real high priest of the family of Aaron." This, however, is most improbable. In historical terms, our literary analysis has suggested that Ezra himself did not include this lengthy genealogy; in terms of the editor, it would be inexplicable that he should either have omitted Ezra from the list of high priests in Neh 12:10–11 or that he should not have included Jeshua the high priest (see *Comment* on 2:2) at this point, had his intention been to make such a claim.

The genealogy compares closely with that in 1 Chr 5:27–41 (6:1–15). Cf. J. R. Bartlett, "Zadok and his Successors at Jerusalem," *JTS* ns 19 [1968] 1–18), though whether our author borrowed directly from Chronicles or from the common source (which must have been widely known in priestly circles) cannot be determined. Comparison shows that the genealogy is defective at two points at least: six names are omitted between Azariah and Meraioth (v 3), and Ezra's father cannot have been the Seraiah of 1 Chr 5:40 (6:14), since he lived before the exile. The first omission is likely to be purely accidental, owing to the repetition of names in the list. Rudolph suggests that the

second omission was also accidental; he thinks that Ezra was really the son
of Seraiah, and that this led to the omission of names between one Seraiah
and the next. While this is a possibility, it is more likely that Ezra belonged
to "a collateral branch of the family" from the Seraiah of pre-exilic times
(Clines), and that the editor was not concerned with the details beyond this
point.

6 The description of Ezra in this verse (cf. v 10 for further details) as
"a scribe who was skilled in the law of Moses" was no doubt influenced by
the use of comparable words in the EM itself (cf. vv 12 and 21), but the
editor responsible for the final form of this paragraph will have meant something rather different. His phraseology here and in v 10 makes clear that
he means a student and expositor of God's written word, and it is as such
that Ezra is now presented to us in the subsequent narrative (cf. especially
Neh 8). This is a role that developed very considerably in importance during
the post-exilic period, as was to be expected with the movement toward the
definition of canonical Scripture and the increasing dependence of Judaism
upon it; cf. H. Stadelmann, *Ben Sira als Schriftgelehrter* (WUNT II/6 [Tübingen:
Mohr, 1980]). The editor's arrangement of the material concerning Ezra and
Nehemiah (cf. *Introduction,* "A Theological Reading") shows that he regarded
this role as one of paramount importance. Did he number himself among
"the scribes," and even model himself upon Ezra?

The word for "skilled" (מהיר) is used elsewhere in this same combination.
From its original meaning of "quick," it developed to refer to the wisdom
and experience of a high court official. (Note, however, that E. Ullendorff,
Ethiopia and the Bible [London: Oxford University Press, 1968], 129, maintains
that the basic meaning of the Semitic root *mhr* was "to be skilled.") This
may be the point of the comparison in Ps 45:2 (1), "my tongue is like the
pen of a ready scribe" (סופר מהיר), though NEB keeps closer to the less
developed sense with its "my tongue runs like the pen of an expert scribe."
Certainly, however, when Ahikar (1:1; *AramP* 212) is described as
ספר חכים ומהיר "a wise and ready scribe," it is clear from the context
that more is involved than the ability to write fast. Thus the expression has
evidently become stereotyped as a term of approval for a scribe in whatever
capacity he functioned (cf. McKane, *Prophets,* 29–36), and it is intended as
such here too. Whatever might be the identity of the law book from which
Ezra himself worked, there can be no doubt that for the editor of this passage
"the law of Moses which the Lord, the God of Israel, had given" refers to
the Pentateuch. No other interpretation is consistent with his description of
Ezra as a scribe in this developed sense.

As noted above in *Form,* the final part of v 6 probably uses the language
of Neh 2:8 ("And the king granted me [my requests] according to the good
hand of my God upon me"; note also the use of בקש "request" in Neh
2:4) in order to compress the fuller account in the original EM. Though we
have no surviving record of what was involved, it is not difficult to imagine
some of the needs Ezra would have faced in undertaking such a journey;
8:22 says only that he specifically did not request an armed escort. Beyond
this, however, the context suggests that permission for the whole venture

was involved, so that the letter of vv 12–26 should also be viewed as part of the king's response.

"According to the hand of the Lord his God upon him"; cf. vv 9, 28; 8:18, 22, 31; Neh 2:8, 18. If this expression derived from the secular sphere in the sense of royal bounty (1 Kgs 10:13; Esth 1:7; 2:18), then its use here will be of particular significance: what appears at one level to be the bountiful grant of the Persian king turns out to be merely a channel through which the bounty of the King of kings reaches his people.

7 In order to fill out a probable first person plural ("we came up") in his *Vorlage,* the editor lists representatives of the main groups of people within the community of his own time. Putting the laity first was not unusual (cf. Neh 7; Ezra 2), but contrasts with the list relevant to the present occasion in 8:1–20. Similarly the expansion of the category of Levite to include singers and gatekeepers (contrast 8:18–19) accords with the situation of later times. Both these factors indicate that this expansion is the work of the editor, and that this list did not stand in the original EM.

For "temple servants," see *Comment* on 2:43, and for discussion of "the seventh year," see *Introduction,* "Chronological Order."

8–9 The information about the length of the journey is not derived from the later account, and since 8:31 states that the actual day of departure was the twelfth day of the first month (there having been some delay while Levites were found; 8:15–16), it is likely that the material as a whole is derived from the EM. The details of what happened are supplied in the following chapter.

Koch, *JSS* 19 (1974) 185–86, finds here several elements that support his view that Ezra undertook his journey "as a second Exodus and a partial fulfilment of prophetic expectations." He notes the use several times of the verb עלה "to go up" and the unusual word מעלה (lit., "going up") in the expression "he had arranged the day of departure." In particular, though, Koch draws attention to the connection between these verses and the next by the causal כי "for, because," and argues that it was from his study of the Torah that Ezra learned on which day he should leave. The first day of the first month points to the Passover festival (Exod 12:2), and hence to the journey as a second Exodus. These observations, when taken with other points to which Koch draws attention, are suggestive. It is not at all certain, however, whether this was Ezra's own understanding of his mission, or whether it is the interpretation of the editor; it seems probable that it was the latter who added v 10 and that it had no equivalent in the EM.

10 The scribe, we should note, was not only a student of Scripture, but explicitly a practitioner and especially a teacher of its requirements. And these qualities we find exemplified in Ezra's ministry. "He is a model reformer in that what he taught he had first lived, and what he lived he had first made sure of in the Scriptures. With study, conduct, and teaching put deliberately in this right order, each of these was able to function properly at its best: study was saved from unreality, conduct from uncertainty, and teaching from insincerity and shallowness" (Kidner). This sense of "study" (לדרוש) no doubt derives from the editor, based on 7:14 (and cf. 10:16), where its meaning is actually rather different.

Explanation

Ezra is introduced to the reader under two main headings, priest and scribe. Both are related to the one great task for which he was subsequently remembered, that of an expositor of the law.

In pre-exilic times, it was especially the priests who were the guardians of the law and who ideally should have taught it to the people. The Levites too were associated with them in this task, though the precise relationship between the two is not always clear. As one who could trace his ancestry back to Aaron himself, Ezra was clearly fully qualified to continue in this tradition.

With the development of Judaism during the period of the second temple, however, the class of scribe as student and teacher of the written Torah came increasingly into prominence. Ezra is portrayed as the first and great example of this class. He thus represents in a unique manner the transition between the different modes of Torah mediation in the pre- and post-exilic periods.

It is probable that in historical terms Ezra's task was more complicated than this (see *Explanation* on 7:11–28). The manner in which he has been presented at this literary level, however, was determinative for later tradition, so that it is not uncommon to find him described in terms of a second Moses, nowhere more so than in 2 Esdr 14, where he is inspired to restore to Israel the Scriptures which, it was thought, had been destroyed when Jerusalem fell. As will be seen again later, the presentation of Ezra in this literature probably had at least as much, if not more, influence on the development of Judaism as did the historical Ezra himself.

The same considerations apply to the hints which have been noted of Ezra's return as a second Exodus. These too derive from the editor rather than the EM, and are part and parcel of the interpretation of Ezra as a second Moses. In this way, personalities and events are drawn into a framework or pattern of familiar saving history, thus facilitating the appreciation of God's ruling over the affairs of humanity, and of his people in particular.

Ezra's Commission (Ezra 7:11–28a)

Bibliography

Bin-Nun, Y. "גְּמִיר." *BMik* 65 (1976) 296–302. **Driver, G. R.** "Studies in the Vocabulary of the Old Testament." *JTS* 31 (1930) 275–84. **Falk, Z. W.** "Ezra vii 26." *VT* 9 (1959) 88–89. **Fruhstorfer, K.** "Ein Alttestamentliches Konkordat (Esr 7.8)." *Studia Anselmiana* 27–28 (1951) 178–86. **Hensley, L. V.** *Documents.* **In der Smitten, W. Th.** *Esra.* **Kapelrud, A. S.** *Authorship.* **Kellermann, U.** "Erwägungen zum Problem der Esradatierung." *ZAW* 80 (1968) 55–87. **Mantel, H.** "The Dichotomy of Judaism during the Second Temple." *HUCA* 44 (1973) 55–87. **Meyer, E.** *Entstehung.* **Mowinckel, S.** *Studien III.* **Nober, P.** "אַדְרַזְדָּא (Esdras 7, 23)." *BZ* 2 (1958) 134–38. **North, R.** "Civil Authority in Ezra." **Noth, M.** *Studien.* ———. *The Laws in the Pentateuch and Other Studies.* Tr. D. R. Ap-Thomas. Edinburgh and London: Oliver & Boyd, 1966. **Porten, B.** "The Documents in the Book of Ezra and the Mission of Ezra" (Heb.). *Shnaton* 3 (1978–79) 174–96. **Rinaldi, G.** "Note." *BeO* 3 (1961) 85. **Rundgren, F.** "Zur Bedeutung von šršw—Ezra vii 26." *VT* 7 (1957) 400–4. **Schaeder, H. H.** *Esra.* **Vaux, R. de.** "Decrees." **Welch, A. C.** *Post-Exilic Judaism,* 245–79.

Translation

[11] *This is a copy of the letter which Artaxerxes gave to Ezra the priest, the scribe, one learned in* [a] *matters relating to the commandments of the Lord and his statutes laid upon Israel:*

[12a] *Artaxerxes, king of kings, to Ezra the priest, the scribe of the law of the God of heaven, all peace!* [b] *And now:* [c]

[13] *I hereby issue an order that any one of the people of Israel or of its priests or Levites in my kingdom who volunteers to go to Jerusalem with you may go,* [14] *for you are sent* [a] *by the king and his seven counselors to conduct an inquiry into the situation in Judah and Jerusalem* [b] *on the basis of the law of your God which is in your hand,* [15] *and to transport some silver and gold which the king and his counselors have freely offered to the God of Israel whose dwelling is in Jerusalem,* [16] *together with any silver and gold which you may acquire* [a] *anywhere in the province of Babylon as well as the voluntary offerings of the people and the priests which they contribute freely* [b] *for the house of their God in Jerusalem.* [17] *Consequently with this money you are specifically* [a] *to buy bulls, rams, lambs,* [b] *and the appropriate meal-offerings and drink offerings,* [b] *and you are to offer* [c] *them on the altar of the house of your* [d] *God in Jerusalem.* [18] *Whatever seems best to you and your brethren to do with the rest of the silver and gold you may do, according to the will of your God.* [19] *The vessels which have been entrusted to you for the service of the house of your God you shall deliver in full before the God of Jerusalem.* [a] [20] *Whatever else is needed for the house of your God which it falls to you to provide, you may provide it from the royal exchequer.*

[21] *I, King Artaxerxes, hereby issue an order to all the treasurers* [a] *of Beyond the River:*

Whatever Ezra the priest, the scribe of the law of the God of heaven, shall request of you is to be provided precisely, [22] *up to a maximum of a hundred talents of silver, a hundred kors of wheat, a hundred baths of wine, a hundred baths of oil, and salt without prescribed limit.* [a] [23] *Whatever the God of heaven commands is to be faithfully* [a] *executed for the house of the God of heaven, lest his wrath fall upon* [b] *the realm of the king and his sons.* [24] *Be it further known to you* [a] *that you have no authority to impose tribute, tax, or dues* [b] *upon any of the priests and Levites, the musicians, gatekeepers, temple servants, or (other) servants* [c] *of this house of God.*

[25] *And you, Ezra, according to the wisdom of your God which is in your hand, appoint magistrates* [a] *and judges to judge all the people in Beyond the River, that is to say* [b] *all those who practice the laws* [c] *of your God; and you* [d] *must instruct any who do not acknowledge them.* [26] *But anyone who does not obey the law of your God and the law of the king, judgment is to be rigorously* [a] *executed against him, whether by death, banishment,* [b] *fine* [c] *or imprisonment.*

[27] *"Blessed be the Lord the God of our fathers who has influenced the king's thoughts in this way* [a] *to beautify the house of the Lord in Jerusalem,* [28] *and who has extended to me his steadfast love before the king* [a] *and his counselors and all* [b] *the powerful royal officials."*

Notes

11.a. Lit., "scribe of." The awkward repetition of ספר and its interpretation in a manner similar to vv 6 and 10 suggest that the second half of the verse is an addition by the editor to the original heading to the document in the EM; see further *Form* below. Rudolph helpfully observes that ספר never means "author," so that attempts on the basis of this verse to relate Ezra to the composition or editing of the Pentateuch, either in whole or in part, are misguided.

12.a. Verses 12–26 are in Aram.

12.b. MT here simply has גמיר "complete, perfect." Various suggestions have been advanced to explain its significance: (i) it may be a bureaucratic note with the meaning "and so on" (cf. Heb. וגומר), indicating either that Ezra's full title or the correct formulae of greeting are to be supplied; (ii) Driver, *JTS* 31 (1930) 283, suggests the meaning "devoted," and thinks it was abbreviated from "Ezra . . . a servant whose heart is devoted to his lord," because such a description would not be well received by the Jewish community; (iii) it may have been originally a clerical note, "dealt with," which has been incorporated from the margin (Rinaldi, *BeO* 3 [1961] 85); (iv) it may refer to Ezra in the sense "learned, accomplished," parallel with מהיר in v 6 (Bin-Nun, *BMik* 65 [1976] 296–302); (v) perhaps the simplest solution is that of Torrey, *Studies*, 197, who restores שלם "peace" before גמיר. (Driver's objection that a king never sends peace to a subject is invalid; cf. 4:17.) It is not certain, however, whether those Vrs that add such a word actually read שלם, or whether they were just translating according to sense.

12.c. Cf. n. 4:10.c.

14.a. Pass ptcp without pronominal subj. Though many wish to emend slightly to a 2 masc sg peil (שְׁלִיחְתָ), this may not be necessary since it is clear by the end of the verse that Ezra is being addressed. (The construction thus differs from the apparent parallel in *AramP* 21:3.) Either way, the meaning is not in doubt.

14.b. For ל as the continuation of another preposition, cf. Torrey, *Studies*, 193[n].

16.a. For the haph of סכם with this nuance, cf. *AramP* 13:5; 42:7, etc.

16.b. BL § 100n.

17.a. Cf. *Notes* 5:8.c.

17.b-b. Lit., "their grain-offerings and their drink-offerings."

17.c. For the use of קרב as a "technical term for presenting an offering," cf. I. Rabinowitz, "Aramaic Inscriptions of the Fifth Century B.C.E. from a North-Arab Shrine in Egypt," *JNES* 15 (1956) 5.

17.d. Somewhat surprisingly, the suff here is pl.

19.a. Though this phrase is not attested elsewhere, that is not necessarily strong enough evidence to conform it to more normal usage by emendation, such as אלה ישראל די בירושלם, "the God of Israel who is in Jerusalem."

21.a. Cf. E. Lipiński, review of A. Lacocque, *Le Livre de Daniel, VT* 28 (1978) 237.

22.a. Lit., "without writing," i.e., written requirement.

23.a. For discussion of this Persian loan-word (אדרזדא), cf. Nober, *BZ* 2 (1958) 134–38.

23.b. Lit., "lest there be wrath against."

24.a. An impersonal pl construction, "(They) inform you that . . ."; cf. BL § 99d.

24.b. Cf. n. 4:13.b.

24.c. J. P. Weinberg, *ZAW* 87 (1975) 366–68, has tried to show that פלחין refers to all the non-cultic members of the community, so that the whole community would have been exempt from tax. However, apart from the inherent improbability of this, Weinberg fails to observe that the word is in the constr before בית אלהא דנה "this house of God," making it certain that cultic officials are involved. Their position in the list suggests that they may be the sons of Solomon's servants; cf. 2:55. Alternatively, the *wāw* may be epexegetic, and the phrase a summary description of the whole of the preceding list.

25.a. שפטין "magistrates" is probably a loan-word from Heb. in the present context, though the root is not completely unknown in Aram. "Magistrates and judges" appear to be synonymous (so that the one might conceivably have been an explanatory gloss on the other), but that is no objection to their presence together here; legal jargon tends to pile up such repetitive phrases. A similar ambiguity exists in the Egyptian Aram. papyri; cf. Porten, *Archives*, 49. 1 Esdr 8:23 supports MT here, but LXX has γραμματεῖς "scribes." Since this could be merely an attempt to avoid an apparent tautology (Batten), it is doubtful whether we should use it as the basis for emendation to ספרין, "secretaries" (Rudolph).

25.b. Cf. 1:5.

25.c. Some find this pl difficult, on account of vv 14 and 26. Though it would be easy to emend to the sing, as the Vrs do, a reference in this context to the individual demands of the law is not out of place.

25.d. Pl, i.e., Ezra and the judges together.

26.a. Alternatively, this word could qualify the earlier "obey."

26.b. It has been argued by Rundgren, *VT* 7 (1957) 400–404, Falk, *VT* 9 (1959) 88–89, and others that this should be translated "flogging," or the like. Rundgren points to סרושיתא in *AD* 3:6, a Persian loan-word meaning punishment, which he then interprets as corporal punishment. He therefore prefers to see the first letter as ס, and thinks that MT arose later as an etymological speculation by the Masoretes (שרש, "to uproot"), giving rise to Vg's *exilium*. However, it should be noted (i) that the step from "punishment" to "flogging" is speculative, and not, apparently, inherent in the meaning of the word; (ii) that Ezra 10:8 may be understood as an early testimony to the interpretation as "banishment"; and (iii) that the Vrs do not support the suggested meaning. LXX παιδείαν "discipline" is nowhere near so specific as "Prügel, Bastonade" "thrashing" (Rundgren), and 1 Esdr 8:24 τιμωρία "punishment" is again general, like the Iranian word. Such generalized senses are inappropriate to the context, however. Driver may therefore be right in his suggestion (*AD*, 99) that "assimilation has taken place, and the Iran.-Aram. סרושי 'punishment' has been used in the sense suggested by the Heb. שֶׁרֵשׁ 'up-rooted'."

26.c. Lit. "punishment of goods."

27.a. Lit., "Who has put thus into the heart of the king." Von Rad, *ZAW* 76 (1964) 184–85, speculates that the idiom may be of Egyptian origin.

28.a. I have defended this rendering against the majority of commentators in "The Sure Mercies of David: Subjective or Objective Genitive?" *JSS* 23 (1978) 38–39.

28.b. Cf. n. 14.b. above.

Form/Structure/Setting

It has been argued above that 7:1–10 represents the rewritten form of an originally first-person narrative. The present section moves over to the direct citation of the edict of Artaxerxes, which in turn leads without further introduction into the first-person benediction of vv 27–28a. It is noteworthy that it is also by way of a prayer that the transition back to third-person narration is eased between chaps. 9 and 10.

Verse 11a supplies a straightforward heading to the following letter, and could have been written up in the EM on the basis of the address in v 12; see *Comment* on 5:6 for a similar procedure. V 11b, however, is attached awkwardly by the repetition of ספר (see *Notes*); its sentiments, phraseology and the use of the tetragrammaton mark it as an addition by the editor. It testifies once more to his reinterpretation of the title "scribe" (see *Comment* on 7:6).

The edict, vv 12–26, takes the form of a letter, and, generally speaking, it conforms to the conventions of epistolary style of the period; see the comments on "form" at 4:6–24 and chaps. 5–6 above. Thus in outline we have address, brief greeting, formula for transition to the substance of the letter (וכענת "and now," v 12), then the various clauses that make up the body of the letter, and finally a warning against infringement of its demands (v 26). In all these elements there is a striking similarity to the other letter from Artaxerxes at 4:17–22 (and see also 6:11–12).

The substance of the letter is made up of four main clauses: (1) Permission for a return to Jerusalem by any Jews who wish (v 13). (2) Commission to conduct an inquiry in Judah and Jerusalem (v 14). (3) Regulations for the transportation and use of certain gifts and grants for the temple cult (vv 15–20). (4) Permission to appoint magistrates and judges for the enforcement (with full legal sanctions, v 26) and the teaching of the law (v 25). For the detailed interpretation of these clauses, see *Comment*.

Thus, from a purely formal point of view, the only intrusive element is the order to the treasurers of Beyond the River in vv 21–24. This order is reasonably self-contained, with its own address, and with Ezra introduced by his full title (cf. v 12) in the third person (contrast v 25). If 8:36 is to be believed, this section will have been composed in such a way as to be able to be used quite independently. This conclusion need not necessarily mean, however, that this paragraph was not included in the original edict. Although some have so regarded it, Kellermann, *ZAW* 80 (1968) 58–60, correctly observes that it is very well integrated into its present setting, with the changes of address clearly indicated in vv 21 and 25. It was therefore probably already found by the editor in its present position in the EM. It cannot be established that it also stood in the original edict (as opposed to having been added by the author of the EM), but there is no reason why it should not have; for the citation of one letter in another, cf. Hensley, *Documents*, 224, and 6:3–12. Ezra would have needed to know the details of the order as much as did the treasurers.

The authenticity of the edict was formerly questioned by a number of scholars (e.g., Batten; Torrey), but is now acknowledged in outline, at least, by nearly all. Historical objections to individual elements will be treated in the comments below, but we may note here the use of Imperial Aramaic which is at home among the texts of the period (though these do not show quite the monolithic uniformity that was once supposed, and some modernization of spelling by later scribes may have taken place), the number of Iranian loan-words, the form of the letter and the general agreement of its terms with Achaemenid policy toward subject peoples (cf. Boyce, *History*, 188–95).

The objection that it shows too close an acquaintance with Jewish technical vocabulary and practice was answered by Meyer, *Entstehung*, 65, with the suggestion that the document would have been drafted by a Jew, probably Ezra himself, in order precisely to ensure accuracy in these matters. Alternatively, we may suggest that it was drawn up in response to a written request by Ezra and so used the language and expressions which he himself had framed. That this was indeed common Persian practice has since been strikingly confirmed by a number of texts discovered after Meyer's work; see *Comment* on 1:2 for details.

Finally, reference should be made to the relationship between the terms of this edict and the actions of Ezra as recounted in the following narrative. The details will be noted at the relevant points of the commentary below, but the overall conclusions may be summarized here. At a surprising number of places there is a close correspondence between the two. Nevertheless, some of the terms of the edict are not referred to later, while others are carried out in ways that differ slightly from what might initially have been supposed.

Noth, *Studies;* Kellermann, *ZAW* 80 (1968) 55–87; and In der Smitten, *Esra,* use these observations to argue first that where there is agreement this is because a later writer (whom they identify with the Chronicler) has written the Ezra narrative as a midrash on the basis of the edict and in the light of other material available to him, such as the NM, and, second, that where there is no such agreement (e.g., v 24) this is because that part has been added to the edict only by a redactor.

This approach runs into two difficulties, however. First, we have already noted evidence from 7:1–10 that an earlier source lay before the editor and that it included more than just the edict of Artaxerxes. Second, not all the correspondences between the edict and the narrative are as smooth as might be supposed. For instance, would anyone working on the basis of v 14 have arrived at the account in Ezra 9–10 with Neh 8–10, or on the basis of v 25a at Ezra 10:8, 14, 16–17, or v 25b at Neh 8:7ff., all as Kellermann supposes?

It may thus be argued that the evidence can be more satisfactorily explained by the assumption that the course of Ezra's work turned out somewhat differently from that envisaged by the king's edict, but that the memoir was drawn up, in part at least, as an attempt to show that its requirements had not been ignored. In some cases, especially as concerns the financial provision, the memoir indeed seems to go out of its way to emphasize that the terms of the edict were carried out to the letter, and this is not surprising; elsewhere, the edict and reality were in general, though not detailed, agreement; while finally, on the evidence available to us, Ezra did not succeed in even starting to put into effect one or two of the points stipulated. If this analysis is correct, it would be a mistake to challenge the unity of this text on the basis of the subsequent narrative alone.

Ezra's benediction, vv 27–28a, is in the simplest form of the declarative psalm of praise (cf. C. Westermann, *The Praise of God in the Psalms* [London: Epworth, 1966], 81–90), namely "shout of praise" followed by "report of God's act." As in the earlier historical books, it arises as an immediate response to God's intervention (Westermann, 87). It is integrally related to its context both by its content (note especially כזאת "in this way") and by the absence of any introductory narrative. (The addition of "Then Ezra said" [NEB] in 1 Esdr 8:25 is clearly secondary.) This latter feature is intelligible within the original first-person account, but would be less easy to explain on the hypothesis that it was part of a later, purely literary, development.

Comment

11 See *Form* above.

12 The title "king of kings" (cf. Ezek 26:7; Dan 2:37), though occasionally used by the Babylonians, was a typical self-designation by the Achaemenid kings; cf. Kent, *Old Persian*, 107–63 passim, and F. M. Cross, *IEJ* 29 (1979) 40–44. It was not, apparently, used by the Hellenistic monarchs, so that its use here is a small pointer towards the decree's authenticity.

For "the priest," see *Comment* on 7:1–5. It has been widely accepted since Schaeder's work that "the scribe of the law of the God of heaven" was an official Persian title, so that some have gone so far as to translate "minister/ secretary of state for Jewish affairs." Further support for this suggestion was advanced by de Vaux, "Decrees," 90, who noted that Neh 11:24 refers to an official who "was at the king's hand in all matters concerning the people."

To this theory, Mowinckel, *Studien III*, 117–24, has objected that the Jews were not such an important element in the Persian empire as to warrant so high-ranking a representative and that Neh 11:24 refers to a representative in Jerusalem, not at the Persian court. This latter point is rejected in the exegesis of Neh 11:24 below. In addition, Mowinckel overlooks two other important factors. One is that, assuming this edict to be genuine, and in view of the powers that it grants to Ezra, the title must still be one that was officially recognized by the Persian authorities; it is unrealistic to suppose that they would have understood it in the sense which it developed only later within Judaism (cf. 7:6). Second, since this decree not only directs Ezra but also invests him with a certain degree of authority, the title could well in fact be that conferred on him only at this time with reference forward to the status that he is to hold in Jerusalem. (Schaeder seems once [*Esra*, 49] to envisage this possibility.) Even on Mowinckel's own view, therefore, de Vaux's comparison with Neh 11:24 could thus be justified, though whether the roles would have been identical, or merely similar, we cannot tell. If these observations are sound, then Mowinckel is correct at least in arguing that we have no means of knowing what Ezra's former status would have been, so that on this point Schaeder's suggestion remains conjectural. (For a severely critical examination, cf. North, "Civil Authority in Ezra." In our view, he rather underplays the degree of authority with which Ezra is invested in this decree.)

While it was argued at 7:6 that the final editor of the Ezra material must have understood "the law of the God of heaven" to refer to the Pentateuch, it is not therefore certain that Ezra himself did. The contents of his law book can only be decided after a study of the actions which he appears to have based upon it. It is therefore best to avoid drawing conclusions until after the relevant texts have been analyzed; cf. *Introduction*, "The Book of the Law," for an attempt at a synthesis.

For "the God of Heaven," see *Comment* on 1:2.

13 In permitting a general return with Ezra, Artaxerxes was merely continuing the policy of Cyrus (cf. 1:3) and probably others of his predecessors too. The use of "the people of Israel" as a term for the laity and the distinction between priests and Levites (and other cultic officials in v 24) are two of the more striking "Jewish" characteristics of this text, explained in *Form* above.

14 The king's "seven counselors" were a group of the monarch's most trusted advisers, allowed full access into his presence; cf. Esth 1:14; Herodotus III §§ 31, 84, 118; Xenophon, *Anabasis* I § 6. Thus Ezra was "sent" by the very highest authority in the empire.

The meaning of the first stated aim of his mission, "to conduct an inquiry (לבקרא) into the situation in Judah and Jerusalem on the basis of the law of your God," is unfortunately not clear to us; it is one of the examples where the orders of this letter do not exactly match the narrative that follows. Elsewhere in Ezra, the verb refers only to searching for records, and is never followed by the preposition על, as it is here (cf. 4:15, 19; 5:17; 6:1). The verb is not attested elsewhere in Imperial Aramaic. The difficulty is compounded by the fact that on the one hand it can hardly be so broadly defined as to mean "teach and enforce the law" (something that is in any case explicitly demanded in vv 25–26), while on the other hand it would be difficult to understand the purpose of simply investigating whether or not the law was being observed.

There are, however, two clues that may help us toward a solution, though even then much remains unclear. First, the continuation of the letter deals in considerable detail with concern for the worship in the Jerusalem temple. In view of the concern of the Achaemenids for the religious well-being of their subject peoples (see *Comment* on 6:9–10), Ezra's inquiry may thus have been primarily aimed at investigating how closely the temple worship related to the Mosaic law (Galling, *Studien,* 170).

Second, it has always seemed puzzling that so much is made in the Ezra narrative of the problem of mixed marriages; indeed, according to the ordering of the material favored in this commentary, it forms the climax of the memoir (chap. 10). It is striking, however, that according to 10:16 the whole affair came to a head with a group of prominent citizens who sat with Ezra "to examine the matter"; cf. Gunneweg, VTSup 32 (1981) 146–61. This suggests the possibility that the first duty Ezra had to perform was to determine precisely who it was that was to be subject to the Jewish law, and that the need for a formal inquiry was envisaged. Naturally, cases of mixed marriage would pose a particular difficulty here.

Finally, it may be noted that both these points may be related to the issue of state aid for the temple cult. The grants placed at Ezra's disposal (see below) would not last so very long. It is reasonable to assume that before any further allowances or concessions were made, Artaxerxes would want to be assured about the state of the cult itself and the condition of those associated with it. Noth, *Laws,* 76–78, argues in addition for the influence of military considerations on the Persian motives, but this is less certain.

The phrase "which is in your hand" should not be pressed to mean that Ezra was literally taking some new law code to Judah; in fact, v 25 suggests that the law should already be known there. Some parts of the Pentateuch, however, had been particularly the concern of priests, of whom Ezra was one, while others may have fallen into neglect because of the changed political circumstances of the Jewish community (see *Comment* on 9:1–2 below). It has been suggested, therefore (cf. Ellison, *EvQ* 53 [1981] 48–49), that part of Ezra's work was to turn the whole Torah into the concern of all the people. But in the context of this letter, "which is at your disposal" (Brockington) conveys the intended sense; cf. *AD*, 49.

15 The offerings of the king and his counselors, as with the grants mentioned later (vv 21–24), may have been made not only to secure good will in general terms but also specifically to support the prayers and sacrifices offered in the temple on behalf of the king and the empire (cf. 6:10).

16 Permission is also granted to transport offerings for the temple from Jews who preferred to remain in Babylon. More surprisingly, reference is made at the start of the verse to gifts from non-Jews. These may have been quite limited, however: 8:25 mentions (in addition to the other groups already covered) offerings from the king's princes. Perhaps, therefore, a few of the nobility followed the royal example almost as a matter of course.

The care with which the following chapter spells out how Ezra carried out these responsibilities suggests that part of the narrative's purpose was precisely to show how obedient he had been to the king's wishes.

17–18 The money is to be spent initially on animals (cf. 6:9 and 17) and accompanying offerings (cf. Num 15:1–16). Since reference is made to what shall be done with the remainder of the money, and since vv 20–24 cover many, if not all, of the needs for the regular daily sacrifices, we must assume that a single celebration is envisaged here, probably in thanksgiving for a safe arrival in Jerusalem (cf. 8:35).

"Your brethren": i.e., fellow-priests. "According to the will of your God": after the strict injunction of the previous verse, it is likely that this is limited to cultic purposes.

19 For the theme of "vessels . . . for the service of the house of your God," see *Comment* on 1:7. There, the vessels were the same as those that had been removed by Nebuchadnezzar prior to the temple's destruction. Here, however, we are clearly meant to presume that they are newly made as part of the king's generous gift; see further at 8:26–27.

20 Finally, provision is made for more general expenses incurred in the running of the temple to be met from public funds. While the following paragraph suggests that recurrent expenditure is envisaged, it was understood by a later writer—at 6:14—to refer rather to further work on the building itself (perhaps under the influence of v 27). For other examples of such financial support, see *Comment* on 6:3–5 and 8.

21–24 On the position of this paragraph within the letter and its address (v 21), see *Form* above. Just as with the building of the second temple (6:3–4), the grant made, though generous, is carefully limited. It takes the form both of an outright grant (vv 21–22) and of a remission of taxes for cultic officials (v 24).

22 It is rarely possible confidently to supply modern equivalents for ancient measures since there can be no complete certainty that they were universally agreed to even in antiquity. It has, however, been estimated that the amounts of wheat (for the cereal offerings), wine (for the drink offerings) and oil (as an accompaniment of other offerings, as an independent offering, and for the temple lamp; cf. Exod 27:20; 29:2; Lev 2:4; 14:10–18; Num 28:5) would have supplied the temple for about two years (cf. A. Bertholet as cited in Rudolph), perhaps the conjectured length of Ezra's mission. A bath is now thought to have been approximately 21 liters or less (cf. D. Ussishkin, "Excavations at Tel-Lachish, 1973–1977," *Tel Aviv* 5 [1978] 87), and a kor contains ten baths (Ezek 45:14). Salt, which was used in much smaller quantities in all sacrifices and which was in any case not such a valuable commodity, could be supplied without limit.

In this list, therefore, "a hundred talents of silver" stands out as a quite disproportionate sum, for each talent weighed about 75 pounds. (Silver was presumably needed for the purchase of sacrificial animals.) According to Herodotus III § 91, the total annual tax levied from the whole province of Across the River amounted to only 350 talents. Unless there has been willful exaggeration here, we must assume that there has been some error in the transmission of the figure (see *Notes* on Ezra 2), perhaps under the influence of the series of units of a hundred which follows.

23 Just as Darius had supported the temple cult in order that prayers might be offered on behalf of the royal household (6:10), so negatively Artaxerxes hopes thus to avert disaster befalling his empire; קְצַף "wrath" is frequently used in the Hebrew Bible of God's intervention in battle (e.g., Josh 22:20; 2 Kgs 3:27; 2 Chr 29:8; 32:25–26), and in view of Judah's strategic importance, the same may be intended here.

24 Exemption from payment of tax for cultic officials by a Persian king is not unprecedented; cf. Herodotus III § 91 and the letter of Darius to Gadatas, condemning him for having "exacted tribute from the sacred cultivators of Apollo" at Magnesia on the Meander; cf. Meyer, *Entstehung*, 19–21; Olmstead, *History*, 156. For the list of officials, which is close to chap. 2, see *Comment* on v 13.

25 The interpretation of this verse is widely debated, and no solution to its problems can claim more than probability.

First, there are some who regard this verse (with or without other verses) as a later addition to the original edict; cf. Galling, *Studien*, 168, 176–77. However, the literary issues have already been treated in *Form* above, and if the content of the verse can be explained satisfactorily within its context, then it would seem preferable to retain the unity of the document.

Second, probably the majority of commentators see this verse as an amplification of the terms of v 14. They argue that, despite appearances, it still refers to the Judean community, since nowhere else in Beyond the River would its terms have been applicable. The reference to the whole province here was occasioned only by its position following the letter to all the treasurers of the province in vv 21–24. This view too, however, is difficult to accept, because it does not adequately explain the differences between the two verses. (i) "To conduct an inquiry" (v 14) is a far more limited exercise than that envisaged here. (ii) It would be surprising in a legal document if no difference were intended between "Judah and Jerusalem" (v 14) and "Beyond the River" (v 25). (iii) Why is this verse separated so far from the passage it is intended to explain? The construction of the letter as a whole makes it look much more as though vv 15–20 explain v 14, and that v 25 (note "And you, Ezra . . .") marks a further step. (iv) Historically speaking, it is highly improbable that there were no groups outside Judah and Jerusalem who did not regard themselves as living under "the law of the God of Heaven" (i.e., basically the Mosaic law, in whatever stage of development).

Third, then, should we go as far as Ackroyd, who suggests that the text envisages "a situation in which the whole province becomes one community, all obedient to the law"? When viewed in historical terms, this suggestion too is hard to accept, for it must be remembered that the province of Beyond the River was a great deal more extensive than the area of the former kingdoms of Israel and Judah. It was populated by many groups of quite varied backgrounds, and even the most visionary of Jews could not have expected them to submit themselves to Jewish law within the Persian empire. (Eschatological hopes are, of course, another matter, but there is no evidence of their inclusion here.) Furthermore, since "all the people" is carefully explained as "all those who practice the laws of your God," it is likely that "any who do not acknowledge them" should be understood to mean "any who do not acknowledge this law, but ought to on account of their background."

Any fresh solution must, therefore, take full account of the differences between this verse and v 14 and yet stay within the bounds of historical possibility. It was argued at v 14 above that Ezra's inquiry, as indicated by the context of the following verses, related primarily to the conduct of the temple cult. This, however, would have been of most relevance to those in Judah and Jerusalem. The religious life of Jews living farther away from the cult center had inevitably to be organized on somewhat different lines. This had already been envisaged by Deuteronomy. It may therefore be suggested that the present verse authorizes Ezra to regulate the lives of such groups according to the law that would have been most applicable to them. Thus we may note that "magistrates and judges" could be intended as the equivalent of the "judges and officers" of Deut 16:18, while teaching, as envisaged here, is also a well-known feature of Deuteronomy.

That this suggestion involves something of a distinction between sacral and civil law is no difficulty, for the next verse does precisely the same ("the law of your God and the law of the king"). Had this program been put into effect, difficulties might have arisen in this area on the ground that the Mosaic law legislates for both areas of life without distinction. Nevertheless, it must be assumed that the Jews in exile had already been living with this problem for well over a century, so that a *modus vivendi* must by now have emerged. Who better, therefore, to establish a similar framework in Beyond the River than a leading representative of Babylonian Jewry? There need certainly be no doubt that, as with later empires, the Persians would have allowed a wide sphere of social, as well as religious, life to be regulated according to the Jewish law.

Finally, it may be noted that such a move as this would not have been unprecedented. There is evidence that when he was in Egypt Darius undertook a similar measure. In 519 B.C. Darius ordered the Egyptian satrap to assemble "the wise men . . . from among the warriors, the priests, and the scribes

of Egypt so that they may set down in writing the ancient laws of Egypt."
Later, the text refers to "the law of Pharaoh, of the temples, and of the
people." It has been argued that in addition to confirmation, some new measures were also introduced. The interest of all this for our purposes is the
fact of Achaemenid respect for the ancient laws of their peoples, including
religious law, and their willingness to see it put into effect as far as possible
even within the boundaries of their own empire. For the text and comments
upon it, cf. W. Spiegelberg, *Die sogenannte Demotische Chronik* (Leipzig: Hinrichs,
1914), 30–32; E. Meyer, *Kleine Schriften* II (Halle: Niemeyer, 1924), 91–100;
N. J. Reich, "The Codification of the Egyptian Laws by Darius and the Origin
of the 'Demotic Chronicle,' " *Mizraim* 1 (1933) 178–85; A. T. Olmstead, "Darius as Lawgiver," *AJSL* 51 (1934–35) 247–49; de Vaux, "Decrees," 73–76.

"The wisdom of your God": it has often been thought, on account of
the parallel expression in v 14, that this is the earliest attestation of the
identification of the Torah with wisdom; cf. Sir 24. If so, it will refer particularly to Deuteronomy on the interpretation suggested here. However, there
is no real reason why it should not simply refer to Ezra's own wisdom.

26 The addition of a penalty clause to such a document is quite usual.
The passive construction suggests that Ezra himself may not have been em-
powered to enact the punishments (see further North, "Civil Authority in
Ezra," 384–85), but rather that the Persian authorities were to support his
work with the force of law. (Note especially imprisonment, which was not a
typically Jewish penalty.) If we do not read of all these penalties being used
later, that is probably because they were not needed: 10:8 suggests that the
threat of using some of the lesser penalties was in itself sufficient to ensure
against the need to invoke the death sentence.

27–28 For this doxology, see *Form* above. Though the edict made no
direct reference to "beautifying" the temple, Ezra may have thought this a
suitable way of spending the remaining funds referred to in v 18; see also
6:14.

Explanation

The first reaction which the recording of Artaxerxes' edict evoked from
Ezra was one of praise and thanksgiving. Momentous as the document was
in terms of the history of the development of Judaism, Ezra sees here only
further provision for the Jerusalem temple, center of his people's worship,
and an expression of God's steadfast love. The conditions might have changed
radically over the centuries since the first call of Abraham with all the promises
that call entailed, but God was still "the God of our fathers" (v 27), who
could move even a Persian monarch and his courtiers to further his purposes.

As understood in this commentary, the document itself was certainly of
great significance in the process of establishing a working relationship between
the Jew and his foreign overlord. God's grace is to be seen in the measure
of freedom and responsibility entrusted to Ezra for the regulation of both
cultic and wider, social affairs concerning his people in the land. Nevertheless,
a new distinction is beginning which carefully distinguishes between "Church"
and "state." "The law of your God" and "the law of the king" are not to

be simply identified as the same, and in the generous provision for the temple's worship there is to be recognized a Jewish responsibility to pray for the well-being of their secular rulers.

Neither for Jew nor for Christian has it ever proved a simple matter to know just where such boundaries should be drawn. Nevertheless, there can be no doubt that a big step was taken in Ezra's time toward the realization of a situation in which the distinction could be observed, at least in principle. Only against such a background could the radical message of Jesus with its call to be citizens of God's kingdom, not of this world, though paradoxically with attendant responsibilities towards the outcast and downtrodden of its society, have ever been received. Ironically, it was also this same division that enabled those who rejected this message to manipulate the distinction between the Sanhedrin and Rome to carry out his crucifixion.

List of Exiles Who Returned with Ezra
(Ezra 7:28b—8:14)

Bibliography

In der Smitten, W. Th. *Esra.* **Koch, K.** "Ezra and the Origins of Judaism." *JSS* 19 (1974) 173–97. **Mowinckel, S.** *Studien I.*

Translation

7:28b So, according to the hand of the Lord my God upon me, I took courage and gathered leading men out of Israel to go up with me.

8:1 These are the heads of families [a] (together with their genealogy) who went up with me from Babylon in the reign of King Artaxerxes:

2 Of the family of [a] Phinehas:	Gershom
Of the family of Ithamar:	Daniel
3 Of the family of David:	Hattush the son of Shecaniah [a]
Of the family of Parosh:	Zechariah, [b] and with him were registered [c] 150 men
4 Of the family of Pahath-moab:	Elihoenai the son of Zerahiah, and with him 200 men
5 Of the family of Zattu: [a]	Shecaniah the son of Jahaziel, and with him 300 men
6 And of the family of Adin:	Ebed the son of Jonathan, and with him 50 men
7 And of the family of Elam:	Jeshaiah the son of Athaliah, and with him 70 men
8 And of the family of Shephatiah:	Zebadiah the son of Michael, and with him 80 men
9 Of the family of Joab:	Obadiah the son of Jehiel, and with him 218 men
10 And of the family of Bani: [a]	Shelomoth [b] the son of Josiphiah, and with him 160 men
11 And of the family of Bebai:	Zechariah the son of Bebai, and with him 28 men
12 And of the family of Azgad:	Johanan the son of Hakkatan, and with him 110 men
13 And of the family of Adonikam the last ones, [a] namely [b] Eliphelet, Jeiel, and Shemaiah, and with them 60 men	
14 And of the family of Bigvai:	Uthai the son of [a] Zabud, [b] and with him [c] 70 men.

Notes

1.a. The 3 masc pl suff anticipates the following העלים "who went up."
2.a. Lit., "sons of," and so throughout the list.

3.a. MT has "of the sons of Shecaniah," which makes it look on the surface as though a name has dropped out after it. However, it is probably the MT that has been mistakenly assimilated to the pattern of the list, whereas the slight emendation of מבני to בן, with the support of 1 Esdr 8:29, conforms the genealogy to 1 Chr 3:22 (emended). It is nonetheless curious that on three related occasions (1 Chr 3:22; Ezra 8:3 and 5) an uncorrected reading of the MT would imply that a son of Shecaniah has consistently been dropped from the lists. (For v 5, see below; at 1 Chr 3:22, "the sons of Shecaniah" is followed by only one name. However, because of the "six" at the end of the verse, it is probable that "and the sons of Shemaiah" should be deleted as a corr dittogr, thereby eliminating the earlier difficulty.)

3.b. The pattern of the following list suggests that the name of Zechariah's father has been lost here.

3.c. Sing verb before pl subj; cf. GKC § 145o: lit., "and with him 150 were registered as males."

5.a. Restored on the basis of LXX and 1 Esdr; the form of the list shows clearly that a name has been lost from the MT. Strictly speaking, MT could be read, "Of the family of Shecaniah: —" (cf. n. 3.a. above), but there is no external evidence to support this alternative.

10.a. Lacking in MT, but restored on the basis of the same considerations as 5.a.

10.b. MT has "Shelomith," but this is a fem name only. The revocalization is favored by several Vrs, and cf. M. Noth, *Die israelitischen Personennamen im Rahmen der gemeinsemitischen Namengebung* (BWANT; Stuttgart: Kohlhammer, 1928), 165.

13.a. Coming without the article, this word is certainly strange. It can hardly mean "those who came later" (RSV) in view of v 1, nor "The last were . . ." (NEB), since the list ends with yet another group in the next verse. Perhaps, therefore, it means the last of Adonikam's family who remained in Babylon.

13.b. Lit., "and these are their names."

14.a. 1 Esdr 8:40 and the following "with him" suggest the emendation of וזבוד, "and Zabbud," to בן־ז', "the son of Z."

14.b. So K (זבוד); Q and some Vrs have Zakkur, favored by RSV. Either form is possible.

14.c. The MSS and Vrs that read "and with them" are to be explained as secondary corrections consequent upon the corr noted in 14.a.

Form/Structure/Setting

Following its heading (v 1), the list falls into three sections, dealing with priests (v 2), the royal line (vv 2b–3a) and laity (3b–14). This contrasts sharply with the earlier list of returning exiles (Ezra 2), with which otherwise this passage shows a degree of contact. It is thus unlikely that the list was fabricated on the basis of Ezra 2 (*contra* Mowinckel, *Studien I*, 122; for further arguments, see below).

The longest section, which deals with the laity, lists twelve families. The clauses have a regular structure to indicate the current head of each "father's house" (see *Comment* on 1:5) and the number of its male members who went with him, his own father, and the name of the father's house itself. That these latter occur also in Ezra 2 should cause no surprise.

The literary setting of this list has been much debated, with no consensus emerging as to whether it is a completely secondary addition, whether it is a genuine but independent piece added only by the main editor of the Ezra material (often identified with the Chronicler), or whether Ezra himself included it in his memoir. The arguments are finely balanced, but it will be suggested here that the list was originally drawn up as an independent document, and then included by the first author of the EM.

Its independent origin is strongly suggested by the inclusion of the words "in the reign of King Artaxerxes" in v 1. If the list had been composed specially for its present setting, this would have been quite redundant. Indeed, it is more general than the dates already supplied in Ezra 7 for these events. Second, there is a degree of verbal overlap between 7:28b and 8:1. This is most probably to be explained by the assumption that the author of 7:28 had 8:1 already before him and was aiming consciously to effect a literary join.

Its inclusion in the original Ezra material is also favored by this latter point, and further by the fact that, as Noth, *Studien,* 125, has shown, 8:15 does not join smoothly with 7:28 (*pace* Mowinckel, *Studien I,* 118); rather, the repetition of the verb "to gather" should be viewed as a "repetitive resumption" (see *Form* at 4:6–24), and so suggests that the intervening material was consciously inserted here by the author of the surrounding narrative. (The suffix on וָאֶקְבְּצֵם, "And I assembled them," in v 15 also supports this conclusion; cf. In der Smitten, *Esra,* 21.) Finally, in view of the many points of contact between the edict of Artaxerxes and the remainder of the Ezra material, we almost expect some such list as this to be included in order to demonstrate the fulfillment of 7:13.

Most of the arguments brought against this conclusion relate, in fact, to the list's authenticity, to be dealt with immediately below, even though they are not strictly relevant to its original literary setting. It should be noted here, however, that it would be utterly anachronistic to argue that it could not have been included in the EM because it interrupts the narrative flow.

If this list was indeed an independent document included by the author of the EM, then there must be a strong presumption in favor of its authenticity. It is reasonable to suppose, on the basis of 8:34, that Ezra first recorded the material shortly after his arrival in Jerusalem, but that when he or another wrote up the full account of his activities it was included at this appropriate point. (If the list was originally completed after the journey, Levites would have been included; they were omitted at this juncture out of narrative considerations, and the part of the list dealing with them became instead the basis for vv 18–20.) The arguments that have been leveled against its authenticity are not compelling. Those advanced by Hölscher have already been answered satisfactorily by Rudolph (see also Michaeli; In der Smitten, *Esra,* etc.).

Not all the names in 8:16 appear in the list. That is true, but they could well have been included among the many men who are numbered, but not named. As will be seen, the text of 8:16 is uncertain; it is already clear, however, from a comparison of 7:28 and 8:1 that all those enumerated in the list (not just those named) are רָאשִׁים "heads, leading men" (7:28 and perhaps 8:16), while those expressly named are singled out in 8:1 as רָאשֵׁי אֲבוֹתֵיהֶם "heads of (their) families." In fact, this apparent discrepancy tells rather in favor of the list's authenticity, for we might otherwise have expected the names to be the same.

The names of the laity are also found in Ezra 2. This objection can be easily answered, for it is not surprising that only some members of the various extended families had journeyed at the first, now to be followed by others. Myers adds two further counterarguments: "First, the priests here are reckoned after the Aaronite line, whereas in Ezra ii they follow the Zadokite line. There was apparently a shift in the priority of priestly authority in Babylon between the time of Zerubbabel and Ezra." Second, the line of Joab, formerly reckoned with the Pahath-Moab family (Ezra 2:6), now enjoys independent status (8:9).

The number of lay families (twelve) is clearly schematic. If this is so, however, it could as well be Ezra's work as another's. Koch, *JSS* 19 (1974) 194, in particular, finds evidence for Ezra's preference for this number, though his explanation for this is questionable (see *Comment*).

Mowinckel, *Studien I*, 116–17, has since added a further argument, for he thinks that Artaxerxes is here called "King of Babylon," which would be improbable in an authentic document. However, as the translation above suggests and as is generally agreed, מבבל "from Babylon" qualifies the verb "went up" and not the title "king"; if it did, the preposition מן would not be necessary (cf. 1:1, 2, 8; 2:1; 3:7, 10; 4:2, 3, etc.). Mowinckel's objection thus rests on an uncharacteristic misreading of the text.

Since there is therefore no substantial objection to the list's authenticity, and since on literary grounds it has been suggested that it is an early composition, it is probable that it reflects accurately the participants in Ezra's return.

Comment

2 The priests are listed first both in contrast with Ezra 2 and in preference to the royal line. The outlook is in this sense comparable with the earlier Ezek 40–48, which also stems from priestly circles in Babylon, and in which royalty is subordinated to the priesthood and an emphasis placed on the fullness of Israel; cf. J. D. Levenson, *Theology of the Program of Restoration of Ezekiel 40–48* (HSM 10; Missoula, MT: Scholars Press, 1976).

Although nothing else is known of Gershom and Daniel, it would seem from v 24 that they were heads of families. (This is not stated with regard to Hattush either; by this device, these first three names are distinguished from the twelve lay families which follow.) Since this was a time of rapid transition in the ordering of the priestly genealogies, lack of reference to them elsewhere is not sufficient evidence to discount their existence (*contra* Mowinckel, *Studien I*, 119). The families of Phinehas and Ithamar point to an Aaronic connection (cf. Exod 6:23–25), and many commentators consider this to be "one of the earliest records we have of the tracing back of the priesthood to Aaron" (Brockington). Ezra's own genealogy was traced back through Phinehas in 7:1–5.

2b–3a Hattush is known as a member of the royal line from 1 Chr 3:22. This is one of the very few allusions to a continuing interest in the Davidic family in these books (cf. the treatment of Zerubbabel in Ezra 2–6), and it is in any case to be attributed to the author of the EM rather than to the final compiler. It is of particular significance here, however, since the list is clearly idealistically arranged, thus demonstrating the abiding, though reduced, attention ascribed to the royal line at this time.

3b–14 Twelve lay families are listed with a total of approximately 1,500 men. The caravan as a whole, including women and children, may thus have numbered some 5,000. As seen above, it is not particularly surprising to find that the names are closely comparable with those in Ezra 2:3–15. There are, however, some differences in detail and in the order in which they are listed.

That there is an element of artificiality in the list is suggested not only by its order and the prominence of the number twelve, but also by the round numbers supplied for each family; multiples of ten are used almost throughout. Like the placing of the priests first, the twelve families fit very well with Ezra's own outlook; cf. vv 24, 35, and Neh 8:4 (Koch, *JSS* 19 [1974] 194). If, as seems likely, it derives from the traditional number of the tribes of Israel, it suggests not so much that Ezra was aiming to reunite all the remnants of former Israel, as Koch supposes, as that he regarded his own more restricted community as the sole legitimate representative and heir of Israel.

Explanation

There can have been little to attract recruits to Ezra's group of returning exiles. Those with a pioneering spirit or strong feeling for the land of Israel would have gone long before, and, although history is silent as to detail, it does not seem probable that reports from those in the land to others of their families in Babylon would have been very encouraging. As the following verses show, some groups in particular lacked any incentive to move.

Nevertheless, a sizable party is assembled, and the manner in which the list is constructed shows clearly that it is regarded as ideal Israel, viewed from a priestly perspective. Though with a somewhat different emphasis from Ezra 1–3, there is nevertheless the definite impression here of a second Exodus, with its arduous desert journey and entry into the land. Thus we find here a further fulfillment of Israel's prophetic hopes for a return from exile, which had themselves drawn on the language and imagery of the Exodus for their expression.

As presented in this book, therefore, the second Exodus is not a solitary event, but a type of experience that successive generations may enjoy. Its promise and hope are not exhausted by the first group who returned, and apparently no blame is attached to those who chose to go only later. The prospect of a new life is ever open, and it confronts each successive generation with its challenge for decision; this is like the repeated exhortations of Deuteronomy, which also encourage second generations to "choose life" (Deut 30:15–20; cf. 5:3 *et passim*). The NT too insists on the importance of eventual repentance rather than on the virtue of preceding others in response to the challenge of the gospel; cf. Matt 20:1–16; 21:28–31; Luke 15, etc.

Ezra's Journey to Jerusalem   (Ezra 8:15–36)

Bibliography

Browne, L. E. "A Jewish Sanctuary in Babylonia." *JTS* 17 (1916) 400–401. **Driver, G. R.** "Babylonian and Hebrew Notes." *WO* 2 (1954–58) 19–26. **In der Smitten, W. Th.** *Esra.* **Kapelrud, A. S.** *Authorship.* **Koch, K.** "Ezra and the Origins of Judaism." *JSS* 19 (1974) 173–97. **Pelzl, B.** "Philologisches zu Esra 8:27." *ZAW* 87 (1975) 221–24. **Snaith, N. H.** "A Note on Ezra viii.35." *JTS* ns 22 (1971) 150–52.

Translation

[15] *I assembled them by the canal which flows to Ahava, and we encamped there for three days. I noted the presence of laymen and priests, but discovered that none of the Levites were there.* [16] *So I summoned* [a] *Eliezer, Ariel, Shemaiah,* [b] *Elnathan, Jarib, Zechariah, and Meshullam, intelligent leaders,* [b] [17] *and sent* [a] *them to Iddo, the leading man at the place Casiphia, giving them a message to relay to Iddo* [b] *and his brethren and the temple servants* [b] *at the place Casiphia that they should bring us ministers for the house of our God.* [18] *Then, according to the good hand of our God upon us, they brought us a man of discretion from the family of Mahli son of Levi, the son of Israel, namely* [a] *Sherebiah, together with his sons and kinsmen: eighteen;* [19] *also Hashabiah and with him Jeshaiah from the family of Merari, his kinsmen* [a] *and their sons: twenty;* [20] *and of the temple servants whom David and the princes had appointed to serve the Levites: 220 temple servants; they were all recorded by name.*

[21] *Then I proclaimed a fast there by the canal Ahava in order that we might humble ourselves before our God so as to ask of him a safe journey* [a] *for ourselves, for our children and for all our goods,* [b] [22] *for I was ashamed to ask the king for a detachment of soldiers and cavalry to help us against enemy attack on the way, since we had already said to the king, "The hand of our God rests in favor upon all those who seek him, whereas his fierce wrath* [a] *is upon all those who forsake him."* [23] *So we fasted and besought our God for this and he heard our entreaty.*

[24] *Then I set apart twelve of the priests' chiefs and* [a] *Sherebiah and Hashabiah* [a] *and with them ten of their kinsmen,* [25] *and I weighed out to them the silver, the gold, and the vessels—the offering for the house of our God—which the king, his counselors, and his chiefs, as well as all Israel who were present, had offered.* [26] *I weighed out into their keeping:*

> *650 talents of silver*
> *100 silver vessels weighing . . . talents* [a]
> *100 talents of gold*
> [27] *20 gold bowls worth 1,000 darics* [a]
> *2 vessels of brightly gleaming copper* [b] *as precious as gold.*

[28] *And I said to them, "You are holy to the Lord, and the vessels are holy; the silver and the gold are a freewill offering to the Lord the God of your fathers.* [29a] *Take the greatest care of them* [a] *until you weigh them out before the chiefs of the priests*

and the Levites and the family chiefs [b] of Israel in Jerusalem in the chambers of [c] the house of the Lord." [30] Thus the priests and the Levites [a] took responsibility for the consignment of [a] silver and gold and vessels, to bring them to Jerusalem, to the house of our God.

[31] We departed from the river Ahava on the twelfth day of the first month to go to Jerusalem; the hand of our God was upon us and he saved us from enemy attacks and from ambush on the way. [32] When we arrived at Jerusalem, we rested there for three days. [33] Then on the fourth day the silver, the gold, and the vessels were weighed out in the house of our God into the care of Meremoth, son of Uriah, the priest, together with Eleazar, son of Phinehas, and assisting them were the Levites Jozabad, son of Jeshua, and Noadiah, son of Binnui. [34] Everything was checked [a] by number and by weight and the total weight was recorded in writing.

[35] At that time [a] those who had come [b] from the captivity, the exiles, offered as burnt offerings to the God of Israel twelve bulls for all Israel, ninety-six rams, and seventy-two [c] lambs (and twelve he-goats as a sin-offering), [d] the whole being a burnt offering to the Lord. [36] And they delivered the king's orders to the royal satraps and governors of Beyond the River who then gave support to the people and to the house of God.

Notes

16.a. Lit., "sent for." Alternatively, ל may introduce the accus; cf. NEB, "So I sent Eliezer. . . ." The Vrs divide over the correct interpretation. Avoidance of duplication with v 16a slightly favors the translation given here.

16.b-b. MT is here represented literally by NEB: "Elnathan, Jarib, Elnathan, Nathan, Zechariah, and Meshullam, prominent men, and Joiarib and Elnathan, men of discretion." The distinction between the two groups could only be justified if "men of discretion" (מבינים) meant "teachers," and hence priests, but there is no apparent reason why they should have been designated in this artificial way. The list of names too poses difficulties: Elnathan occurs three times and its equivalent Nathan once, while Jarib and Joiarib are merely variants of the same name. If different people were referred to, we would expect the inclusion of patronymics to make the distinctions clear. It is thus probable that "and Joiarib and Elnathan" should be deleted as a misplaced marginal gl on the earlier part of the list, thus joining מבינים and ראשים together; this is represented still in 1 Esdr 8:44. The confusion that provoked the gl had apparently already taken place by the time of 1 Esdr, however, so that we are reduced to conjecture. Presumably, as the gl implies, one occurrence of Elnathan and that of Nathan should be deleted as early corrections or variants. (Rudolph [80], alternatively, suggests on the basis of six MSS that one occurrence of Elnathan should be read as Jonathan. This is not supported by the early Vrs, however, and therefore probably represents a secondary attempt to improve on the repetitive MT.)

17.a. So K (וָאוֹצְאָה), Q has וָאֲצַוֶּה, "I commanded them." The meaning is not seriously affected, though it is not strictly legitimate to combine them in translation (e.g., NEB, "with instructions to go to").

17.b-b. Read ואחיו והנתינים, with support (for the most part) from 1 Esdr 8:46. The conjunction will have been lost in each case by haplogr. The MT ("Iddo his brother the temple servants") makes no sense, and any emendation must avoid the implication that Iddo, a leader with authority over Levites, was one of the temple servants. K, הנתונים, can be construed as "who were appointed." It would fit well with the suggestion that there was a sanctuary of some sort in Casiphia (see *Comment*), and it enjoys a measure of versional support. Nevertheless, Q is to be preferred on the basis of the following list. K may have arisen once the loss of the conj brought it into relation with "his brethren" and so made "temple servants" inappropriate; it could then have been understood as "dedicated, devoted,"

18.a. Explicative *wāw*.

19.a. MT, rendered literally above, is certainly expressed rather strangely, but is not therefore impossible. Nevertheless, many commentators favor repointing אחיו ("his kinsmen") as אָחִיו, "his brother," and moving it up to qualify Jeshaiah.

21.a. Lit., "a straight, level way."

21.b. See *Comment* on 1:4.

22.a. Hendiadys.

24.a-a. Read ושרביה וחשביה with 1 Esdr. It is clear that they should not be linked with the priests in the first half of the verse both because they were Levites (vv 18–19) and because of the numbers involved: as reconstructed, the text gives us twelve priests and twelve Levites.

26.a. The numeral has dropped out, as the parallel structure at the beginning of v 27 shows. Many (e.g., Ehrlich, *Randglossen;* Bewer; Rudolph; NEB) simply repoint the word for talents as a dual, לְכִכָּרָיִם "of two talents," though there is no evidence for this. LXX and Vg omit "talents" altogether, while 1 Esdr (followed by RV) incorrectly links מאה "one hundred" with "talents" rather than with "silver vessels."

27.a. Cf. Williamson, *TynB* 28 (1977) 123–25. The LXX suggests the alternative possibility that this text originally read "drachmas," as at 2:69.

27.b. Cf. Pelzl, *ZAW* 87 (1975) 221–24, who argues that טובה should be construed adverbially, "brightly."

29.a-a. Lit., "Watch and keep."

29.b. It is possible that this unusual use of שרי "chiefs of" has mistakenly replaced the expected (and orthographically not totally dissimilar) ראשי "heads of," under the influence of the preceding phrase; but cf. *Comment*.

29.c. MT here has the def art on a noun in the const. Suggestions for emendation may be unnecessary if Rudolph is right in regarding the whole phrase as an accus of place with this word as an intentional "mixed form" of לְשָׁכוֹת and הַלְּשָׁכוֹת.

30.a-a. Lit., "received the weight of."

34.a. The verb is added in translation for smoother reading. In the MT, "by number, by weight to the whole" qualifies "were weighed" in the previous verse.

35.a. In the MT this phrase concludes the previous verse, where it would have to be translated "at the same time." The otherwise abrupt opening of the present verse, together with the transition to third-person narrative for vv 35–36, favors taking the phrase as its introduction. LXX may support this, but the evidence is ambiguous.

35.b. There is no evidence to support Ehrlich's conjectural emendation, repeated in *BHS*, רבבאם "and when they arrived."

35.c. MT has "seventy-seven," but all the other figures are multiples of twelve, and 1 Esdr supports the emendation. The error may have arisen by a combination of homoioarchton and the influence of the previous word.

35.d. Snaith, *JTS* ns 22 (1971) 150–52, suggests this use of brackets to avoid the impossible suggestion that a sin-offering could be part of a burnt offering.

Form/Structure/Setting

Although this section is made up of several smaller, episodic units, it is nevertheless afforded an overall unity by its concentration on the preparations for, and immediate sequel to, the journey to Jerusalem. It is framed both by the care for the temple offerings (vv 24–30, 33–34) and by the period of three days for muster before the journey (v 15) and for the mention of rest at its conclusion (v 32). The narrative continues in an uninterrupted manner throughout. It is, however, set apart from the preceding list (vv 1–14) by the repetitive resumption in v 15 (see *Form*, 7:28b–8:14) and from the following events by the third-person summary in vv 35–36.

Three levels of composition may be discerned within the passage. First, there are two short lists, both of which were probably committed to writing at or soon after the time of the events concerned. This is indicated for the summarizing list of Levites and temple servants by the conclusion in v 20, "they were all recorded by name." In other words, the author of our present text extracted his material from a more extensive antecedent source. As with 8:1–14, a number of scholars regard this list as a much later, secondary expansion (e.g., Noth, *Studien*, 125; Mowinckel, *Studien III*, 29; Kellermann, *Nehemia*, 64). Their reasons are very weak, however, and certainly cannot stand apart from similar conclusions for comparable passages such as 8:1–14 above. However, it was suggested above (*Form* on 7:28b—8:14) that these two lists may originally have been one (cf. the comprehensive heading in 8:1, suggesting a list of all who came to Jerusalem, which eventually included Levites), and that they were only separated because of the demands of the narrative. Our conclusions regarding the literary integrity and authenticity of 8:1–14 will therefore apply here also.

The second list, that of the offerings for the temple (vv 26–27), is also said to have been recorded in writing at the time of these events (v 34). As the narrative states, this would have been necessary for accounting purposes both before and after the journey, at which points responsibility for the offerings changed hands. The preservation of such a list in the temple archives is inherently probable.

Both these lists are of a type already familiar, and they show no noteworthy peculiarity or development of form except that the manner of registering Levites differs slightly from that of the laity; see *Form* on 8:1–14 and (for the list of offerings) *Form* on 1:7–11.

The bulk of the passage, into which the two lists have been woven, is again the EM. Its unity at this point is widely recognized and there is no reason to deny that it represents a single composition here. A decision about its general setting and authenticity will therefore be largely dependent upon our overall assessment of the Ezra material (see *Introduction*, "The Ezra Memoir").

However, there are one or two features of this passage which themselves contribute to that assessment. First, there are two place names, Ahava and Casiphia, which are not otherwise known. Some have seen in them names of once-prominent Jewish centers that would have been known to a later writer. It seems more likely, however, that here, as with the names in 2:59, they reflect local knowledge by one who was involved in the events described. This is a further small pointer to the authenticity of the EM.

Second, as was noted at 7:1–10, the curious relationship between the dates in the two passages is best explained on the theory that antecedent material lay before an editor in 7:1–10. Naturally this suggestion points to the prior and independent composition of the present section.

Finally, it has been observed in combating this suggestion that there are several features in this narrative that echo elements in the NM, but in such a way as to suggest that this account was deliberately written up in order to exalt Ezra over Nehemiah (cf. In der Smitten, *Esra*, 22–23). The individual points will be examined in *Comment* below. We may summarize our conclusion here by maintaining that the evidence is not strong enough to support the case: a number of the examples simply derive from the demands of narrative, not to say historical, convention, and do not therefore demand direct dependence. In addition, the case cannot look to 7:1–10 (or 8:35–36; see below) for support, since it was argued there that those verses were in their present form to be attributed to the later editor who could certainly have borrowed from his knowledge of the NM. Third, it has been well said that "if much of the narrative in Ezra vii–x and Neh. viii–xiii was invented by the Chronicler with the aim of making Ezra overshadow Nehemiah, it is surprising that the task was not fulfilled more efficiently" (J. A. Emerton, review of Kellermann, *Nehemia; JTS* ns 23 [1972] 183). The few examples not already covered by our first two categories are not sufficiently sustained to maintain the case for conscious modeling on Nehemiah and must be attributed to the historical coincidence of two men undertaking similar ventures at the same general historical period.

A third and final level of composition may be seen in the third-person account of vv 35–36. Without dealing fully at this point with the question of the changes in person in the EM (see discussion on chap. 10 below), it seems probable that a later editor is responsible for this section. While it would not be unreasonable to expect the material to come from the EM, such a postulate is not strictly necessary: v 35 is general enough to be based on what the editor expected in the light of the cultic practices with which he would have been familiar, while v 36 may have been suggested by 7:21 and by Neh 2:9, which of course the editor would have known. Rudolph may well be right in arguing that the editor contributed this passage as part of the same operation of removing the next section of the EM to Neh 8 (q.v.).

Comment

15–20 The lack of Levites in the assembled company is remedied.

15 The narrative is consciously resumed from the end of chap. 7 after the incorporation of the preceding list, but with the additional information now that the assembly took place "by the canal which flows to Ahava." This has not been identified, though it appears from v 21 that both the canal (lit., "river") and the locality shared the same name. We must assume from the context that it was a large open space close to Babylon. Babylon itself was built on the Euphrates river from which flowed a number of artificial canals and waterways for defensive purposes (cf. *IDB* 1, 334–38; Ezek 1:1; Ps 137:1). Ahava was no doubt one of these.

During the "three days" of assembling and preparation (the figure may be somewhat conventional, though it is in itself eminently reasonable; see *Comment* on v 32), the complete absence of Levites was noticed. The reasons may have been the same as those noted at 2:40. Since there were already Levites active back in the land, Ezra's concern at this point cannot have been dictated primarily by his estimate of future needs. Rather, as Koch, *JSS* 19 (1974) 187, observes, the delay in order to involve at least a token group of Levites is intelligible "only against the background of the order of the march through the desert after the original Exodus. In accordance with the P source (Num x.13ff.), there must be Levites with special tasks, as well as priests and laymen, with Ezra also."

16–17 Since Ezra seems to have had no hesitation in sending a substantial delegation of leaders specifically and directly to Casiphia (otherwise unknown), it has been suggested that there must have been a cult center or even sanctuary there (cf. Browne, *JTS* 17 [1916] 400–401). Support for this suggestion is further found in the repeated use of "the place" (המקום) as a qualifier: it is used on occasion for "sanctuary" (cf. A. Cowley, "The Meaning of מקום in Hebrew," *JTS* 17 [1916] 174–76), while Bowman's suggestion that it is used here only "as a determinative, an aid in reading, as in Akkadian" is an unconvincing guess because it is not an attested usage in Hebrew. Centers of Jewish worship did undoubtedly develop in the exile, as elsewhere in the diaspora, and the existence of a temple at Elephantine is well known. Thus the suggestion is reasonable, though not proved. The precise nature of Iddo's function remains unknown, however. "His brethren" would, of course, be the Levites, while for "the temple servants" see discussion of 2:43–58.

18–19 Thirty-eight Levites responded. This might seem very few, but in view of the speed with which they would have had first to decide and then to prepare for so momentous a move, quite apart from the reasons already noted for the difficulties of securing any levitical support whatever, Ezra regarded their presence as a mark of God's special grace, indicating again his blessing on the whole undertaking.

Sherebiah recurs several times in the Ezra narrative; cf. v 24; Neh 8:7; 9:4, 5; 10:12; 12:8, 24. Within the Levites ("son of Levi") he came from the line of Mahli, a grandson of Levi through Merari, a family that traditionally was responsible for carrying the Tabernacle (Num 3:33–37; 4:29–33). If the title "son of Israel" means "son of Jacob," it is unique in Ezra-Nehemiah, though the use of Israel for Jacob is regular in Chronicles. Alternatively there may be textual corruption here (so Batten) or it may simply mean "an Israelite," just as "son of Levi" is virtually equivalent to "Levite."

20 As at 2:43–58, a larger number of temple servants were willing to return. A full list of their names is said to have been available to the writer. This is the only passage that tells us explicitly of their origins. Probably by analogy with "the sons of Solomon's servants" (cf. 2:55–57) they are said to have been appointed by David and his princes to serve the Levites. This is in line with the general tendency of the period to legitimize the inevitable development in cultic institutions beyond Pentateuchal prescriptions by attributing the changes to David. Several examples are to be found in Chronicles (cf. 1 Chr 15–16; 23–27), though significantly this particular group is referred to there only in passing at 1 Chr 9:2, and what may be inferred of their origins in Chronicles differs from this verse; cf. S. Japhet, *VT* 18 (1968) 351–54. It has been suggested that the use of the relative particle שׁ here, rather than the more regular אשׁר, indicates that the clause is a later addition. This is unnecessary, however; the particle was beginning to gain currency in Judah at this time but is not yet used consistently by any single writer (e.g., for the Chronicler, cf. 1 Chr 5:20; for the priestly redactor of Chronicles, cf. 1 Chr 27:27, but both writers normally use אשׁר. Later, Ecclesiastes uses שׁ sixty-eight times and אשׁר eighty-nine times, etc.). Ideologically there is no reason to doubt that this view of the origins of the temple servants could have been adopted as early as Ezra's time.

21–23 The final preparations for the journey are divided between general religious exercises to entreat God's favor (vv 21–23) and practical steps to ensure the safe delivery of the considerable treasures earmarked for the temple (vv 24–30).

21 The practice of fasting seems to have become particularly widespread among the Jews of the post-exilic period (e.g., 10:6; Neh 9:1; Esth 4:3, 16; Isa 58:3; Joel 1–2; cf. *IDB* 2, 241–44), partly as a means of reinforcing the supplications of an individual or community. There is thus no reason whatsoever to regard this verse with In der Smitten, *Esra,* 22, as dependent on Nehemiah's fast (Neh 1:4, 2:1), which in any case was not undertaken as preparatory to the journey itself.

By thus "humbling" themselves (lit., "afflicting" themselves; note that, significantly, a different word is used from that used regularly with the same translation in Chronicles), the community aimed to put themselves directly under the protection of God, who had so often shown his particular care for the afflicted. This protection was necessary both because of their physical weakness (note the reference to "children") and because of the treasure they were carrying.

22 In particular, however, they needed divine protection because Ezra had specifically renounced the possibility of asking for an armed escort, as an act of witness to his faith in God's personal care for his people. The words cited are probably a traditional couplet, with antithetic parallelism and the enemy described as "those who forsake him," which is not strictly appropriate to the brigands who might be expected on the journey; for comparable formulae, cf. 1 Chr 28:9 and 2 Chr 15:2; many of the Psalms express similar sentiments. It is thus not impossible that Ezra had used familiar liturgical language in expressing his confidence to the king and was now suddenly brought to realize the extent to which a faith so glibly expressed was to be tested; for a similar challenge, cf. Isa 40:21–23. In that case, the intention would not have been "to avoid unduly attracting the attention of their future neighbors whose enmity might be further aroused thereby" (Myers), since the letters that Ezra brought from the king could hardly have allowed his arrival to be kept secret. Still less would there have been a boast here to demonstrate Ezra's spiritual superiority over Nehemiah, who did have an armed escort for his journey; cf. Neh 2:9 (Kapelrud, *Authorship,* 50–51; In der Smitten, *Esra,* 22). This would be the most telling of such points of contact from within the EM itself (cf. *Form* above), but in fact it is far from a boast on Ezra's part: as interpreted above, it is to be seen as a somewhat embarrassed explanation of why he took such an enormous risk. It thus provides a good example of "the expected contrast between the realistic and practical administrator Nehemiah and the religious idealist Ezra" (Bowman).

23 Ezra, looking back after the conclusion of the journey, gratefully records that the people's prayers were answered; see *Comment* on v 31 for further detail.

24–30 Finally, provision is made for the safe transportation of the freewill offerings for the temple.

24 Responsibility is vested in twelve priests and twelve Levites, specially selected for the task. This is in accord with the Pentateuchal legislation for the care and movement of the tabernacle furnishings (Num 3–4). It may also be that the number twelve is symbolic of all Israel, as elsewhere, perhaps, in the EM, but this is less certain in the present case since all those referred to were members of the one tribe of Levi.

25 Since Ezra was handling other people's sacred offerings, he was scrupulously careful both to ensure that none was lost or stolen and to guard against any claim that he had made personal gain from them. The items were weighed out (and, we infer, receipted in writing; cf. v 34) both before and after the journey so that a careful check and record could be made at every stage of their movement. The contributors are listed in conformity with the edict of Artaxerxes in 7:15–16.

26–27 As at 1:9–11, the list of vessels is presented in an orderly manner (silver followed by silver vessels; gold followed by gold vessels; special items), though the second item shows clearly that, as in chap. 1, there has been some textual corruption. As it now stands, the text presents a curious mixture of the historically credible and the incredible. The last two items are perfectly reasonable: assuming the gold daric is intended (generally reckoned at about 8.4 grams), the bowls will have been worth rather less than 20 pounds of gold; this was by no means excessive in the ancient world. The value of the second item is uncertain because of textual corruption, but if "two talents" was the correct reading (see *Notes*), it too would be reasonable. This leaves the first and third items—silver and gold, presumably in ingots—as defying belief, if only because of the physical weight involved: if a talent weighed approximately 75 pounds, then the silver would have weighed more than 24½ tons, and the gold some 3¾ tons. Pavlovský's solemn attempt, *Bib* 35 (1957) 297–301, to calculate the purchasing power of such a sum merely serves to underline its unreality. The situation is closely similar to 7:22, where again "talents of silver" was the disproportionately large item in the list. It is thus probable that an originally "reasonable" list has been transmitted inaccurately, either out of a desire to magnify the glory of the temple by exaggerating the value of the offerings or, more probably in view of the second item and the evidence of chap. 1, by an error through misunderstanding of figures or weights. The evidence clearly does not favor the view that the list is simple fabrication, in which such improbabilities could be expected.

The exact nature of the two bowls with which the list ends is not known, though apparently they were regarded as exceptionally precious. Driver, *WO* 2 (1954–58) 24–25, maintains, on the basis of a translation "copper of tawny ware," that they were made of orichale, an alloy of copper highly prized in the Ancient Near East, while Pelzl, *ZAW* 87 (1975) 221–24, defends the view that it is to the brilliance of the copper that reference is made.

28–30 Holiness is a characteristic of God himself and hence by extension of anyone or anything dedicated to him. This was especially true of priests (Exod 29:1; 39:30; Lev 21:6), Levites (Num 3:12–13) and of the Tabernacle and its equipment (Exod 29:36; 30:29; 40:9, etc.), of which the vessels mentioned in these verses would have been regarded as a continuation. Now, as G. J. Wenham, *Leviticus* (Grand Rapids: Eerdmans, 1979) 22, has it, "Contact between uncleanness and holiness is disastrous. They are utterly distinct in theory, and must be kept equally distinct in practice, lest divine judgment fall." Precisely this ideology underlies Ezra's strict injunction, and it applies in two directions: God, the Holy One, may be relied upon to protect from outside attack that which is his own, especially as it is now in the care of holy men. At the same time, members of Ezra's own company who heard his words would appreciate the fearful consequences that would ensue should they themselves be tempted to steal any of the treasures.

29 The absence of "the family chiefs of Israel" from v 33 has led some commentators to suppose that they have been inserted here only secondarily. However, their addition at a later stage is no easier to understand than their original inclusion in the EM. It is, perhaps, a mistake to look for so precise a consistency. The "chambers" of the temple (cf. 10:6; Neh 10:38–39; 13:5, 8) were rooms around the edges of parts of the temple area used both for administration and storage and for the priests' personal convenience.

31–34 The journey and safe arrival in Jerusalem are briefly recorded. However, both in this and the preceding verses considerably more detail is supplied about the undertaking than in Nehemiah's case (Neh 2:8–11), so that there is no need to regard the one as having influenced the other (*contra* In der Smitten, *Esra*, 23). Further detail beyond that already supplied concerning the journey itself would have served no useful purpose in the EM.

31 Whereas in 7:9 the departure date was said to have been intended for the first day, here the actual date is given as "the twelfth day of the first month." The delay was doubtless caused by the unexpected need to send for Levites (vv 15–20). The date of the arrival in Jerusalem is not given here because it had already been supplied in 7:9. It was suggested there that 7:1–10 was a rewritten, and possibly abbreviated, form of the original introduction to the EM. There is thus no need to suppose that the date has been deliberately omitted here by an editor in the light of 7:9; probably it was never included here.

God's goodness, already noted as punctuating crucial points in the preparations, was evidenced again by his protection on the way. The extent of this protection is not quite clear, however. Are we to understand that there were no attacks at all, or that God rescued the travelers when there was an attack? The word "saved" would normally imply the latter, whereas the general context suggests rather the former. The translation given above, "he saved us from enemy attacks," consciously reflects this ambiguity.

32 The journey lasted some four months. Since the route is unknown, we cannot calculate accurately the rate of progress, but it is generally estimated at about nine miles per day, sustained over approximately nine hundred miles. On the network of roads maintained by the Achaemenid empire and their regular supervision by protective patrols, cf. R. N. Frye, *The Heritage of Persia* (London: Weidenfeld and Nicholson, 1962), 102–3. Under these conditions, this suggested rate of progress appears feasible.

A three-day rest on arrival seems hardly unreasonable in the circumstances. The figure may be somewhat stereotyped ("a few days"); cf. Josh 3:1–2; Neh 2:11, while it has also been suggested that they arrived shortly before the Sabbath, so necessitating a rest period; cf. A. Jaubert, "Le Calendrier des Jubilés et de la Secte de Qumrân: Ses Origines Bibliques," *VT* 3 (1953)

261. In any event, this does not constitute evidence of literary dependence on Nehemiah. It arises out of the demands of the narrative at this point.

33–34 The following day the treasures, which have really been the focus of attention throughout the description of the journey, are again transferred to new custodians (see *Comment* on v 25). The rather ponderous emphasis in v 34 is certainly suggestive of someone who is on the defensive regarding his stewardship; see *Form* on 7:11–28a above.

Two priests and two Levites receive the offerings at the temple. (For the question of whether they formed a standing committee earlier established by Nehemiah, see *Comment* on Neh 13:13.) As usual, the question of identifying individuals remains uncertain. Of the Levites, a Jozabad is mentioned in Neh 11:16 as one who was in charge of the external affairs of the temple, while in Ezra 10:23 a Levite Jozabad is included in the list of those who married foreign wives. Does this account for the slightly less responsible position implied by Neh 11:16, assuming the identity of the three individuals? Noadiah is mentioned only here, but his family is probably referred to in the list of homecomers at 2:10.

Of the priests, Eleazar may be mentioned again at 10:18, but the name is sufficiently common to preclude certainty. The case of "Meremoth son of Uriah the priest" has given rise to much discussion, however. At Neh 3:4 and 21, Meremoth son of Uriah, son of Hakkoz, is listed as an energetic wall-builder. He is not there called a priest, but comes in a portion of the list that appears to be dealing with either Levites or priests. The name Hakkoz in Neh 3:4 and 21 further points us back to Ezra 2:61 where the name is mentioned as one of the priestly families unable at that time to prove their descent. There are at least four reasonable ways of explaining these data:

Since both the names Meremoth and Uriah are quite common, no identification need be made; cf. Kellermann, *ZAW* 80 (1968) 69. The reference to Hakkoz in Neh 3 could well link with Ezra 2, and the fact that in Neh 3 he is not specifically called "the priest" may suggest continuing uncertainty about his family's status. In the present verse, however, Hakkoz is not mentioned and Meremoth is designated "the priest."

The data have been used as evidence for reversing the order of Ezra and Nehemiah: in Nehemiah's time, the family had still not received priestly recognition, but Meremoth's outstanding efforts on the wall-building led sooner (Rudolph) or later (i.e., 398 B.C.) to their reinstatement, as evidenced by the present verse. Against this view, however, it must be observed that the use of the title "priest" here probably points to him as a leading, if not the supreme, priest (Koch, *JSS* 19 [1974] 190–91); on Rudolph's view, could he have been elevated so quickly to such prominence (Schneider, 69)? According to the more usual view, if 2:61 implies that Uriah was already alive at the time of the first return, then Meremoth would have been impossibly old by 398 B.C. (In der Smitten, *Esra*, 133).

Koch argues for Meremoth's demotion rather than for his promotion, and thus retains the traditional order of Ezra before Nehemiah. In the present passage he appears as the supreme priest; in Neh 10:6 there is a Meremoth listed eleventh among the priests, while in Neh 3 he is classed as a layman.

"It seems as if Ezra acknowledged Meremoth at the time of the arrival in Jerusalem, but deposed him shortly afterward while carrying out his investigation in Jerusalem by means of the law he had brought with him." This is somewhat speculative, however, particularly as there is no mention of Meremoth in chap. 10.

On the assumption that the same man is referred to both here and in Neh 3, it is not difficult to believe that the traditional order is nevertheless correct. Although Meremoth is not given the title of "the priest" in Neh 3, his position in the list suggests that he was one in fact, as even Rowley, "Order," 167, is happy to agree. Others in the list are probably also priests, though not designated as such. Thus he could well have been temple treasurer when Ezra returned in 458 B.C. (it is by no means certain that "the priest" must mean "the high priest"; he is not listed as such in Neh 12) and still easily have been able to act as a section leader in the wall-building thirteen years later.

In view of the uncertainties, the case of Meremoth clearly cannot help settle the issue of the order of Ezra and Nehemiah either way. The first and last possibilities listed above face the fewest difficulties, and the coincidence of both name and patronymic strongly favors the last.

35–36 The origin of this paragraph was discussed at *Form* above. While it probably comes from the final editor, it is nevertheless reasonable to suppose that Ezra and his associates would have offered sacrifices both as a means of thanksgiving and for the repayment of vows undertaken before the journey. After all, they had not had opportunity to sacrifice previously, while in Babylon. The sin-offerings were for the cleansing from ritual defilement, inevitably contracted on so prolonged a journey. In all this, the fulfillment of the terms of Artaxerxes' edict (7:17) is being presented.

The repeated emphasis on the number twelve is doubtless due to the final editor. Once again, therefore (see on 7:1–10), it is to him rather than Ezra himself or the EM that the more ideologically weighted interpretation of the events is to be ascribed. The returning community is the heir of all Israel, and this is probably to be read, as elsewhere in these books, as an exclusive attitude.

In accordance with the implications of 7:21–24, letters are delivered to the Persian administrators of the province. The absence of a reference to the governor of Judah is not surprising: he was a Jew with responsibility only for local affairs, whereas the kind of support to which Ezra was entitled required authority at a higher level.

36 The expression "satraps and governors" is strange, since while a satrapy (such as Beyond the River) might have a number of districts or provinces each with its own governor (פחה, a word whose use appears to be quite flexible), it would have only one satrap. Unless "satraps" is being used loosely with "governors" as an explanatory comment on it, it is probable that this inexactitude points again to the editor of the Ezra-Nehemiah material rather than to the first-hand EM itself.

The important point of the verse is that once again the Persian officials are shown to be fully supporting the properly authorized and constituted temple worship in Jerusalem.

Explanation

There are three main elements in the narrative of this section, and by reference to God's good hand upon Ezra and his companions, each is marked out as having been carried through under the blessing of divine providence (vv 18, 22 and 31). These three elements are the gathering of Levites, the care for the treasures to be presented at the temple, and the journey itself, with all its attendant dangers. Small wonder that sacrifices of thanksgiving were offered at its conclusion!

In each case, the grace of God is highlighted by the initial unlikelihood of success in the venture. In the case of the Levites, not a single one joined Ezra at first. This makes clear the fact that such a move was particularly unattractive to them. Yet, if Ezra's caravan was in any way to match Pentateuchal legislation, with its insistence on Levites to carry the sacred vessels, their participation, no matter how small the numbers, was imperative. The speed with which thirty-eight did eventually respond is attributed to more than merely human persuasion.

As far as the journey is concerned, success in terms of a safe arrival also seemed unlikely at the start because of Ezra's refusal to ask for an armed escort (v 22). There is the suggestion that he later regretted this as a rash move. However, his initial boast that "the hand of our God rests in favor upon all those who seek him" proved to be well-founded.

It is concern for the transportation of the costly offerings for the temple, however, which dominates most of this section. It is at the center of attention from v 24 onwards, but even before that it may, as noted, have prompted Ezra to seek the support of the Levites. Moreover, the very fact that the caravan was carrying such wealth must have made it peculiarly vulnerable to ambush. But here again, "the hand of our God was upon us" to deliver (v 31).

Now in all this, it might appear as though a "spiritual" approach was being contrasted with a more "practical." Indeed, the view has gained some currency that this is part of a deliberate attempt to present Ezra as superior to Nehemiah. In fact, however, this is not the case. Ezra made careful arrangements for the delegation to gather Levites, as may be seen from vv 16–17, and in the case of the temple vessels the elaborate precautions which he took against theft or loss have been noted at vv 25–30 and 33–34. In these two cases, at least, the goodness of God was operative through human channels and resources, not despite them or in contrast with them. Only in the matter of the absence of an armed escort is this not obviously so, but we have seen Ezra's embarrassment over this. Finally, the concluding note of the chapter reminds us that the temple worship too was supported by the Persians, and this is clearly welcomed as a further indication of divine blessing.

God's grace and human effort thus go hand in hand. Early biblical narrative often tends to oppose them: "stand still, and see the salvation of the Lord" (Exod 14:13) could be written over many accounts, including a number in the near-contemporary books of Chronicles (e.g. 2 Chr 20). Such a text reminds us of the necessary truths of the sovereignty of God and man's inability to save himself apart from grace. Alongside that, however, we see, as in this chapter, the developing emphasis on the equally necessary theme that God's grace is usually operative through human channels, a theme which reaches its definitive climax in the incarnation itself (John 1:14). This should be an encouragement to believing readers to submit themselves afresh under the good hand of this gracious God in order that, whether recognized by the world at large or not, he may continue through them to work for blessing and the extension of the kingdom of his love.

A Report of Mixed Marriages and Ezra's Response (Ezra 9:1-15)

Bibliography

Bossman, D. "Ezra's Marriage Reform: Israel Redefined." *BTB* 9 (1979) 32–38. **Braun, R. L.** "Chronicles, Ezra, and Nehemiah: theology and literary history." VTSup 30 (1979) 52–64. **Eichhorst, W. R.** "Ezra's Ethics on Intermarriage and Divorce." *Grace Journal* 10 (1969) 16–28. **Emerton, J. A.** "Review of Vogt, *Studie.*" *JTS* ns 18 (1967) 169–75. **Fernández, A.** "La Voz גָּדֵר en Esd. 9, 9." *Bib* 16 (1935) 82–84. ———. "Esdr. 9, 9 y un Texto de Josefo." *Bib* 18 (1937) 207–8. **In der Smitten, W. Th.** "Die Gründe für die Aufnahme der Nehemiaschrift in das chronistische Geschichtswerk." *BZ* N.F. 16 (1972) 207–21. **Kaupel, H.** "Die Bedeutung von גדר in Esr. 9, 9." *BZ* 22 (1934) 89–92. ———. "Zu גָּדֵר in Esr. 9, 9." *Bib* 16 (1935) 213–14. **Lohfink, N.** "Enthielten die im Alten Testament bezeugten Klageriten eine Phase des Schweigens?" *VT* 12 (1962) 260–77. **Plöger, O.** "Reden und Gebete im deuteronomistischen und chronistischen Geschichtswerk." *Festschrift für Günther Dehn.* W. Schneemelcher (ed.). Neukirchen: Verlag der Buchhandlung des Erziehungsvereins, 1957, 35–49. **Rad, G. von.** "Gerichtsdoxologie." *Gesammelte Studien zum Alten Testament*, vol. 2. Munich: Chr. Kaiser, 1973, 245–54.

Translation

[1] *When these things were finished, the chiefs approached me and said, "The people of Israel, including* [a] *the priests and Levites, have not kept themselves separate from the peoples of the lands,* [b] *but have acted according to the abominations of* [b] *the Canaanites, the Hittites, the Perizzites, the Jebusites, the Ammonites, the Moabites, the Egyptians, and the Amorites.* [c] [2] *For they have taken some of their daughters as wives for themselves and their sons, so that the holy seed has become mixed with the peoples of the land;* [a] *what is more, the chiefs and officials have led the way in this unfaithfulness."* [a]

[3] *When I heard this I rent my garment and cloak, pulled hair from my head and beard and sat in a state of severe shock.* [4] *Then all who trembled at the words of the God of Israel gathered* [a] *round me on account of the exiles' unfaithfulness while I continued sitting in a state of severe shock until the evening offering.*

[5] *Then at the time of the evening sacrifice* [a] *I got up from where I had sat in humiliation* [a] *and, with my garment and cloak torn, I bowed down on my knees and spread out my hands to the Lord my God* [6] *saying, "O my God,* [a] *I am too utterly ashamed* [a] *to lift up my face to you, O my God, for our iniquities have increased* [b] *until they are higher than our heads* [b] *and our guilt has mounted up to heaven.* [7] *From the days of our fathers until this very day we have been in great guilt. Because of our iniquities we, our kings, and* [a] *our priests* [b] *have been at the mercy of* [b] *the kings of the lands, of sword, captivity, pillage, and open shame, as we are today.* [8] *But now for a brief moment grace has been shown by the Lord our God in leaving us a remnant, and in giving us a secure hold* [a] *in his holy place, so that our God brightens* [b] *our eyes and gives us* [c] *a measure of revival in our bondage.* [9] *For though indeed we are slaves, our God has not abandoned us in our bondage, but has extended*

to us his steadfast love ª before the kings of Persia in reviving us ᵇ to erect the house of our God and to repair its ruins and in giving us a protective wall in Judah and Jerusalem.

¹⁰ *"And now, O our God, what can we say after this? Only that* ª *we have neglected your commandments,* ¹¹ *which you gave through your servants the prophets, when they said, 'The land which you are going in to possess is a land polluted by the impurity of the peoples of the lands with their abominations whereby they have filled it with their uncleanness from end to end.* ¹² *So now do not give your daughters in marriage to their sons nor marry their daughters to your sons, and never seek their peace or welfare, so that you may be strong and eat the good things of the land and bequeath it to your children for ever.'*

¹³ *"After all that has happened to us because of our evil deeds and our great guilt—although, O our God, you have punished us less than our iniquity deserved* ª *and have given us a remnant like this—* ¹⁴ *shall we again break your commandments and intermarry with the peoples who practice these abominations? Would you not be angry with us to the point of completely destroying us without remnant or survivor?* ¹⁵ *O Lord, God of Israel, you are in the right! Yet we are now left as an escaped remnant. Here we are before you in our guilt, though in such a condition no one can stand before you."*

Notes

1.a. Cf. Vogt, *Studie,* 136–38, who regards the conjunction as a *wāw premens* or *wāw concomitantiae* (cf. GKC § 154a¹; Joüon, *Grammaire* §§ 150p and 151a) which draws particular attention to one section of a complete group. Less probably, העם "the people" could be construed absolutely, with the three following words as a parenthetical explanation: "Israel (= the laity), the priests and the Levites," or again the whole phrase העם ישראל "the people (of Israel)" could stand for the laity, followed by "the priests and the Levites" (Rudolph).

1.b-b. Lit., "according to their abominations to the . . ." Thus "have acted" is added for a smoother rendering in English. The pronominal suff הם "their" is regarded here as anticipatory, with the following list being opened either with the so-called *lāmed* of introduction or with *lāmed* to indicate the gen (GKC §129).

1.c. Many commentators follow 1 Esdr 8:69 in reading והאדמי "and the Edomites" but this is unnecessary; see under *Comment.*

2.a-a. Lit., "the hand of the chiefs and officials has been first in this unfaithfulness."

4.a. The verb is in the impf. Being followed by a circumstantial clause, this suggests that the crowd gradually continued to grow throughout the time that Ezra sat.

5.a-a. Lit., "I arose from my humiliation."

6.a-a. Lit., "I am ashamed and humiliated."

6.b-b. למעלה here has its normal meaning of "upwards," and ראש follows as an adverbial accus, "with regard to the head." Thus there should be no confusion with the idiosyncratic use of למעלה by the Chronicler to mean "exceedingly." To find that here would involve the conjectural and unnecessary addition of 'מֵעַל הָ "above the" (Rudolph; *BHS*). S. Japhet, *VT* 18 (1968) 357–58, conjectures that the text may have originally read מֵעַל הָרֹאשׁ, but that the words were wrongly divided in the course of transmission. Once that had happened, the *lāmed* was added to make sense. This conjecture, which is possible though not necessary, may be partly supported by the Masoretes. Quite anomalously, they have put a *daghesh* in the *rēsh;* was this a device whereby they sought to indicate that they wanted the *hē* to be understood as the definite article?

7.a. The conjunction may have been lost by haplogr, though it is not absolutely necessary; cf. Vogt, *Studie,* 23–24.

7.b-b. Lit., "given into the hand of."

8.a. For this image, see *Comment.* There is thus no need to emend (with one MS) to יֶתֶר "remnant."

8.b. Cf. GKC § 116k.

8.c. In theory, the verbal suff could be construed as a dir obj; hence "and make us" (cf. Keil; Vogt, *Studie,* 23–25), but cf. *Comment.*

9.a. I have defended this rendering in *JSS* 23 (1978) 38–39.

9.b. Lit., "to give us a revival." Unlike at v 8.b., the use of the preposition *lāmed* eliminates ambiguity. Although such repetition is not surprising in a liturgical setting, an alternative understanding has been advanced by Emerton, *JTS* ns 18 (1967) 174–75 (following a suggestion of G. R. Driver), which has the effect of introducing a play on words with regard to מחיה. It is held on the basis of 1 Chr 11:8 and Neh 3:34 (4:2) that the piel of חיה may mean "to restore" or "to rebuild." The cognate noun could then be rendered here "rebuilding" or "restoration." In my opinion, however, this view rests on a misunderstanding of 1 Chr 11:8 (see my commentary *ad loc.*), while the heavily sarcastic tone of Neh 3:34 (4:2) (q.v.) suggests that we should be wary of basing a new meaning of the piel of חיה upon its usage alone.

10.a. Or, "because, for."

13.a. Lit., "you have withheld (*sc.* our punishment) below our iniquity." Alternatively, מעוננו might be the direct object of חשׂכת (with partitive מן), למטה being used adverbially; cf. BDB 641A: thou "hast kept back, *downward,* part of our iniquity (prevented it from appearing, and being counted against us)." There is no need conjecturally to emend to לְמֶּה (e.g., "you have withheld the rod from our iniquity," with ל to introduce the accus).

Form/Structure/Setting

It is generally recognized that Ezra 9–10 forms a single, extended narrative unit dealing with the question of mixed marriages. The change of person between the chapters is not of great significance in this regard (see *Form,* chap. 10 below). Indeed, K. Baltzer, *The Covenant Formulary* (tr. D. E. Green, Oxford: Blackwell, 1971) 47–48, argues that together these chapters describe a single ceremony of covenant renewal, though if he is right, it would appear to be at the historical level rather than at the level of the present text itself. Within this unit, however, there are several well-defined sections. For convenience only, therefore, chap. 9 may here be treated on its own.

Regarding the narrative framework (vv 1–5), in common with many other commentaries, the view is adopted here that places Ezra's reading of the law between Ezra 8 and Ezra 9 (see *Form* on Neh 8). Thus within the original Ezra narrative it was the community's understanding and acceptance of that law which pricked their leaders' consciences into bringing their confession to Ezra.

There is, moreover, some evidence to suggest that an account of Ezra's ministry following the reading of the law has been omitted by our editor. First, 10:3 indicates that the events recorded here were not the first that Ezra knew or spoke about with regard to the problem of mixed marriages. Second, the dates involved (see *Comment* on v 1) leave an awkward gap between the reading of the law and this chapter. If we may suppose that during this period Ezra was pressing home the law's teaching on a matter that vitally concerned the fulfillment of his commission (see *Comment* on 7:14), then the gap and the people's ultimate confession are both explained. Third, we have seen that the editor regularly reverts to third-person narrative when he is summarizing or otherwise "interfering" with the text of the original EM. While 8:35–36 may already be adequately explained by the fact that he is covering over the transposition from here of the material now found in Neh 8, it would be a contributing explanatory factor if he were also glossing over some other material that he did not feel necessary to include in his account. Was he, perhaps, embarrassed that it took the Jews so long to respond to Ezra's ministry?

In the rearranged narrative of the finished work, while the presentation of the law is given climactic significance, the present passage is left without adequate introduction and the motivation for the leaders' confession remains unexplained. Its "setting" has therefore shifted dramatically. In the original narrative it opened the final scene of the account of Ezra's work, leading toward the fulfillment of the demands of 7:14 in the next chapter (see especially 10:16). Now, however, it has become merely one in a sequence of events undertaken by both reformers, Ezra and Nehemiah, whose fulfillment is presented rather as the reading and acceptance of the law.

Apart from this major qualification, the passage takes its place without difficulty in the EM. It neither adds to nor detracts from the evidence already accumulated above for the view that the final editor of Ezra-Nehemiah had such a source before him. Naturally, those scholars whose understanding of the origins of the material in Ezra 7–8 differs from that adopted here will represent similar opinions with regard to the present passage. They particularly follow Torrey, *Composition*, 14–21, and Kapelrud, *Authorship*, 59–63, in maintaining that the style is identical with that of the Chronicler, and that he alone is therefore to be regarded as responsible for the composition here. (Note, however, Kapelrud's admission, *Authorship*, 63, with regard to vv 3–5 that "the choise [sic!] of words does not seem to be so close to Chr's especial vocabulary as it was in previous sections.") This argument, however, is not securely based; for instance, the syntax of the first verse should be regarded as characteristic of late biblical Hebrew generally, not just of the Chronicler, while מעל, "unfaithfulness" (vv 2 and 4) is used in a way significantly different from that in Chronicles. For these points, see Williamson, *Israel*, 49 and 53.

The content of Ezra's prayer, vv 6–15, shows that it was written specially for its present context. Unlike, for instance, Dan 9:4–19, with which it otherwise has a number of points in common, the references to the current circumstances in vv 8–9 and 11–14 are too specific for it to have been an independent prayer inserted in its present position by a later editor who thought that it might be appropriate. Furthermore, the verses immediately before and after the prayer lead us to expect its inclusion, while without it the transition from first- to third-person narrative between the two chapters, however it might be explained, would be impossibly harsh. We may thus conclude that the prayer was an integral part of the literary composition from the earliest stage of its formation. For the present commentary, this means that it would have been included in the original EM.

This conclusion is reinforced by the observation that from a form-critical perspective the prayer is unique. In outline, it may be analyzed as follows: general confession, including transition from singular to plural penitential lament (vv 6–7); reflection on God's present mercies (vv 8–9); specific confession (vv 10–12); statement of future intent (vv 13–14); and concluding general confession (v 15).

Reflection on this outline reveals first that it comprises confession only, with no supplication in the imperative or jussive whatsoever; cf. In der Smitten,

BZ N.F. 16 (1972) 217–20. This not only distinguishes the passage from the penitential psalms of lament (cf. S. Mowinckel, *The Psalms in Israel's Worship,* vol. 1 [Tr. D. R. Ap-Thomas; Oxford: Blackwell; New York and Nashville: Abingdon, 1962], 193–224), but even from such passages as Neh 1:5–11; 9:6–38; Dan 9:4–19; and Bar 1:15—3:8, with which it is frequently compared. Second, however, we should note that within the confession there are elements that could be more accurately described as hortatory, as though Ezra were very conscious of the audience who surrounded him. Both these observations support the view that this is a special composition for the present context, and in consequence that it may be treated as a unity (*contra* O. H. Steck, *Israel und das gewaltsame Geschick der Propheten* [WMANT 23; Neukirchen-Vluyn: Neukirchener Verlag, 1967], 111).

Having said that, we may, of course, observe that the general style of composition is not unfamiliar in its period. It stands in common with the passages listed in the previous paragraph in that it is written not just in the style of late biblical Hebrew prose, but "high" prose at that. (For a reconstruction of the Hebrew text of Baruch, cf. E. Tov, *The Book of Baruch* [Missoula, MT: Scholars Press, 1975].) In particular, these passages are marked by frequent and liberal citation of earlier scriptural texts. In addition, however, we should note such a phrase as צדיק אתה "You are in the right!" which von Rad used as one of his main criteria for grouping these texts under the category of "Gerichtsdoxologie" ("a doxology of judgment"; see *Comment* on v 15), and the concentration on familiar themes such as the gift of land (v 11) which govern the scriptural texts cited. (Some of these parallels too are noted in the comments below.) It is thus probable that such linguistic comparisons as have been drawn between this passage and the Chronicler are due to the style of the period as employed particularly in liturgical usage. Certainly, in terms of the ideology of retribution the thoughts expressed in this passage mark it as a composition utterly separate from that of Chronicles; cf. Braun, VTSup 30 (1979) 53–56; Koch, *JSS* 19 (1974) 178.

Comment

1 The long and important passage relating Ezra's handling of the problem of mixed marriages is given only a vague chronological introduction, "When these things were finished." As the text stands, this appears to refer back to Ezra's arrival in Jerusalem and the attendant ceremonies of thanksgiving. This, however, occurred in the fifth month (cf. 7:9), whereas we know from 10:9 that the present events took place only in the ninth month, some four months later.

It is possible that this interval was partly filled with the events recorded in Neh 8, dated in the seventh month (see Neh 8, *Form*). Even so, it would be surprising if, four months after his arrival in Jerusalem, this was the first that Ezra knew about the problem of mixed marriages. There is, however, an indication in 10:3 that Ezra was not only already aware of the problem, but had even outlined proposals for a solution. Significantly, he waited until the people themselves came forward in confession and with a willingness to act rather than forcing a solution on a reluctant population.

It was noted in *Form* above that an account of this ministry may have originally been included in the EM. If so, the chronological introduction, once quite specific, has now been purposefully left imprecise (cf. 7:1!) in order to gloss over the community's somewhat tardy response to the preaching of the law.

The identity of "the chiefs" is not revealed, though the addition of "officials" in v 2 to indicate the general leadership of the community suggests that they were a relatively small group. The context clearly presupposes that they were the leaders of those already in the land and not part of the group who returned with Ezra. Thus the suggestion that they were district governors (cf. Neh 3:9 etc.) is attractive. There is no evidence to support Ellison's conjecture (*From Babylon to Bethlehem*, 49) that they were some of the judges whom Ezra had appointed in conformity with 7:25.

The substance of the confession is that members of the religious community (basically, Jews whose families had previously returned from exile, together with those who, though not having been in exile, had nevertheless wholeheartedly thrown in their lot with them; cf. 6:21), including even their spiritual leaders, had both married ("not kept themselves separate from" is explained in v 2), and adopted some of the religious practices of, the rest of the Palestinian population ("the peoples of the lands"; see *Comment* on 3:3). Needless to say, Welch's suggestion, *Post-Exilic Judaism*, 247–49, that only those who had recently returned with Ezra were involved in these mixed marriages, is ruled out by chronological considerations.

It should be noted that marriage with foreigners in itself was not forbidden in the Mosaic law, and indeed not a few of the patriarchs and other heroes of the faith of Israel are said to have contracted such marriages (see, e.g., Gen 16:3; 41:45; Exod 2:21; Num 12:1; 2 Sam 3:3, etc.). However, there was recognized the particular danger that affinity by marriage with the indigenous population of Canaan would almost certainly lead to religious apostasy or syncretism; cf. Exod 34:11–16; Deut 7:1–4; 20:10–18. Such marriages were therefore expressly forbidden, and it is of interest that even the patriarchs are portrayed as being aware of this danger (Gen 24; 28:1–9). There can be no doubt that the subsequent history of the monarchical period showed how apt this warning was.

In the present verse we see how, once conditions had changed beyond the point where the law could be literally applied, its principle was nevertheless upheld. Three points concerning this "exegesis" may be observed. First, laws dealing with the indigenous population of Canaan (see the list at the end of the verse) are now interpreted by reference to the contemporary "peoples of the lands." Ethnically, there was no exact equation, but the intention of the law, that the chief religious danger comes from those closest at hand, is accurately represented. Note, however, that the text is careful not to identify "the peoples of the lands" as "Canaanites" etc. The list at the end of the verse qualifies "abominations," and is thus meant only as a stereotyped formula, adopted from the law. Thus it is correct to speak here of interpretation of the biblical text.

Second, the confession keeps in step with the law at this point (though contrast v 2 below) in regarding the evil of a mixed marriage as being religious, not racial. The partner is led astray "according to the abominations of the Canaanites." ("Abominations" is by now simply a technical term, taken over from the Pentateuchal texts, for foreign religious practices; cf. P. Humbert, "Le substantif *toʿēbā* et le verb *tʿb* dans l'Ancien Testament," *ZAW* 82 [1960] 217–37.)

Finally, the list of peoples is itself revealing. Such lists recur a number of times in the OT with slight variations between them; cf. R. North, "The Hivites," *Bib* 54 (1973) 43–62, and T. Ishida, "The Structure and Historical Implications of the Lists of Pre-Israelite Nations," *Bib* 60 (1979) 461–90. None exactly parallels the present one, however. The first four names and the last doubtless come from Deut 7:1, since Deut 7:3 is cited later on. Two of the remainder, the Ammonites and the Moabites, are for a similar reason drawn from Deut 23:3 (note the citation of 23:6 in v 12 below). Thus we find in this list an early example of drawing together comparable Scriptures, and allowing the one to interpret the other, for Deut 23 actually says nothing about intermarriage.

Two problems remain. Some commentators wish to read "Edomites" at the end of the list with 1 Esdr 8:69 instead of "Amorites." This is unlikely, however, for in the continuation of Deut 23:7–8 Edomites are set in a category distinct from the Ammonites and Moabites just before: "Thou shalt not abhor an Edomite; for he is thy brother." Despite the bitter hostility which the Edomites incurred because of their actions against Judah during the exile, it seems unlikely that the law would have been stood on its head at this point. It is, moreover, worth noting in this connection that, according to J. Van Seters, "Amorites" may have been understood by this period as "Arabs," who were an equally contemporary threat to the community; cf. J. Van Seters, "The Terms 'Amorite' and 'Hittite' in the Old Testament," *VT* 22 (1972) 74. (For other arguments, cf. A. R. Hulst, *OTS* 9 [1951] 92–95.)

Second, however, why are "the Egyptians" mentioned in this list, since for similar reasons they too cannot be derived from Deut 23:7? Most probably we see here reflection on yet a further passage of the Pentateuch, namely Lev 18. This chapter, which deals with all kinds of forbidden marriage relationships, is introduced in v 3 by "After the doings of the land of Egypt, wherein you dwelt, you shall not do; and after the doings of the land of Canaan, whither I bring you, you shall not do." Since Deut 7:1–5 made clear that in regard to the population of Canaan this danger was to be avoided by forbidding intermarriage, it may well have been concluded that the same principle should be extended to the Egyptians.

The chiefs' confession thus betrays an advanced level of exegetical reflection on several legal texts. This again may point to the nature of Ezra's teaching ministry during the preceding months.

2 A citation from Deut 7:3 is followed by an explanation of the dangers of mixed marriages which, although it has a biblical sound to it, is in fact not justified in Scripture. As already noted, the Pentateuch sees the danger in the possibility that the foreign wife may entice the husband away from firm loyalty to God. Of course, if, as in the story of Ruth, the wife was converted to the religion of her husband, the problem did not arise. Such a solution is not envisaged here. Instead, appeal is made to the laws of holiness which forbade the mixing of unlike animals, crops, or material (Lev 19:19). It is thus difficult to avoid the conclusion that the community here regards itself as racially distinct from its neighbors. The concept of the seed of Abraham, elect by God as a "holy people" not because of any superiority but in order to be his servant for the blessing of the nations (e.g., Gen 12:1-3, 7; Deut 7:6-7) has now been twisted by the misapplication of a quite separate law into an idea of racial, as distinct from religious, separation. The contrast is well illustrated by one of the few other examples of the use of התערב "become mixed," namely Ps 106:35, where intermarriage with the Canaanite population is condemned in the following verses on exclusively religious grounds.

The description "holy seed" fits this explanation. Unlike the Deuteronomic "holy people," it concentrates on the physcial transmission of holiness. It may have been coined by a mental combination of the frequent use of the phrase "the seed of Abraham," the use of the cognate verb, "(sow) seed," in Lev 19:19, and the term "holy people." If so, the phrase is likely first to have been used in the present historical setting, and its use in the gloss to Isa 6:13 will be a direct reflection of this.

That the emphasis in this explanation lies on the word "holy" is shown by the description of the offense at the end of the verse as מעל "unfaithful-ness." This word is used for sin against God either by trespassing onto holy things or by violating an oath sworn in God's name; cf. J. Milgrom, *Cult and Conscience* (SJLA 18; Leiden: Brill, 1976), 16-35 and 71-73, who argues that the speakers (not Ezra himself, as Milgrom seems to think) have "spun a midrash" between Deuteronomy's description of Israel as "a holy people" and Jer 2:3, which uses the point metaphorically to threaten destruction to Israel's enemies if they desecrate her. The present passage takes this further to redirect the metaphor literally against Israel, endangered by the desecration of contact with "unholy" Gentiles.

The problem facing the community was compounded by the fact that its leaders had hitherto been the worst offenders. For "chiefs," see *Comment* on v 1. There is no reason why they should not be confessing their own failure in this matter. "Officials" (סגנים) is a word of wide range, so that it can here easily refer to lesser leaders. The two terms together could then be paraphrased "the whole leadership."

3 It has been argued above that the news about the mixed marriages came as no surprise to Ezra. In one sense, therefore, his reactions have to be regarded as somewhat stylized or symbolic. This need not mean, however, that he was merely play-acting. The leaders' confession had for the first time brought the matter out into the open as a religious problem with serious consequences for the whole community. Ezra's response should therefore be regarded not so much as an expression of personal grief as an attempt to act representatively on behalf of all the people. His prayer later on continues as a similar embodiment of this corporate response, while the fact that he remained in a prominent public place ("before the house of God," 10:1 and 6) further supports this interpretation. As such, his actions may be regarded as utterly sincere and genuine; see also *Comment* on 10:6.

Taken together, the three actions here described should be regarded as expressive of the rites of mourning for the dead, even though separately any one of them may be found in other contexts also. The tearing of clothes was a stylized way of stripping oneself naked to express grief in the face of death; cf. Gen 37:34; 2 Sam 1:11; Job 1:20; Mic 1:8, etc., and M. Jastrow, "The Tearing of Garments as a Symbol of Mourning with Especial Reference to the Customs of the Ancient Hebrews," *JAOS* 21 (1900) 23–39. That Ezra tore not only his outer cloak but also his inner garment, or tunic, indicates the intensity of his actions.

Mourning was frequently accompanied by the shaving (at least partially) of the hair and beard (cf. Job 1:20; Isa 22:12; Jer 16:6; 41:5; Ezek 7:18; Amos 8:10, etc.). This, however, was condemned by the law (cf. Lev 19:27–28; Deut 14:1), and so in stricter circles, such as Ezra's, it was replaced by a token pulling of hair from the head and beard instead.

Finally, Lohfink, *VT* 12 (1962) 265–67, has noted that sitting in stunned silence for a period was also a recognized part of ritual mourning; cf. Job 2:13; Ezek 26:16.

In acting thus, Ezra intends to give expression to the repentance already implied in the leaders' confession and explained more fully in the prayer following. Because of its sin, the community deserves the judgment of death. One aspect of repentance includes an acceptance that the individual or group is "in the wrong," and that its condemnation—even to death—is justified; cf. vv 14–15. God is "in the right!" By enacting mourning, as it were, for the death of the community, Ezra shows that he and they accept this verdict upon them.

4 Ezra's handling of the problem of mixed marriages is noteworthy in that, quite unlike Nehemiah (cf. Neh 13:23–27), he used no direct coercion, but rather he encouraged the people to see the problem for themselves and so formulate their own response (cf. v 1 above and 10:1–4, 7, 14 below). However, his actions would have been partly intended to assist this process, and the success of his approach is to be seen in the present verse.

"All who trembled at the words of the God of Israel" is shown by 10:3, Isa 66:2 and 5 to be a stereotyped expression in the post-exilic community for strict observers of the law. As the news of what was happening spread, these Jews gradually gathered around Ezra both to express support and, no doubt, to await developments now that they sensed that his ministry of teaching over the past months was nearing its climax.

"The evening offering" is probably to be identified with the ninth hour (i.e., 3:00 P.M.), "the hour of prayer" of Acts 3:1. It was thus an appropriate time for Ezra to break his silence.

5 "Humiliation" is a general word to cover all that has gone before. In later Judaism, this was expressed by fasting, but that does not justify such a translation here (*contra* RSV). Clearly Ezra would not in fact have eaten during this period, but, unlike at 8:21 or 10:6, attention is not directed to that fact at this point.

The OT knows of no single posture for prayer. Ezra here took up one appropriate to the confession he was about to offer: he prayed on his knees as a sign of humility and self-abasement, and with his hands spread out as a gesture of need.

6–15 For a general introduction to Ezra's prayer, see *Form* above. It was noted there that it was an original part of the EM. This cannot, however, ultimately answer the question whether or not Ezra himself really spoke this prayer or something like it. Many have thought that he did, e.g., Rudolph, who observes that he had long enough during the period of his "humiliation" to think out carefully what he was going to say, and so to recall it accurately afterwards. This is possible, but in view of the undoubted fact that authors in antiquity did sometimes put into the mouths of their characters speeches which they deemed appropriate for the occasion, the issue must remain an open one.

6 In this opening and general confession of guilt, Ezra first establishes his solidarity with the community by use of the first-person singular before switching to the first-person plural for the remainder of the prayer as the means by which he could speak representatively to the best advantage. This is characteristic of many of the "public" prayers of confession in the OT, even when, as here, it is evident that the speaker himself is not to be regarded as having been personally involved in the sin; cf. Neh 1:6; 9:33; Dan 9:5–19, etc.

7 This solidarity not only exists among contemporaries; it also spans generations. Israel's history of sin resulting in the judgment of exile is the history of the present community too. "The days of our fathers" refers to the pre-exilic period; cf. Zech 1:4–6. The Deuteronomic historian had patiently shown how, despite the warnings of the prophets, Israel had accumulated guilt to the point where there could be no remedy; see especially 2 Kgs 17:7–23. This awareness is continued by Ezra: the fundamental distress of the people of God is that they remain in that same exilic condition; "sword, captivity, pillage and open shame" are just the forms which judgment takes in the Deuteronomic History; cf. Judg 2:14; 1 Kgs 8:44–50; 2 Kgs 17:20, etc. In fact, however, Ezra is going to go on to make the point that really the present generation's guilt is even greater because of the measure of relief which they have already experienced. Thus, "while Ezra does not blame the evils of the present on the sin of former generations, he sees the men of his own generation as united in a sinful solidarity with their fathers" (Clines).

This theology, which certainly contrasts sharply with that of Chronicles, is often set against Ezekiel's teaching about the importance of individual responsibility. In fact, however, there is no real difficulty here. Ezekiel too is aware of the solidarity of guilt which spans his people's history; cf. Ezek 16, 20, and 23. His point in the celebrated chap. 18, however, is twofold. First, the present generation cannot claim immunity from judgment on the ground that, unlike its ancestors, it is completely innocent. Second, the invitation to turn and live confronts each individual immediately; the sin of the past, whether of a man or of his father, is no barrier to the greater and overriding grace and forgiveness of God; see W. Zimmerli, *Ezekiel 1* (tr. R. E. Clements; Philadelphia: Fortress, 1979) ad loc. It is precisely the first of these two points which Ezra is here making, and there is no reason to deny that he would have endorsed the second, although that is not his present concern.

"The kings of the lands": the kings of Assyria, Babylon, and Persia; cf. Neh 9:32. "As we are today": this is attached loosely and adds little to the sense of the verse, which has already included the words "to this very day." Ezra would have been thinking partly of the fact that many of his co-religionists remained in exile or dispersion and partly of the depressed conditions of those in the land; cf. v 9.

8 In turning to the present in this and the following verse, Ezra outlines the community's recent experiences of the grace of God not so much as an encouragement to faith as to underline just how culpable they really are (vv 10–11). By saying that this grace has been shown "for a brief moment," he intends only to contrast the eighty years since the decree of Cyrus with the long centuries of oppression by the Assyrians and Babylonians. No implication of grudging ingratitude is intended.

This grace was seen first in the leaving of "a remnant," for strictly speaking, God would have been justified in destroying his people entirely. In these books, as generally in the post-exilic period, "remnant" has acquired the rather specialized meaning of the community of those who have returned from the Babylonian exile. It therefore implies a positive act of restoration on God's part, whereas in earlier and secular uses it meant simply someone or something who had escaped from a disaster.

There follow several phrases introduced by לתת "to give." It has been argued by Vogt, *Studie*, 23–43, that these are arranged chiastically, that the verbs should be translated rather as "to make us," and that "tent-peg," "reviving," and "wall" are therefore, like "remnant," titles of the community. This view has been carefully refuted, however, by Emerton, *JTS* ns 18 (1967) 169–75, who successfully shows that it is neither necessary linguistically (both since a suffix on a verb may express the indirect object and since, in any case, by analogy with Ps 21:7, "to make us a reviving" may mean the same as "to make us revive, to revive us") nor probable exegetically (since the lack of symmetry in the passage makes it unlikely that a chiasmus is intended). We may therefore proceed on the basis that the nouns in these verses are intended as expressions of the gracious gifts of God to the community. (Against Emerton's own alternative proposal, see n. 9.b.)

Ezra mentions first יתד, which literally means "a tent peg," but is translated above as "a secure hold" in an attempt to catch its metaphorical application. Two possible ways of understanding this have been advanced. The first refers to the nomadic way of life, in which a tent peg securely driven in meant stability for the tent and hence its occupants; this image is used for the restored community in Isa 54:2. Alternatively, reference has been made to Isa 22:23, where (with the use of the same word) Eliakim is compared to a "nail" fastened "in a secure place," on which the community can depend. Whichever interpretation is preferred, the result comes to much the same thing. The temple, "his holy place," is regarded as a guarantee of the community's security and stability. We may thus note with interest the comparison which Clines draws with the use of pegs or nails as an element in certain foundation deposits in ancient Mesopotamia. The symbolism of this is disputed, but it may relate either to the stability of the building or to the fixed agreement between man and the deity; cf. R. S. Ellis, *Foundation Deposits in Ancient Mesopotamia* (New Haven and London: Yale University Press, 1968), 46–93; E. A. Speiser in R. C. Dentan (ed.), *The Idea of History in the Ancient*

Near East (New Haven and London: Yale University Press, 1955), 47, and *ANET*, 356a.

This measure of restoration results in a "brightening of the eyes." Literally, this refers to the rapid sense of physical revival which refreshment can bring following a period of hunger and thirst; cf. 1 Sam 14:27. Its metaphorical application in the present context is clear. The following phrase makes the same point more directly, but adds (together with v 9a) that the final consummation is by no means yet reached. "Bondage" and "slaves" must refer to the fact that the Jews had not yet attained political freedom, but were subject to their Persian overlords, no matter how enlightened the latter's policies might be. It is thus of interest to observe that political aspirations were still regarded as an integral part of Jewish religious hope. It would be quite anachronistic to argue that, even at this late stage in the OT, blessing is entirely spiritualized and removed from the realm of God's promise of a land for the patriarchs and their descendants; cf. Neh 9:36–37.

9 This verse largely repeats the substance of v 8, the reference to the rebuilding of the temple being this time more direct. The positive role of the "kings of Persia" is also acknowledged, and it is probable that it is their protection which is viewed metaphorically in the new element which this verse introduces at the end, the "wall in Judah and Jerusalem."

Certainly, a number of scholars have argued that this should be taken to refer to a literal wall—the city wall of Jerusalem—and have then used this verse to argue that Ezra must be dated later than Nehemiah (though the one does not necessarily involve the other; cf. Bowman); for a full listing of the secondary literature, cf. Rowley, "Chronological Order," 147–51. However, a metaphorical interpretation is by no means impossible in the present context, where several of the phrases have already been seen to fall into this pattern (and cf. Ps 80:12), and indeed two considerations make it more probable. First, the qualifying phrase "in Judah and Jerusalem" would be very odd if the reference were merely to the city wall. Second, the word used here (גדר) is not at all the normal word for a city wall (חומה). It usually refers to a wall or fence around a vineyard or along a road. Only in one other passage could it even possibly mean "city wall" (Mic 7:11), and even there it is not completely certain that this is what is meant (see most recently K. Jeppesen, review of B. Renaud's *La Formation du Livre de Michée: Tradition et Actualisation, VT* 29 [1979] 255). In any event, the writer was more concerned, in a prophecy of restoration, to use a term "that refers to the enclosure of a vineyard, a traditional metaphor for Israel in their enjoyment of a healthy relationship with Yahweh" (L. C. Allen, *The Books of Joel, Obadiah, Jonah and Micah* [NICOT; Grand Rapids: Eerdmans, 1976], 396–97). Thus it is hazardous to argue on the basis of Mic 7:11 that Ezra's words would have been appreciated as referring to a city wall.

Finally, we should note that others, such as Myers, press the metaphorical meaning even further: the word גדר occurs on some stamped jar handles from Gibeon with the extended meaning of the vineyard itself; cf. J. B. Pritchard, *Hebrew Inscriptions and Stamps from Gibeon* (Philadelphia: University of Pennsylvania, 1959), 9–10; H. Michaud, "Review of Pritchard's *Inscriptions,*" *VT* 10 (1960) 103. In light of this, Myers compares our passage with Isa 5:5–6 and concludes, "Revived Israel is the vineyard of Yahweh with its enclosure." However, the interpretation of the word on the jar handles from Gibeon is so uncertain that we should hesitate before adopting this suggestion; cf. J. C. L. Gibson, *Syrian Semitic Inscriptions* 1 (Oxford: Clarendon Press, 1973) 56.

10–12 After this summary of God's present mercies to the restored community, Ezra turns straight to the particular unfaithfulness of the contemporary generation, thus highlighting by contrast the ingratitude which it represents.

In order to make the point, Scripture is cited. Two items of wider interest arise here. First, the citation does not come from a single passage, but is rather a mosaic of many passages and scriptural allusions. This is understandable in a liturgical context, but also is of significance as a pointer to the emergence of a view which came to regard Scripture as a unity and hence of uniform authority. Second, the quotation is attributed to "your servants the prophets," an outlook very similar to Dan 9:6, 10. (For the phrase itself, cf. 2 Kgs 17:23, a passage whose influence on this prayer has already been noted; 2 Kgs 21:10; Jer 7:25, etc.) However, since it is mainly the Pentateuch which is cited, Ezra would appear not only to be regarding Moses as a prophetic figure (cf. Deut 18:15; 34:10), but also to be blurring the sometimes too rigid distinction between law and prophecy by subsuming the whole under the category of the spoken, prophetic word of God.

Some of the phraseology used is quite widespread in the OT, but the principal passages to which allusion is made are Deut 7:1–3; 11:8; 23:6; 2 Kgs 21:16; Isa 1:19. The idea that the land had been "polluted by the impurity of the peoples of the lands with their abominations" is expressed more forcibly here than in earlier texts (cf. especially Lev 18:24–30), but "we may see this as a quite logical development from the thought of the land as previously possessed by nations whose religious practices were regarded as improper" (Ackroyd).

13–14 The homiletic tone of the prayer is at its strongest here. Israel experienced a measure of God's judgment in the exile, and the very fact that any were spared at all was solely due to his mercy. How can they have either the ingratitude or the presumption to risk the total annihilation that might follow a further flouting of the divine commands?

15 Ezra makes few concessions as he finishes his prayer: the confession is unqualified and rouses little expectancy of divine clemency. In a condition such as that of his fellows, none can "stand," i.e., be acquitted, before God. The only positive hint comes in the recurrence of the remnant theme. This has been used throughout the prayer as a token of God's mercy, and there is no reason to regard it here as meaning anything different. Is it possible, Ezra seems to suggest, that even at this eleventh hour they might still survive as an "escaped remnant"? "The tense emotional scene is psychologically contrived to induce just such action as is described in ch. 10" (Bowman).

The climax of the confession is to be seen in the opening phrase of the verse: צדיק אתה, lit., "You are righteous." This acknowledgment comes at an equivalent point in other comparable prayers (Exod 9:27; 2 Chr 12:6; Neh 9:33; Dan 9:14; cf. Ps 119:137; 129:4). The righteousness of God takes many forms in the OT, including sometimes his mighty acts of salvation on behalf of his people. In such contexts as the present one, however, it is used rather with forensic overtones. Even if God should utterly destroy his people, they acknowledge that he would be fully justified. They have broken the commandments, which are perhaps regarded as an integral part of the covenant between God and people, while he has remained consistent in his adherence to that relationship. This little phrase thus constitutes the highest form of worship: an acknowledgment of God, even though at the same time it accepts that the worshiper has forfeited his or her right to live before God. God is thus praised solely for who he is, and not merely for what the worshiper hopes to gain from him.

Explanation

The explanation of this chapter is included with that on chap. 10 in view of their common attention to the problem of mixed marriages.

¹² *Then the whole assembly shouted in reply,* ¹³ *"Yes! We must do as you say. But there are a lot of people and it's the rainy season;* ᵃ *we can't go on standing around outside.* ᵇ *In any case it will take longer than a day or two,* ᵇ *for we have been exceedingly unfaithful in this affair.* ¹⁴ *Let our chiefs act for the whole assembly, and let all in our towns who have married foreign women come at appointed times, together with the elders and judges each of his own town, so as to* ᵃ *turn away from us God's fierce anger concerning* ᵇ *this affair."* ¹⁵ *(Only Jonathan the son of Asahel and Jahzeiah the son of Tikvah, supported by Meshullam and Shabbethai the Levite, opposed this.)* ᵃ

¹⁶ *So that is what the exiles did. Ezra the priest selected* ᵃ *various men, heads of families to represent their families, designating each of them by name. They held their first sitting to investigate* ᵇ *the affair on the first day of the tenth month,* ¹⁷ *and they finished (dealing) with all the men* ᵃ *who had married foreign women by the first day of the first month.*

¹⁸ *Of the families of priests there were found the following who had married foreign women:*

Of the family of Jeshua the son of Jozadak and his brothers:

> *Maaseiah*
> *Eliezer* ᵃ
> *Jarib*
> *Gedaliah.*

¹⁹ *They pledged themselves to divorce* ᵃ *their wives and each to offer as a guilt offering* ᵇ *a ram of the flock for their guilt.*

²⁰ *Of the family of Immer:*

> *Hanani*
> *Zebadiah*

²¹ *of the family of Harim:*

> *Maaseiah*
> *Elijah* ᵃ
> *Shemaiah*
> *Jehiel*
> *Uzziah*

²² *of the family of Pashhur:*

> *Elioenai*
> *Maaseiah*
> *Ishmael*
> *Nethanel*
> *Jozabad*
> *Elasah.*

²³ *Of the Levites:*

> *Jozabad*
> *Shimei*
> *Kelaiah (that is, Kelita)*
> *Pethahiah*
> *Judah*
> *Eliezer.*

²⁴ *Of the singers:*

> *Eliashib.*

The Problem of Mixed Marriages Resolved (Ezra 10:1-44)

Bibliography

Blidstein, G. J. "Atimia: a Greek parallel to Ezra x 8 and to post-biblical exclusion from the community." *VT* 24 (1974) 357–60. **Cogan, M.** "The Men of Nebo—Repatriated Reubenites." *IEJ* 29 (1979) 37–39. **Cross, F. M.** "A Reconstruction of the Judean Restoration." *JBL* 94 (1975) 4–18. **Gray, G. B.** "Nebo as an Element in Hebrew Proper Names." *ExpTim* 10 (1898–99) 232–34. **In der Smitten.** *Esra,* 28–35. **Mowinckel, S.** " 'Ich' und 'Er' in der Ezrageschichte." *Verbannung und Heimkehr: Beiträge zur Geschichte und Theologie Israels im 6. und 5. Jahrhundert v. Chr.,* ed. A. Kuschke. Tübingen: J. C. B. Mohr, 1961, 211–33. ———. *Studien I,* 124–35. ———. *Studien III,* 75–94. **Porter, J. R.** "Son or Grandson (Ezra x.6)?" *JTS* ns 17 (1966) 54–67. **Williamson, H. G. M.** "The Historical Value of Josephus' *Jewish Antiquities* xi.297–301." *JTS* ns 28 (1977) 49–66.

Translation

[1] *While Ezra was praying and confessing, weeping and prostrate [a] in front of the house of God, a very large crowd [b] of Israelites—men, women and children—gathered around him, for the people [c] were weeping very bitterly. [d]* [2] *Then Shecaniah the son of Jehiel, one of the family of Elam, [a] responded by saying to Ezra, "We have been unfaithful to our God in marrying [b] foreign women from the peoples of the land, but now there is some hope for Israel in this matter.* [3] *Let us now make a covenant before [a] our God to send away all our wives [b] and the children born of them, according to the advice of my lord [c] and of those who tremble at the command of our God, and let it be done according to the law.* [4] *Arise! for it is your duty to deal with this matter, but we will support you. Take courage and act."*

[5] *So Ezra arose and made all the chiefs of the priests, the Levites and all Israel swear an oath that they would act according to this suggestion; and they took the oath.* [6] *Then Ezra departed from in front of the house of God and withdrew to the room of Jehohanan the son of Eliashib, and he spent the night [a] there without eating any food or drinking any water because he was still mourning over the unfaithfulness of the exiles.*

[7] *A proclamation was then made throughout Judah and Jerusalem summoning all the exiles to gather in Jerusalem;* [8] *anyone who did not come within three days might, on the decision of the chiefs and elders, have all his property forfeited and he himself be excluded from the assembly of the exiles.*

[9] *So within the three days all the men of Judah and Benjamin gathered in Jerusalem; it was the twentieth day of the ninth month. All the people were sitting in the square in front of the house of God, trembling because of the affair [a] and because of the heavy rain. [b]* [10] *Then Ezra the priest stood up and said to them, "You have been unfaithful in marrying foreign women, thereby adding to Israel's guilt.* [11] *But now, make confession [a] to the Lord, the God of your fathers, and do his will. Separate yourselves from the peoples of the land and from the foreign women."*

 Of the gatekeepers:
  Shallum
  Telem
  Uri.
 [25] *Of Israel:*
  of the family of Parosh:
  Ramiah
  Izziah
  Malchiah
  Mijamin
  Eleazar
  Malchiah [a]
  Benaiah
 [26] *of the family of Elam:*
  Mattaniah
  Zechariah
  Jehiel
  Abdi
  Jeremoth
  Elijah [a]
 [27] *of the family of Zattu:*
  Elioenai
  Eliashib
  Mattaniah
  Jeremoth
  Zabad
  Aziza
 [28] *of the family of Bebai:*
  Jehohanan
  Hananiah
  Zabbai
  Athlai
 [29] *of the family of Bani:* [a]
  Meshullam
  Malluch
  Adaiah
  Jashub
  Yishal [b]
  Jeremoth
 [30] *of the family of Pahath-Moab:*
  Adna
  Kelal
  Benaiah
  Maaseiah
  Mattaniah
  Bezalel
  Binnui
  Manasseh

31 *of the family* [a] *of Harim:*
    Eliezer
    Isshijah
    Malchiah
    Shemaiah
    Simeon [b]
32 *Benjamin*
    Malluch
    Shemariah
33 *of the family of Hashum:*
    Mattenai
    Mattattah
    Zabed
    Eliphelet
    Jeremai
    Manasseh
    Shimei
34 *of the family of Bani:* [a]
    Maadai
    Amram
    Joel [b]
35 *Benaiah*
    Bedeiah
    Keluhu [a]
36 *Vaniah* [a]
    Meremoth
    Eliashib
37 *Mattaniah*
    Mattenai
    Jaasau
38 *of the family of Binnui:* [a]
    Shimei
39 *Shelemiah*
    Nathan
    Adaiah
40 *of the family of Azzur:* [a]
    Shashai
    Sharai
41 *Azarel*
    Shelemiah
    Shemariah
42 *Shallum*
    Amariah
    Joseph
43 *of the family of Nebo:*
    Jeiel
    Mattithiah
    Zabad

Zebina
Jaddai
Joel
Benaiah.
⁴⁴ *All these had married foreign women,* ^a *and some of the women had even borne children.* ^a

Notes

1.a. Lit., "throwing himself down." However, the whole of this introductory clause clearly describes the circumstances of Ezra's prayer and does not mark any fresh action, so that this verb may be regarded as loosely parallel with 9:5.

1.b. Though this is probably the best translation of קהל in the present context, it is likely that it consciously includes overtones of religious assembly or congregation.

1.c. Rudolph, finding a non sequitur in this clause, emends radically. However, if "the people" refers to those who had already gathered before Ezra started to pray (9:4), then MT presents no difficulty.

1.d. Lit., "with much weeping."

2.a. So with Q and most Vrs against K "Olam."

2.b. Lit., "cause to dwell (in one's house)." This expression occurs a number of times in this chap. and Neh 13, though it is not the usual word for "to marry." It has its opposite in "send away" (v 3), again different from the usual שלח (piel), "to dismiss, divorce." For the possible implications, see *Comments*.

3.a. Not "with," as usage elsewhere shows that this would carry the absurd implication that the people were the dominant partner in a relationship with God. The people enter rather into a solemn commitment to which they invoke God as a witness; it is thus effectively the same as the oath in v 5; cf. S. Japhet, *The Ideology of the Book of Chronicles and Its Place in Biblical Thought* (Heb.; Jerusalem: Bialik, 1977) 101–3.

3.b. Read נשינו for MT's unqualified נשים "women," with LXX^L and 1 Esdr 8:90(93). The error probably arose by a scribe misreading the *nūn* and *wāw* joined by ligatures as a final *mēm*; cf. R. Weiss, "On Ligatures in the Hebrew Bible (נו = ם)," *JBL* 82 (1963) 188–94.

3.c. MT אֲדֹנָי, "the Lord," is improbable because (i) he does not advise in such matters, but commands (Rudolph); (ii) there is no "advice" about such situations in the Bible; (iii) God's involvement is mentioned rather at the end of the verse; and (iv) Shecaniah consistently refers to the Lord as "our God." The increasing use of אֲדֹנָי for "the Lord," however, makes this mistaken pointing of אֲדֹנִי ("my lord," implied by 1 Esdr and LXX^{A,B}) understandable.

6.a. MT, "went," repeating the same word from earlier in the verse. It is better to follow the Vrs which presuppose the orthographically very slight emendation to ויל.

9.a. Joüon's suggestion, *Bib* 12 (1931) 85, that הדבר "the affair" should be emended to הברד, "the hail," is unlikely to be correct. Hail is not mentioned in the parallel v 13, whereas דבר is used several times in the passage to refer to the whole affair of the mixed marriages (e.g., vv 13 and 14).

9.b. Heb. "rains," a pl of intensity; cf. GKC § 124d-e.

11.a. Lit. "give praise"; see *Comments*.

13.a. Cf. GKC § 141d.

13.b. Lit., "and the work is not for one day or for two." For the use of this idiom to denote a somewhat indefinite numerical value, cf. W. M. W. Roth, "The Numerical Sequence x/x+1 in the Old Testament," *VT* 12 (1962) 300–11.

14.a. עד ל can be either temporal ("until") or final; despite most English translations, the latter seems to make much better sense here.

14.b. MT, "as long as this matter lasts" (Keil), coordinate with עד להשיב "so as to turn away." This, however, is extremely awkward, especially if the preceding clause is correctly interpreted as final. The Vrs (and two Heb. MSS) show that an original על־הדבר has been corrupted under the influence of the preceding עד ל.

15.a. For possible alternative translations, see under *Comments*.

16.a. MT can scarcely be construed as it stands: "Ezra the priest, men, heads of families . . . were separated (i.e., set apart for the work)." Sense can only be obtained by inserting a prep, such as "with," before "men"; cf. LXX[A,B] and Vg. However, we are then not told who appointed the commission, and the procedure rather runs counter to Ezra's tactics up to this point; we would not expect him personally to decide the disputed cases, but rather to initiate a course of action that would encourage the community's own leaders to accept full responsibility. All these points can be resolved by following 1 Esdr 9:16, LXX[L] and Syr. in reading ויבדל "and he selected," possibly followed by לו "for himself" (in which case MT would have arisen by haplogr). This is the solution favored by most moderns.

16.b. לדרוש must be read with some MSS and Vrs. MT ("of Darius") is only slightly different (the addition of a *yōd*), and is probably to be explained as the work of a careless scribe who expected such a reference after the date.

17.a. The general meaning is not in doubt, but the grammar is uncertain, since אנשים "men" is anarthrous. It may be an accus of nearer definition, but the particular construction here would be unusual in prose (cf. GKC § 127b-c). Most add the art (בכל־האנשים "with all the men"), though Rudolph prefers בָּכֹּל לָאֲנָשִׁים, since the error can then be more easily explained (haplogr).

18.a. Throughout the list, the names are often joined with the copula, but this has been consistently omitted here.

19.a. See *Note* and *Comment* on v 2.b.

19.b. MT, "(being) guilty," words which, Ryle suggests, "sound like the sentence of the commission, after investigating each case." We would then have expected the sg, however. Most prefer to repoint either to אֲשָׁמִים "guilt offerings," or to אֲשָׁמָם "(as) their guilt offering." Either "to offer" has to be supplied to make sense, or, perhaps, the force of ויתנו "and they gave" ("to give one's hand" = "to pledge") is carried over from the first half of the verse.

21.a. For the first attestation of this name on a seal, cf. C. Graesser, "The Seal of Elijah," *BASOR* 220 (1975) 63–66.

25.a. There is no particular reason why two members of the same extended family should not have the same name. In this case, however, 1 Esdr 9:26 presupposes חשביה "Hashabiah," and since it is difficult to see how this could have arisen apart from a variant text, RSV may well be right to adopt it.

26.a. Cf. n. 21.a.

29.a. Bani recurs as a family name in v 34; one occurrence must therefore be corrupt. Binnui would be the simplest emendation, did it not recur in v 38. The reading בגוי "Bigvai" (cf. 2:14), has therefore been proposed for one or the other verse. בֻּנִּי would be an alternative proposal, but it does not occur in Ezra 2.

29.b. Read ישאל for MT's improbable ושאל "(and) Sheal"; cf. Bewer.

31.a. The unvarying pattern of the list, the Vrs and many MSS support the emendation of ובני to ומבני "and from the family of."

31.b. For a suggestion that the reintroduction of this patriarchal name indicates the incipient stages of Gr. influence, cf. N. G. Cohen, "Jewish Names as Cultural Indicators in Antiquity," *JSJ* 7 (1976) 97–128.

34.a. Cf. n. 29.a.

34.b. A probable emendation (יואל) for MT אואל "Uel."

35.a. So Q, though it is an odd form of name. K has כְּלוּהִי or כְּלוּהַי, also strange. Possibly a corr of כליה.

36.a. Rudolph here wishes to emend to ומבני, "(and) of the family of . . . ," with the patronymic lost. However, there is no real evidence for this, while the name Vaniah appears to be acceptable (cf. *AramP* 22:40). Were Rudolph right, there would be a restored thirteen, rather than twelve, families represented in the list.

38.a. MT, ובני ובנוי, "and Bani and Binnui," should certainly be emended to the very similar ומבני בנוי; cf. LXX and 1 Esdr[L]. Also, without this emendation, the list of the family of Bani (v 34) would be disproportionately long.

40.a. MT מכנדבי, apparently intended as a proper name, "Maknadebai." This would be inexplicable, however, and Gray's emendation to מכרנבו "possession of Nebo" is unconvincing; *ExpTim* 10 (1898–99) 232–34. 1 Esdr 9:34 suggests that we have here the start of another family list, and itself presupposes ומבני עזור. This seems reasonable (see *Notes* to 2:16), though admittedly ומבני זכי "of the family of Zaccai" (cf. 2:9), would be orthographically closer to MT.

44.a-a. It is difficult to know what to do with this celebrated crux. (i) Though problematic, MT is not impossible: "And there were of them (masc) wives, and they (masc) bore children."

For שׁים = "bear (of children)," see now the Arabic parallel cited by L. Kopf, "Arabische Etymologien und Parallelen zum Bibelwörterbuch," *VT* 9 (1959) 276. The use of a masc pl verb with fem pl subj is likewise not unprecedented, especially in late biblical Heb.; cf. GKC §§ 135o and 145p. MT is supported by LXX[L] and Vg and probably by Syr and LXX[A,B], though they do not translate so literally. The translation offered above attempts to render MT in a manner fitting to the context. (ii) Perhaps the majority of scholars follow 1 Esdr 9:36 and so emend to וישלחום נשים ובנים "and they dismissed them, wives and children together." This makes excellent sense in the context, and it is not impossible to reconstruct how MT might be a corruption of it (Bewer). (iii) Schneider ingeniously inverts the order of two words in MT (though not adjacent words) to read וישימו מהם נשים ויש בנים "and they put their wives from them, even if there were children." However, though Clines tentatively favors this view, he correctly observes that שׁים is not otherwise attested as a divorce formula.

It appears that these three proposals are the best among the many that have been advanced (e.g., against Zimmermann's view that the problem has arisen because the Hebrew is a mistranslation of an Aram. original, cf. S. P. Brock, review of Zimmerman, *Biblical Books Translated from the Aramaic, JSS* 22 [1977] 97–98). If we tentatively favor MT, it can only be because of the principle that, provided sense can be made of the text, *lectio difficilior potior;* in other words, it is easier to suppose that 1 Esdr 9:36 might be a free rendering according to sense and context than that MT has been corrupted from the easier text of 1 Esdr. But when all is said and done, ancient MSS were sometimes corrupted in the course of transmission, so that dogmatism in the present instance is quite out of the question.

Form/Structure/Setting

It was noted at the start of *Form* on chap. 9 that the narrative here, 10:1–17, 44b, continues without interruption. At a formal level, however, there is a significant difference in that following Ezra's prayer the narrative is cast in the third person, rather than the first person. This was also the case in material relating to Ezra at 7:1–10 and 8:35–36, and it will recur again at Neh 8. For reasons which will become apparent, however, it is on the present chapter that discussion of this phenomenon has generally focused. It should be noted, moreover, that this discussion is quite independent of the question of the authenticity and historicity of the Ezra material.

Mowinckel (" 'Ich' und 'Er' "; *Studien III*, 75) lists four possible explanations: (i) two separate sources, one first-person and the other third-person, may have been combined; (ii) an original first-person narrative has been later changed in a number of passages into the third person; (iii) an original third-person narrative has been later changed into the first person for much of its extent; (iv) the difference is original, having been intended from the first by the author. A fifth possibility, favored by G. Fohrer, *Introduction to the Old Testament* (tr. D. Green; London: S.P.C.K., 1970) 243, may be added, namely that Ezra 10 was composed *de novo* by the Chronicler after the pattern of the Memoir which he inherited.

The first possibility is generally associated with the name of O. Eissfeldt (cf. *The Old Testament: an Introduction* [tr. P. R. Ackroyd; Oxford: Blackwell, 1966], 544), and he is followed tentatively by Myers. The difficulty with this view is that it can appeal to no further supporting evidence beyond the change in person. It might conceivably be possible to argue that 10:1 overlaps with 9:4, but no one has done so because in every other way there is an uninterrupted narrative flow and because 10:1 can be understood quite naturally as the direct sequel of what precedes.

The third possibility may also be quickly eliminated. It has never been seriously proposed by anyone, not least because the procedure envisaged would be without motivation or reason. It would have involved a highly conscious decision by the narrator (one might guess that he wished to align the Ezra material with that of Nehemiah), but then it remains inexplicable that he did not carry through his purpose consistently.

Fohrer's suggestion (the fifth possibility mentioned above) is unfortunately difficult to evaluate, because he does not support it with any substantial arguments. He agrees that Ezra 7:11—9:5 (less 8:1–14) goes back to Ezra, but does not discuss the continuation of this material; no one could suppose that a document finished at 9:5! It seems incredible that a later editor would have composed a conclusion to an account without any reference to that account's own conclusion with which, *ex hypothesi*, he was familiar. Assuming Fohrer is willing to accept at least some connection between Ezra 10 and the continuation of the Ezra material after 9:5, his proposal becomes only a variant of the second of Mowinckel's four possibilities.

Mowinckel himself favors the fourth possibility, namely that the change in person was intentionally present for stylistic reasons from the very first. Torrey, *Ezra Studies*, 244–46, held a similar view, although, unlike Mowinckel, he argued that the Chronicler was the author. Mowinckel's argument is basically twofold. He seeks first to eliminate the other possibilities (including the majority view, the second listed above), and then goes on to suggest that such changes in person are not unparalleled in the literature of the Ancient Near East. This Mowinckel considers sufficient to establish his case, for he then proceeds to discuss the effects the author hoped to achieve by using this method of composition.

In evaluating Mowinckel's proposals, it is clear that his case rests in large measure on his success in eliminating all rival theories, and it will be argued below that in fact he has not succeeded in this. On the positive side, his proposed parallels for a narrative in which changes of person occur could only establish the possibility, but not ever the probability, that this was also the case with regard to Ezra. As it is, however, it may even be questioned how apt his comparisons are. In most cases (including, apparently, Ahikar, though the text is not sufficiently well preserved for us to be certain of this), they are texts in which a third-person narrative or heading is used to introduce a first-person account or document. This is not at all noteworthy, and indeed the introduction to the NM (Neh 1:1) provides a very brief example of the same feature. It may be that the EM also once had a similar heading. When we look for examples of texts that switch back and forth between first and third persons, the best parallel Mowinckel can adduce is the Book of Tobit. This book is certainly later than Ezra, however, and it is not impossible that it may be dependent upon it for this particular stylistic device. It does use similar devices to effect the transition, though other narrative considerations, not present in Ezra, may also have played a part; cf. D. C. Simpson in *The Apocrypha and Pseudepigrapha of the Old Testament in English*, Vol. 1: *Apocrypha*, ed. R. H. Charles (Oxford: Clarendon Press, 1913), 195. Similar points might be made about Mowinckel's (and Torrey's) other later examples. We may thus conclude that while it is possible that the change in person is original to the memoir it would be most unusual at the time of composition to find such changes taking precisely the form that they do.

We come finally, then, to consider the view that the changes in person are a reflection of editorial work exerted over a consistently first-person account. It may be suggested that some features of the material already studied demand this explanation, others are best explained by it (though alternative explanations would be possible), and third, that arguments brought against this view are not convincing.

Under the first category come especially the points already examined at 7:1–10 above and also the indications noted in *Form*, chap. 9, that some material has been omitted from the original EM. In addition, it seems probable from the wording of v 16 of this chapter that the editor has chosen to omit a list of names at that point (contrast *Form*, 8:15–36), and that a few sentences have been removed from a point between vv 15 and 16 to the opening of Neh 9; see *Form*, Neh 9. Finally, it will be suggested later that the list in the second half of the chapter has been subjected to editorial rearrangement.

Next, we must observe that this hypothesis provides an adequate explanation of the phenomena: it was argued that the third-person passage in 7:1–10 occurred through editorial abbreviation, and 8:35–36 through editorial insertion, perhaps partly to cover the removal of Neh 8. Neh 8 itself, of course, had to be cast in the third person because of its new literary setting. Otherwise it could not be distinguished by the reader from Nehemiah's own account. It is probable, therefore, that similar considerations affected Ezra 10: the same device, prayer, is used to cover over the change in person (compare 7:27–28 and 9:6–15); editorial abbreviation may again have taken place (e.g., vv 3 and 15), and last, an adequate motive may be found in the desire to round off the Ezra material in the style adopted for its opening.

Finally, we must consider the principal objections raised against this conclusion by Mowinckel. First, he thinks that this issue is bound up with the view that Ezra himself wrote the first-person material. Mowinckel has no difficulty in adducing examples of texts cast in the first person that were not in fact written by the subject of the narrative. In response to this argument, it may be readily agreed that most scholars have assumed that Ezra himself was the original author. However, that conclusion is not necessarily relevant to the point at issue. The EM could for these purposes be a total fabrication cast in the first person, and yet still have been edited in the manner maintained here. It does not follow that if Ezra was not the author then first- and third-person passages must always have stood side by side.

Second, Mowinckel maintains that the evidence for redactional work in the Ezra material is slight, limited to odd phrases or sentences that can easily be detached and ascribed, in his view, to the Chronicler. Nothing apart from the change in person argues for redactional activity in Ezra 7:1–10; 10; and Neh 8. A response to this argument is unnecessary at this point, since the contrary case has already been set out earlier in this section and elsewhere. The case with regard to Neh 8 is slightly different, since Mowinckel argues that it was only moved to its present position from one following Ezra 10 at a very late stage in the books' composition. According to the view favored in this commentary, however, it originally followed Ezra 8 and was moved by the editor responsible both for combining Ezra and Nehemiah and for editing the Ezra material. According to this view its position alone is an argument for more extensive redactional activity than Mowinckel allows.

Finally, the apparent uniformity of style throughout the Ezra material is inconclusive as an argument. Most of the elements usually discussed in this connection are simply examples of the style of late biblical Hebrew generally, while the editor is in any case likely to have been influenced in his choice of style by that of the text on which he was working. Moreover, the sample for analysis in this particular case is so small that no firm results are likely to emerge; cf. Rudolph, 163–65; Williamson, *Israel,* 37–59; R. Polzin, *Late Biblical Hebrew* (Missoula, MT: Scholars Press, 1976).

We may conclude this discussion, therefore, by affirming that the change of person in this chapter results from editorial activity but that otherwise the narrative continues smoothly from chap. 9. Reasons why the editor's hand should be more apparent here than previously have been advanced, and arguments against this conclusion have been found unconvincing.

The main part of the list in 10:18–44a is carefully ordered. Cultic officials come first, arranged according to seniority: members of the high priest's family (v 18), other priests (vv 20–22), Levites (v 23), singers and gatekeepers (v 24). Then follow the laity, probably in twelve family divisions, though the text is not completely certain at this point. There are thus a number of formal contacts with the list at the start of chap. 8.

As there, the setting of this list has been much debated, with little agreement as to the stage in the development of the text at which it was included, whether it was originally an independent list, and, if so, whether it was once more extensive than it now is.

We may start by observing that from a narrative point of view the list is, in fact, extremely well integrated into its present context. While v 18 starts the list, it is followed in v 19 by a narrative element essential for the understanding of what happened. Yet it cannot be argued that v 19 was once joined immediately to v 17 because that would involve an impossibly harsh change of subject between ויכלו "and they finished" (v 17) and ויתנו ידם "they pledged themselves" (v 19), as In der Smitten, *Esra,* 34, rightly emphasizes. Nor, on the other hand, can we accept Kellermann's view (*Nehemia,* 68) that v 18 was part of the original narrative but not the following list, which in his view, therefore, started only at v 20. Verses 18 and 20 clearly belong together as parts of the same list. In addition, it may be noted from a negative point of view that the list lacks any feature such as those noted at 8:1–14 which would enable us to regard it in its present form as a fully independent piece that had been added in here as a purely secondary literary exercise. We must conclude, therefore, that by the time of the redaction of the Ezra-Nehemiah material this list had assumed its present setting.

Since it has been argued above that the editor responsible for this redaction undertook rather more extensive rewriting of this chapter than of those immediately preceding, it cannot be confidently asserted that it was not he who thus integrated the list into its context. Nevertheless there are four considerations that make it probable that it was in fact included in the EM. As argued at 7:12–26, the investigation of the issue of mixed marriages turned out to be a major element of the task that Ezra was instructed to undertake. That it is not so regarded in the present text, where it is overshadowed by Neh 8, and yet that it remains so prominent despite this, is a strong argument in support of the issue's great importance in the original memoir. This ties in well, therefore, with the view already frequently noted that part of the purpose of the memoir was to show how Ezra had fulfilled the tasks entrusted to him. In that case, the inclusion of the list in the memoir would have been a virtual necessity, even more so than in the case of 8:1–14.

It is probable that in its present form the list is altered somewhat from its original form (cf. Rudolph and *Comment* below). It is attractive to suppose that this is the work of the final redactor, who may have felt that to give the list in its full form would have unbalanced his work as a whole. It has already been suggested that he abbreviated elsewhere in Ezra 9–10. In that case it would be hard to understand his motives if he had in fact introduced this list from elsewhere. It is more probable that he was following a consistent editorial policy with regard to a single *Vorlage*.

Comparison of this list with 8:1–14 has indicated a number of general similarities. These, together with the independent evidence that the EM included the list of 8:1–14 from the start, lend further support to the view that this passage would have been fully at home in the original memoir.

The list uses the same distinctive terminology in relation to mixed marriages as does the rest of the EM: להוציא, להושיב, "to marry, to send away" and נשים נכריות "foreign women." This consistency makes it probable that these sections always belonged together, rather than having been joined by later editorial activity.

We may thus conclude that the list was included in the EM from the start. There is no evidence to indicate whether it was composed first for that setting, or may originally have been drawn up independently. Its present form, however, may owe something to later editorial activity. The likelihood of the authenticity of the original list follows from this conclusion, though if it has been reshaped editorially we must recognize that it may present a rather distorted picture for purposes of historical reconstruction.

Comment

1 It has already been noted in chap. 9 that Ezra's prayer was both a genuine confession of sin to God and at the same time aimed at giving a lead to the people so that they might respond out of conviction rather than coercion. In this latter purpose Ezra clearly succeeded. Drawn by the wailing of those who had already gathered, and no doubt sensing that a long-standing problem was nearing its climactic solution, a large crowd gathered expectantly. The qualification "men, women, and children" draws attention to the unusual size and comprehensive composition of the crowd. It also introduces a note of tragic gravity as it reminds the reader of the possible social consequences of the proceedings about to be initiated, a point recapitulated in the last verse of the chapter.

Only now are we told that Ezra had been praying "in front of the house of God," i.e., probably in one of the outer courts of the temple, a setting that adds to the solemnity of the occasion.

2a Shecaniah belonged to a family (Elam) that had returned to Judah from Babylon at the first opportunity (cf. 2:7). Since it was this group that was primarily involved in the mixed marriages (see *Comment* on 9:1), he was well qualified to act as spokesman. He is not, however, included in the list of offenders in vv 18–44. Unless this is the result of editorial abbreviation (which would seem improbable in this case), we will have to understand his following confession as representative, just as Ezra's was.

This raises the possibility that Shecaniah was not speaking purely spontaneously. He may in fact have been one who was influenced by Ezra's early ministry (cf. v 3) and who had previously agreed with him to lead the people's response. At any rate, it is noteworthy that the radical solution that he proposes finds general agreement. Did the original account include some reference to prior consultation to establish that he might thus act as spokesman?

Comparison with v 26 suggests that Shecaniah's own father, Jehiel, may have been involved in a mixed marriage. This in itself would not necessarily have prevented Shecaniah from speaking out: Clines's argument that then he would have been advocating his own excommunication is uncertain, for Jehiel could well have married twice, while the children excommunicated with their foreign mothers were probably minors. Despite his postulated mixed origins, Shecaniah, who is clearly an adult, could have become a member of the Jewish community in his own right; cf. 6:21. Despite this, however, Jehiel is a common enough name to preclude certainty of identity, even within a single extended family.

2b–4 Shecaniah starts by echoing the confessions already made in chap. 9. He sees more hope than was expressed in Ezra's prayer, however, provided that quick action is undertaken to eliminate the problem. Finally, he urges Ezra to take the lead in this task.

2b On "unfaithful," cf. 9:2. The expression for "to marry" used in this chapter and in Neh 13 (but nowhere else in the OT) is the hiph of ישׁב, literally, "to cause to dwell," i.e., "to give a home to." It applies only to mixed marriages. Witton Davies, noting that the word for "foreign" which immediately follows is used in Proverbs to describe a harlot, suggests that the usage implies "that the union in question was not true marriage . . . ; the women whom they had living with them were harlots, not wives."

3 In contrast with the gloomy conclusion of Ezra's prayer (note that "in this matter," על־זאת, v 2b, explicitly picks up the identical phrase from the end of 9:15, translated above as "in such a condition"), Shecaniah can envisage a plan that might rescue the endangered community. There has been no hint of this in the previous chapter, but he still refers to it as "the advice of my lord" (i.e., Ezra) and "of those who tremble at the command of our God," quite explicitly the group who gathered round Ezra in 9:4 (q.v.). It is thus evident that Ezra had previously given some instruction on the matter, and that he had won the following of a limited section of the community (see also *Comment* on 9:1). The significant development here, therefore, is the wider acceptance of this plan, including acceptance by those who were directly involved.

The proposal was simple: all the members of the community should enter a binding agreement (see *Notes*) to send away the foreign wives and their children. The word used here (להוציא) is again not the usual one for divorce, and may reflect the same pejorative attitude to these unions noted in v 2.

The force of the final clause in the verse is not clear. Divorce is permitted under certain circumstances by Deut 24:1–4, and some elementary procedures are laid down. Possibly, therefore, under the influence of Ezra's teaching (see *Comment* on 9:1–2), the husbands now regarded the foreign origins of their wives to constitute "something unseemly, shameful" (ערות דבר, a phrase of uncertain meaning in Deut 24:1) and so felt justified in proceeding to a divorce. If those procedures were followed, then at least the wives would have been free to marry again. Alternatively, the clause may be no more than a general encouragement to return to a state of conformity with the law as then understood, i.e., with no mixed marriages.

4 It is not surprising that Shecaniah looked to Ezra for leadership, even though later Ezra showed a reluctance similar to that noted in the previous chapter to take matters further than the community had previously expressed itself willing to go. Shecaniah draws on the form and phraseology of the "installation genre" (cf. H. G. M. Williamson, "The Accession of Solomon in the Books of Chronicles," *VT* 26 [1976] 351–61), familiar from such passages as Deut 31:23; Josh 1:6, 9b; 1 Chr 22:11; 28:10 and 20. It is clear, however, that this is purely a matter of convention and carries no official significance whatever, for there is no element of succession in office involved here, and the usual element in the genre giving assurance of divine aid is here replaced by a promise of support by the community.

5 By making the people swear to follow the suggested course of action while feelings were still running high, Ezra ensured that there could be no turning back at a later stage. For the time being he contented himself with this assurance; it would have been quite impractical to proceed immediately, as the length and thoroughness of the eventual investigation demonstrates.

6 Ezra continued mourning and fasting after he had withdrawn from public view. This shows that not all his display in the previous chapter was purely for effect. It was precisely because he felt so deeply about the situation that he was prepared to use even his emotions to help stimulate what he regarded as the necessary response.

The reference to Ezra withdrawing to "the room of Jehohanan the son of Eliashib" has featured prominently in discussions of the date of Ezra. Briefly, the facts are these. Eliashib is a common name. There are three men of that name in the list later in this chapter alone. It was carried by the high priest in Nehemiah's time (Neh 3:1, etc.), and he is no doubt to be identified with the man of that name in the list of the high priestly family in Neh 12:10–11, in the list of high priests in Neh 12:22, and in Neh 13:28. It is not agreed whether he is also to be identified with "Eliashib the priest, who was appointed over the chamber of the house of our God" (Neh 13:4, 7). It is not agreed either whether Ezra 10:6 refers to the same or another Eliashib.

Jehohanan (and its variant Johanan) is also a common name. For instance, one is mentioned in a list of priests in Neh 12:13. Of particular note is its occurrence in the list of high priests in Neh 12:22–23, and since he is mentioned next but one after Eliashib, the high priest in Nehemiah's time, it seems virtually certain that he is to be identified with the Jehohanan who is referred to in one of the Elephantine papyri as high priest (*AramP* 30:18).

The letter is dated in 408 B.C. and indicates that Jehohanan was active as high priest three years earlier. It should be noted, however, that Neh 12:22–23 is a simple list of high priests, with no family relationships mentioned. Where such relationships are the subject of attention, however (Neh 12:10–11), we find that the line runs through Eliashib–Joiada–Jonathan and that there is no reference to any Jehohanan.

Finally, a number of scholars have held a story told by Josephus to be relevant to this discussion, for it recounts the murder of Jesus by his brother Joannes (Johanan), the high priest, in the temple, and the consequent imposition of a tax on the daily sacrifices by Bagoses the governor. I have argued in detail elsewhere, however, that this account should be dated to the reign of Artaxerxes III Ochus (358–338 B.C.); cf. *JTS* ns 28 (1977) 49–66. This is long after any conceivable date for Ezra. It should therefore, in my view, be omitted from any consideration of the date of Ezra, despite the fact that it has frequently featured in such discussions. It will not be treated further here, nor will arguments that others have based upon it.

The facts listed above have given rise to a variety of explanations, of which the most significant are listed here. (a) The Eliashib of the present verse has been identified with the high priest of Nehemiah's time and the Johanan of the present verse with the high priest of Neh 12:22–23 and the Elephantine papyri. This is then regarded as one of the strongest arguments in favor of dating Ezra after Nehemiah, and so in the seventh year of Artaxerxes II, 398 B.C.; cf. Rowley, "Chronological Order" 153–59; Bowman.

If these identifications are correct, then the conclusion may follow. It is not at all certain, however, that they are correct. First, the argument is usually taken a step further, though this is not absolutely necessary for the case. It is assumed from Neh 12:22 that Johanan was Eliashib's grandson, with the result that first a scribal error of Jonathan for Johanan is postulated for Neh 12:10–11, where Jonathan is certainly Eliashib's grandson, and second "son" in Ezra 10:6 and Neh 12:23 is taken to mean "grandson." Neither of these points is securely based, however. There is no evidence for the textual emendation in Neh 12:10–11 (where in fact the name Jonathan occurs twice), and although "son" can sometimes have the more general meaning of "descendant," this is usually in contexts where there is good reason for such terminology, as with the descendant of the founder of a dynasty. Since such reasons are absent here, Johanan should indeed be regarded as the son of Eliashib; cf. Mowinckel, *Studien I,* 158–60; Porter, *JTS* ns 17 (1966) 54–67.

Even so, it would still be possible to argue that the Johanan of Ezra 10:6 was the high priest of later times. However, he is not given the title which we would expect, and we have seen that it is illegitimate to appeal to the story in Josephus as a possible explanation for this (*contra* Rowley). The way is thus opened to some of the alternative explanations noted below, and also to the possibility that, despite the coincidence of names, the high priestly family is not in fact being referred to here at all. Other considerations will further support this view; cf. (e) below, Scott *ExpTim* 58 (1946–47) 265, and Tuland, *AUSS* 12 (1974) 55–59.

(b) Still maintaining the identities assumed above, the probability that Johanan was indeed the son, not the grandson, of Eliashib, and that one of

Eliashib's grandsons was already married in Nehemiah's time, according to Neh 13:28, together with the fact that he is not called the high priest in Ezra 10:6, allows the possibility that he was a young man in Ezra's time, albeit one who had his own room in the temple precincts. This would then permit an earlier date for Ezra, whether in 428 b.c., as Bright, *History,* 391–402, proposes, in 433 or 432 b.c., as Rudolph suggests, or even in 458 b.c., the traditional date for his journey to Jerusalem. Furthermore, there is no particular reason to suppose, as some have, that Ezra could have retreated only to a room of the high priest.

(c) Yet a third possibility which maintains these same identities is to suggest that in the writer's own time that particular room was known under this name because of its former association with a famous high priest. Since this view is generally held by those who favor an early date for Ezra, they suggest that the room was not so named in the EM, but that the later editor substituted this better known equivalent for whatever lay in the original text. No conclusion for the date of Ezra could then be drawn from this reference; cf. Meyer, *Entstehung,* 91; Ryle; Siegfried; In der Smitten, *Esra,* 98.

(d) We move next to a suggestion that proposes a different set of identifications but still maintains that the high priestly family is here referred to. It has for some while been observed that the list of high priests in Neh 12 is probably defective since there are not enough names to fill the time concerned; for references, cf. Williamson, *JTS* ns 28 (1977) 62–63. From this, Cross, *JBL* 94 (1975) 4–18, has sought to fill in the gaps on the assumption that the high priest's family adopted the practice of papponymy (naming a child after his grandfather). Other evidence renders this a likely assumption. One consequence is that Cross, followed most recently by Clines, includes an Eliashib and Johanan *before* the Eliashib of Nehemiah's time. They may be referred to here, demanding the traditional date for Ezra.

Cross's theory has been severely criticized by Widengren in "The Persian Period," 506–9, on the grounds that it is "based on so many uncertainties and reconstructions, as well as one fundamental mistake." Nevertheless, Cross's starting point—that the list of high priests is defective—is fully justified in my view. Clearly we cannot be sure how it should be filled out. In that case, the possibility of an earlier Johanan, son of Eliashib, should not be lightly dismissed.

(e) Finally, it should be questioned whether the intention of the text is to refer to the high priest's family at all. As a number of commentators have correctly observed (e.g. Bertholet; Rudolph) and as was stressed above, both names in question were extremely common at this time.

In my opinion, there is one piece of evidence which has not been adequately recognized which would favor the view that in fact some other family is intended here. In Neh 13:4 we read of an "Eliashib the priest, who was appointed over the chamber of the house of our God." This definition seems intended to identify Eliashib, and may therefore be presumed to *distinguish* him from Eliashib the high priest. We would not expect the high priest to function as a caretaker. This Eliashib's association with a "chamber" in the temple immediately links back to our verse, Ezra 10:6 (the same word, לשכה, is used), and suggests that reference may be being made to this family, not to the high priests. If so, Ezra could still, of course, be dated after Nehemiah if the Eliashib in the two verses is the same. Equally, however, since it may be regarded as established that papponymy was widely practiced, the Eliashib of our verse could easily have been the grandfather of the one in Neh 13:4, thus allowing an early date for Ezra.

All the proposals mentioned here have some points in their favor as well as difficulties to face. It is clear that the issue is too uncertain to be admitted as evidence for the dating of Ezra, despite the fact that it has become a major plank in the platform of those who would put him after Nehemiah. That question should be settled on other grounds (see *Introduction*, "Chronological Order"). On the whole I slightly favor the last proposal listed, though the evidence is insufficient to allow more than a tentative preference.

7–8 All members of the Jewish community are summoned to Jerusalem in order to resolve the problem. There is no indication of how much time may have elapsed following the events of the previous paragraph, but it is unlikely to have been very long. The post-exilic province of Judah was quite small in geographical extent, so that the summons to appear "within three days" would not have caused any hardship.

It appears from v 8 that the proclamation was issued by "the chiefs and elders" (i.e., the local leaders) rather than by Ezra himself. This fits with what has already repeatedly been seen of the manner in which he encouraged the community itself to come to terms with its shortcomings rather than impose solutions by external authority. Nevertheless, the sanctions threatened for failure to obey (v 8b) are sufficiently severe to suggest that Ezra lent his authority to what was being done.

The threatened penalties coincide with the second and third options available to Ezra under the terms of his commission by Artaxerxes in 7:26. The death sentence mentioned there may have been regarded as somewhat severe in the circumstances, while imprisonment does not seem to have been a form of punishment to which the Jews normally resorted. The two referred to, however, could be drawn approximately into line with punishments included in Pentateuchal legislation, and so would have suited Ezra's style and purpose rather better.

For property being "forfeited," the text employs the root חרם, which is used in various ways in the biblical texts; cf. M. Greenberg, "Herem." *EncJud* 8, 344–50. It is best known in connection with the accounts of Israel's early settlement in Canaan, where at Jericho, for instance, the city was to be "devoted" or "put to the ban," "even it and all that is therein, to the Lord" (Josh 6:17; cf. 6:21 and 7:1, 11, 13 etc.). It can also refer, however, to property devoted privately and permanently for temple and priestly service; cf. Lev 27:28; Num 18:14; Ezek 44:29. The punitive use of the ban within Israel is attested in Exod 22:19 (20). It is likely that these various laws have been interpreted in the light of one another (for a comparable process, see *Comment* on 9:1–2) so that they could be linked with confiscated property being dedicated to temple use (as 1 Esdr 9:4 rightly understands) and with the individual concerned being excommunicated. This latter development could only take place, of course, in the context of the sharp delineation of community membership which, we have argued, it was part of Ezra's commission to initiate.

Banishment as such was not a punishment envisaged in the Pentateuch, but one may clearly see here the beginnings of the process whereby the death penalty was later interpreted in this way. A Greek parallel is suggested by Blidstein, *VT* 24 (1974) 357–60.

9 The threat of these sanctions was apparently sufficient to win the people's full cooperation. The ninth month, Kislev, approximates our December. This is the season of the early winter rains in Palestine, and they can be very heavy. For those who had had to travel some distance, this would have made the occasion uncomfortable enough. However, the solemnity of the occasion, perhaps heightened by the fact that they were meeting in the same square as that where two months previously they had gathered to hear Ezra read the law (cf. Neh 8:1), was the overriding factor that led to their apprehension.

10–11 Wasting no time, Ezra first recapitulates what has already been said in chap. 9. For the language and thought of v 10, see *Comment* on 9:1–2, 7, and 15. He then urges them to confess and to conform to God's will by redrawing the community's lines of demarcation.

To "make confession" is literally to "give thanks/praise to" (נתן תודה ל'); cf. H. Grimme, "Der Begriff von hebräischen הודה und תודה." *ZAW* 58 (1940–41) 236–37. This expression occurs in only one other comparable context, Josh 7:19, where Joshua urges Achan to confess his sin. There, it is actually parallel with שים כבוד ל' "give glory to." The thought is very much in line with what was noted at 9:15 concerning the acknowledgment in confession that God is "righteous." Just as in ascribing praise to God the worshiper is perforce accepting his own sinfulness and God's judgment upon it, so conversely to express that acceptance openly glorifies God as the righteous judge. " 'Praise' was given to God by the utterance of confession. The penitent who renounced his sin and threw himself upon the mercies of God rendered that true praise of trust and love, from which 'confession' springs" (Ryle).

12–14 The consensus which emerged, no doubt, from some form of discussion is here summarized. It may well be that the depressing physical conditions speeded the deliberations considerably. The people agreed that action must be taken, but urged that it would be impractical to do so on the present occasion: the number of cases meant that it would take some time to complete the inquiry satisfactorily, and it was clearly out of the question for all those who had travelled to Jerusalem, the majority of whom were in any case not directly involved, to stay longer without adequate accommodation in such weather.

The suggestion about how to proceed was a sensible one. A representative commission of "chiefs" (שרים, a vague word in such a context, probably meaning high-standing and well-regarded members of the community in general) was to be established, presumably in Jerusalem. Times would be set when the individuals involved should appear before them, accompanied by their local civic leaders. The latter would be best placed to testify for or against their fellow citizens. (They are not, of course, to be identified with the "magistrates and judges" of 7:25; see *Comment* on that verse.) Though not explicitly stated, the possibility of local, preliminary hearings to establish where there was a *prima facie* case to answer, may have been envisaged.

Ezra had spoken of the possibility of God's wrath falling upon the community because of their faithlessness (9:14). The people therefore conclude by expressing the hope that they may have done enough to avert any such disaster.

15 The significance of this verse is disputed. The word translated above as "opposed" is literally "stood on, against." This has led some to believe that it actually means "supported." This is improbable, however, since the majority apparently supported the proposals. There would seem to be no reason to single out these four individuals for particular mention, and the particle אך at the start of the verse leads us to expect a contrast with the foregoing. Rudolph points out that the misunderstanding, present already in several of the Vrs, derives from the failure to observe that this whole verse should be regarded as parenthetical, with v 16 directly continuing the narrative from v 14.

An alternative approach is to suggest that "stood" links back to the same word in v 14, translated above as "act for." According to this view, the present verse would list the first members of the commission. This interpretation is also improbable, however. It too fails to do justice to the force of אך. The two occurrences of עמד "stand" are followed by different prepositions in vv 14 and 15, which suggests that they should not necessarily be taken together. And appointment to the commission comes later in the narrative (v 16).

It is thus probable that the verse is expressing opposition; but opposition to what? To the resort to divorce, or to the plan suggested for accomplishing that end? The former would indicate that the opposition was by a "lax" group, the latter that it was by a group of rigorists who wanted the matter dealt with more quickly or more severely. This second suggestion seems most probable: note should be made first of the likelihood that Meshullam and Shabbethai supported Jonathan and Jahzeiah. Some have argued that the second half of the verse is to be read as a contrast to the first half, so that "supported" would have the proposals of v 14 as its object. Against this, however, the 3 masc pl suff on עזרם (lit. "they helped them") is most naturally referred to Jonathan and Jahzeiah as its antecedent; if the proposals were intended, we would have expected either a fem sing suff, referring to the previous זאת, or a masc sing suff, referring to לדבר הזה. This being so, v 15 must be understood to say that all four individuals mentioned here were united in their opposition. Now, Shabbethai is expressly called a Levite, and since Meshullam (a very common name) is not otherwise designated, it seems most reasonable to link him with the prominent Meshullam of 8:16. No Shabbethai is listed among the Levites who had married foreign wives in 10:23, and since Meshullam travelled with Ezra, he can hardly have married in the brief time since their arrival in Jerusalem; he is therefore not to be linked with the Meshullam in v 29. Neither of the other two appear in that list either. No reason is thus apparent why these should have opposed the plan of divorcing the foreign wives, while Meshullam's position and Shabbethai's Levitical status (plus the probability that it is they who are mentioned as firm supporters of Ezra's policy in Neh 8:4 and 7, which, historically speaking, precedes the present passage) tip the balance of probability in favor of the view that they took a more rigorous line than that which was eventually adopted.

For a suggestion that some material has been removed from here by the editor, see *Form* at Neh 9.

16–17 The establishment and work of the commission are briefly recorded. Once again it is noteworthy (assuming the text is correctly restored above) that Ezra takes no more personal involvement than is absolutely necessary. He prefers to delegate the actual decision-making to the community's own leaders. The members of the commission are not named here, but the wording suggests that they were in the original account.

Their work was simply "to investigate the affair." The decision about what to do with their findings had been agreed separately and beforehand by the community as a whole, and was apparently accepted by those involved (v 19). The commission itself is thus presented in the Memoir as the fulfillment of Ezra's primary duty according to the edict of Artaxerxes. Surprising as this may seem at first sight, it probably conforms rather more closely to what Artaxerxes intended than is generally recognized: see *Comment* on 7:14.

The work lasted for some three months, concluding exactly a year after the first date associated with Ezra (cf. 7:9). Rudolph estimates that this represents approximately 75 working days, which he regards as rather slow for the 110 (109 according to Rudolph) cases listed later in the chapter. Even allowing that some cases investigated may have been dismissed, he still uses this as part of his argument that the following list is incomplete. This is highly speculative, however. Considering the difficulties of communication and transport during the winter season in those days, delays may well have occurred, with the result that the commission could not sit on every available working day. We do not know how many cases were investigated only to be dismissed or left undecided, nor have we any notion of the commission's procedures. The figures involved do not, therefore, seem to be so much out of line as to demand the conclusion that the following list is particularly misleading.

18–44 For general, introductory remarks on this list, see *Form* above. Consideration of the original form of the list, however, has been held over until now.

Scholars who have broached this question have generally argued that the final editor has abbreviated the original list. It will be suggested here, however, that the editor is more likely to have rearranged the list than abbreviated it to any considerable degree, with the exception that he has eliminated a repetitious element.

Rudolph may be taken as representative of those who argue for abbreviation. He advances two arguments. First (in addition to the speculative point noted at the end of *Comment* on vv 16–17 above), he feels that many more people must have been involved with the problem of mixed marriages. He notes that, by comparison with Ezra 2, the lower classes, both lay and cultic (i.e., the temple servants), are not mentioned here, even though he thinks they would have been equally as likely to involve themselves in these marriages.

This argument is to be rejected, however. We have no right to determine how long the list must have been, for in Ezra's ideology any mixed marriages, however few, posed an acute threat to the community (see *Comment* on 9:1–2). Furthermore, it is not at all surprising that the problem is largely confined to the higher levels of society (the fact that the temple servants may ultimately have been of foreign origin—cf. 2:43–58—would no longer be of any relevance at this stage). The lower classes, if involved at all in mixed marriages, would only be likely to have married local inhabitants who could well have been assimilated to the prevailing cultural and religious conditions; cf. 6:21. The real danger came from those who were in a position to maintain their alien cultural identity and religion, either because they in fact came from abroad or because they were, by their financial position, somewhat detached from the general conditions of society. This view is further supported by the numbers involved in vv 20–24; see *Comment* below. A final possible explanation has been provided by Ackroyd, who links the composition of the list with the fact that the OT often enjoins stricter laws of purity for the priesthood than for the laity. He suggests that this is here extended to a top stratum of Israelite society as a whole, where it was important to preserve the faith firmly. In lower strata, such considerations were of less significance. "What is important is that there should be an absolute assurance of fitness at the centre, for without this, the community would be at risk." Thus while the considerations that follow allow the conclusion that the list may have been "trimmed" here and there, it may nevertheless be maintained that it approximates closely its original extent.

Rudolph's second argument is of a different nature, and carries more weight. The procedure in the first half of v 19 applies to everyone in the list, not just the representatives of the high priest's family. Since there is no reason to suppose that this verse has been transposed from elsewhere, its position suggests that a comparable statement must originally have followed each group of names (cf. Num 7 for a similar structure) but was omitted for stylistic reasons by a later editor. This reasoning appears to be sound, and it will be argued at v 19 below that in fact it applies to the whole verse, not just its first half.

The text-critical work set out above enables us to add a further suggestion not available to Rudolph. He believed that members of thirteen lay families were listed, but our reconstruction has produced only twelve. It seems likely that this is the result of an artificial arrangement. It could, of course, have been present from the first, as in 8:1–14. However, we have noted a number of places where such typological schematization is the work of the later editor (e.g. 7:1–10; 8:35–36). Since other evidence has already been accumulated that points to heavy editorial activity in this chapter, it is attractive to attribute this schematization to him as well. There are thus two points that favor editorial arrangement, rather than strict abbreviation, of this list, whereas there is no good reason to suggest why he should have shortened it to any significant degree (cf. Mowinckel, *Studien I*, 127–29, *contra* Rudolph).

18   This verse lists relatives of the high priest, other priests following in v 20–22.

19   The procedure followed is first to give a solemn undertaking to divorce their wives and, second, to make an offering to expiate their trespass. Some have held that this latter applied only to the priests, and that this explains why this verse is not repeated for the other groups. However, J. Milgrom, *Cult and Conscience* (SJLA 18; Leiden: Brill, 1976), 71–73, has argued that this is unlikely. The sin of intermarriage is several times referred to as מעל, "unfaithfulness"; see *Comment* on 9:2. For this—trespass upon the Lord's *sancta*—the correct offering is an אשם, "guilt offering," according to Lev 5:14–16. "It would not make sense that all Israel is guilty of *maal* for intermarriage (9:2, 4; 10:2, 6, 10; Neh 13:27) but only the priests are required to bring an *asham*" (Milgrom, 73).

20–24 The remaining cultic officials are listed in the conventional order. The decreasing numbers as one goes down the scale speak in favor of our explanation above for the absence of any members of the lowest class, that of temple servant.

25–43 The laity are divided into twelve family groups. As with the divisions of the cultic personnel, the groups are familiar from Ezra 2, sometimes in contrast with the situation in Ezra 8. This is to be expected, since the problem related to those who had been back in the land long enough to enter into such marriages. The relationship with Ezra 2 cannot thus be turned against the list's authenticity.

43 Cogan, *IEJ* 29 (1979) 37–39, finds a connection between the names of this verse and those of 1 Chr 5:4–8 as part of his argument that these were Reubenites who returned after the exile to their Trans-Jordanian homeland. Whatever the merits of his general suggestion, it has to be admitted that the onomastic argument is tenuous and could simply be the result of coincidence.

44 The text of this verse is so uncertain (see *Notes*) that it would be unwise to build much on it. If it is true that in the original list v 19 or its equivalent was repeated at the end of each of the list's main sections, then perhaps its equivalent once stood after this verse too. In that case, there is no need to emend this verse into a statement that the wives were dismissed (as 1 Esdr 9:36 does), and MT may stand as an indication that the narrator was not insensitive to the personal tragedies he was recording.

The narrative breaks off abruptly, to be followed immediately by the account of Nehemiah's work. For some discussion of this, cf. *Introduction*, "The Achievements of Ezra and Nehemiah." It is there maintained that, though this may not represent the precise original ending of the EM, yet not much is likely to have been lost. For alternative proposals, see *Form*, Neh 8 and Neh 9.

Explanation (chaps. 9–10)

The treatment described in these two chapters of how Ezra tackled the problem of mixed marriages is among the least attractive parts of Ezra-Nehemiah, if not of the whole OT. Responsibility dictates that we should endeavor first to understand the reasons that justified it in the participants' own eyes before going on to evaluate it in the light of Scripture as a whole.

The Jewish community in Judah and Jerusalem to which Ezra returned found itself in an ambivalent situation, trapped between a political and religious sense of identity. The edict of Artaxerxes that provided Ezra with his mandate was intended, in our view (see *Comment,* 7:11–26 above), to encourage the development of Judaism as a religious community. That being so, the qualifications for membership had to be redefined; otherwise, there was (or at least was felt to be) a danger that the distinctive elements of the Jewish faith would be watered down, perhaps beyond the point of recognition, by assimilation to the surrounding cultures.

This danger was heightened by the economic power wielded by some of those who are here labeled "the peoples of the lands." During the exile foreign landlords had apparently assumed control of a good deal of the territory of Judea, and the difficult economic circumstances that the returned exiles faced could soon have placed them at the mercy of these powerful neighbors.

Against this precarious background, five points may aid an understanding of why events took the turn that they did. The Mosaic law, which by now was the constitutional foundation, as it were, for this emerging community, gave no direct guidance on the central issue that Ezra had to face. In consequence, as our exegesis of 9:1–2 has tried to show, he taught, and the community accepted, an interpretation of the law according to its "spirit," as he understood it. We may not agree with certain aspects of Ezra's interpretation, but his motivation and method here remain ones we would still acknowledge as valid today.

We have noted in connection with the list in the second half of chap. 10 that only the leadership of the community was directly involved in these proceedings. The survival of the whole stood no chance at all if the center became "soft." Israel's election was not merely for her own comfort, but so she might shine as a witness to the nations for God and his standards (see Gen 26:4). This could not be achieved without the maintenance of her distinctive self-identity, and this was thought to be threatened by mixed marriages.

It appears from Mal 2:10–16 (from roughly the same period) that in some cases the men had already divorced their Jewish wives in order to enter into these new partnerships. Though not mentioned here, knowledge of this fact may have reduced the sympathy of the majority for the families concerned. It also serves to remind us that divorce was in any case regarded in a rather different light than it is today when the Church has had its expectations of marriage raised by Jesus' high estimation of its value.

We have emphasized repeatedly that Ezra did not impose his solution from above upon an unwilling population. He may in the meantime have been teaching them his interpretation of the law, but the initiative for response and action throughout the narrative comes from the community itself and its leaders. According to the record we have, there is not even an expression of opposition from the parties most directly involved.

Finally, it should be noted that no indication is given of what provision may have been made for the divorced families. The concerns of the narrative lie elsewhere, and what we regard as mitigating factors may have been considered irrelevant by the author.

It is thus evident that in the circumstances the divorce of foreign wives was considered the lesser of the two evils. However, while a commentator should make every effort to understand his text, he need not accept it uncritically in its entirety. These chapters are descriptive. That does not automatically make them prescriptive for the Christian faith. Consideration of the wider context of Scripture brings other conflicting voices into play.

First, it appears from 9:2 that the clinching factor in deciding the course of action to be followed was racial. This is not taught directly in Scripture, but was part of the interpretation derived by combining various passages in a way which we today must reject. The passages in Deuteronomy prohibiting mixed marriages do so on religious grounds alone—the danger of the Jewish partner being enticed away from faithful observance of the law. In a case like that of Ruth, where the foreign partner was converted to Judaism, the situation was naturally rather different. The present passage, however, shows no awareness of such a possibility. It misinterprets the principle of the law along racist lines. The OT's own rejection of this standpoint is strongly reinforced in the NT (e.g., Acts 17:26; Gal 3:28; etc.).

Second, in the most nearly analogous situation in which a Christian is ever likely to find himself or herself—namely, married to an unbelieving partner—the NT explicitly rules out divorce as an available option (1 Cor 7:12–13). Indeed, 1 Cor 7 and 1 Pet 3:1–7 encourage, rather, a life-style by the believer of such a manner as may win their unbelieving partner to the faith.

Nevertheless, concentration on the narrow, racist aspects of this passage should not blind us to the more general biblical teaching that for a believer to enter marriage with an unbeliever is likely both to endanger his or her faith and to weaken their marriage, since they cannot share together those things which one partner holds most dear. This was the intention of the Deuteronomic laws already referred to, and it remains true for the Christian as well (e.g. 2 Cor 6:14).

Finally, there are a number of separate points raised in these two chapters that are of abiding value and that should not be overlooked in any general evaluation.

The nature of Ezra's leadership repays careful study. While we may not fully agree with the direction in which he was taking the community, we may nevertheless learn from the manner in which, by teaching, patience, and example, he was able to bring the people without coercion to make for themselves the decisions he considered beneficial, even though they might be painful in the short run.

Clines has rightly drawn attention to the creative interplay between community and Scripture. On the one hand, we have seen how circumstances led them to an interpretation of Scripture that we do not accept; this should act as a solemn reminder that acceptance of the authority of Scripture is only the start of the problem of setting the guidelines that should govern our actions. On the other hand, however, "the biblical text is not only the object of the community's interpretation, but also an active subject in the life of the community." It is astonishing the extent to which Scripture as then understood became the creative element in the formation of Judaism.

Ezra's prayer of confession, and the people's response to it, is free of any taint of pride or self-justification. This is noteworthy in view of the exaggerated sense of election by race which underlies their self-awareness. Their unaffected humility still speaks to those who are conscious of an election by grace through Christ.

Also lessons may be learned from the presentation of repentance as a unified step of confession and action to eliminate the wrong perceived.

Finally, if we may overlook for the moment the details of how Ezra worked out the principle of Jewish distinctiveness, his underlying concern was absolutely right. Israel's mission could only make headway if she maintained the servant identity that separated her from the nations to whom she should mediate the revelation of God. In just the same way, Christians individually and collectively as the Church are called to be "light" and "salt," elements that function effectively precisely because of their difference from the setting in which they are placed; "But if the salt has lost its savor . . ." (cf. Matt 5:13–16).

Nehemiah

Nehemiah's Vocation   (*Neh 1:1–11*)

Bibliography

Ararat, N. "Nehemiah's Only Arrival in the Twenty-Fifth Year of Ezra's Arrival (433 B.C.E.)" (Heb.). *BMik* 65 (1976) 293–95. **Bickerman, E. J.** "En marge de l'Écriture. I.—Le comput des années de règne des Achéménides (Néh., i, 2; ii, 1 et Thuc., viii, 58." *RB* 88 (1981) 19–23. **Deliceto, G. de.** "Epoca della partenza di Hanani per Gerusalemme e anno della petizione di Neemia ad Artaserse. Neem. 1, 1 e Neem. 2, 1." *Laurentianum* 4 (1963) 431–68. **Kellermann, U.** *Nehemia*, 8–11, 84–86, 154–59. **Mowinckel, S.** *Studien II*, 14–20. **Rowley, H. H.** "Nehemiah's Mission and Its Background." *Men of God*, 211–45. ———. "Sanballat and the Samaritan Temple." *Men of God*, 246–76. **Saley, R. J.** "The Date of Nehemiah Reconsidered." *Biblical and Near Eastern Studies. Essays in Honor of William Sanford LaSor*, ed. G. A. Tuttle. Grand Rapids: Eerdmans, 1978, 151–65. **Tuland, C. G.** "Hanani—Hananiah," *JBL* 77 (1968) 157–61. **Vogt, H. C. M.** *Studie*, 43–46. **Yamauchi, E. M.** "Was Nehemiah the Cupbearer a Eunuch?" *ZAW* 92 (1980) 132–42.

Translation

[1] *The words of Nehemiah, son of Hecaliah:*
In the month Kislev of the twentieth year, while I was in the fortress of Susa,
[2] *Hanani, one of my brothers came with some other men from Judah. I asked them about the Jews—those who, having escaped, were left of the captivity—and about Jerusalem.* [3] *They told me, "The remnant who are left of the captivity there in the province are in great trouble and disgrace. The wall of Jerusalem has been broken down and its gates burned with fire."* [4] *When I heard this news I sat down and wept; for days I was in mourning; I fasted and prayed to the God of heaven.*
[5] *I said, "O Lord God of heaven, you great and awe-inspiring God, who keeps covenant and faith* [a] *with those who love him and observe his commandments,* [6] *let your ear be attentive and your eyes open to hear your servant's prayer which I now* [a] *pray before you night and day on behalf of your servants the sons of Israel. I confess the sins of the sons of Israel which we have committed against you; even I and my father's house have sinned.* [7] *We have acted very* [a] *corruptly towards you: we have not observed the commandments, the statutes and the ordinances which you commanded your servant Moses.* [8] *Remember the command which you gave to your servant Moses when you said, 'If you* [a] *are unfaithful, I will scatter you among the nations,* [9] *but if you return to me and observe my commandments by keeping them, then, even if those of your number who have been banished are at the farthest horizon,* [a] *yet I will gather them from thence and bring them to the place which I have chosen as a dwelling for my Name.'* [10] *They are your servants and your people whom you redeemed by your great power and your mighty hand.* [11] *O Lord, let your ear be attentive to your servant's prayer and to the prayer of your servants who delight to reverence your name and grant success to your servant today by giving him favor in this man's presence." Now I was the king's cupbearer.*

Notes

5.a. In this formula it is usual for חסד "faith" or "loyalty" to have the def art; cf. Deut 7:9 and Dan 9:4. Many MSS may therefore be right in reading it here too, though it is not absolutely essential.

6.a. Lit., "today," but this would be an inappropriate rendering following v 4 and preceding "day and night." The word is being used in an entirely stereotyped manner.

7.a. Inf const instead of the inf abs usually used in such cases. This is not unparalleled, however, so that we should pause before emending the vocalization; cf. GKC § 113x; Joüon, *Grammaire* § 123q.

8.a. The 2 pl is used here and in the remainder of vv 8–9.

9.a. Lit., "at the end of the heaven/sky." This may be simply hyperbolic language, but it is attractive to suppose that the furthest visible part of the sky, i.e., the horizon, is intended, as in the comparable English idiom.

Form/Structure/Setting

It is almost universally agreed that most of, if not all, the first-person material in the book of Nehemiah is taken directly from the Nehemiah Memoir, a work whose general form requires separate discussion (cf. *Introduction*, "The Nehemiah Memoir). Three items in the present chapter, however, require individual attention.

The first of these is the heading. It is most unlikely that the opening of the original Memoir coincided exactly with v 1. Most telling is the unqualified date, "the twentieth year." While this raises problems of its own (see below), there must once have been a reference to the king's reign (cf. 2:1). Since there is no textual evidence to suggest that this has subsequently dropped out (*contra* Rudolph), we must conclude that this points to the hand of the editor of the Ezra-Nehemiah material. When he combined the accounts of their activities, he assumed that, following Ezra 7:1, 7, etc., there was no need here to specify the reign again.

What precisely was included in the original heading is thus unknown to us. Many suppose that the information about Nehemiah's status, now preserved in v 11b, must have stood at the start. In particular, Mowinckel, *Studien II*, 15, argues in favor of this conclusion on the basis of Ancient Near Eastern royal inscriptions with which he compares the NM. While this view is certainly possible, it must not be concluded that v 11b itself can be removed; it provides a necessary and effective literary link between Nehemiah's prayer and the subsequent narrative in chap. 2.

Since the opening words of the chapter include information about Nehemiah's father not otherwise known to us, they too must have been part of the material inherited by the later editor. It is impossible now to tell, however, whether they were part of the memoir itself or a clerical note attached to it at an early time. Either way, however, influence from prophetic books, as suggested by Ackroyd, is unlikely at so early a stage in the composition.

We conclude, therefore, that with only a minimum of interference, the editor of the Ezra-Nehemiah material made clear the transition from one account to the other before following his new source very closely.

The second item of concern is Nehemiah's prayer, vv 5–11a. A number of scholars, such as Hölscher, Mowinckel (*Studien* II), Noth (*Studien*), and

Schneider, have argued that this must be a later insertion into the NM; it is generally supposed to be the work of the Chronicler. Kellermann, *Nehemia*, 9, has conveniently gathered and summarized their reasons: (i) The prayer deals generally with the question of exile and return rather than with the specific situation of this chapter; (ii) the use of היום, "today," in v 11 contradicts the long period mentioned in v 4 and already presupposes the account of chap. 2; (iii) the heavily Deuteronomic style betrays the hand of the Chronicler; (iv) the close comparison with Ezra 9 and Dan 9 rules out authorship by Nehemiah; (v) the divine name יהוה (v 5) and the expression בני ישראל "the sons of Israel" (v 6) are uncharacteristic of Nehemiah; (vi) the reference to "this man" in v 11 is inappropriate in such a memoir; (vii) the prayer is long by comparison with Nehemiah's otherwise rather clipped style; (viii) some lexical items are thought to be typical of the Chronicler; and (ix) Mowinckel, *Studien II*, 18, finds the retranslation of a brief prayer in Josephus' account more suitable to the present context.

Many of these points are to be explained by the use of liturgical language in the prayer. (Others are dealt with in *Comment* below.) There is no adequate reason to doubt that at least as early as the time when he wrote the memoir—and perhaps even in the historical situation itself—Nehemiah could have used such stereotyped phraseology; indeed, this would be the type of material on which we would expect him to draw in order to gain orientation in a time of crisis. Some of the most striking parallels and citations will be pointed out in *Comment* below.

Alongside this must be set the fact that the prayer does not fit easily into any formal category known to us. Though sometimes compared, for instance, with the community laments, it in fact lacks the most characteristic feature of that genre—the complaint in its various forms (e.g., against God, with the characteristic questions "Why?" and "How long?", the complaint about the trouble and the shame it brings, and the accusation against the enemy). Similarly, the prayer switches uncharacteristically between first person singular and plural speech.

In outline, the prayer is comprised of an expanded address (v 5; cf. especially Dan 9:4), an appeal for a hearing (v 6a; cf. 1 Kgs 8:28–29; 2 Chr 6:40; 7:15; Ps 130:2; Isa 37:17), a confession (vv 6b–7), and an appeal to God's covenant promises (vv 8–9), followed by supplication for the people (v 10) and for Nehemiah's personal situation (v 11a). While none of these elements except the last one is unfamiliar, their combination in this manner is unparalleled. This too suggests a special and individual composition by one thoroughly conversant with Israel's liturgical tradition but not bound by it; the prayer is used creatively to suit the current situation of national disgrace (v 10, which, despite the objection of the commentators listed above, is a reasonable response to the report of v 3) and pressing personal need (v 11a).

Cult-historically, however, the occurrence of such a prayer at this period should not cause surprise. It may be compared with Ezra 9; Neh 9; Dan 9 and Bar 1:15—3:8 (see *Form* on Ezra 9 above), where we find other expressions of penitence each with distinctive elements. As Westermann observes, once Israel became a province within an empire, the place of the old liturgical observances which gave rise to the communal psalms of lament was "taken over by the service of penitence, such as the one described programmatically in Ezra 9. The prayer transmitted there exemplifies the transition from the psalm of lament to the prayer of repentance"; C. Westermann, *The Psalms: Structure, Content and Message* (tr. R. D. Gehrke; Minneapolis: Augsburg, 1980), 31.

Finally, the length of the prayer is not remarkable. It is intended as a summary of the substance of Nehemiah's petition over several months and as such combines his general response to the news of v 3 and his particular prayer (v 11) when an opportunity to approach the king arose. This is just what we would expect when Nehemiah came later to record his exploits; the anticipation of chap. 2 by v 11 is thus fully intelligible. Moreover the setting of this prayer bears no comparison with that of his brief petitions later, uttered in the heat of feverish activity. Lastly, it is most improbable that Josephus bears witness to an alternative, and more original, Hebrew text. So far as can be judged, he had only our biblical books and 1 Esdr on which to construct the detail of his history of this period; cf. Williamson, *Israel*, 21–29.

In connection with the setting, two chronological problems are raised by v 1 when it is taken in conjunction with 2:1. Which Artaxerxes is referred to? And can sense be made of the sequence of months involved?

Since the publication of the Elephantine papyri, nearly all scholars have accepted the view that Nehemiah served under Artaxerxes I; see the full summary in Rowley, "Nehemiah's Mission." In particular, it is noted that while according to *AramP* 30 (408 B.C.) Sanballat was still governor of Samaria, his two sons were primarily responsible for the actual administration of affairs. This suggests that Sanballat was elderly at that time, which would fit with his active opposition to Nehemiah a few decades earlier. The name of Johanan as high priest in the same letter also fits this chronology well (see *Comment* on Ezra 10:6 above).

This consensus has recently been challenged by Saley, "The Date of Nehemiah," on the basis of evidence from the Wadi ed-Daliyeh papyri. They demonstrate that there was another Sanballat who served as governor of Samaria during the reign of Artaxerxes II; cf. F. M. Cross, "Aspects of Samaritan and Jewish History in Late Persian and Hellenistic Times," *HTR* 59 (1966) 201–11. Postulating the wide-spread practice of papponymy at this period, Saley is able also to accommodate the names of priests associated with Nehemiah to this later date.

As Saley himself freely admits, however, he has only demonstrated the formal possibility of dating Nehemiah to the reign of Artaxerxes II. It can no longer be said that the Elephantine papyri *prove* a date under Artaxerxes I. Nevertheless, the latter remains more probable, in my view, because of the difficulties otherwise in finding a suitable background for 1:3–4 (see below), because the reference to Sanballat as "the Horonite" (cf. 2:10 and 19, etc.) suggests that he may have been the first in his family to hold the office of governor, because Geshem the Arabian, one of Nehemiah's opponents, should be dated to the middle of the fifth century B.C. (see *Comment* on 2:19), and because of the excessive and unlikely gap in our knowledge of the history of the Jews in the fifth century B.C. which Saley's view demands. Furthermore, his suggestion rests on a postulated reconstruction of high priests, whereas the earlier date involves only securely attested evidence. There seems to be no positive reason whatsoever for favoring the later date, despite the arguments of a few earlier scholars in that direction, such as C. C. Torrey, "Sanballat 'the Horonite,'" *JBL* 47 (1928) 380–89. Torrey's views were carefully examined by Rowley, "Sanballat," and found unconvincing on other grounds also. Nehemiah should therefore most probably be dated in the reign of Artaxerxes I.

A further problem is raised, however, when one compares the date of Neh 1:1 with 2:1, for according to the Babylonian calendar used by the Persian administration and generally thought to be followed also by the Jews at this time, the month Nisan (2:1) was the first month of the year, and so could not possibly follow Chislev, which was the ninth month (1:1). Several explanations of this discrepancy have been advanced, though not all are equally plausible.

It has been suggested that Nehemiah used a calendar in which the new year was reckoned from the seventh month, Tishri. This may have been Judean practice in the pre-exilic period; if so, "is it not reasonable to suppose that Nehemiah was acquainted with the custom formerly followed by the kings of Judah to begin their regnal years with Tishri and, in a spirit of intense nationalism, applied the customary Jewish practice even to a Persian king?" (E. R. Thiele, *The Mysterious Numbers of the Hebrew Kings* [Exeter: Paternoster, 1966], 30). Without any explanation, this would be a confusing procedure, however, for it runs counter to all known Jewish practice of the period. In addition, doubt has been cast on whether this was indeed the situation in pre-exilic Judah; cf. D. J. A. Clines, "The Evidence for an Autumnal New Year in Pre-exilic Israel Reconsidered," *JBL* 93 (1974) 22–40; it is hazardous to appeal to an uncertainty in order to explain our difficulty.

An alternative form of the same theory appeals to the much later Jewish liturgical practice of celebrating the New Year in the autumn. Here again, however, we have no evidence that this was practiced as early as Nehemiah's time.

Rudolph has suggested that the difficulties can be overcome only by textual emendation. He conjectures that the date in 1:1 originally read שנת תשע עשרה לארתחשסתא המלך, "in the nineteenth year of Artaxerxes the king." He suggests that the words were lost because of the similarity of the last two letters of כסלו, just before, and המלך, and that the gap was then filled "mechanically" from 2:1. This explanation is not very convincing, however, and since it rests upon pure conjecture it should be adopted only as a last resort.

It has been noted above that 1:1 betrays evidence of editorial intervention. The suggestion has therefore been advanced that the editor, who of course lived later than Nehemiah, was influenced by subsequent Jewish liturgical practice and so provided this date by a comparison with 2:1 consistent with the calendar of his day. This is a more reasonable suggestion, but runs into the difficulty that the Nehemiah material was apparently edited quite early, and certainly before Ezra 1–6 (cf. *Introduction*, "Composition"). In that case there can still be no certainty that the autumnal new year had already been introduced. Clines, "The Evidence for an Autumnal New Year in Pre-Exilic Israel Reconsidered," *JBL* 93 (1974) 34–36, manages to overcome this objection, however, by reckoning that "an original 'nineteenth year' was altered to 'twentieth year' by an editor of the Greek period used to reckoning royal years on the Seleucid system of an autumn new year" (cf. Schneider).

Ararat's far more radical version of this theory, *BMik* 65 (1976) 293–95, suggesting that the date was originally "the twenty-fifth year of Ezra('s arrival)," and that it was added by the editor of the Ezra-Nehemiah material, is certainly to be rejected. His appeal to Josephus, *Antiquities* 11:168, is invalid because he fails to observe that Josephus, for reasons of his own, dates Nehemiah to the reign of Xerxes, not Artaxerxes. Moreover, it is arbitrary to reject the united testimony of Neh 1:1; 2:1 and 5:14 in favor of the speculative view that Nehemiah came only once to Jerusalem in the thirty-second year of Artaxerxes' reign (cf. 13:6). Scarcely more convincing is de Deliceto's proposal, *Laurentianum* 4 (1963) 431–68, that the editor of 1:1 intended the twentieth year to refer to Hanani's original departure from Susa for Jerusalem.

Finally, the possibility may be considered that the reference is to the regnal, not the calendar, year. Commentators have generally rejected this suggestion because the month of Artaxerxes' accession was unknown and because there was no evidence to support the view that such a method of reckoning was employed. Recently, however, Bickerman, *RB* 88 (1981) 19–23, has endeavored to answer both objections. He argues that in court circles, in which Nehemiah moved, it would not have been unusual to follow the regnal rather than the calendar year, and he cites an independent example from Thucydides (8:58) to support this claim. In addition, he maintains that Artaxerxes ascended the throne in the month of Ab (22 July–20 August). In a regnal year based on this date, Kislev would be the fifth month and Nisan the ninth. Thus 1:1 would refer to December 446 B.C. and 2:1 to the following spring.

If Bickerman's arguments are sound, his suggestion clearly provides the neatest explanation of the difficulty. In so personal a composition, Nehemiah may be allowed to have used the calendar most familiar to himself, since he was not primarily addressing his Jewish compatriots in his memoir. The best alternative solution is one which sees the confusion arising at some stage during the editorial handling of the material (cf. above).

Comment

1 For the form of the heading and the date, see *Form* above. "Nehemiah" ("the Lord has comforted") was a not uncommon name both in its full form (cf. Ezra 2:2; Neh 3:16) and in such abbreviated forms as Nahum. It is attested in both pre- and post-exilic extrabiblical sources, most recently as the name of a slave on one of the Aramaic papyri (fourth century B.C.) from Wadi ed-Daliyeh; cf. F. M. Cross, *BA* 26 (1963) 111–12. The much less common name of Nehemiah's father, "Hecaliah," remains unexplained, however.

"The fortress of Susa" was a winter residence of the Persian kings (for Ecbatana as their summer residence, cf. Ezra 6:1), though in fact Artaxerxes spent much of his time there; cf. Olmstead, *History*, 352. Whether he was absent at this stage, or whether Nehemiah's duties did not require him to have direct dealings with the king during the following months, is not stated.

2 The account of Nehemiah's meeting with a group of Jews recently arrived from Judah is likewise restricted to essentials. Thus we are given no indication, for instance, whether they were residents of Judah or had simply been on a visit there, perhaps precisely to investigate the effects of Artaxerxes' decree recorded in Ezra 4:17–22, nor whether Nehemiah received them as an official delegation specifically to request that he press the Jewish case at court or whether he learned of the conditions in Jerusalem following a merely casual inquiry and thereafter took the initiative himself. If we are right in supposing that Nehemiah already had family and economic interests in Jerusalem (see Neh 2:3 and 8), his concern would in any case be understandable enough.

A prominent member of the group was Hanani (a shortened form of Hananiah), "The Lord has been gracious." Although "one of my brothers" need mean no more than "a fellow Jew," it seems likely from 7:2 that the word should here be taken literally, assuming that the same man is referred to. This is not absolutely certain, however, for the name was common at the time (e.g., 3:8 and 30; 12:36; Ezra 10:20 and 28). There can thus be even less certainty that he should be identified with the Hanani/Hananiah who features prominently in some of the Elephantine papyri, as suggested by W. R. Arnold, "The Passover Papyrus from Elephantine," *JBL* 31 (1912) 30–31, and pressed further by Tuland, *JBL* 77 (1958) 157–61.

While Nehemiah clearly asks about the welfare of Jerusalem and its inhabitants, his description of the latter is less easily understood: does he refer to Jews who had returned from Babylon to Jerusalem or to those who had escaped ever going into exile in the first place? Opinion has been fairly evenly divided over this issue. Bertholet, for instance, argues that שׁבי "captivity," must be given the meaning it has elsewhere in these books, namely the Babylonian exile, while נשׁארו "who are left," is taken in the technical sense of "belonging to the remnant." The phrase is thus understood to mean "those who have escaped from the exile in which they once were, and so now belong to the Remnant." To this Rudolph replies that according to this view Nehemiah would not yet regard himself as part of the remnant; he therefore thinks that reference is made to Jews who were never taken into exile. This does not rule out an early return from Babylon (Ezra 2), as the memory of that event would have long since faded.

This latter point is questionable, however. Ezra 4:12 shows that memories of a return from exile (whether early or more recent) were very much alive in official circles at the time, and Neh 7:6 may point to Nehemiah's own awareness of the same thing. Moreover, on the assumption that his memoir was written up after his return to Jerusalem, his ignorance of the return would be even less likely. It is thus more probable, as Vogt, *Studie*, 45, suggests, that no such distinctions are intended in this and the following verse. The context is sufficient to make clear that the remnant terminology is applied loosely by Nehemiah to all surviving Jews in Judah (elsewhere in his memoir he does not draw any rigid distinction between those who survived the exile in Judah and those who returned from Babylon), and this is supported by the addition of the words "there in the province" to the answer in v 3. The phrase cannot, therefore, be turned into an argument against the return of Ezra some years previously. The possibility remains, of course, that the later editor took the phrase in its more restricted sense (cf. Ezra 9).

3 Nehemiah's reaction to the news (v 4) is so strong that this report cannot refer to the destruction of Jerusalem by Nebuchadnezzar some 140 years previously. A recent event, as yet unconfirmed in Susa, must be intended, and for this the destruction mentioned briefly in Ezra 4:23 presents itself as the ideal, and indeed only possible, candidate. If this conclusion is sound, and if Ezra's journey to Jerusalem is to be dated to 458 B.C., then it follows that the events of Ezra 4 could have taken place while Ezra was present. For the possible bearing of this on historical reconstruction, cf. *Introduction,* "The Achievement."

4 Nehemiah's response is described in terms that are to some extent stereotyped (cf. Ezra 9:3–5), but the sequel shows that they nevertheless express genuine emotion. Moreover, his persistence in prayer over several months (cf. Neh 2:1) demonstrates how fully involved he became in the fate of his fellow Jews. Fasting was added to intercession as "an effective means of strengthening the force of a prayer"; cf. H. A. Brongers, *OTS* 20 (1977) 11 and Ezra 8:23. For "the God of heaven," see *Comment* on Ezra 1:2.

5–11a An outline of Nehemiah's prayer and discussion of the major problems it raises have been supplied in *Form* above. It is particularly important to bear in mind that it combines Nehemiah's personal intercession for his forthcoming encounter with the king with more general prayer and confession in regard to the whole state of his people, of which he has just been informed.

Much of the prayer is a mosaic of earlier biblical phrases which had no doubt been absorbed into liturgical patterns and so were thoroughly familiar to Nehemiah. He need not, therefore, have been particularly conscious of their specific origin. The predominance of Deuteronomic language is here an indication of the widespread and pervasive influence of Deuteronomy, especially in lay circles, in the post-exilic period, rather than an indication of its peculiar importance for Nehemiah personally.

The closest parallels elsewhere in the OT are as follows: v 5—Deut 7:9, 21; 10:17; Dan 9:4. This latter verse is almost identical, indicative of the stereotyped language of prayer; v 6—see the liturgical references listed in *Form* above; v 7—Deut 6:1; v 8—Deut 4:27; 28:64; v 9—Deut 30:1–4; 12:5 etc; v 10—Deut 9:29; Exod 32:11. In addition, many more minor parallels, such as the linking of "the commandments, the statutes, and the ordinances" (v 7), are listed by Ryle.

5 "There is more than rhetoric in this elaborate opening. It deliberately postpones the cry for help, which could otherwise be faithless and self-pitying. It mounts immediately to *heaven* (as the Lord's prayer does), where the perspective will be right, and it reflects on the character of God" (Kidner). The "awe-inspiring" aspect of God's character, together with the reminder at the end of the verse of his demand for love and obedience, leads Nehemiah into confession, while consciousness of God's covenant faithfulness will enable him later to move to petition on the basis of earlier promises. Overarching all is the title "God of heaven," with its suggestion of great power to implement God's purposes towards his people.

6a It was normal to appeal to God in this way for a hearing. The superficially curious juxtapositioning of "eyes" and "hearing" provides a fully intelligible metaphor, known also from 1 Kgs 8:52.

6b–7 Nehemiah's confession is extremely general, the phraseology of v 7 amounting to a comprehensive summary of the whole law. Yet he is explicit in admitting his family's and his own personal responsibility, as had Ezra before him (cf. Ezra 9:6). The expression "I and my father's house have sinned" in no way implies that Nehemiah was a member of the Davidic royal family (so Kellermann, *Nehemia*, 157), as Tob 3:3 shows. See further *Comment* on 2:3 and 6:6 below.

8–10 In moving forward toward the first element in his petition, Nehemiah is conscious that the exile and the continuing depressed conditions in which the Jews now find themselves are evidence that God had already fulfilled his word to punish the people's persistent sin. (The words for "great trouble and disgrace" in v 3 are perhaps suggestive of a typological broadening of what is understood as "exile" to cover many other situations of distress.) In line with the Deuteronomic theodicy, Nehemiah therefore sees these conditions as tokens of God's power, not of his weakness. Therefore, he pleads, God is equally able, now that he and the people generally (v 10) are showing signs of repentance, to restore their fortunes.

It has been argued that this petition is inappropriate in the context because it speaks of return from exile whereas the prevailing situation (v 3) is of distress among those who have already returned. This argument overlooks two factors, however. First, vv 8–9 are not themselves petition. They are a promise indicating that God will change his attitude toward his people when they repent. Nehemiah applies the underlying theology, rather than the letter of the promise, in his implied petition in v 10. There, he brings the people before God with the reminder that God has formerly redeemed them, and then leaves God to draw his own conclusions, so to speak. Second, it is probable that Nehemiah would in any case have believed that far more was involved in the promise of v 9 than simple movement from exile to Jerusalem. Implicit in the promise is restoration; a return "to the place which [God had] chosen as a dwelling place for [his] Name" implies the Divine Presence dwelling with the restored community. It is precisely that, according to Nehemiah, which the currently prevailing conditions show yet to lie in the future.

11a Nehemiah's second petition is for his own success as he prepares for an audience with the king. Presumably, the prayer as a whole represents a summary of all that Nehemiah might have prayed over several months. It is thus not inappropriate to include at its end a petition that looks forward to the specific events of chap. 2. We need not suppose that this too was repeated "night and day" (v 6).

The petition is quite generally expressed. Nehemiah was no doubt aware that if he was to have any success, Artaxerxes would need to overturn his previous decree (Ezra 4:21); to make such a request could be highly dangerous, even for a royal favorite (cf. Esth 4:11–16). He therefore wisely refrains from determining his approach in advance, but leaves God to open the way in an appropriate manner. The sequel shows with what boldness Nehemiah was to move once he saw that opening made.

Much has been made of the expression "this man" as a way of referring to the king. Does it betray Jewish disdain for a pagan monarch (Rudolph)? Is it even legal terminology, indicating that Nehemiah's memoir was drafted as the case for his defense when he was accused of disloyalty to the Persians (Kellermann, *Nehemia*, 85–86)? Such speculations are unnecessary. As the memoir was written, Nehemiah could no doubt vividly recall his apprehension as he took wine to the king (2:1) and he simply reproduced the otherwise quite neutral words which, both in the historical setting and later, came most naturally to his mind. "Neh. i.11 is used of the Persian king in a context in which reference to an opponent in a lawsuit is inappropriate. The context is a prayer to God that the king will grant Nehemiah's request, and it appears in the narrative describing how Nehemiah approached the king" (J. A. Emerton, review of Kellermann's *Nehemia*, *JTS* ns 23 [1972] 175).

Finally, there is no problem in the fact that "this man" has no antecedent. Rather, an effective narrative crescendo is achieved as "this man" is identified later in the verse as "the king," and in the next verse is further identified as Artaxerxes. The reader's developing awareness of just how precarious Nehemiah's situation was successfully carries him forward into the next episode of the narrative.

11b The parenthetical explanation that Nehemiah was "the king's cupbearer" not only builds up the reader's anticipation of the reference to Artaxerxes in the next verse (see above), but also, with the greatest economy of words, tells us all we need to know in preparation for the following scene. We at once understand Nehemiah's access to the king and his status at court.

Royal cupbearers in antiquity, in addition to their skill in selecting and serving wine and their duty in tasting it as proof against poison, were also expected to be convivial and tactful companions to the king. Being much in his confidence, they could thus wield considerable influence by way of informal counsel and discussion. Texts and pictures from many Ancient Near Eastern sources (including Achaemenid) supporting this statement have been helpfully collected by Yamauchi, *ZAW* 92 (1980) 132–42. The portrayal fits admirably with the sequel in chap. 2. It may be noted also that the office of cupbearer could be combined with other important offices. Cf. Tob 1:22: "Now Ahikar was cupbearer, keeper of the signet, and in charge of administration of the accounts, for Esarhaddon had appointed him second to himself."

Beyond this, however, many scholars have claimed that Nehemiah was a eunuch, and support for this is found in LXX[B,S], which here read εὐνοῦχος "eunuch." This, however, is clearly no more than a scribal error for οἰνοχόος "cupbearer," attested by LXX[A]. The various other arguments in favor of the theory are examined by Yamauchi, and none is found to be convincing. For instance, although there is evidence that some cupbearers of the period were eunuchs, there is equally strong textual evidence to show that not all were by any means. Similarly, reference to the queen in 2:6 does not prove that Nehemiah must have been a eunuch, for in the book of Esther, where eunuchs are explicitly referred to, Haman, who was the king's chief minister and had access also to the queen, was certainly not a eunuch (cf. Esth 7:8). Moreover, texts from both Assyrian and Achaemenid times distinguish between cupbearers and eunuchs and outline how those at court who were not eunuchs should behave in the presence of women and even in the harem.

As well as the complete silence of the text on Nehemiah's condition as a eunuch, there are a few considerations which actually militate against such a supposition. For instance, despite Isa 56:4–5, it is most unlikely, in view of Deut 23:2 (1), that as a eunuch Nehemiah would have been accepted as a Jewish leader, and one who undertook various cultic reforms at that. As Ackroyd observes, "since Nehemiah's opponents are shown as making all manner of attacks on him, we might have expected there to be some reference to this which could well have discredited him in the eyes of some members of his own community." Thus, while the possibility that Nehemiah was a eunuch must be held open in view of the lack of completely compelling evidence to the contrary, it is very improbable that in fact he was, and recent commentators are rightly cautious in this regard (e.g., Ackroyd, Coggins, Michaeli, North, Kellermann, *Nehemia,* 154–55). It follows from this conclusion that Nehemiah need not have written his memoir as a memorial to his name in place of children.

Explanation

When we are first introduced to Nehemiah as cupbearer to Artaxerxes, there is no indication whatever that he had ever previously thought of relinquishing his comparatively exalted status in order to throw in his lot with his fellow Jews in the remote and insignificant Jerusalem.

As presented in the biblical narrative, the news of a catastrophe which has recently overtaken that city reaches him almost accidentally. The effect of this news on Nehemiah is so overwhelming that it can only be described as a sudden realization that God was calling him to a radically new sphere of service, for which, all unknowing, his position and training had uniquely equipped him. Only thus can we explain the determined purpose which now overtakes him, the strong sense of identity with his people, evident in his prayer, and the durability which he will later show in the face of stiff opposition. These are the marks of a true divine vocation, seen in their fullness in the ministry of Jesus Christ himself, but known too in humble and exalted spheres alike by all who enter the service of God in whatever capacity.

Nehemiah first answers his vocation not with action, but, as is right, with prayer—and prayer lasting some four months at that! This period of waiting upon God is not to be regarded as a sign of weakness on his part. From the later narrative we know that he was a dynamic man of action. But if a true vocation has been received to serve God, such a testing time of waiting is often to be expected; prayer during such a period will be an indication of whether the call has been genuine and whether commitment to it is unwavering.

Beyond this, it should be remembered that it was vital to the success of Nehemiah's mission that he approach the king at the right time. Wisely, therefore, he awaited an indication that it was God's time for him to move. Meanwhile, he had faith to pray not only for a restoration of his people's fortunes, based on his knowledge of God's covenant mercies, but also for the specific reversal of the king's previous edict (compare v 11 with Ezra 4:17–22). There is the sense that success here would finally· seal his vocation and so afford his later activities that sense of purpose from which he never wavered.

Nehemiah's Commission   (Neh 2:1-10)

Bibliography

Alt, A. "Judas Nachbarn zur Zeit Nehemias." *KS* 2, 338–45. **In der Smitten, W. Th.** "Erwägungen zu Nehemias Davidizität." *JSJ* 5 (1974) 41–48. **Jepsen, A.** "Pardes." *ZDPV* 74 (1958) 64–68. **Kellermann, U.** *Nehemia*, 11–13, 156–59, 166–70. **Mazar, B.** "The Tobiads," *IEJ* 7 (1957) 137–45, 229–38. **McCown, C. C.** "The ʿAraq el-Emir and the Tobiads." *BA* 20 (1957) 63–76. **Torrey, C. C.** "Sanballat 'The Horonite.' " *JBL* 47 (1928) 380–89.

Translation

[1] *In the month of Nisan of the twentieth year of Artaxerxes the king* [a]*when wine was before him,* [a] *I took the wine and gave it to the king.* [b] *Now I had not previously appeared sad in his presence,* [b] [2] *and so the king asked me, "Why do you look so sad? You're not ill, are you? This is nothing but sadness of heart!" Then I was much afraid,* [3] *but I replied to the king, "May the king live* [a] *for ever! How can I help looking sad* [b] *when the city, where my ancestors' graves are, lies in ruins and its gates have been destroyed by fire?"*

[4] *The king then said to me, "What is it that you want?" So I prayed to the God of heaven* [5] *and said to the king, "If it pleases your majesty and if your servant has found favor before you, that you would send me to Judah, to the city where my ancestors' graves are, so that I may rebuild it."*

[6] *Then, with the queen consort sitting beside him, the king asked me, "How long would your journey last, and when would you return?" Thus it pleased the king to send me,* [a]*when I had told him how long I should be.* [a]

[7] *I also said to the king, "If it pleases your majesty, let letters be given* [a] *me addressed to the governors of Beyond the River so that they grant me a safe conduct until I reach Judah,* [8] *and a letter too for Asaph, the keeper of the king's park, so that he may supply me with timber to make beams for the gates of the temple fortress, for the city wall, and for the residence which I shall occupy."* [a] *The king granted my requests, according to* [b] *the good hand of my God upon me.*

[9] *Then I came to the governors of Beyond the River and delivered the king's letters to them. The king had sent army officers and cavalry to accompany me.*

[10] *When Sanballat the Horonite and Tobiah the Ammonite servant heard about this, they were extremely annoyed that someone had come to promote the welfare of the Israelites.*

Notes

1.a–a. A circumstantial clause in further definition of the preceding date. LXX introduces the clause with καί "and" (and cf. Vg *et al.*). Many commentators therefore wish to restore a *wāw* before ייך "wine," explaining its loss as haplogr before the *yōd.* Though the meaning is unaffected, this is not strictly necessary, however, as nominal circumstantial clauses are not infrequently attached without the copula; cf. GKC § 156c. Such a clipped style would not be

inappropriate for the third phrase of the introductory temporal statement. "Before him" (לְפָנָיו)
is also frequently emended on the basis of LXX and Syr. to לְפָנַי; lit., "before me" (e.g., "when
I had charge of the wine," Myers). It is argued that MT must be at fault since Nehemiah does
not bring the wine until later in the verse, and the error is explained as a dittogr. The objection
to MT is not cogent, however; the clause merely defines the general occasion on which Nehemiah
appeared before the king; cf. Ryle: "the Hebrew text gives with great minuteness the full circumstances of the event: (1) the month and year; (2) the time of day, at the dinner; (3) the stage
at the dinner, when the cupbearer offered the king wine. It distinguishes between 'wine . . .
before him,' the occasion of the repast, and 'I took up . . . the wine,' the act of presenting
the royal cup." In addition, לְפָנַי, "before me," is not a natural way of saying "when I had
charge of"; the passages Rudolph cites in his support (Num 8:22; 1 Sam 3:1; 1 Chr 24:6) all
refer to people serving "in the presence of" other people, and so are not exact parallels. For
implications of this for the background understanding of the passage, see *Comment* below.

1.b–b. MT, "And I was not sad before him," which is clearly out of keeping with the following
verse. Equally, however, the use there of רַע in the sense of "sad" rules out such translations
of this phrase as "I was not out of favor with him" (Batten). Furthermore, the Vrs which omit
the negative (or regard it as asseverative; cf. Myers) are most likely to be explained as later
attempts to ease the difficulty. It is better to follow Bertholet in restoring לְפָנִים "formerly."
He, however, proposes this as a correction of לְפָנָיו "before him; in his presence." The whole
clause reads more easily if we postulate that both words were originally present, and that one
was accidentally omitted because of similarity to its neighbor. Note that in some forms of Hebrew
script, the use of ligatures makes the letters ם and יו look extremely alike; cf. R. Weiss, *Studies
in the Text and Language of the Bible* (Heb.; Jerusalem: Magnes, 1981), 14–16.

3.a. It is unlikely that the impf of a *lamedh he* verb in this position should be distinguished
from the more usual juss; cf. GKC § 109a². Despite Syr. and Vg, it hardly seems necessary to
emend to the imperative חְיֵה, as proposed by Joüon, *Bib* 12 (1931) 85–86; they are probably
just imitating the common formula found frequently in Dan. P. A. H. de Boer, "Vive le Roi!,"
VT 5 (1955) 225–31, by contrast, argues that the juss in the common parallel expression יְחִי הַמֶּלֶךְ
should be taken as indicative.

3.b. Lit., "why should I not look sad?" For the vocalization of the verb, cf. GKC § 67dd.

6.a–a. Lit., "and I set (gave) him a time," but the logic of the sentence presupposes the
translation supplied; cf. Keil. In view of the king's questions in the first half of the verse, there
is no need to follow Syr. with its "he set me a time."

7.a. Impers pl for pass.

8.a. It is unnecessary to emend with Joüon, *Bib* 12 (1931) 86, to אֶבְנֶה לִי "and for the
house which I shall build." MT poses no serious difficulty as it stands; see further *Comment*
below.

8.b. Cf. *Notes* on Ezra 7:6b.

Form/Structure/Setting

The date in 2:1 indicates the start of a new paragraph. It has already
been seen in the comments on 1:11, however, that an effective literary join
has been achieved between these two chapters. There is therefore no need
to attempt to reconstruct a further join on the basis of Josephus, as Mowinckel,
Studien II, 19–20, does.

Although Neh 2 has a certain unity in its continuous narrative, a division
is indicated in v 10 by reference to the initial reaction of Nehemiah's enemies.
They are clearly an important element in the memoir as a whole, as is seen
by the fact that when they are mentioned Nehemiah often recalls his prayers
at the time or appeals directly to God as he looks back over his achievements.
Thus Neh 2 is neatly divided into two by reference to these enemies in vv
10 and 19–20. This conclusion is reinforced by the observation that vv 10
and 19 both begin with identical wording; see also *Form* on 3:33 and 4:1
(4:1 and 7).

Occasional voices have been raised against the originality to the NM of vv 6–9a and 10, but they have failed to convince the majority; contextual considerations adequately account for most of the supposed difficulties (cf. Kellermann, *Nehemia*, 11–13). Arguments based on the vocabulary and phraseology of the passage carry little weight, since part of the evidence is more probably to be explained as influence from Nehemiah on a later editor (see *Form* on Ezra 7:1–10). The only serious remaining difficulty is v 6b; see *Comment* below.

The main part of the paragraph consists of Nehemiah's conversation with the king. In realistic fashion, the king is portrayed as direct in his approach and yet totally relaxed, initially displeased at an apparent breach of etiquette (v 2), but then almost carelessly pleased to gratify a court favorite. Meanwhile Nehemiah, for his part, is initially fearful, subservient in his speech until sure of his ground (vv 2–6) and exceedingly careful in his choice of words in the opening exchanges. Once his basic request is granted, however, his more natural forthright boldness shines through as he presses home his advantage with the king (vv 7–8) and moves directly on to record the execution of the first requirements of his new commission (v 9).

Comment

1 For the date, see *Form*, 1:1–11. "When wine was before him" simply means on an occasion, such as a banquet, when wine was served; cf. Esth 7:2; 1 Esdr 3; and Herodotus 9:110–11 for some examples. This seemingly curious mode of expression is used in order to provide a smooth connection of thought into the subsequent narrative: following 1:11b, it leads the reader to expect Nehemiah's encounter with the king.

Adoption of the LXX reading (cf. *Notes* above) has led many commentators to suppose that this was the first time since Hanani's visit, some four months previously, that Nehemiah had appeared before the king, perhaps because the latter had been away, or because of some rota system. But there is no indication of this in the text, and, as Ryle says, "it does not seem likely that a cupbearer, who enjoyed the favor of the king, should have appeared so rarely in his presence as this view supposes." If, on the other hand, we retain MT, as in the translation above, then (the restored) "previously" later on in the verse may refer specifically to the period since Hanani's visit. Despite his prayer and fasting, Nehemiah had hitherto "kept up appearances" when attending the king. Now he allowed his emotions to show through. Was this by design? It is just possible that the date—Nisan, the start of the new year— is a hint that it was. Herodotus (9:110) speaks of a custom of the Persian king showing particular generosity at a certain feast in the year. He describes it as "the law of the feast, which required that no one who asked a boon that day at the king's board should be denied his request." The feast is said to be "in celebration of the king's birthday," but it is not impossible that it was held at the start of the new year, or that a similar practice was in effect on other occasions; cf. Esth 2:18; 5:6; 1 Esdr 5:6 with 4:42, and, more remotely, Mark 6:22–23; see also Kellermann, *Nehemia*, 151–52. One may at least ask, therefore, whether Nehemiah did not choose his moment with considerable care.

2 Even if this were the case (and much more so if not), Nehemiah was conscious that he was exposing himself to considerable danger. Artaxerxes would not lightly revoke his previous decree (Ezra 4:21), while a gloomy appearance, as well as lack of courtesy, might well be interpreted as evidence of plotting against the king. The king's initial probing questions suggest such a suspicion on his part, making Nehemiah's fear understandable enough.

3 Nehemiah's respectful reply carefully leaves the initiative for a second time with the king. It could be taken as a sufficient answer to the king's question or could open the way for a further inquiry, as in fact happened. Behind his cautious approach may lie a desire to determine whether this is also God's time for action.

Nehemiah admits that Artaxerxes has correctly analyzed his frame of mind, but explains its cause in a way most likely to elicit the king's sympathy. Respect for ancestral tombs was universal in the Ancient Near East, and especially among the nobility and royalty. At the same time he avoids a direct reference to Jerusalem or to its walls, either of which might have been immediately counterproductive in recalling the correspondence of Ezra 4.

The expression here and in v 5 has been taken by Kellermann, *Nehemia*, 156–59, as an indication that Nehemiah came not just from an old and probably wealthy (cf. v 8 and chap. 5) Judean family, but from a branch of the royal, Davidic family. However, it must be observed in reply, with J. A. Emerton, review of Kellermann's *Nehemiah*, *JTS* ns 23 (1972) 177, and In der Smitten, *JSJ* 5 (1974) 41–48, that it is not a necessary inference from the text that the graves were inside the city walls. We have already seen that Nehemiah was guided by other circumstances to refer to his ancestors' graves, while the unparalleled form of expression (lit., "house of the graves of my fathers") may also be due to Nehemiah's apologetic concern. In the case of Cyrus, the Achaemenid royal tomb was very much in the design of a house (cf. Galling and In der Smitten; for a full description, cf. D. Stronach, *Pasargadae* [Oxford: Clarendon, 1978] 24–43). Darius and several of the later kings including Artaxerxes were, it is true, buried in a rock tomb at Naqš-i-Rustam, but even here the façade was carved with a representation of the palace portico (cf. Olmstead, *History*, 228).

4–5 The king's open invitation for Nehemiah to state his request marks the turning point in the conversation. From now on it is Nehemiah who takes the initiative, not just by spelling out his basic concern, but also by pressing on uninvited to request all the material and moral support he needs.

Conscious of this turning point, Nehemiah gathers up in a flash his prayers of the past months (note the link by way of the title "the God of heaven" with 1.4 and 5) and simultaneously (the division between vv 4 and 5 is unfortunate) presents his petition to his earthly lord. The implications of his initial statement—to rebuild the city—will be filled out subsequently (v 8). A statement of principle is enough for this opening request.

6 This verse raises three problems: why is the queen suddenly referred to; how seriously were the king's questions meant to be taken; and is the last clause a later gloss?

"The queen consort" (cf. NEB) is an attempt in translation to retain something of the ambiguity of the Hebrew שֵׁגַל, Aramaic שֵׁגַל. Though it occurs rarely, enough is known to suggest that it is not the straightforward equivalent of "queen" (מלכה). Ps 45:10 (9) shows that she may stand in a category apart from the women of the harem, and this is supported by the distinction in Dan 5 between women of this class and "concubines" (לחנה). There, however, the word is nevertheless used in the plural, so that again "queen" would be misleading. (Note that in Dan 5:10 מלכה apparently refers to the queen mother.) Evidently there is a certain flexibility in the word's use, leaving us with no certain basis on which to decide whether the reference here (singular with the definite article) is to Artaxerxes' legitimate queen, Damaspia, or to some personal favorite from the harem.

At all events, her presence at this scene indicates that it was probably an intimate and private occasion; it would have been unusual for her to appear at a public banquet (cf. Esth 1, but contrast Dan 5; cf. Bowman for supporting references in classical sources). We may then understand this reference in one of several ways. (1) Most commentators hold that Nehemiah was a favorite of hers, and that she was therefore supporting him in his request. It is frequently observed that feminine influence was strong during Artaxerxes' reign (cf. W. W. Tarn, "Xerxes and His Successors: Artaxerxes I and Darius II," in *CAH* 6, 2–3) and the suggestion of prior agreement is advanced by some. Needless to say, even this extreme theory does not oblige us to conclude that Nehemiah was a eunuch (see *Comment* on 1:11b). (2) It is possible, with Batten, to hold that "the suppliant sees in her presence an obstacle to his plans." The king might have been distracted by her, but in spite of this and as a further token of God's grace towards him, Nehemiah is heard out to the end. (3) Since direct evidence in support of either of these views is lacking, a third possibility may be suggested, namely, that the phrase is intended to signify a shift of scene from a public banquet (see *Comment* on v 1) to a more private occasion. The latter would be the appropriate setting in which to discuss the details of an agreement made previously in principle. However, for the sake of thematic continuity Nehemiah chose not to spell this out more fully when, much later on, he wrote his account.

It has been suggested that the king's questions were no more than playful jibes at a favorite courtier, in which case no response would be called for. This in turn leads to the suggestion that the final clause of the verse is a gloss, added by a later scribe who misunderstood the point of the questions.

This is an improbable interpretation, however. The whole scene is recounted with maximum economy; it is unlikely that Nehemiah would have retained purely inconsequential remarks in his account. If the suggestion made above about a change of scene is correct, then this argument is reinforced still further. There is no suggestion, moreover, that Nehemiah is here being appointed as governor of Judah. Rather, he is requesting permission to undertake a specific task, and it is therefore not unreasonable that an agreement should be reached about the time involved (cf. Kellermann, *Nehemia*, 11–12, *contra* Mowinckel, *Studien II*, 20–21). Quite clearly a comparatively short time is envisaged, certainly not the twelve years of Nehemiah's first term as governor (cf. 5:14). This must be linked with internal considerations of content when seeking to understand the original purpose and setting of the NM; cf. *Introduction*, "The Nehemiah Memoir."

7 Now that Nehemiah is sure of his ground, he presses on uninvited with further requests. First, he needs letters to the various regional officials serving under the satrap of "Beyond the River"; see *Comment* on Ezra 4:9–10 and 5:3. As the remainder of the book shows, they could often act as "a law unto themselves," so that Nehemiah not unreasonably required some assurance of safe conduct. Schneider suggests that an example of the kind of letter involved has been preserved for us in *AD* 6, though it must be emphasized that not all the circumstances are by any means the same. Perhaps the escort mentioned in v 9 was also arranged at this stage.

8 Nehemiah's second request is for supplies of timber for the work to be undertaken. This again required an authorizing letter to the responsible official (cf. Ezra 7:21–24; 8:36), whom Nehemiah already knew by name: "Asaph, the keeper of the king's park." This latter word, פרדם, is a Persian loan-word, occurring otherwise only at Cant 4:13, where trees are also mentioned in the context, and Eccl 2:5. The context clearly indicates that it here refers to the royal domain or estates.

The location of the king's park is disputed. Some immediately think of Lebanon, since supplies of timber for the first and second temples had come from there. However, Asaph's (Jewish) name is suggestive of a setting more local to Judah. Thus the coastal plain referred to as having timber in 1 Chr 27:28 is suggested, or alternatively some unknown site nearer Jerusalem (cf. Hag 1:8 and Josephus, *Ant* 8:186). Jepsen, *ZDPV* 74 (1958) 64–68, hazards the more specific proposal that the name is preserved in the modern *dschebel ferdēs*, a district around Herodium which, he maintains, could have supported timber growing in antiquity. Clearly, certainty is unattainable without fuller evidence, especially as much larger areas of Palestine were forested then than now; cf. B. S. J. Isserlin, "Ancient Forests in Palestine: Some Archaeological Indications," *PEQ* 86 (1955) 87–88.

The timber was required for three specific projects. First, it was needed "for the gates of the temple fortress," which receives its earliest mention here, but whose existence at this time is confirmed by 7:2. Little is known about it at this stage, but it is to be regarded as a forerunner of the later "Antonia" fortress, built by Herod the Great on the north side of his reconstructed temple (and cf. 1 Macc 13:52). Its purpose was to guard that vulnerable approach to the temple mount, and so it was doubtless located within the city walls. Bowman thinks that the Tower of Hananel and perhaps the Tower of the Hundred (3:1) were part of it.

Second, timber was required for the city wall, which, tactfully, had not previously been brought into the conversation. In particular, it would be necessary for the wall's gates and towers, the remainder of the construction being largely of stone (cf. 3:33–38 [4:1–6]).

Finally, Nehemiah speaks of his own residence. There is no need to think here of a completely new building, especially if at this stage he was not contemplating an extended stay. On the assumption that Nehemiah came from a Judean family of some means with property in the province (see *Comment* on 5:10, 14, 17–18), the repair to an existing house would be a reasonable concern. There is no need to assume that Nehemiah did not also consult with Hanani (1:2) about private family affairs in Jerusalem, so that he would have known what the requirements were.

For the attribution of the granting of these requests to "the good hand of my God upon me," see *Comment* on Ezra 7:6.

9 No details of the journey are recorded, only the carrying out of the plans just described. The second half of the verse is an excellent example of the use of "dischronologized narrative" (cf. W. J. Martin, " 'Dischronologized' Narrative in the Old Testament," VTSup 17 [1969] 179–86) for heightened narrative effect. Chronologically, of course, it belongs with v 7, but Nehemiah holds back the reference to this point in order to give an almost cynical, but utterly characteristic, comment on the delivery of letters requesting safe conduct. To suggest that the intervening material must therefore be a later addition is to betray a woeful lack of literary sensitivity.

10 The paragraph ends with the first ominous note of the opposition which Nehemiah will have to face time and again. That religious as well as purely political opposition is involved is suggested by the rather ponderous and certainly uncharacteristic use of the old, association-laden expression בני ישראל, lit., "sons of Israel," for the inhabitants of Judah.

Two opponents are mentioned here, and a third will be added in v 19. The first, "Sanballat the Horonite," appears to have been the prime mover against Nehemiah. His name is Babylonian—*Sin-uballiṭ*, "Sin (the moon god) gives life"; cf. its spelling in *AramP* 30:29, סנאבלט. (For the probable identity of these two, cf. *Form*, 1:1–11.) This, however, tells us nothing of his origins, status or faith (cf. Zerubbabel!). Of the latter we know little, except that he gave his sons Yahwistic names (Delaiah and Shelemiah, *AramP* 30:29), suggesting that he regarded himself, at any rate, as an adherent to the Israelite cult.

According to the Elephantine papyri, he was the governor of Samaria (פחת שמרין) in 408 B.C., but was apparently elderly by then, as his sons were acting for him. Since Nehemiah never credits him with this title, we cannot be sure that he had risen to that status as early as 445 B.C. His approach to Nehemiah in Neh 6, however, appears to be that of one equal to another, so that the probability is that he was already governor. Indeed, if he was acting in some sort of "caretaker" capacity over Judah—perhaps after the death or removal of Nehemiah's predecessor following the events of Ezra 4—his jealousy from the outset would be more easily explained.

Instead of giving him a title, Nehemiah regularly calls him "the Horonite," a designation of uncertain significance. The main proposals are (a) that he came from, or was a resident in, either upper or lower Beth-Horon (Josh 16:3 and 5), some miles north of Jerusalem. This is probably the majority view (cf. Rowley, "Sanballat," 246; Rudolph, who observes that analogy with הפלטי, "the Paltite" [2 Sam 23:26], generally assumed to come from בית פלט "house of Pelet" [Josh 15:27], shows that Sanballat would not need to be styled בית החרני "house of the Horonite"; Torrey, *JBL* 47 [1928] 380–89, as part of an otherwise rather unconvincing theory). It has been argued against this view that we expect some term of abuse here to parallel that for Tobiah and to explain why Nehemiah preferred this designation to that of "governor of Samaria." Both points carry some weight, but are not sufficiently conclusive to eliminate this possibility altogether. (b) In order to answer these last two points, other scholars (most recently Kellermann, *Nehemia*, 167) link the name with Horonaim in Moab (cf. Isa 15:5; Jer 48:3). This would make Sanballat a Moabite, just as Tobiah is an Ammonite, thereby excluding both from "the assembly of God"; cf. Neh 13:1–3 with Deut 23:4–7 (3–6). Nehemiah's action in 13:28 also implies that he was of foreign origin, although for Nehemiah that might have applied to any non-Judahite. This proposal has obvious attractions, but fails to explain why Sanballat was not simply styled "the Moabite." Would contemporary readers have readily understood the allusion? Neither of these two suggestions is therefore free of difficulty, so that it is not possible in the present state of our knowledge to decide between them. (c) Either, however, is preferable to the other suggestions that have been advanced, such as revocalizing to הַחָרָנִי and so linking Sanballat with Harran in Mesopotamia, a center for the worship of the god Sin (cf. S. Feigin, "Etymological Notes," *AJSL* 43 [1926–27] 58, and Galling), associating him with Hawan, east of Galilee (*BMAP*, 107–8) or even that he was a devotee of the god Horon. (This last view is erroneously attributed by several commentators to J. Gray, "The Canaanite God Horon," *JNES* 8 [1949] 27–34. In fact Gray only collected evidence about this deity, and I am unable to determine who first suggested the association with Sanballat.)

"Tobiah the Ammonite servant" has frequently been linked with the influential Trans-Jordanian Tobiad family known from later times. It is then argued that he was in fact governor of Ammon, and that Nehemiah plays on the ambiguity of עֶבֶד, "servant," which can be used for an important official, but which Nehemiah means pejoratively; cf. Alt, *KS* 2, 338–45; McCown, *BA* 20 (1957) 63–76; Mazar, *IEJ* 7 (1957) 137–45, 229–38; Bowman; Myers, etc.

Rudolph, and Kellermann, *Nehemia*, 167–70, rightly point to difficulties which suggest that an alternative solution should be sought. First, were the majority view correct, we should certainly have expected עֶבֶד to be used in the construct state before "Ammon," rather than with "Ammonite" as its adjective. Second, in 3:35 (4:3) Tobiah is simply called "the Ammonite." This shows that the adjective is indeed intended to describe his origin (parallel with "Sanballat the Horonite"), and not just his sphere of activity. Third, we have no direct evidence that there existed a separate province of Ammon at this time, and even if it did it would be curious to find that its governor had such close ties with certain circles in Jerusalem, as the sequel shows he had, and difficult to explain the motive for his involvement in the opposition to Nehemiah. Finally, it should be remembered that the name itself is a common one, and that Mazar's attempt to link this Tobiah with the one whose name is carved twice in the scarp of the rock façade of a cave-tomb at ʿAraq el-Emir in Trans-Jordan must now be discounted on paleographic grounds; cf. J. Naveh, *The Development of the Aramaic Script* (Jerusalem: The Israel Academy of Sciences and Humanities, 1970) 62–64.

It therefore seems preferable to see in Tobiah a junior colleague of Sanballat; "the servant" can equally well be explained as an ironical play on the word's ambiguity according to this view. "The Ammonite" will then indeed relate to his ancestry, while his Yahwistic name in such a setting poses no difficulty. The description is certainly meant pejoratively by Nehemiah in the light of Deut 23:4 (23:3), and contrasts, of course, with "the sons of

Israel" (see above) at the end of the verse. Finally, we should note Kellermann's further suggestion that he is to be equated with the Tabeel of Ezra
4:7. (The Aramaic form of the name there is to be explained by its setting
in a letter in Aramaic, and does not therefore militate against Kellermann's
suggestion, *pace* W. Th. In der Smitten, "Nehemias Parteigänger," *BO* 29
[1972] 155–57.) He appears there as some kind of official from Samaria;
perhaps, therefore, after the forcible stopping of the building work in Jerusalem (Ezra 4:23), he was appointed to temporary authority in Judah under
the jurisdiction of Samaria until the next full governor should be appointed.
This is, of course, a pure guess, but it does account well for his involvement
with Sanballat and for his close associations with Jerusalem; see especially
Comment on 6:10–13 and 17–19.

Explanation

Practically all that takes place in this paragraph has already been covered
by the prayer of chap. 1. Consequently, we find Nehemiah moving with a
certain confidence through the various stages which bring him to Jerusalem
(contrast vv 11–20).

This confidence is seen first, paradoxically, in his willingness to wait for
God's time to answer his prayer. Those months of private intercession must
have been a peculiarly testing time for so active a man as Nehemiah, but
for him to have forced the issue with the king could have proved disastrous
to his whole enterprise. Instead, he shows that his confidence is supremely
in God. Thus, although there is the suggestion in the opening verses of
the chapter that Nehemiah gave the king a "lever" to open his inquiry, he
nevertheless is diffident and ambiguous in his initial response, presumably
to ensure that this was indeed the right time to act.

Second, as soon as he realizes that it is, Nehemiah is confident enough
to ask in a forthright manner for exactly what he wants and needs. It is
evident that he has thought all this out in some detail during the previous
months, so that he is able to fix a timetable and to know just what provision
he will require.

Finally, because his confidence is in God, he has no hesitation in accepting
all that the king offers both materially and by way of protection for the journey.
(Contrast Ezra's embarrassment at Ezra 8:22.) Recognizing that ultimately
all was due to God's "good hand" upon him in response to his prayer, he
did not reject on pseudo-pietistic grounds the human channels through which
God chose to make good his supply.

The whole paragraph is thus a model of the balance that needs to be
maintained between the total sovereignty of God, with prayer as its proper
response, and human responsibility with its counterpart in wise and thoughtful
activity. In the practicalities of the situation, Nehemiah appears unaware of
any clash between these two, for he needed to know the truth of both if he
was to make any substantial progress.

Nehemiah's First Steps in Jerusalem
(Neh 2:11-20)

Bibliography

Adan, D. "The 'Fountain of Siloam' and 'Solomon's Pool' in First Century C. E. Jerusalem." *IEJ* 29 (1979) 92–100. **Alt, A.** "Das Taltor von Jerusalem." *KS* 3, 326–47. **Avi-Yonah, M.** "The Newly-Found Wall of Jerusalem and Its Topographical Significance." *IEJ* 21 (1971) 168–69. ———. "The Walls of Nehemiah—a Minimalist View." *IEJ* 4 (1954) 239–48. **Braslavi, J.** "En-Tannin (Neh. 2:13)" (Heb.). *EI* 10 (1971) 90–93. **Burrows, M.** "Nehemiah's Tour of Inspection." *BASOR* 64 (1936) 11–21. **Cross, F. M.** "Geshem the Arabian, Enemy of Nehemiah." *BA* 18 (1955) 46–47. **Dumbrell, W. J.** "The Tell el-Maskhuta Bowls and the 'Kingdom' of Qedar in the Persian Period." *BASOR* 203 (1971) 33–44. **Heller, J.** "Die abgeschlagene Mauer." *CV* 11 (1968) 175–78. **In der Smitten, W. Th.** "Nehemias Parteigänger." *BO* 29 (1972) 155–57. **Kaupel, H.** "Der Sinn von הַמְּלָאכָה עֹשֶׂה in Neh 2, 16." *Bib* 21 (1940) 40–44. **Kenyon, K. M.** *Digging up Jerusalem.* London and Tonbridge: Benn, 1974. **LaSor, W. S.** "Jerusalem." *ISBE* 2, 998–1032. **Rabinowitz, I.** "Aramaic Inscriptions of the Fifth Century B.C.E. from a North-Arab Shrine in Egypt." *JNES* 15 (1956) 1–9. **van Selms, A.** "The Origin of the Name Tyropoeon in Jerusalem." *ZAW* 91 (1979) 170–76. **Simons, J.** *Jerusalem in the Old Testament.* Leiden: Brill, 1952. **Ussishkin, D.** "The Original Length of the Siloam Tunnel in Jerusalem." *Levant* 8 (1976) 82–95. **Wilkinson, J.** "The Pool of Siloam." *Levant* 10 (1978) 116–25. **Williamson, H. G. M.** "Nehemiah's Wall Revisited." *PEQ* 116 (1984) 81–88.

Translation

[11] *After I had reached Jerusalem and had been there for three days,* [12] *I set out by night, taking only a few men with me and without having told anyone what my God was prompting me* [a] *to do for Jerusalem. Moreover I took no animal with me except the one which I myself was riding on.* [13] *I went out through the Valley Gate by night, past* [a] *the Dragon Spring and as far as the Dung Gate. As I went* [b] *I inspected* [c] *the wall* [d] *of Jerusalem which had breaches there* [e] *and whose gates had been destroyed by fire.* [14] *I passed on to the Spring Gate and to the King's Pool, but then there was no room for the animal which I was riding* [a] *to pass.* [15] *So I went up the valley (instead)* [a] *by night and inspected the wall before turning back* [b] *and re-entering through the Valley Gate; so I returned.*

[16] *Now the officials did not know where I had gone or what I was doing; I had not yet told the Jews, the priests, the nobles, the officials, or the rest of the administration.* [a] [17] *So I said to them, "You can see the plight which we are in—how Jerusalem is in ruins and its gates are burned with fire. Come, let us rebuild the wall of Jerusalem, so that we are no longer an object of reproach."* [18] *Then I told them about how good the hand of my God had been upon me and also what the king had said to me. "Let us start to rebuild," they replied, and thus they encouraged themselves in preparation for the good work.* [a]

[19] *When Sanballat the Horonite and Tobiah the Ammonite servant and Geshem* [a] *the Arabian heard about it, they jeered at us with contempt. "What's this you are*

up to?" they asked; "are you in rebellion against the king?" [20] I answered them by saying, "The God of heaven will give us success. We, his servants, will start to rebuild; but you have no share, right, or traditional claim in Jerusalem."

Notes

12.a. So NEB; lit., "what my God was putting (pres ptcp) in my heart." For parallels, cf. von Rad, "Die Nehemia-Denkschrift," ZAW 76 (1964) 176–87.

13.a. Or, "in the direction of," depending on the location of the Dragon Spring (see Comment below) and with אֶל־פְּנֵי understood as equivalent to עַל־פְּנֵי. The prep אֶל־פְּנֵי normally means "in front of," so that without further evidence we should assume that Nehemiah passed "in front of" the spring. (The wāw before the prep precludes the suggestion that it was the Valley Gate which stood opposite or in front of the spring.) Alternatively, the preposition may be being used eliptically for "to a point on the wall opposite the Dragon Spring"; cf. Burrows, BASOR 64 (1936) 13–14, following Dalman.

13.b. These words are used in translation in order to catch the syntactical sense of the circumstantial clause which follows.

13.c. This verb, used only here and in v 15, is probably not to be associated with the more common שבר, used in the piel for "wait, hope." Its general sense is clear from the context, however, and is supported by most of the Vrs. (LXX's συντρίβων cannot be right, but is nevertheless valuable as a witness to the consonants of the MT.) The etymology of the word is uncertain; for alternative suggestions, cf. Rudolph (following Gesenius) and G. R. Driver, "Studies in the Vocabulary of the Old Testament VII," JTS 35 (1934) 382–83. A completely different approach is taken by Heller, CV 11 (1968) 175–78. He notes the textual evidence in favor of pointing שָׁבַר, and then links it with the use of this verb in some other passages to mean "breaking down" cultically defiled objects. He therefore conjectures that the breaches in the wall had had notices inserted in them, warning people not to pass under threat of divine judgment ("amulettartige Warnungen, die im Namen Jahwes denen mit dem Bann gedroht haben, die die Mauerlücken betreten würden"). Later, the word was reread as שׂבר for pietistic reasons. This intriguing suggestion is unlikely to be correct, however. While it would explain Nehemiah's initial furtiveness, we would have expected some allusion to what he had done in the meeting that followed (contrast the complaints in Judg 6:25–32) or elsewhere in the context. Second, it is only in the piel that שבר carries the particular meaning that Heller wants, whereas here it is clearly qal, and in the qal שבר is never followed by the prep ב to introduce the direct, definite object. Nehemiah's readers would therefore have been unlikely to detect the allusion that Heller finds here. Finally, on Heller's view it is not really the wall that Nehemiah smashes—and indeed it would be hard to see how he could have done with so little help and without attracting attention. It is therefore curious that it is expressly the wall that is the obj of שבר.

13.d. Repoint to sing חוֹמַת with LXX, Vg, and some MSS (and cf. 1:3 and v 15 following) in the light of the following.

13.e. Both K, הַמְפוֹרָצִים "which had been breached," and Q הֵם פְּרוּצִים "they had been breached," are extremely difficult because they are masc whereas their antecedent ("walls") is invariably fem. An additional difficulty for K is that the relative אשר preceding is redundant. It is easiest with many modern commentators to adopt Klostermann's emendation שם פרצים "breaches there." MT may then be explained as a partial corr under the influence of 1:3, and its pl pointing of "walls" (see n. 13.d. above) as being made necessary by the pl form of the resulting corr.

14.a. Lit., "under me."

15.a. For this explanatory addition, cf. Burrows, BASOR 64 (1936) 19–20.

15.b. The use of שוב here is ambiguous. It can either mean "and I turned back and entered by the Valley Gate," as translated above, or be used, as often, as a verbal hendiadys, which we might render "before reentering through the Valley Gate." It is thus not immediately clear whether Nehemiah completed the circuit of the walls or turned back the way he had come when the going became too hard; cf. Comment below.

16.a. Cf. 1 Chr 29:6; Dan 8:27; Esth 3:9 and 9:3, which suggest that this phrase can refer to civil administration (Kaupel, Bib 21 [1940] 40–44). The use of יתר "rest" shows that this group should be in the same category as those preceding, and hence be officials of some kind.

To link מלאכה "work" here with the future work of wall-building is an unnecessary anticipation.

18.a. Lit., "and they strengthened their hands for the good." The exact meaning is not quite clear. Many commentators think that "they began this good work" (NIV), but the following two verses are suggestive rather of preparation only.

19.a. In 6:6 the same name is spelled "Gashmu." The latter is closer to the postulated original form Gušamu, the final vowel representing the nomin case ending. After this was dropped in Heb., the resulting consonantal cluster was resolved, as so often, by a segholate formation.

Form/Structure/Setting

There is no good reason to doubt that the literary setting of this paragraph is within the NM or that its historical setting is that which it most naturally appears to be—the immediate sequel to Nehemiah's arrival in Jerusalem. The arguments of the tiny minority who challenge this consensus rest in large measure on faulty exegesis (for one example see n. 16.a. above). Most recently, Kellermann, *Nehemia*, 13, has added stylistic considerations in favor of this conclusion. Nor is it necessary (e.g., with Mowinckel, *Studien II*, 22–23) to argue that material that can be restored by appeal to Josephus has been lost between vv 16 and 17; it may be conceded that Nehemiah's narrative is terse here, but then so is it generally in his memoir: only the bare essentials are recounted. Within that limitation, however, the sequence of events is clear enough, and he no doubt relied on his readers' imagination to supply matters of prosaic detail.

The paragraph is in three sections: Nehemiah's secret investigation of the task confronting him (vv 11–15), his invitation to his fellow-citizens to cooperate with him in rebuilding the wall (vv 16–18), and a further comment about the opposition. The conclusion is thus parallel to that of the first half of the chapter. If this factor invites further comparison with 2:1–10, it will be noted that there is a contrast in Nehemiah's approach. We saw there that he was able to move with considerable confidence because all that transpired was covered by his earlier prayer. Now, however, he is entering unknown territory, and it will be seen that his approach is one of considerably greater caution.

Comment

11 For a rest of three days after the journey to Jerusalem, see *Comment* on Ezra 8:32. Nehemiah may have had certain formalities to dispense during this period and may have also needed to attend to his family's affairs (on the assumption that he already had interests in Jerusalem; see *Comment* on chap. 5) and to familiarize himself with the general situation (not least political) in the city.

12 It is not difficult to understand Nehemiah's concern for secrecy as he first turned his attention to the question of the wall that had been destroyed. He would have known of the opposition that led to its destruction (Ezra 4) and was doubtless aware that Sanballat and Tobiah had allies in the city who would quickly report on his movements. Until he gauged the size of the problem, decided how to tackle it, and was ready to start, he did not want to stir up trouble which would pose difficulties enough at any stage of the work, as the sequel shows, but which would be most threatening of all to the project before the work had begun. One by-product of this concern is a passage of exceptionally enthralling narrative.

The need to work "by night" was self-evident, whatever practical difficulties it posed. As Rudolph parenthetically observes, it is to be hoped that it was at least a moonlit night. The "few men" who accompanied him must have been privy to his plans, so perhaps they were members of his household, those resident in Jerusalem who could act as guides and those who had accompanied him from Babylon whom he could trust for counsel. The one animal he allowed himself was doubtless a donkey or mule—surefooted and generally silent.

13–15 The identification of the places that Nehemiah names here has long been the subject of lively debate. The passage cannot be studied in isolation, but has to be linked with the data of chaps. 3 and 12, where considerably more detail is supplied about the walls and gates of Jerusalem.

As well as disagreement about the location or identification of the individual places referred to, there is a more fundamental dispute about the whole size and shape of Jerusalem at this time. In the late pre-exilic period, the city had already spread from the eastern hill, the "City of David," to the western hill (confusingly known today as Mount Zion). There is debate, however, whether the whole area was included in the restored city of the post-exilic period, or whether habitation (or at least fortification) was again restricted to the eastern hill. This in turn will fundamentally affect our estimation of the line of the wall that Nehemiah's wall followed. In the former case, the "Valley Gate" would be located to the south of the western hill (cf. 3:13); in the latter case, it would be located some way up the western side of the eastern hill, overlooking the central valley. (This is generally known, following Josephus, as the Tyropoeon Valley, on which see A. van Selms, *ZAW* 91 [1979] 170–76.)

Since a full discussion of this issue would outstrip the confines of the present commentary, it has been necessary to devote a special study to it; cf. *PEQ* 116 (1984) 81–88. It is there concluded, on the basis of a wide variety of evidence, that Nehemiah's city did not include the Western hill, but was restricted to the eastern ridge alone, together with the Temple Mount to its north. This conclusion is presupposed in the following discussion as well as at chaps. 3 and 12.

13 Nehemiah went out of the city through the Valley Gate. On our understanding, this is to be placed overlooking the Tyropoeon Valley, 1000 cubits from the Dung Gate (cf. 3:13). A gate at about this spot was found by J. W. Crowfoot in 1927; cf. J. W. Crowfoot and G. M. Fitzgerald, *Excavations in the Tyropoeon Valley, Jerusalem, 1927* (London: APEF for 1927, 1929) 12–23. Its date is uncertain, but it could come from Nehemiah's time; cf. Kenyon, *Digging up Jerusalem,* 194–95. Even if it does not, it is at least evidence that a gate at this point is eminently reasonable.

The next reference is to "the Dragon Spring" or well, which is mentioned nowhere else. This has most frequently been identified with En-rogel (modern *Bîr Ayyûb,* "Job's Well"), some 210 meters south of the confluence of the

Hinnom and Kidron Valleys. It is then suggested that Nehemiah went "toward, in the direction of" this well or spring. This explanation is most implausible, however. We already know from the mention of the Dung Gate in which direction Nehemiah was heading, and it is in any case most unlikely that he would indicate his direction by a landmark so far off. Nor can it mean "that he passed the wall at a point opposite the well" (Bowman), because En-Rogel lies (south-) east of the Dung Gate. It is far more probable that it was a spring or well along the east side of the Tyropoeon Valley between the two gates mentioned and that it has since dried up and been forgotten (see also n. 13.a.). Was it perhaps linked in some way with the overflow from the Pool of Siloam? Indeed, Braslavi, *EI* 10 (1971) 90–93, has even suggested that it was Siloam itself, which acquired increasing importance as the city's main water supply when Gihon, from which it is fed through Hezekiah's tunnel, became more difficult to reach because of the destruction on the eastern side of the city. This suggestion, of course, would provide further evidence against an identification of the King's pool with the pool of Siloam in the next verse. Alternatively, as LaSor reminds us (*ISBE* 2, 998–1032), the phrase could legitimately be translated "the Dragon's Eye," and so refer to some landmark other than a spring or well.

"The Dung Gate," it is generally agreed, was at the extreme southern end of the City of David, allowing rubbish and refuse to be dumped into the valley below. It is usually identified with the Potsherd Gate of Jer 19:2. The final clause of the verse suggests by its construction (auxiliary verb and participle) that Nehemiah was inspecting the wall all the way along between the two gates.

14 Nehemiah passed on next "to the Spring Gate and to the King's Pool." We assume that the Spring Gate was a gate leading to a spring of water. Since Gihon is ruled out by its association with "the water gate on the East" (3:26), it is most likely En-Rogel that is in question. Its location (see *Comment* on v 13 above) is suitable for a gate near the southeastern corner of the city, where we assume Nehemiah now to be after the Dung Gate. The need for this gate quite close to the Dung Gate was determined by the incompatibility of their respective functions.

The location of the King's Pool is more difficult to resolve, and no agreement about it exists at present. First, some believe that it is the Pool of Siloam at the end of Hezekiah's tunnel. On this view, Nehemiah must have gone inside the city through the Spring Gate in order to inspect the southwestern section of the wall from the inside. (Kenyon, *Digging up Jerusalem,* 181, followed by Kidner, seems to think that Nehemiah passed by the Pool of Siloam on the outside, but this seems impossible in view of its occurrence in the description after the Spring Gate.) Alt, *KS* 3, 326–47 thinks that he then went straight back to the Valley Gate along the inside of this wall. This is difficult to accept, however, because it would involve נחל "the valley" of v 15, being the Tyropoeon Valley, whereas it elsewhere always refers to the Kidron Valley. To accommodate this latter point, it would be necessary to suppose that Nehemiah came back out through the Spring Gate and so on up the Kidron Valley (van Selms, *ZAW* 91 [1979] 170–76), but of this there is no hint in the text.

Similar problems attend the attempts to relate the King's Pool to the modern Birket el Ḥamra which, according to Wilkinson, *Levant* 10 (1978) 116–
25, may well have been the site of the original "Pool of Shiloah," the receiving
pool for the water of the pre-Hezekian hillside channel from Gihon down
the Kidron Valley (see further *Comment* on 3:15).

We expect, then, on the basis of the textual evidence, a pool outside the
walls in the Kidron Valley near the Spring Gate. The existence of such a
pool has been conjectured for several—and not always compatible—reasons;
see especially Simons, *Jerusalem in the Old Testament*, 192–93; Ussishkin, *Levant*
8 (1976) 82–95; Wilkinson, *Levant* 10 (1978) 116–25. It is thought that there
must have been a pool to catch the overflow from the Pool of Siloam, which
is channeled out in that direction (Ussishkin, indeed, believes that this was
an integral part of Hezekiah's tunnel), and that such a conjecture would best
explain Josephus' reference to a "Pool of Solomon" in the same area. The
names suggest that they could well refer (at an interval of several centuries)
to the same pool. Most recently, parts of a plastered pool have been discovered
on this very spot, measuring just over 18 meters in length (the width could
not be determined); cf. Adan, *IEJ* 29 (1979) 92–100. The present pool is
certainly dated by its associated pottery to the first Christian century, and
is an excellent candidate for Josephus' "Pool of Solomon." However, since
it appears to have been fed from the much older water system, it raises the
possibility that it replaced an older pool on approximately the same site.
While at present this remains hypothetical, it seems to present the most satisfactory explanation of "the King's Pool." Its name may have derived originally
from its association with the nearby "King's Garden."

We must suppose, therefore, that when he reached the Spring Gate, Nehemiah was obliged by either the steepness of the hillside or by the rubble to
leave the exact line of the wall and to move slightly downhill into the valley;
hence his reference to the King's Pool. Thereafter, as he tried to move north-
ward, the conditions became even worse, so that he had to start picking his
way over the rubble on foot. Kenyon, *Digging up Jerusalem*, 182, corroborates
this hypothesis.

15 Instead of following the line of the wall, as before, Nehemiah now
had to move along the valley floor itself, some way below (see n. 15.a. above).
How far he went in this northerly direction up the Kidron is not stated. No
doubt he soon realized that it would take too long to attempt to rebuild
this section of the wall, and that time would be saved by marking out a
new line along the crest of the ridge (see *Comment* on 3:16–31).

The Hebrew text is not altogether clear as to what happened next (see
Notes). Nehemiah could have gone on to complete the circuit of the walls.
Those who hold this view argue that the northern and northwestern parts
were not so badly damaged, and thus Nehemiah did not deal with them
here in such detail.

It must be said, however, that the lack of any reference whatsoever tells
heavily against this view. If it had been Nehemiah's intention to go right
around, he may have been forced to change his plans because of the danger
of proceeding in the dark in the evidently appalling conditions along the
eastern side. More probably, however, he had accomplished his purpose once

he reached this point. He could already have discovered a good deal about the state of the wall in such public areas as the northern part of the city without attracting any undue attention during the preceding days. What he could not do secretly, however, was to inspect the state of the terracing that was so vital to the previous line of the wall along this east side. That had to be done at night in order to maintain secrecy; in the light of his survey he could then draw up plans, which, as noted, were quite radical for this part of the city. Only then would he be ready to reveal his hand to his fellow-citizens.

16–18 No indication is given of how soon after Nehemiah's nocturnal inspection he shared his plans with the inhabitants of Jerusalem. In view of the curiosity and consequent rumors which his arrival may have stimulated, it is likely that he proceeded with all possible haste.

16 Despite its appearance later in the verse, סגנים, "officials," is a sufficiently flexible word to stand at the start of the verse as a general term for the leaders of the community; see *Comment* on Ezra 9:2 and J. van der Ploeg, "Les Chefs du Peuple d'Israel et Leurs Titres," *RB* 57 (1950) 51–52. "The Jews" refers to the population at large; cf. 3:33–34 (4:1–2). There is no need to restrict it to the leaders who are enumerated in the following list.

"The priests," we know, assumed an increasingly significant role in the administration of Judah in the post-exilic period, especially as large parts of the small province's economy were dominated by the temple. The next two groups, "nobles" and "officials," can scarcely be distinguished on the basis of our present knowledge; indeed, comparison of 13:11 with 13:17 and of 5:7 suggests the similarity, if not identicalness, of their roles. The usage in Neh 13, together with the continuation here ("the rest of the administration"), indicates that for Nehemiah the titles refer to function rather than nobility, whereas the latter aspect—in continuation of pre-exilic usage—is more prominent in Neh 5. Kellermann's attempt, *Nehemia,* 161, to limit "the nobles" to local leadership of the cultic community and "officials" to administrative officials of the Persian empire, is thus somewhat speculative.

17 As Nehemiah now shares his plans with his fellow-Jews, he first describes their plight in terms identical with those used in 1:3. The impact upon his own life of the news received on that occasion was so great that he expects it to have a similar effect on others. As Kidner points out, his perspective on their situation is significant: "it is the *disgrace,* not the insecurity of their position, which strikes him." The word "reproach" (חרפה), in particular, is heavy with overtones of the punishment of the exile, behind which lies the disrepute brought upon God's name among the nations by those who should have been his servants.

18 Man of forceful action though he was, Nehemiah's correct perspective is seen here again as he points first to God's favor as the cause for their change in fortune (cf. 2:8 and Ezra 7:6), and only secondly to the king as God's instrument. The people's united and eager response to his words must have been taken by Nehemiah as a further confirmation of his vocation.

19 The section ends with another note about opposition. The speed both here and later on with which Nehemiah's opponents reacted to events in Jerusalem suggests that they had sympathizers there who kept them informed

of developments. From initial displeasure (v 10), they turn to scorn and ridicule with just a hint of political accusation against Nehemiah, both of which
tactics are taken a good deal further in subsequent chapters. It should be
noted in particular here that for many of the inhabitants of Jerusalem the
charge of "rebellion against the king" had resulted not long before (Ezra
4) in the prevention by force of their attempts to rebuild the walls. Even
though the force of the jibe may have been lost on Nehemiah, Sanballat
and his colleagues no doubt reckoned that a reminder of the earlier debacle
would be sufficient to dissuade many from supporting him in his renewed
attempt.

To Sanballat and Tobiah (cf. v 10) the name of a third enemy is added,
"Geshem the Arabian." The occurrence of his name on a silver vessel dedicated by his son Qainū to the goddess Han-ʾIlat and found at Tell el-Maskhūṭa
in Lower Egypt, together with a probable reference to him in a Liḥyanite
inscription found at Arabian Dedan testifies to the very extensive power this
monarch wielded (he is styled "king of Qēdār"); cf. Rabinowitz, *JNES* 15
(1956) 1–9, and Cross, *BA* 18 (1955) 46–47. This conclusion is reinforced
by Dumbrell's provisional account of Qedarite history in the Persian period;
BASOR 203 (1971) 33–44: "Her confederate or allied peoples were distributed
from the Syrian desert to North Arabia and were found in the Persian period
to the south of Palestine and in the Delta region" (p. 44). While nominally
under Persian control, the geographical sphere of Geshem's influence is such
that he probably enjoyed a substantial measure of *de facto* independence.
He thus posed a severe threat to Judah from the south and east. The reasons
for his hostile attitude towards Nehemiah are not fully clear, for it is unlikely
that he had the personal vested interest in the affair which we have postulated
for Sanballat and Tobiah (see v 10 above). It is thus no surprise to find
him mentioned less frequently than the other two. Though Nehemiah could
not possibly have posed any significant threat to his authority, he may have
been unhappy at the prospect of a strengthening of Persian influence in a
neighboring province.

20 Rather than retaliating in like fashion, Nehemiah merely states his
confidence in God's power to give him success. By his use of the title "the
God of heaven," he points us back to his earlier prayers (cf. 1:5; 2:4), and
so demonstrates whence he believes his ultimate authority derives.

The concluding words of the chapter give the impression of deriving from
legal terminology. "Share" refers to a physical stake in the nation. Its use
in some other passages for a division of land is inappropriate here; rather,
it is used more metaphorically, as when, in declaring a rebellion, someone
might say that he no longer had any "share" in the nation as presently constituted (cf. Brockington's reference to 2 Sam 20:1 and 1 Kgs 12:16). "Right"
may refer to legal rights either within or over the province. The former would
be another way of denying any form of citizenship, while the latter would
discount any authority that Sanballat and Tobiah, in particular, may have
wished to exercise. Finally, we come to the difficult word זִכָּרוֹן, "traditional
claim"; for the variety of possible meanings, cf. *TDOT* 4, 77–79. Its frequent
association with the cult has led some to think of a specific act in the temple
commemorating the leaders' sovereignty. More probably in the present con-

text it refers to a denial of the right of participation in the cult generally; cf. Ezra 4:3. On this understanding, Nehemiah is denying to his opponents civic, legal, and cultic rights in the Jerusalem community. His emphasis, however, is positive: come what may, "we . . . will start to rebuild."

Explanation

In the discussion of the first half of this chapter, it was suggested that Nehemiah acted with a confidence based on the fact that his dealings with the king had been prepared for by the prayer of chap. 1. The second half of this chapter provides a complete contrast with this: Nehemiah has now moved into the unforeseen, and his activity is marked accordingly by a greater reserve and diffidence.

His first recorded activity on arrival in Jerusalem is therefore to take a hard look at the difficulties of the task in hand in order to make a realistic appraisal of its demands. This he does secretly, in the privacy of the night. There is something affecting about this man of action, so assured of his vocation, nevertheless refraining from speaking of his proposals until he has engaged physically with the enormity of the task and no doubt prayerfully counted the cost of proceeding; cf. Luke 9:57–62; 14:28–32.

In the second paragraph of this section (vv 16–18), Nehemiah's approach to his people is comparable. He does not simply announce what he intends doing, nor force his own will on his audience. Rather, with the emphasis firmly laid on theological considerations, as explained in *Comment* above, he invites the people's participation in the fulfillment of God's call. He even uses language identical with that which had so touched him at the first (compare v 17 with 1:3). The remarkable unanimity of the people's response will have served as confirmation that he was on the right path. Similarly in the Church, it is to be expected as a general rule that an individual vocation to whatever task will be acknowledged by the community of faith at large; cf. Acts 13:1–2.

Finally, even in his dealings with his opponents, Nehemiah responds to their jibes not with rash retaliation but with a firm expression of God's ability to prosper his cause. Rather than being deflected from his primary task, he asserts positively that "We, his servants, will start to rebuild" (v 20). At this early stage, he is content to leave God with responsibility for the negative handling of opposition. This, too, is one of the hardest lessons for any church or individual to learn; cf. Rom 12:19; 1 Pet 2:21–23; 4:19.

Rebuilding the Walls   (Neh 3:1–32)

Bibliography

Burrows, M. "Nehemiah 3:1–32 as a Source for the Topography of Ancient Jerusalem." *AASOR* 14 (1933–34) 115–40. **Cook, S. A.** "Notes on 1 Kings x.25; Neh. iii.19." *ExpTim* 10 (1898–99) 279–81. **Grafman, R.** "Nehemiah's 'Broad Wall.'" *IEJ* 24 (1974) 50–51. **Kellermann, U.** *Nehemia,* 14–17. **Kenyon, K. M.** *Digging up Jerusalem.* London and Tonbridge: Benn, 1974. **Mowinckel, S.** *Studien I,* 109–16. **Simons, J.** *Jerusalem in the Old Testament.* Leiden: Brill, 1952. **Tuland, C. G.** " ʿzb in Nehemiah 3:8. A Reconsideration of Maximalist and Minimalist Views." *AUSS* 5 (1967) 158–80. **Wilkinson, J.** "The Pool of Siloam." *Levant* 10 (1978) 116–25.

Translation

[1] *Then Eliashib the high priest and his fellow priests started to build the Sheep Gate. They boarded it [a] and set up its doors.* [b] *. . . and as far as the Tower of the Hundred; they consecrated it. . . . as far as the Tower of Hananel.* [b] [2] *And next to him [a] the men of Jericho built. And next to them [b] built Zaccur, son of Imri.* [3] *The sons of Hassenaah built the Fish Gate; they laid its beams and put its doors, bolts, and bars in place.* [4] *Next to them repaired Meremoth, son of Uriah, son of Hakkoz. Next to them [a] repaired Meshullam, son of Berechiah, son of Meshezabel. Next to them repaired Zadok, son of Baana.* [5] *Next to them the men of Tekoa repaired, but their nobles would not stoop [a] to serving their lord.* [b]

[6] *Joiada, son of Paseah, and Meshullam, son of Besodeiah, repaired the Mishneh Gate; [a] they laid its beams, and set its doors, bolts, and bars in place.* [7] *Next to them there repaired Melatiah the Gibeonite and Jadon the Meronothite with [a] the men of Gibeon and of Mizpah, the [b] seat of the governor of Beyond the River.* [8] *Next to them [a] Uzziel, son of Harhaiah, one of the [b] goldsmiths, repaired. Next to him Hananiah, one of the perfumers, repaired, and they left out (part of) [c] Jerusalem as far as the broad wall.* [9] *Next to them there repaired Rephaiah, son of Hur, ruler of half the district of Jerusalem.* [10] *Next to them Jedaiah, son of Harumaph, repaired opposite [a] his own house. And next to him Hattush, son of Hashabniah, repaired.* [11] *Malchiah, son of Harim, and Hasshub, son of Pahath-Moab, repaired a second section, including [a] the Tower of the Ovens.* [12] *Next to them [a] there repaired Shallum, son of Hallohesh, ruler of half the district of Jerusalem, he and his daughters together.*

[13] *Hanun and the inhabitants of Zanoah repaired the Valley Gate; they rebuilt it, and set its doors, bolts, and bars in place, and they repaired [a] a thousand cubits of the wall as far as the Dung [b] Gate.* [14] *Malchiah, son of Rechab, ruler of the district of Beth-hakkerem, repaired the Dung Gate; he rebuilt [a] it, and set its doors, bolts, and bars in place.* [15] *Shallun, [a] son of Col-hozeh, [b] the ruler of the district of Mizpah, repaired the Spring Gate; he rebuilt it, roofed it, and set [c] its doors, bolts, and bars in place. He also repaired [d] the wall of the Pool of Shelah of [e] the King's Garden, and as far as the steps which go down from the City of David.*

[16] *After him Nehemiah, son of Azbuk, ruler of half the district of Beth-zur, repaired*

to a point opposite the tombs of David, as far as the artificial pool and the House of the Warriors. ^a ¹⁷*After him the Levites repaired—Rehum, son of Bani, (and) next to him Hashabiah, ruler of half the district of Keilah, repaired on behalf of his district.* ¹⁸*After him their brethren repaired: Binnui,* ^a *son of Henadad, ruler of half the district of Keilah;* ¹⁹*and beside him Ezer, son of Jeshua, ruler of Mizpah, repaired a second section,* ^a*opposite the ascent to the armory by the buttress.* ^a ²⁰*After him Baruch, son of Zabbai,* ^a *repaired* ^b *a second section, from the buttress to the door of the house of Eliashib the high priest.* ²¹*After him Meremoth, son of Uriah, son of Hakkoz, repaired a second section, from the door of Eliashib's house to the end of Eliashib's house.*

²²*After him the priests from the surrounding region* ^a *repaired.* ²³*After them* ^a *Benjamin and Hasshub repaired opposite their own house. After them* ^a *Azariah, son of Maaseiah, son of Ananiah, repaired next to his house.* ²⁴*After him Binnui, son of Henadad, repaired a second section, from Azariah's house to the buttress and the corner.* ²⁵*(After him there repaired)* ^a *Palal, son of Uzai, from a point opposite the buttress and the upper* ^b *tower which projects from the king's house, and which belongs to the court of the guard. After him Pedaiah son of Parosh* ²⁶*and the temple servants who were living* ^a *on Ophel (repaired)* ^b *as far as a point opposite the Water Gate to the east and the projecting tower.* ²⁷*After them* ^a *the men of Tekoa repaired a second section, from a point opposite the great projecting tower to the wall of Ophel.* ²⁸*Above the Horse Gate the priests repaired, each one opposite his own house.* ²⁹*After them* ^a *Zadok, son of Immer, repaired opposite his house. And after him Shemaiah, son of Shecaniah, keeper of the East Gate, repaired.* ³⁰*After him* ^a *Hananiah, son of Shelemaiah, and Hanun, the sixth son of Zalaph, repaired a second* ^b *section. After them* ^c *Meshullam, son of Berechiah, repaired opposite his own room.* ³¹*After him* ^a *Malchiah, one of the goldsmiths,* ^b *repaired as far as the house of the temple servants and the merchants, opposite the Muster Gate, and as far as the upper room at the Corner.* ³²*And between the upper room at the Corner and the Sheep Gate the goldsmiths and the merchants repaired.*

Notes

1.a. This verse poses several textual difficulties which cannot be treated in complete isolation: the word קִדְּשׁוּהוּ "they consecrated it" occurs twice, and raises separate problems on each occurrence. Some have found the whole idea out of place, because it is not repeated anywhere else in the list and because it seems out of keeping with the later consecration of the whole wall in chap. 12. Neither objection is compelling, however: it is possible that the high priest conducted a representative consecration of his section which was not repeated elsewhere. Furthermore, in view of the originally independent composition of this list (see *Form* below), full consistency with Nehemiah's account is not necessarily to be expected, as the detail about the gates makes clear (contrast 6:1). Despite this, however, the word raises quite separate difficulties. On its first occurrence, it is mentioned between the building of the gate and the setting up of the doors. This is most unlikely, and in the parallel accounts relating to gates (vv 3, 6, 13, 14, 15) we find instead a verb dealing with some aspect of the construction. On the basis of vv 3 and 6, some commentators therefore emend to קֵרוּהוּ, "they laid its beams," since this is orthographically quite close to קִדְּשׁוּהוּ. Vv 13, 14, and 15, however, show that other verbs of similar meaning can also be used in this part of the formula, so that the suggestion of Ehrlich, *Randglossen* vii, 188, to read קֵרְשׁוּהוּ "they boarded it" is even more attractive. Though not attested elsewhere in the OT, it is postulated as a piel denominative of קֶרֶשׁ "board," just as קֵרָה is from קָרָה. The error may simply have arisen by confusion of the very similar letters ד and ר. Perhaps, however, a scribe's eye was deflected from הַמֵּאָה קֵרְשׁוּהוּ "they boarded it" to הַמֵּאָה קִדְּשׁוּהוּ "the Hundred, they consecrated it" later in the verse.

1.b-b. The second occurrence of קדשׁוהו also raises difficulties. Lit., the whole phrase reads, "And they consecrated it as far as the Tower of the Hundred as far as the Tower of Hananel." The masc suff, "it," would seem to refer to the Sheep Gate, but this makes for nonsense. It cannot refer to the wall, as might at first be supposed, because חומה is fem. In addition, "as far as the Tower of Hananel" lacks any connection with what precedes. It cannot be epexegetical of "the Tower of the Hundred," since 12:39 (where the towers occur in reverse order, appropriately for the direction of the procession there) shows that there were indeed two separate towers. Sense can be made of the MT only if "they built" is mentally repeated twice from the first half of the verse, the verbal suff then being made to refer to "the Tower" (Keil, and cf. NEB): "they built to the Tower of the Hundred; they consecrated it; and they built further, to the Tower of Hananel." This, however, is a most unlikely form of composition, and even then we would have expected the conj before קדשׁוהו and before the second עד "as far as." Finally, the most widely proposed emendation—to delete קדשׁוהו and add a wāw "and" to the second עד—is unconvincing; it does not explain how the present text arose, and it still leaves "and they built" to be supplied to complete the sense. A new approach is therefore demanded. It is surprising that none of the commentators has noted the evidence that suggests something may have been lost from the text at this point. (i) This is the only reference to the repair of a gate that does not have the words מנעוליו ובריחיו, "its bolts and bars," after דלתתיו, "its doors." (ii) Although the location of many of the places referred to in this list is uncertain, the section undertaken by the priests in the present form of this verse seems disproportionately large by comparison with the fact that two sections are mentioned in v 2 for rebuilding between the Tower of Hananel and the Fish Gate. (iii) The start of v 2, ועל-ידו, "And next to him," leads us to expect an individual as its antecedent, not a large group as at present. The list is usually careful to distinguish between sg and pl in this regard (and v 12 is probably not an exception to this; see notes *ad loc.*). This argument is not completely convincing, as the second half of v 2 shows (unless there has been further damage there), but it is at least a contributing factor. (iv) Although the list describes the complete circuit of the walls, it is agreed that some items have been lost from it (see *Form* below). It should therefore not surprise us to find traces of these losses. Since any reconstruction of the damaged text cannot be other than totally conjectural, it seems best to translate as above, indicating where there may have been a loss and simply suggesting that the name of one or more of those who are later told built a second section may originally have stood here. Alternatively, one or both of the two halves of v 2 may have been misplaced.

2.a. For the sg suff, see previous note. As the text stands, it refers to Eliashib. The phrase used throughout the first half of the list is literally "at his (their) hand," hence "beside," and so "next to" when occurring in a list such as this.

2.b. MT here has a sg suff, which can be variously explained: it may be collective, but that would be exceptional in this passage. It may testify to further textual loss, though there is no other evidence of this. Possibly, therefore, once the present form of vv 1–2a had developed, a scribe altered an originally pl suff under the impression from v 2a that this was the expected form.

4.a. The pl suff here and on several other occasions in the list suggests that the individual named before it was acting as head of a group, perhaps of his family. This makes the sg suff in v 2 stand out as all the more exceptional.

5.a. Lit., "did not bring their neck into the service of." The image is suggestive of pride (cf. "stiff-necked") rather than lack of enthusiasm. The apparently similar English idiom, "to put one's back into," would thus be an inappropriate rendering.

5.b. Pl of "majesty" (Rudolph), with reference, apparently, to Nehemiah; cf. Ezra 10:3.

6.a. "The Old Gate" is not an acceptable translation, because שׁער "gate" is masc, but ישׁנה is a fem form of the adj. Additionally שׁער lacks the def art, which would be grammatically impossible in such a construction. It must therefore be in the const. Many, therefore, regard ישׁנה as a proper name, "Jeshanah" being a town in the neighborhood of Bethel. The def art is then unexplained, however, and it would be odd to have a gate named after a relatively obscure town. Probably, therefore, we should make the very slight emendation to המשׁנה. A proposal that would, topographically, be of similar import would be to assume that this was "the Gate of the Old City," the word "city" (a fem noun) being understood (Brockington).

7.a. We must supply the conj (cf. Syr.); has a wāw been lost by haplogr after the yōd of the previous word? The phrase cannot be in apposition with what precedes (*contra* NIV), as it would be tautologous as regards Melatiah. Rather we are to understand that he led some of his fellow townsmen. By analogy, therefore, Meronoth must be somehow linked with Mizpah; perhaps it was a town in the district of Mizpah (cf. vv 15 and 19).

7.b. The use of the prep ל rules out the interpretation that they repaired "as far as the residence of the governor," because this list always uses עד for such a construction. We do not, therefore, have any evidence that the governor had a residence in Jerusalem. The phrase is intended, rather, to distinguish which of the several places called Mizpah is meant: "the Mizpah which pertains to the seat of . . ." See also *Notes* on Ezra 1:5.a. It is therefore no doubt the Mizpah mentioned in 2 Kgs 25:23 and Jer 40:5–12 as an administrative center after the fall of Jerusalem.

8.a. MT's sg suff refers to Melatiah as leader of the preceding group. Note that the verb in v 7 is also sg; cf. n. 12.a.

8.b. MT, "son of Harhaiah, goldsmiths." Since the name is found nowhere else, some wish to emend it to בן־חבר הצ׳, "one of the company of the goldsmiths." This represents quite a drastic and unattested emendation, however, while nowhere else in this list are members of guilds so introduced. It is simpler to restore בן־ח׳ after Harhaiah (cf. Syr.) to give the form of expression we expect (cf. vv 8b, 31). Perhaps it was lost after the similar בן־ח׳ that immediately precedes. Alternatively Cook, *ExpTim* 10 (1898–99) 279–81, suggests deleting חרהיה as an intrusive corr gl from vv 19–20 (cf. 19.b.), which he thinks stood in an adjacent column to this verse. This suggestion would restore a text exactly parallel with the following clause, and may find some support in the suggestion made at 10.a. below.

8.c. Lit., "abandoned." Since good sense can be made of this in the context (see *Comment* below), there is no need either to emend or, with the majority of commentators and modern translations, to think of any root other than the common עזב. The problem for all such approaches is that they fail to explain why the object is "Jerusalem" rather than "the wall." Although there are meanings close to that suggested here in languages cognate with Heb., it has yet to be established that they existed in Heb. too; see *Notes* on 3:34 (4:2) below. Since the usual meaning of the Heb. verb makes excellent sense here (cf. *Comment* below), there is in any case no need to look for a hypothetical alternative root; see also Tuland, *AUSS* 5 (1967) 158–80.

10.a. MT has the copula before נגד "and opposite." While this may be for emphasis, it should more probably be deleted with LXX^L and Vg. It is noteworthy, however, that this is the only occurrence of this phrase on the western side, whereas it is frequent on the eastern (cf. vv 23, 28–30). It is possible that it may have come in erroneously from there: if it was added in the margin as a correction to one column, it could have been mistakenly transferred to an adjacent one.

11.a. Ehrlich, *Randglossen* vii, 190, followed by Rudolph, prefers to delete the *wāw* and to take את as the prep "with," hence, "by," while LXX suggests reading ועד "and as far as." Since we have no way of knowing the precise relationship of the tower to the wall (it is mentioned elsewhere only at 12:38), it is impossible to decide. In such cases, it is prudent to keep close to the MT.

12.a. The sg suff of MT is again to be explained by the fact that Malchiah's prominence in the previous verse is emphasized by the use there of the verb in the sg; cf. v 8.a.

13.a. The verb is not expressed in the MT; it has to be understood as a continuation from the first part of the verse.

13.b. The next verse makes clear that this is the intended gate. MT, however, has השפות for the expected האשפות. There are several possible explanations for this: (i) it may be a simple scribal error; (ii) it may be a variant form arising from syncopation of the א with article; cf. GKC § 35d; (iii) it may be a euphemistic title, "the cheese gate" (Rudolph, who aptly compares Josephus' term, "the Tyropoeon Valley"; see also A. van Selms, *ZAW* 91 [1979] 170–76).

14.a. There is no need, with some earlier commentators, to emend with LXX "and his sons." The translators were no doubt confused by the surprising use of the impf tense here and in the next verse (*yaqtul concomitans;* cf. König, *Syntax* § 154) and so misread יבננו "he rebuilt it" (supported by בנוהו "they rebuilt it" in the equivalent position in v 13) as ובניו "and his sons." And this in turn obliged them to add a further verb after, for which they understandably turned to the similar formula earlier in the chapter.

15.a. This is the same name as Shallum, which is read by several Vrs and MSS.

15.b. I.e., "All-seeing" or "everyone a seer." It is clearly a family name that derives from a profession.

15.c. In K, this verb has a pl form. This is clearly anomalous, however, since all the other verbs in the verse are sg, as we would expect. The pl should not, therefore, be used as a basis for further emendation, but we should read the sg, ויעמיד, with Q.

15.d. Cf. n. 13.a.

15.e. The prep ל has a wide range of meaning. Its correct translation here ("of, by, at, towards") depends upon fuller knowledge of the topography than we possess; cf. *Comment*.

16.a. I.e., "barracks," unless reference is to the tombs of some heroes of the past.

18.a. MT should be emended slightly to בְּנָי; cf. v 24 and some Vrs and MSS.

19.a-a. The translation of this phrase is quite uncertain. The meaning of the individual words is disputed, and their syntactical relation to each other is not clear; compare, for example, NEB, "opposite the point at which the ascent meets the escarpment." "The Buttress" (cf. vv 20, 25, and 2 Chr 26:9), here construed as an accus of place, is distinguished from הפנה, "the Corner" (vv 24 and 31). Hence the usual translation—"the Angle"—may be misleading.

20.a. The MSS and Vrs are divided between reading Zabbai and Zaccai.

20.b. MT adds החרה, usually interpreted as "earnestly, zealously." This is not a legitimate meaning of the hiph of the verb ("to burn, be kindled, of anger"). It is better deleted either as a corr dittogr of אחריו, or as a misplaced and corr marginal gl (ההרה, "uphill") that originally referred to the last phrase of v 19; cf. Cook, *ExpTim* 10 (1898–99) 279–81.

22.a. הככר "surrounding region," which basically has to do with something round, has a wide range of meaning, and could even be the proper name of a district or area. In the lack of more specific evidence, 12:28 must be determinative for the present context, and there it is glossed with the words "round Jerusalem."

23.a. Sg suff. In fact, the prep אחרי is never used with a pl suff in this list, so that its usage is not to be set alongside that of על־יד in the first half of the chapter. Nor should we conclude that something has necessarily dropped out from the preceding verse which would supply a sg antecedent, as some have supposed.

25.a. The words in parentheses have to be supplied to make sense. Whether we should actually restore אחריו החזיק "after him there repaired" to the MT is less certain, though possible; note that החזיק is also missing later in the verse and cf. nn. 13.a. and 15.d.

25.b. Grammatically, this could qualify either "tower" or "the king's house." Those who take it with the latter explain that it was an alternative royal residence to "Solomon's palace" in pre-exilic times. However, it is difficult to see how this one could be called "upper," since we seem to be at a point still well south of the palace-temple complex.

26.a. MT has "And the temple servants were living on Ophel," which interrupts the definition of Pedaiah's section, and provides information quite gratuitous to the present context. Many commentators delete it altogether as a misplaced gl on v 27 from 11:21. However, the wording is not identical, and there is in any case no apparent reason for such a gl. Ehrlich, *Randglossen* vii, 190, neatly suggests joining the two words to read הישבים, as translated above.

26.b. Cf. 25.a. above.

27.a. Cf. 23.a.

29.a. Cf. 23.a.

30.a. K, "after me," cannot be right. With Q, many MSS, and the Vrs we must restore אחריו.

30.b. Read שנית.

30.c. Cf. n. 23.a.

31.a. Cf. 30.a.

31.b. Reading בן־הצרפים, lit. "son of the goldsmiths," an idiomatic way of expressing membership of a class.

Form/Structure/Setting

The list of those engaged in the rebuilding of the walls of Jerusalem moves section by section round the wall in a counter-clockwise direction, making a full circuit from and to the Sheep Gate (vv 1 and 32). There is variety among the descriptions of each section, but at their fullest they indicate the connection with the previous section, the names and associations of those engaged in the section, the starting and finishing point of the section along the wall, and any noteworthy items included in it. Despite general similarity, the variety is so great that no attempt to impose a greater uniformity on each element would be justified.

Although a complete circuit of the walls appears to be described, it is clear that the list has not been preserved in its entirety. A number of individuals or groups are said to have repaired "a second section." In some cases, their first section is mentioned earlier in the list (compare vv 21 and 4; 24 and 18; 27 and 5) but not always (cf. vv 11, 19, 20 and 30). This suggests that a reference to them earlier may have been lost, and independent evidence in support of such a conjecture was advanced in the *Notes* to v 1 above. (Others note that the Ephraim Gate is not mentioned here, though we expect it on the basis of 12:39, and so postulate a similar lacuna before v 8; this is less certain, however, as the commentary *ad loc.* points out.) Sections could easily be lost in the course of transmission by a scribe's eye jumping from one section to the next because of the identical wording with which they start. This probability that the list is not complete, despite appearances, should warn us against overconfidence in topographical conclusions based solely upon it.

In the first half of the list (vv 1–15) Burrows, *AASOR* 14 (1933–34) 115–40, has argued that "the workers fall into six groups, corresponding to the six gates which are rebuilt." The groups are vv 1–2, 3–5, 6–12, 13, 14, and 15. The first person or people mentioned were the leaders of the whole of the following section, which, Burrows suggests, helps to explain why the suffixes in the expression "next to him/them" do not always agree with their immediate antecedent. Similarly, only one "terminus" of the work is mentioned for each group, rather than for each separate section, as might otherwise be expected.

This ingenious proposal does not stand up to closer scrutiny, however. First, since vv 13, 14 and 15 have only one section each in any case, nothing can be based on them with regard to Burrows' theory. For the rest, Burrows has to admit that his theory does not, in fact, fully resolve the problems raised by the expression "next to him/them," and there are equally plausible alternative suggestions that might be preferred; see nn. 2.a. and 2.b. above. Finally, the strongest point that Burrows makes concerns the "terminus" of each group's work. However, the first group has two, not one, and the second has none at all. For the third, Burrows thinks there are two, whereas on the understanding represented in the translation above there is again none; neither understanding supports Burrows' theory.

We must therefore reject the suggestion that some of the sections are parts of larger groups. Each section represented in the text was an independent unit, joined to other units by geographical succession alone.

Burrows has made a much stronger case in favor of his division of the chapter into two halves. In vv 1–15 the sections are joined by the phrase עַל־יָד (lit., "at [his] hand") but in vv 16–32 by the preposition אַחֲרָיו, "after him." Similarly, the description of the rebuilding of the gates is confined to the first half. This raises the possibility that the list was originally composite, compiled from two separate sources or completed by a later writer. Intriguing hypotheses could be suggested. For instance, does the prominence of Eliashib (v 1) by comparison with Nehemiah's critical attitude to him in 13:4–9 indicate that the first half of the list is a relic of the record of the earlier wall-building (Ezra 4)?

In fact, however, Burrows is right to reject such a radical division and to hold to the list's essential unity. The references to some who undertook work on two different sections (see above) cut across the two halves of the chapter, which would be impossible if they referred to two separate occasions. Similarly, characteristic words and phrases, such as "ruler of half the district of" and החזיק "repaired," come in both halves, while even those who later fell foul of Nehemiah (by implication at least) occur in both halves; in addition to Eliashib (v 1), see *Comment* on Meshullam in v 30. The break in the pattern of description in the last verse, v 32, suggests that the writer was here consciously returning to his starting point. Finally, there is apparently neither geographical gap nor overlap between the two halves.

How, then, should the differences between the two halves be explained? Burrows thinks they are purely stylistic. It may be suggested, however, that a more convincing explanation can be found. The change in style comes at the very point where the description of the line of the wall begins to be carefully defined by reference to topographical features which are not part of the wall itself. This will be seen in the comments below to be the point where Nehemiah could no longer follow the line of the old wall, but had to strike out along a completely new line, higher up the ridge along the eastern side of the City of David. The compiler of the list may have used על־יד to mean "next to, along the line of an old wall" (for even where the immediately pre-exilic wall was not followed on the western side, we may presume that some earlier line was followed, either from much earlier days or from the efforts mentioned in Ezra 4) and אחריו to mean "after him" with reference to a completely new wall.

As far as the distribution of the gates is concerned, the same considerations will apply to some extent: clearly, on the eastern side there was no point in repairing earlier gates, since they no longer formed part of the new wall. Where gates are mentioned in these verses, it is for the purpose of identification, not because the gates themselves were being rebuilt.

It is generally agreed that Nehemiah did not originally compile this list. Its standpoint is that of the work completed, with the "doors, bolts, and bars" of the gates all in place. In the first person account by Nehemiah, however, the work is not completed until chap. 6, and even there it is explicitly stated that "at that time I had not yet hung the doors in the gates" (v 1: cf. 7:1). Second, the account is in the third person, whereas Nehemiah's account is always in the first person. Third, the use of אדירים, "nobles," contrasts with Nehemiah's own ways of referring to the local leaders; cf. 2:16. Finally, there is a probable reference to Nehemiah as "their lord" in v 5, which again contrasts with his style elsewhere.

This strong evidence for the independent origin of the list raises two questions with regard to its setting: the first is historical, for it relates to the setting of the list's composition; the second is literary, for we must ask whether Nehemiah used the list in his memoir, or whether it was inserted in its present position by a later editor.

Only very few scholars—principally Torrey, *Composition*, 37–38, and *Ezra Studies*, 225 and 249—have denied the historical authenticity of the list by making it the fictional creation of a later editor, but this extreme view has been rightly rejected by all recent writers. Nor, in view of the list's unity, can we attribute it to any other enterprise than the successful completion of the task under Nehemiah's leadership. The prominence given to Eliashib the high priest (v 1) suggests that the list was originally drawn up under priestly influence, and so is likely to have been preserved in the temple archives. It is of further interest to note the use of "their lord" in reference to Nehemiah (v 5). The same title was used for Ezra in 10:3 on the lips of one whose family had participated in the first return many years earlier (Ezra 2). An origin for our present list in the same circles is not unlikely. It may be suggested as a speculation that, in view of the prominence of Eliashib, and the reference to Meshullam, who was related by marriage to Tobiah (see *Comment* on v 30), the list may have been drawn up originally at the instigation of those who later became antagonistic to Nehemiah in an attempt to claim from him much of the credit for the successful completion of the task.

Opinion is more sharply divided over the question of when the list was given its present literary setting. The fullest case for regarding it as the work of a later editor is advanced by Mowinckel, *Studien I*, 109–16. His principal argument is that it interrupts the connection between 2:20 and 3:33 (4:1). He believes that 2:18 describes the start of the work, and that the theme then switches to the difficulties that the builders faced. 3:1–32 is thus an intrusion. Mowinckel further maintains that such an objective description of the wall-building serves no purpose in the NM. He also believes that Josephus had access to a copy of the memoir that did not yet include the list. He therefore attributes its inclusion to a very late stage of redaction. Mowinckel's general position is adopted by commentators such as Batten and Hölscher.

The alternative view is represented by Kellermann, *Nehemia*, 14–17, cf. Noth, *Studien*, 127; Rudolph; Galling; Schneider; Michaeli, etc. He maintains that it would be suitable for inclusion in the memoir because of the brilliant light it sheds on Nehemiah's organizational abilities. Furthermore, we know from 2:13–15 and 12:31–39 that Nehemiah could show great interest in the detail of Jerusalem's topography when it served to point up his achievements. Third, Kellermann maintains that without the list 2:20 and 3:33 (4:1) would not join smoothly but would rather present the reader with a jarring doublet. He accepts the view that the end of chap. 2 concentrates on the preparations for building, so that some account of the building itself is demanded by the context. 2:18 and 20 are hardly sufficient as descriptions of Nehemiah's most outstanding achievement. Finally, the pattern of initiative by Nehemiah followed by a negative response by the opposition can be maintained only if 3:1–32 was included in the original memoir.

It seems clear that a decision on this matter rests ultimately on the reader's opinion whether 3:33 (4:1) should be regarded as the direct continuation of 2:20. To the present writer, 2:18–20 appears to deal mainly with the preparations to build, and not with the start of the building proper, as Mowinckel maintains. In that case the immediate transition to 3:33 (4:1) would certainly be harsh without an intervening account of the building. Accepting the premise that Nehemiah had access to an independent record of the work (whose precise details he may not have been able to recall in their entirety later on), there seems, therefore, to be no good reason why he should not have made use of it at this point.

The topography of Jerusalem will be discussed in *Comment* below. It is worth here, however, reproducing the substance of Rudolph's careful observations on what this list reveals of the wider politico-geographical situation of the province of Judah at this period. See also fig. 1 below. He observes on the basis of the use of the word "ruler" that five administrative centers are mentioned: Jerusalem, Beth-hakkerem, Mizpah, Beth-zur, and Keilah. These are no doubt related to the administrative divisions of the province by the Persians, though we have no means of telling for sure whether there were others that are not included.

Thus although some other towns, such as Jericho, Tekoa and Gibeon, are mentioned independently, not too much should be made of the lack of reference to a town like Bethlehem; rather than indicating that its inhabitants refused to cooperate with Nehemiah, it may have included them in the district of Beth-hakkerem.

The evidence of place names further suggests that the southern boundary of the province ran between Beth-zur and Hebron, as established already by Nebuchadnezzar. Zanoah and Keilah indicate a boundary to the west which is roughly the same as that envisaged by Ezra 2 (though the Lod, Hadid, and Ono trio of Ezra 2:33 are not mentioned here; see also *Comment* on 6:2 below), while the inclusion of Jericho to the east points to the river Jordan as the natural border. Thus Rudolph estimates that the province was no more than 40–50 kilometers wide, less than half as large as the pre-exilic kingdom of Judah.

Finally, Rudolph observes that the Persians left the administrative leadership of the province in local hands, so far as the evidence of personal names goes, and that, as Meyer, *Entstehung*, 166–68, has observed, these leaders appear for the most part to come from families who had never been in exile (though a few reappear from the list in Ezra 2). Nehemiah's caution in chap. 2 is thus explained, and his success in winning such widespread support becomes all the more remarkable.

Comment

1 In the present form of the text this chapter is closely associated with the foregoing by the use of וַיִּבְנוּ . . . וַיָּקָם, lit., "and he arose . . . and they built," following the people's וּבָנִינוּ . . . נָקוּם, "let us arise and build," in 2:18. The initiative is taken here by "Eliashib the high priest," grandson of Jeshua (cf. 12:10–11). Later (13:28) Nehemiah was to clash with a member of his family for his association with Sanballat, and this suggests that there may have been deep-seated differences between the two men over the policy which should be adopted towards Judah's neighbors. This does not, however, make his presence in this list unduly harsh: Nehemiah came with the full backing of the court for his enterprise. His policy on other matters may not have been known yet—or, indeed, even formulated; it is reasonable to suppose

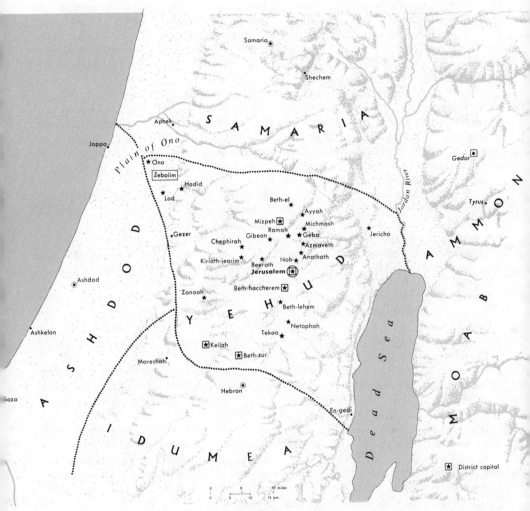

Fig. 1 The Post-exilic Province of Judah (After Aharoni and Avi-Yonah)

that the opposition he encountered may have had considerable influence on him.

"The Sheep Gate" (v 32; 12:39) was in the northeastern corner of the city wall (cf. its proximity to the pool of Bethesda in John 5:2), and probably derived its name from the sheep that were brought through it for sacrifice in the temple nearby. The interest of the priests in this section is thus self-evident. The emphasis on "building," rather than just "repair," in these opening verses is quite marked, and might suggest more extensive destruction along this vulnerable section than elsewhere. However, the fact that "repaired" is used also for the devastated eastern side later in the chapter shows that not too much weight should be put on the variation in vocabulary.

The text of the rest of this verse is poorly preserved (see *Notes*), and suggests that it may only be our ignorance which prevents us from passing a similar judgment on later parts of the list. 12:39 confirms, however, that there were two separate towers called "the Tower of the Hundred" and "the Tower of Hananel" along the northern wall. They are likely to have been related in some way to the temple fortress; see *Comment* on 2:8. The former is not referred to outside these two passages, but the latter, the more westerly of the two, is mentioned also at Jer 31:38 and Zech 14:10. These references indicate that it was a prominent landmark and could be used in definition of the overall extent of the city. It is often deduced from Zech 14:10 that it may have marked the most northerly point on the wall.

3 "The Fish Gate" (cf. 12:39; Zeph 1:10; 2 Chr 33:14) cannot be certainly located. While it may well have been the way through which fish came into the city's fish market, we do not know whether that was from Galilee to the north or the Mediterranean coast to the west. Zeph 1:10 brings it into association with the Mishneh, while both here and in 12:39 (restored text) it is the gate next to the Mishneh Gate. Finally, according to 2 Chr 33:14, Manasseh "built an outer wall, on the west side of Gihon, in the valley even to the entering in at the fish gate." If these associations are all to be taken at face value, the Fish Gate must have been near the point where Nehemiah began to follow the "original" city wall rather than the late post-exilic one. A setting near the northwest corner, or just to the south of it, fits all the evidence best.

The construction of each of the gates is described in stereotyped manner. The hanging of the doors was evidently one of the final stages in the process; cf. 6:1; 7:1. The "bolts and bars" are presumably finishing touches linked with the doors themselves, the means for securing them when shut. The preceding element (here "they laid its beams") varies from one description to another; by comparison of the various verses with each other (cf. vv 1, 6, 13, 14, 15) it can be deduced that it relates to the substantial structure within which the doors were hung. This part of the "gate" sometimes included a series of guardrooms, and even in smaller towns was adequate to accommodate the groups of elders who passed judgment "in the gate."

4 For Meremoth, see *Comment* on 8:33–34.

5 No reason is given for the unwillingness of the leaders of the Tekoites to serve. The form of expression used, however (see *Notes*), is indicative of a resentment against the new leadership. This is in no way surprising. The return of exiles from Babylon at any time is bound to have caused tensions with those who had remained in the land, particularly in the matter of relationships with other inhabitants of the land. The location of Tekoa makes likely the influence of Geshem—for good or ill. The viewpoint of Ezra-Nehemiah is such that these tensions are often glossed over or presented in a rather different light (cf. the treatment of mixed marriages). A verse such as the present one is thus a valuable reminder that sharp differences of opinion within the wider Jewish community were never far beneath the surface.

6 The "Mishneh Gate" was a gate which opened through the original

Israelite city wall into the new quarter of Jerusalem which grew up to the
west of the city during the period of the monarchy and which was finally
walled in during the reigns of Hezekiah and Manasseh. This quarter was
known as the Mishneh (cf. 2 Kgs 22:14; 2 Chr 34:22; Zeph 1:10; Neh 11:9),
derived from the root related to "two; second; to repeat." The gate must
therefore have been on the west side of the city. 12:39 probably distinguishes
it from the Ephraim Gate, but it could be identified with the Corner Gate
of 2 Kgs 14:13.

7 The main issues for the interpretation of this verse are discussed in
the *Notes* above. That Mizpah is defined as "the seat of the governor of
Beyond the River" does not mean that he was permanently resident there;
rather, when he did visit the province of Judah (cf. Ezra 5:3 for an example)
it was at Mizpah that he had his official residence.

8 The reference to "goldsmiths" and "perfumers" (and "merchants" in
v 31) is to be explained by the fact that, whereas most of those engaged in
the work did so in groups determined by family or geographical ties, some
did so rather on the basis of their professional guilds; the participation of
priests and Levites provides a loose analogy. There is evidence that from
much earlier times those with particular skills lived and worked together;
cf. I. Mendelsohn, "Guilds in Ancient Palestine," *BASOR* 80 (1940) 17–21.
They probably formed the middle class of Judean society (Fensham). They
will have had a vested interest in the security of the city. Unlike at v 31,
there is no immediately obvious explanation for their participation on this
stretch of the wall, unless it be that in pre-exilic times they had established
their trade in the originally extramural Mishneh market which, on our understanding, cannot have been far from the section here described.

The last clause of the verse, "they left out (part of) Jerusalem as far as
the broad wall," has been interpreted in several ways. Taking the words at
face value, the clause will offer further evidence for the view that Nehemiah's
wall cut inside part of the pre-exilic city. Since we know that this was not
where the divergence began, we may assume that it marks the point where
the lines of the walls converged again. The "they" will then refer in a general
and summarizing way to a number of the preceding sections. On this view,
then, the lines of the wall diverged at or near the northeastern corner and
rejoined some way down the western side, still to the north of the Valley
Gate (v 13). It is noteworthy that this coincides quite closely with the hypothetical reconstruction of Kenyon, *Digging up Jerusalem,* 146 (fig. 26). It does not,
of course, rule out the possibility of habitation further to the south on the
western hill; it suggests only that an earlier wall once enclosed only the northern sector of the western side of the city, the Mishneh.

An alternative view of the same general theory is advanced by Grafman,
IEJ 24 (1974) 50–51. He argues, however, that "the broad wall" enclosed
virtually the whole of the western hill. We may accept his first conclusion,
that "the broad wall" does not refer to its thickness but rather to its widespread
and extensive nature, enclosing a substantial section of the city. His more
precise identification of the line of that wall faces certain difficulties, however:
no explanation is offered as to why the clause under discussion comes at
just this point, at neither the start nor the finish of "the broad wall." This

difficulty becomes insuperable once we reach 12:38, for there the procession must have had contact with the broad wall between "the Tower of the Ovens" and the Ephraim Gate. This would not be possible on Grafman's view. In addition, we may make the more general point that there is no physical evidence for the southern extension of the broad wall. The segment unearthed by Avigad in the modern Jewish Quarter of the Old City of Jerusalem is accommodated by Kenyon's conjecture. Meanwhile, it is curious to observe that most of the sites on the western hill that have yielded Iron Age remains in fact lie outside even Grafman's suggested line; cf. the plotting of the sites and proposed line of the wall in M. Broshi, "The Expansion of Jerusalem in the Reigns of Hezekiah and Manasseh," *IEJ* 24 (1974) 24. Finally, even if H. Geva, "The Western Boundary of Jerusalem at the End of the Monarchy," *IEJ* 29 (1979) 84–91, has correctly identified elements of the pre-exilic wall to the west of the line proposed by Kenyon (and this is not certain), the line could still have cut back along approximately the line of the present southern wall of the Old City to join the City of David at about the point we are suggesting. Geva has produced no evidence to prove that it must have continued as far south as the southern tip of the City of David.

9 This verse contains the first of a number of references to rulers of districts or half districts; cf. vv 12, 14, 15, 16, 17 and 18, where Jerusalem, Beth-hakkerem, Mizpah, Beth-zur and Keilah are mentioned. The word in question, פלך, is not used elsewhere in the Hebrew Bible with this meaning. Since many terms in Hebrew for administration entered the language under Assyrian and, later, Babylonian influence, it is probably cognate with the Akkadian *pilku*, whose primary meaning is "region, district" (cf. *AHW* 863). Since a distinction is drawn in vv 15 and 19 between "the ruler of the district of Mizpah" and the "ruler of Mizpah," it would appear that it refers to the administration of the territory around the urban center (and this could be subdivided into two) rather than the town itself. Support for this view comes from the fact that even so (apparently) insignificant a town as Keilah had two districts (vv 17 and 18). Whether these five districts represent all the administrative subdivisions of the province of Judah is not stated.

Bowman, by contrast, argues that *pilku* can sometimes mean an "assigned portion" in building work (cf. the fifth meaning, "Bauabschnitt," in *AHW*). He therefore thinks that our expression means the foreman responsible for half the town's assignment of work on the wall. This suggestion, however, demands the emendation of both vv 15 and 19 to "foreman of half the assigned portion of Mizpah," and for this there is no evidence whatsoever.

10 For the expression "opposite his own house," see *Comment* on vv 20–21, but cf. *Notes*.

11 "Malchiah, son of Harim": cf. Ezra 10:31. If both verses refer to the same man, as is *prima facie* most likely, there is a small pointer here against the probability of a late date (i.e., 398 B.C.) for Ezra. For "a second section," see *Form* above. "The Tower of the Ovens" is mentioned elsewhere only at 12:38, where its location agrees with that implied by the present text, i.e., between the Valley Gate and the broad wall. It can therefore make no independent contribution to a discussion of the line of the wall. The ovens in question were of the sort used for baking.

12 The reference to participation by Shallum's daughters is interesting. The temptation to emend to "sons" should be resisted: it will have been precisely because this was something rather unusual that the fact was recorded in the first place. Nor can we interpret this as a reference to the (daughter-) villages of Jerusalem, since the suffix, "his," is masculine. If Shallum had no sons, "it would be natural for the daughters to help on an occasion like this, since they would inherit his name and property" (Brockington, with reference to Num 36:8).

13–14 "The Valley Gate" and "the Dung Gate": see *Comment* on 2:13–15. The distance between them is set at "a thousand cubits." The precise length of a cubit varied over the course of time, but the distance here is generally reckoned at about 500 yards. Again, there is no need to doubt the figure on "common sense" grounds of how much wall each group could repair (as does Burrows, *AASOR* 14 [1933–34] 131, for instance); it was only recorded here because it was so unusually long. Presumably the wall here was in a better state of repair: it was not the side from which an attack on Jerusalem usually came in antiquity. In addition, it is possible that it had been repaired in part not long previously (cf. Ezra 4).

15 The "Spring Gate" was discussed at *Comment* 2:14 above. "The wall of the Pool of Shelah of the King's Garden" is more difficult to identify, especially as it apparently need not necessarily have been part of the city wall itself. We should note in addition that according to the next verse there was another pool, called "the artificial pool," a little further to the north.

It is probable that one of the two pools mentioned in this chapter should be identified with "the King's Pool" of 2:14. The difference in nomenclature is not a problem in view of the independent origin of this chapter. Both possibilities have been entertained in the recent past (see the articles referred to in *Comment* on 2:14). Because "the Pool of Shelah" is closely linked with "the King's Garden," it is attractive to suppose that it could also be called "the King's Pool" (later, Solomon's Pool). In that case, the wall referred to here cannot be more closely identified, but its repair would be intelligible if damage to it was causing an unnecessary waste of water. "The artificial pool" will then be some otherwise unknown feature.

The alternative is to identify the King's Pool with the artificial pool. This would then enable us to locate the Pool of Shelah further south, and in fact to regard it as the same as "the Pool of Shiloah"; the consonants are identical in each case. It has been well argued by Wilkinson, *Levant* 10 (1978) 116–25, that in OT times this was located at the site of the modern Birket el Hamra. If so, "the most natural interpretation [of our phrase] would be the wall along the scarp at the south of the city above Birket el Hamra" (p. 120).

Both identifications have their attractions, but in view of the unlikelihood of the existence of two pools close to each other whose names were differentiated by vocalization alone, the second is to be preferred. This means that Shallun must have repaired a section of wall to the west of the Spring Gate, in order to accommodate the evidence presented above. The conclusion of his section northwards is uncertain, however. "The steps which go down from the City of David" are usually thought to have led through the Spring gate itself, in which case it is an odd way of describing Shallun's portion in a context which has already referred to the Gate. Since, however, this is the very point at which Nehemiah abandoned the line of the earlier wall (see below), it may be suggested that from the Spring Gate Shallun started work on the new wall, following the line of the steps up the hill into what had formerly been part of the city itself.

16–31 As noted already in *Form* above, the style of description is rather different in this second half of the chapter. It is clear that we are no longer following the course of a previously existing wall, with its gates and other features. Rather, a new course for the wall is carefully defined by reference to local landmarks, familiar no doubt to the writer's contemporaries, but completely unknown to us in nearly every case. The archeological evidence coincides with this impression, for the wall that Kenyon identified as belonging to this period is considerably higher up the eastern slope than the line of the pre-exilic walls; cf. *Digging up Jerusalem*, 183–84. The reason for this is clear. The eastern slope is very steep. The walls had suffered badly and the whole area can have been little more than a formidable mass of tumbled rubble. To clear this and reterrace the slope would have been a major undertaking, beyond the means available to Nehemiah in the time at his disposal, and in fact unnecessary at this stage in view of the city's reduced population.

16 For "the artificial pool," see *Comment* on v 15. "The tombs of David" (i.e., of David and his descendants) are often identified with some large, rock-cut tombs uncovered by Weill in the southeastern part of the City of David. This is very uncertain, however, and although their location was still known in NT times (cf. Acts 2:29) they may have been obliterated by the later extensive Roman quarrying in the area. Kenyon, however, argues that burial within the city was not semitic practice, that it is not necessarily demanded by passages like 1 Kgs 2:10, that the so-called tombs are in fact cisterns, and that the royal tombs should be sought outside the walled city, on the opposite slopes of the surrounding valleys (*Digging up Jerusalem*, 31–32). This disagreement well illustrates how little we know with any certainty about the topography of this part of the chapter.

"The House of the Warriors" could refer to some barracks originating from David's time, if "the warriors" were originally those of David listed in 2 Sam 23:8–39, and mentioned elsewhere too; but cf. *Notes*. Its location is unknown.

17 It is not clear how far the list of Levites who participated is intended to stretch. It has clearly ended by v 22 and in v 21 Meremoth was probably a priest (cf. Ezra 8:33). But the text does not read at all smoothly in these verses, and explanatory material may have been lost. It emerges, however, that some Levites were prominently involved in civil administration. Perhaps some of their number who remained in the land during the exile turned to this in the absence of any form of temple service.

19 The details at the end of this verse are quite uncertain; cf. *Notes*. It should be observed that, despite 2 Chr 26:9, הַמִּקְצֹעַ, "the buttress" (but frequently rendered "the Angle"), cannot be a specific location, since it recurs in vv 24–25. Also, it never occurs on its own in this list, but is always more closely defined by some other specific element. Thus some commonly occurring but distinctive feature is probably intended. It seems to mean "a place where something is cut off or ends abruptly." "Buttress" would thus be suitable if it is an architectural feature, and "escarpment" (NEB) if it is a natural feature. More cannot be said in the present state of knowledge.

20–21 Now a section of the list begins in which the line of the wall is traced by reference to private houses. Usually, Nehemiah allocated these parts of the wall to the relevant householders themselves, since they had the greatest interest in ensuring that the work was done well. In the case of Eliashib, however, his position demanded his participation on the strategically vital northern wall, close to the temple. Meremoth's "second section" seems to have been very short. This may be a reflection of the scale of devastation along the eastern side of the city.

22 In some way no longer clear to us, "from the surrounding region" must distinguish these priests from those of v 1.

24 See *Comment* on v 19. "The corner" presumably means a sharp change in the direction of the wall, even though it is still running mainly in a line from south to north.

25 The section described in this verse is clearly located by reference to the palace, and is apparently slightly to the south of the section overlooking the Gihon spring (v 26). The "court of the guard" was included in the palace, according to Jer 32:2. The tower should not, as has often been supposed, be brought into connection with the pre-exilic wall (e.g., as part of the Water Gate, or by reference to 2 Chr 26:9). It too was part of the palace. Since the latter doubtless had several towers, it is further defined as the one adjacent to the court of the guard.

26 For "the temple servants," see *Comment* on Ezra 2:43–58. Although "Ophel" is the name commonly applied to the whole of the southeastern hill, it seems originally to have been the name of only one specific area (cf. Isa 32:14; Mic 4:8). The word derives from a root meaning "to swell"; as the southeastern hill continues to rise towards its northern end (the point which the description has now reached), a location for the Ophel here is appropriate.

The "Water Gate" must refer to a gate in the pre-exilic wall immediately above the Gihon spring and used for access to it. This, of course, was not rebuilt by Nehemiah. Whether he included a gate in his new wall at this point is not stated; perhaps direct access down the hill to Gihon was blocked by the tumble of rubble. The definition "to the east" could refer either to the gate itself—perhaps to distinguish it from the Spring Gate "in the south"— or more probably to the fact that the gate was "to the east" of the new line of the wall. In the latter case, we should supply "to the west" for "the projecting tower" (the same one as in v 25?). An east-west line between the gate and the tower thus defines the northern limit of this section.

27 For "Ophel," see on v 26 above. The "wall of Ophel" (cf. 2 Chr 27:3) does not appear from the context to be part of the wall being rebuilt. Rather, it is likely to have been a wall running roughly east-west around the northern side of Ophel. This was the line of the northern wall of the city until Solomonic times, when the city was extended northwards to include the temple site. Nehemiah's new wall must have crossed this line at about the point reached here in the list. Topographically this suggestion makes better sense than attempts to relate the wall to that mentioned in 2 Chr 33:14.

28 There is disagreement over whether "the Horse Gate" was a gate in the pre-exilic city wall or merely some gate within the temple-palace complex. At first sight, 2 Kgs 11:16 suggests the latter, but it is not certain that "the way of the horses' entry to the king's house" is the same as the Horse Gate. By contrast, Jer 31:40, which makes explicit mention of the Horse Gate, provides strong evidence in favor of the alternative view; cf. Simons, *Jerusalem*, 338–40. It was therefore probably a gate in the city wall on the east side, in the vicinity of the temple. This in turn furnishes a satisfactory explanation for the residence of priests in this area ("each one opposite his own house") and for the use of the preposition "above": the line of the new wall is clearly still higher up the slope than the old one.

29 The East Gate is generally considered to have been a gate into the temple and not in the city wall. It is mentioned here only as an aid to the closer identification of Shemaiah, its "keeper." He was therefore presumably a Levite. The need to make this clear may have arisen in order to avoid confusion with another "Shemaiah, son of Shecaniah," who was a member of the post-exilic Davidic family (cf. 1 Chr 3:22).

30 The translation above keeps as close to the MT as possible, though even so two small emendations are demanded (see *Notes*). While there is no substantial textual evidence to support further emendation, there are two other curious features in the verse, suggesting that the whole may have been confused in the course of transmission: (i) reference to Hanun as "the sixth son of Zaleph" is without parallel in this list, and indeed there seems to be little point in the remark. Moreover, if the mention of "a second section" directs our attention back to v 13, we find there that Hanun is not given a family name, but is linked rather with "the inhabitants of Zanoah." Many commentators believe that the latter was the original reading in our verse as well. (ii) "Meshullam, son of Berechiah" has already been mentioned at v 4. It has therefore been suggested that "a second section" originally belonged to this second half of the verse. In the present state of knowledge it is not possible to do more than observe these curious features; we have already noted evidence to suggest that the list has suffered quite badly in places; cf. *Form* above.

The unexpected use of "his own room" is suggestive of some official chamber, such as those in the temple (cf. Ezra 10:6; Neh 12:44; 13:4–9). Indeed, it may be more than a coincidence that Tobiah, who was related to Meshullam by marriage (cf. 6:18) was himself given the use of such a chamber in the temple later (13:4–9).

31 For "the goldsmiths," see *Comment* on v 8. The "temple servants" (cf. Ezra 2:43–58) are said to have lived elsewhere (cf. v 26); the house mentioned here was therefore probably for their use when on duty at the temple. That they shared it with "the merchants" (cf. Rudolph for the construction here) is to be explained by the likelihood that the latter also contributed to the service of the temple by the sale of necessary supplies for sacrifice etc. to the worshippers on their way in.

The "Muster Gate" cannot be clearly located. The meaning of the word translated "muster" is uncertain: "inspection" and "appointed place" have also been suggested. Nor is it known whether it was a temple gate or a city gate. If the latter, it appears to have been at the northernmost point on the eastern side, and its identification with the Benjamin Gate (Jer 37:13; 38:7; Zech 14:10) would be attractive (and possibly also with "the Gate of the Guard," 12:39).

32 "The upper room at the corner" presumably marked the northeastern corner of the city. The section along the north wall to complete the circuit by joining again with the Sheep Gate (cf. v 1) was carried out by "the goldsmiths and the merchants," no doubt because just inside this wall was a market for the convenience of those on their way to the temple.

Explanation

Almost inevitably, the comments on this chapter have focused on topographical concerns and related matters. In concluding, it is worth standing back from such a plethora of detail in order to reflect on the nature of the achievement which it represents.

We are struck first by the *unity of intention* which is here displayed. Some forty or more sections are mentioned in the list, most of them, we must suppose, working simultaneously. This, it should be remembered, includes extensive areas where a completely new line for the wall was being followed. Moreover, we learn in the next chapter that the work was done sufficiently quickly to take Sanballat by surprise.

This undoubtedly testifies to a remarkable feat of organization and leadership, though nothing is said directly about that in the text. It is emphasized, nevertheless, by the evidence presented above, which suggests that there may have been considerable strains between those of different political and religious outlook among the people who worked on the wall. The very length and detail of the list demonstrates the evident willingness unselfishly to cooperate which each individual and group displayed. Without a determination to submit personal pride and ambition to the larger task, the work could never have been accomplished so swiftly and successfully. As will be seen in a moment, this is not by any means to overlook the many points which differentiate one group from another. It is simply to observe that without a common commitment to the specific task in hand, the result would have been a self-defeating chaos.

The pattern which thus emerges is one which may be profitably contemplated as an exemplary illustration of much NT language about unity in the Church. In the Johannine literature, the prayer of Jesus for his followers "that they may all be one, Father, just as you are in me and I am in you" (John 17:21) is clearly not to be read ontologically; the oneness described is that of intention, for the qualifying clauses point us back to 10:28–30, where the statement of the equality of the purpose of Father and Son alike in guarding the sheep is concluded with the saying, "I and the Father are one." If Father and Son are at one in their purpose of love for the disciples, so should the latter be in turn in their aim to serve God and their fellow men.

The Pauline epistles present a similar concept though with the use of different language and imagery. Note, for instance, how 1 Cor 12:4–6 and Eph 4:1–6, with their heavy emphasis on unity, are immediately followed by passages that underline the value of and, indeed, necessity for variety of gift. Many contributions are needed to promote the common goal of the building of the Church in love, but without that unity of intention, the wall will have serious gaps along its length.

As already indicated, however, unity and uniformity should not be confused; the list speaks eloquently of the *diversity of interest* of those engaged in the work. We may note, for instance, that some participated on the basis of family association, others as individuals, some in district associations, some on the basis of their standing or position within the community, and yet others because of professional association. Moreover, it seems that Nehemiah allowed each group to be responsible, so far as possible, for the section of wall in which they had the greatest vested interest—because it protected their home, place of business, or the like.

Here too we need not be afraid of seeing an example for the diversity of involvement within the Christian Church, be it at the local level or more widely. We may have the faith to believe that God has made us as we are because, as we are controlled by his Spirit, he has a use for our individual gifts and abilities. Nor need we be disquieted if we find that it comes most easily, and with the greatest sense of motivation, to channel those gifts in areas closest to our own concerns.

Finally, we should briefly note the *variety of involvement* displayed. There were some, we observed, who because of pride and proprietary interest refused to take part at all. Most, we know, labored effectively at the task allotted to them, while a few even managed "a second section." By this testimony, the chapter stands as a permanent challenge to all readers in their own spheres of service.

Renewed Opposition (Neh 3:33–37 [Evv 4:1–5])

Bibliography

Bauer, J. B. "Der 'Fuchs' Neh 3, 35 ein Belagerungsturm?" *BZ* N.F. 19 (1975) 97–98. **Burrows, M.** "The Origin of Neh. 3:33–37." *AJSL* 52 (1935–36) 235–44.

Translation

3:33(4:1) *When Sanballat heard that we were building the wall he became angry and was very indignant.* 34(2) *He heaped scorn upon the Jews, saying*[a] *in front of his allies and the army of Samaria, "Whatever do those*[b] *feeble Jews think they are doing? Will they commit their cause to God?*[c] *Will they simply offer some sacrifices? Do they hope to finish this very day?*[d] *Can they raise stones to life*[e] *from the heaps of rubble, all burnt as they are?"*[f] 35(3) *Tobiah the Ammonite, who was beside him, said, "Whatever they try to build, if a fox*[a] *climbs up, it would break down their stone wall."*

36(4) *Hear, O our God! For we have become an object of contempt. Turn their reproach back on to their own heads and deliver them up as plunder in a land of captivity.* 37(5) *Do not forgive their iniquity or blot out their sins from your sight, for they have provoked you to anger*[a] *right in the presence of the builders.*

Notes

3:34(4:2).a. MT repeats ויאמר "and he said" as a variation on the more usual formula ויאמר . . . לאמר, "and he spoke . . . saying."

34.b. For an explanation of the LXX, cf. Rudolph. It is not necessary, however, to follow him in restoring האלה "these" after האמללים "feeble." This would imply that Sanballat was speaking within sight of Jerusalem, but for this there is no evidence. "Those" is supplied in the translation merely for the sake of English idiom.

34.c. This phrase, היעזבו להם, has caused considerable difficulty. The main proposals are well summarized already by Ryle, though it is now possible to bring some additional considerations to support both his negative and his positive conclusions. Three general, introductory points need also to be borne in mind: (i) The Vrs support the MT, but do not offer a unified or compelling tradition of interpretation. Their solutions are generally open to the criticisms of the more modern proposals noted by Ryle. (ii) This question is followed by three others. Since in each case they are heavily sarcastic, as the context demands, this first one should be so understood as well. (iii) Since the Jews are the subj of all the other pl verbs in this verse, it is likely that they are here too. These considerations rule out the older translation, "Will men let them alone?," i.e., will the government or the neighboring peoples allow the Jews to build? Many recent translations and commentaries find here a second root, עזב. It is thought to refer to the work of building in some way or other; thus RV: "Will they fortify themselves?" RSV: "Will they restore things?" NEB: "Do they mean to reconstruct the place?" NIV: "Will they restore their wall?" etc. The use of the same root at 3:8 is usually cited in support. It is certain that there was a root with this sort of meaning in Ugaritic and in epigraphic South Arabian which would be cognate with עזב II if it existed in Heb. Moreover, the occurrence of מעזיבה "plaster, restoration," in post-biblical Heb. could be held to support the view that it was also known in biblical Heb. Such a supposition must first establish, however, that the common meaning of עזב, "to leave, abandon," is less suitable to the context than the postulated alternative. We have already seen, however, that this is not the case at 3:8. Nor, we would now affirm, is it fully appropriate here either, because there is no particular sarcasm behind the question in this case. Better, therefore, is the approach of Keil, who observes on the basis of Ps 10:14 that עזב followed by ל may have the meaning "to leave, to commit a matter to any one," giving the sense here of "Will they leave the building of the fortified walls to themselves?," i.e., "Do they think they are able with their poor resources to carry out this great work?" This certainly gives acceptable sense in the context, and is no doubt the best way of taking MT as it stands. Nevertheless, the expression is awkward and arouses suspicion, as the difficulty most scholars have experienced with it shows. For this reason, Bertheau, followed by Ryle, Witton Davies, and others, proposed emending להם to על־אלהים or לאלהים, to give a translation "Will they commit themselves to God?" Bertheau in fact eventually discounted this suggestion, but it can be developed further and a possible explanation for the present text be suggested. First, the use of עזב in this way is clearly attested by Job 39:11, ‏התבטח־בו כי רב כחו ותעזב אליו יגיעך: , "Wilt thou trust him, because his strength is great? Or wilt thou leave to him [i.e., commit to him] thy labor?" (AV). The parallelism here makes clear that "leave to" means "commit to." In Ps 10:14b, the parallelism again suggests a similar meaning, but this time with an elipse of the object: עליך יעזב חלכה יתום אתה היית עוזר: . RV supplies a reflexive object ("the helpless committeth himself unto thee; Thou hast been the helper of the fatherless"), but on the basis of Job 39:11 we might equally well supply an object such as "his cause." This would then furnish a close parallel for the proposed emendation in our verse, to be rendered as in the translation above. It is most appropriate in the context, as the following verb shows, and 2 Kgs 18:30, 32, and 35 are often cited as a comparable example of such scorn of Jewish faith by a threatening enemy. The elipse may be explained as due to Sanballat's terse tones reflected also in the following two clauses. How, then, did the error arise? Rather than postulating simple textual corruption, as those who have previously adopted this emendation have supposed, we may suggest that it was a theologically motivated correction by a pious scribe, in the manner of the Tiqqun Sopherim. Because of the terse form of expression, and in a period when, under Aramaic influence, ל often introduced a direct object, היעזבו לאלהים was misunderstood as "Will they abandon God?" Finding such a thought unacceptable, להם was substituted, and understood in the way Keil explains (see above). A parallel for this substitution exists in the Tiqqune Sopherim of להם for אלהים at 1 Sam 3:13. That such corrections not included in the usual list of Tiqqune Sopherim may nevertheless be found in the MT is acknowledged by C. McCarthy, *The Tiqqune Sopherim and Other Theological Corrections in the Masoretic Text of the Old Testament* (OBO 36; Freiburg: Universitätsverlag, and Göttingen: Vandenhoeck & Ruprecht, 1981).

34.d. ביום, "in the day." The demonstrative force of the art is accepted for היום "this day" (cf. GKC § 126b), and this may have influenced the construction here, "in this day," i.e., "today, directly." Both this clause and the preceding one have been amplified slightly in the translation for the sake of English idiom; literally, "Will they sacrifice? Will they finish this day?"

34.e. The tone of the passage and the qualification "from the heaps of rubble" suggest that חיה "live" is here being used with its normal meaning applied sarcastically to the stones; cf. *Notes* on Ezra 9:9.b. for some further comment. The use of the same root in one Phoenician inscription (cf. Gibson, *SSI* 3, 18) with the meaning "to restore" hardly justifies our translating it thus here.

34.f. המה for הנה, as in a number of other passages; cf. GKC § 32n. For the force of this circumstantial clause, see *Comment* below.

35.a. Bauer, *BZ* N.F.19 (1975) 97–98, suggests that "fox" may be a name for a siege weapon. He notes a number of examples of animal names used in this kind of way, and argues that only so can פרץ "break down" be properly understood. While the suggestion is a possibility, it robs Tobiah's comment of the element of sarcasm which we expect from the context.

37.a. Most modern translations take "the builders" as the dir obj of the verb, but לנגד "in front of" seems to stand as an insuperable difficulty for this view; it can hardly be understood adverbially, as NEB implies: "they have openly provoked the builders." הכעיס "to provoke" can, however, be used without the object expressed of provoking God to anger; cf. 1 Kgs 21:22; 2 Kgs 21:6; 23:19; Hos 12:15 (14); Ps 106:29 (it is unlikely that textual corr has affected all these passages, though it has independently been held responsible for them all by various commentators). This gives a suitable meaning in the context (cf. *Comment* below, *contra* Rudolph), and allows לנגד to have its usual meaning.

Form/Structure/Setting

In chap. 2 a literary pattern was observed whereby each major step forward in the narrative was marked by a reference to the opposition of Sanballat and his colleagues. That this was intentional was considered probable on the basis of the identical formulae at the start of 2:10 and 19. This pattern continues with the present paragraph: the major advance recorded by the inclusion of 3:1–32 is here countered by a further notice of opposition (33–35). Again, the identical openings of 3:33 (4:1) and 4:1 (7) are suggestive of a careful patterning by the author. If this paragraph is rather longer than 2:10 and 19, then that is to be explained by the fact of the greater length of 3:1–32 and its particular importance for the fulfillment of Nehemiah's mission.

Nehemiah's response, vv 36–37 (4:4–5), also shows expansion over the pattern in chap. 2: in 2:10 no response at all was recorded; in 2:20 Nehemiah contented himself with a curt dismissal of their charge. Now he turns at greater length to God for vindication, and in subsequent paragraphs this element in the structure (i.e., Nehemiah's handling of the opposition) will come increasingly to dominate the whole. Thus the literary structure reflects the growing intensity of the struggle and the consequent need on Nehemiah's part to devote more energy and attention to containing its threat.

The form of Nehemiah's prayer (vv 36–37 [4:4–5]) is generally compared with that of the psalms of lament, and indeed there are points of close contact; cf. C. Westermann, "The Structure and History of the Lament in the Old Testament," *Praise and Lament in the Psalms* (tr. K. R. Crim and R. N. Soulen; Edinburgh: T. & T. Clark, 1981), 165–213: the drawing into relationship of God, the one who laments, and the enemy; the elements of address (with introductory petition), lament, and petition, and so on. This, however, is only to be expected. We have already seen in chap. 1 that Nehemiah adopted quite naturally the liturgical language of his day when in prayer, and of course it goes without saying that the form of a prayer arises out of what needs to be said rather than *vice versa*. It is thus in no way surprising to find common elements between Nehemiah's prayer here and the psalms of lament. No significant conclusion about purpose or setting can legitimately be drawn from this observation.

Nearly all commentators are satisfied that this paragraph forms an integral part of the original NM. The remarks made above about its place in the overall structure of the narrative strongly support this view, especially once it is accepted that 3:1–32 was itself included by Nehemiah, if not originally written by him. A contrary opinion is expressed by Torrey, *Ezra Studies*, 225–26, Batten, and Burrows, *AJSL* 52 (1935–36) 235–44, who regard either part or the whole of the paragraph as due to editorial activity by the Chronicler. Their starting point, however, is, first, the view that 2:19 and 3:33–35 (4:1–3) overlap and repeat each other, rather than saying anything new and, second, the opinion that 3:1–32 was added only later. Neither presupposition is shared here, however; see the comments on the relevant sections. For further counterarguments, cf. Kellermann, *Nehemia*, 17.

Comment

3:33 (4:1)   3:1–32 was included to indicate that work had now started in earnest on rebuilding the wall. Sanballat's reaction to this development is more severe than at the end of chap. 2. There, it looks as though the ridicule is from a position of contemptuous superiority and confidence that Nehemiah's plans are a mere pipedream. Here, by contrast, the emphasis on his extreme anger indicates the start of desperation on his part that Nehemiah may, after all, succeed. Moreover, as the next verse shows, his scorn is voiced, not merely in the hearing of the wall-builders, but in the presence of his allies; it is his way of boosting morale among his own people now that he sees that the threat is taking on serious proportions.

34 (2)   The setting of Sanballat's remarks is first clarified: they were as much for "home consumption" as for the intimidation of the Jews. His "allies" seems to be the most appropriate translation of a word that literally means "his brothers." Physical brothers would clearly be too narrow a meaning, while "fellow Samarians" would be less easy to differentiate from the following group. Thus the reasonably attested meaning of "allies" (cf. Amos 1:9; *TDOT* 1, 191) fits best, especially in view of the presence of Tobiah mentioned later. The "army of Samaria" is not more specifically defined. Was it an official Persian garrison, or a local militia group? At any rate it is certain that the governor of Samaria had some kind of troops under his command (cf. 4:2 [8]; Ezra 4:23). Thus Sanballat uses ridicule as a means of avoiding loss of face in the presence of his supporters and subordinates.

Sanballat's first question simply contrasts his estimate of the Jews as "feeble" with the magnitude of the task, implying that they are incapable of accomplishing it. אמללים "feeble" occurs only here in the Hebrew Bible. It is related to a verbal root meaning "to be weak, languish," which can refer to a wide variety of animate and inanimate objects with a general sense of weakness through failure of the normal strength-giving agencies.

Sanballat's following questions are rather obscure; see *Notes* above. As translated here, they are grouped in two pairs. The first pair ridicule the suggestion that God can be cajoled into prospering the work as if by the wave of a magic wand. Naturally, the complete contrast this makes with Nehemiah's mature awareness of human responsibility deriving from divine sovereignty (see *Explanation* on chap. 2) will not have troubled Sanballat or been noted by his audience.

The second pair of questions implies that the Jews are hopelessly overoptimistic: the task is larger than they suppose, and it will take longer than they have calculated. This is reinforced by the final clause of the verse: not only would stones blackened by fire be less than satisfactory for the rebuilding, but inasmuch as it was limestone, it would have been considerably weakened and may even have crumbled. In effect, the ruins were beyond repair.

35 (3)   Tobiah's jest chimes in with Sanballat's sarcasm, neatly combining the suggestion that the Jews are not up to such a major task with the implication that the materials they are using are inadequate.

36–37 (4–5)   This is the first of Nehemiah's brief prayers which are so characteristically included in his memoir (cf. 5:19; 6:9b, 14; 13:14, 22, 31). They add a vivid contemporaneity to the account. For their position within the composition, cf. *Introduction,* "The Nehemiah Memoir."

36 (4) The language and sentiment are somewhat stereotyped, but it is noteworthy nonetheless that a man of action such as Nehemiah should reply to such an incitement by resorting to prayer—"Hear, O our God!"—rather than to direct action. By characterizing himself and his fellows as "an object of contempt" (בוזה), he is not only recalling the initial motivation for his mission (cf. 1:3), but is also using a word that is calculated to secure divine response: "he who carries out a *bazah* against one chosen by Yahweh is himself condemned to insignificance" (M. Görg, *TDOT* 2, 63). Since God cannot be despised with impunity (the word is often used for offense against his express will), neither, by extension, can his representatives. His honor is at stake in the present confrontation.

This thought is then made explicit in the remainder of the verse: let them suffer what they prescribe for others! And more—may they in fact endure the penalty from which the Jews have only so recently found relief. The whole prayer is reminiscent of such Psalms as 44, 74, and 79, and in particular of the situation which Hezekiah faced when threatened by Sennacherib; cf. his prayer in 2 Kgs 19:14–19.

37 (5) Nehemiah now makes his own the imprecatory prayer of Jer 18:23. The word used for "forgive" here is, literally, "to cover," and the image, if not the word, is, together with that of to "blot out," part of the standard OT approach to an understanding of atonement; cf. F. D. Kidner, "Sacrifice—Metaphors and Meaning," *TynB* 33 (1982) 119–36 (127–28). However, Nehemiah wishes to have this denied to his enemies for, as he returns to the opening thought of his brief prayer, it is God himself whose honor is here impugned; see further under *Explanation* below.

"Right in the presence of the builders": this is the first indication we have that this whole scene has been played out within earshot of the builders. By withholding this information until now, Nehemiah certainly gives it maximum dramatic impact: the exchanges are not behind the isolation of closed doors but at a point of close psychological encounter. The parallel with the Rabshakeh's embassy to Hezekiah is thus heightened; cf. especially 2 Kgs 18:26, where the Jerusalem leaders try to persuade the Rabshakeh to speak "in the Aramaean language, for we understand it; and speak not with us in the Jews' language, in the ears of the people that are on the wall." Note also the Chronicler's heightening of the underlying theological conflict in this episode in his later retelling of it in 2 Chr 32:1–23; cf. my *1 and 2 Chronicles* 378–85.

Explanation

Insecurity expresses itself in a surprising variety of ways, perhaps the least common of which is real timidity. When that insecurity is brought into the sphere of the divine, its expression can be truly appalling.

The present short passage demonstrates this in two different ways. The

case of Sanballat and his allies is the more straightforward. The use of mocking
sarcasm in the face of what one suspects underneath may truly be a work
of God is illustrated time and again in Scripture and in the experience of
the people of God throughout the centuries of Church history right down
to our own day. Moreover it is known both at the personal and at the institutional level. Perhaps it was never linked with such poignant irony as when
Jesus heard it said, "He saved others; himself he cannot save. . . . He trusted
in God; let him deliver him now, if he will have him" (Matt 27:42–43, kjv).

More difficult to handle is Nehemiah's prayer for vengeance against his
enemies in the last two verses. Clearly, it belongs in spirit with the so-called
psalms of imprecation (e.g., Pss 35, 58, 59, 69, 109, and 137), a group of
passages that have often been a source of embarrassment to Christian readers;
for helpful attempts at understanding with some guidelines for use, cf.
C. S. Lewis, *Reflections on the Psalms* (London: Geoffrey Bles, 1958), 20–33;
and F. D. Kidner, *Psalms 1–72* (TOTC. London: Inter-Varsity, 1973), 25–32.

On the one hand, it is possible to adopt an apologetic stance with regard
to the sentiments expressed, seeking to understand them in their context,
and so to soften their offensive impact. We may say with a degree of justification that Nehemiah regards the insults as directed as much against God as
against himself, and thus hands over the need for vindication to his Lord;
that he deemed it better to express his wrath in prayer rather than in physical
action against his opponents; that his words demonstrated a keener awareness
of the ultimate moral values of right and wrong than we frequently display;
and that, after all, he was not outstripping the conventions of his time, as
comparison with Jer 18:23, as well as with the psalms of imprecation, makes
clear. What is more, we should not underestimate the degree of provocation
to which Nehemiah and these other writers had been subjected.

These points are helpful as far as they go, but in the last resort they are
inadequate as a full statement for the Christian, whose New Testament teaches
the need to "bless them that persecute you; bless and curse not," to "recom-
pense to no man evil for evil," to "avenge not yourselves, beloved, but rather
give place to wrath," to feed an enemy who is hungry and to "overcome
evil with good" (Rom 12:14–21, kjv; cf. Matt 5:43–48; Luke 23:34; Acts 7:60;
1 Tim 2:1–4). Similarly, there is the persistent call to forgive beyond the
point of reason (e.g., Matt 18:21–22) and finally the example of Jesus himself
whose passion paves the way of enduring unjust accusation and treatment
for his followers (1 Pet 2:20–23). What is more, these values were not unknown
even to those of Old Testament times: it is from Prov 25:21–22 that Paul
quotes in Rom 12, and cf. Exod 23:4–5; Lev 19:17–18; Prov 24:17. Perhaps,
therefore, we should realize that expressed in Nehemiah's prayer there is
also an underlying insecurity—an insecurity that was inevitable until the cross
revealed the full extent of God's unquenchable love for a humanity that as
a whole stood in enmity against him, until the empty tomb could proclaim
his triumph over evil through love, and until the inauguration of the Kingdom
of God could give an assurance that righteousness will ultimately be vindi-
cated. Those who have entered into that assurance have therefore a security
within which the practice of the Christian ethic becomes possible. Few, if

any, will feel that they have attained that ideal, and honesty will compel us to admit that we have breathed the atmosphere of Nehemiah's prayer more often than we should; but by that very confession we testify to our conviction that since the coming of Christ there has been opened before us the vision of a better way.

Further Opposition and Countermeasures (*Neh 3:38—4:17 [Evv 4:6-23]*)

Bibliography

Alt, A. "Judas Nachbarn zur Zeit Nehemias." *KS* 2, 338–45. **Warner, H. J.** "A Simple Solution of Nehemiah iv. 23 (Heb. verse 17)." *ExpTim* 63 (1951–52) 322.

Translation

3:38(4:6) *So we built the wall and the whole wall was joined up to half its height,* [a] *for the people had a will to work.*
4:1(7) *When Sanballat, together with Tobiah, the Arabs, the Ammonites, and the Ashdodites, heard that the restoration of the walls* [a] *of Jerusalem was going ahead (and) that the parts which had been broken down were beginning to be stopped up, they became very angry.* 2(8) *So they all conspired together to come and fight against Jerusalem and to cause confusion,* [a] 3(9) *but we prayed to our God and posted a guard over the city* [a] *day and night because of them.*
4(10) *Then, however, it became a saying in the Judean community:* [a]
The strength of the porters is failing,
There is so much rubble!
On our own we shall never be able
To rebuild the wall.
5(11) *Meanwhile, our adversaries said, "Before they know anything about it or realize what is happening we shall come amongst them and kill them and so make the work stop."*
6(12) *When the Jews who lived near them came and said to us time and again* [a] *from all sides, "You must return to us,"* [b] 7(13) *then I took up a position* [a] *in the lowest parts of* [b] *the space behind the wall in an exposed place* [c] *and I made the people stand* [d] *by families with their swords, their spears, and their bows.* 8(14) *Then I reviewed them and immediately spoke* [a] *to the nobles, the officials, and the rest of the people: "Do not be afraid of them; remember the Lord, who is great and awesome, and fight for your brothers, your sons, and your daughters, your wives and your homes."*
9(15) *When our enemies heard that all was known to us and that God had frustrated their plan,* [a] *we all returned to the wall, everyone to his own work.*
10(16) *From that day on half my men were engaged in the work while the other half held the shields, the spears,* [a] *the bows, and the coats of mail. Meanwhile the officers* [b] *were (stationed) behind all the house of Judah* 11(17) [a] *who were building the wall.* [a] *The basket-carriers* [b] *did their work* [c] *with one hand supporting the load* [d] *and one holding a weapon.* 12(18) *As for the builders themselves, each one had his sword fastened* [a] *at his side as he built, while the man who sounded the trumpet stayed close to me.* 13(19) *Then I said to the nobles, the officials, and the rest of the people, "The work is very spread out* [a] *and we are widely separated from one another along the wall.* 14(20) *In whatever place you hear the sound of the trumpet, rally to us there: our God will fight for us."*

15(21) *Thus we progressed with the work '. . . .*)ᵃ *from the crack of dawn until the stars came out.* 16(22) *At the same time I also said to the people, "Let every man and his servant spend the night in Jerusalem, so that they can act as guards for us by night and as workmen by day."* ᵃ 17(23) *So neither I nor my kinsmen nor my men nor the men of the guard who supported me ever took off our clothes; each man kept his weapon at his right hand.* ᵃ

Notes

3.38(4:6).a. Lit., "its half." In view of the context, it must be the wall's height rather than circumference that is being referred to. It is mere pedantry to object that this is not possible because not all sections of the wall needed to be rebuilt.

4:1(7).a. The wall is generally spoken of in the sg in Nehemiah, and there is considerable MS and Vrs support for such a reading here too; the transposition of one letter only is involved (חומת sg Syr., Vg, for חמות, pl MT). The pl is grammatically possible, however, as in the English idiom, and it is simpler to suppose that the MSS and Vrs that read the sg here have been assimilated to the practice elsewhere rather than that the exceptional reading has arisen purely by accident.

2(8).a. MT here adds לו "to it" (masc sg). This cannot refer to Jerusalem, which would have to be fem, and it is doubtful whether it can refer to its inhabitants as a collective sg. Some conjecture reading לי "to me" or לנו "to us" but there can be no certainty about this. Did a later scribe unconsciously assimilate one of these to a third-person account, with reference to Nehemiah? Fortunately, English idiom allows us to omit the word without loss of clarity.

3(9).a. MT, "against them . . . because of them," while not completely impossible (cf. Ryle), seems improbably repetitive. The simplest emendation is that of Ehrlich, *Randglossen*, who reads עליה "over her" for עליהם "over them," the fem suff referring to Jerusalem. This reading is supported by Vg, whose *super murum* no doubt reflects an interpretation of the same suff as referring to חומה "wall."

4(10).a. Lit., "And Judah said," where Judah stands for the whole post-exilic community.

6(12).a. Lit., "ten times," which appears to be the expression of a round number. In the context, it is clearly the frequency of the summons that is being emphasized.

6(12).b. The second half of the verse is uncertain, and many solutions have been proposed. The Vrs offer little help, as they apparently presuppose the present text; cf. Rudolph. Any solution must take into account the fact that this whole verse is a subordinate clause to the following one in which Nehemiah takes protective countermeasures. There must, therefore, be an adequate cause-and-effect relationship between them. This rules out the traditional understanding of MT (cf. Keil; Ryle, etc.) in which the Jews in question "express apprehension on their own account and for their own homes. Deprived of the able-bodied men who had been sent to work at the walls on [*sic!*] Jerusalem, these little towns and villages could not hope to defend themselves against the gathering foe. Wherefore they address themselves through the leaders to their fellow-townsmen sojourning in Jerusalem, 'Ye must return unto us.' " (Ryle). It is not clear, however, how Nehemiah's stationing of a guard in Jerusalem would meet this fear; nor is there any suggestion in the text that towns other than Jerusalem were under threat. The same translation can make good sense, however, if those who came felt that Jerusalem's plight was hopeless and they were therefore encouraging their fellows to abandon it and to "evacuate" to the safety of other towns. Syntactically, the relative pronoun אשר introduces direct speech. Aram. has a comparable idiom, and the usage is attested elsewhere in biblical Heb.; cf. GKC § 157c. Similarly, the interchange of the preps אל־ and על־ is not at all unusual, especially in late biblical Heb.; see, for example, 2 Chr 30:9. Rudolph's objection that "us" would then refer to different groups of people within the same verse is correct as an observation but of no weight since a switch of reference is inevitable with the introduction of direct speech; there is no ambiguity. It goes without saying that an intelligible rendering of the MT is to be preferred to an emendation. Many such have been proposed, but only the most influential need be briefly noted here: (i) Insert יעלו before עלינו; cf. NIV, "Wherever you turn, they will attack us." However, שוב cannot mean "turn" in this way; cf. W. L. Holladay, *The Root šûbh in the Old Testament* (Leiden: Brill, 1958). (ii) The same with the additional emendation of תשובו to

ישבו: "from all places where they live they will attack us" (Bertholet); in addition to being further removed from MT, this fits less easily with the preceding "they said to us ten times." (iii) Read כל־המזמות אשר חשבע עלינו "all the schemes which they were devising against us" (Rudolph, adapting Ehrlich). This makes good sense, but is entirely conjectural. (iv) The same applies to NEB, which adds יעלו after פעמים (with possible LXX support, but see above), emends תשובו to ישבו and ואעמיד in the next verse to ויעמרד: "they warned us many times that they would gather from every place where they lived to attack us, and that they would station themselves on the lowest levels below the walls, on patches of open ground. Accordingly, I posted my people by families . . ." An additional difficulty for this view is that it implies very curious military tactics on the part of the enemy.

7(13). The first half of this verse is again very difficult, so that the possibility of some physical damage to the text of vv 6b–7a at an early stage of its transmission cannot be ruled out. Again, it seems best to stay as close as grammar and sense will allow to the form of the text which we have in the absence of any firm evidence for alternative readings. The suggestion of some LXX MSS, favored by some commentators, that the first verb should be referred to the enemy is ruled out by the words "behind the wall."

7(13).a. I propose reading ואעמוד for MT ואעמיד "and I stationed." The latter is a transitive verb, but no obj is expressed. Attempts to find an obj in the next word are unconvincing, either because they are too fanciful and implausible in the historical context (e.g., Bertheau, מחשבות or חשבונות or מטחויות, all referring to some kind of catapult) or because there is no reason for isolating them from the second half of the verse (e.g., Rudolph, מתי חנית "spearmen"). Nor is it plausible to argue that את־העם "the people" later in the verse is the obj, since syntactically it is too far removed from the verb, and there would be no reason for the repetition of the verb in that case either. Finally, the view that one occurrence of ואעמיד has arisen by dittogr from the other (e.g., Fensham) is also unlikely: it must have come before את־העם later in the verse; how then could the "dittograph" have worked backwards to the start of the verse? Nonetheless, the repetition remains awkward. When it is coupled with the lack of a dir obj in the first half, the simplest solution seems to be to make the tiny alteration proposed above (in effect it does no more than alter the vocalization). Internally, Nehemiah needed to boost his people's morale as much as take actual defensive measures. This verse and the next describe how he did it; see further Comment below.

7(13).b. The construction (מן . . . ל) may be analogous to the related compound prep מתחת ל; see also מאחרי ל following.

7(13).c. Q, בצחיחים, is generally thought to derive from צחח "be dazzling," which gives rise to an adj, צח, that can have the meaning "clear" (of speech), and the noun צחיח, used at Ezek 24:7, 8; 26:4 and 14 in the expression צחיח סלע "bare rock." For the use of the pl with reference to place, cf. GKC § 124b. Such a meaning gives good sense in the context (see Comment below) though it cannot be certain and other renderings are possible.

7(13).d. עמד hiph is usually translated "stationed," which is also possible. As understood here, however, Nehemiah is mustering all the people to one open space rather than distributing them around the walls. This interpretation is supported by his address that follows and by the need as much to encourage his own people as to impress the enemy; see further Comment below.

8(14).a. Lit., "And I saw and arose and said," which conveys a sense of urgency. This is enough to account for the fact that the object of "saw," obvious from the context, remains unexpressed.

9(15).a. Rudolph here proposes the addition of וישובו ממנה "they desisted from it" (i.e., their plan). There is no evidence whatsoever for such a restoration, however; the text as it stands may be considered to imply this thought without its having actually to be spelled out.

10(16).a. MT has "held and the spears, the shields . . . ," which clearly cannot be right: there cannot be a conjunction on the first item of the list, whereas there should be one on the second. To insert "swords" at the start of the list would solve only the first of these problems, not the second. In addition, it does not fit well with the view that this group was set apart specifically to carry the weapons which the wall builders could not carry, for we are told in v 12 (18) that swords were carried by all. Most commentators, therefore, transpose the conjunction from the first word to the second (הרמחים והמגנים "the spears and the shields"), citing various MSS and Vrs in support. The latter evidence is not strong, however: how else could they translate MT? A more satisfactory solution is to reverse the order of these two words—המגנים והרמחים, as translated above. The transposition of words during the course of transmission is a well-attested phenomenon, resulting from the writing back in of a word that has been accidentally omitted at first; cf. my "Word Order in Isaiah xliii.12," *JTS* ns 30 (1979) 499–502. In favor of the conjecture here is the observation that in other lists of armor, shields usually precede spears; cf. 2 Chr 26:14 for an especially close parallel. Also, in v 7 (13) of this chapter, spears and bows are listed next to one another.

10(16).b. There is no substantial textual evidence to support the proposed deletion of this word as a dittogr. Since good sense can be made of the passage (see *Comment* below), it should be retained.

11(17).a-a. Sense and the Vrs demand that these two words should be taken with v 10 (16). Otherwise we are left with the absurd picture of the builders working with a weapon in one hand! As taken here, the basket carriers each carried a weapon, which is reasonable, while the builders (v 12[18]) had theirs girded by their sides.

11(17).b. For this translation, cf. M. Held, "The Root *zbl/sbl* in Akkadian, Ugaritic and Biblical Hebrew," *JAOS* 88 (1968) 90–96.

11(17).c. עמש is to be regarded as a variant of עמס, which is well attested in cognate languages and Hebrew as "carry"; cf. Held (*JAOS* 88 [1968] 90–96). No object is expressed, but it is clear from the context, and the verb is used elliptically in other passages too. For the use of נשא and עמס in close conjunction, cf. Isa 46:3. The translation supplied above is thus based on a literal rendering, "The basket-carriers carried (their loads)." There is therefore no need to follow the lead of LXX in emending to חמשים "armed." The translators probably experienced difficulty with MT and so assumed a variation between the similar sounding ע and ח.

11(17).d. As it stands, MT may be rendered literally as "with one hand (each man) engaged in the work" (which in the context must mean supported the load he was carrying). There is an awkward switch to the distributive sg, however, and the parallel with the following clause is lost. Rather than restore איש "man" before עשה "made" (Rudolph; but this does not answer the second difficulty noted), I propose repointing the verb עֹשָׂה, to agree with יד: "with one of his hands engaged in the work . . ." The present pointing was an inevitable consequence of the faulty verse division noted earlier; once that had happened, the present verse was given its major division at עמשים (note the *'athnāḥ*) with the consequence that עשה was understood verbally, and so required a subject (clearly "workman" understood), rather than adjectivally in dependence on יד "hand."

12(18).a. For the syntax, cf. GKC § 116k².

13(19).a. הרבה ורחבה (lit. "great and expanded") is to be understood as a hendiadys.

15(21).a. MT here has "and half of them holding the spears." The phrase is, however, extremely awkward. (i) Since the narrative context is in the first person, the suff on the first word (וחצים, "and half of them") has no antecedent. (ii) It is not true that half the builders held their spears; contrast v 12(18). (iii) Nowhere else is there a reference to a group armed with spears alone. (iv) The words are suspiciously repetitious of the same phrase in v 10(16). Moreover, the two previous words in each verse are the same (עשים במלאכה "engaging in the work"). It is thus probable that the phrase originated by a scribe erroneously copying from the wrong place (Bowman. This seems preferable to Rudolph's view that it started as a marginal correction to v 10. The slight difference between the two passages may be explained by the accommodation of v 15 to the more common idiom ב החזיק at a subsequent stage of transmission).

16(22).a. Lit., "guardianship by night and work by day," the abstracts serving for the concrete "guards" and "workmen" (Keil). It is true that הלילה and היום usually mean "tonight" and "today" respectively, but cf. GKC § 118i for the syntax here. There is thus no need for emendation (*contra* Joüon, *Bib* 12 [1931] 85, and Rudolph).

17(23).a. MT: "a man his weapon the water." Despite numerous attempts both in antiquity (cf. the Vrs) and since, it has not been possible to make sense of this text as it stands; cf. Ryle for a long list of proposals. Thus AV (following Vg) repointed שלחו as a verb: "saving that every one put them off for washing," though even this rendering is forced; RV, "every one went with his weapon to the water," has to supply a good deal and even then gives an unsatisfactory connection with the remainder of the verse. It looks, therefore, as though the corr is very early, and that attempts to emend on the basis of later Vrs (e.g. Syr., "each one with his weapon in his hand for a full month of days," linking המים with הימים) are unlikely to succeed. In such a case, the most convincing emendation is the one that stays closest to the MT, makes sense, and can explain how the error arose. Here, therefore, following Böttcher (Keil and Rudolph), we restore ה(י)מינו. The confusion of נ and ם is not infrequent and may have arisen because

of the use of ligatures in the script; cf. R. Weiss, "On Ligatures in the Hebrew Bible (נ = ם)
JBL 82 (1963) 188–94, for discussion and examples. The verb is a rare denominative hiph
from ימין, for which the meaning "to keep at one's right hand" seems reasonable. איש "man"
and the suff on שלחו "his weapon" are then to be regarded as distributive sgs. Beside this
view, Warner's proposal, *ExpTim* 63 (1951–52) 322, to read שַׁלֹּחַ, "at the discharge of the
waters," or "at Siloam" (justified on the grounds that this was the customary place for washing
clothes), seems less plausible.

Form/Structure/Setting

No one seriously doubts that this passage derives from the NM and that
its setting is to be taken at face value: a crisis point that was successfully
passed during the building of the walls.

There are those, however (principally Hölscher and Mowinckel, *Studien
II*, 24–26), who find that the passage has been extensively glossed by a later
hand with one particularly important historical consequence: an original *internal* mutiny against Nehemiah has been transformed into an external threat.
Much will depend, however, on whether coherent sense can be made of the
passage as it stands; on this, see *Comment* below. Meanwhile, Kellermann,
Nehemia, 18–20, has examined the arguments advanced for each phrase which
has been taken as a gloss and has rightly rejected most of them.

Two observations about the structure of the passage further support the
majority view. First, it continues the pattern already noted as characteristic
of the memoir (cf. *Form* on 3:33–37). A step forward in the narrative, 3:38
(4:6), is met by opposition, introduced by the formula "When Sanballat . . .
heard." Nehemiah's countermeasures then follow. In a variation on this same
basic pattern, 4:9 (15) repeats the formula ("When our enemies heard that
all was known to us . . .") as an indication that this form of frontal opposition
had finally failed; Nehemiah and his people are now able to continue the
work unhindered—albeit with necessary precautions. This reversal of structure
neatly brings one section of the narrative to a close; when the enemies reappear
in chap. 6, their tactics will be quite different.

It may be noted briefly at this point that the increasing emphasis on Nehemiah's countermeasures noted already at 3:33–37 (4:1–5) is here continued.
Indeed it completely dominates by comparison with the introductory positive
statement of 3:38 (4:6). This too, therefore, points to a certain climax in
the narrative, for this development has now reached its furthest possible
extent.

Second, Kellermann, *Nehemia*, 18, has observed that throughout 4:1–14
(7–20) there are points of contact with the laws for and descriptions of the
"holy war" in earlier, particularly Deuteronomic, texts; cf. G. von Rad, *Der
Heilige Krieg im alten Israel* (ATANT 20; Zürich: Zwingli-Verlag, 1951). Though
not all the elements serve quite the same function as in the earlier sources,
he notes the following points: the enemy band together against Jerusalem;
the people pray before arming themselves; the human resources for defense
are slender; the forces are a conscript militia rather than a standing army;
the leader proclaims God's involvement in the battle and calls for faith and
fearlessness; the enemy is discouraged; and the trumpet blast is the signal
for battle. It may well be, therefore, that the author was influenced to some

extent by the earlier, stereotyped descriptions of the preparation for battle and the engagement itself. If so, the even distribution of these elements throughout the main part of this passage tells in favor of its unity and coherence.

Comment

3:38 (4:6) Though a generalization, this verse may stand as a broadly accurate description of the work to date. Only a few held back from involvement (3:5), and the taunts of Sanballat and Tobiah do not seem to have had much impact. Their change of tactics to the threat of frontal assault in the next paragraph immediately had a demoralizing effect, however. From this high point of progress and enthusiasm, therefore, Nehemiah has not only to counter "fightings without," but also, and potentially more debilitating, "fears within."

4:1 (7) The renewed opposition comes, literally, from all sides. Sanballat, of course, represents Samaria to the north. For the remainder, cf. Alt, *KS* 2, 338–45, who suggests that "the Arabs" were, in the Persian provincial system, Judah's immediately southern neighbor, the Idumaeans (Edomites) being included with them. On Geshem as their leading official, see 2:19. "The Ammonites" were immediately to the east of Judah, though we have no evidence whether they too were a separate Persian province or whether Nehemiah is here speaking less specifically. In the case of "the Ashdodites," however, he uses precise terminology again for Judah's western neighbor: after the capture of this Philistine territory by the Assyrians in 711 B.C., Ashdod was the name given to the new province which they there established, and this name was evidently taken over by the Persians.

For "Tobiah," see *Comment* on 2:10 above. The order of the list in this verse gives further support to the view advanced there that he should not be associated with the administration of the Ammonites. He is mentioned here because of his particular personal interest in Judah, and his place in this list is determined by the fact that Sanballat championed his cause.

The "restoration of the walls" is referred to by way of a metaphor derived from the healing of a wound. The expression is found also at 2 Chr 24:13, so that it may have been a regular idiom. It is tempting, nevertheless, to see in it something of Nehemiah's intense concern for the health and well-being of the city. More prosaically, he then explains that those parts where the wall had been completely breached were now partially filled in ("were beginning to be stopped up": i.e., to half their full height; cf. 3:38 [4:6]).

2 (8) It is a moot point whether the alliance was in earnest in its stated aim of coming to "fight against Jerusalem," later explained in v 5 as to "kill them and so make the work stop." On the one hand, such action by local officials would clearly not have been tolerated by their seniors—the satrap and the court itself. Especially was this so when Nehemiah's authorization was so clear. On the other hand, they may have thought that if they acted quickly enough and so presented their seniors with a *fait accompli,* there would be few, if any, reprisals. After all, they were only doing what they had been authorized to do shortly before, according to Ezra 4:21–23. More importantly, however, those in Jerusalem who had experienced that earlier set-back (and that must have been the vast majority) would not have paused to consider the legalities of the threat: enough for them that recent history appeared to be about to repeat itself! Sanballat and his allies may have been relying on this reaction, just as Nehemiah had to counter it with an equally resolute-looking response.

3 (9)   We have already noted on several occasions that it was characteristic of Nehemiah to regard prayer and action as the necessary and complementary ways to face each developing situation.

The chronology of these verses is not fully clear. Should each episode be regarded as following temporally upon that which is recounted before it, or is this verse intended as a summary statement whose details are elaborated in the remainder of the chapter? The impression through vv 2–6 (8–12) is of a generally deteriorating situation, with external threat merely fueling the internal discouragement. Then in v 7 (13) Nehemiah makes a fully decisive response after which the arrangements described in the later part of the chapter presumably lasted until the work was finished.

4 (10)   If "bad news travels fast," so does the discontent which often attends it. In this case the process was hastened by a mournful jingle that rapidly caught on. The verse couplet has the *qinah*, or lament, meter (3+2; 3+2), indicative of the despair of melancholy. Most unusually for biblical verse, there is also internal rhyme (נוכל . . . הסבל); this gives an inconsequential, almost trite impression, thereby echoing the futility which the words express. At this halfway stage in the work and with external pressure mounting, the sentiment is clear enough: "We shall *never* be able to finish."

5 (11)   See *Comment* on v 2 (8) above. By spreading a rumor (see the next verse) that a surprise attack was planned, the enemy made the builders yet more unsettled and on edge.

6–7 (12–13)   The main problem in these verses concerns the understanding of the Hebrew text; once that issue is decided, the interpretation follows naturally. The problems have been discussed above in *Notes*, with some attention to alternative views. The picture which emerges is reflected in the translation.

As we know from the list in chap. 3, many of the outlying˜villages and towns of Judah had sent representative groups of workers to assist the rebuilding of the wall. Just where the enemy "coalition" was mustering we do not know, but we may be sure that it will not have been without a sufficient show of strength to impress all who saw it. Furthermore, they no doubt made sure that these same Jews were under the clear impression that their design was only upon Jerusalem and its wall-builders. Any who returned home to their townships would not be threatened. Thus it was that "time and again" groups of concerned relatives and fellow villagers were coming to Jerusalem to implore their menfolk: "You must return to us."

Faced with the likelihood of a mass desertion if he made no response, Nehemiah found a way both to encourage his own men and to impress the enemy with his determination. The usual view is that Nehemiah immediately stationed his men at various strategically chosen points around the walls (see, for instance, RSV: "So in the lowest parts of the space behind the wall, in open places, I stationed the people . . ."). The translation and notes above, however, seek to defend an understanding which appears more appropriate in the context. On this view, Nehemiah gathered the people together in full battle order in the manner of the ancient conscript army and addressed them in a way reminiscent of the preparation for a "holy war"; see *Comment* on v 8 (14) below. By calling together into a show of strength all those who had been scattered in small groups along the length of the wall, he was quickly able to restore morale.

At the same time, Nehemiah was careful to choose a spot for this gathering that would not go unnoticed by the enemy. Observation of his preparations would assure them that they could not catch the wall-builders by surprise and that their attempts to undermine support for Nehemiah had failed.

8 (14) The people were not particularly well armed—the previous verse mentions only such light weapons as might have been owned by members of a basically rural population for hunting and so on; nor had they any experience, so far as we know, of armed combat. Nehemiah capitalizes, however, on two quite separate, but equally valuable, assets. Most simply, he motivates them with concern for their families and homes: "fight for your brothers, your sons and your daughters, your wives and your homes." This exhortation will have been the more effective for the fact that he had already marshaled them according to family association (cf. v 7).

More important even than that, however, Nehemiah sets the whole enterprise within the context of the religious tradition of his ancient people's struggle for freedom within the land promised to them, a struggle which, indeed, had been waged not merely by their ancestors but, according to the biblical tradition, by God himself fighting on their behalf. This tradition was, of course, well known to Nehemiah and to his people. Nehemiah is therefore able to speak in stereotyped language which not only carries meaning within itself but is further reinforced by the recollections it would evoke of the past victories of God for his people's sake; see in particular Exod 14:13–14, together with many other references listed in von Rad, *Heilige Krieg*, 6–14, and *Form* above.

9 (15) Nehemiah modestly recounts the success of his tactics in a matter-of-fact style: while it seems to have been Nehemiah's demonstration that he was aware of the enemies' plans which caused them to withdraw, the credit is nevertheless ascribed to God, who had "frustrated their plan"—a parallel to the confusion and despair into which God had often cast his people's enemies of old (Exod 15:14–16; 23:27–28; Deut 2:25; 11:25, etc.). With the immediate danger now past, therefore, the people (apparently without dissension) return to their work.

10 (16) The next paragraph outlines the defensive precautions which Nehemiah took and which were to last until the completion of the wall-building. He describes first the disposition of "my men" (נערי). This does not refer to the builders in general, but to a small group of trained men who, for whatever reason, owed personal allegiance to Nehemiah. Something of their social standing (clearly higher than that of a normal "servant"), significance and loyalty may be gauged from 4:17 (23); 5:10 and 16; 13:19, while a similar picture emerges from the use of the same word in connection with other leading citizens of Jerusalem or Samaria at 4:16 (22); 5:15; 6:5; for the remainder of the OT, cf. J. MacDonald, "The Status and Role of the Naʿar in Israelite Society," *JNES* 35 (1976) 147–70, and especially H.-P. Stähli, *Knabe-Jüngling-Knecht: Untersuchungen zum Begriff* נער *in Alten Testament* (BET 7. Frankfurt am Main: Peter Lang, 1978), who on pp. 162–67 suggests that the נערים were placed at Nehemiah's disposal, *ex officio*, in his capacity as governor, and for the evidence from seals, cf. N. Avigad, "New Light on the *Naʿar* Seals," in F. M. Cross, W. E. Lemke and P. D. Miller (eds.), *Magnalia Dei: the Mighty Acts of God* (Garden City: Doubleday, 1976) 294–300. Until now, they had apparently all been involved in the building work (perhaps in a supervisory capacity [cf. 5:16], though this is not stated for certain). Now, however, half were to serve as a picked cadre to give the lead if combat became inevitable. Note how their armor was more refined than that of the people's militia (v 7[13]). No doubt the sight of this well-armed troop would have also inspired the builders with confidence.

Next, Nehemiah mentions certain "officers" who stood back from the work of building itself. These we must understand to be the divisional commanders of the people's militia (see the use of the same word at Deut 20:9), which in earlier times, at least, was organized on a largely family and clan basis. They stood apart from the work in order to keep watch, to be in communication with Nehemiah (cf. v 14[20]), and to be ready at a moment's notice to direct their men from building to defense. Thus we may see that, even with the few men at his disposal, Nehemiah appears to have maintained on a modified scale something of the distinction attested in the period of the monarchy between a professional standing army and a people's conscript army or militia; cf. de Vaux, *Ancient Israel*, 218–28.

11–12 (17–18) Even though the bulk of the work force continued to concentrate on building, they were in a state of constant armed readiness. "The basket-carriers," who removed rubble and collected materials, had a hand free to carry a weapon with them—and this may well have been necessary as they moved in more exposed places outside the walls. The word used here, שלח, suggests some kind of a missile. "It would seem quite natural for men who work among the rubble to pick up a stone (missile) and carry it in one hand to defend themselves" (Fensham).

"The builders themselves," of course, needed both hands free for their work, but could nevertheless have their swords girded at their sides.

13–14 (19–20) With his men spread so thinly around the circumference of the wall, Nehemiah needed to be able to summon them quickly to any given spot where an attack might come. He solved this problem by preparing the people to listen for a trumpet blast as a signal which he could order to be sounded at any moment. In his instructions to the people on this matter, he again made use of the language of the traditional "holy war" (see *Comment* on v 8 and *Form* above). Not only was the trumpet blast the signal for action in earlier times too (cf. Judg 3:27; 6:34; 7:18; 1 Sam 13:3), but Nehemiah's concluding words of encouragement, "our God will fight for us," exactly echo the stereotyped formula of previous accounts; cf. Exod 14:14; Deut 1:30; 3:22; 20:4; Josh 10:14, 42; 23:10. Kidner aptly draws attention to Ps 127:1b: "Unless the Lord watches over the city, the watchman stays awake in vain."

16 (22)   Two reasons may have motivated the emergency measure of having the whole workforce sleep in Jerusalem. At the simplest level, it would save the time otherwise spent in traveling back home to the surrounding villages. At the same time, however, it would prevent any drifting away from commitment to the task at the point where the going was most tough. The psychological pressure analyzed at vv 6–7 (12–13) above was no doubt maintained throughout this period.

For "his servant," see *Comment* on v 10 (16) above. This would imply that the men ("every man") involved were leading citizens. Nehemiah's move to prevent this particular group returning home each evening may well have been popular among the people at large, especially in view of the sequel in chap. 5.

The language of this and the previous verse is naturally to be understood as a generalization. No doubt a shift system ensured that everyone also had some sleep!

17 (23)   Whether awake or asleep, however, Nehemiah and his immediate entourage (again, see v 10[16]) set an example of constant vigilance. With a weapon to hand and dressed at all times for action, they could not be accused of laying harder burdens on others than they themselves were willing to shoulder.

Explanation

For all its apparent triumph, the opening verse of the section sounds an ominous note: the halfway stage has been reached. In all major undertakings this is often a point for critical reflection. Initial enthusiasm has worn thin and the end is not yet sufficiently within sight to encourage a final effort. Nehemiah's leadership thus faced a crisis as sentiments of despair rapidly passed from mouth to mouth, aided by an expressive ditty that did nothing to relieve the gloom (v 4 [10]).

To make matters worse, the tactics of the enemy were having an increasingly unsettling effect. The unholy alliance of v 1 (7) meant that Judah was effectively surrounded by hostile powers whose threats, whatever their legality in fact, will have seemed far from empty to those most closely involved. Had Nehemiah allowed these twin dangers to go unchecked, there was a serious likelihood of mass desertions, resulting in the probable abandonment of the whole project.

His response, however, was a model of perceptive leadership. He apportioned no blame, but yet confronted each cause of discontent head on. First, against the external threat he displays a *common-sense flexibility*. He is prepared to interrupt the building for a while in order to prepare his people and put on a determined face, to redeploy some of those previously engaged in building as full-time guards, to slow the pace of the work somewhat by introducing the encumbrance of weapons, and to institute an effective means of communications.

Second, he responds to the people's unsettled nervousness with an *appeal to tradition*. This is seen by his introduction of measures which had been found trustworthy at many times through Israel's long history. His organizing of the popular militia and his words to them were, as has been seen in *Comment* above, couched in such a way that the people would be filled with confidence: "our God will fight for us" was known from past experience to be no empty saying. By thus imposing a familiar interpretative framework on his people's sense of confusion, Nehemiah succeeded in using their very fear itself as a ground for renewed faith. And here we should further note that, as has been seen several times already in Nehemiah's account, there is no room for a dichotomy between faith and responsible action: prayer and trust in God go hand in hand with sensible organization of what resources were available. Indeed, the words "watch and pray" could be written large over this chapter. Without doubt, Nehemiah will have calculated that his practical measures, such as the use of the trumpet to ensure that none felt isolated in his work, would materially assist, not stand as an alternative to, the builders' faith.

Finally, the temptation to give up because of the difficulties of the work was met with the response of *leadership by example*. The closing verse of the chapter is, of course, most explicit here, but it is likely to be behind the preceding verse too, on the understanding advanced above, while throughout the narrative Nehemiah seems to be tireless in efforts to ensure that the work could proceed unhindered.

And Jesus said . . . , "No man, having put his hand to the plough, and looking back, is fit for the kingdom of God" (Luke 9:62, KJV).

"Grant us, O Lord, to remember that it is not the undertaking of any great matter, but the continuing of the same until it be thoroughly finished, which yieldeth the true glory."

Internal Difficulties (Neh 5:1–19)

Bibliography

Alt, A. "Die Rolle Samarias bei der Entstehung des Judentums." *KS* 2, 316–37. **Avigad, N.** *Bullae and Seals from a Post-Exilic Judean Archive.* Qedem: Monographs of the Institute of Archaeology 4. Jerusalem: Institute of Archaeology, The Hebrew University, 1976. **Cohen, A.** "ה'צפרים 'בארוחת נחמ'ה." *B Mik* 12/3 (1966/67) 139–40. **Kellermann, U.** *Nehemia,* 19–21, 154–66. **Kippenberg, H. G.** *Religion und Klassenbildung im antiken Judäa. Eine religionssoziologische Studie zum Verhältnis von Tradition und gesellschaftlicher Entwicklung.* SUNT 14. Göttingen: Vandenhoeck & Ruprecht, 1978. 54–77. **Kreissig, H.** *Die Sozialökonomische Situation in Juda zur Achämenidenzeit.* Schriften zur Geschichte und Kultur des alten Orients 7. Berlin: Akademie-Verlag, 1973. **McEvenue, S. E.** "The Political Structure in Judah from Cyrus to Nehemiah." *CBQ* 43 (1981) 353–64. **Neufeld, E.** "The Rate of Interest and the Text of Nehemiah 5.11." *JQR* ns 44 (1953–54) 194–204. **North, R.** *Sociology of the Biblical Jubilee.* AnBib 4. Rome: Pontifical Biblical Institute, 1954. ———. "Civil Authority in Ezra." (See *Main Bibliography.*) **Pons, J.** *L'Oppression dans l'Ancien Testament.* Paris: Letouzey et Ané, 1981. **Smith, M.** *Palestinian Parties and Politics that Shaped the Old Testament.* New York: Columbia U. Press, 1971. chap. 6 and pp. 193–201 (= "Appendix: Alt's Account of the Samaritans"). **Stern, E.** *Material Culture of the Land of the Bible in the Persian Period 538–332 B.C.* Warminster: Aris and Phillips, 1982. 196–214. **Vogt, H. C. M.** *Studie,* 108–17. **Watson, W. G. E.** "Reclustering Hebrew *l'lyd -.*" *Bib* 58 (1977) 213–15. **Yamauchi, E. M.** "Two Reformers Compared: Solon of Athens and Nehemiah of Jerusalem." *The Bible World. Essays in Honor of Cyrus H. Gordon,* ed. G. Rendsburg, R. Adler, M. Arfa and N. H. Winter. New York: Ktav and The Institute of Hebrew Culture and Education of New York University, 1980. 269–92. **Zimmermann, F.** "The Root *KAHAL* in Some Scriptural Passages." *JBL* 50 (1931) 311–12. **Zwaan, J. de.** "Shaking out the Lap." *The Expositor* vii/5 (1908) 249–52.

Translation

[1] *Then there arose a great outcry of the people and their wives against their fellow Jews.* [2] *There were some who said, "With our sons and daughters we are numerous;* [a] *so let us have* [b] *some grain so that we may eat and live."* [3] *Others said, "We are mortgaging our fields, our vineyards, and our houses to get* [a] *some grain during the famine."* [4] *Still others were saying, "We have had to borrow money on* [a] *our fields and vineyards for the royal tribute."* [b] [5] *"Now,* [a] *we are of the same flesh and blood as our brothers* [b] *and our children are as their children. But we are on the point of bringing our sons and daughters into the bondage of slavery; indeed, some of our daughters are (already) enslaved, and we are powerless to do anything about it,* [c] *for our fields and our vineyards belong to others."*

[6] *I was very angry when I heard their outcry and these words.* [7] *After turning the matter over in my mind* [a] *I contended with the nobles and officials and said to them, "Each of you is acting the creditor* [b] *against his own brother." I summoned a great assembly* [c] *because of them,* [8] *and said to them, "As far as possible, we have been buying back our fellow Jews who had to sell themselves to the Gentiles, whereas you*

are selling off your brethren with the result that they will have to be sold back ᵃ *to us again.'' At this they were silent, unable to find a word in reply.* ⁹ *So I continued,* ᵃ *"What you are doing is not good. Will you not walk in the fear of our God in order to avoid the reproach of our Gentile enemies?* ¹⁰ *Yes, I too, my brothers and my men have been advancing them loans of money and grain; let us now abandon this practice of loans.* ᵃ ¹¹ *Return to them today their fields, their vineyards, their olive groves, and their houses and the percentage on* ᵃ *the money, grain, new wine, and oil which you are loaning to them.''* ¹² *"We will return them,'' they said, "and we will not exact anything from them. We will do as you say.'' So I called the priests and made them swear to act accordingly.* ¹³ *Then I shook out the fold of my garment and said, "Thus may God shake out* ᵃ *from his house and property any man who does not keep this promise; thus may he be shaken out and left empty!'' The whole assembly said "Amen,'' and praised the Lord, and the people did as they had promised.*

¹⁴ *Moreover from the day when I was appointed* ᵃ *to be governor* ᵇ *in the land of Judah—from the twentieth to the thirty-second year of King Artaxerxes, twelve years in all—neither I nor my brothers ate of the governor's food allowance.* ¹⁵ *The earlier governors who came before me laid a heavy burden* ᵃ *on the people and exacted from them* ᵇ *for their daily ration* ᵇ *forty shekels of silver. Their retainers too used to lord it over the people. Out of reverence for God, however, I have not acted like that.* ¹⁶ *On the contrary, I stuck to the work on this wall, even though we* ᵃ *acquired no land: all my men were gathered there for the work.* ¹⁷ *As for the Jews* ᵃ*—there were* ᵇ *150 officials together with any who came to us from the surrounding nations, at my table.* ¹⁸ *What was prepared each day at my expense* ᵃ *was: one ox, six choice* ᵇ *sheep, and some poultry,* ᶜ *and, at ten day intervals,* ᵈ *wine of every kind in abundance.* ᵉ *Yet for all this I never claimed the governor's food allowance because the service weighed so heavily on this people.*

¹⁹ *Remember in my favor, O my God, all that I have done for this people.* ᵃ

Notes

2.a. MT is tersely expressed ("our sons and our daughters we are many"), but not necessarily impossible (*contra* Rudolph) if this indeed represents a cry of desperation. There is no formal textual warrant for emendation (Vg's addition is interpretative, not a witness to a different text). If sense can then be made of MT in context, it should be accepted; cf. *Comment* below. A number of commentators, however, prefer the slight conjectural emendation (first proposed in 1753) of ערבים for רבים; cf. NEB: "Some complained that they were giving their sons and daughters as pledges for food to keep themselves alive." It is maintained that MT does not fit the context of v 1 and was not alleviated by the measures which Nehemiah took, whereas the emended text gives a closer parallel with v 3. This latter point is vitiated by the lack of parallel between v 3 and v 4, however, while the emendation has the disadvantage of anticipating v 5 where the selling of children into debt-slavery is, perhaps, threatening as the ultimate indignity.

2.b. The *wāw* may be construed as introducing the apodosis, followed, as sense here demands, by a cohortative.

3.a. Or "We are about to mortgage . . . , so let us have." The construction is identical with the previous verse. Verse 11, however, gives some grounds for favoring the translation given above.

4.a. Unless שדתינו וכרמינו "our fields and our vineyards" has been erroneously repeated from the previous verse, לוה "borrow" must here be construed with a double accus. Others favor the addition of the prep על "upon," with no difference in meaning. Lack of an exactly parallel usage precludes certainty.

4.b. This word does not occur elsewhere, but cf. Ezra 4:13 for a note on its Aram. equivalent.

5.a. The use of ועתה suggests that this verse may represent a summing up of all the previous complaints rather than merely a continuation of v 4.

5.b. Lit., "our flesh is like the flesh of our brothers."

5.c. While the meaning of this phrase is not in doubt, its precise explanation is disputed; for parallels, see Gen 31:29; Deut 28:32; Mic 2:1; Prov 3:27; Sir 5:1; 14:11. Usually, אל is said here to have the meaning "power," and hence "there is no power to our hands." Recently, however, F. M. Cross, *TDOT* 1, 260–61, and Watson, *Bib* 58 (1977) 213–15, have independently proposed redividing the words as אין לא לידנו and understanding לא as "power." While this would ease the syntax, the existence of this word in Heb. is not certain, though it occurs in a number of cognate languages. It would also be curious if the MT so consistently divided the consonants incorrectly.

7.a. Cf. *mlk* in Aram. and Akk., and H. R. Cohen, *Biblical Hapax Legomena in the Light of Akkadian and Ugaritic* (SBLDS 37; Missoula: Scholars Press, 1978), 143; "my heart took counsel upon it." NEB, "I mastered my feelings," links מלך with the denominative verb "to reign," but this is nowhere attested in the niph, and the sense is not particularly borne out by the sequel.

7.b. The precise nature of Nehemiah's accusation is disputed (see also *Comment*). It is not certain that the practice involved was strictly illegal (Nehemiah had himself been involved according to v 10) so much as inappropriate; this may account for the unusual word order. Heb. has other words for "to lend" and "to exact interest"; it looks, therefore, as though נשא may mean to loan on pledge (see also Exod 22:24; Deut 24:10). This, at least, would fit the accusation to the complaints of the previous verses. Rudolph's proposal to read משא and נשאים and to translate "Each one of you is imposing a burden upon his brother" (Myers) is implausible. נשא means "to carry, remove," not "impose," and the preposition ב (rather than expected על) is a further difficulty to this view.

7.c. Although קהלה is used in place of the more common קהל "assembly," its meaning seems to be guaranteed by v 13. Zimmermann, *JBL* 50 (1931) 311–12, suggested "rebuke" on the basis of an Arab. cognate; he is followed (independently?) by Brockington and NEB: "I rebuked them severely." However, NEB correctly keeps the usual meaning at Deut 33:4 (the only other place where the word occurs), and this makes its rendering of the present passage less likely. Finally, in Sir 7:7 קהלה is clearly parallel with עדה (*contra* Zimmermann), providing further confirmation of the traditional rendering.

8.a. Rudolph objects that the sequence of thought here is unexpected; he therefore proposes reading ונכרו, "so that they will have to be bought back." Nehemiah is clearly playing on the word מכר, "to sell," however; if the niph may be allowed a fully passive meaning here (rather than reflexive as earlier in the verse), it is preferable to retain MT.

9.a. Read ואמר with Q and the Vrs.

10.a. Fensham thinks that Nehemiah's proposal goes even further: "Let us absolve this loan!" This is a possible, though apparently unattested, use of עזב. In any case, it becomes clear in the next verse that Nehemiah also has this in mind.

11.a. This is the only use of מאת (lit., "a hundredth of") in this technical sense. It is generally taken to mean 1% (probably monthly), i.e., an annual rate of interest of 12%. Without other examples of the usage, however, we should not rule out the possibility of the more general rendering "percentage." Either way, that interest on the loans is intended seems to be clear from the response of the people in the next verse (cf. Keil; Ryle). The widely adopted emendations to מַשָּׁאת "debt" or מַשֹּׁאת "burden" or perhaps "income" (NEB) are thus unnecessary. Kidner prefers the latter translation ("the income derived by the creditors from the property they have taken in pledge"), but I am unable to follow his reasoning when he seeks to defend this as an interpretation of MT ("The word *hundredth* could presumably denote this yield, and fix the assessment of it"). If the problem had arisen quite recently, it is probable that the interest had not yet been paid; this again is the implication of v 12. In that case, השיבו "return" has to be understood by zeugma to mean "remit" before the second half of the verse; cf. Neufeld, *JQR* ns 44 (1953–54) 201.

13.a. On this piel (for qal earlier in the verse), cf. E. Jenni, *Das hebräische Piʿel* (Zürich: EVZ Verlag, 1968) 136–37.

14.a. As it stands, MT either has an unusual impers sg construction ("one appointed me") or expects "the king" to be understood as subject. Neither construction is very likely, so that Rudolph's conjecture (צויתי = צואתי) is attractive.

14.b. Read פחה with one MS, Vg and Syr. While one might have thought of an anticipatory suff in this late biblical Heb., that would require פחתם. In view of the overall context, North's attempt ("Civil Authority in Ezra") to exploit the problems of the MT of this verse so as to deny that Nehemiah was governor (he proposes reading בהם for פחם) must be rejected.

15.a. MT here uses the hiph of כבד absolutely, with an elipse of the expected object. As there is no parallel for this construction, however, many prefer to conjecture that על "a yoke" has been lost by haplogr before על; cf. Joüon, *Bib* 12 (1931) 87, who compares 1 Kgs 12:10, 14, and the Lucianic reading here: κλοιόν.

15.b-b. As Joüon correctly observes, MT's אחר "after" is impossible, and יין "wine" should not be singled out for particular mention. Following the indication of v 18, read ליום אחד "for one day" (cf. Vg). לחם may then be understood in the general sense of "food," hence "ration," and the prep ב may be retained before it (*contra* Rudolph *et al.*) as a form of the ב *pretii* (cf. GKC § 119p) as at Gen 29:18, אעבדך שבע שנים ברחל, "I will serve you seven years *for* Rachel."

16.a. Apparently an anticipation of the following clause; not surprisingly, however, some MSS and Vrs have a 1st pers sg.

17.a. "The Jews" can hardly be a title for one group within society. Rather it is to be taken as a *casus pendens* followed by a *wāw apodosis* (cf. GKC § 143). There is thus a nice contrast made with the previous verse: Nehemiah's men, who might be expected to be taking their ease, worked on the wall, while representatives of the local population were lavishly entertained at the governor's table.

17.b. This has to be added for the sake of English style. The Heb. construction is a somewhat involved nominal clause.

18.a. It is generally agreed that this must be the force of לי. The syntax of the first half of the verse is in any case somewhat idiosyncratic. A lit. translation would give: "And what was prepared for one day (was) one ox, six choice sheep and poultry; they were prepared for me." Several modern translations (e.g., rsv and neb) seek to ease this by dividing the verse before "poultry": "Now that which was prepared for one day was one ox and six choice sheep; fowls likewise were prepared for me. . . ." The Masoretic accents rightly tell against this, however, for despite the syntax the poultry are to be included as part of the general provision, and לי "at my expense" is intended to qualify the whole list.

18.b. The fact that ברדים is not used elsewhere for animals is no reason to emend to בריות (for בריאות "fat"), as suggested by Joüon, *Bib* 12 (1931) 87–88. Nehemiah's style in this verse (to go no further!) can clearly not be pressed into a stereotyped mold.

18.c. There is no compelling reason to emend to צפרים, "goats," *contra* Cohen, *BMik* 12/3 (1966–67) 139–40.

18.d. בין must here be understood substantivally; cf. L. Köhler, "Hebräische Vokabeln III," *ZAW* 58 (1940–41) 229.

18.e. It is usual to emend to נבלי יין or כלי יין "skins *or* vessels of wine." Neither proposal removes the chief difficulty, namely, that the exact quantity is not specified. It therefore seems better once more to retain MT (which has the unanimous support of the Vrs) as a further example of Nehemiah's idiosyncratic style. The verb is, of course, understood from the previous clause. For the partitive use of ב, cf. GKC § 119m.

19.a. For a grammatical analysis of this recurrent formula in Neh, cf. my "The Sure Mercies of David: Subjective or Objective Genitive?," *JSS* 23 (1978) 37–38, and W. Schottroff, *"Gedenken" im Alten Orient und im Alten Testament* (WMANT 15; 2nd ed.; Neukirchen-Vluyn: Neukirchener Verlag, 1967), 218–19 and 222.

Form/Structure/Setting

The chapter divides into two unequal halves. In the first (vv 1–13), Nehemiah deals with a particular socioeconomic problem that probably arose during the course of the wall-building. In the second (vv 14–18), he reflects in defensive mood on his practice in such matters throughout the period of his (first) term as governor. In a concluding verse he appeals to God to remember his good deeds with favor.

Very few doubt that the chapter forms an original part of the NM. The first-person narrative, the formula in the final verse, and the style of presentation are all said to speak strongly in favor of this conclusion (Kellermann, *Nehemia,* 19–21). The possibility of a few later additional glosses has been entertained (e.g., see *Comment* on v 14 below), but these do not materially affect the position and are, in any case, by no means certain.

In my opinion, for reasons arising from a wider consideration of the *genre* and composition of the NM as a whole, the final paragraph is to be regarded as having been added by Nehemiah at a later stage to his original account. The matter is discussed in the *Introduction,* "The Nehemiah Memoir." This helps to account for the evident chronological discontinuity between the two parts of the chapter. Since the paragraph was nevertheless composed by Nehemiah for its present setting, the results of this literary-critical conclusion for exegesis are only slight.

A major point of disagreement among the commentators concerns the setting of vv 1–13. A substantial minority maintain that they must have come from a time much later during Nehemiah's term of office, probably towards its close. Thus Batten (and cf. Ackroyd and Michaeli) argues that (i) the time of the wall-building was too short for such a major crisis to arise, (ii) the text does not link the crisis to the work on the wall, (iii) Nehemiah would not have stopped work on the wall for such an issue, and (iv) v 14 indicates that a much longer time span is in view. Finally, (v) Bowman suggests that Nehemiah may have placed the chapter here out of its current chronological sequence in order to mark the passing of time while the wall was being built.

In fact, however, it is the literary setting of the chapter that forms the strongest argument in favor of the alternative view (Pons, *Oppression,* 135–36). Since there is no evidence that the chapter has been misplaced, there is really no good reason to doubt that Nehemiah recorded it at this point simply because it took place here. Bowman's suggestion to the contrary falls down in the face of the arguments that there has already been quite enough material in chaps. 3 and 4 to mark the passing of time and that in any case the whole point about the wall-building was that it was accomplished so quickly.

The other difficulties, too, are more apparent than real. Taking them in reverse order, (iv) it is conceded that vv 14–18 reflect on a longer period, but this is made clear in the text and has no bearing on the setting of the incident in vv 1–13. The setting of vv 14–18 is a separate issue, discussed in the *Introduction,* "The Nehemiah Memoir," and should not prejudice consideration of vv 1–13. (iii) There is every indication that Nehemiah had no choice but to deal with the issue as soon as it arose—and the stoppage need not have lasted long. Had he taken no action, it is likely at best that he would have lost the service of many of his workers, and at worst that civil unrest would have developed. (ii) The lack of explicit reference to the wall-building in vv 1–13 is of no significance. The connection is already apparent from the literary context, and the complaints are best understood when read at face value against that background. (i) The only argument of any substance concerns the question whether the crisis could have developed so quickly. Here, however, it should be remembered that for the majority of those who were dependent on small farms alone, there were no reserves of capital or supplies on which they could draw. All the evidence we have points to the difficulties that this class faced in simply maintaining a level of subsistence for themselves and their families; the failure of even a single year's harvest could spell disaster for many. It is not unlikely, therefore, that an economic malaise had been simmering for some time. Now, there is good reason to believe that the commitment Nehemiah demanded of the builders was enough to spark the unrest described in the opening verses of the chapter. (i) As Neufeld, *JQR* ns 44 (1953–54) 203–4, has observed, the wall was completed on the twenty-fifth day of Elul, and the complaints may have been raised shortly before that date (August/September). "We are justified in assuming that the complaint came at a moment when the harvest of all important products of the soil had come to an end. That was the time when the creditors exacted their capital and interest." Neufeld may have slightly overstated his case, for it is doubtful if all aspects of harvesting would have finished so early. Nevertheless, if the implications of the situation were beginning to become clear at this time, his main point may still stand. (ii) Since, according to 4:16 (22), Nehemiah had forbidden the men to return home from Jerusalem while the wall was being built, the farms may have been severely understaffed during the crucial period of ingathering. (Among other factors, this may help account for the prominence of the wives in v 1.) The consequences of Nehemiah's resolve on the economy of many families may have thus become quite suddenly apparent. (iii) While the details of vv 2–5 are not as clear as we could wish, it nevertheless appears that the situation was not yet completely desperate, but rather that many could foresee disaster if prompt action was not taken. (iv) For the landless classes who are referred to in v 2, a period of even a few weeks without gainful employment would have had particularly harsh consequences. All in all, therefore, we may conclude that the wall-building could have brought matters to a head in the way described here. Indeed, Nehemiah's failure to invoke the laws of release (e.g., Deut 15) favors the view that the immediate situation developed suddenly rather than being the expression of a longer-term problem.

It remains finally to note that parallels have been drawn by several writers (most recently Kippenberg, *Religion und Klassenbildung;* Smith, *Palestinian Parties;* and Yamauchi, "Two Reformers") between Nehemiah's reforms as here described and those of Solon in Athens over a century before. There is no suggestion of direct influence, however, and indeed, as Kippenberg has pointed out, the differences in the nature of the two societies need also to be kept clearly in view. It is important, therefore, when undertaking such comparisons, first to understand the work of each reformer in his own right. An exegesis of Neh 5 on its own terms thus remains the first priority, and to this we must therefore now turn.

Comment

1 For the chronological setting of the chapter, see *Form* above. The somewhat unusual reference to the wives may not so much reflect the intensity of the suffering, as is generally thought, as it does the fact that they were more conscious of the approaching calamity because they were having to manage at home while their husbands were engrossed in the wall-building.

2 Three groups are distinguished in vv 2–4 by the introductory formula, ויש אשר אמרים "and there were some who said," which is repeated at the start of each verse. Their complaints were related by the fact that they were all falling into serious debt, but the reasons for this and the background against which it was happening varied from one group to another. It is probable that these groups are intended to be representative of a general problem rather than an exhaustive listing of every individual complaint.

The first group we take to refer to families who owned no land. They were dependent on wages from laboring of whatever sort. Since we have no evidence that Nehemiah paid wages to the builders, the families of these men were becoming destitute. Not unreasonably, they asked for basic sustenance to be provided.

Many commentators have found difficulties with this account and so wish to emend the text. The purely textual evidence is set out in *Notes* above, but the wider issues must be touched on here. First, it is argued that Jews would never complain about the size of their families because children were regarded as a mark of God's blessing. In reply it must be said that this is not the point of the text as it stands; the number of children is mentioned simply to underline the seriousness of the situation and perhaps also to evoke greater sympathy. Second, and more significantly, it is thought that the measures Nehemiah took later in the chapter do not answer to this particular complaint. However, on the one hand it is likely that in order to survive these families would have had either to borrow on the security of their children or even sell them into slavery, so that they would come under the general summary in v 5, and on the other hand, the list of complaints here is to be taken as representative, as already noted. It would be a mistake to try to tie up too closely every detail of the two parts of the chapter. Furthermore, the reference later to Nehemiah's personal generosity may well point to the solution of this particular difficulty.

Finally, it may be noted as a corollary of retaining the MT that the three groups in vv 2–4 are certainly separate and are not to be regarded as three successive stages along the path to debt-slavery, as proposed by Kippenberg, *Religion und Klassenbildung*, 56–57, in dispute with Kreissig, *Sozialökonomische Situation in Juda*, 78–79.

3 The second group are clearly differentiated from the first in that they owned land that they could use as security against a loan to tide them over the period of difficulty. (An instructive, and nearly contemporary, parallel is provided by *BMAP* 11, a legal document dealing with just such a loan.) However, the danger was now looming, we must suppose, that they would not be able to repay these loans because of the added burden imposed by the wall-building. In these circumstances they would probably choose first to sell their children (see the summary in v 5 and Kippenberg, *Religion und Klassenbildung*, 57). Harsh as this may seem, they would then still own their means of livelihood which would enable them to redeem their children. Once their land was forfeit, however, irreversible debt-slavery would soon inevitably follow.

This verse alone mentions "the famine" as a cause of the problem. While this might be another way of referring to the shortages caused by the preoccupation with the wall, it is more likely that it refers to a more general time of need. (These were clearly a recurrent problem; cf. Hag 1; Mal 3.) While normally such families would have expected to be able to repay their debts after the harvest, this year they would not be able to do so if the ingathering was seriously affected by Nehemiah's demands.

4 The situation of the third group was yet again slightly different: they too were evidently landowners who were falling into debt, but this time because they needed to borrow in order to pay their taxes. No mention is made of a food shortage, so that we may infer that their plight was not so immediately threatening. Nonetheless, if conditions continued unaltered, they too would apparently have to resort to the unhappy remedy of v 5.

For "the royal tribute," cf. Frye, *The Heritage of Persia,* 112–14, who observes that since the time of Darius there was a fixed annual land tax assessed "on the basis of an average yield from the land, for each satrapy, taking into account, of course, the kind of cultivation as well as the average amount of the yield." Despite this reform, the burden of taxation was nevertheless heavy, and its effects appear to have grown more severe as time went on and resort had increasingly to be made to creditors; cf. Olmstead, *History,* 297–99; Yamauchi, "Two Reformers Compared."

5 Together with other considerations already noted, the lack of a further introductory formula suggests that this verse does not describe a separate fourth group. Either it continues the complaint of the third, or, more probably, it summarizes the position of all three. Because (in cases where they owned them) their fields were already mortgaged, the debtors were on the point (הנה + participle) of having to sell their children into debt-slavery; indeed, the process was already starting, as some of their daughters had already been "enslaved." This word, נכבשות, has sexual overtones at Esth 7:8, and the singling out of daughters here suggests some treatment separate from debt-slavery. It is thus probable that they were having to gratify the creditors' lusts as payment for delaying foreclosure on the loans.

The loaning of money on pledge and the practice of debt-slavery were not illegal as such; cf. Exod 21:2–11; 22:24–26 (25–27); Lev 25; Deut 15:1–18; 24:10–13. (It is the practice of such loans that is primarily in view here rather than hardship caused by interest payments; cf. n. 7.b.) The laws, however, are concerned to protect the minimal rights of the very poor. Some of their stipulations were clearly unsuitable for the present emergency. For instance, the "year of release," if it was ever regularly observed, was evidently not sufficiently soon to offer the prospect of speedy alleviation; such a possibility simply passes without mention. Alongside these institutional safeguards, however, there was an attempt to build into Hebrew law a more general sense of justice and propriety regarding the treatment of fellow-Israelites. This comes to expression, among other means, by the repeated use of the term "your brother" in Lev 25, and it is on this that the complainants here base their plea. (Further allusions to Lev 25 are noted in vv 8 and 9 below.) They argue that the Jewish "brotherhood" involves codes of behavior that go further than legal stipulation. This had also, of course, been an important element in the preaching of the eighth century prophets, and it was apparently this which touched Nehemiah's conscience. (For the importance of Jewish "brotherhood" at this period, cf. Vogt, *Studie*, 106–117, and E. Neufeld, "The Prohibitions against Loans at Interest in Ancient Hebrew Laws," *HUCA* 26 [1955] 355–412, though, curiously, Neufeld does not draw this verse into his discussion of what he terms the "concept of theocratic brotherhood.") Despite this, it should be noted in conclusion, there is no indication that the people complained, or that Nehemiah reacted, on the specific basis of the law of Lev 25. As North, *Sociology*, 205–6, correctly observes, Nehemiah acted immediately and absolutely, apparently, therefore, on his own authority and without invoking any of the specific legal stipulations. If the parallels noted with Lev 25 are conscious allusions, then we must conclude that Nehemiah acted within the spirit, not the letter of the law.

6–7 When, after due reflection on the best way to proceed, Nehemiah enters into a quasi-legal dispute (אָרִיבָה "I contended with") with those who were acting as creditors, "the nobles and officials," he shows by his initial statement that it was an underlying concern with morality, rather than with the niceties of legal observance, that had touched his conscience. He picks up the reference of the complainants to the grievance that they were being treated in this way by their brothers—their fellow Jews and Judeans.

Nehemiah's wisdom in restraining his initial impulse to an angry outburst now becomes apparent: to a charge so carefully aimed there is no response, and so he is able to summon a public gathering to witness his elaboration both of the charge and its solution. By thus involving the population at large, the creditors would find it less easy to go back on the pledge that they are about to make. At the same time he managed to avoid personally alienating this group who were, after all, the leaders of the community, men on whom he relied for support in his administration.

8 In amplifying his charge, Nehemiah first points out the moral absurdity of what has been going on. In line with the procedure envisaged in Lev 25:47–48, the Jewish community had been rescuing by payment of a redemption price as many of their fellows who had had to sell themselves to the Gentiles as their limited resources allowed. It was considered quite unacceptable that Jews should be sold to foreigners if it could possibly be avoided. But now, Nehemiah observes, these creditors are, in effect, undoing with one hand the work they were seeking to establish with the other! They, no doubt, would have defended themselves by asserting that being sold to a fellow Jew was not at all the same as to a Gentile. Nehemiah undercuts this position, however, by asserting, first, that it still puts the same burden on the community and, second, that, from the point of view of the poor Jewish "brother," it is even more degrading.

This interpretation of the passage assumes that it is a particularly Judean custom which is here referred to. Other commentators maintain rather that Nehemiah is recalling the practice of the Jewish community in Babylon. Since the practice is not referred to elsewhere, there can be no final certainty in this matter. Nevertheless, the logic of the case Nehemiah is pressing is far more effective if he is pointing to the self-contradictory nature of the Jews' actions. This suggests that it was not only Nehemiah's personal practice to redeem enslaved Jews from the Gentile neighbors; after all, he had hardly been in Jerusalem for a sufficiently long time. We conclude rather that this verse preserves in passing a heartwarming insight into the humanitarian concerns of the Judean community stretching back over some considerable period.

9 Nehemiah turns secondly to religious considerations: with a further possible allusion to Lev 25 (cf. vv 36 and 43) he urges that a proper reverence, or "fear," of God would lead to a greater concern for maintaining his honor in the sight of the nations even at the expense of personal gain.

10 Finally, Nehemiah candidly admits that he, his family ("my brothers" seems here to be a separate group from the remainder of his entourage; see also 1:2), and his personal followers ("my men"; see *Comment* on 4:10 [16]) have also been involved in these practices. By this confession, Nehemiah probably succeeded in maintaining the unity of the community. At the same time it serves as further confirmation (see *Comment* on 2:3 and 8, and at vv 14–18 below) that Nehemiah belonged to one of the wealthy land-owning families of Judah.

Nehemiah's first and general statement of intent is also expressed in the first person: "let us now abandon . . ." It may be significant that he continues in the next verse in the second person. Perhaps his involvement was less extensive than the others, and it was certainly less advanced. The exposition of v 11 below will further show that conditions had gone much farther than could have happened in the personal case of Nehemiah since his arrival in Jerusalem. Thus, although for political reasons he associates himself with the culprits, yet he is clear that the longer-term problems, and hence their solution, are the responsibility of others.

11 Nehemiah now makes two specific proposals. The first is clear: any land that has been seized either as collateral or because the debtors had been unable to repay what they owed is to be returned to them unconditionally. The meaning of the second proposal is disputed. The main suggestions are summarized in *Notes* on this verse above, where it is concluded in the light of the following verse that the return (or waiving) of interest on the loans is intended. The question of interest has not been raised previously, because the fundamental problem was the practice of loans on pledge. That is no reason, however, to conclude that interest was not also levied. It is true that Exod 22:24 (25) and Lev 25:35–37 prohibit the exacting of interest on loans to poor Israelites and that Deut 23:20–21 (19–20) raises this into an absolute prohibition of interest on any loan to any Israelite, but it is clear that these laws were by no means universally observed.

The expression used here by Nehemiah is not found elsewhere with the same significance. If, as the majority of commentators believe, it means literally "one hundredth," and if this is then to be understood as the interest due each month, it would indicate an annual rate of interest of 12 percent. This would be very low by international standards of the time. The generally accepted minimum during the Persian period was 20 percent, though much higher rates are attested too; cf. R. P. Maloney, "Usury and Restrictions on Interest-Taking in the Ancient Near East," *CBQ* 36 (1974) 1–20. Perhaps, therefore, the word refers to "interest" more generally.

On this view, then, Nehemiah demands the return of property taken in pledge (or more probably seized in lieu of loan repayment) and the interest due on the original loan. It appears, therefore, that nothing is said about the repayment or cancellation of the original loan itself. (Verse 10 does not cover this either; see *Notes*.) However, if property that had been seized in lieu of repayment was to be returned, it is clearly implied that this also involves cancellation of the original loan. Nehemiah "sees now that the depth of poverty had called for gifts, not loans" (Kidner).

To summarize: as an immediate measure to meet the present crisis, Nehemiah demands the cancellation of all debts and interest due and therefore the return of any property that had been used in repayment. In the longer term, he demands the abandonment of this form of loan on pledge (v 10), which could so easily lead to loss of property and debt-slavery. He does not specify what should happen if anyone required a loan in the future, but shows rather by his own example (vv 14–18) that within the community generosity is to be preferred to personal gain.

12 The creditors accept Nehemiah's two specific demands and, apparently, his general statement of intent: "We will do as you say." Nehemiah then summons the priests, before whom the creditors take an oath to this effect. It is not stated whether this was because they showed some reluctance or whether Nehemiah wanted to impress the populace that the problem really had been dealt with so that they could now return without preoccupation to their work. Either way, there is no evidence to support the view that this is part of a covenant-renewal ceremony, as suggested by D. J. McCarthy, "Covenant and Law in Chronicles-Nehemiah," *CBQ* 44 (1982) 25–44, even though, in fairness, McCarthy qualifies his position with the words, "the object is not covenant as a whole but a single stipulation which touches a social, not a cultic duty, not even indirectly" (p. 33). Elements such as repentance, oath-taking and an acted-out curse (v 13) may have more than one solitary social or cultic setting.

13 With a gesture reminiscent of the prophets' "symbolic acts," Nehemiah enacted a curse against any who would violate the oath just taken. Small personal items were carried in a fold of the long, flowing garments, and kept secure by a belt or girdle. This Nehemiah emptied out and simultaneously pronounced his threat; for a somewhat far-fetched parallel, cf. Zwaan, *The Expositor* vii/5 (1908) 249–52. Such enacted words were believed to have a particular power in the ancient world; the people could therefore rest assured that God would guard the agreement just made. Their response thus shows not only concurrence in what Nehemiah had done ("Amen") but a sense of true relief that this burdensome problem had been resolved: they "praised the Lord!"

The last clause of the verse is ambiguous. It could be that the whole congregation "did according to this thing" (כדבר הזה), i.e., shook out their garments in imitation of Nehemiah. However, the use of the same phrase at the end of v 12 and a parallel one in the middle of v 13 (translated above as "this promise") makes it more likely that the paragraph concludes with a statement that Nehemiah's proposals were in fact carried out. The wide description, "the people," is possibly used because not only the creditors but also the debtors were involved in seeing the restitution through.

14 Not surprisingly, Nehemiah later found this to be a suitable point at which to include a note about the question of his personal financial generosity throughout his term as governor; see *Introduction*, "The Nehemiah Memoir." In the context it serves to show how he led the way by example toward a greater sense of social responsibility among the more wealthy residents of Judah. It is thus implied that under his leadership the internal strains that the wall-building operation revealed found a long-term solution. In particular, he gave a measure of relief from the taxation that had contributed to the problem in the first place (v 4).

At the same time, this paragraph contains interesting information for the reconstruction of the province's political history. First, only now are we told directly that Nehemiah was appointed "governor." The flexibility of the word used—פחה—has already been noted several times (e.g., at Ezra 5:3 and at 8:36). There is general agreement here, however, that it means governor of the small but independent province within the satrapy of Beyond the River. It is instructive to note that there is no record of this appointment, whether at the time of Nehemiah's initial commission, as seems most probable, or shortly after. This fact underlines the silence of our sources on many matters that we automatically regard as central. We should therefore beware of other arguments from silence that have featured prominently in discussions of the political status of Judah prior to Nehemiah (see below).

Second, the duration of Nehemiah's (first) term is clearly stated: "from the twentieth to the thirty-second year of King Artaxerxes, twelve years in all." The first half of this statement has been regarded by several commentators as a later gloss, though its information is not thereby necessarily challenged (cf. Rudolph). The text of this verse is not above suspicion (cf. *Notes*); nevertheless, as it stands, the syntax points away from the phrase in question being a gloss: the verse starts . . . גם מיום, "Moreover, from the day . . ." The use of the preposition מן, "from," does not prepare smoothly for the temporal phrase "twelve years in all." Such a phrase requires the later "from . . . to" construction as its antecedent to be intelligible. However, those who regard the dates as a gloss nevertheless have to retain the temporal phrase, because without it, they maintain, the gloss would not have been added in the first place. The resumption of מיום "from the day" by משנת "from the . . . . year" and the need of the latter to prepare for the temporal phrase "twelve years in all" combine to favor the integrity of the text at this point.

Third, we learn that, as we should expect, the governor was entitled to draw his salary from the taxation that he levied from the province on behalf of the Persian throne. This, however, Nehemiah waived, despite his wide responsibilities (see below), confirming again that he enjoyed a considerable personal income. To that extent, his position may be compared with that of Arsames, the satrap of Egypt, as revealed to us by his letters published in *AD*. They are to be distinguished, however, by the fact that Arsames' estates were back home in Babylon, whereas we have argued that the estates of Nehemiah's family were probably in Judah itself.

15 Fourth, we learn that there had been other governors before Nehemiah. The precise significance of this continues to be fiercely debated, however. On the one hand there are those who argue that this shows that Nehemiah's appointment did not herald any fundamental change in Judah's political status: Nehemiah succeeded to an office that had a long previous history. On the other hand, there are those who affirm on separate evidence that until Nehemiah's time Judah was governed as part of the province of Samaria; only with Nehemiah was Judah granted her separate provincial status. On this view, the present verse refers to governors who were resident in Samaria.

This latter position was given its fullest expression by Alt in his essay "Die Rolle Samarias bei der Entstehung des Judentums." Elaborations and restatements of it are made by, *inter alia,* Galling, *Studien;* Rudolph; Kellermann, *Nehemia* 154–66; and most recently, McEvenue, *CBQ* 43 (1981) 353–64. Archeological support is claimed by Stern, *Material Culture,* chap. 7. The evidence for Samaria's administrative authority over Judah remains, however, a hypothesis by which to explain the history of previous relations between the two districts. Our exposition of the relevant passages, especially Ezra 4, has not revealed the necessity of the hypothesis for an adequate understanding. The danger of arguments from silence in this area has been noted at v 14 above (and this danger is reinforced by the fact that there may be good reasons to explain the silence in Ezra 1–6; cf. Japhet, *ZAW* 94 [1982] 66–98), while on the other hand we should not hastily dismiss the ascription of the title "governor" to both Sheshbazzar (Ezra 5:14) and Zerubbabel (Hag 1:1, 14). Further, we have argued at Neh 2:10 that after the forcible stopping of building work in Jerusalem (Ezra 4:23), Tobiah, a junior colleague of Sanballat, may have been appointed to temporary authority over Jerusalem until Nehemiah's arrival. This would be sufficient to explain Samaria's opposition to Nehemiah's appointment. Finally, there is no doubt that Nehemiah did institute a number of reforms in various aspects of Judah's political life and carve out for her a more resolutely independent stance. This, it may be suggested, could be enough to account for the evidence that Stern, *Material Culture,* 209–13, advances from the change in the style of seal impressions.

The alternative view has been defended in recent times by (*inter alia*) Smith, *Parties and Politics;* Widengren, "Persian Period," *Israelite and Judean History,* 509–11; and Avigad, *Bullae and Seals.* Avigad's evidence, we must concede at once, is ambiguous. He has published a bulla and a seal which probably contain the name and title of a governor of Judah, and he links this with others excavated at Ramat Raḥel. The date of these stamps is not sufficiently secure, however, to affirm conclusively that they are earlier than Nehemiah. Avigad has to rely on evidence from paleography alone to determine this date. On the basis of material currently available his arguments are strong, and so would tend to confirm the presence of governors in Jerusalem before Nehemiah. Avigad is aware, however (p. 36), that to base chronology on paleography alone is always somewhat hazardous, being open to revision as new finds are made. Nonetheless, no substantial arguments have yet been advanced by those who dispute his conclusions (e.g., Stern and McEvenue; the latter's treatment of Avigad's discussion, especially at the end of n. 22 on p. 362, is wholly inadequate and appears to be based on only a cursory and superficial reading of the evidence presented). Thus, while these new finds can in no way support Alt's view, they may prove to be irrelevant to the present discussion altogether.

We are reduced, therefore, to the evidence of the present text, and here Smith's point has not been answered by McEvenue, namely, that Nehemiah's claim loses much of its force if like is not being compared with like. Since there is no clear or compelling evidence to the contrary, we may conclude that Nehemiah's appointment did not signify a fundamental change in the status or administration of Judah. We would qualify this only with the new evidence that he restored Judah's position following the hiatus after the events of Ezra 4:23 and that his personal style and favored status with Artaxerxes may have led to a heightened projection of Judah's independence.

The governors of Judah who preceded Nehemiah, then, burdened the people with taxation, much of it for their personal gain. This may receive revealing illustration if Avigad, *Bullae and Seals,* 34–35, is right in linking the many "yehud" jars with this period: "an efficient tax-gathering apparatus using special jars." Such collections in kind were on top of monetary revenue, set at "forty shekels of silver." While modern equivalents of such figures are rarely meaningful, the very recording of the exact figure suggests that the reader is intended to be impressed by its size.

Finally, the governor's retainers (נער; see *Comment* on 4:10 [16]), that is to say, his officials who also owed him personal allegiance, abused their authority by lording it over the people. There is another clear contrast here with Nehemiah's behavior, as emphasized in the following verse; see *Comment* on 4:10 (16) and 17 (23).

Nehemiah attributes his different approach to "reverence for God." Here, Kidner's comment deserves citation in full: "He reveals his twofold motivation: first, filial reverence for God, which restrained him from 'lording it over the people' (15b), and made heaven's verdict all-important to him (19); and second, brotherly compassion, 'because the servitude was heavy upon this people' (18). In his own brusque style he exemplified the two great commandments."

16 A parenthetical statement comments on Nehemiah's conduct while the wall was being built. It interrupts somewhat the general characterization of his term as governor, but is intelligible enough in the overall context. Its purpose is to highlight both the difference between himself and the former governors and that of their respective officials.

Nehemiah himself seems to have kept on the move among the wall-builders, directing, encouraging, and keeping watch for any external threat; see especially 4:12b (18b) with 14 (20). For the distribution and involvement of Nehemiah's men, see 4:10 (16).

Nehemiah emphasizes that neither he nor his men made any personal gain from the operation. The verb used, קנה, can mean "to buy," but often has a much wider application; underlying it, therefore, may be the sense of "to acquire by whatever are the appropriate means in the circumstances." The suggestion in the present context must, therefore, be that Nehemiah did not come into the possession of any property from those to whom he had advanced loans but who were unable to repay.

17–18 Nehemiah's waiving of the expenses to which he was entitled was the more remarkable in view of the extensive entertaining that he had regularly to undertake. The meals provided for the 150 Jewish officials were no doubt part of their salary, and to these had to be added a steady stream of foreign diplomatic visitors such as characterize all government activity down to the present day.

The most costly provisions (i.e., meat and wine) are listed to exemplify Nehemiah's generosity. They may not have matched the lavishness of Solomon's court (cf. 1 Kgs 5:2–3 [4:22–23]), but they remain as an impressive witness to the extent of Nehemiah's personal wealth.

The second reason (for the first, see v 15) for Nehemiah's unusual approach was his appreciation of the burden (עבדה "service") that the people already had to bear. This probably does not refer to the work on the wall, for which a different word, מלאכה, was used in v 16, but to the burden of taxation by the Persians. There is a comparable attitude to the lack of full political autonomy, to the need to pay taxes to foreigners and to the consequent feeling of the Jews that they are "slaves," עבדים, at 9:36–37.

19 This is the first of Nehemiah's brief prayers that God will "remember" him. Previously, his prayers were a vivid part of the narrative itself (cf. 3:36–37 [4:4–5]). Now, however, he is standing back from his work and, at a later time, seeking God's favor in view of all that he has accomplished and sacrificed. As Rudolph observes, the addition to the similar prayer at 13:22 of the words "and spare me according to the greatness of your mercy" shows that Nehemiah was well aware that favor and forgiveness cannot be "bought" from God, but are the gifts of his grace. At the same time, however, for whatever reason (cf. *Introduction*, "The Nehemiah Memoir"), Nehemiah prays in detail that his work and self-sacrificial generosity may stand as an eternal memorial to his purity of motive and dedication in service both to God and his fellow Jews.

Explanation

There are few issues so divisive of a harmonious community as extreme disparity in personal wealth and income. In the chapter under review sheer desperation was compounded by a sense of frustration that the prospect of economic ruin was brought about in large part by those who were supposedly their "brothers." And it was this factor that evidently struck Nehemiah so forcibly. Somewhat characteristically, he made no direct appeal to the law. Although it made some humanitarian provision for those in such straits, it was never Nehemiah's style to be content with a legalistic minimum once his conscience and passion were aroused. Rather, he must cut through to the spirit that lay behind the law and work positively to rectify the damage that had been caused.

Three further qualities of his leadership are revealed in his handling of the situation. First, he displays a disarming candor in admitting his own involvement, even if it was not particularly extensive. No one could accuse him of taking a superior or privileged attitude. Second, his proposals, though costly, were practical and simple. He left no room for casuistic maneuverings but confronted the wealthy with a direct challenge to charity and generosity.

Finally, in the closing verses of the chapter, he showed how he was willing personally to take on a greater burden than that which he asked of others. It is a classic illustration of the obvious truth that leadership means going further than those one is leading.

The attitude displayed by Nehemiah finds many echoes and counterparts in the NT. Here too, it is not so much that legislation can determine attitudes as a simple assumption like that in 1 John 3:17 that is most clearly expressed: "If anyone has material possessions and sees his brother in need but has no pity on him, how can the love of God be in him?" In the light of Jesus' own lifestyle and attitude to the poor, which has been so frequently documented in recent years; in the light of the evidently Spirit-led attitude of the earliest Jerusalem church (whose spontaneous desire to share everything together is presented as part of the outcome of that Pentecostal experience as much as were signs and wonders, prayer, fellowship and evangelistic success [Acts 2:43–47], even if their practical expression of that desire was less than successful); in the light of the consistent apostolic injunctions to make no distinctions on the grounds of wealth and social standing (e.g., Jas 2:1–13); and in the light of the persistent, urgent appeal of the NT writers to do good to all men indeed, but "especially to those who belong to the family of believers" (Gal 6:10; see among numerous other passages Rom 12:13; 2 Cor 8; Phil 4:10–19; Heb 13:16; Jas 5:1–6, etc.)—there can be no answer to John's searching question other than the kind of practical response that Nehemiah exemplified.

The Completion of the Wall   (Neh 6:1-19)

Bibliography

Bewer, J. A. "Josephus' Account of Nehemiah." *JBL* 43 (1924) 224–26. **Ivry, A. L.** "Nehemiah 6, 10: Politics and the Temple." *JSJ* 3 (1972) 35–45. **Kutsch, E.** "Die Wurzel עצר im Hebräischen." *VT* 2 (1952) 57–69. **Löw, I.** "טובתיו Neh 6:19." *ZAW* 33 (1913) 154–55. **Paul, S. M.** "Nehemiah 6:19—Counter Espionage." *Hebrew Annual Review* 1 (1977) 177–79. **Schiemann, R.** "Covenanting with the Princes: Neh vi.2." *VT* 17 (1967) 367–69.

Translation

¹ *When Sanballat, (Tobiah),* ᵃ *Geshem the Arabian and the rest of our enemies heard* ᵇ *that I had rebuilt the wall and that no breach remained in it (though at that time I had not yet hung the doors in the gates),* ² *Sanballat and Geshem sent me a message: "Come and let us meet at Hakkephirim* ᵃ *in the plain of Ono." Their scheme was to harm me, however,* ³ *so I sent messengers to them to say, "I am involved in some important work; I am therefore unable to come down lest* ᵃ *the work should stop while I leave it* ᵇ *to come down to you."* ⁴ *Four times they sent me a message of this sort and each time I replied to them in the same way.*

⁵ *On the fifth occasion, Sanballat sent his servant to me in the same way, but this time he carried an open letter.* ⁶ *In it was written, "It is reported among the nations—and Gashmu* ᵃ *confirms it—that you and the Jews are plotting a revolt and that that is why you are rebuilding the wall.* ᵇ *According to these reports* ᵇ *you are about to become their king,* ⁷ *and you have even appointed prophets to proclaim in Jerusalem with reference to you that 'There is a king in Judah!' Now, the king will hear of these reports; so then come, let us confer together."*

⁸ *I sent him a reply as follows: "Nothing like what you say has happened; you are just fabricating* ᵃ *it in your own mind,"* ⁹ *for they were all trying to intimidate us, thinking,* ᵃ *"Their resolve to do the work will weaken* ᵃ *and it will not get done," but in fact I continued with even greater determination.* ᵇ

¹⁰ *Later, I went to the house of Shemaiah, son of Delaiah, son of Mehetabel, who was looking extremely worried.* ᵃ *He said:*

> *"Let us meet at the house of God, right inside the temple,*
> *Let us shut the doors of the temple, because they are coming to kill you,*
> *They are coming to kill you by night!"*

¹¹ *But I replied, "Should a man in my position run away? Or who in my state would enter the temple and live?* ᵃ *I will not go in."* ¹² *I realized that it was not God who had sent him, but that he had uttered this prophecy against me because* ᵃ *Tobiah and Sanballat* ᵇ *had hired him,* ¹³ *(. . .)* ᵃ *intending that I should take fright, act as he suggested, and so fall into sin. Then they would have a bad name with which to discredit me.*

¹⁴ *Remember Tobiah and Sanballat,* ᵃ *O my God, according to these deeds of theirs,* ᵇ *and also Noadiah the prophetess and the rest of the prophets who have been trying to intimidate me.*

¹⁵ *So the wall was completed on the twenty-fifth of Elul, in fifty-two days.* ¹⁶ *When our enemies heard of it, all the nations who were round about us were afraid* ª *and much deflated in their self-esteem;* ᵇ *they realized that this work had been accomplished by (the power of) our God.*

¹⁷ *Furthermore, throughout that period* ª *the nobles of Judah were sending many letters* ª *to Tobiah and Tobiah's letters were coming to them,* ¹⁸ *for many in Judah had sworn allegiance* ª *to him since he was the son-in-law of Shecaniah, son of Arah, while his son Jonathan had married the daughter of Meshullam, son* ᵇ *of Berechiah.* ¹⁹ *They also used to keep telling me about his good deeds* ª *and then reporting my words back to him.* ᵇ *Tobiah (however) wrote letters to intimidate me.*

Notes

1.a. It is disputed whether "and Tobiah" should be regarded as part of the text or as a later gl by an editor who found his absence from this list surprising. In favor of the latter conclusion it is observed that he is not mentioned in v 2, and that his name alone is not introduced with the prep ל. On the other hand, none of "the rest of our enemies" features in v 2 either, while the fact that Sanballat and Geshem are listed again in v 2 suggests that there is meant to be some kind of distinction between the two lists. V 1 may serve as an introduction to the chap. as a whole rather than to the incident immediately following alone. Furthermore, the absence of the preposition may be variously explained. The evidence is thus finely balanced.

1.b. ל . . . נשמע is a Heb. form of the Aram. idiom שמיע ל, itself an Iranian calque. "It was heard to me" is simply a periphrastic construction for "I heard"; cf. E. Y. Kutscher, "Two 'passive' constructions in Aramaic in the light of Persian," in *Hebrew and Aramaic Studies* (Jerusalem: Magnes Press, 1977), 70–89, and Driver, *AD*, 100. That Nehemiah's language should have been influenced by Eastern idiom is not surprising. Semantically, the phrase is thus identical with that found at 3:33 (4:1) and 4:1 (4:7).

2.a. Confronted by this otherwise unknown place-name, it is not surprising that LXX and Vg should have read it as כְּפָרִים, "(one of) the villages." On this view, Sanballat and Geshem might be thought to be concealing their intentions by offering Nehemiah a wider choice of places to meet. A completely different approach is suggested by Schiemann, *VT* 17 (1967) 367–69. He observes (i) that the MT could equally well be rendered "with the lions," and that at Nah 2:12–14 and Ezek 19:2–6 "lions" means "princes," and (ii) that the phrase "let us meet together" could mean "let us covenant together" (cf. v 7 and the parallelism at Ps 83:6 [5]). Vg, indeed, renders our phrase this way. Schiemann therefore interprets the text to mean "let us covenant together with the princes" (meaning local chiefs). This is unlikely, however, for (i) "lions" could hardly mean "princes" without any contextual indication. Note its absence from the wide-ranging consideration of such usage by P. D. Miller, "Animal Names as Designations in Ugaritic and Hebrew," *UF* 2 (1970) 177–86. The passages Schiemann cites in his support are both extended metaphors where the meaning is made quite obvious by the context; and (ii) a proposal that Sanballat, Geshem, and Nehemiah should make a covenant with some other party ("the princes") would imply that they were themselves already closely associated with each other and shared common political aims; the case, however, was (and was known to be) exactly the opposite.

3.a. This meaning of למה (usually "why?") is common in Aram. (cf. Ezra 4:22; 7:23), and may be found more frequently in Heb. than is generally supposed; see the list of passages at BDB 554a and Ehrlich, *Randglossen* 1, 133.

3.b. Emendation is unnecessary, *pace* Batten, and Joüon, *Bib* 12 (1931) 88.

6.a. Cf. *Notes* on 2:19.a. for this spelling. The fact that it is closer to the postulated original form than the more common Heb. spelling "Geshem" suggests that we should not entertain any proposed emendation here.

6.b-b. This phrase is usually deleted as "a senseless, disturbing intrusion from vs. 7" (Bowman). However, as rendered above the words have a different nuance from v 7 and are appropriate to the context. This has now been recognized by both NEB and NIV.

8.a. For the etymology of בדא (otherwise only at 1 Kgs 12:33), cf. L. Kopf, "Arabische Etymologien und Parallelen zum Bibelwörterbuch," *VT* 8 (1958) 165. For the vocalization and retention of the elided א, cf. GKC §§ 23c and 74i.

9.a-a. Lit., "Their hands will drop from the work."

9.b. The translation of the final clause is disputed. Many of the Eng. versions take it as a brief prayer: "and now, strengthen my hands!" They show their unease, however, by adding such words as "O my God," or "But I prayed," for which there is no textual support. The objections to this approach are: (i) It was not so understood by the ancient Vrs. When they present a united tradition of interpretation, they should be considered carefully. (ii) Nowhere else is God the subject of "to strengthen the hands." For Nehemiah's use of the phrase, cf. 2:18 (Ehrlich, *Randglossen* 7, 197). (iii) While it is true that sometimes Nehemiah does include in his memoir the prayers that he must have offered in the historical setting rather than as he wrote (cf. 3:36–37 [4:4–5]), they are clearly marked by the inclusion of the vocative "O my God." Without some such indication, there is nothing to mark this as a prayer at all. חזק "strengthen" is thus to be construed as an inf abs doing service for a finite verb; cf. GKC § 113y–gg, which includes as part of its explanation the use of this construction for "hurried or otherwise excited style . . . in order to bring out the verbal idea in a clearer and more expressive manner." The use of ועתה, "and now," further contributes to this impression.

10.a. והוא עצור, usually rendered "who was shut up" (rsv), or the like. Various explanations have been suggested: (i) Shemaiah was in a state of ritual impurity, and therefore could not go out (e.g., Bertholet, who compares Jer 36:5). If that were so, however, he could not have contemplated an immediate visit to the temple, as Jer 36:5 itself makes clear. (ii) Shemaiah had shut himself indoors as a symbolic act, to underline how Nehemiah should shut himself up in the temple (e.g., Keil). However, as Rudolph observes, if this were the case we would expect the text to say so more explicitly. (iii) Hölscher and others have maintained that the reference is to seizure by prophetic ecstasy, but the root is never used in this sense in the OT. (iv) Rudolph thinks the phrase is included to explain why he, the governor, visited the prophet in his home rather than vice versa. It is difficult to see, however, what could have hindered the prophet from going to Nehemiah's house but did not hinder him from visiting the temple. (v) Others prefer to admit ignorance, and then to guess that Shemaiah may have been pretending to be in danger as he said Nehemiah was (Bowman). (vi) Finally, in the course of a discussion of the meaning of the root עצר as a whole, Kutsch, *VT* 2 (1952) 57–69, has linked the present occurrence with its meaning in some contexts of "oppressed." From this he postulates a developed sense of "harassed, worried" (*"bedrückt, gequält"*). This, at least, has the merit of fitting the context very well: Shemaiah puts on the right act for the lie he is about to perpetrate. LXX, συνεχόμενος, may support this interpretation; cf. Luke 8:37, etc. The difficulty for this view, which Kutsch does not face at all, is that we have no real evidence for this metaphorically developed meaning of the root; it seems to rely more on the range of meaning of the German *"bedrückt"* than the Heb. Nevertheless, the suggestion is not impossible, and it is favored here—with considerable hesitation—as the only one advanced so far that makes any real sense in the context.

11.a. יחי is ambiguous. In some contexts (e.g., Gen 3:22) it expresses purpose, and that would not be impossible here ("to save his life"). However, the translation supplied above "and live" is more normal, particularly in cases where unguarded human contact with the divine sphere is involved; see, e.g., Exod 33:20; Deut 5:24. The counterargument of Rudolph, Fensham, etc., that in v 13 Tobiah expected only disgrace to follow for Nehemiah is overscrupulous; after all, Uzziah is said in 2 Chr 26:16–21 to have trespassed in just this way and to have suffered disgrace for a considerable period of time as a result, while from a theological point of view it may be maintained that his uninvited intrusion into the sphere of the sacred led to the loss of his life.

12.a. For causal clauses introduced by the *wāw* copulative, cf. GKC § 158a.

12.b. Because Sanballat is unusually listed after Tobiah, many commentators think that his name has here been added secondarily. However, (i) the same order is found in v 14; it is less plausible to suppose that an addition was made in both places; (ii) the sg verb following (שְׂכָרוֹ "had hired him") is by no means decisive, as Rudolph agrees; he compares 5:14, which suggests it may have been a mark of Nehemiah's style (but see n. 13.a.); (iii) both the first two points are to be explained in a positive way as indicating Nehemiah's desire to stress Tobiah's prominence in organizing this particular plot (just as Sanballat and Geshem initiated the one at the start of the chap.). There are excellent reasons for this (see *Comment* below). Sanballat's role on this occasion was subordinate and supportive.

13.a. MT here becomes repetitive, and in order to salvage any sense normal syntax has to be disregarded. The verse starts למען שכור הוא "in order that he might be hired." Since this is tautologous after v 12, it has to be taken with what follows, the second למען serving in a resumptive capacity; cf. RV, "For this cause was he hired, that I should be afraid." This, however, is an unparalleled use of למען, which otherwise always qualifies what precedes, and it can scarcely be accepted. The passage makes excellent sense without the disputed phrase. It probably did not arise as a simple case of dittogr, as many commentators state. Rather, as Rudolph, following H. Guthe (*The Book of Ezra and Nehemiah* [Baltimore: Johns Hopkins Press, 1901]), suggests, שכור הוא למען and שכרו למען are doublets; it is thus likely that the second started as a marginal comment: שְׂכָרֻדהֻ למען, "they hired him in order that . . ." This will have been intended as a correction or alternative reading to the sg verb שָׂכָרוֹ, v 12; cf. n. 12.b. (ii) above. This reading was then added to the text rather than its being corrected. The identification of this gl leaves open the possibility that the text was read in accordance with it in some MSS in antiquity, the proto-MT having then been "collated" against them; if so, the argument for deleting "and Sanballat" in v 12 because of the sg verb following is further weakened; textually, שכרו may itself be a corr of an original שכרוהו.

14.a. Cf. n.12.b.

14.b. Cf. GKC § 126y for the absence of article on אלה. For the formula as a whole, see n. 5:19.a.

16.a. So MT, as the *methegh* makes clear. It is supported by the *plene* spelling of several MSS (וייראו) and the Vrs. It is contextually appropriate because (i) the root ירא is a key-word in this chapter (see *Form* below), and (ii) Nehemiah often records the emotions of his adversaries; cf. 2:10, 19; 3:33 (4:1); and 4:1 (7). The alternative is to ignore the *methegh* and to translate, "When our enemies heard of it and all the nations who were round about us saw it, . . ." Though favored by a number of modern translations and commentaries, this not only ignores the above considerations, but introduces an artificial distinction between "our enemies" and "the nations" (contrast 5:9). It is absurd to suggest that "the nations" lived close enough to see the walls, but that Sanballat and his allies had to rely on hearsay (e.g., Bowman). "Our enemies" means the Gentile leaders (Sanballat, etc.), as 6:1 shows (cf. Vogt, *Studie*, 150), while "the nations" refers to their peoples generally. As the leaders heard of Nehemiah's success, so their followers grew downhearted.

16.b. The Heb. expression here has no exact parallel, but is comparable with phrases like נפלו פנים, "(his) countenance fell," and נפל לב, "(his) heart sank." There remains some ambiguity, however: it may be that "they (the leaders) fell in their (the nations') estimation"; more likely, however, since previously Nehemiah has several times implied considerable arrogance on the part of Sanballat, Tobiah, and the others, he here takes some pleasure in seeing their pride deflated. Several commentators follow Klostermann, however, in emending ויפלו to ויפלא, "they thought it a very wonderful achievement" (NEB; Ehrlich, *Randglossen* 7, 200, adds a reference to Ps 118:23 by way of comparison). This is an unsupported and unnecessary conjecture, however. Indeed, despite the grudging acknowledgment of the following clause, it is most unlikely that the nations would have taken so positive a view of the achievement as the root פלא normally implies (see the dictionaries).

17.a-a. Lit., "the nobles of Judah were making many their letters (which were) going . . ." This is slightly awkward, especially as one would normally expect the participle (מרבים) to follow its subject (חרי יהודה). That does not make the phrase impossible, however, especially in late biblical Heb., written by Nehemiah at that. At the most, one might wonder whether the art (serving as the relative) has been lost before הלכות by haplogr, but even this is not certain. Despite this, slight emendations have been proposed to ease the text, the most popular being יהודה (haplogr) מחרי (dittogr) גם בימים ההם רבים, "Also in those days, as for many of the nobles of Judah (*casus pendens*), their letters were going . . ." The difference in meaning is thus minimal.

18.a. Cf. GKC § 128u.

18.b. Only about six times in the Heb. Bible does the const בן appear thus without *maqqeph*.

19.a. Several emendations of MT have been proposed, e.g., by Bertholet, (סטוביה "about Tobiah") and Löw, *ZAW* 33 (1913) 154–55, reviving a suggestion of Geiger (מבותיו "rumors about him"; cf. Aram., טבָא), while R. Gordis, "The Text and Meaning of Hosea XIV 3," *VT* 5 (1955) 88–90, has suggested that there may be a second word טוב in Heb., meaning "speech" (but cf. J. Barr, *Comparative Philology and the Text of the Old Testament* [Oxford: Clarendon Press, 1968], 16–17). MT is quite satisfactory in the context, however (see *Comment* below), and is favored textually by (i) the word play on the name Tobiah, and (ii) the congruity with the following clause (*contra* Rudolph), once it is remembered that דברי "my words" may, in Heb., include "my deeds."

19.b. Paul, *Hebrew Annual Review* 1 (1977) 177–79, adduces Akk. parallels to suggest the rendering "and they divulged my secrets to him," but this may be a little too precise in the present context.

Form/Structure/Setting

In setting, Neh 6 represents the continuation of the NM. It resumes the theme of opposition to the work after the specific problem treated in chap. 5. Similarly, it is clearly separated from chap. 7, in which, with the walls now completed, Nehemiah turns to organizing other matters within the community.

No one doubts that it is of a piece, from a literary point of view, with the narrative of the previous chapters. Nehemiah's characteristic style is everywhere apparent (see the comments on the chapter's structure below), and the content too fits exactly what we know of the outlook and character of the memoir from elsewhere. Torrey, *Ezra Studies*, 226 and 248, ventured the opinion that vv 16–19 were an editorial addition by the Chronicler, but since he declined to give any reasons for this suggestion, it need not be taken seriously. More weighty is the view of Rudolph, developed by Kellermann, *Nehemia*, 22–23, that verses 11–13 have been editorially glossed; see *Comment* below for discussion. Either way, the results for our overall appreciation of the chapter's setting remain unchanged. The possibility of other isolated glosses has been treated in *Notes* above.

Broadly speaking, the structure of the chapter falls into a pattern already familiar from chaps. 2–4; note especially how the first and third main sections are introduced by the familiar formula ויהי כאשר נשמע ל "When X heard . . ." (v 1) and ויהי כאשר שמעו "When X heard . . ." (v 16); cf. 2:10, 19; 3:33 (4:1); 4:1(7) and 9 (15); and how the second section is concluded with the זכרה "Remember!" formula. (The position of this formula within the NM as a whole is discussed in the *Introduction*, "The Nehemiah Memoir." It is seen there that the present verse fits least well with our proposals as a whole. Two possible explanations are advanced to account for this, one of which would allow this verse to have been part of the NM from the start. If, however, it was added later, then the discussion in the present paragraphs would point to its having been more thoroughly integrated into its new context than we could otherwise have realized.)

Within this regularity, however, there are some interesting variations. First, each of the three sections concludes with a note that the enemy tried to "intimidate" (piel of ירא) Nehemiah; cf. vv 9, 14, and 19. This unusual form at once indicates the unity of the chapter and the structural integrity of the text as it stands. It also serves as a pointer to the correct division of the chapter into sections, namely, vv 1–9, 10–14, and 15–19.

Second, within this overall unity, the first two sections are closely linked together, while the third is somewhat more isolated. At the formal level, this may be seen from the use of the זכרה formula at v 14 between the second and third sections, and by the fact that the introductory formula occurs only with the first and third sections, not with the second. Similarly, the content of the sections points to the same conclusion: sections one and two have Sanballat and Tobiah respectively as the main protagonists, and these two are drawn together in v 14. The third section, by contrast, focuses mainly on "the nobles of Judah"; if Tobiah is mentioned, that is only because of their league with him.

It may be suggested that the reason for this arrangement is that, while vv 15–19 are clearly to be taken together with vv 1–14 (the theme of opposition and the use of "intimidate" demonstrate this), yet at the same time they are intended to serve as a transitional paragraph to the remainder of the memoir which, so far as can be judged from chaps. 7–13, treated reforms internal to Judah and Jerusalem for the most part. Such a transition is appropriate after the climactic statement of v 15 that "the wall was completed."

A final point on the structure of the chapter relates to the position of vv 15–16. A minority of commentators (e.g., Mowinckel, *Studien II*, 29; Myers) believes that they should be transposed to follow verses 17–19. On the one hand, it is maintained, there are close links between the content of vv 17–19 and 1–10, whereas on the other hand vv 15–16 are connected with the start of chap. 7 by the notice of the completion of the walls. In reply, it should be said that whereas from a purely historical point of view there is obviously a degree of truth in these observations, there can be no justification at the literary level for actually transposing vv 15–16. It is certain that verses 16–19 stand in their correct order, as the introduction (ויהי כאשר שמעו . . .) and conclusion (לירׇאׅנׅי) show clearly; see the analysis above. Verse 15 is necessary as the antecedent for שמעו "(they) heard" in v 16, and does not attract particular prominence in this account as it stands; it thus plays the same literary role as, for instance, 3:38 (4:6), q.v. Finally, the movement from v 16 to v 17 (a general statement of the reaction of the enemies outside the community to the attitude of some within the community) represents precisely the transition which this paragraph serves in the composition as a whole.

The form of the chapter as a whole is not to be distinguished from its structure just analyzed. Two details within it, however, call for a brief comment.

In vv 6–7 we are presented with what purports to be a transcript of Sanballat's letter to Nehemiah. Study of Hebrew epistolography (as with Aramaic) has advanced rapidly in recent years, especially because of the increasing numbers of actual examples of the genre, usually on ostraca, unearthed by archeological excavations. Despite this, not a great deal may be said about the present example, because the narrative in which the letter is set will have absorbed most of the formal characteristics such as address and greeting. What little remains for analysis may be cited from D. Pardee, *Handbook of Ancient Hebrew Letters* (SBLSBS 15; Chico, CA; Scholars Press, 1982), 179: "The relationship of the correspondents was apparently that of equals, though there are no lexical markers of relationship. The main part of the letter is declarative with an imperative and a cohortative at the end. The marker of transition *wĕ^cattâ* occurs twice in v 7; but, as in Jer 29:27, its function here is not specifically epistolary." In fact, the possibility that Nehemiah is not quoting but writing more freely on the basis of his memory, cannot be ruled out; the use of גוים "nations" (v 6), is suggestive of this conclusion.

In v 10, Shemaiah's words are couched in poetic form, as befits a prophet, whether true or false. Metrically, the lines may be analyzed as 3 + 2; 3 + 2; 3. This is the rhythm normally associated with the lament, which Shemaiah perhaps deemed appropriate to the substance of his message. The parallelism within the first line is clear enough, the second half in fact intensifying the first ("at the house of God" → "right inside the temple"). The second line has no formal parallelism, but it lays the basis for another climactic parallelism with the last line, whereby ולילה (lit., "and by night") receives particular emphasis. Finally, the form of the saying itself is unremarkable: an imperative/ cohortative followed by substantiation introduced by כי "because" is common enough in later prophetic collections. It is thus probably not necessary to omit any of the repetitious elements in the text as later accretion, even though, it must be said, the passage is more of a jingle than poetry. There is thus no need to defend the text's integrity on the basis of style; its banality is just what might be expected in view of Shemaiah's duplicity.

Comment

1 The digression caused by chap. 5 from the description of the wall-building enables the reader to accept without difficulty that the task has progressed quite markedly in the meanwhile. The narrative resumes almost at the point of completion: the wall itself was complete (contrast the position at 4:1[7], where a word from the same root as that here translated "breach" is used), and only some finishing touches on the gates were outstanding. This parenthetical remark is necessary to the account because the whole of vv 1–14 presupposes that the task is not yet quite complete; cf. especially vv 3 and 15. At the same time, it gives us useful firsthand information about the detailed progress of the work that enables us to deduce the literary independence of chap. 3; cf. *Form* of chap. 3. On the construction of the gates themselves, see *Comment* on 3:3.

For Sanballat and Tobiah, see *Comment* on 2:10, and for Geshem, see *Comment* on 2:19. "The rest of our enemies": we may assume that the other groups listed at 4:1(7), at least, will have been included. Comparison with v 16 below and the three individual names in this chapter suggest that it is particularly the leaders of the surrounding peoples who are in view. The work was now so far advanced that they must have realized that their taunts and threats had not succeeded; they therefore changed their tactics and concentrated instead on eliminating Nehemiah himself from the scene.

The verse serves to introduce the chapter as a whole. All the chief protagonists are mentioned, and they will be taken up separately in what follows: Sanballat and Geshem in vv 1–9, Tobiah in vv 10–13, and "our enemies" in v 16.

2 No particular reason for the proposed meeting between Nehemiah, Sanballat, and Geshem is given, but Nehemiah suspected that it was to harm him personally. Ackroyd reminds us that we have only Nehemiah's account of the matter; seen from the other side, there may have been a desire to

defuse the situation, since the Persians would not have welcomed squabbling between their provincial officials.

Several points should be remembered in evaluating this suggestion. First, had the desire been one of genuine concern, Sanballat could have offered to come to Jerusalem itself when his first proposal was declined. Second, neither his attitude before nor after (vv 5–9) looks like that of someone who is committed to reconciliation. Third, and most important, if we follow Ackroyd's lead and really try to see things from Sanballat's point of view, we shall surely conclude that it was Nehemiah himself whom he will have regarded as the chief stumbling block to peace. Prior to his coming, if our surmise about Tobiah is correct (cf. 2:10), relations between Samaria and Jerusalem will have been established on an excellent footing after the debacle of Ezra 4. It seems from the end of our present chapter as though Tobiah had succeeded well in getting himself accepted in Jerusalem. Now Nehemiah had arrived with his blatantly separatist and aggressive policies. If one could eliminate him, good relationships would soon be restored.

If this line of thought represents Sanballat's reasoning to any degree, we may conclude that Nehemiah's suspicions were indeed well-founded.

The site of Hakkephirim is uncertain. It is said to be in the plain of Ono, not mentioned elsewhere in the Bible, but identified in the Talmud (on the basis of 11:35) with "the Valley of the Craftsmen"; cf. J. Simons, *The Geographical and Topographical Texts of the Old Testament* (Leiden: E. J. Brill, 1959) § 1091. Clearly it must be linked with the town of Ono (see *Comment* on Ezra 2:33) and yet be considerably more extensive than it, since it apparently accommodated separate settlements besides. This will locate it to the northwest of Jerusalem in an area whose political status at this time has been much disputed.

Two main views are held at present. One follows Alt, *KS* 2, 343, in believing that the Plain of Ono was a neutral territory between the provinces of Ashdod and Samaria, administered directly by the Persians. It thus made a suitable setting for such a meeting. The evidence for this particular aspect of Alt's theory is slender, however; indeed, as he presents it, it is largely based on his understanding of this verse itself, though few who have followed him seem to have observed this.

The alternative view believes on the basis of Ezra 2:33 and Neh 11:35 that Ono was within the province of Judah at this time (though some argue that it may not always have been); cf. Simons, *Geographical and Topographical Texts*, § 1095, and the various views summarized in Stern, *Material Culture*, 245–49. In addition to textual evidence, Stern adds new archeological considerations to bolster his conclusions, namely the place of discovery of a number of seal impressions which he believes belonged to the Judean administration and of coins bearing the legend $yh(w)d$ (Judah). As regards Ono, he locates this within a district that he calls "north-west Shephelah" centered on Gezer, where such finds have been made. Unfortunately, however, this sort of evidence cannot at present finally settle the issue, for Ono would, on this view, be situated in the extreme northwest corner of the province of Judah (see fig. 1 on p. 203). This is quite some distance from Gezer, so that unless finds come specifically from that area, we cannot be sure exactly where the border lay. We are thus left with the literary evidence alone. This points unanimously to the inclusion of Ono within the province of Judah, which may seem geographically a little odd, but which was defended on historical grounds at Ezra 2:33. (The absence of Ono from the list in Neh 3 does not necessarily tell against this conclusion: as seen in the commentary on that chapter, the list is not complete and the builders volunteered on the basis of several possible reasons besides district representation. In addition, the distance of Ono from Jerusalem may have played a part.)

If, then, the town of Ono was near the provincial border, we would offer the speculation that the plain of Ono may have straddled it, and that Hakke-phirim might have been a border town. (There can then be no question of identifying it with the similar sounding Chephirah of Josh 9:17; 18:26; Ezra 2:25, because this lies in Benjamite territory some way to the east of Ono.) This would be a reasonable setting for a conference, though sites nearer Jerusalem that filled the same conditions could have been found. If the remote-ness of Hakkephirim was precisely what roused Nehemiah's suspicions in the first place, he was able to make a virtue of it in his response.

3–4 To some extent, Nehemiah's response was an excuse to avoid an unwanted meeting: according to v 1, the work was on the point of completion, and it is not certain that it would have stopped if Nehemiah had absented himself for a few days. Perhaps, however, he was himself seeking to be less provocative than would have been the case with a flat refusal. Unless Sanballat accepted his reply in this spirit, it is difficult to see what motive could have induced him to renew the invitation with such persistence. For Nehemiah, however, this will have only confirmed his worst suspicions.

5–9 Unable to secure a meeting with Nehemiah, Sanballat changed his tactics. He sought to achieve the same end by a form of blackmail based on unfounded rumor.

5 We learn for the first time that Sanballat had been using his נער (unsatis-factorily translated above as "servant") to act as an intermediary. For this word, which appears to have some official overtones in Nehemiah, see *Comment* on 4:10 (16). On this occasion—his fifth journey to Jerusalem—he carried an "open letter." The significance of this is much as it would be today: anyone could read it, and therefore Nehemiah would realize that the spotlight of official suspicion was already on him, no matter how unjustified.

The physical form of an open letter is less certain; the use of an ostracon or unsealed papyrus has been suggested, and either seems reasonable. Less plausible is the suggestion that we should read this in the light of Jer 32:11–14 and the spasmodically attested Ancient Near Eastern practice of making two copies of legal texts, the one open for quick reference, the other sealed for consultation in cases of dispute. This appears to apply to a number of cuneiform tablets, which were encased in a clay "envelope" bearing a copy of the original, and much later (second century A.D.) to some documents discovered in the Judean desert. In the latter case, however, the sealed and open texts were both part of the same scroll; see the detailed description by Y. Yadin, "Expedition D—The Cave of the Letters," *IEJ* 12 (1962) 236–37. Despite the assertion of several commentators on Nehemiah and on Jere-miah, the practice is probably not attested at Elephantine. The view that it was seems to derive from a remark of Cowley in the introduction to *Aram P* (p. xxix), where he attempts to explain the duplicate papyri nos. 2 and 3 against the background of Jer 32. As Cowley admits, however, there are some differences between these two similar documents, and his suggestion has not been followed as an explanation for their similarities. It is thus quite misleading to talk of it as a general practice by which one may explain an uncertain biblical passage.

In the present case, then, the following points tell against understanding "open" to imply a "closed" counterpart: (i) The practice was used for legal texts, understandably enough. We have no evidence for its use in the case of letters. (ii) Whereas the word פתוחה is used here, at Jer 32:11 and 14 (and perhaps compare Esth 3:14 and 8:13) we find גלוי. (iii) There is no extrabiblical attestation for this practice in the case of papyri in anything remotely approaching the period of Nehemiah.

6 Sanballat reports to Nehemiah what he claims to have heard as a widespread rumor "among the nations," i.e., the neighboring provinces. The use of this word (גוים) has led to the suspicion that Nehemiah is here summarizing Sanballat's message in his own words, for גוים is frequently translated "Gentiles," and is thus most appropriate to Jewish speakers. While this has already been acknowledged as a possibility in *Form* above, it must also be remembered (i) that גוי has a wider significance than "Gentile," and indeed is sometimes referred to Israel herself; cf. R. E. Clements, *TDOT* 2, 426–33; and (ii) we have very little evidence about how this word might have been used outside Jewish circles. Its attestation in the Mari dialect of Akkadian (*gāwum/gāyum*) shows that it was not limited to Hebrew. It is not impossible that it might have been used without any religious overtones by a speaker of Hebrew in Samaria at this time.

Gashmu (Geshem) was involved with Sanballat's plans from the start (v 2). Sanballat could therefore refer to him to add verisimilitude to his report and at the same time rely on him to back up his story if challenged.

There are two related elements in Sanballat's report, followed by a thinly veiled threat with a final invitation to meet with Nehemiah. The first point is that the wall-building was in preparation for a revolt against the Persian authorities. Sanballat doubtless knew that precisely this charge had been (falsely) made during the attempt to rebuild the walls not so very long before; cf. Ezra 4:7–16. On that occasion, the charge had succeeded in securing an order from the king that the work should cease (vv 17–22). He may have thought that history could repeat itself in the last resort. More immediately, however, since he intended the content of his letter to become public knowledge (v 5), he doubtless hoped that the prospect of a repetition of the previous debacle would cause such disquiet among those still living in Jerusalem who had experienced it that they would put irresistible pressure on Nehemiah to compromise.

7 The related accusation Sanballat brings is that, as part of the revolt, Nehemiah was preparing to have himself proclaimed as king. The reference to prophets may suggest knowledge of their role as king-makers in pre-exilic times (e.g., Samuel with Saul and David in 1 Sam 9–10 and 16; Nathan's dynastic oracle in 2 Sam 7; Elisha with Jehu in 2 Kgs 9, etc.). We know very little of prophetic activity in Jerusalem at this later period, however, though the following paragraph suggests that there must have been some. Perhaps particular reference is made to the earlier oracles of Haggai and Zechariah regarding Zerubbabel. Of that episode, too, nothing developed in royalist terms, and there are even some who have suggested that Zerubbabel may have been removed as a messianic pretender. This view was discounted as improbable at Ezra 5:1–2 above, though if there were any truth in it, it would make an excellent parallel with Sanballat's first point as analyzed in the previous verse.

Finally, it may be noted in passing that no reference is made to any association of Nehemiah with the Davidic family. Had such been known to Sanballat, we would have expected him to make something of it in the present context. The fact that he does not adds further weight to our earlier arguments that Nehemiah was not of Davidic descent (see *Comment* on 2:3). The argument that he would have to have been in order for Sanballat's words to gain any credibility is unconvincing. The rest of his accusations are equally far-fetched, and in any case usurpers or claimants who were not of royal birth were by no means unknown in the Persian empire.

Sanballat concludes by hinting that if Nehemiah does not respond to his invitation for a conference, letters will soon be on their way to the Achaemenid capital. Again, the reflection of, and even deliberate play on, the events of the latter part of Ezra 4 are apparent. Sanballat seems to have overlooked the considerations (i) that a secret meeting with Nehemiah in such circumstances might itself be construed as collaboration in rebellion, and (ii) that to seek a secret consultation after sending an open letter was somewhat self-contradictory.

8 Nehemiah's response was characteristically forthright. Knowing his innocence full well (and we have no reason whatever to doubt this), and confident that no charges of this nature against him could possibly withstand investigation by the royal court, he deemed that a flat denial would be the best way of rallying any of his supporters who might have begun to weaken. To have met Sanballat and sought a compromise might easily have been mistaken as a partial admission of guilt.

9 Nehemiah's personal analysis of Sanballat's motives and his own calculations as to how best to respond are here spelled out. We have accepted them at face value and worked their substance into the exegesis of the exchange in *Comment* above. Nehemiah concludes that far from weakening his own and his followers' resolve, these threats if anything had the opposite effect of driving him back to the task in hand with even greater determination.

10–14 In this second main paragraph of the chapter, Tobiah emerges as the chief protagonist, probably because of his close contacts in Jerusalem. Though working in collaboration with Sanballat, he was in a better position to arrange for Nehemiah to be discredited within his own community. Although several difficulties surround the detailed interpretation of the narrative, it looks as though the purpose of the scheme was again to isolate Nehemiah; as described at v 2 above, he was regarded as a divisive troublemaker. Consequently, Tobiah tried to drive a wedge between him and the priesthood in particular. He was on close terms with the priests (cf. 13:4), and they in turn exercised considerable influence over the native population of Jerusalem.

10 This verse raises several questions that cannot be answered in the present state of our knowledge. First, Shemaiah is otherwise unknown to us. He acts as a prophet (v 12), and both his name and that of his ancestors are reasonable in the context (though Mehetabel occurs only here as a man's name). To attempt to say more would be mere speculation.

Second, it is not stated why Nehemiah visited him in the first place. Did Shemaiah write to Nehemiah to say that he had a word from the Lord for him? We cannot be certain, but something of the sort seems plausible in view of the fact that Shemaiah evidently wanted Nehemiah to visit him; the plot will hardly have depended upon the offchance of Nehemiah encountering him in private.

Third, the meaning of עצור is very uncertain, as discussed already in *Notes* above. In view of all these points, together with other unexplained allusions in v 14, it might be thought that there has been some textual loss from the narrative (so, for instance, Batten). Far more probably, however, Nehemiah is writing with vivid memories, and, as often happens in such cases, does not appreciate that he is assuming knowledge of certain pieces of background information that have thus been lost to us beyond recall.

Shemaiah's message is that "they" (he leaves Nehemiah to infer that assassins hired by Sanballat are implied) are coming one night to murder him; Shemaiah will therefore help Nehemiah to hide behind closed doors in the temple. We may notice that this was not intended as a simple case of taking sanctuary. The need for asylum was recognized by the law (cf. Exod 21:13–14), but it was to be taken at the altar which stood in the open court in front of the sanctuary itself (1 Kgs 1:50); only priests were allowed into the "temple" or sanctuary proper. (There may be a hint in this that Shemaiah belonged to a priestly family.) In any case, there was no guarantee that assassins would respect the law of asylum (cf. 1 Kgs 2:28–34), nor was Nehemiah in one of the carefully defined situations to which the laws of sanctuary applied. Shemaiah urged Nehemiah, therefore, quite simply to hide in the temple, where no one, presumably, would think of looking for him.

At this point, we should take note of the quite different interpretation of this verse by Ivry, *JSJ* 3 (1972) 35–45. He thinks that Shemaiah was urging Nehemiah to commandeer and take possession of the whole temple site in order to turn it into a camp or fortress. This could be done without violating the sanctity of the holy place itself. "Of course with the soldiers and their commander present, the character of the temple would be altered, the priests' status would diminish and Nehemiah's prestige and power would rise. The priestly class would thus be neutralized politically, without any religious changes being necessary." Ivry thus sets the incident within the wider context of Nehemiah's struggle to gain complete support within Jerusalem. The charge to which it would then lay him open, however, would be that he was acting like a king.

This interpretation is improbable, however. First, Nehemiah's response in v 11 ("should a man in my position run away?") clearly understands Shemaiah's suggestion to imply avoidance of danger rather than an offensive move; but to turn the temple into a fortress would not only be unnecessary to escape assassins but actually counterproductive as it would draw attention toward, rather than away from, Nehemiah. Second, Ivry reads a great deal into this text that simply is not there. There is no mention, for instance, of Nehemiah's men accompanying him; on the contrary, Shemaiah's whole approach is secretive. Third, Ivry starts by arguing against the view that Shemaiah was urging Nehemiah to take sanctuary in the normal way. We have already seen, however, that this was not Shemaiah's purpose, but rather that he was encouraging Nehemiah to hide. The difficulties that Ivry thus finds in these verses disappear, eliminating the need for more speculative interpretations. Fourth, Ivry maintains that in this passage היכל "temple" does not refer to the sanctuary but to the temple area as a whole. He concedes, however, that היכל *may* refer to the sanctuary when the context so demands—and it may be urged that this is the case here: (i) the form of parallelism (cf. *Form* above) in the first line of Shemaiah's oracle suggests penetration to a point "right inside the temple"; (ii) reference to shutting "the doors of the temple" is most naturally understood of going inside the sanctuary rather than merely the courts and temple chambers; (iii) Nehemiah's words in v 11, "who in my state would enter the temple and live?" implies a close contact with the divine sphere (cf. n. 11.a. above), and so suits the sanctuary best. For these reasons among others, Ivry's interpretation of v 10 is to be rejected.

11 In the translation defended above, Nehemiah refuses Shemaiah's invitation on two grounds. First, it would be demeaning for "a man in my position" to run away. As legally appointed governor, Nehemiah should not show such fear and self-interest; indeed, we have already had ample evidence that this would run counter to his own character and style. Second, Nehemiah is conscious of his lay status. The sanctuary was reserved for the priests because of its proximity to the symbolic dwelling place of God himself in the inner sanctuary, the Holy of Holies. Not only would Nehemiah have been legally in danger of death (cf. Num 18:7), but he apparently shared the view (as the form of wording he chooses—וחי "and live"—suggests) that direct contact with the divine sphere when in an unprepared state would lead to death (see, e.g., Exod 20:21; 33:20; Deut 5:25; Judg 13:22; 2 Chr 26:16–21, etc.). The verse thus sheds rare but welcome and revealing light on Nehemiah's respect and humility in relation to God.

Rudolph and others argue that Nehemiah cannot have originally intended his answer to have this twofold aspect, and this has consequences too for the interpretation of v 13. However, once again Rudolph's starting point is an insistence that Shemaiah was urging Nehemiah to seek asylum in a legal and legitimate manner, but this we have seen to be false (a view not contradicted by Ps 27:5, *pace* Rudolph; 1 Macc 10:43 is indecisive, since it is part of a letter by Demetrius suggesting a widening of the biblical law of asylum in accordance with Greek practice and so not applicable as evidence to the time of Nehemiah). There is therefore no need to take the second element in Nehemiah's reply as equivalent to the first, or to argue that it is a later gloss (Kellermann, *Nehemia*, 22–23).

12 If, as argued here, Shemaiah was encouraging Nehemiah to act in defiance of the laws regarding the sanctity of the holy place, it would explain why he was able so quickly to discern that the prophecy could not have come from God. It would then not be difficult to work out its origins.

13 Tobiah's intention (about whose involvement Nehemiah may have learned more after interrogating Shemaiah) again has two elements (see *Comment* on v 11 above), but we see now how they are related: he hoped that Nehemiah's instinct for self-preservation would lead him to fall into the trap of cultic trespass; this would certainly give him a "bad name" or reputation with the priesthood, and once discredited in their sight, his standing in the community at large would be in jeopardy. It follows from this interpretation that וחטאתי "and (so) fall into sin" need again not be taken as the work of a later glossator (see *Comment* on v 11). The passage as a whole has a coherence and logic of its own that should not be disturbed.

14 For the "remember" formula, see *Introduction*, "The Nehemiah Memoir," and for the place of this verse (with its catch phrases at the beginning and end) in the structure of the chapter as a whole, see *Form* above. Previously, Nehemiah has prayed with similar words that God will be mindful of his service toward both God and his fellow Jews. Now, rather than take the law into his own hands, he prefers to invoke by implication the repeated biblical teaching that vengeance is the prerogative of God alone (e.g., Deut 32:35; Ps 94:1; Rom 12:19). Not surprisingly, in view of the two preceding paragraphs, Tobiah and Sanballat are mentioned first. Curiously, however, instead of a reference to Shemaiah, there are then listed "Noadiah the prophetess and the rest of the prophets." The background to these references is completely unknown. Evidently we are expected to appreciate that the Shemaiah incident was far from unique; it was but an example of a whole series of devices by which Nehemiah's enemies had endeavored to ensnare him.

15 Although within the literary structure of the chapter this verse serves only to introduce the third main section (cf. *Form* above), it contains historical information of great interest. Elul was the sixth month of the Jewish year, so that the work was finished during the autumn. There is some dispute as to the exact date, most older authorities asserting or implying a time in mid-September. Recent commentators, however, have followed R. A. Parker and W. H. Dubberstein, *Babylonian Chronology 626 B.C.—A.D. 75* (Brown University Studies 19; Providence, RI: Brown University Press, 1956), on whose reckoning the date would be 2 October. Either way, less than six months had passed since Nehemiah first received his commission (cf. 2:1), and the work itself took only fifty-two days. (It is now generally agreed that the two years and four months mentioned in Josephus as the time taken does not rest upon independent knowledge and so should be disregarded. It may have arisen by textual corruption within the transmission of the Greek text; cf. Bewer, *JBL* 43 [1924] 224–26.)

Many factors contributed to this astonishing speed, not least the enthusiasm and commitment that Nehemiah's leadership inspired. In addition, it may be remembered that not all the previous work of restoration had necessarily been completely destroyed, that on the worst affected eastern side of the city Nehemiah saved much time by relocating the line of the wall along the crest of the hill (see *Form* on chap. 3) and that the work does not all appear to have been of an especially high standard; cf. K. M. Kenyon, *Digging up Jerusalem* (London & Tonbridge: Benn, 1974), 183. Parallels for such feats in antiquity are cited by several commentators; cf. Bowman; Schneider;

Fensham; and W. Vischer, "Nehemia, der Sonderbeauftragte und Statthalter des Königs," in H. W. Wolff (ed.), *Probleme biblischer Theologie* (Munich: Chr. Kaiser Verlag, 1971), 603–10.

16 The speed with which the work was completed receives further emphasis from the reactions of those who had opposed it. The main difficulties in understanding the details of this verse have had to be discussed in the *Notes* above. Our conclusions were that "our enemies" refers to Sanballat and his fellow leaders, and that "the nations" refers to their peoples. As news of Nehemiah's achievements filtered down from leaders to people, they were awe-struck at this evident manifestation of God's power exerted on behalf of his people. Those in particular who had taken the lead in opposing Nehemiah were naturally demoralized at their loss of face.

17–19 This paragraph is not to be regarded as following the preceding two verses in strict chronological order but rather, as the opening words of v 17 make clear (גם בימים ההם "furthermore, throughout that period"), as describing further the kind of intrigues of the period as a whole. It owes its present setting, therefore, to quite other considerations, analyzed in *Form* above.

The exchanges of letters between Tobiah and the Judean aristocracy were no doubt part of the way in which Nehemiah's enemies were kept so well informed of developments in Jerusalem. The personal ties referred to add weight to the case argued at 2:10 above that although Tobiah was an official under Sanballat in Samaria, he had at some point been resident in Jerusalem. It was most likely during such a period that he and his son had married into Jewish families (for the family of Arah, cf. Ezra 2:5; for Meshullam, son of Berechiah, cf. Neh 3:4 and 30, where it was suggested that he was an important official. It would appear from chap. 3 that Meshullam was a firm supporter of Nehemiah's building program. This shows that the situation may not have appeared so straightforward to everyone as it did to Nehemiah. Some may have been happy to see the city repaired without committing themselves in the least to the more separatist policy of which Nehemiah regarded the wall as a major symbol; see *Comment* on 3:5 for an even more extreme attitude). But Tobiah's links were much wider than those of marriage. Quite why many should have "sworn allegiance to him" is uncertain, but the fact itself makes clear that there was an influential Tobiad party in Jerusalem with whom Nehemiah must have had difficulty in dealing, even though it rarely surfaces in our texts. Perhaps they wished to continue with an open policy toward Judah's neighbors in the interests of commerce and trade.

19 For whatever reason, this group tried to encourage a more positive attitude by Nehemiah toward Tobiah (assuming the text here to be sound; cf. above). The rift was damaging to their interests, and so they tried to mediate. Ironically, however, Nehemiah records that the only direct communications he had from Tobiah belied the genuineness of their intentions.

Explanation

As the work on the walls nears its completion, so the enemy abandons all former tactics and concentrates instead on attempting to eliminate Nehemiah from the scene. Not only is this a personal attack in its intention, but in vv 5–9 it similarly becomes a personalization of the more general charges leveled against the community as a whole in 2:19. Because God's work in the world is, generally speaking, entrusted to his people, the dangers to which Nehemiah was thus exposed are ones which, in varying degrees, any disciple has to be prepared to face. As so often, the example of Jesus himself stands out as supreme: while no two witnesses could be found to agree touching any specific charge brought against him, he was immediately condemned once his true identity became the subject of examination (Mark 14:53–64).

Needless to say, Nehemiah did not seek or purposely encourage such a challenge. Where possible, he avoided it with conciliatory words (v 3) or outright rejection (v 8), though where a risk became unavoidable, he faced the danger realistically (v 11). In this case, however, his overriding purpose was his desire to obey God's law; faced with the alternative of saving his own skin at the cost of disobedience, he had no hesitation in the ordering of his priorities. It is in this light that we should read his committal of his cause to God (v 14). Clear in his conscience that he had followed the path of God's choosing, revealed in past Scriptures as much as in present guidance, Nehemiah can, it seems, almost relax in the confidence that God will do what is right both by him and by his opponents.

The last part of the chapter is introduced by the matter-of-fact statement that "the wall was completed." Modestly, it serves only as a foil to the following verses, but what an achievement is thereby revealed! Explain away the speed of the work as we will, the fact remains that in little over seven weeks Nehemiah had overcome internal despair and external opposition to raise not just a physical wall but also the self-respect of his people in the eyes of the surrounding nations.

It is instructive to observe, however, that the narrative does not pause for self-congratulation. Bricks and mortar, or any other aspect of institution, can never provide more than a framework; the substance depends on the attitudes and activities of the people concerned. In this case, the walls alone would not be sufficient to offer protection against the dangers threatened by those in personal alliance with one who had set himself to oppose all the values for which Nehemiah stood (vv 16–19). Thus the narrative itself points the way forward to what follows, giving attention from now on to the people of Jerusalem and their spiritual welfare.

The Need to Populate Jerusalem
(Neh 7:1–72a [Ev 73a])

Bibliography

See the bibliography to Ezra 2. The following works are, in addition, of particular relevance to Neh 7.

Barr, J. "Hebrew עד, especially at Job i.18 and Neh. vii.3." *JSS* 27 (1982) 177–88. **Driver, G. R.** "Forgotten Hebrew Idioms." *ZAW* 78 (1966) 1–7. **Gunneweg, A. H. J.** "Zur Interpretation der Bücher Esra-Nehemia—zugleich ein Beitrag zur Methode der Exegese." VTSup 32 (1981) 146–61. **Haupt, P.** "Batim lo benuyim." *Johns Hopkins University Circulars* 13 (1894) 108–9. **Schaeder, H. H.** *Esra der Schreiber,* 15–26.

Translation

[1] *When the wall had been built and I had hung the doors, the gatekeepers, singers, and Levites were appointed.* [2] *Then I put my brother Hanani and* [a] *Hananiah the governor of the fortress in charge of Jerusalem, the latter being a trustworthy man* [b] *and one who feared God more than most,* [3] *and I said* [a] *to them, "The gates of Jerusalem are not to be left open during the heat of the day,* [b] *but while they are still on duty* [c] *they must shut the doors and secure* [d] *them; and arrange* [e] *rotas of guard duty for* [e] *the inhabitants of Jerusalem, some* [f] *at their sentry-posts and some in front of their own homes."*

[4] *Now, the city was large and spacious, but the people within it were few, without (enough)* [a] *rebuilt houses.* [5] *So my God gave me the idea of gathering the nobles, the officials, and the people to be registered by families. I found the genealogical record* [a] *of those who had come up at the first. I found written therein:*

[6a] *These are the people of the province who came up from the captivity of the exiles whom Nebuchadnezzar king of Babylon had taken into exile and who returned to Jerusalem and Judah, each to his own town.* [7] *They came with Zerubbabel, Jeshua, Nehemiah, Azariah, Raamiah, Nahamani, Mordecai, Bilshan, Mispereth, Bigvai, Nehum, (and) Baanah.*

The list of the men of the people of Israel:

[8] *The family of Parosh*	2,172
[9] *The family of Shephatiah*	372
[10] *The family of Arah*	652
[11] *The family of Pahath-Moab, namely the families of Jeshua and Joab*	2,818
[12] *The family of Elam*	1,254
[13] *The family of Zattu*	845
[14] *The family of Zaccai*	760
[15] *The family of Binnui*	648
[16] *The family of Bebai*	628
[17] *The family of Azgad*	2,322

¹⁸ *The family of Adonikam*   667
¹⁹ *The family of Bigvai*   2,067
²⁰ *The family of Adin*   655
²¹ *The family of Ater, that is, of Hezekiah*   98
   [*The family of Azzur*   432
   The family of Hodiah   101]
²² *The family of Hashum*   328
²³ *The family of Bezai*   324
²⁴ *The family of Hariph*   112
²⁵ *The family of Gibeon*   95
²⁶ *The men of Bethlehem and Netophah*   188
²⁷ *The men of Anathoth*   128
²⁸ *The men of Beth-Azmaveth*   42
²⁹ *The men of Kiriath-jearim, Kephirah, and Beeroth*   743
³⁰ *The men of Ramah and Geba*   621
³¹ *The men of Michmas*   122
³² *The men of Bethel and Ai*   123
³³ *The inhabitants of (the other) Nebo*   52
³⁴ *The inhabitants of the other Elam*   1,254
³⁵ *The inhabitants of Harim*   320
³⁶ *The inhabitants of Jericho*   345
³⁷ *The inhabitants of Lod, Hadid and Ono*   721
³⁸ *The inhabitants of Senaah*   3,930
³⁹ *The priests:*
   The family of Jedaiah, namely the house of Jeshua   973
⁴⁰ *The family of Immer*   1,052
⁴¹ *The family of Pashhur*   1,247
⁴² *The family of Harim*   1,017
⁴³ *The Levites:*
   The family of Jeshua, namely of Kadmiel, of the family of Hodaviah   74
⁴⁴ *The singers:*
   The family of Asaph   148
⁴⁵ *The gatekeepers:*
   The family of Shallum
   The family of Ater
   The family of Talmon
   The family of Akkub
   The family of Hatita
   The family of Shobai   total: 138
⁴⁶ *The temple servants:*
   The family of Ziha
   The family of Hasupha
   The family of Tabbaoth
⁴⁷ *The family of Keros*
   The family of Sia
   The family of Padon
⁴⁸ *The family of Lebanah*

The family of Hagabah
[The family of Akkub
The family of Hagab]
The family of Salmai
⁴⁹ *The family of Hanan*
The family of Giddel
The family of Gahar
⁵⁰ *The family of Reaiah*
The family of Rezin
The family of Nekoda
⁵¹ *The family of Gazzam*
The family of Uzza
The family of Paseah
⁵² *The family of Besai*
[The family of Asnah]
The family of the Meunim
The family of the Naphishim
⁵³ *The family of Bakbuk*
The family of Hakupha
The family of Harhur
⁵⁴ *The family of Bazlith*
The family of Mehira
The family of Harsha
⁵⁵ *The family of Barkos*
The family of Sisera
The family of Temah
⁵⁶ *The family of Neziah*
The family of Hatipha
⁵⁷ *The sons of Solomon's servants:*
The family of Sotai
The family of Sophereth
The family of Peridah
⁵⁸ *The family of Jaalah*
The family of Darkon
The family of Giddel
⁵⁹ *The family of Shephatiah*
The family of Hattil
The family of Pochereth-Hazzebaim
The family of Amon
⁶⁰ *Total of the temple servants and the sons of Solomon's servants:* 392
⁶¹ *The following came up from Tel-Melah, Tel-Harsha, Kerub, Addon, and Immer,*
but they were unable to demonstrate that their family or their descent were of Israel:
⁶² *The family of Delaiah*
The family of Tobiah
The family of Nekoda 642
⁶³ *And of the priests:*
The family of Hobaiah

The family of Hakkoz
The family of Barzillai. (The latter had married one of the daughters
of Barzillai the Gileadite and was called by his name.)
⁶⁴ These searched for their registration (among) those who had been enrolled by
genealogy but it could not be found so they were debarred from the priesthood as
unclean. ⁶⁵ And the governor ordered them not to eat of the most holy food until
a priest should arise who could consult Urim and Thummim.
⁶⁶ The whole assembly together: 42,360
⁶⁷ (apart from their 7,337 menservants and maidservants; and they also had 200
men and women singers).
⁽⁶⁸⁾ [Their horses   736
Their mules   2]45
⁶⁸⁽⁶⁹⁾ Their camels   435
Donkeys   6,720
⁶⁹⁽⁷⁰⁾ Some of the heads of families gave to the work. The governor gave to the
treasury 1,000 drachmas of gold, 50 bowls, 30 priestly vestments, and 500 minas
of silver. ᵃ ⁷⁰⁽⁷¹⁾ Some of the heads of families gave to the treasury for the work
20,000 drachmas of gold and 2,200 minas of silver, ⁷¹⁽⁷²⁾ while the remainder
of the people gave 20,000 drachmas of gold, 2,000 minas of silver and 67 priestly
vestments. ⁷²⁽⁷³⁾ The priests, the Levites, the gatekeepers, the singers, some of the
people, and the temple servants, even all Israel, settled in their own towns. ᵃ

Notes

2.a. It would theoretically be possible to understand the conj here as an explicative wāw,
and so to translate, "Then I put my brother Hanani, that is Hananiah the governor of the
fortress, in charge of Jerusalem." Hanani might then be regarded as a familiar, family form of
the name, while the fuller form, Hananiah, was used in public life; cf. Tuland, "Hanani—Hananiah," JBL 77 (1958) 157–61, but see Comment on 1:2 above. One factor in favor of this interpretation is the sg explanatory clause later in the verse, lit., "for he was a trustworthy man . . . ,"
although, as the translation supplied above seeks to show, this can be understood either way;
perhaps Nehemiah assumed that his readers would appreciate his own brother's good qualities
whereas those of a new character in the account would require explanation. V 3, however,
strongly favors the view that two men are mentioned here, since Nehemiah addresses "them"
(pl). The only way to avoid this conclusion would be to refer the pl "them" to the gatekeepers
mentioned in v 1. However, the orders given refer to a third party, themselves most easily
understood as the gatekeepers. It is thus most probable that Nehemiah is here addressing the
two leaders.
2.b. For the Kaph veritatis, cf. GKC § 118x.
3.a. Read וָאֹמַר "and I said" with Q and the Vrs, exactly as at 5:9. K, וַיֹּאמֶר, "and he
said," might be thought to favor the view that only one person was appointed in v 2, and that
he is the subject of the verb here. The final point made at n. 2.a. above tells against this,
however, even though such an understanding by a scribe in antiquity may explain how the K
reading originated.
3.b. The expression עַד־חֹם הַשֶּׁמֶשׁ is usually rendered "until the sun is hot," and the whole
phrase interpreted to mean that the gates were to be opened not at first light but when
the sun was fully up. Elsewhere, however, the phrase clearly refers to the hottest part of
the day, when most activity generally ceased; see particularly its equivalence at 1 Sam 11:9 with
עַד־חֹם הַיּוֹם, "until the heat of the day" two verses later, and the use of the latter expression at Gen 18:1 and 2 Sam 4:5, both of which show that this was the time for a siesta. Since
it would be absurd to open the gates at such a time (and, indeed, to keep them closed
until then), we should here take עַד to mean "while, during," and translate as above; this
meaning of עַד is well recognized by the lexicons for a number of passages, and is given

further, philological support for the present passage by Driver, *ZAW* 78 (1966) 4–6 (see also *WO* 1 [1947–52] 238 and 412–13). Note, however, that Driver does not argue from the meaning of the phrase as a whole, nor does his interpretation of the following clause agree with ours.

3.c. This clause has generated much debate. Since the first part of the verse is generally thought to refer to the time when the gates should first be opened in the morning, this clause would then refer to when they should be shut in the evening. A wide variety of alternatives is offered by the major translations and commentaries, with or without emendation. On our understanding of the first part of the verse, however, such an approach is misguided. The two clauses are to be regarded as referring to the same time, both being introduced by עד. The subject of the clause, הם "they," may be taken either as indefinite, or to refer loosely to the gatekeepers of v 1 with no difference in meaning. עמדים, "standing," is used to contrast with sitting or reclining during the siesta which is about to follow; hence, "while they are (still) on duty." (Driver's suggestion that it means "standing about inactive" seems improbable as a way of passing the hottest period of the day.) Normally, the gates would have been left open throughout the day. Because he was ordering such an unusual procedure, Nehemiah spelled out carefully exactly what was to happen. A similar approach to the problems of this verse has now been advanced by Barr, *JSS* 27 (1982) 177–88.

3.d. For this meaning of אחז, "secure," which comes close to Aram. אחד, cf. Rudolph, and Segert, *ArOr* 24 (1956) 391. The use of the impv mood is strange, however. Two MSS suggest reading the inf abs, וֶאֱחֹז "and secure," and this is preferred by Rudolph, *inter alia*. I propose merely repointing MT as a *wāw*-consecutive with the perf (following the impf יְגִיפוּ "shut"): וְאָחֲזוּ "and they shall secure."

3.e-e. A slightly loose rendering of the const of משמרות. In the pl, this word generally means "divisions" for service of whatever sort; "rotas of guard duty" thus seems appropriate in the context.

3.f. ואיש . . . איש "a man . . . and a man" distributive sing, hence "some . . . and some."

4.a. Lit., "There were no (re)built houses." It is clear from the previous verse, to go no further, that there were some houses! There is no doubt, however, that when the context so demands אין may have the meaning of "there is/was not enough" (and similarly יש "there is/was enough"); see, for instance, 2:14. There is therefore no need to emend (*contra* Joüon, *Bib* 12 [1931] 88, who proposes רבים "many" instead of בנוים "rebuilt"). An alternative interpretation of the text, first advanced by Haupt, *Johns Hopkins University Circulars* 13 (1894) 108–9, and followed by a number of recent commentators, observes that both בית "house" and בנה "build" can be used in the context of families being established. The translation "the families were not built up/large" is thus proposed. While possible, this seems less likely in the context.

5.a. The present text is difficult, if not impossible, syntactically, since the masc pl העולים "those who had come up" cannot be related to the preceding ספר היחש "genealogical record." Unless we regard the whole section following העולים as a later editorial addition (see *Form* below), we should probably adopt the widely accepted slight emendation (loss of one letter by scribal error) of היחש to התיחש, which may then be construed as a verbal noun (cf. Ezra 8:1) in the const to yield the translation supplied above.

6.a. Textual notes relevant to Neh 7 have already been incorporated into the notes on the parallel Ezra 2.

69(70).a. Despite several English translations, the last part of this verse should not be rendered "Five hundred and thirty priests' garments," since in that case the hundreds would have to come first. Rather, the text as it stands reads "thirty priests' garments and 500 . . ." On the basis of the following verses, Keil (*ad* Ezra 2:68–70, followed by most commentators since) correctly proposed restoring מ׳ נתן וכו׳, translated as above.

72(73).a. See the full discussion in *Comment* below.

Form/Structure/Setting

From chap. 7 onwards, the literary history of the Book of Nehemiah becomes extremely complicated. While we may hope to clarify the issues at stake, the solutions favored can be but tentative since frequently decisions must perforce be taken on less than substantial evidence.

The opening verses of the present chapter clearly continue the narrative of the NM. Whether the list which follows (and hence its introduction in v 5b) was also included is far less clear.

One group of scholars dismisses the list from the NM because they believe that it is borrowed here from Ezra 2. Since such a borrowing would have to include the opening words of the narrative after the list (because they are parallel with Ezra 3:1), and since it is agreed that this narrative is not from the NM, it follows that the borrowing could not have been made by Nehemiah himself, but must be attributed to a later editor. This view, however, was examined in detail in my "The Composition of Ezra i–vi," *JTS* ns 34 (1983) 2–8 and rejected. There is thus no a priori reason to deny the list to the NM.

If, with the majority of commentators, we accept 7:1–5a at least as from the hand of Nehemiah (and its style strongly favors this conclusion), then we must surely agree that the *narrative* continuation of this chapter is found in Neh 11. This conclusion holds despite the fact that Neh 11 is not itself from the NM (see *Form* on chap. 11 for the details). Only there do we find a concern with the settlement of the people including the movement of some to Jerusalem in a way that answers the problem of 7:4–5. The *literary* link, however, between Neh 7 and 11 is to be found at 7:72a (73a) and 11:1, not 7:5 (*contra* Talmon, *IDBSup*, 322; see the commentary on the verses in question). The simplest approach, therefore, is to suggest that the NM was broken off at 7:72a (73a), and that its substance (though not its wording) was resumed in chap. 11.

Those who disagree with this conclusion do not always advance particular reasons. One assumes that they do so out of a sense that this long list is not quite appropriate to the style of the NM. Here, however, it should be remembered that Nehemiah has already included the list of chap. 3; this serves as a warning that feelings of literary propriety may not have been the same in antiquity as today. Besides, Nehemiah may have felt that it showed up his care as an administrator.

We may mention at this point the interesting view of Schaeder, *Esra*, 15–26, that the list originally formed part of the Ezra Memoir, being transferred to its present position (along with Neh 8–9) from a point following Ezra 8:34. Rudolph, 13, has brought cogent arguments to bear against this suggestion, however, and it has not been taken up again by more recent writers; it is therefore not necessary to deal with it here again in detail.

A fuller case against our position is argued by Kellermann, *Nehemia*. Curiously, however, he denies any connection of thought between chap. 7 and chap. 11, affirming rather that the most natural continuation of 7:5 is with the account of the dedication of the walls at 12:27–43. Now, it is true that 12:31 is the next point at which we again find Nehemiah writing in the first person, but Kellermann offers no explanation of the connection between "I found the genealogical record" in 7:5 and the dedication ceremony. It would be more logical, with Kaufmann, *History*, 377 (cf. Appendix x) to dissociate Nehemiah's concern with the genealogical record from the problems of the unpopulated city altogether, believing that 7:4 is added as an explanation for the measures of 7:1–3. Kellermann, however, does not do this; indeed, he insists that the words "and I found the genealogical record" must have stood in the NM in order for the list subsequently to have been added here. But, as we have said, this completely destroys any putative connection with 12:27.

Kellermann's other arguments against the list are also weak. Several derive from contradictions between elements found in it and the situation as it had developed by Nehemiah's day. This is irrelevant, however. Although some of the narrative has been lost to us (see *Form* on chap. 11), it is clear that this list was to serve only as a basis for further action. Similarly, it is no objection to its use in this capacity that those who had come more recently to the province (Ezra 8:1) were not included. 7:5 is quite clear: Nehemiah wished to register all the people. As he set about this task, he found an older list. From this, we are clearly intended to understand that he used the list as a basis for his revised register. In copying out the list at a later date, however, he will have continued it to the end, untroubled by the fact that the last few verses were not strictly relevant to his purpose at the time he was taking action.

We conclude, therefore, that both what precedes the list (7:5) and what follows (the literary connection between the end of chap. 7 and the beginning of chap. 11) argue for its inclusion in the NM. It served as the basis for Nehemiah's next great step of ordering the life of the city whose walls he had rebuilt. Questions relating to the form, structure, and historical setting of the list itself were treated at Ezra 2 above.

One other point deserves mention here, and that is the setting of the list within the present, canonical shape of the book of Ezra-Nehemiah, for undoubtedly the fact that the same list occurs twice in so short a work is surprising. However we explain the fact from the point of view of literary criticism, what can be said about this phenomenon as we find it now? To answer such a question, we need do no more than point to the perceptive treatment of Gunneweg, VTSup 32 (1981) 156. He observes the importance of stressing that the community that here appears toward the end of the period of reconstruction and purification (Ezra 9–10) is the self-same community as that which returned "at the first" to undertake the initial rebuilding of the temple. Indeed, he goes so far as to see here a counterpart to the list of those recorded in the heavenly "book of life" of the apocalyptic visionaries. "Ist das göttliche Heil präsent, so müssen auch die Namen derer, die es erlangten, namhaft gemacht werden können, wohingegen das apokalyptische Buch des Lebens erst 'an jenem Tage' geöffnet werden wird."

Comment

1 Though the walls were now fully completed (cf. 6:15 and contrast 6:1), there was a continuing need for watchfulness, as the concluding verses of the previous chapter emphasized. Nehemiah, in all probability, left the detailed arrangement of the guards to the leaders mentioned in the next verse; it is unlikely, otherwise, that "were appointed" would be cast in the passive mood.

It is widely held that "singers and Levites" is a later gloss on "the gatekeepers." If so, השוערים "the gatekeepers" will not be cultic officials at all (contrast the use of the same word at v 45 below and frequently elsewhere), but rather lay guardsmen. A later reader, misunderstanding the word because of its more familiar cultic associations, glossed it in accordance with vv 43 and 44. This is a possible explanation. Nevertheless, the order is curious: we would expect the Levites to come first even in a gloss. Ryle, therefore, may be right in his suggestion that "in the unsettled state of affairs, . . . Nehemiah entrusted the protection of the whole city to this body of trained 'police,' [i.e., the temple gatekeepers] and augmented their force by other available trained bands, i.e., the musicians and the main body of Levites." These were emergency arrangements only, therefore. In favor of this explanation, it should be observed that the lay population of Jerusalem are dealt with separately as regards their guard duty in v 3 below.

2 Perhaps backtracking slightly, Nehemiah now notes his appointment of two prominent citizens to be responsible for the general administration of the city. It becomes clear from v 3 that these duties included the supervision of the guards just mentioned. How they related to (or whether they replaced) the officials named in 3:9 and 12 is not stated. However, there need have been no direct clash, since it was argued at 3:9 that the latter's responsibility was for the territory around the urban center rather than for the city itself.

For "my brother Hanani," see *Comment* on 1:2. His appointment is understandable enough, and so receives no further explanation. Hananiah, however, is mentioned only here. For "the fortress," cf. 2:8. As its governor, Hananiah was evidently well qualified in military terms to supervise the guarding of the city. Added to that, however, was his character as a man who could be relied on by his fellows and who himself had a right attitude towards God. The characteristics Nehemiah deemed significant in others reflect creditably on his own scale of values.

3 The basic exegetical problems of this verse are dealt with under *Notes* above. The few hours from approximately midday onwards were ones of particular vulnerability, owing to the sleepy atmosphere familiar even today in Mediterranean countries. Indeed, Driver, *ZAW* 78 (1966) 4, is able to supply two examples from Roman history of just this danger; cf. in particular the capture of Rome in A.D. 410 when the Salarian gate was rushed "just at midday, when all those [*sc.* the guards] who should seize them were, as usual, dozing after a meal" (Procopius, *de Bell. Vandal.* I.ii.17. = *History of the Wars*, Book III, ii § 17).

As a further precaution during the emergency, the lay inhabitants of the city were also conscripted for guard duty on a rota-system. Some, whose homes abutted the city wall, were to keep watch at those very points: motivation would be excellent here, as it had been in similar circumstances for the wall-building; see *Comment* on 3:20–21. Others were to man sentry posts to cover the remaining stretches of the wall.

4 At this point, we might have expected the account of the dedication of the walls (12:27–43); for a discussion of the point, see *Form* of the commentary on that paragraph, where it is concluded that an account of the ceremony may possibly have been transposed by the editor from here (or, less probably, from 6:19) for thematic purposes of his own. At all events, the narrative here moves on to a major new consideration, namely, the reduced population

of the city, whose resolution is not presented until chap. 11. Only Kaufmann, *History,* 377, seeks to avoid this conclusion by interpreting the present verse as an explanation of the emergency measures in vv 1–3 and by understanding the remainder of the chapter as a move by Nehemiah to support Ezra's handling of the issue of mixed marriages. Of this latter, however, there is no hint whatsoever in the context. Without such a gratuitous assumption, it becomes impossible not to link v 4 with what follows. Taken in this way, it provides an obvious motive for Nehemiah's concern and his subsequent action: the best solution to the city's vulnerability was to see it well populated. Now that self-respectability and the potential for defense had been reestablished, the possibility of encouraging some of the Jews to live there was realistic. The question was—who?

5 Prompted, as he saw it, by divine guidance (cf. 2:12), Nehemiah gathered the leaders of the people together. The list is close to that in 2:16; 4:8 (14), 13 (19); and 5:7 and is typical of Nehemiah's style; contrast 11:1. In fact, there is scarcely a word in common between these two verses, whereas v 72 (73) is linked with 11:1 both in thought and vocabulary; see further below. This tells strongly against Talmon's suggestion (*IDBSup* 322) that 11:1 is a repetitive resumption of the present verse.

The purpose of the gathering was to draw up a census of the population, on the basis of which an equitable decision could be taken as to who should be moved into the city. To help with this, Nehemiah had at hand the list of the first returnees. The chronological sequence is not quite clear at this point: it may be suggested that "I found" is being drawn into the sphere of the divine prompting rather than that it necessarily followed chronologically upon the gathering together (ואמצא . . . ואקבצה . . . ויתן); if so, "for I had found" would be a possible translation. At all events, the list was clearly suited to Nehemiah's purpose, because it included indications of the population's original places of settlement. For "at the first," see the concluding paragraph of *Form* on Ezra 2.

6–72(73)a Most of the issues raised by this list have been dealt with at Ezra 2. Here it is necessary only to add a few remarks concerning its divergent ending.

69(70) This is the first of the verses which were summarized by Ezra 2:69. Although it was therefore clearly in place by the time Neh 7 was borrowed at Ezra 2, Mowinckel, *Studien I,* 31, has made a strong case for regarding it as one of the latest elements in the composition of the original list: note the clumsy repetition of the opening of the verse at the start of the next, the unlikely inclusion of "the governor" (see *Comment* on Ezra 2:63) among "the heads of families," and the placing of "minas of silver" at the end of the list, against the order in the next two verses. The verse may have been added either by Nehemiah himself or by the editor of the Ezra and Nehemiah material, since both worked prior to the author of Ezra 1–6. It is attractive to speculate that Nehemiah may have added the comment in order to glorify the role of his first predecessor in office and hence to show himself in a measure as a worthy successor because of his own care, demonstrated later, for the temple cult.

72(73)a A literal translation of the MT of this verse is supplied above, as is one of the parallel passage at Ezra 2:70. Comparison of the two at once shows that there has been some textual confusion: "the gatekeepers" and "some of the people" are swapped over, while Ezra has an additional "in their own towns" after "the temple servants." In consequence, neither text is likely to be original: Nehemiah's curious order is suspicious, while the text in Ezra is unlikely, because of its unnecessary and stylistically clumsy repetition.

Most commentators follow (with greater or less precision) the lead of 1 Esdras. At 5:45 (46) its rendering of Ezra 2:70 may be translated, "And the priests and the Levites and some of the people settled in Jerusalem and the neighborhood, whereas the singers and the gatekeepers and all Israel (settled) in their towns," and its rendering of Neh 7:72a (73a) at 9:37, "And the priests and the Levites and some of Israel settled in Jerusalem and the neighborhood (on the new moon of the seventh month) and the children of Israel in their settlements." On this basis, many restore "in Jerusalem" to the MT, in order to draw a distinction between those who settled in the capital and those who settled elsewhere; see, for example, RSV of Ezra 2:70, "The priests, the Levites, and some of the people lived in Jerusalem and its vicinity; and the singers, the gatekeepers, and the temple servants lived in their towns, and all Israel in their towns."

There are, however, three objections to this solution. (i) Textually, it is extremely unlikely that "in Jerusalem" should have survived in both passages until the time of 1 Esdr and then been lost from both. (ii) There are several other differences between MT and 1 Esdras which the commentators dismiss as secondary. It is not good method, however, to pick and choose in this fashion what appears to suit the sense one requires. (iii) The resulting text does not give good sense in any case, since it is clearly stated elsewhere that some, at least, of the temple servants lived in Jerusalem (cf. 3:26, 31; 11:21), if not all (cf. 11:3) while equally some of the senior cultic officials are said to have lived outside the city (11:3). It is thus far more likely that 1 Esdr was disturbed by the same problems we have already noted and, particularly because of the distinction between "some of the people" and "all Israel," felt the need to make two parallel clauses out of the list by the insertion of "in Jerusalem." 7:6 (Ezra 2:1) may have provided the necessary clue. (That the later ancient Vrs conform to MT is neither surprising nor particularly significant.)

An alternative approach, developed especially by Rudolph, suggests that 7:72a (73a) is the result of a confused conflation of both the conclusion of the list and a note about the settlement of Ezra's caravan which would have originally stood at the end of Ezra 8 but which was transferred here together with the other material now found in Neh 8. While such a confusion is possible, the reconstruction of the textual process by which it came about is far too speculative in detail to inspire confidence.

In my judgment, the MT of Neh 7:72a (73a) is not far from the text that left the hands of the final editor, but the process by which he arrived at that text needs fresh examination. It should be noted first (as the author of 1 Esdr may have done) that the heading to the list (7:6) already specifies that some of those who returned went to Jerusalem and that others went elsewhere in Judah, "each to his own town." The division of the population for which Nehemiah (and the modern commentators!) was seeking was already present in the text without the problems that the solution of 1 Esdr has been shown to raise.

Second, it must be observed that the verse under discussion is not really part of the list at all, and further that if it says that various people lived "in their own towns" this will, according to 7:6, include Jerusalem in any case. There is therefore again no need for major emendation.

Third, we should take note of the start of chap. 11, where the words וישבו and העם recur and where the narrative of the present chapter is also continued. It is thus probable that this is intended to serve as a repetitive resumption.

On the basis of these observations, we may now formulate a hypothesis as to how our present verse developed: (i) It did not feature in the earliest form of the list, that which Nehemiah found. The point was already made by the list's introduction. (ii) When Nehemiah incorporated the list in his memoir, he continued into his subsequent narrative (the precise form of which has now been overlaid by the later editor; see *Form* on chap. 11) with the relevant note that "The priests, the Levites and some of the people settled in their towns" (וישבו הכהנים והלוים ומן־העם בעריהם). He then continued to say (as we deduce from chap. 11) that the leaders of the people dwelt specifically in Jerusalem. (iii) When the editor of the material concerning Ezra and Nehemiah spliced the work of these two men together, it was, for reasons that will become apparent in the next chapter, at this point that he broke into the NM. While leaving sufficient evidence to make clear the link between this chapter and chap. 11, he nevertheless wished the verse in its present isolated position to serve more strongly as a summary conclusion to the preceding list. He therefore added the minor cultic officials on the basis of vv 41, 42, and 43, probably originally in that order (though curiously, note 10:29). He may also have added "Even (and) all Israel" as a resumption of his now expanded list, under the influence of his later "all Israel" ideology. His text, then, will have read: וישבו הכהנים והלוים ומן־העם והמשררים והשוערים והנתינים וכל־ישראל בעריהם: "The priests and the Levites and some of the people, and the singers and the gatekeepers and the temple servants, even all Israel, settled in their towns." For an appreciation of the meaning of "some of the people" at this textual level, cf. Gunneweg, VTSup 32 (1981) 157. (iv) When this text was copied by the author of Ezra 1–6, he was puzzled by the distinction between "the people" and "all Israel," since in such a context he probably thought that "Israel" referred to the laity in any case; for this usage in passages with which he was familiar, cf. Ezra 10:5; Neh 12:47 (and less exactly Ezra 7:7 and Neh 11:20). He therefore added בעריהם "in their towns" before "and all Israel" in order to make some sort of distinction between the two. (v) The text of Neh 7:72a (73a) suffered a slight later corruption in that ומן־העם and והשוערים somehow became inverted, a not uncommon type of occurrence. (vi) Confused in particular by the new text of Ezra 2, the author of 1 Esdr sought to clarify the situation by reference back to the introduction to the list. From a textual point of view, however, his reading is entirely secondary.

Explanation

The previous chapter concluded with an indication that the completion of the walls was not in itself an adequate defense for Jerusalem. It provided the framework, but ultimately only a thriving population could ensure that no outsiders would lightly seek sovereignty over it. Thus, as a short-term, emergency measure, Nehemiah ordered that an unusually strict guard should be mounted. He then moved on at once to deal with the more fundamental problem.

Whereas he may have regarded the discovery of a list of the families who made up the core of the population as administratively fortuitous, we should not overlook its present, theological statement: those who should populate the city of God stand in direct continuity with the community who had earlier experienced God's redemption in the second Exodus. We, too, do well to remember that, necessary as bricks and mortar or organizational structures may be, the Church of Christ is neither founded on nor maintained by these alone; it is they who have experienced the grace of God for themselves who become members of Christ's bride, the new Jerusalem (Rev 21:2; see also Eph 2:19–22; 1 Pet 2:5).

Covenant Renewal   (Neh 8–10)

Bibliography

Ahlemann, F. "Zur Esra-Quelle." *ZAW* 59 (1942–43) 77–98. **Baltzer, K.** *The Covenant Formulary.* Tr. D. E. Green. Oxford: Blackwell, 1971. 43–47. **Childs, B. S.** *Introduction,* 624–38. **In der Smitten, W. Th.** *Esra,* 35–53. **Kaufmann, Y.** *History.* Appendix vii, 638–49. **Kellermann, U.** *Nehemia,* 90–92. **McCarthy, D. J.** "Covenant and Law in Chronicles-Nehemiah." *CBQ* 44 (1982) 25–44. **Mowinckel, S.** *Studien I,* 50–59. **Schaeder, H. H.** *Esra,* 5–26. **Torrey, C. C.** *Composition,* 29–34. ————. *Ezra Studies,* 252–84.

Form/Structure/Setting

The composition of Neh 8–10 lies at the heart of the literary and historical problems relating to these books. Not surprisingly, therefore, the very widest spectrum of opinions is to be found represented in the works listed above and the commentaries. There are those, such as Kaufmann, who defend the unity of the three chapters as a whole and maintain that they are in their correct historical setting. Others, such as Torrey, also maintain that the chapters are a unity but at the same time insist that they are misplaced both in terms of literary setting and, in consequence, from the historical point of view (though Torrey himself did not rate their historical value at all highly). Then again there are those who wish to keep chaps. 8–9 together, but to locate them after Ezra 8, and to put chap. 10 after Neh 13; others who keep chaps. 9–10 together but without reference to chap. 8 (e.g., Baltzer); and finally, yet others who argue that all three chapters are originally of independent origin.

A further area of disagreement centers on the process which has led to the present text and its setting within the Nehemiah narrative. Clearly, since Ezra now suddenly moves into the foreground and Nehemiah's first person account is suspended, these chapters (together, in my view, with chaps. 11 and 12:1–26) are in some sense an interruption. But is this intended, or is it simply the result of a mechanical error at some stage in the transmission of the text, or again, is it the result of only late redactional activity on these books that obscures their originally intended shape? Weighty proponents of each view could be cited.

At first sight, this diversity of opinion may seem bewildering and lead to skepticism with regard to a critical approach itself. This would be unjustified, however. The issues involved are, in fact, unusually clear, and careful attention has been paid to them in the sections on *Form/Structure/Setting* in connection with each of the individual chapters below. Naturally, there is room for discussion over how the evidence should be weighed and evaluated, so that readers must make up their own minds on the basis of the case presented, but that the exercise itself is legitimate, and, indeed, demanded by the nature of the material itself, none can reasonably deny.

It will be argued in this commentary that each of chaps. 8, 9, and 10 has
an independent literary and historical origin. The purpose of these introductory remarks is, however, to affirm emphatically that they have not come
together by the random processes of chance or error in transmission, but
rather that they have been carefully assembled and thoughtfully located by
the editor responsible for combining the Ezra and Nehemiah material.

The question of the place of these chapters in the books as a whole is
briefly treated in the *Introduction,* "A Theological Reading." The issue of
their coherence is more conveniently handled here, however. We may start
with the observation that, although the length of time involved shows that
the events cannot historically have taken place on a single occasion, and
though there are some intrusive elements, such as the celebration of the
Feast of Tabernacles, which the editor has retained in faithfulness to his
sources and for other purposes, yet the overall shape of these three chapters
follows a recognizable and intelligible pattern, often referred to as covenant
renewal. In his pioneering study of this form, Baltzer, *Covenant Formulary* 43–
47, reckoned with only chaps. 9–10. Recognizing certain differences between
this text and others of the pre-exilic period, he nevertheless maintained that
chap. 9 was intended as the antecedent history, whose recall necessarily preceded the renewal of the covenant in the pledge of chap. 10. McCarthy,
"Covenant and Law" has refined this broad analysis, and insisted that the
reading of the law (chap. 8) is a necessary, introductory part of covenant
renewal. Finally, Kellermann, *Nehemia* 90–92, has drawn attention to other
texts that share this threefold structure: proclamation of the law—confession—
renewal of commitment to the covenant with general and specific stipulations.
He cites Ezra 9–10; 2 Chr 15:1–18; 29–31; 34:29—35:19.

In my opinion, there can be little doubt that the chapters have been molded
into a unity that is satisfying from a theological point of view. The various
stages develop naturally from one another, and there can be no doubt that
this is how the editor intended them to be read. We shall, however, be wise
to suspend judgment on the question whether this is truly based on a formal
procedure of the cult which the editor knew and sought to imitate. A study
of the texts listed by Kellermann reveals a number of differences that preclude
the conclusion that a rigid form is being followed. For instance, only in 2
Chr 34–35 is there a reference to a reading from the law of God (elsewhere
we find a prophet, or prophetic-like spokesman). Yet there can be no doubt
that this element is a cornerstone of the present narrative. For similar reasons,
we do not find it necessary to ascribe all the texts listed to a single author.
Rather, there is a theological inevitability about the way the narrative unfolds.
This may well, therefore, also have come to expression on occasions in the
cult and have produced analogies in other texts. The evidence is not sufficiently striking to permit further speculation.

The Reading of the Law
(Neh 7:72b [Ev 73b]—8:18)

Bibliography

Driver, G. R. "Studies in the Vocabulary of the Old Testament. II." *JTS* 32 (1931) 250–57. **Emerton, J. A.** "Did Ezra Go to Jerusalem in 428 B.C.?" *JTS* ns 17 (1966) 1–19. **Falk, Z. W.** "Hebrew Legal Terms: III." *JSS* 14 (1969) 39–44. **In der Smitten, W. Th.** *Esra,* 38–47. **Kapelrud, A. S.** *Authorship,* 80–94. **Kellermann, U.** *Nehemia,* 26–32. **Landersdorfer, S.** *Studien zum biblischen Versöhnungstag.* Alttestamentliche Abhandlungen 10/1. Münster: Verlag der Aschendorffschen Verlagsbuchhandlung, 1924. 60–67. **Le Déaut, R.** *Introduction à la literature targumique.* Rome: Pontifical Biblical Institute, 1966. 23–32. **Mosis, R.** *Untersuchungen,* 215–20. **Mowinckel, S.** *Studien III,* 7–11 and 44–61. **Pohlmann, K.-F.** *Studien,* 127–48 and 151–54. **Schaeder, H. H.** *Esra,* 7–26. **Springer, S.** *Neuinterpretation im Alten Testament.* SBB. Stuttgart: Katholisches Bibelwerk, 1979. 78–83. **Torrey, C. C.** *Composition,* 29–34. ———. *Ezra Studies,* 252–84. **Weinberg, W.** "Language Consciousness in the OT." *ZAW* 92 (1980) 185–204. **Welch, A. C.** *Post-Exilic Judaism,* 262–75.

Translation

72(73)b *When the seventh month came and the Israelites were in their own towns,* 8:1 *all the people assembled as one man to the open space in front of the Water Gate, and they asked Ezra the scribe to bring out the Book of the Law of Moses which the Lord had commanded for Israel.* 2 *So on the first day of the seventh month Ezra the priest brought out* a *the Law before the assembly which was made up of both men and women and of any capable of understanding what they heard.* 3 *He read aloud from it to the men, women, and those who could understand as he faced the open space in front of the Water Gate from first light until midday while all the people listened attentively* a *to the Book of the Law.*

4 *Ezra the scribe stood on a high wooden platform* a *which had been made* b *for the purpose while beside him to his right stood* c *Mattithiah, Shema, Anaiah, Urijah, Hilkiah, and Maaseiah, and to his left Pedaiah, Mishael, Malchiah, Hashum, Hashbadana, Zechariah, (and) Meshullam.* d 5 *Then Ezra opened the Book in the sight of all the people (for he was above all the people), and as he opened it, all the people stood up.* 6 *Ezra blessed the Lord, the great God, and all the people responded, "Amen! Amen!," lifting up their hands and then bowing down and worshiping the Lord with their faces to the ground.*

7 *The* a *Levites—Jeshua, Bani, Sherebiah, Jamin, Akkub, Shabbethai, Hodiah, Maaseiah, Kelita, Azariah, Jozabad, Hanan, (and) Pelaiah—helped the people to understand the Law while the people remained in their places.* 8 *And they read from the Book of the Law of God paragraph by paragraph* a *giving the sense, and so they understood* b *the reading.* c

9 *Then* a *Ezra, the priest and scribe, and the Levites, who were helping the people to understand, said to them all, "This day is holy to the Lord your God; do not mourn or weep"—for all the people had been weeping as they listened to the words of the Law.* 10 *Then he said to them, "Go and partake of rich fare and sweet drinks,*

and send helpings to any who have nothing ready, [a] *for this day is holy to our Lord. Do not grieve,* [b] *for it is the joy of the Lord* [c] *that is your protection."* [11] *The Levites too calmed all the people down by saying, "Hush!* [a] *for this day is holy, so do not grieve."* [12] *Then all the people went away to eat and drink, to distribute portions and to celebrate with great joy, for they understood the words that had been declared* [a] *to them.*

[13] *On the second day the heads of families of all the people, together with* [a] *the priests and the Levites, gathered around Ezra the scribe in order to study* [b] *the words of the Law.* [14] *They found written in the Law which the Lord had commanded through Moses, that the Israelites should live in booths during the feast of the seventh month,* [15] *and that* [a] *they should proclaim the following words and spread them throughout their cities and Jerusalem: "Go out into the hill country and bring branches of olive and of oleaster, of myrtle, palm, and leafy trees* [b] *in order to make booths, as prescribed."*

[16] *So the people went out and fetched them and made booths for themselves, each on his own roof or in their courts, or in the courts of the house of God, or in the open space by the Water Gate or in the square by the Gate of Ephraim.* [17] *Thus the whole congregation of those who had returned from the captivity made booths, and they lived in the booths, something that the Israelites had not done from the time of Jeshua the son of Nun until that day, and there was very great rejoicing.* [18] *Moreover, he read from the Book of the Law of God each day from the first day until the last while they kept the feast for seven days; and then on the eighth day there was a solemn holiday, according to the ordinance.*

Notes

2.a. Cf. GKC § 74l.

3.a. Lit., "While the ears of all the people were towards. . . ."

4.a. "A wooden tower," מגדל not being used elsewhere in a comparable context. The general sense is clear, however; the adj "high" must be added to convey the intended nuance, while "platform" is generally chosen for translation because of the number of those who stood beside Ezra.

4.b. Impers act pl serving for pass.

4.c. A sg verb preceding a pl subj; cf. GKC § 145o.

4.d. There is disagreement in some of the Vrs about one or two of these names, e.g., is חשבדנה "Hashbadana" one name or two? And should Meshullam be included in the list? In addition, against normal practice, neither of the last two names is prefixed by the copula (this is necessarily obscured in the translation above), while it has been suggested that Meshullam could either have been introduced secondarily from Ezra 8:16 (Rudolph) or have arisen as a corr dittogr of the similar-looking משמאלו "to his left." Finally, some find it curious that six men are mentioned as standing to Ezra's right but seven to his left. In view of this, a number of different suggestions have been, or could be, made: (i) increase the first half to seven (with some versional support) to balance the second half; (ii) reduce the second half to six to give a total of twelve by omitting Meshullam; (iii) omit Meshullam but retain seven names in the second half by reading Hashub and Badanah for Hashbadana since the total of thirteen is supported by the same number in v 7; etc. It should by now be self-evident that no suggestion has a stronger claim to probability than another, nor is any superior to MT.

7.a. In Heb., והלוים stands at the end of the list. The explanation of the copula that it is an explicative *wāw* ("even the Levites") is not convincing here; it is better simply omitted, with some of the Vrs. Perhaps it owes its origin to a scribe who mistakenly thought that הלוים was the final name in the list.

8.a. Cf. Ezra 4:18.a. The traditional rendering, "clearly, distinctly," would make much better sense here than there, and so cannot be ruled out as a possibility; cf. Driver, *JTS* 32 (1931) 251–53, and Kapelrud, *Authorship*, 83–84. However, on the same linguistic basis as Driver, Falk has argued rather in favor of the rendering given above; cf. *JSS* 14 (1969) 42–43; for further support, cf. Siegfried, Bertholet, and Schneider. Schaeder (*Esra*) maintained that here too the word is a technical term for extempore translation, and he has been followed by, for instance, Rudolph, Fensham, and Le Déaut, *Introduction,* 23–32. However, in addition to the literature with arguments against Schaeder's view cited at Ezra 4:18.a., see *Notes,* with particular reference to the present context, In der Smitten, *Esra,* 42–43, and Weinberg, *ZAW* 92 (1980) 188–89. The syntax of the word is best explained as a ptcp used as an adverbial accus (GKC § 118p); functioning like an adj, the ptcp may then be sg, even though strictly speaking it is governed by a pl (GKC § 118o). Emendation, therefore, is not required (*contra* J. Skinner, *The Divine Names in Genesis* [London: Hodder and Stoughton, 1914] 225–28). The following inf abs, שׂום "establishing, giving," supports this conclusion.

8.b. The absence of a dir obj (contrast vv 7 and 9) suggests that ויבינו "they understood" is not a hiph, but a qal, with "the people" as its subj; cf. v 12.

8.c. Cf. E. Kutsch, "מִקְרָא," *ZAW* 65 (1953) 247–53.

9.a. MT here has נחמיה הוא התרשׁתא, "Nehemiah, who was the governor." (See *Note* Ezra 2:63.a. for the title.) We regard these words not just as an addition by the editor of the Ezra-Nehemiah material in its final form (see *Form* below), but as a wholly secondary addition, and therefore no part of the original text. The reason for this is not that the verb in the present verse is sg (that is grammatically permissible when the verb precedes a composite subj; cf. GKC § 145o), but because the next verse also begins with a sg verb. In the light of the chap. as a whole, there can be no doubt that Ezra is the subj there (*contra* Kidner, 148–50), but he could not be if Nehemiah were mentioned first in the present verse; cf. Rudolph; Emerton, *JTS* ns 17 (1966) 15, etc. Further, it is curious in any case to find Nehemiah suddenly appearing here in this manner. Now, 1 Esdr 9:49 has no equivalent for "Nehemiah," and LXX has no equivalent for "who was the governor." While various explanations in terms of detail are possible as to how this textual state of affairs developed (cf. Williamson, *Israel,* 31–32), it looks very much as though the phrase came in later (perhaps in different stages) by a harmonistic scribe (or scribes). It may be noted that Nehemiah's title is usually הפחה, not התרשׁתא. The latter may be used here under the influence of 7:69 (70).

10.a. Cf. GKC §§ 152v and 155n.

10.b. Rudolph (and hence *BHS*) needlessly suggests the addition of בו "in it." This would have the effect of linking the clause back to what precedes, whereas in fact there is a break in sense before it (as rightly noted by the Masoretic *'athnaḥ*), and the clause stands in perfect contrast with the words that follow it.

10.c. The context makes clear that this is an obj gen (i.e., Israel's joy in God), a construction that has to be variously rendered to catch its intention (cf. GKC § 128h). The exact meaning may not be so easy to grasp (cf. *Comment* below), but that does not give us grounds for emendation (*contra* Ehrlich, *Randglossen* 7, 203–4, and Joüon, *Bib* 12 [1931] 88–89). The Vrs that differ do so on the basis of misunderstanding rather than a divergent *Vorlage;* cf. Rudolph.

11.a. Though inflected like a verb here, הס is no more than an onomatopoeic interjection; cf. GKC § 105a.

12.a. Strictly speaking, Ezra and the Levites are the subj of this (act) verb, but to translate so would be somewhat inelegant.

13.a. The Masoretic accentuation implies that all the priests and Levites, not just the heads of their families (contrast the laity) were involved; cf. Springer, *Neuinterpretation,* 81.

13.b. The syntax is uncertain, though all possibilities lead to the same interpretation: (i) epexegetic *wāw,* "and even to . . ."; (ii) *wāw* + *lāmed* + inf constr to continue a previous finite verb but with the nuance of intention; cf. GKC § 114p; (iii) delete the *wāw* (Rudolph, though his appeal to the Vrs for support is worthless since they need not have represented it in their own languages in order to arrive at an accurate rendering). For אל + להשׂכיל, cf Ps 41·9

15.a. There are no textual grounds for the deletion of ואשׁר "and that," despite the difficulties that it appears to raise. These must therefore be solved exegetically; cf. *Comment.*

15.b. In accordance with Heb. idiom, the text actually says "branches of olive and branches of oleaster and . . ." etc.

Form/Structure/Setting

Although it is accepted that Neh 8–10 has been compiled as a unit to portray something like a covenant renewal by the restored community (see the introduction to chaps. 8–10 immediately above), it is nevertheless evident that Neh 8 represents a discrete element within this unit. Its opening is indicated by the new date in 7:72b (73b) and by the conscious conclusion to the preceding section; for its separation from what follows, see *Form* for chap. 9.

Within itself, however, Neh 8 is to be regarded as a unity: (i) The date is given in full in v 2, while v 13 presents itself as a direct continuation of the narrative by its initial phrase "on the second day." (ii) There is a unity of theme in the chapter, namely Ezra reading and explaining the Law (with Levitical assistance) and the people responding willingly to its demands. It is this that binds the second half of the chapter (vv 13–18) so closely to the first, the celebration of the Feast of Tabernacles being subordinated to this major theme; vv 13, 14, 15, and 18 all relate directly to Ezra and the Law, while in vv 16 and 17 the only point made about the Festival is that the people observed the prescriptions which had been relayed to them in a manner unprecedented for centuries before. No other aspect of the festival receives so much as a mention. These two unifying factors within the chapter, it will be observed, separate it both from what precedes and from what follows.

Within this overall unity, questions have frequently been raised as to whether some elements should not be regarded as secondary or redactional intrusions. In principle this is not unlikely, given our conclusion (see below) that this chapter represents an edited version of an original part of the EM. In practice, however, the isolation of such elements is extremely difficult. Thus, for instance, it has been maintained by some that vv 3 and 5 cannot both be original since chronologically v 5 would have preceded v 3; but, as Kellermann, *Nehemia*, 27, has rightly replied, v 3 is to be regarded as a summary heading to the whole of the following narrative, so that no difficulty arises. It has been further claimed that the list of names (v 4) and in particular the introduction of the Levites (v 7, the plural verb in v 8, parts of v 9 and v 11) are to be ascribed to the later editor. The latter is frequently identified with the Chronicler, whose interest in the Levites is well known. Such proposals are difficult to assess. There is no conclusive grammatical or syntactical argument to be raised against these passages, while Ezra himself, as we know from Ezra 8:15–20, was concerned that Levites should accompany his return. Moreover, their subordinate role in this chapter contrasts quite sharply with their dominance in the next. All in all, therefore, it seems best to conclude that this chapter certainly has passed through the hands of the editor of the Ezra-Nehemiah material and that at the very least he must have been responsible for casting it in the third person (a necessary step once he had moved the chapter to follow the Nehemiah narrative), but that he has covered his tracks sufficiently well to preclude our being able to isolate particular elements which might be his own contribution. (For the only outstanding exception to this conclusion, cf. n. 8:9.a.)

Within the overall unity of this chapter, there are, however, subsections, which may be quite simply indicated in tabular form (following Pohlmann, *Studien*, 132–35, except that we prefer, with the Masoretes, to divide the second paragraph after v 15, thus retaining the parallelism of ככתוב "as prescribed" and כמשפט "according to the ordinance," at the end of vv 15 and 18 respectively).

a) The assembly on the first day of the seventh month, 1–12
   (i) The reading of the Law, 1–8
   (ii) The dismissal of the congregation, 9–12
b) The Feast of Tabernacles, 13–18
   (i) The preparations, 13–15
   (ii) The celebration, 16–18

The limits of these sections are marked by repetitions of ideas that have the effect of emphasizing heavily the major theme of the chapter. Thus we find that both major sections begin with a voluntary gathering (אסף, vv 1 and 13) to hear the Law and its explanation, and that each ends with a note concerning the joy that was consequent upon obedience to Ezra's exposition (שמחה גדולה, vv 12 and 17).

In similar fashion, there is a parallel between the conclusion of each minor section: vv 8 and 12 both end with a reference to the people understanding what they heard (בין), while vv 15 and 18 are clearly twinned by their concluding words, ככתוב "as prescribed" and כמשפט "according to the ordinance."

There is thus set out in schematic form what has already been noted of the chapter's fundamental thought: reading with explanation leads to understanding, and this is a source of joy; understanding, however, should issue in obedience, and this in turn will end in joy.

While the general narrative shape of this passage has already been outlined, the view should be mentioned here that vv 1–12 reflect the pattern of a synagogue service from the writer's own time; cf. K. Galling, "Erwägungen zur antiken Synagoge," *ZDPV* 72 (1956) 163–78; Kellermann, *Nehemia*, 29–30; Pohlmann, *Studien*, 136; In der Smitten, *Esra*, 38–47. Although this opinion is generally accompanied by a scepticism concerning the historical value of the passage, the two are not inevitably combined. It is possible to argue that Ezra and the congregation were following already established liturgical practice; conversely, Rudolph maintains that later synagogue services drew their inspiration from this passage.

In support of this kind of analysis of vv 1–12, In der Smitten lists the following formal elements: assembly; request for a reading from the Torah; opening of the Torah-scroll; standing by the people; blessing of the community; response by the community; prostration (?); sermon; reading of the Torah; oral Targum with exhortation; departure (for an *agape* meal?). These elements, In der Smitten claims (p. 40), provide an intelligible liturgical ritual, from which, without further argument, he deduces that they form a synagogue service (p. 44).

This whole hypothesis is open to a number of serious objections, however. First, we have no evidence whatever for the nature of synagogue services (assuming they existed!) at any time during the pre-Christian era; indeed, the NT (e.g., Luke 4:16–27 and Acts 13:14–43) provides some of the earliest written testimony on this matter. The theory is thus conspicuously more speculative than its proponents acknowledge.

Second, our passage lacks several elements of a synagogue service as we know of it from later times; cf. P. Billerbeck, "Ein Synagogen-gottesdienst in Jesu Tagen," *ZNW* 55 (1964) 143–61; S. Safrai and M. Stern (eds.), *The Jewish People in the First Century* II (Assen/Amsterdam: Van Gorcum, 1976), 914–33; E. Schürer, *The History of the Jewish People in the Age of Jesus Christ (175 B.C.—A.D. 135)* II, ed. G. Vermes, F. Millar, and M. Black (Edinburgh: T. & T. Clark, 1979), 447–54. The earliest evidence available points to the following elements as important items in the regular liturgy of the synagogue: the recitation of the *Shemaʿ*, prayer (including the recitation of the *Shemoneh ʿEsreh*, the Eighteen Benedictions), the reading of the Torah (with Targum), the reading of the prophets, address, and priestly blessing.

Comparison of this list with Neh 8 reveals that the latter makes no reference to the first two items. The significance of this is, of course, uncertain, for it is not known when the *Shemaʿ* and the *Shemoneh ʿEsreh* became fixed in the liturgy; however, the lack of any prayer whatsoever (apart from Ezra's blessing on opening the scroll) points away from the liturgical nature of the gathering. Next, on the interpretation given here, the reading was not accompanied by a Targum, although the running exposition which was supplied will have fulfilled part of the function of the later Targums. More significantly, there is no record of a reading from the prophets, no final blessing, and it is questionable whether vv 9–10 are to be understood as an address, since they are not in any sense based on what had been read.

Third, there are elements present in Neh 8 that we should not expect to find in a synagogue service: the gathering came together explicitly to invite Ezra to read to them (v 1); the reading was prolonged (v 3), and it was undertaken by a group of people, while another group was responsible for the interpretation (vv 7–9; it is true that there may be some later elements included in these verses, but it is generally held that, if anything, the chapter has been moved closer to, rather than away from, synagogue practice).

Finally, it should be observed that there is really only one focus of attention in this passage, namely, the reading of the Law. Everything else, including the most obviously liturgical elements, which are found in vv 5–6, is subordinated to this. These individual items are therefore better understood as being borrowed from current liturgical practice for a specific occasion rather than being part of a synagogue service in their present setting. To this extent only, therefore, may this chapter be used as evidence for early liturgical worship away from the temple. Thus, whereas Safrai (in Safrai and Stern, *The Jewish People*, 912–13) sees the synagogue as developing directly out of this and other similar public assemblies under Ezra, we would rather conclude that some form of liturgy already existed and that it influenced the procedures on this occasion, but that the passage neither describes, nor takes the form of, a literary description of a synagogue service of any kind.

In discussing the setting of Neh 8, it is extremely difficult to hold literary and historical considerations apart. Although it is not denied that the actual course of events will have been a major influence on the shape of the literature, there are some pressing factors in this particular instance that make it imperative to deal with the literary issues first. This may be illustrated by the observation that no year is mentioned in the chapter, only days and the month. If, then, it is concluded that this material was originally composed together with that in Ezra 7–10 and separately from Neh 1–7, it will follow as an inevitable consequence that the events described cannot have taken place, as a superficial reading might imply, some thirteen years after Ezra's arrival in Jerusalem. Attempts to explain this thirteen-year interval in historical terms (e.g., Kidner, 150–52), are thus completely beside the point (and are in any case unconvincing, in my view). For a further argument against this position on its own terms, see *Comment* on 7:72b (73b) below.

Among those who discuss the literary evidence, several agreed points emerge, leaving one item for major discussion. The only significant exception to this consensus is Pavlovský, "Die Chronologie der Tätigkeit Esras: Versuch einer neuen Lösung (I)," *Bib* 38 (1957) 275–305, 428–56. His idiosyncratic rearrangement of both the literature and the history of the period is highly speculative, however, being based at important points on no more than circumstantial evidence and with a number of doubtful, if not mistaken, observations as well; for a response to some of these, cf. Emerton, *JTS* ns 17 (1966) 1–19.

First, then, we may recall that the final editor of the Ezra and the Nehemiah material used the device of repetitive resumption to indicate that Neh 8–10 has been inserted between Neh 7 and 11 (see *Form*, Neh 7). Commentators are also generally agreed that Neh 11 continues the narrative begun in Neh 7. Whereas the status of Neh 9 and 10 has to be left open at this stage, it may nevertheless be concluded that Neh 8 has been inserted in its present position from somewhere else.

Second, this conclusion is reinforced by comparison of the style and content of the chapter with what precedes. For instance, Nehemiah's first-person account here gives way to a narrative cast in the third person; Ezra, not mentioned previously in Nehemiah, now occupies the center of attention, while it is doubtful whether Nehemiah himself was originally mentioned here at all, and the method of dating (numbered day and month) contrasts with Nehemiah's method of naming the months (e.g., Neh 1:1; 2:1; 6:15); for further stylistic considerations, cf. Kellermann, *Nehemia*, 26.

Third, if we look for an original literary setting for the chapter, our attention is immediately drawn to Ezra 7–10. The theme of Ezra and the Law is central there as here; the presentation of Ezra's character and style are the same (note how he waits for the people to make the first move—Neh 8:1 and Ezra 9:1; and how he takes problems gradually, allowing plenty of time in between for reflection; Neh 8:9–10, 13 and Ezra 9:3–4; 10:6, 16); the system of dating fits Ezra 7–10 exactly; and so on. Because of all these factors, there is a widespread and wholly correct scholarly consensus that Neh 8 belongs, from a literary point of view, with Ezra 7–10.

The question then arises, however, as to where precisely within those chapters Neh 8 originally stood. From one point of view, this dispute is of secondary importance. For the interpretation of the text in its present form, it is enough to have established that Neh 8 (and 9–10) has been added editorially. Nevertheless, the question we have posed is of significance in an attempt to reconstruct the course of Ezra's mission and so to evaluate his achievement.

For a few scholars, of course, the question is an improper one. They are those, such as Kapelrud, *Authorship*, and Kellermann, *Nehemia*, 32, who believe that the Chronicler (be he an individual or a school) both composed the material about Ezra himself (whether or not on the basis of some earlier source) and edited the Nehemiah material. On this view, Neh 8 never stood in any other than its present position; it was composed by the final editor. This view seems implausible, however. We have already argued that there was an original EM, and suggested that it was not so heavily worked over as this view implies. Further arguments in favor of this conclusion are accepted in any case for the present chapter by Kapelrud. The fundamental basis for this approach—namely, the isolation of the Chronicler on the ground of style—is highly questionable (cf. Williamson, *Israel*, 37–59); and the harsh transition between Neh 1–7 and 8 is better explained by an interweaving of originally separate sources than by the view that Neh 8 was specifically composed for its present setting. We must therefore proceed to inquire after its original setting.

One of the first scholars to consider this question in depth was Torrey. His proposal was that Neh 8 should be fitted between Ezra 8 and 9; cf. *Composition*, 29–34; *Ezra Studies*, 252–84. His main reasons were that the closing verses of Neh 7 (which he included with Neh 8) fitted the theme of giving in Ezra 8:33–34, that the reading of the law was the main reason that Ezra came to Jerusalem in the first place, that the dates in the Ezra material fit smoothly in sequence on this view, and that the events of Ezra 9 presuppose a knowledge of the Law, and therefore could only follow Neh 8. Torrey believed that the displacement occurred by a scribal error which transferred Neh 7:70—8:1 to its present position because of its similarity with the end of Ezra 2 (much of which is parallel with Neh 7). So confident was Torrey in his proposals that he even went so far as to reconstruct what he called "The Ezra Story in Its Original Sequence."

With minor differences, Torrey's view was followed by many other scholars in the following decades, notably Schaeder, *Esra*, 7–26, Ahlemann, *ZAW* 59 (1942–43) 77–98, and Rudolph. The differences centered chiefly over the position of Neh 9–10, which will be dealt with later in this commentary, and the point at which the change from the Nehemiah to the Ezra material is to be found in Neh 7 (for some discussion of which see *Form* on chap. 7 above). This latter point leads to consequentially different explanations of the mechanics of how and why the transposition occurred.

In recent years, however, an alternative view has gained considerable popularity. Although it is found in some older works, such as Bertholet's commentary, this view is upheld in detail by Mowinckel, *Studien III*, 7–11 (and cf. *Studien I*, 7–61), and he has been followed, with some additional arguments, by Pohlmann, *Studien*, 127–48; In der Smitten, *Esra*, 35–47; Koch, *JSS* 19 (1974) 179, and Mosis, *Untersuchungen*, 215–20. On this view, Neh 8 originally followed Ezra 10 rather than Ezra 8. The main positive reasons for this are that this is the order now found in 1 Esdr which, Mowinckel and Pohlmann believe, represents the original ending of the Chronicler's work, and that Neh 8, with its emphasis on festivity and joy, is more suitable as a climax to the account of Ezra's work, an account which would otherwise tail off lamely. Negatively, points are raised against the position of Torrey and Rudolph, principally that they start from the mistaken view that Neh 8 describes the presentation of a new Law by Ezra; once it is realized that his Law was already known in Judah, one of the main reasons for placing Neh 8 before Ezra 9 falls away. Finally, other arguments, such as that from the dates within the EM, are shown to be inconclusive.

In seeking to evaluate this discussion, it should be said first that both in this commentary and elsewhere I have repeatedly argued against the view that 1 Esdr represents the original ending of the Chronicler's work. It is a secondary compilation, whose ordering of events is not to be accepted uncritically. This was the chief plank in the second view outlined above, and the only one in either view that appealed to external testimony. Without it, we are free to ask, simply, where Neh 8 fits most satisfactorily.

Certainly, as Mowinckel realized, the dating scheme favors the first view: Ezra arrives on the first day of the fifth month (= 1.5; cf. Ezra 7:9), reads the Law on 1.7 (cf. Neh 8:2) and deals with the mixed marriages issue during months 9–10 (cf. Ezra 10:16). On Mowinckel's view, by contrast, the reading of the Law would follow some nine months later, in the second year. He seeks to explain this by arguing that Ezra waited until the following New Year as the appropriate time to proclaim the Law in a covenant renewal. This, of course, is a historical, not a literary, explanation; it thereby shows its less appropriate nature in the context, and leaves us wondering why there is no note to show that it relates to a different year from the other dates in the Ezra material. It is also an attempt to counter a forceful argument, and not a reason in itself to prefer Mowinckel's suggestion.

Next, while we would fully agree that the Law which Ezra read to the people was probably not completely new to them, it does appear that he offered a new interpretation of it in such a way that the people came suddenly to appreciate its relevance to their own situation in a fresh way. The details with regard to the present chapter are dealt with in *Comment*, vv 13–18, below, but see also *Comment* on Ezra 9:1–2 for a similar impact of the law on the people with regard to mixed marriages. (Further, though not directly related to Ezra, see *Comment* on Neh 10 below.) The account of a teaching ministry by Ezra would thus fit very well before Ezra 9, and for this, Neh 8 is the only candidate.

Third, our discussion both of the structure and of the form of this chapter above led to the conclusion that the presentation of the Law is a major focus—more so than Mowinckel, Pohlmann, and In der Smitten allow. We saw that the stress was less on the Feast of Tabernacles itself. Similarly, it is not correct to deny that the edict of Artaxerxes (Ezra 7:12–26) leads us to expect a promulgation of the Law by Ezra: 7:14 and 25–26 both imply that reference to the Law is likely to be prominent in the following narrative, and that there are those to whom it will need to be taught. This need not mean that the Law was totally new; Ezra 7:25 suggests that it was not, but rather that it had fallen somewhat into neglect. Taking these two complementary points together, we may conclude that Neh 8 is more appropriate as an introduction to Ezra's work in Jerusalem, less appropriate as its conclusion. Moreover, it must be remembered that in its present position Neh 8 forms a part of the climax that the editor has supplied to the work of both Ezra and Nehemiah. The atmosphere of climax that some commentators feel at this point may therefore be due more to editorial handling than to original composition.

Finally, it should not be forgotten that the last two verses of Ezra 8, being cast in the third person, were considered an editorial insertion into the EM. It is possible that this is a small pointer to the fact that it was necessary to cover over an uneven join left there by the removal of Neh 8.

We may thus conclude that the original literary setting of Neh 8 was between Ezra 8 and 9. Its historical setting, of course, follows directly from this conclusion. The present arrangement is not accidental, however; see the introduction to Neh 8–10 as a whole above. The precise point for the insertion of this material into the NM was chosen by the considerations explained immediately below.

Comment

72(73)b One of the factors that first led scholars to the view that this chapter originally formed a sequel to Ezra 8 was the observation that we miss there a reference to the settlement in Judah of those who had accompanied Ezra from Babylon. Such a reference is summarized in the present verse. A similar notice also concludes the list in Neh 7. When, therefore, the editor wished, for theological reasons, to include Ezra's reading of the Law in his account of the climax of the work of both Ezra and Nehemiah, his attention was drawn to this particular point by this close similarity. There is enough overlap of content between the two halves of this verse as they stand to account for his choice of setting once it is accepted that he was consciously seeking a point of connection. It is then unnecessary to postulate the loss of a previously more extensive overlap, as Rudolph has to, because of his opinion that this was a much less highly motivated transfer by a later scribe. The possibility remains, of course, that the editor also omitted some further material on the settlement of the people because it was no longer relevant to this new context. In its present setting, the circumstantial clause "and the Israelites were in their own towns" serves both as a link with the previous chapter and as a prelude to the opening act of assembly in this one.

The date is given as the seventh month, and this is later defined (8:2) as the first day of that month. The last date mentioned in Nehemiah (6:15) was the twenty-fifth of Elul, when the wall was completed. Since Elul is the sixth month, it is apparent that the editor has managed to retain a chronological sequence here. Historically, however, the handful of days involved would clearly not be long enough, after all the rigors of the wall building, for the people to return home, for Nehemiah to gather the leaders for the census (7:5), for them too to return home (as the present verse implies) and for arrangements to be made for "all the people" (8:1) to reassemble in Jerusalem to invite Ezra to read the Law. This is therefore a further small argument against the historicist's position (cf. *Form* above).

Within the sequence of Ezra 7–10, however, it fits extremely well two months after Ezra's arrival in Jerusalem (cf. Ezra 7:9); we need not doubt that he had already started work with the intention of using this day for the formal presentation of the Law and his program based upon it. The date chosen, we should note, was entirely appropriate for such a gathering, suggesting careful prior arrangement. Not only was it the start of one of the, if not the, most important months in the religious calendar (cf. Lev 23:23–26, listing (i) the Feast of Trumpets on the first day; later this was certainly New Year's Day, but there is much debate as to whether it was so also at this time; (ii) the Day of Atonement on the tenth day; and (iii) the Feast of Tabernacles for a week beginning on the fifteenth day). But more particularly it was the month in which, according to Deut 31:10–13, there should be every seventh year, during the Feast of Tabernacles, a proclamation of the Law, which many have seen as the basis for a covenant renewal ceremony. The emphasis both in Deuteronomy and here on the gathering of a full assembly of the people and the general similarity of the procedure and its purpose (at least as seen by the editor of Neh 8–10 as a whole) suggests that Ezra intended his activity to comply with this law.

8:1 The initiative for the gathering is attributed to the people. Clearly, however, such things do not happen completely spontaneously. We are thus reminded of the procedure noted in Ezra 9, and may assume a comparable background and preparation.

The assembly gathered in a large open space near the Water Gate, mentioned otherwise in vv 3 and 16; 3:26; and 12:37. Its precise location is a matter of dispute, since some scholars (e.g., Pohlmann, *Studien,* 151–54) suggest that it was associated with the temple in some way; this is part of the wider theory that Neh 8:1–12 describes a regular religious service. In support, appeal is made especially to the implications of Neh 12:37 and 40.

It was argued at 3:26 above, however, that the Water Gate lay to the east (and so outside) of the new line that Nehemiah's wall took along the crest of the Kidron Valley. Its name, in addition, suggests association with the Gihon Spring to which it probably provided access; cf. J. Simons, *Jerusalem in the Old Testament* (Leiden: Brill, 1952) 121–23. This does not necessarily mean that it was directly above the spring (cf. Burrows, "Nehemiah 3:1–32 as a Source for the Topography of Ancient Jerusalem," *AASOR* 14 [1933–34] 115–40), though it may have been. On the assumption that Ezra preceded Nehemiah, it will thus have stood—possibly in ruined condition—on the line of the eastern city wall. The text of Neh 12 is fully compatible with this, since it gives the Water Gate only as the point at which the procession left the wall to go into the temple; it does not imply that the Water Gate itself led into the temple.

In view of the topography of the area and the badly damaged state of the masonry and terracing (cf. 2:14–15), we would suggest that this meeting place was outside (לפני = "in front of," i.e., facing from outside) the city wall of Ezra's time, a little down the slope in the general vicinity of the spring itself. No doubt a certain amount of clearance had had to be undertaken here to give access to the spring, and the ground itself would have been less steep.

Whether or not this precise location is accepted, we may still profitably note Ellison's words, *From Babylon to Bethlehem,* 47, at this point: "In the choice of site we have Ezra's deliberate proclamation that the Torah was greater than the Temple and its sacrifices, indeed that the Torah as such was above anything it might contain"; see further *Comment* on v 4.

For a discussion of "the Book of the Law," cf. Introduction, "The Identifica-

tion of the Book of the Law." The clear association of it here with Moses
suggests strongly an identification with either all or part of the Pentateuch;
it is hardly credible that a book associated with Moses and given such prominence in the post-exilic community would have been entirely lost; it would
certainly have been preserved along with the other "Mosaic" legislation (*contra*
Houtman, *OTS* 21 [1981] 91–115).

2 The assembly that gathered to hear Ezra read from the Book of the
Law comprised not only men but, worthy to note, women and children as
well. It seems likely that the latter are referred to by the words "any capable
of understanding what they heard" (cf. the similar expression in v 3). The
gathering at Ezra 10:1 was similar (cf. Vogt, *Studie*, 79–80), although there
the children were mentioned directly (יְלָדִים) in order to highlight part of
the consequences of the action that was about to be initiated. Here, however, the emphasis is different. The root used, בּין "understand," recurs later
in the chapter to describe the work of the Levites (vv 7, 8 and 9). All of an
age to benefit by their activity were present. See also 10:29 (28). From a
wider canvass, Kidner, 105, reminds us that "The Law had always envisaged
'a wise and understanding people,' taught from childhood not only the words
of God but what the words and rituals meant (Ex. 12:26f.; Dt. 4:6; 6:6ff.;
31:12f.). Mindless superstition was the mark of paganism ('they cannot understand,' Isa 44:18f.), and had been the downfall of an apostate Israel (Ho.
4:6: 'My people are destroyed for lack of knowledge')."

3 In the manner characteristic of Hebrew narrative style, this verse supplies a summary heading to the more detailed description which follows.
The overlap in content thus poses no difficulty. We learn here that the reading
lasted for some six or seven hours. The participation of others alongside
Ezra later in the chapter is thus not surprising; indeed, it would have been
a virtual necessity. Even allowing for some interpolated explanation, it is
evident that the Book of the Law was a substantial document. This is emphasized by the fact that probably only extracts were read (קָרָא בּ, "read from,"
rather than קָרָא + accus, "read"; so also *Comment* on v 8 below). The attentive
listening of the people is an important element in the theme of the chapter
as a whole; naturally, therefore, it cannot be used as evidence that the Law
was completely new to them.

4 Details of the occasion are now filled in. The first point mentioned
shows again that some preparatory work had preceded the gathering, for a
large platform had been specially made for the occasion (לַדָּבָר = "for the
purpose"; "for the word," i.e., for the presentation of the Word of God,
would be a linguistic anachronism). Though sometimes compared with the
"bema" of the synagogue (so translated here, naturally enough, by LXX and
1 Esdras), its antecedents lay rather in the platform Solomon used at the
dedication of the first temple (2 Chr 6:13; cf. G. Widengren, "King and Covenant." *JSS* 2 [1957] 11). With so large a crowd assembled, it was imperative
that the leaders should have such a high platform in order to be seen and
heard. Our attention is thus directed once more to the unique nature of
the occasion.

We are given no clue as to the identity of those who stood on either
side of Ezra. This in itself makes it more likely that they were leading or

representative members of the laity, since priests and Levites are usually specifically designated as such. As was shown in *Notes* above there can be no complete certainty about their number, so that speculations based on this (e.g., twelve, to represent the twelve tribes) are worthless. Nor is anything said about their role in the proceedings. It may be that they were prominent supporters of Ezra whose very presence added weight to his authority. Alternatively, they may have been leaders who would inevitably be at the front of such community gatherings. Matt 23:6 is often cited as a parallel for this, though naturally there is no direct connection of any sort. Finally, they may have been representatives chosen to help Ezra with the reading, a task not restricted to priests or Levites in post-exilic Judaism. If these deductions are correct, the fact that Ezra chose members of the laity to assist him with the reading will be highly significant. Coupled with the choice of location (see *Comment* on v 1), Ezra was boldly proclaiming that the Torah was for all people, not just for a few privileged by either birth or particular ability.

Little can be gleaned from the names themselves either, especially as no family associations are mentioned. It is therefore prudent not to speculate either for or against the historical value of the list. Of the less common names, Rudolph points to two that occur elsewhere (Hashum in 7:22 and Anaiah in 10:23) as heads of families. Perhaps of more significance, several recur in the list of those who divorced their wives in Ezra 10 (Mattithiah in v 43; Maaseiah in v 18; Malchiah in v 25); if any of these could be identified, it would be an additional small point in favor of a literary setting for Neh 8 before, rather than after, Ezra 10.

5–6 For some general comment, see p. 282, *Form* above. "Opened the book" (ויפתח הספר): strictly speaking, unrolled the scroll; before the invention of the codex the phrase was inevitably understood so. "Stood up": a mark of respect (cf. Judg 3:20; Job 29:8; Ezek 2:1).

A benediction before the reading of Scripture has been customary for as long as we have evidence, and there is no reason that it should not have been so as a matter of course in Ezra's time. It was presumably a brief and simple expression of praise. האלהים הגדול "the great God" is an unusual title in Hebrew. It is not found elsewhere, though the similar האל הגדול is found at 1:5; 9:32; Deut 10:17; Jer 32:18. For some comment on its Aramaic and Persian equivalent, see *Comment* on Ezra 5:8. Its occurrence also in *AramP* 72:15 has suggested to Bowman the possibility of an ultimate origin in Neo-Babylonian (*ilu rabû* and *bēlu rabû*). Its significance is self-explanatory.

The people's response was threefold, and may have followed a customary pattern. Their cry of "Amen! Amen!" (repeated for emphasis) expressed their concurrence in Ezra's words (cf. 5:13); the raising of their hands demonstrated their sense of need and dependence (cf. Ezra 9:5; Ps 28:2; 134:2), no doubt with the thought that God would meet that need through the Scripture soon to be read; and their prostration demonstrated both their worship, as stated, and humble adoration. We are left to infer that they stood up again for the reading itself.

7–8 If we take these two verses as they stand, there appears to be some confusion. The Levites help the people to understand the Law. Only then (v 8) are we told that "they," presumably the Levites again, read from the

Book and gave it its sense. Apart from the oddity of mentioning interpretation before proclamation, it is strange to find the Levites now reading when it was clearly stated earlier that Ezra did the reading. A number of commentators therefore regard v 7 as an insertion by the Chronicler, who felt that insufficient attention was paid to the Levites in his *Vorlage*. Verse 8 will then originally have referred to Ezra and perhaps the others listed in v 4.

More recently, especially among those who do not recognize two stages in the composition of this chapter, an attempt to explain these anomalies has been made along the line of that already favored at v 3 above. V 7 is regarded as an anticipatory introduction to the following narrative. The explanation is not so convincing here, however, not least because v 7 in fact gives more detail than v 8.

Now, it was suggested in *Form* above that Neh 8 does in fact represent the editorial reworking of an earlier source, but that the editor has not left clear tracks to enable us to distinguish his own contribution in specific detail. It was further stated as probable that Ezra himself already included a reference to the Levites in his account at this point. Our suggestion, therefore, for understanding the overall shape of these two verses is as follows: (i) We are left to assume from all that has gone before that Ezra started to read aloud after the introduction in vv 5–6. No one reading the chapter could doubt that this is what happened next. (ii) The Levites gave explanations to the people (v 7; see further below). (iii) V 8 is a *summary* of the preceding paragraph—"they" (Ezra and those with him) read; "giving the sense" (an infinitive absolute expression which therefore has no subject expressed) may refer both to the way the reading was conducted and to the work of the Levites, with the result that "they" (the people; cf. n. 8.b.) understood the reading. This final conclusion is, of course, the culmination and climax of the whole paragraph. Though these changes of subject may appear confusing, in reality they are not so, provided each action is allowed to be understood in the light of the foregoing passage. Taken as a summary, the verse at once becomes quite clear.

7 Thirteen Levites are mentioned, on our understanding of MT (cf. *Notes*). While there appears thus to be some correspondence with v 4, again no explanation for this particular number is forthcoming. The names themselves are generally familiar from other contexts, though without further details we cannot propose any identifications.

These Levites, then, "helped the people to understand the Law." In this, they were fulfilling a function that the OT recognizes as peculiarly theirs (cf. Deut 33:10; 2 Chr 17:7–9; 35:3; and G. von Rad, *Deuteronomium-Studien* [Göttingen: Vandenhoeck & Ruprecht, 1948]; ET, *Studies in Deuteronomy* [tr. D. Stalker; SBT 9; London: SCM Press, 1953]). How they achieved this on the present occasion is not clear. However, since it is expressly stated that "the people remained in their places," there is a hint that the Levites in fact moved around. It is probable, therefore, that after each section of the Law had been read (cf. v 8), the Levites moved from group to group among the people making sure that all had understood what they had heard.

8 By establishing that this verse is a concluding summary, we have already fixed the general parameters for its interpretation, namely the subjects for each verb, and the fact that the actions recorded are the same as those already explained, rather than fresh developments. For "paragraph by paragraph," cf. *Notes.* (Note that the other possible translation, "clearly," would not significantly alter our approach to this verse.) Continuous reading would have been exhausting for reader and audience alike. As it was, the text was broken down into sensible units. This gave opportunity for others to share the physical task of reading with Ezra and for him to select those portions of the Law that he deemed most appropriate. Coupled with the ministry of the Levites, this all leads to the climax of this portion of the chapter, that the people "understood the reading." This will find its parallel at the end of v 12 as well.

9 The reading of the Law caused the people to weep. According to a number of scholars, this was a regular part of the ritual celebration of the New Year, and its origins may be traced back to Canaanite influence; cf. Mowinckel, *Studien III,* 47–59; N. H. Snaith, *The Jewish New Year Festival* (London: S.P.C.K., 1947), 151; F. F. Hvidberg, *Weeping and Laughter in the Old Testament* (tr. and ed. F. Løkkegaard; Leiden: Brill, 1962), 101–2; Pohlmann, *Studien,* 136–37; J. C. de Moor, *New Year with Canaanites and Israelites,* Part I (Kampen: J. H. Kok, 1972), 23–25. While this suggestion cannot be either proved or disproved, it must certainly be stated that it is inadequate as a full explanation in the present case. As Mowinckel, *Studien III,* 52, himself maintains, many of the elements that he associates with the celebration of the New Year are missing here because the author has selected only those matters of particular relevance to his theme; he could assume his readers' familiarity with the remainder. Now, we have already established that the author (or editor) has selected and arranged his material in this chapter in order to highlight Ezra's presentation of the Law and the people's response. It follows, therefore, that at the literary level we are to understand this weeping along the lines of remorse for failure adequately to observe the demands of the Law, rather than as the account of a regular or quite normal occurrence.

This need not mean that the Law was totally new to those who heard it. It is not unusual for individuals or a whole congregation to be struck in a fresh way by the seriousness of God's demand and their shortfall in meeting it. This is all the more likely to have been so on this occasion because of the explanation (and, no doubt, application) which was provided. It was noted at Ezra 9 (and see further below) that a characteristic of Ezra's hermeneutic was to make relevant in unexpected ways the requirements of historically outdated laws.

As the reading drew to a close, however, Ezra did not wish the people to depart in this frame of mind. From one point of view their response was appropriate—and the editor has noted and reinforced this by his juxtaposition of chap. 9 with chap. 8; however, two other factors served to overrule this consideration on the present occasion: first, the day was "holy" to the Lord. This is stated in Lev 23:24 and Num 29:1–6 with regard to the Feast of Trumpets, and it may also have been implied with regard to the promulgation of the Law in the covenant renewal ceremony every seven years (Deut 31:9–13). Such feast days are regularly associated with joy in the Old Testament (e.g., Deut 12:12; 16:11), perhaps particularly because they are linked with a memorial of God's grace towards his people in historical acts of redemption.

10 This leads on directly to the second reason Ezra gave the people not to depart weeping: "It is the joy of the Lord that is your protection." In this context, "protection" must be against the judgments that the Law proclaims against transgressors (e.g., Lev 26; Deut 27–28). Since these are themselves the judgments of God, it follows that on occasions when God's earlier acts of salvation were recalled it was appreciated that grace was an overriding characteristic of his nature. "The joy of the Lord" was the joy each Israelite felt at these festivals as he identified himself afresh with the community of God's people and so appropriated in his own generation the salvation once bestowed upon his ancestors. In this act of identification— which took the form of joyful celebration and worship—lay his protection from the judgment that might otherwise fall on those outside of the covenant. Naturally, the sacred recital of the original event formed a vital part of this process. Ezra, therefore, encouraged the people to regard his reading of Scripture in this light. Though it might challenge their consciences, it was to be regarded first and foremost as a declaration of God's grace to his people.

In order, therefore, that the people might demonstrate this festival joy, Ezra dismissed them to share in a special meal. The importance of the fellowship meal in the Old Testament has perhaps been underestimated simply because it was so natural and frequent an occurrence; it lay behind one of the commonest of the regular sacrifices (Lev 3), but is mentioned also on numerous special occasions, e.g., 2 Sam 6:19; 1 Chr 12:40–41 (39–40); 29:22; 2 Chr 7:8–10; 30:21–26, etc. "Rich fare" (משמנים) is literally "the fat pieces," not those parts forbidden by the sacrificial law (e.g., Lev 3:17), but the most choice and sumptuous portions—those "little luxuries that can turn a meal into a feast" (Kidner). The intention of the "sweet drinks" must be similar, though a precise identification is not possible. ממתקים occurs elsewhere only at Cant 5:16, where the metaphorical usage sheds no light on the specific nature of the drink. Finally, the people are to be generous in sharing their meals so that all may participate. We are not told why some were unprepared; it may be that they were too poor, and that here again the Deuteronomic law is being invoked (cf. Deut 14:29; 26:12, etc.). Alternatively, it has been suggested that laxity or ignorance concerning the Law meant that some had not realized that they should prepare for so auspicious a day. Either way, there is a further tacit recognition in the phrase that this whole occasion was not entirely spontaneous. The emphasis, however, is on the importance of ensuring that all might participate in the celebration.

11 While some commentators regard this verse as an editorial insertion, this is not a necessary conclusion, despite its somewhat repetitive nature. The Levites take up one of Ezra's reasons for urging the people not to grieve, though without, apparently, the depth of reasoning that lay behind his formulation. On the other hand, it may be that the editor intends us from this partial repetition to understand that the Levites conveyed the whole of Ezra's message to the people.

12 The section ends with emphasis on the joy that accompanied obedience to his words; for its place in the structure of the chapter as a whole, cf. *Form* above. It is noteworthy that the parallel between the conclusion of this verse and that of v 8 has the effect of virtually putting Ezra's interpretation ("the words that had been declared to them") on the same level as the Law itself. In this late period, when circumstances had changed so much from the time of the original law-giving, there had arisen the danger that the Law would slip into being a document of only antiquarian interest. It was Ezra's hermeneutic that brought it to life again for the community. Although in theory the text of Scripture alone was normative, in practice it could only be that text as it came to be interpreted that would shape the future mold of Judaism.

13 A comparison of vv 12 and 15 suggests that the majority of the population returned home. This would have been a busy time of year for many. Since the day following the first day of the seventh month ("the second day"; see *Comment* on 7:72b [73b]) was not a feast day, few had the luxury of spare time for further study. A number of the leaders did, however; the general quickening of religious consciousness on the previous day may have roused both the lay readers (cf. Deut 6:6–9) and the religious leaders (see *Comment* on v 7 and the prophetic condemnations such as Hos 4:6; Jer 8:7–9; Mal 2:7–8) to a renewed determination to carry out their responsibilities more faithfully, while they had already recognized in Ezra one with the ability to teach with authority. They therefore gathered around him for more intensive study, no doubt in a more practical setting.

14–15 In their study, they found (or were directed to) legislation relating to "the feast of the seventh month," immediately identified with the Feast of Tabernacles. These verses raise three particular questions.

First, there is no reference to the Day of Atonement, even though in the religious calendar of Lev 23 it comes on the tenth day of the month, between the Feast of Trumpets on the first day and the Feast of Tabernacles, which started on the fifteenth; cf. vv 26–32. Several suggested explanations have been advanced to solve this puzzle. Some argue that in Ezra's time there still was no Day of Atonement, this being one of the latest additions to the Priestly legislation in the Pentateuch. Others conjecture that relationships were so strained between Ezra and the high priest, whose participation in the ritual was, of course, essential, that Ezra withheld his approval for its celebration. A third possibility is that it was unnecessary because of the penitence to be expressed in chap. 9.

For none of these theories is there any evidence in the text, however. We would suggest, therefore, that we again tackle this problem in the light of the single-minded theme of this chapter already noted. The Day of Atonement bears no close relationship to the reading, teaching, or application of the Law. Moreover, its celebration at this time was very much a priestly affair, largely conducted within parts of the temple from which the laity were excluded. It is thus difficult to see what relevance it would have had to the description of Ezra moving the Law out of its priestly preserve into the realm of the people. It is therefore better not to speculate about its absence from this chapter where, as we have already seen, even matters that come closer to its theme are omitted unless absolutely essential.

Second, it has sometimes been argued that because of the date in v 13, "the second day," the Feast of Tabernacles must on this occasion have been

celebrated from the third to the tenth days of the month, instead of the
fifteenth to the twenty-second days of Lev 23:33–36. For this conclusion too,
however, there is no warrant in the text. We are not told how long the leaders
continued in conference with Ezra, and in any case, since the people had
gone home after the first day (see *Comment* on v 13), it is not possible that
they could all have reassembled in Jerusalem with the materials for their
booths on the third; cf. de Vaux, *Ancient Israel,* 500. Although there is again
no explicit reference in the text, there is equally no reason to believe that
the feast was not celebrated on its appointed days; indeed, the careful conformity with other aspects of the Levitical legislation makes it most likely that
it was.

The third problem which these verses raise concerns the detail of what
"they found written in the Law." The emphasis in this clearly lies on the
command "that the Israelites should live in booths [סכות, sometimes translated 'tabernacles'] during the feast of the seventh month," for this is recapitulated also at the end of the passage with the words "to make booths, as
prescribed." Of all the Pentateuchal passages that deal with this feast (Exod
23:16; Lev 23:39–43; Num 29:12–38; Deut 16:13–15), it is only the one in
Leviticus that makes this stipulation (although the influence of Deuteronomy
is probably to be detected in a separate detail below). It is a natural assumption, therefore, that this is the passage referred to.

However, there is an important feature of the feast in Lev 23 in which
the laity should take part but which is not mentioned here; and, conversely,
there appears to be a citation from the Law here that has no counterpart in
Leviticus. Some scholars have used this evidence in favor of their conclusion
that Ezra's law book was quite separate from the Pentateuch and has subsequently been lost (cf. *Introduction,* "The Book of the Law").

The first point refers to the legislation in Lev 23:40 that fruit and branches
are to be taken from the trees as part of the celebration. It is known from
later texts (e.g., 2 Macc 10:6–8; Josephus, *Ant.* 3 § 245; 13 § 372) that the
celebrants would process "bearing in their hands a bouquet composed of
myrtle and willow with a branch of palm, along with fruit of the persea,"
or that it was "a custom among the Jews that at the Festival of Tabernacles
everyone holds wands made of palm branches and citrons." Of this, however,
there is no mention here, the branches to be cut being used only for the
erection of booths. There are two possible responses to this. On the one
hand, it is commonplace to observe the clearly composite nature of Lev 23
itself; cf. de Vaux, *Ancient Israel,* 472–73 and 496–97; K. Elliger, *Leviticus* (HAT;
Tübingen: Mohr, 1966) 304–7. It is possible, therefore, that the detail about
fruit and branches belongs to the latest phase in the chapter's growth and
so was not yet found in the text which Ezra was reading (so de Vaux). This
view is attractive in its neatness, but has to rest on the uncertainty of the
literary analysis of Lev 23 and the assumption that later writers would have
felt free to add to a text that is already presented and expounded as authoritative. What we have seen above, and will see again, of the handling of biblical
Law in Ezra and Nehemiah suggests that they are already working with a
fixed text where application to the present must be made by means other
than literary innovation. The second response to the difficulty, therefore,

takes seriously the silence of our present text. For some reason, the description concentrates entirely on the booths; perhaps, since this feast was a celebration of harvest, it had long been the practice to bring fruit to the ceremony. Ezra, therefore, concentrated only on that aspect of the Law that had not previously been observed. Support for this comes from the many other aspects of the festival (e.g., the sacrifices of Num 29), which equally go without mention here because they are not relevant to the theme of the laity's reception of and response to the Law.

We come finally to the difficulty that although v 14b may be regarded as closely dependent upon Lev 23:42, v 15 seems to have no foothold in the earlier Law. (It was observed in the *Notes* that attempts to avoid this difficulty by emendation are textually unwarranted.) Here, several points need to be taken together in order to solve the problem. First, although the wording of v 15 is not found in the Law, the gist of what was said can easily be deduced from Lev 23:2 and 4 ("These are the set feasts . . . which you shall proclaim in their appointed season"). Readers for whom this law was to be observed in its detail must have asked what they were to proclaim— and v 15 could well represent Ezra's answer. It is a further example, therefore, of his making ancient Scripture practical and relevant for his own day. Second, there is a suggestion here which the following verses confirm that the proclamation summoned the celebrants to Jerusalem. While there is no mention of this in Lev 23, it will have been the natural deduction from Deut 16:15. The influence of one passage on another ("Scripture interpreting Scripture") is a further characteristic of Ezra's exegesis demonstrated elsewhere, and thus it takes its natural place here too. Third, the concluding words of the verse—"as prescribed" ("written"; ככתוב)—demonstrate clearly that the words spoken are not intended as a literal quotation from the law, but are a summary of its contents. This is reinforced by the mention of "Jerusalem," which no one can have supposed was in any book attributed to Moses. The text itself thus leaves adequate indications that we would be mistaken to look for these words as a direct citation from the law. Finally, the continuation of the narrative shows that there has been a subtle shift from an account of what was "found written" to an account of what the leaders actually did about it. The style of writing may be compact, but it is fully acceptable in terms of the overall emphasis of the chapter.

We may conclude, therefore, that Ezra's teaching concentrated on Lev 23, though with influence from Deut 16, and that, despite the lack of verbal correspondence, there is no need to look further for the text of his Law.

"Palm" and "leafy trees" are found also in Lev 23:40, but not the other trees mentioned, while Lev 23:40 itself contains others not mentioned here. If our general analysis above is correct, however, this should pose no difficulty. The present proclamation is dealing with materials for the making of booths, and thus need not be expected to correspond with the separate stipulations concerning produce for the festival.

"As prescribed": see *Form* for the importance of this in the structure of the chapter and its contribution to the dominant theme.

16 The final paragraph in this chapter starts with a note of how precisely and promptly the people moved to obey the law whose stipulations had long ceased to be observed (v 17). The residents of Jerusalem evidently erected their booths on or beside their own houses, while those who travelled in from the countryside found various open spaces they could use—in the temple courts, by the Water Gate (see *Comment* on v 1), or by the Gate of Ephraim (see *Comment* on 12:39).

17 The wording of this verse suggests that the living in booths was regarded as a deliberate re-enactment of the Israelites' wandering in the desert following the Exodus. This comes to light first from the phrase השבים מן־השבי, "those who had returned from the captivity." This description is not used elsewhere in the chapter, but seems to be introduced here in order to draw a parallel between the first Exodus and the more recent experience of a "second Exodus" by those who had returned from Babylon (see *Comment* on Ezra 1:6; 7:9, etc.). Second, the reference back to Joshua also finds part of its application here; as Myers explains, "To recall the time of Joshua is to associate the Festival of Booths with the wilderness period when Yahweh dwelt in a tabernacle and the people in booths (Lev xxiii.43; Hos xii.9), and to dissociate it from the vintage customs related to the agricultural festivals that proved to be so attractive to Israel."

These observations are important in determining the significance of the second half of the verse. Many commentators have argued that the very name of the festival shows that the use of booths was integral to it and cannot have been neglected. In addition, we have good evidence that the festival was regularly celebrated in ancient Israel (e.g., Judg 21:19; 1 Sam 1:3; 1 Kgs 8:2, 65; Zech 14:16; Ezra 3:4, etc.). It is therefore suggested that the new element on this occasion was the centralized celebration in Jerusalem.

This widespread interpretation cannot be correct, however; first, it could not be said that this "had not been done from the time of Jeshua the son of Nun," since Jerusalem was not the central sanctuary in his day; second, the text in fact states explicitly that it was the dwelling in booths that was the newly revived element.

The answer to this puzzle lies in the observations made above: even if booths were erected at the festival before Ezra's time, they were merely part of the harvest aspect of the festival. They were a reflection of the booths that the harvesters used in the fields during this season (if, indeed, the very same booths were not used). Now, however, the significance of the booths in terms of Israel's history was reintroduced. For the first time in centuries (in the author's view, at any rate), they were erected in Jerusalem as a reminder of the wilderness wanderings. It is thus striking to observe that this historicizing treatment of the booths is another of the elements unique to the prescriptions of Lev 23 (cf. v 43). Our interpretation here thus dovetails neatly with our conclusions on verses 14–15.

"Jeshua": this is a unique spelling for Moses' successor, usually called Joshua. The spelling is used several times in these books for the High Priest at the time of the first return (cf. Ezra 2:2). The patronymic, "the son of Nun," precludes confusion, even though some modern commentators persist in seeking to muddle what the writer has thus made clear. As interpreted above, the reference makes excellent sense and need not be changed. For the element of "rejoicing," cf. *Form* and *Comment* on vv 9, 10, and 12 above.

18 This verse also shows the influence of both Deuteronomic and Priestly legislation. The former is found in the daily reading of the Law; cf. Deut 31:9–13. Whether that means, as some have sought to deduce, that this was therefore a year of release, or whether this reading became part of an annual covenant renewal ceremony, can hardly be determined from the evidence of the present passage. Needless to say, however, it fully coincided with the author's concern in the chapter as a whole.

Influence from the Priestly law, on the other hand, is clear from the length of celebration—not now just seven days, as in Deut 16:13, but with the addition of an eighth day, "a solemn holiday, according to the ordinance" of Lev 23:36 and 39 and Num 29:35–38. The use of the rare word עצרת in all these passages is strongly indicative again of direct dependence on this particular law. It has often been translated "solemn assembly." Kutsch, *VT* 2 (1952) 65–67, has shown, however, that this is too limited a translation, and that at its basis lies the idea of cessation, from work in particular. Thus it is not only the specific gathering, but the whole day which is referred to.

Explanation

Our analysis has shown that the dominant theme of this chapter is the declaration of the Law of God, its explication, and the people's consequent response. After summarizing the chapter's presentation of these themes, it will be necessary to call attention to a major problem for modern hermeneutics that the passage poses.

The scene opens with a happy confluence of a congregation anxious to hear the Law of God read to them and a teacher willing to match their demands. On the side of the people, it should be noted that they first anticipated the reading with reverent expectation (vv 5–6); second, that they listened attentively throughout the long morning as it was read and explained to them (v 3); and third that they were responsive both to the reading itself, as their weeping showed (v 9b), and to its interpretation (v 12). The same themes are to be traced in the second part of the chapter (vv 13–18), as our analysis of the structure made clear. However we formulate our doctrine of the Word of God in detail, it is abundantly clear both from this chapter and from many others that orthodoxy in this realm is of little practical benefit if the proclamation of that Word is not met by such an attitude as is here exemplified; even the ministry of Jesus himself was frustrated on occasions by a lack of responsive faith, e.g., Mark 6:1–6; Matt 23:37. Expectancy should mark our approach to the reading of God's Word, and responsiveness our leaving it to reenter our daily lives, if it is ever to be allowed to accomplish its primary purpose.

From Ezra's side, we cannot fail to note his willingness to meet the people's request. They took the initiative, but several indications have been observed that suggest that he was already prepared—waiting and anxious for the invitation when it came. More significantly, he chose both to read the Law in an easily accessible public place away from the sacred precincts of the temple, so that none might be barred from attending, and to associate laymen with him in the whole enterprise (v 4). Similarly, he was anxious that those who

listened should understand clearly what was read. There was to be no place
here for a purely liturgical reading that could wash over the consciousness
of the congregation. Finally, the prominence of the lay leaders is noteworthy
in v 13, as a smaller group gathered around Ezra after the initial reading
for a more detailed exposition. Perhaps more than in anything else, Ezra's
importance lies in the fact that he put the Bible of his day into the hands
of the laity; it was no longer the exclusive preserve of the "professionals."
Much of the shape of Judaism thereafter was determined by this fundamental
achievement.

A problem arises, however, when we move on to consider the results of
this activity. It is highlighted by the intentional parallelism between the end
of verses 8 and 12: when the people "understood the reading," they wept
(v 9b). This was not, however, the result Ezra desired. When he explained
why, they celebrated "with great joy, for they understood the words that
had been declared to them" (v 12). How is this acute contrast to be explained?

To answer this question fully, we must recall first that in all probability
the Law being read was not completely new to the people. Many of its regulations, however, had fallen into disuse because of the changed political circumstances of the community. How could regulations relating to a sovereign
state in which the revealed will of God could be built straight into the law
of the land be observed and practiced now that the people were but part
of the population of a small province in the mighty Persian Empire? As we
have seen both in vv 13–18 of this chapter and in Ezra 9–10, Ezra addressed
himself to such problems and introduced a hermeneutic whereby the principle
of the Law could continue to be observed even when its letter was deadened
by changed circumstances. We need not doubt that what caused the people
to weep was the fresh realization that they had been neglecting parts of the
Law whose relevance to their lives was being emphasized to them in a fresh
way.

That this was not the result for which Ezra was looking has been demonstrated in our exegesis of vv 9–10. In understanding the details of the Law,
the people were left with a sense of failure and frustration; only when Ezra
raised their vision to encompass the message of the Law in its totality—a
message of grace and salvation to their ancestors first and to themselves by
faith in consequence—did their sorrow turn to joy. Thereafter, their rectification of individual abuses (vv 13–18) served only to reinforce that joy.

From this experience, we cannot escape the observation that between the
theory and the practice of the authority of Scripture there is a considerable
gulf. Protestant orthodoxy has generally held to the belief that the Bible
alone should regulate faith and conduct for the Christian, and to this human
reason and Church tradition are frequently opposed. This chapter, however,
should give us pause on two counts. First, of what value is an authority if it
is not correctly understood? The cultural differences between the biblical
world and our own, together with the fragmentation of Christendom, suggest
that this question cannot be ignored. Second, what happens when individual
texts are understood, but in ways that run counter to the prevailing teaching
of Scripture as a whole? In other words, text without an acceptable hermeneutic runs into the danger of becoming no more than a fossilized object of

veneration. Ezra's activity in the present chapter suggests that the interplay of all three sources of authority, among which the text is the first both in time and in weight, is inevitable. In an unending process within the life of the believing community, each must play its part in a hermeneutical spiral whereby the insights of one constantly check and reform the statements of another. The text is the basis; reason is applied for interpretation; and tradition serves to ensure that all is done within the larger framework of appreciation that God's final word is one not of exclusion and judgment, but of grace and invitation.

Confession (Neh 9:1–37)

Bibliography

Ackroyd, P. R. "God and People." *La notion biblique de Dieu*, 145–62. **Ahlemann, F.** "Zur Esra Quelle." *ZAW* 59 (1942–43) 77–98. **Baars, W.** "Einige Bemerkungen zu einem altlateinischen Text von Nehemia." *VT* 8 (1958) 425. **Couroyer, B.** "'Avoir la nuque raide': ne pas incliner l'oreille." *RB* 88 (1981) 216–25. **Driver, G. R.** "Forgotten Hebrew Idioms." *ZAW* 78 (1976) 1–7. **Fensham, F. C.** "Neh. 9 and Pss. 105, 106, 135 and 136. Post-exilic Historical Traditions in Poetic Form." *JNSL* 9 (1981) 35–51. **Gilbert, M.** "La place de la Loi dans la prière de Néhémie 9." *De la Tôrah au Messie. Mélanges Henri Cazelles*, ed. J. Doré, P. Grelot and M. Carrez. Paris: Desclée (1981) 307–16. **In der Smitten, W. Th.** *Esra*, 47–51. **Kellermann, U.** *Nehemia*, 32–37. **Kühlewein, J.** *Geschichte in den Psalmen*. Calwer Theologische Monographien 2. Stuttgart: Calwer Verlag, 1973. **Liebreich, L. J.** "The Impact of Nehemiah 9:5–37 on the Liturgy of the Synagogue." *HUCA* 32 (1961) 227–37. **Mowinckel, S.** *Studien I*, 50–59. **Noth, M.** *The Laws in the Pentateuch*. Tr. D. R. Ap-Thomas. Edinburgh and London: Oliver & Boyd, 1966. ———. *Überlieferungsgeschichtliche Studien*. **Rad, G. von.** "Gerichtsdoxologie." *Gesammelte Studien zum Alten Testament*, vol. 2. Munich: Chr. Kaiser (1973) 245–54. **Rehm, M.** "Nehemias 9." *BZ* N.F. 1 (1957) 59–69. **Schaeder, H. H.** *Esra der Schreiber*. **Torrey, C. C.** *Composition*, 31–33. ———. *Ezra Studies*, 252–84. **Welch, A. C.** "The Source of Nehemiah ix." *ZAW* 47 (1929) 130–37. ———. *Post-exilic Judaism*, 26–46.

Translation

[1] *On the twenty-fourth day of this month the Israelites assembled, fasting, wearing sackcloth, and with earth upon their heads.* [2] *Those of Israelite descent separated themselves from all foreigners. They stood to confess their sins and the iniquities of their ancestors.* [3] *They stood in their places and read from the Book of the Law of the Lord their God for a quarter of the day while they spent a further quarter confessing and worshiping the Lord their God.* [4] *On the stairs of the Levites* [a] *there stood Jeshua and Binnui,* [b] *Kadmiel, Shebaniah, Bunni, Sherebiah, Bani (and) Chenani; they cried out loud to the Lord their God.* [5] *Then the Levites—Jeshua and Kadmiel, Bani,* [a] *Hashabniah, Sherebiah, Hodiah, Shebaniah (and) Pethahiah—said, "Stand up and bless the Lord your God:*

> [b] *May you be blessed, O Lord our God,* [b] *from everlasting to everlasting, And may your glorious name be blessed,* [c] *although* [d] *it is exalted above all blessing and praise.*

> [6] *You alone are the Lord;*
> *You have made heaven,* [a] *even the highest heaven,* [b] *with all its host,*
> *The earth and everything on it, the seas and everything in them;*
> *You preserve them all, and the host of heaven worships you.*
> [7] *You are the Lord God who chose Abram,*

Who brought him out of Ur of the Chaldees and gave him the name of Abraham;

8 *When you found that he intended* a *to be faithful to you, you made a covenant with him,*

To give to his descendants b *the land of the Canaanites, the Hittites, and the Amorites,*

The Perizzites, the Jebusites, and the Girgashites;

And you kept your promise, because you are righteous.

9 *You saw the suffering of our ancestors in Egypt; you heard their cry at the Red Sea.*

10 *You performed signs and portents against Pharaoh, against all his servants and all the people of his land,*

Because you knew how arrogantly they had treated them, so you made a name for yourself, as it remains to this day.

11 *You split the sea open before them so that they passed through the sea on dry land;*

But you hurled those who were pursuing them into the depths, like a stone into mighty waters.

12 *You guided them with a pillar of cloud by day and with a pillar of fire by night,*

To light up the way for them in which they should go.

13 *You came down upon Mount Sinai and spoke with them from heaven;*

You gave them right judgments and true laws,

Statutes and commandments which were good. a

14 *You informed them of your holy Sabbath,*

And gave them your commandments, statutes, and laws through Moses, your servant.

15 *You provided them with bread from heaven when they were hungry*

And brought water out of the rock for them when they were thirsty;

You told them to come in and take possession of the land

Which you had sworn to give them.

16 *But they, our ancestors,* a *acted arrogantly; they became stubborn* b *and would not obey your commandments,*

17 *They refused to obey and did not remember the miracles which you performed among them.*

They became stubborn and appointed a leader a *in order to return to their slavery in Egypt.* b

But you are a God more than willing to forgive, c *gracious and compassionate,*

Long-suffering and unwavering in your faithful love; d *you did not abandon them—*

18 *Even when they made for themselves a bull calf of cast metal*

And said, 'This is your god who brought you up from Egypt,'

Or when they committed colossal blasphemies,

19 *Still in your great compassion you did not abandon them in the desert,*

By day the pillar a *of cloud did not cease guiding them in the way*

Nor did the pillar of fire cease by night to light up the way b *for them in which they should go.*

20 *You gave your good Spirit to instruct them.*

You did not withhold your manna from them, and you gave them water when
they were thirsty.

21 For forty years you sustained them in the desert (where) they lacked nothing;
Their clothes did not wear out, neither did their feet become swollen.

22 You gave them kingdoms and peoples and assigned them as a boundary; a
Thus they took possession of the land of Sihon, b king of Heshbon,
And the land of Og, king of Bashan.

23 You made their descendants as numerous as the stars in the sky;
You brought them into the land which you had told their ancestors to enter
and possess.

24 These a descendants entered and took possession of the land, while you subdued
before them
The Canaanites, who inhabited the land, handing them over into their power,
Their kings and the peoples of the land alike, that they might do with them as
they pleased.

25 They captured fortified cities and fertile land;
They took possession of houses filled with all manner of good things,
Cisterns ready hewn, vineyards, olive-groves and orchards in abundance;
They ate till they were satisfied and grew fat; they revelled in your great goodness.

26 Despite this they became disobedient and rebelled against you; they turned their
backs on your law a
And killed your prophets who had solemnly warned them so as to bring them
back to you;
They committed colossal blasphemies.

27 So you handed them over into the power of their adversaries, who oppressed
them,
But when in their oppression they cried out to you, you heard from heaven,
And in accordance with your great compassion you gave them saviors who rescued
them from the power of their adversaries.

28 However, no sooner were they enjoying a respite than they again started doing
what you considered evil.
So you abandoned them to the power of their enemies who dominated them; but
when they again cried out to you
You heard from heaven and rescued them many times a according to your compassion.

29 You solemnly warned them so as to bring them back to your law, but they became
arrogant and would not obey your commandments;
They sinned right against your judgments—the very ones which bring life to
the man who keeps them;
They turned a stubborn shoulder, grew obstinate a and would not obey.

30 You bore patiently with them in your faithful love a for many years;
You solemnly warned them by your Spirit through your prophets,
But they paid no attention, and so you handed them over into the power of the
peoples of the lands.

31 In your great compassion, however, you did not eliminate them,
Nor did you abandon them, because you are a gracious and compassionate God.

32 Now therefore, O our God, O great God, mighty and awe-inspiring,

Who keeps covenant with loving loyalty, do not belittle all the hardship[a]
Which has befallen us—our kings[b] *and princes, our priests and prophets, our*
ancestors and all your people—
Ever since the time of the kings of Assyria until today.
[33] *You have been in the right with regard to whatever has happened to us,*
Because you have acted faithfully whereas we have done wrong.
[34] *Our kings,*[a] *our princes, our priests, and our ancestors have not kept your law,*
Nor heeded your commandments and solemn warnings which you gave them.[b]
[35] *Even while they were in their own kingdom, enjoying the great goodness with*
which you favored them,
Even while in the spacious and fertile land which you gave them,
They did not serve you nor repent of their evil ways.
[36] *And so now today we are slaves.*
Yes! we are slaves
Here in the land which you gave to our ancestors so that they might eat its
fruit and its good fare.
[37] *Its produce piles up to the benefit of the kings whom you have set over us because*
of our sins;
They rule over our bodies and do as they please with our livestock whilst we
are in great distress.

Notes

4.a. NIV fails to observe that מעלה "stairs" must be in the constr because of its vocalization and (in this context) because it lacks the def art. Its rendering, "Standing on the stairs were the Levites," is thus inadmissible.

4.b. MT has Bani, which recurs later in the verse. While it is not impossible that there were two men of the same name present, comparison with 10:10 (9) strongly favors emending to בנוי, as proposed by Rudolph. Apart from the general similarities between the two lists, Jeshua, Binnui, and Kadmiel are clearly set apart slightly (as leaders?) in 10:10 from the other Levites who follow. In the present passage, Jeshua and Kadmiel head the list in v 5, so that Jeshua and Binnui are a likely combination in this verse. We should note in support of this that the first two names are linked with the copula in both verses 4 and 5, whereas the others follow without any conj. Thus, here too, the same three are set apart from the others, if the emendation is correct. This last observation also tells strongly against an alternative proposal (following LXX) to repoint to וּבְנֵי, "and the sons of." In addition, the relationships that such an emendation would involve would not fit easily with those suggested by 10:10–11 (9–10).

5.a. Or "Binnui," by analogy with the list in v 4, though the case is not strengthened here by a repetition of the name later. Because five of the eight names in the two verses are the same, it has often been suggested that the two lists were originally identical. However, there would then have been no need to repeat the list (Rudolph), while the second half of each verse suggests a different role in each case. Nor must it be overlooked that a good deal of the overlap concerns the leaders of the Levites, and thus is hardly surprising; cf. Torrey, *Ezra Studies*, 279–80, for the alternative viewpoint.

5.b-b. It is widely agreed that there has been some textual loss at the beginning of the prayer, because by the final line of this verse the address has already passed over to the 2nd pers. Moreover, "from everlasting to everlasting" which follows is clearly a characteristic of God, not of the worshipers. Torrey, *Ezra Studies*, 280–82, observed that this formula also occurs at the end of Pss 41 and 106 (and cf. 1 Chr 29:10), where it is preceded by "Blessed be the Lord God of Israel." This, he argues, gives us the clue for a possible reconstruction here (I omit his inclusion of "And Ezra said" for reasons which will follow): ברוך אתה יהוה אלהינו "blessed are you, O Lord, our God." We may observe that (especially if אתה was spelled defectively, as in v 6) the words in an unpointed text are almost identical with the preceding phrase:

ברכו את יהוה אלהיכם "Bless ye the Lord, your God."
ברוך את יהוה אלהינו "May you be blessed, O Lord, our God."

The loss of the phrase by scribal error would thus be understandable. Alternative suggestions that have been made seem less probable. Kidner, admitting that there is "some roughness of style," nevertheless attempts to defend MT with the proposal that at the transition to the 2nd pers "the Levites at this point lifted their hands heavenwards, with a gesture that gathered up the congregation's response." As well as being a conjecture for which the text offers no evidence, this proposal does not deal with the difficulty of the words "from everlasting to everlasting" in their present setting. NEB translates ". . . thy glorious name is blessed," reading ברוך "is blessed" instead of ויברכו "they blessed" on the basis of Syr.; see also G. R. Driver, ZAW 78 (1966) 6–7. The resultant word order is strange, however, and no explanation is offered as to how the error arose. Finally, Torrey himself, and several of those who have followed him, made the additional suggestion that ויאמר עזרא "and Ezra said" should also be included in the emendation and so prefaced to the prayer. It is observed that it introduces v 6 in the LXX. This further emendation is to be rejected, however: (i) By interrupting the two otherwise almost identical phrases, it makes an explanation for the difficulty less plausible. (ii) It is inappropriate to the context. Comparison with chap. 8 shows that if Ezra were leading the confession, he would have been mentioned prominently in the introductory narrative. Instead, however, attention is focused entirely on the Levites, whom we therefore expect to find continuing as the speakers. (iii) The evidence from LXX is worthless, both because it does not relate to this verse, and because it is so clearly a secondary addition by someone who thought, in view of the sequence of chaps. in the present text, that Ezra must have been involved. The alternative view (Stade; Bertholet; Schaeder, *Esra*, 9), that the words were omitted from the MT because such a confession should have been made by the high priest (Lev 16:21), is quite beside the point: the resultant text takes the confession further away from the high priest. Ezra at least belonged to the high priestly family (Ezra 7:1–5), whereas the Levites did not.

5.c. Impers pl for pass.

5.d. The previous note shows that, syntactically, we cannot render "blessed and exalted." In view of the following words, Rudolph is therefore probably correct to construe as a concessive circumstantial clause; cf. GKC §§ 141e; 142d.

6.a. In theory, this could also refer to the sky, in which case the following phrase might refer to heaven; the semantic range of שמים "heavens" is problematic; cf. E. Levine, "Distinguishing 'Air' From 'Heaven' in the Bible," ZAW 88 (1976) 97–99. The contrast with the earth in the following line, together with the last line of the verse, which implies that שמים is the abode of spiritual beings, favors the rendering supplied above.

6.b. For "the use of a substantive in the construct state before the plural of the same word" as a means of expressing the superlative, cf. GKC § 133i.

8.a. Lit., "And you found his heart faithful before you." The heart relates to the mind in Heb. anthropology, so that intention and resolve are expressed in this idiom.

8.b. Because of the long list of names, the inf const is repeated before the indir obj. This may have misled the versions into supposing that a second indir obj (לו, "to him") had dropped out. It is quite unnecessary to restore it, since the fulfillment of the promise came only long after Abraham's own day.

13.a. Being masc pl טובים "good," this adj must qualify both nouns in the line (since מצות "commandments" is fem); this is most clearly rendered in Eng. by a relative clause.

16.a. Explicative *wāw*.

16.b. Lit., "they stiffened their necks"; see also vv 17 and 29. This idiom is generally explained in terms of a stubborn animal. Couroyer, RB 88 (1981) 216–25, however, has contrasted the idiom rather with the phrase "to incline the ear" (see especially Jer 7:26; 17:23) and so sees in it a human image of refusal to listen to what is being said. Couroyer's main objection to the traditional interpretation relates to the refusal to submit to the yoke; he does not, however, deal fully with the possibility that it refers to the refusal of an animal to go in the direction its master wishes. (It is not necessary, of course, for the animal to be mounted, a comparatively late custom; it could as well apply to a donkey carrying a load with the master walking beside it.) This latter would seem more appropriate in v 29 of this chapter, in view of the additional reference there to "shoulder," less appropriate (except as an image) to human stubbornness. Fortunately, the imagery is not significantly affected by this dispute.

17.a. Several commentators think that נתן ראש is an idiom for "to determine." However, this passage is clearly based on Num 14:4, where exactly the same phrase must mean "to appoint a leader." The fact that there it expresses the people's intention whereas here it is represented as having happened must not color this conclusion. Besides, there are frequently differences of a much larger order than this between prose and verse accounts of the same incident in the OT.

17.b. MT: "In their rebellion." This is intelligible, but several MSS and LXX suggest that here too the text was originally close to Num 14:4 in reading במצרים (loss of one letter), "in Egypt."

17.c. Pl of amplification (intensive pl); cf. GKC § 124e.

17.d. The *wāw* before חסד is to be deleted with Q, many MSS and the Vrs.

19.a. This is one of the classic examples of the particle את appearing to introduce a so-called nomin; see also vv 32 and 34. Since the meaning of the passage is not materially affected by the discussion of this phenomenon, it is unnecessary to enter the debate here. For bibliography and discussion, cf. J. Hoftijzer, *OTS* 14 (1965) 1–99.

19.b. Deleting ו "and" with some MSS and the Vrs, but cf. Baars, *VT* 8 (1958) 425; the emendation brings the line exactly into accord with the corresponding line in v 12. MT is represented by RV: "to show them light, and the way wherein they should go." However, this demands that להאיר "to give light to" or "to light up" be understood intransitively in the first clause but transitively in the second, which is extremely harsh. The present text may have arisen under the influence of ואת earlier in the verse.

22.a. Not certain; פאה is normally a "corner" or "side," though Akk. *pāṭu* has the meaning of "border" (*AHW* 851), and this is not unreasonable in the context (Rudolph). NEB renders "allotting these to them as spoils of war," apparently on the basis of an Arab. cognate (cf. Brockington). While this clearly makes good sense, it is difficult to accept without a full presentation of the evidence and discussion of the appropriateness of admitting a new root to the Hebrew lexicon on the basis of this passage alone.

22.b. MT has "Sihon, even the land of the king of Heshbon." (Since Sihon was king of Heshbon, the *wāw* must be explicative.) However, ואת ארץ is better deleted, with 1 MS and LXX, as the parallelism with the following line suggests.

24.a. Lit., "the sons." The lack of pronominal suff and use instead of the def art shows that reference is to the same group as in the previous verse; hence "these" in English.

26.a. So NEB; it captures well with an Eng. idiom the force of the Heb.: "They cast your law behind their back."

28.a. The pl of the adj רב occasionally precedes its noun; cf. Joüon, *Grammaire* § 141*b*. The gender and lack of def art preclude ambiguity. See also Baars, *VT* 8 (1958) 425.

29.a. Cf. n. 16.b. above.

30.a. Ellipse of חסד; cf. Pss 36:11 (10); 109:12; Jer 31:3.

32.a. Cf. n. 19.a. and GKC § 117*aa*.

32.b. Compare the use of ל at Ezra 1:5.a.

34.a. Cf. n. 19.a.

34.b. For an alternative understanding, cf. T. Veijola, "Zu Ableitung und Bedeutung von *hēʿid* im Hebräischen," *UF* 8 (1976) 343–51.

Form/Structure/Setting

We shall deal here first with matters relating solely to the prayer in vv 5b–37 before turning to the setting of the chapter as a whole.

In the translation above, the lines have been set out according to the proposals in *BHS* which, following Rudolph's commentary, regards the prayer as poetic. Certainly, there are several reasons that may be thought to justify this: parallelism occurs (e.g., v 15a and b), there are sections of acceptable meter (e.g., vv 6–7), and there are examples of poetic syntax, such as the

carrying forward of the force of a verb from one line to the next (e.g., v 6b
and c). On the other hand, none of these features is sustained throughout,
while in addition prosaic elements such as the particle אֵת and the relative
אֲשֶׁר occur frequently; it would be difficult in consequence to justify the poetic
nature of a verse such as v 19.

The passage thus poses problems of classification even with regard to so
basic a question as whether it is prose or poetry. It undoubtedly comes closer
to poetry than Ezra 9:6–15 or Neh 1:5–11, with which it otherwise has many
points of similarity, and yet it falls far short, from a formal point of view,
of most of the poetry in the Psalter. We must therefore be content with
calling it rhythmic liturgical language and recognize that it has been much
influenced both in style and in phraseology by other poetic passages. For
convenience, however, we shall use the language of poetic analysis in what
follows (e.g., stanza).

The question of *Gattung* is equally difficult to define with precision. The
prayer starts in hymnic fashion with a call to praise God—first in the narrative
introduction, then in a blessing construed in the passive mood (according
to our reconstruction of v 5), and finally with a transition to the jussive.
There is no formal connection with what follows (e.g., כִּי, "for"), but it is
clear that the whole of the following historical retrospect (vv 6–31) is intended
to serve as a substantiation in narrative style. At v 32, however, the strong
adverb וְעַתָּה, "and now," indicates the start of a fresh section that is much
closer to the communal lament. There is an element of veiled petition (v
32) as well as of confession (vv 33–35) and lament proper (vv 36–37).

As in the case of the prayers of Ezra 9 and Neh 1, no exact parallels to
this passage are to be found. Nevertheless, the mixing of several components
here is not haphazard; each serves in its own way to make of the prayer as
a whole a most powerful combination of confession by the community and
request for full restoration.

First, we must take note of Gilbert's study of this chapter, "La place de
la Loi dans la prière de Néhémie 9," in *Tôrah au Messie*. Observing that the
overall structure of the prayer is confession, transition by וְעַתָּה "and now,"
and petition, he denies that we should look to prophecy (*contra* Gunkel) or
the Psalter (e.g., Pss 38; 51; 106; 130) for analogies. Rather, he finds many
brief examples of this pattern in both individual and collective confessions
in the historical books; cf. Num 22:34; 1 Sam 15:24–25; 2 Sam 24:10; Exod
10:16–17 (individual) and Num 21:7 (without וְעַתָּה); Exod 32:31–32; Judg
10:15; 1 Sam 12:10. This is sufficient to suggest that we are dealing in Neh
9 with a form of confession deeply rooted in Israelite life, not restricted to
the cult, as narrowly defined. Here, however, the form is elaborated under
the influence both of the cult, as the setting and language show, and of the
Law, which has now begun to replace God himself as the party against whom
sin has been committed.

Second, however, it would be churlish to deny all contact with the Psalter.
The extended historical restrospect at once invites comparison with a number
of the Psalms; cf. Fensham, "Neh. 9 and Pss. 105, 106, 135 and 136: Post-
exilic Historical Traditions in Poetic Form," *JNSL* 9 (1981) 35–51. In particu-

lar, Neh 9 is often compared with Ps 106 precisely because both passages use historical recollection as a vehicle for confession and as a ground on which to base an appeal for mercy; cf. Kühlewein, *Geschichte in den Psalmen,* 122–25. In other words, it is inadequate to rest content merely with examples of historical recital. When we press beyond this to inquire after the purpose of the recital, it is immediately to the fact of confession that we are again drawn.

Third, Neh 9 is included by von Rad among the group of texts that he categorizes as "Doxologies of Judgment"; cf. "Gerichtsdoxologie," *Gesammelte Studien.* For some discussion, cf. Ezra 9, *Form,* and the *Comment* on v 15 of that chapter. Von Rad grouped these texts in particular because of their formulaic confession אתה צדיק "you are in the right." This occurs in v 33 of the present chapter (its occurrence in v 8 serves a quite different purpose; see below), where its function is precisely to acknowledge, as an act of worship, that God is justified in his judgment on the worshiper. As von Rad's name for this type of prayer makes clear, it constitutes the most exalted, because most objective, form of confession that the OT knows.

Fourth, it is thus not by chance that the passage is introduced in hymnic form, as was pointed out above. This reinforces the effectiveness of the confession for once again it is set within a context of praise. This separates our chapter from several of the other doxologies of judgment (e.g., Ezra 9; Dan 9), but draws it closer not only to Ps 106, as already seen, but in particular to the doxologies in the book of Amos (4:13; 5:8–9; 9:5–6); cf. J. L. Crenshaw, *Hymnic Affirmation of Divine Justice* (SBLDS 24; Missoula: Scholars Press, 1975). According to Crenshaw, these doxologies "seem to have been used on special days of penitence and confession" during the exilic or early post-exilic period (p. 143). In view of the present literary setting of Neh 9, there is no reason why our author should not in fact have used material drawn directly from its original life-setting in the cult.

Finally, the closing verses of the chapter have, not unnaturally, been compared with the psalms of communal lament.

It is thus apparent that to press Neh 9 into the mold of a single *Gattung* would be to miss much of its forcefulness. Probably adapting material from a liturgy of public penance, our author has woven together several elements that were all associated with confession. In their combined effectiveness, they well serve his purpose in this central climax of the book between the presentation of the Law in chap. 8 and the covenant renewal in chap. 10; see the introduction to chaps. 8–10 above.

The question of how to divide the long historical retrospect will be more easily handled in *Comment* below. Suffice it therefore here to summarize that the principal divisions are:

6	Creation
7–8	Abraham
9–11	Exodus
12–21	Wilderness period
22–31	The land.

This will be justified on the basis of content, structure, and vocabulary. It will also be shown that each section focuses upon one particular characteristic of God, usually expressed in a well-known phrase whose significance is thus elaborated by the recital, e.g., אתה הוא יהוה לבדך "You alone are the Lord" (v 6); צדיק אתה "you are righteous" (v 8), etc.; see *Comment* on vv 6, 8, 10, 17 and 31. Finally, it will be observed that the first three sections deal with the background and formation of the people. Though they are longer, only the final two deal with the life of the people, and each has a similar structure: account of God's grace, the people's rebellion, and statement of God's continuing mercy. Even within confession, therefore, there remains a strong memory of the grace of God as expressed in the nation's history, and this forms the rationale for the appeal in the chapter's closing verses.

We must now deal with the literary and historical setting of the chapter as a whole. From v 1 it would appear at first glance that the narrative continues directly from chap. 8 with only a very brief interval. The Feast of Tabernacles would end on the twenty-second day of the month (see *Comment* on 8:14–15), and our chapter continues "On the twenty-fourth day of this month." Many commentators have therefore assumed that no new setting is presupposed.

Further investigation shows, however, that this presupposition cannot be justified; in addition to the discussions in the standard commentaries and monographs on Ezra-Nehemiah, cf. Welch, *ZAW* 47 (1929) 130–37 (and *Postexilic Judaism*, chap. 2), and Rehm, *BZ* N.F. 1 (1957) 59–69. Naturally, the arguments brought forward depend in part upon conclusions reached concerning the original setting of Neh 8. In what follows, however, an attempt will be made after the immediately succeeding paragraph to include some points that stand regardless of this particular issue.

First, on our view that Neh 8 originally followed Ezra 8, it is at once apparent that Neh 9 could not have been its sequel. The separation from foreigners (v 2) and confession would be completely out of place before the events of Ezra 9–10 (*contra* Schaeder, *Esra*, 12, and Michaeli).

The sequel between Neh 8 and 9 is itself extremely harsh, however. Many have observed the sudden and unconvincing change of mood from joy to mourning, and attempts to explain this away are unconvincing. Torrey, *Composition*, 31–33, first drew attention to this fact, emphasizing the difficulty posed by the explicit command of 8:9–11 that the people should not mourn. If someone were composing freely in these chapters, as Noth, *Studien*, 148–49; Kellermann, *Nehemia*, 32–37; and In der Smitten, *Esra*, 47–51, for instance, suppose, we should not expect such an unmotivated change of mood. It would have been more natural, for instance, to put the confession earlier, perhaps on the Day of Atonement, the tenth day of the month, and to conclude with a joyful celebration; this is certainly the liturgically expected order (so Mowinckel, *Studien I*, 52). If, on the other hand, this were a historical account, then, in addition to the oddity of the change after the command not to mourn, we may note Welch's observation: "A day of repentance might well usher in the time when Israel became anew confirmed in its national law and its national festival: it was scarcely in place after these had been renewed" (*ZAW* 47 [1929] 131).

Next, the absence of Ezra from our chapter is striking. After his prominence in chap. 8, we seem to move into a different world in chap. 9, where the Levites collectively lead the gathering.

The bearing of the people too is markedly different. In chap. 8 they appear to be ignorant of the procedures for even the most important of all the national festivals. Here, however, they need no instruction, but gather spontaneously—and yet quite correctly—for a day of mourning and confession.

The statement in v 2a has long puzzled those who hold to the unity of Neh 8 and 9. There is no adequate reason for the people now to separate themselves from all foreigners; it should either have come at the start of chap. 8 or not at all. Coming where it does, however, it strongly suggests that the gathering described was quite independent of any preceding celebration.

Finally, the confession in Neh 9 is expressed in very general terms. There is no allusion to any of the specific ills of which we read elsewhere in Ezra and Nehemiah. In this it contrasts sharply with the confession in Ezra 9. Any connection with the EM which it would have to have if it were a direct sequel to Neh 8 is thus rendered less probable.

Those who recognize the force of these arguments have made several suggestions as to the chapter's original setting. Welch (*ZAW* 47 [1929] 130–37), for instance, suggested that "The chapter has preserved a litany written for the worship of Northern Israel on the occasion of a day of fasting, confession and prayer," and so dated it to late pre-exilic times, whereas Rehm (*BZ* N.F. 1 [1957] 59–69) thought rather that it belonged with the Nehemiah material. The majority, however, again following Torrey, suggest that it fits best as a sequel to Ezra 10.

In seeking to evaluate such suggestions, we should, in my opinion, keep the following factors in mind: (i) The contrasts between chaps. 8–9 already outlined suggest that, although their juxtaposition was acceptable to the final editor in the interests of his wider purposes, there must be seen here too the constraints of antecedent sources. Entirely free composition would have surely led to a smoother narrative. (ii) The wording of 9:2 points to some connection with Ezra 9–10. The use of זֶרַע, literally, "seed," here and at Ezra 9:2 is especially striking (see *Comment* on the earlier passage) and comes nowhere else with this particular nuance. וַיִּבָּדְלוּ, "And (they) separated themselves," is a verb that also comes several times in connection with Ezra's treatment of mixed marriages. (iii) The absence of Ezra himself from our chapter makes it unlikely that we have here an extensive extract from the Ezra source, as Torrey supposed. (iv) Combined with this is the probability that the prayer is of independent origin. We have seen that it has uncharacteristically little to do with its immediate context, but it was of considerable importance for the final editor's purpose. It is therefore likely that he himself introduced it from his background knowledge of contemporary liturgy. (v) Only a fragment of vv 1–5 need therefore have come from some point in Ezra 9–10, and even then some editorial changes are not unlikely, as noted elsewhere already.

This is close to Rudolph's conclusion, though his summary of it rather overshadows this view by referring again to "Neh 9" as though the whole, rather than two or three verses, were involved. He places the fragment after Ezra 10. Clearly by this point, argument in detail becomes more than a little speculative. Precisely because of this, however, we may wonder whether Rudolph's solution is the best. Would the people have waited three weeks before coming together for confession after the separation of their foreign wives (compare the dates at Ezra 10:17 and Neh 9:1)? And what is meant now by v 2, since the foreign wives have already been divorced? There is much to be said for reviving a modified form of Ahlemann's theory, *ZAW* 59 (1942–43) 89, that the material originally stood between Ezra 10:15 and 16. There is no need to follow his emendation of v 15, but it is of interest that v 16 is certainly textually corrupt (see *Notes*), and that the opening of that verse lacks an effective antecedent.

On this suggestion, the dates fit admirably. On the twentieth day of the ninth month the men of Judah and Benjamin came to Jerusalem to initiate proceedings over the question of mixed marriages (Ezra 10:9). On the twenty-fourth, they gathered for confession (Neh 9:1) before leaving the commission to sit from the first day of the tenth month onwards (Ezra 10:16). This means that the entire recorded work of Ezra is fitted into exactly one year.

The verses extracted are to be seen in part as a heading to the rest of the narrative in Ezra 10. Understood thus, v 2a makes excellent sense: it is a general statement, the detail of which is supplied in Ezra 10:16–44. Exactly the same style of composition has been noted elsewhere, e.g., at Neh 8:3. Finally, if Pethahiah in v 5 is to be identified with his namesake at Ezra 10:23, a setting for our passage before the separation proceedings would clearly be more suitable.

Naturally, it is futile to attempt a precise reconstruction of the wording of the original passage, since in both cases there has been some editorial reworking. It is sufficient to establish in general terms the most likely original setting for this material. The reasons that the editor moved it to its new position will be both positive—to aid his general purpose in this new section (see the introduction to Neh 8–10)—and negative—to avoid any anticipation of the climax that he wished to reserve for this present section alone. He may also have been influenced by the coincidence of date already noted on p. 308 above.

The suggestion advanced here is admittedly hypothetical. Our general conclusions regarding the composition of Neh 9 are close to those of Rudolph and many others and they are not affected in any way by the more speculative issue of the original setting of the material drawn from the EM.

Comment

1 For the date, see *Form* above. נֶאֶסְפוּ "assembled": this may be the editor's vocabulary; cf. 8:1 and 13. Ezra 10 uses the synonymous root קבץ. The people came "fasting, wearing sackcloth, and with earth upon their heads." See in part on Ezra 8:26. We have noted before the connection in biblical thought between mourning and confession; the same association is attested here (and see v 3 below); for sackcloth as a sign of repentance, cf. Dan 9:3; Jonah 3:5, 8; 1 Chr 21:16, and for earth on the head in a context of mourning, cf. 1 Sam 4:12; 2 Sam 1:2 and Job 2:12.

2 As already noted in *Form,* the first half of the verse is to be explained historically in the context of Ezra 9–10. There, it was probably part of a summarizing introduction to the agreement to divorce foreign wives. In its new context, it reads curiously after chap. 8, but was no doubt retained to stress the purity of the community who entered into the covenant renewal. Its exclusively racial understanding of "Israel" is made clear by the use of זרע "seed" (see *Comment* on Ezra 9:2) and by the separation from "all foreigners" without distinction. This attitude is found elsewhere only in Ezra 9–10, and contrasts markedly with Ezra 6:21 etc.

The second half of the verse provides an apt introduction to the following confession with its reference both to "their sins" (vv 33–37) and those of "their ancestors" (vv 16–30).

3 This verse is often regarded as an editorial addition. The subject of the plural verbs should, strictly speaking, be the Israelites of the previous verse, whereas we expect the Levites to read. The purpose of the verse seems to be to "correct" v 2 in order to make the pattern of events conform more closely with chap. 8. In view of our analysis of this chapter, such a conclusion is not impossible: editorial activity is likely at almost any point, and we could understand the desire to impose a similar pattern on the events of chaps. 8 and 9. Nevertheless, the conclusion is not necessary once the original purpose of v 2 as a summary heading is appreciated. This verse would then reflect the start of the more detailed description of events. Jer 36 shows that reading was not out of place on such an occasion. The verbs may be understood as impersonal plurals, and we have no reason to dismiss the possibility of a reading before confession and worship. According to this approach, the opening words may refer to the Levites, though cf. 8:7. It is of interest to note the varying titles for the Book of the Law in these chapters; cf. 8:1, 2, 8, 14, 18; 9:3. The reference is clearly the same in each case, so that the changes must be ascribed to stylistic considerations alone. "A quarter of the day": approximately three hours.

4–5 מעלה הלוים "the stairs of the Levites" have not been identified. Harmonistic attempts to link the phrase with the platform of 8:4 are to be rejected, for that was a temporary structure whereas the wording here suggests "a well-known cult apparatus used by the Levites on such occasions" (Bowman; Kidner suggests that they may have been steps leading from one courtyard of the temple to another, with reference to *m. Mid.* 2:5). This gives us a hint that the gathering may have taken place in a different location from that in chap. 8.

On the two lists of Levites, see *Notes* above. The leading of public worship by Levites was usual; in this respect it is chap. 8 that stands out as exceptional. It is quite likely, therefore, that these verses owe more to the final editor than to the EM. His concern was that the confession leading to covenant renewal should be an affair of the whole community, not just of a prominent individual.

The distinction of function between vv 4 and 5 is explicit in the text, but not clear to us now in detail. זעק בקול גדול "to cry out loud" is generally used of a cry of distress in time of need (see v 28 below). It is most unlikely, therefore, that the Levites here "burst forth into some well-known psalm of adoration to the God of Israel" (Ryle). More likely, it refers to some public

display of grief before this was put into words with the prayer of confession
led by the second group.

5b–37 A full exegesis of this prayer, with word studies of its rich theological vocabulary and discussion of all the incidents to which allusion is made,
would far exceed the limits of the present commentary. Our purpose must
be restricted to the significance of the material for the confession itself. We
shall, however, cite the most important of the many biblical parallels, some
of which will have served as sources for the present text. (For a much fuller
list, cf. Myers. One clear conclusion to emerge in this respect will be the
fact that even on the standard critical analysis of the Pentateuch the author
must have known the books of Moses in substantially their present form. In
common with his contemporaries, as von Rad, *Geschichtsbild,* has shown, he
is particularly drawn to Deuteronomy, but he makes use too of the other
sources, as usually defined.) From these references, readers should have
little difficulty in tracing discussions of the matters which are here passed
over.

5b For the hymnic introduction to the prayer, see *Notes* (where some
biblical parallels are noted) and *Form.* Compare also Ps 72:19.

6 Like the Bible itself, the prayer starts with an uncompromising acknowl-
edgement of the uniqueness of God: "You alone are the Lord." This is explained by reference to creation—so that nothing in heaven or on earth can
challenge God's supremacy—and to the fact that "the host of heaven worships
you." Whether this refers to stars or to heavenly beings, both of which were
objects of reverence in some of the surrounding cultures, they are here clearly
subordinate to the one God. This throws into sharper relief the grace which
chose Abram (v 7), and Israel through him. In addition, Schneider suggests
that the context is already being set for the gift of the land to Israel, a theme
that dominates much of the rest of the prayer.

It is possible that the second line of the verse draws on Gen 2:1
(וכל־צבאם, "and all their host," comes in both passages). If so, it will be
of particular significance, in that this is probably one of the latest parts of
the Pentateuch. For the remainder of the verse, cf. Deut 10:14; 1 Kgs 8:27;
2 Kgs 19:15, 19; Isa 37:16; Ps 86:10.

7–8 The section on Abraham starts with the same words as v 6
(אתה הוא יהוה "You alone are the Lord"), thereby emphasizing the power
and greatness of the God who called Abraham. The main point of the section
comes at its close, however: כי צדיק אתה "because you are righteous." Not
only is God creator, but his character is such that he must fulfill what he
has promised; "righteous" conduct in relation to speech involves complete
faithfulness and truth; cf. Deut 32:4.

The brief survey of events from the Abraham narrative in Genesis builds
up steadily towards this climax. No event is self-contained or without purpose,
but each is preparatory to the next; this inspires a confidence that God will
not allow his promises to go by default: election, deliverance (the implication
of והוצאתו, "You brought him out"), change of name, covenant. This last
is elaborated in terms of the gift of the land, and so draws into prominence
the major focus of the remainder of the prayer; cf. Ackroyd, "God and People,"
Notion Biblique, 154–60, and Gilbert, "Néhémie 9," *Tôrah au Messie.* Despite

God's gift, the people constantly rebelled; and yet, because of God's "righteousness," they still dare to appeal to unfulfilled aspects of the original promise (cf. vv 32–37). "And you kept your promise" (lit., "you established your words"): as well as leading directly to the statement concerning the character of God, this clause points forward to the following paragraphs, thereby demonstrating a profound appreciation of the unity of God's purposes in the history of Israel. It would thus be quite mistaken to regard either the whole (Welch, *ZAW* 47 [1929] 130–37) or part (Bowman) of this section as a later addition. It establishes a momentum that continues right through to the final appeal.

The writer draws on the following passages in Genesis: 15:6, 7, 18–21; 17:5. Here again, 17:5 is of importance, because it is generally attributed to P; it is no response to speculate with Witton Davies that "J must also have had this." We must work from what evidence is available to us when it is adequate to account for the facts. The writer is not a slave to the letter of his sources, however, but draws out implications which he believed they justified. Thus only here is Abraham the object of בחר "to choose," though it is implied by Deut 4:37; 10:15. Also, the list of names of the inhabitants of Canaan differs from Gen 15:19–21 in line with post-exilic practice; cf. T. Ishida, "The Structure and Historical Implications of the Lists of the Pre-Israelite Nations," *Bib* 60 (1979) 461–90.

9–11 The mentions of the oppression in Egypt and the deliverance at the Red Sea mark the limits of this section. Verse 12 moves beyond this framework with its reference to the wilderness tradition.

Embedded in the heart of how God delivered his people is the expression ותעש לך שם כהיום הזה "you made a name for yourself, as it remains to this day." God's revealed character and abiding reputation ("name"), therefore, is not just that of mighty creator (v 6) or gracious promise-maker (vv 7–8) but of savior of his people, one who has acted in concrete terms to bring his word to realization. This is the third and last stanza of the poem to speak without qualification of God's achievements for his people; from now on they will be qualified by the accounts of rebellion. This high point in the account is therefore singled out by כהיום הזה "as it remains to this day," a confession which contrasts sharply with the evil plight of the people "today" (היום) in vv 32 and 36.

This particular paragraph is almost a pastiche of quotations from the Exodus account; cf. Exod 3:7 (4:31); 14:10; Deut 6:22 (7:19); Exod 9:16 (Isa 63:12); 14:21–22; 15:5, 9–10, 19.

12–21 Commentators have completely failed to observe the careful structure of this long but unified section. Though the whole relates to the wilderness period, the author abandons a strict biblical sequence in order to present the following scheme:

(a) God's gracious provision of
    (i) guidance on the journey (the pillar and cloud, v 12)
    (ii) good laws for guidance in all aspects of their lives (vv 13–14)
    (iii) material provision for life in the wilderness (v 15a)
    (iv) renewal of the promise of the land (v 15b).

(b) The people's ungrateful rebellion, rejecting both God's laws and his provision in their desire to return to Egypt (vv 16–18; note that this is introduced with הזידו "they acted arrogantly," a rare verb with this meaning, but used of the Egyptians in v 10).

(c) God's continuing mercy, so that he did not remove the provision made previously, namely,

    (i) the pillar and the cloud (v 19)
    (ii) his Spirit "to instruct them" (להשכילם, v 20a, used elsewhere to express the results of study and practice of God's law, e.g., Josh 1:7–8)
    (iii) material provision for life in the wilderness (vv 20b–21).

It will be noted that only (a) (iv) is not recapitulated; this is because it is made the subject of a complete section in the following verses (note the frequent repetition in vv 22–25 of the key words of v 15b: ירש "take possession," הארץ "the land," and נתן "to give"). By this device, the stress of the whole prayer is given renewed emphasis (see *Comment* on vv 7–8 above. We should note here that a similar effect is achieved in v 17a by singling out as a major example of faithlessness the story of the people's refusal to enter the land from Kadesh).

At the very center of this long stanza, sandwiched between descriptions of the people's rebellion, we find the words

ואתה אלוה סליחות חנון ורחום
ארך אפים ורב ( )חסד

"But you are a God more than willing to forgive, gracious and compassionate,
Long-suffering and unwavering in your faithful love."

This, then, is the key statement in this section, revealing a further aspect of the character of God over those already noted in the first three sections. It is followed immediately with the words "you did not abandon them," unexplained at first, but recapitulated in v 19a as an introduction to the description of God's continuing mercy.

Although, as noted above, the biblical order of events is subordinated to the overall structure, the Pentateuchal allusions continue to be manifest: for v 12, cf. Exod 13:21–22; Num 14:14; Deut 1:33; for vv 13–14, cf. Exod 19:18, 20; 20:22; the descriptions of the law are widespread and stereotypical, but the reference to "your holy Sabbath" (perhaps singled out because of its importance to the post-exilic community; cf. Neh 10:31; 13:15–22) is probably due to priestly influence. The only phraseological parallel is in Exod 16:23, generally thought to be very late; for v 15, cf. Exod 16:4; 17:6; Num 14:30; 20:8; vv 16–18 summarize much of the account of the wilderness rebellions (often with Deuteronomic phraseology), but with particular reference to Num 14:4 and Exod 32:1–6. The description of God's character echoes Exod 34:6–7; vv 19–20 recapitulate vv 12 and 15, but v 21 is clearly based on Deut 8:4.

22–31 The fifth and final stanza of the historical period deals with entry into, and life in, the land. In broad terms, its structure corresponds with that of the previous section, for it too starts with a passage that speaks entirely of God's goodness in providing for his people (vv 22–25), a central passage that includes much talk of rejection and rebellion, and a conclusion that ends on a renewed note of God's continuing mercy (v 31). Indeed, the final words of all, אתה ורחום חנון אל כי "because you are a gracious and compassionate God," provide the brief statement of that aspect of God's character which the whole section reveals, a feature we have observed in every preceding stanza. In this case, its similarity with vv 12–21 is further to be seen in the repetition of the words עזבתם לא "You did not abandon them," exactly as at the end of v 17, the verse which contained the comparable statement about God in the previous stanza.

Within this broad similarity, however, there is one point of crucial distinction. It demonstrates the author's complete mastery of his material and shows that he used literary structure to serve his theological purpose, never allowing it to take control and so determine arbitrarily his form of composition. This distinction concerns the shape of the passage dealing with the people's rebellion and God's response to it. Accepting the interpretation of his people's history expounded in the Deuteronomic writings, he did not feel able to speak of a single act of rebellion; he wished rather to expose the almost cyclical view seen so clearly in the Book of Judges, but carried forward in more muted terms right down until the Babylonian exile. In order to express this artistically, therefore, the writer appropriately presents us with three cycles on the pattern rebellion: handing over to foreign power, cry for help, and response by God in mercy and deliverance (vv 26–27, 28, 29–31; on the apparent lack of a cry for help and divine response in the final cycle, see *Comment* on vv 32–37 below).

Two points should be added by way of further clarification. First, the conscious aim to portray the description in cyclical terms is made clear by the use of comparable phraseology. For instance, the statement of God's handing over of his people to foreign powers is similar in each case: צריהם ביד ותתנם (v 27; "So you handed them over into the power of their adversaries"), איביהם ביד ותעזבם (v 28; "you abandoned them to the power of their enemies"), and הארצת עמי ביד ותתנם (v 30; "you handed them over into the power of the peoples of the lands"). Similarly, the first two cycles are linked by the repetition of תשמע משמים ואתה "You heard from heaven," in vv 27 and 28, the first and third by the repetition of the theme of prophets sent solemnly to warn the people in vv 26 and 30 and of God's desire to warn (העיד) the people so as to bring them back (להשיבם) in vv 26 and 29, and so on.

Second, however, I believe it possible that the author intends us to see an intensification, if not of the people's rebellion (though vv 29–30 certainly contain the strongest statement in this regard), yet at least of the severity of God's judgment. Verse 28b is markedly more forceful than v 27a, but what of v 30c? While at first glance it seems milder, it is in fact probably to be understood, in the light of the following verse, as a statement about the Babylonian conquest and exile; it is difficult to see otherwise the force of כלה עשיתם לא, "you did not eliminate them," and the fact that this stands at the very end of the historical retrospect adds some support to this conclusion. So too do the structural considerations advanced at vv 32–37 below. The contrast with Ezra 9:14b may also be instructive. If, then, it is correct that the author has presented these three cycles somewhat in the form of a downward spiral, then the effect will be to give added emphasis to the all-important statement of v 31b.

22–25 These verses are clearly a single unit, bound together by a common theme (the conquest as fulfillment of God's promise to give the land) and vocabulary: as already noted in connection with v 15 above, the roots ירשׁ "possess," נתן "give," and ארץ "land" are used with great frequency. In the interests of his rather simple line analysis of the prayer, Rudolph deletes v 22 as a later addition; he considers that it anticipates v 24. This is quite unjustified, however. Stylistically, there is nothing to distinguish v 22 from its context; all three key words appear in it. Nor is it out of place thematically: it speaks only of the conquest of the Trans-Jordanian territories, achieved, in the biblical perspective, under Moses. Then follows (v 23) a note about the increase in the Israelite population, with emphasis on the word בניהם/הבנים ("(their) descendants/children," vv 23 and 24). This is appropriate as an introduction to the entry into the land proper (v 24) because of the biblical emphasis that it was not the generation of Moses but that of their children who should take the land (cf. Num 14:29–31; Deut 1:35–39). The sequence of these verses is thus wholly satisfactory, and no reason whatever exists for the deletion of v 22.

The events to which these verses refer are described in Num 21:21–35 (Deut 2–3); Num 26; Josh 1–12; Deut 6:10–11; 8:7–10, though the phraseology finds many parallels elsewhere (cf. Myers).

26–31 Although the material in these verses, already analyzed above, reflects an outlook based on the Deuteronomic view of history, expressed clearly, for instance, in Judg 2:11–23, 2 Kgs 17, and some of the sermon material in Jer, and though many of the phrases used may be paralleled elsewhere, it cannot be said that the author is here following particular biblical passages in the way that was apparent earlier. It is more appropriate to handle this material in terms of traditio-historical (rather than literary-critical) methods; for one detailed example with reference to the treatment of the prophets in vv 26 and 30, cf. O. H. Steck, *Israel und das gewaltsame Geschick der Propheten* (WMANT 23; Neukirchen-Vluyn: Neukirchener, 1967). The other particularly noteworthy feature of the passage is the prominence given to the law (for which a variety of terms is used, perhaps in a way that points explicitly to the whole of the Mosaic law, not just the Decalogue; note the use of Torah in an absolute sense for the first time in v 26; cf. Gilbert "Néhémie 9," *Tôrah au Messie*). At times it can stand virtually alongside God himself: to reject the one is to reject the other (vv 26a, 29), while to return to the one is to return to the other (vv 26b with 29a). This strongly suggests that Welch was wrong to date the prayer to the pre-exilic period; rather, it belongs to the time when the Torah was approaching, at the very least, its canonical form; the influence of this prayer on synagogue liturgy, analyzed by Liebreich, *HUCA* 32 (1961) 227–37, is thus not surprising; see also Noth, *Laws*, 81–83.

32–37 In discussion above regarding the structure of the three cycles that conclude the long historical retrospect, it was observed that the elements of a cry to God for help and what follows it were lacking in the third cycle (vv 29–31). The reason for this now becomes apparent. It was suggested that v 30 brought us down to the period of the exile. Not considering that the restoration from that severe judgment was yet complete, our author could not record the historical fulfillment of the final cycle, but rather includes himself and his contemporaries within it as he here actualizes the cry for help in words of confession, petition, and lament which arise from his present situation (cf. Gilbert, "Néhémie 9," *Tôrah au Messie*, 313). In this way, the preceding stanza is joined to the present one by way of the development of an element lacking in the pattern, just as vv 12–21 were joined to vv 22–31.

The effect of this move is very powerful in terms of the prayer's intercessory aspect. The cyclical repetition with its grounding in the revealed character of God means that there is a strong confidence underlying the lament that God will not fail once again to "hear from heaven" and respond with deliverance. The commentators who have made much of the expression of frustration and despair in the final verses have generally overlooked completely this complementary aspect of hope with which the prayer looks towards an open future.

At the same time a further device is employed to reinforce this position. As will be noted below, many of the key words and themes of the historical survey are picked up again here. The gift of the land with the attendant enjoyment of all its produce, for instance, has been noted as the leading topic of the prayer so far. It formed the basis of the covenant with Abraham, the goal of the Exodus and the purpose of the conquest. The author has therefore only to hold up to God the present situation of life in the land under a foreign power which creams off its benefits (vv 36–37) for the irony of the contrast between divinely determined history and current short-fall to make its inherent request most pointedly apparent. The same holds true for the repetition of the description of God's character in vv 32–33. And so too, when the prayer concludes with the words וּבְצָרָה גְדוֹלָה אֲנַחְנוּ, "we are in great distress (affliction)," it is impossible to miss the echo of v 27, where there is considerable play on what the author in all probability took to be the same word group:

וַתִּתְּנֵם בְּיַד צָרֵיהֶם וַיָּצֵרוּ לָהֶם
וּבְעֵת צָרָתָם יִצְעֲקוּ אֵלֶיךָ וְאַתָּה מִשָּׁמַיִם תִּשְׁמַע
וּכְרַחֲמֶיךָ הָרַבִּים תִּתֵּן לָהֶם מוֹשִׁיעִים וְיוֹשִׁיעוּם מִיַּד צָרֵיהֶם

"So you handed them over into the power of their *adversaries*, who *oppressed* them,
But when in their *oppression* they cried out to you, you heard from heaven,
And in accordance with your great compassion you gave them saviors
    who rescued them from the power of their *adversaries*."

32 The transitional verse (וְעַתָּה, "And now") contains the only explicit request of the whole prayer; it appears to be slight, but in the context it says all that is required: "do not belittle all the hardship which has befallen us." The God to whom this prayer is directed is addressed first in words that would have been suitable (though they are not found) in the description of the creator (v 6), but this is immediately qualified by a reference to his covenant faithfulness (cf. v 8, where the covenant is expanded in terms of the promise of the land to Abraham and his descendants) and his "loving loyalty" (חסד), echoing v 17.

The days of "the kings of Assyria" are mentioned, not because they are still the oppressors (*contra* Welch), but because from the time when they overran the northern kingdom, God's people never again knew true freedom from subservience in greater or lesser degree to foreign powers. In this context, עד היום הזה "until today" makes its point by contrast with the similar כהיום הזה "as at this day" in v 10, where it refers to the reputation as savior which God gained at the Exodus.

33 ואתה צדיק "You have been in the right" is here pure confession; see section on *Form* above, and Ezra 9:15. It contrasts, however, with the use of the same words in v 8, where they were used in appreciation of God's faithfulness to his promise of the land.

34 The confession continues in words that echo several of the historically descriptive passages earlier (e.g., vv 26 and 29–30).

35–37 For purposes already noted, the gift both of the land and of its good produce is recalled; cf. vv 8, 15 and 22–25. Two further ironies are introduced, however: first, because the fathers "did not serve you" (v 35), "now we today are slaves" (v 36, twice). Second, whereas God "gave" the land to the ancestors, now he has "given" (="set up") foreign kings to be over the people "because of our sins" (v 37). In both contrasts, the author shows his appreciation that the service of God is in reality true freedom.

Ending quotation marks should not close this prayer because, in the present text, the direct speech continues immediately into the next chapter.

Explanation

We have seen that Neh 8–10 was put together from a variety of sources. It is nevertheless entirely appropriate that as events move toward the people's reaffirmation of the covenant in the next chapter, the author should have resisted the temptation to have either Ezra or Nehemiah predominate in the great confession to which the present chapter is devoted. By concentrating instead upon collective leadership by the Levites, he drew attention as far as was possible to the people's solidarity in acknowledging their responsibility before God, just as the prayer in turn makes clear that they identified themselves with both the blessings and the failures of previous generations. While these books have many important lessons to teach about the value of strong and effective leadership for God's people, this must never become an excuse for individuals to abdicate their own personal responsibility or involvement, lest by doing so they also forgo the very security that membership of the community is intended to ensure.

It is to be hoped that the major theological emphases of the prayer itself have already become clear from the exegesis offered above. It offers no excuses for the past conduct of the nation, but rather combines many elements of form, all quite familiar to the people from their Scriptures and liturgy, with direct expressions of confession to acknowledge that Israel had sinned both against the known character and the revealed will of God. At the same time, however, it aligns the present generation with those who in the past had thrown themselves similarly onto the mercy of their God—a God who, powerful as creator, had bound himself to them in a covenant promise that he had moved in deliverance to uphold and realize. He had thereby gained for himself a name, a reputation (v 10), in which the people gloried until this present day. While they therefore offered no excuse on their own behalf, they appealed to the contradiction between their present circumstances and what they perceived as God's immutable purposes toward them. The future might still be open, but in its own way the conclusion of the prayer breathes an atmosphere of strong faith and hope in spite of all the present, contradictory circumstances.

To us, the concentration on the gift of the land and its bounty may seem crudely materialistic. If that is so, it is only because the Christian Church has learned to add a fourth stanza to the first three of this prayer, a stanza in which God moved once more, and this time with finality, in an act of unmerited and unmotivated grace towards his people. We are surely not mistaken, therefore, in adding to the characteristics of God that this prayer summarizes the crowning glory of God revealed as unutterable love in the cross of Christ (Rom 5:8). With that perception, however, there is linked the realization that the ultimate bondage is not to the rule of worldly potentates, but to the rule of that other "law in my members . . . , bringing me into captivity under the law of sin" (Rom 7:23). So too, for those who, with Paul, find themselves crying out of their distress "O wretched man that I am! who shall deliver me from the body of this death?" there is vouchsafed a passage into his responsive cry of triumph, "I thank God through Jesus Christ our Lord" (vv 24–25, KJV).

A Pledge to Keep the Law
(Neh 10:1–40 [Evv 9:38–10:39])

Bibliography

Brin, G. "The Firstling of Unclean Animals." *JQR* 68 (1978) 1–15. **Clines, D. J. A.** "Nehemiah 10 as an Example of Early Jewish Biblical Exegesis." *JSOT* 21 (1981) 111–17. **Eissfeldt, O.** *Erstlinge und Zehnten im Alten Testament. Ein Beitrag zur Geschichte des Israelitisch–Jüdischen Kultus.* BWANT 22. Leipzig: J. C. Hinrich, 1917. **Ibáñez Arana, A.** "Sobre la colocación original de Neh. 10." *EstBib* 10 (1951) 379–402. **Jepsen, A.** "Nehemia 10." *ZAW* 66 (1954) 87–106. **Kaufmann, Y.** *History*, 382–89. **Kellermann, U.** *Nehemia*, 37–41, 100–103. **Kippenberg, H. G.** *Religion und Klassenbildung im antiken Judäa. Ein religionssoziologische Studie zum Verhältnis von Tradition und gesellschaftlicher Entwicklung.* SUNT 14. Göttingen: Vandenhoeck & Ruprecht, 1978, 69–77. **Liver, J.** "The Half-Shekel Offering in Biblical and Post-Biblical Literature." *HTR* 56 (1963) 173–98. **Moscati, S.** "I sigilli nell'Antico Testamento." *Bib* 30 (1949) 314–38. **Mowinckel, S.** *Studien I*, 135–45; *Studien III*, 142–55. **Welch, A. C.** "The Share of N. Israel in the Restoration of the Temple Worship." *ZAW* 48 (1930) 175–87. ———. *Post-Exilic Judaism*, 69–86.

Translation

10:1(9:38) *"In spite of all this, we are making a firm agreement in writing;* [a] *on the sealed document* [b] *(are the names of) our leaders,* [c] *our Levites (and) our priests.*
2(1) *On the seals* [a] *(are the names of) Nehemiah, son of Hecaliah, the governor,* [b] *and*

> Zedekiah.
3(2) *Seraiah*
> *Azariah*
> *Jeremiah*
4(3) *Pashhur*
> *Amariah*
> *Malchiah*
5(4) *Hattush*
> *Shebaniah*
> *Malluch*
6(5) *Harim*
> *Meremoth*
> *Obadiah*
7(6) *Daniel*
> *Ginnethon*
> *Baruch*
8(7) *Meshullam*
> *Abijah*
> *Mijamin*

$^{9(8)}$ *Maaziah*
Bilgai
Shemaiah. These are the priests.
$^{10(9)}$ *The Levites: Jeshua,* [a] *son of Azaniah,*
Binnui of the sons of Henadad
Kadmiel
$^{11(10)}$*And their fellow-Levites:* [a] *Shebaniah* [b]
Hodiah [c]
Kelita
Pelaiah
Hanan
$^{12(11)}$ *Mica*
Rehob
Hashabiah
$^{13(12)}$ *Zaccur*
Sherebiah
[a] *Shebaniah*
$^{14(13)}$ *Hodiah* [a]
Bani
Beninu. [b]
$^{15(14)}$ *The chiefs of the people: Parosh*
Pahath-Moab
Elam
Zattu
Bani
$^{16(15)}$ *Bunni*
Azgad
Bebai
$^{17(16)}$ *Adonijah*
Bigvai
Adin
$^{18(17)}$ *Ater*
Hezekiah
Azzur
$^{19(18)}$ *Hodiah*
Hashum
Bezai
$^{20(19)}$ *Hariph*
Anathoth
Nebai [a]
$^{21(20)}$ *Magpiash*
Meshullam
Hezir
$^{22(21)}$ *Meshezabel*

Zadok

Jaddua

23(22) Pelatiah

Hanan

Anaiah

24(23) Hoshea

Hananiah

Hasshub

25(24) Hallohesh

Pilha

Shobek

26(25) Rehum

Hashabnah

Maaseiah

27(26) Ahiah a

Hanan b

Anan

28(27) Malluch

Harim a

Baanah.

29(28) *The rest of the people—the priests, the Levites, the gatekeepers, the singers, the temple servants, and anyone who has separated himself from the peoples of the lands for the sake of the Law of God, together with their wives, their sons and their daughters, all who are capable of understanding* a— 30(29) *now associate themselves* a *with their noble brothers* b *and enter into a curse and an oath* c *to live by God's Law which was given through Moses, the servant of God, and carefully to obey all the commandments, judgments, and statutes of the Lord our Lord,* 31(30) *and in particular that:* a

We will not give our daughters (in marriage) to the peoples of the land, nor will we take their daughters for our sons.

32(31) *If* a *the peoples of the land bring merchandise or any corn* b *to sell on the Sabbath day, we will not buy from them on the Sabbath or any other holy day.*

c *We will forgo (the produce of) the seventh year and every loan made on pledge.* cd

33(32) *We hereby pledge ourselves to keep the commandments to give* a *a third of a shekel each year for the service of the house of our God,* 34(33) *for the showbread and the regular grain offering and for the regular burnt offering, the Sabbaths, the New Moons, and for the appointed festivals, and for the holy offerings and for the sin-offerings to make atonement for Israel, and (for) all the work of the house of our God.*

35(34) a *And we—the priests, the Levites and the laity* a—*have cast lots in the matter of the wood offering, (to arrange) to bring it to the house of our God by families at the appointed times each year, to burn upon the altar of the Lord our God, as it is written in the Law.*

36(35) *(We pledge ourselves) to bring to the house of the Lord the first-fruits of our land and the first-fruits of every kind of fruit tree each year,* 37(36) *and the first-*

born of our sons and of our cattle, as it is written in the Law, and to bring the first-born of our herds and flocks to the house of our God, to the priests who serve in the house of our God. 38(37) *We will bring to the priests at the storerooms of the house of our God the best of our dough, of our sacred contributions, of the fruit of every kind of tree, of new wine and of oil; and (we will bring) a tithe of (the produce of) our land to the Levites. It is the Levites who collect the tithes in all the towns where we work.* a 39(38) *An Aaronite priest* a *shall be with the Levites when the Levites collect the tithes,* b *and the Levites shall bring up a tenth of the tithes to the house of our God, to the storerooms of the treasury.* 40(39) *For the Israelites and the Levites are to bring the contribution of corn, new wine, and oil to the storerooms where the sanctuary vessels are kept, and where the ministering priests, the gatekeepers, and the singers are.*

We will not neglect the house of our God."

Notes

1.a. Lit., "and writing." This unattached ptcp is clearly to be taken as parallel with כרתים "making a firm agreement," and so understood to have the same subj and obj.

1.b. "Something sealed," used of a sealed document in Jer 32:11 and 14. NEB, however, understands the force of the preposition על "upon" rather differently so as to yield ". . . witness the sealing."

1.c. Or "our princes," but without royal overtones. The title in v 15 suggests the present translation.

2.a. MT, ועל החתומים "and on the sealed documents." It is sometimes suggested that more than one copy of the agreement would have been made, or that more than one document would have been required for all the names. This does not, however, explain why the pl is used here when the sg apparently sufficed in the previous verse. Emendation to the sg is poorly attested (1 MS only); the Vrs clearly read a consonantal text close to MT, and certainly with a pl ending on this word. In addition, LXX attests the presence of the prep על, whereas the absence of its equivalent in Vg may mean no more than that the translator was unsure what to make of it. The proposal to emend it to ואלה on the basis of Syr. and the Arab. version (cf. Rudolph) is thus poorly supported. LXX and Vg suggest a consonantal text ועל החותמים, and they took the second word to be a pl ptcp, "those who signed." Perhaps, however, we should vocalize rather הַחוֹתָמִים "on the seals" (cf. Schneider; Galling?). It is not difficult to see how the present vocalization could have arisen under the influence of the previous verse, while this approach has the advantage of retaining על. The reference, then, is to the names stamped on (or conceivably written "beside") the seals of the individuals named. Many examples of seals with personal names are known; see, e.g., N. Avigad, *Bullae and Seals from a Post-Exilic Judean Archive* (Qedem 4; Jerusalem: The Institute of Archaeology, The Hebrew University, 1976), and cf. Exod 28:21.

2.b. For "the Tirshatha," cf. *Notes* on Ezra 2:63.a. The position of this title between personal name and patronymic has led many to delete it as a later gl; this is unnecessary, however, because the word order is attested in several primary sources; cf. A. T. Clay, *Business Documents of Murashû Sons of Nippur Dated in the Reign of Darius II (424–404 B.C.)* (The Babylonian Expedition of the University of Pennsylvania, Series A, Vol. x; Philadelphia: Department of Archaeology and Palaeontology, 1904), nos. 5 and 8; C. C. Torrey, "A Few Ancient Seals," *AASOR* 2–3 (1921–22) 107–8; see also Schneider and Myers.

10.a. The conj ו makes no sense before Jeshua; it should be deleted with the Vrs and a number of MSS.

11.a. Lit. "And their brethren."

11.b. The same name occurs later in this list (v 13). Were there two Levites with the same name, we should expect them to be distinguished by the use of a patronymic. Normally, we should emend one or other occurrence to the orthographically very similar שכניה "Shecaniah." Some MSS and Vrs do so either here or at v 13 (as for the priest of the same name in v 5, and the Levites in 9:4 and 5). In this case, however, it should be observed that on each occasion the name is followed by Hodiah. This raises the suspicion that both owe their presence in one verse or the other to accidental repetition.

11.c. See the previous note. Some, however, prefer to read הוֹדַוְיָה (cf. Ezra 2:40 and LXX) "Hodaviah," or הוֹדִוְיָה "Hodujah," either here or at v 14.

13.a.-14.a. Cf. nn. 11.b. and 11.c. above.

14.b. Not otherwise attested as a personal name. That does not of itself rule it out, however. Many prefer to make the slight emendation to כנני "Chenani," on the basis of 9:4, though this is entirely conjectural. The other similar-looking Levitical names—בני "Bani" and בנוי "Binnui"—have already appeared earlier in the list, and so should not be considered here.

20.a. So Q; K: נוֹבַי "Nobai." Versional evidence is divided. Brockington wonders whether it is an error for נבו "Nebo," a place name mistakenly regarded here as a personal name from Ezra 2:29, exactly like Anathoth before it, in his view, from Ezra 2:23. A more plausible alternative is the suggestion that some families adopted the name of the town in which they settled (cf. Meyer, Entstehung, 156).

27.a. This is the only name in the list to be preceded by the conj "and." Most Vrs (and hence modern commentators) omit it, understandably enough.

27.b. This name has occurred already in v 23. One of the two might be read חנני "Hanani." However, on both occasions the name is followed by another that is quite similar (ענַיָה "Anaiah" in v 23 and ענן "Anan" here). Perhaps there has consequently been some further accidental repetition; cf. n. 11.b. above.

28.a. Exactly these two rare names occur next to each other in the list of priests in vv 5–6 above. There must certainly be a suspicion of a further copyist's error.

29.a. For the complementary verbal idea expressed by a ptcp, cf. GKC § 120a-b.

30.a. The hiph of חזק + על usually means "to prevail over," but this would clearly be unsuitable here. The verb has an underlying idea of strength or firmness, hence, "hold fast to, cleave to." The syntax of these verses has been confused by the insertion of the long list of names. The translation above represents the probable intention of the MT. However, for the passage's original syntax, see Form below.

30.b. Lit., "their brothers, their nobles," an apposition expressing "nearer definition."

30.c. These two terms are construed as a hendiadys ("a penalty-fraught oath") by H. C. Brichto, The Problem of "Curse" in the Hebrew Bible (JBLMS 13; Philadelphia: SBL, 1963/1968), 33–34.

31.a. ואשר. It is clear that the general statement of v 30 is now to be amplified with regard to certain particulars in the following clauses. For ו used to express emphasis (= "and especially") cf. GKC § 154a fn. 1(b), and on אשר to introduce such object clauses (in this case, therefore, carrying forward the force of the infs const in v 30), cf. GKC § 157.

32.a. In Heb., the sentence is not strictly conditional but a statement introduced by a long casus pendens which is then resumed by מהם "from them." However, a literal rendering of this construction would be extremely awkward in Eng.

32.b. The conj is sometimes understood to mean "especially," as at 31.a. above. However, there seems to be no particular reason why it should have been more serious to buy corn than any other goods on the Sabbath. The conj could conceivably be epexegetic ("even"), but then מקחות "merchandise" would be completely redundant. Part of the problem is that מקחות is a h.l., so that we cannot be sure of its exact meaning. The rendering above seeks to keep an intelligible distinction between it and שבר "corn."

32.c.-c. This clause is tersely expressed, so that some commentators wish to add תבואת "produce of" after את (parablepsis), ונשא before משא and בה at the end of the verse, to give "and in it we shall remit every debt." It is doubtful, however, whether the text needs such emendation: נטש "forgo," may be used eliptically, and the meaning of the final clause is clear in the context.

32.d. See Notes and Comment on 5:7 and 10. The addition here of יד "hand" is because of the legal phrase found in Deut 15:2, but makes no difference to the sense. It refers to "that hand which holds a document proving debt" (Bowman).

33.a. Omit עלינו with some MSS and Vrs. It is an accidental repetition of the same word earlier in the verse. MT means "to lay upon ourselves the third of a shekel"; sense can be made of this, but it is unnecessarily repetitious of the first clause.

35.a-a. These words are awkwardly placed in the MT, and may be a later addition. The context of the chapter as a whole in fact makes clear that these three groups are involved throughout.

Perhaps they were added to spell this out because some had questioned whether this particular pledge related to lower-ranking temple staff (and laity?) alone.

38.a. Rudolph objects to this translation that the tithe law applied to all towns—even Jerusalem—without distinction. He therefore proposes "our cult cities" (cf. Myers). It stands to reason, however, that tithes would not be collected from areas that did not observe the Jewish law. The phrase seems rather to refer to the main agricultural areas of the province where such centers of collection were needed; those who lived near Jerusalem could, of course, bring their tithes directly to the temple.

39.a. The generic art (cf. GKC § 126l-t); there were many more than one Aaronic priest.

39.b. בעשׂר is generally thought to be a hiph inf with elision of the ה (בְּהַעֲשֵׂר); cf. GKC § 53k. Such an elision is common in post-biblical Heb., and may also be found at Deut 26:12. Alternatively, we may repoint as a qal inf (בַּעְשֹׂר, "when (they) receive the tithes") or as a piel inf (בְּעַשֵּׂר, "when they collect the tithes"). The latter is to be slightly preferred on the basis of the previous verse.

Form/Structure/Setting

This chapter is a first-person account of a one-sided agreement into which the community entered to observe the Law of God. After the introduction (1) comes a list of those who signed the document (2–28). The rest of the community (29) joins with them in agreeing to observe the law (30). Of this, several particular requirements are singled out for special mention (31–40).

At first sight, there appears to be a smooth connection with the previous chapter, as the alternative chapter division in the Evv already shows. The opening words, ובכל־זאת "In spite of all this" require some kind of antecedent; the first-person narrative may be held to continue that of the prayer in chap. 9; and, contrary to the opinion of earlier commentators such as Bertholet, it is theologically appropriate for such an affirmation to follow confession. Within the present complex of Neh 8–10 and their purpose in the books as they now stand, chap. 10 thus takes its place quite naturally.

Recognition of this fact does not by any means involve us in holding that the chapter's present setting is therefore original either from the literary or the historical point of view. As regards the former, we have already seen that most of Neh 9 is of independent origin. Since the narrative setting of the prayer is thereby recognized as a secondary development, it follows automatically that the join with Neh 10 must also fall into the same category. As regards historical considerations, the present sequence fails to explain why the particular laws mentioned in vv 31–40 were singled out at this time; if this were a sequel to the events in chaps. 8 and 9, we should have expected a greater concentration on the lapses which there receive attention. Similarly, the lack of reference to Ezra would also be surprising in this case. These points also tell against those such as Kellermann, *Nehemia,* 37–41, who think that this chapter was composed *de novo,* and without any historical basis, explicitly for its present setting.

Analysis of the chapter must begin, therefore, with the hypothesis that its literary and historical origins are to be sought in some setting other than that which it has now been given. This hypothesis will find support in some of the further matters discussed below.

We must turn next to the list of names in vv 2–28, because nearly all scholars now recognize that it has been inserted secondarily into its present position. (The question whether it nevertheless is the list of those who signed the agreement is separate, and will be dealt with below.) Suspicion is roused by the unusual feature of having a list of signatories at the head of a document, by the fact that the order of the list differs from that of the heading in v 1b, and by the roughness of the join between vv 1 and 2, accentuated by the partial repetition. Conclusive evidence, however, comes from the fact that the list interrupts the single syntactical construction of vv 1 and 29–30 (Rudolph). The infinitives in v 30 (ללכת "to walk = to live"; לשמור ולעשות "carefully to obey") depend not only on the subject and participles of vv 29–30a but also, according to plain sense, on the subject and verbs in v 1; it was not only the rest of the people but also the leaders who agreed to obey the law. Verses 29–30a were therefore originally a circumstantial clause (lit., "while the rest of the people . . . associate themselves . . .") embedded in the continuous narrative of vv 1 and 30b.

In view of this conclusion, it will be simplest to complete a study of this list before returning to consider the remainder of the chapter. Questions of structure, authenticity, and setting are closely intertwined. We shall therefore proceed, against our usual practice, by summarizing and evaluating three representative and detailed studies.

1. Jepsen, ZAW 66 (1954) 87–106, begins with the observation that the list of priests (vv 3–9) is closely parallel with 12:1–7 and 12–22. He regards the latter as earlier because it includes the names of individuals and families, whereas the former treats the family names as though they were names of individuals. Indeed, he thinks that 12:12–22 is closer to the original form of the list of signatories, because this would account for its preservation and because we expect individual as well as family names in such a list. He therefore postulates that the list was written in parallel columns of individual and family names according to the pattern לשריה מריה ("of Seraiah, Meraiah") and that in the form of text which lies behind Neh 10 the whole of the lefthand column was lost. The ל then had necessarily to be omitted from before each of the remaining (family) names in the right hand column, so giving rise to the present list.

Jepsen next applies his conclusions to the other two parts of the list. As regards the laity (vv 15–28), he observes that the first half parallels part of the list of family names in Ezra 2, whereas the second half is made up of individual names. He therefore thinks that originally parallel columns (after the pattern of the priests) have been read successively rather than together.

This pattern is found also for the list of Levites. It is unnecessary to describe here the more complicated process of reconstruction, but we should note that the first two names in the list follow a slightly different pattern ("a son of b," "c of the sons of d," against the usual "of x, y") and that three names of individuals are appended to the list without a family connection.

Finally, as far as our present interest is concerned, Jepsen moves on to compare his reconstructed list with that of Neh 3. He finds several names in common, but observes that in each case those listed in Neh 10 are fathers (or, in one case, a grandfather) of those engaged in the wall-building of Neh 3. He therefore concludes that Neh 10 is earlier than Neh 3 by a generation (cf. "in the days of Joiakim" at 12:12). He devotes the remainder of his article to showing that Neh 10 would not be out of place in connection with Ezra's work, and that this could have preceded the time of Nehemiah.

Jepsen's study is one of the most detailed ever devoted to this chapter, and so far as I am aware it has never received a full critical evaluation either positively or negatively, though cf. Schneider, 40–41, and Kellermann, *Nehemia*, 102. Its great strength is that it proposes a coherent solution to the problem raised by the juxtaposition of family and individual names. However, because it depends on conjecture at so many points, one is entitled to ask whether it presents the most plausible explanation of the facts. For instance (i) is it not strange that exactly one column relating to the priests should have been lost? Damage is seldom so respectful. (ii) If the columns originally followed the pattern Jepsen suggests, the ל before each name on the righthand side would have at once made clear that it should be followed by the name on the left. It was a curious scribe indeed who, when copying the list of laity, was obtuse enough not to understand this but careful enough to remove every ל before each of the twenty-two names in the righthand column. (iii) No explanation is offered for the fact that the first two names in the list of Levites follow a pattern different from that in the rest of the lists. Again, would not these names—which the scribe evidently understood aright!—have given the clue for the correct interpretation of the remainder? (iv) The three "unattached" Levites in Jepsen's reconstruction are an obvious embarrassment to his position. (v) Jepsen seeks to eliminate Nehemiah and Zedekiah from the head of the list by a radical emendation in partial and slight dependence on Syr. This is a mark of desperation and completely unconvincing. Syr is itself most probably secondary. (vi) The conclusion drawn from the comparisons with Neh 3, on which Jepsen's dating of the list is based, is not convincing. If, for the sake of the argument, Neh 10 were a little later than Neh 13, it would be no more than fifteen years after the wall-building. It is not difficult to suppose that those three or four mentioned as fathers of active builders should still have been alive and so able to sign the list as senior, indeed leading, members of their families. A further possibility, which Jepsen does not consider, is that papponymy has confused the picture, while finally the evidence from single names alone is precarious because of the possibility that different individuals are involved. Only one individual can be certainly identified in each list, the Levite Binnui of the sons of Henadad (3:18 and 24; 10:10). In this case, however, the builder and signatory are the same, not father and son.

We must, therefore, reject both Jepsen's reconstruction of the structure of this list and his historical setting for it.

2. In his commentary, Rudolph adopts a more conservative position with regard to the list. He believes that it was the original list of those who signed the agreement, and that the compiler added it in its present new setting. In favor of this conclusion, he argues (i) that Nehemiah is mentioned at the head of the list. For reasons to be noted below, Rudolph regards this as historically correct. Were the list fabricated, however, Ezra would have been mentioned; (ii) Zedekiah, who follows Nehemiah, is otherwise unknown. If the list were invented, we would expect someone whose name we know; (iii) as is to be expected in a document from the temple archive, a high

priest heads the list—albeit as a family name, Seraiah (cf. Ezra 7:1, etc.); (iv) this list was already known to the "Chronicler," who borrowed names from it at 9:4–5. Against alternative positions, Rudolph argues that we can make nothing of the numbers of those listed (multiples of seven, in Torrey's view) because of the probability of textual loss. He also follows the majority view with regard to the mixture of family and personal names (cf. Smend, *Listen*, 13; Meyer, *Entstehung*; Myers, etc.): observing the same parallels with other lists as Jepsen (and these are closer than appears at first sight owing to alternative forms of names and occasional slight corruption), these scholars maintain that many of those who signed did so, not in their own names, but in those of the families whom they represented. In the list of laity, this is clear for vv 15–21a by comparison with Ezra 2. The remainder are new families that had either returned later, developed in the meantime, or had never been in exile. A similar conclusion emerges for the priesthood, though we have not yet quite reached the developed stage of the twenty-four courses listed in 1 Chr 24, while the Levitical list is mixed, reflecting their smaller numbers.

Though Rudolph has advanced arguments in support of the genuineness of this list, his arguments are not, in reality, particularly strong: since the final editor of this material clearly wished to show how the work of Ezra and Nehemiah led up to a unified climax, the presence of Nehemiah's name in the list is to be expected, whereas, within the context of chaps. 8–10 as a whole, Ezra will have been omitted as the instigator of the proceedings. The name of Zedekiah could be derived from the "Zadok the scribe" of 13:13, and so on. We must, therefore, move on to examine a third and more radical view.

3. Mowinckel discussed Neh 10 in several parts of his monographs on Ezra-Nehemiah, most notably in *Studien I*, 135–45, and *Studien III*, 142–55. In this latter passage, he accepts the premise that an originally independent official document underlies the chapter. In the earlier study, however, he argues strongly that the list itself is pure fabrication by the editor. His first point is the weakest; he suggests that the list was originally signed by the שׂרים "leaders" alone, and that the Levites and most of the priests would have been included among "the rest of the people" of v 29. This is far from certain, however, and depends largely on the elimination of the words "our Levites and our priests" from v 1, but for this no substantial reasons are offered.

More weight, however, attaches to Mowinckel's discussion of the names in the list themselves. First, he observes (as is universally agreed) that many of the names are family rather than personal names. However, they are presented in the list as though they were individuals; cf. "the chiefs of the people," v 15, the first two names in v 10 (and we could add Nehemiah himself), some of the names of the Levites, which it is agreed are personal, and Daniel (v 7), who nowhere appears as the name of one of the priestly courses or as a family name in other lists of priests. This demonstrates the artificial nature of the list. Mowinckel questions besides whether extended families had their own seals (seals usually carry personal names) and whether they were such readily identifiable social units as the usual theory presupposes.

Next, Mowinckel moves on to observe that the list is no more than a compilation from other lists in Ezra-Nehemiah. (It should be noted here that even scholars who do not accept Mowinckel's conclusions agree that these correspondences are closer than appears at first because of subsequent corruption. Thus, for instance, Adonijah in v 17 is almost certainly the same as Adonikam in 7:18; Ezra 2:13.) For the list of priests, see Neh 12, with some additions from elsewhere. (There are, of course, some variations in spelling.) This is not too surprising, however, since we know from later times that the priestly families were generally presented in a fixed order; cf. my "The Origins of the Twenty-Four Priestly Courses," VTSup 30 (1979) 251–68. A similar case obtains for the Levites; cf. 12:8; 8:7; 9:4–5. In fact, the list collects almost all the names of Levites from elsewhere in Ezra and Nehemiah. With the lay leaders, however, a similar explanation is hardly feasible. For the first half of the list, which effectively follows the list of family names in Ezra 2 together with four of the geographical names from Ezra 2:20–35 in vv 20–21a, such an explanation might still be possible. Then, however, from Meshullam on comes a separate group of twenty-three names. Of these, no less than thirteen are found in Neh 3 in the same order (though in neither case are they a continuous group). To Mowinckel's synopsis, I add the relevant verse numbers in parentheses:

Neh 3		Neh 10	
Meshullam	(4)	Meshullam	(21 [20])
Meshezabel	(4)	Meshezabel	(22 [21])
Zadok	(4)	Zadok	(22 [21])
Joiada	(6)	Jaddua	(22 [21])
Melatiah	(7)	Pelatiah	(23 [22])
Hananiah	(8)	Hananiah	(24 (23))
Hasshub	(11)	Hasshuh	(24 [23])
Hallohesh	(12)	Hallohesh	(25 [24])
Rehum	(17)	Rehum	(26 [25])
Hashabiah	(17)	Hashabnah	(26 [25])
Ananiah	(23)	Hanan	(27 [26])
Hanun	(30)	Anan	(27 [26])
Malchiah	(31)	Malluch	(28 [27])

There are some points Mowinckel does not take into account; for instance, in Neh 3:17, Rehum is clearly a Levite, while Baanah (10:28) also occurs in Neh 3:4 and so does not conform to his order. Nevertheless, even allowing for the apparently random selection of names from the long list in Neh 3, it is doubtful if the evidence he has produced can all be explained away as coincidence. The significance of this should not be overlooked: unlike the other lists, this cannot be explained as a traditional order by which families were arranged, for quite obviously other principles determined the order in Neh 3. When this point is linked with his argument about family names being presented as personal names, and when none of the arguments in favor of the list's authenticity stands up to scrutiny (see above), the conclusion must be drawn that the list is an artificial literary compilation, based on other material in Ezra and Neh. (Note that this need not argue for its composition

later than Ezra 1–6, since the list in Ezra 2 will already have been known to
the editor from Neh 7.)

Mowinckel argues only for this negative conclusion. While in the present
state of knowledge it appears to me to do most justice to the evidence, we
must also ask why the editor compiled and included this list. Elsewhere, we
have argued for the genuineness of the lists included in these books, and
there must have been a good reason to make up this further one in view of
the fact that the work already includes so many.

It may be suggested that, in accordance with our understanding of Neh
8–10, this agreement was regarded as the climax of the work of Ezra and
Nehemiah. Consequently, the author was concerned to demonstrate the united
and wholehearted support of all the people for what was proposed. He therefore compiled a comprehensive list of nearly all the families and individuals
whom he regarded as being of good standing within the community and
set it first, before the terms of the agreement, in order to emphasize that
all the people were in accord with the stipulations that follow. For similar
reasons, he probably also expanded the summarizing v 29 (see *Comment* below).

We must now turn to deal with the rest of the chapter (vv 1, 29–40; the
possibility that some later glosses have been included in these verses is considered in *Comment* below). We have already taken note of its form and outline
structure, its original independence from chap. 9, and the consequent unlikelihood of its being a special composition for its present setting. In favor of
the last conclusion, we may now add the evidence from the addition of the
list in vv 2–28. If, as I have argued, this was added by the editor of Neh 8–
10, then the material into which he inserted it must have had an independent
prior existence.

With regard to the passage's literary setting before it was inserted into
its present context, I must concur with those who find no place for it within
either the Ezra or the Nehemiah material. The style of presentation is quite
conclusively against such a direct borrowing (cf. Mowinckel, *Studien III*, 142–
55), while there is no evidence to suggest that such material has here been
editorially adapted. Equally, there is no break in the other material from
which this passage could have been extracted. We are therefore left with
the conclusion that this was (part of?) an originally independent document.
Its affinities with the temple archives are suggested by (i) the use of אדיריהם,
"their nobles" (v 30), which is to be compared with 3:5 and our remarks
about the likely origin of that chapter (cf. *Form* on Neh 3); (ii) the conclusion
of the chapter with a note of strong support for the temple; and (iii) the
temple as the most likely place in which the secondary material in v 40(39)a
would have been added.

Finally, we must consider the chapter's historical setting. We can immediately discount Welch's proposal, *ZAW* 48 (1930) 175–87 (and cf. *Post-exilic
Judaism*, 69–86), that it comes from the exilic period because, among other
considerations, it definitely presupposes the existence of the temple (so Rudolph). Since Bertholet's time, scholars have generally been impressed by
the similarity of subject matter between this chapter and Neh 13 (though

cf. Jepsen [*ZAW* 66 (1954) 87–106], whose views were examined above, and Ibáñez Arana, *EstBib* 10 [1951] 379–402). These include principally:

mixed marriages	(10:31 [30]; 13:23–30)
Sabbath observance	(10:32 [31]; 13:15–22)
the wood offering	(10:35 [34]; 13:31)
first-fruits	(10:36–37 [35–36]; 13:31)
Levitical tithes	(10:38–39 [37–38]; 13:10–14)
neglect of the temple	(10:40 [39]; 13:11).

We are therefore left with a choice between the views that (i) after these abuses had been exposed and Nehemiah had taken some steps to deal with them, the community then entered into a solemn agreement to prevent their recurrence; and (ii) after the community had agreed to observe certain stipulations precisely those points of the law were later abused. In agreement with the majority of scholars, the former possibility seems much the more probable. Accordingly, Neh 10 followed Neh 13 from a historical point of view.

In justifying this view, two final factors need to be borne in mind. First, since this document was never a part of the NM, the differences between it and Neh 13 need not surprise us. Some points not mentioned there (e.g., the temple tax) may have been included in the agreement for reasons that have nothing to do with Nehemiah himself. Also, in some cases Nehemiah may have sought to convey the impression that he dealt with some abuses in a more final way than was actually the case. Some of the points that have been raised in regard to such details are treated in *Comment* below. Second, that such an agreement was made following Nehemiah's initial activity is entirely consistent with what we know of his procedures elsewhere: in chap. 5, he first rectified the abuse (vv 11–12) and then required those involved to take an oath to this effect (v 12b) while he enacted a curse against any future offenders (v 13). This would be exactly the pattern of Neh 10 following Neh 13; cf. especially 10:30 (29). A similar procedure seems to lie behind 13:25 with regard to mixed marriages; indeed, we may wonder whether in both these passages Nehemiah is not claiming for himself the credit for the agreement of Neh 10.

Comment

10:1 (9:38) The opening words clearly serve in the present text to link this chapter with chap. 9. Whether they were added by the editor for this purpose, or whether they imply that the document which lies behind chap 10 was originally more extensive, cannot now be determined.

אנחנו כרתים אמנה, "we are making a firm agreement." The MT here uses an unparalleled idiom. The verb is כרת "to cut," familiar from the expression כרת ברית "to make a covenant." In place of ברית, however, we find אמנה "something firm, true, or faithful." There are those, therefore, who maintain that these two phrases are virtually synonymous; cf. P. Kalluveettil, *Declaration and Covenant* (AnBib 88; Rome: Biblical Institute Press, 1982),

51, inaccurately citing J. Barr, "Some Semantic Notes on the Covenant," in H. Donner, R. Hanhart, and R. Smend (eds.), *Beiträge zur Alttestamentlichen Theologie* (Göttingen: Vandenhoeck & Ruprecht, 1977), 23–38. While it is certainly the case that כרת could be used on its own with covenantal overtones (cf. 1 Sam 22:8; 2 Chr 7:18, *contra* Batten), the present overall context suggests that אמנה here adds a specific nuance to the phrase, namely, that of a voluntarily entered and unilaterally binding promise or agreement. "Binding agreement" (NIV) is thus a more suitable alternative rendering to "firm covenant" (RSV) as usually understood within discussions of biblical theology (though cf. Barr for a possibly acceptable analogy from modern English usage).

The force of the agreement is attested by the fact of its being set in writing and sealed as a guarantee of its authenticity and to preserve against subsequent tampering; cf. Moscati, *Bib* 30 (1949) 320; the present verse neither demands nor precludes the view that the leaders who added their names did so with seals only rather than signatures. That view derives from the next verse, whose historically secondary nature has already been suggested.

The order of leaders (presumably laity), Levites, and priests is unparalleled. This argues against, rather than in favor of, editorial expansion of an original שרינו "our leaders" alone. Whatever be the explanation, it adds further support to the arguments for the literary independence of the document. As already noted, the list itself follows a different order, though Nehemiah and Zedekiah may come first as lay leaders. A further distinction is introduced by the phrase ראשי העם "the chiefs of the people" in v 15. While the order priests, Levites, and laity is conventional (cf. Ezra 8 and 10), a closer parallel to the order in the list itself is to be found at *AramP* 30:18–19, where there is the record of a letter addressed to "your lordship (i.e., the governor) and to Johanan the high priest and his colleagues the priests . . . , and to Ostanes the brother of ʿAnani, and the nobles of the Jews." (The Levites were naturally not included in that context.)

2–28 (1–27) The compiler of the list apparently believed that each person signing the document did so by means of his personal seal, though the text is not certain; cf. n. 2.a. above. The list of priests begins not with Zedekiah (*contra* Bertholet) but with Seraiah, as all the parallel lists demonstrate. Why אלה הכהנים "These are the priests" should follow its section when the other titles precede is unclear. It may even be a later addition, an original heading to the list of priests (presumably just הכהנים "the priests") having been lost in the course of transmission.

For comments on the list itself, cf. *Form* above.

29 (28) As seen above, this verse was originally the direct continuation of v 1 and, as such, was a circumstantial clause. While a developed subject would not be impossible in such a construction, it is nevertheless probable that "the rest of the people" once stood alone. The expansion through the remainder of the verse is to be attributed to the editor, who here shows the same concern for a comprehensive definition as he has in a different way in the list itself. There, he gathered most of the names known to him; here, he amasses every way of describing the people already found in the preceding chapters in order once more to emphasize that the agreement was undertaken by the whole community without exception. Thus the full listing of the cultic officials recalls 7:72, which serves now as part of the introduction to the reading of the law in chap. 8. From the latter chapter itself comes the emphasis on men, women, and children, together with the highly characteristic description at the end of the verse, "all who are capable of understanding" (cf. 8:2 and 3), while the remaining, central phrase—"anyone who has separated himself from the peoples of the lands"—echoes 9:2 quite closely. This verse gives strong support, therefore, to the view that Neh 8–10 did not come together accidentally, but was consciously molded into a unity by the final editor, who saw in this agreement the climax of the reforms of Ezra and Nehemiah.

30 (29)   This verse constitutes a general statement of intent. Appropriately, the law is given a comprehensive description with terminology familiar, in particular, from the Deuteronomic literature. As well as swearing to their intention with "an oath," the people reinforced their words by entering into "a curse." This was probably the ritual enactment of some form of judgment which they accepted would justly fall upon them if they transgressed the terms of their undertaking.

31–40 (30–39)   This general statement is followed by a number of particular stipulations. They are not to be regarded as additional to the law just mentioned, as though the law did not legislate for these areas, for all of them can be related to it more closely than this view would imply. Rather, they spell out a few matters where the community is particularly conscious of having lapsed, either through neglect or through having failed to appreciate the full significance of the law's requirements. This awareness is to be largely, though not exclusively, explained against the background of Neh 13; cf. *Form* above and the further comments below.

A most helpful and suggestive study has been devoted to this passage by Clines, *JSOT* 21 (1981) 111–17. He maintains that although each of the particular stipulations includes novel material, they nevertheless also represent "the result of exegetical work upon previously existing laws." These laws are to be identified with those now found in the Pentateuch. They were worked on, however, by priestly or Levitical lawyers, who drew up the document as "a set of halakot" which was "thereafter assented to by the populace." If Clines is right, this chapter would testify to the continuing influence of that approach to biblical law for which, we have argued, Ezra was largely responsible. It may be noted in passing that allusion is made to all the major strands of Pentateuchal law, so that once again it would seem that the Book of the Law is itself the Pentateuch in more or less its completed form; cf. Mowinckel, *Studien III*, 145–52.

Clines finds five types of legal development underlying these halakot, based upon four exegetical principles. These five types are (a) creation of facilitating law, enabling earlier regulations to be carried out; (b) revision of facilitating law; (c) "creation of a new prescription from a precedent in Pentateuchal law"; (d) "re-definition of categories, always in the direction of greater comprehensiveness"; and (e) the integration of separate legal prescriptions. The exegetical principles that underlie this approach are much as we would expect, namely, that the law is authoritative and so can be harmonized into univocal directives. To aid in this, there is need sometimes for supplementary law and sometimes for reapplication by way of the law's intent rather than explicit requirement. The comments below will generally follow Clines's guidelines.

There is no agreement as to the number of clauses to which assent is given; Kaufmann, *History*, finds eighteen, but this seems artificially atomistic. It seems preferable to group these verses into six clauses, of which some have subsidiary or explanatory requirements. The closing words of the chapter are, of course, a generalizing summary rather than a separate clause. For some comments on the passage from a sociological perspective, cf. Kippenberg, *Religion und Klassenbildung*, 69–77. He finds here a coalescing of Persian state interests with the Judean peasant and temple-loving community against a more internationally minded and urban-based aristocracy who looked more to Greek civilization for their inspiration.

31 (30) The first clause forbids intermarriage with foreigners. The legal background for this was examined at Ezra 9:1–2. The problem posed by the law was that it referred to nations that had long since ceased to exist, but it was noted that it was possible to overcome this by various exegetical moves. The issue there was largely foreign wives (9:2, though cf. 9:12), as it was later in Nehemiah's time (cf. 13:23). Nehemiah, however, contented himself largely with an oath that such behavior would not be repeated, referring to the marriage of either foreign men or women (13:25). A similar commitment is undertaken here. This represents, therefore, a "revision, or rather updating, of the law" (Clines, *JSOT* 21 [1981] 111–17). In order to retain the vitality of the older laws (originally given, as we have seen, for quite a different purpose), the specific list of names is replaced with the more timeless "peoples of the land." Ezra's exegesis was therefore "codified" in the pledge, and this sets the pattern for the clauses which follow.

32 (31) It is generally thought that it is possible to trace a developing severity in the Sabbath laws of the OT whereby the original prohibition of occupational work spreads to cover other spheres of activity also (cf. Exod 20:8–11; 23:12; 34:21, etc.). This law was already understood to forbid trading (Amos 8:5), but the later period, with its closer relations between Jew and foreigner, gave rise to a new problem, whether it was forbidden to buy from a non-Jew on the Sabbath or "any other holy day" to which the conditions of Sabbath observance applied. Nehemiah had contended that this too was forbidden by the law; cf. 13:16–22. This extension, then, of the law to cover unforeseen circumstances is again codified in the pledge. That this is the intention of the present verse is reinforced, according to Clines (*JSOT* 21 [1981] 111–17), by the observation that nothing is said of the violations mentioned in 13:15—"the reason can only be that it was clear in those cases what the law was, whereas in the case of buying the question of its inclusion within the category of 'work' had not been previously resolved."

The third clause of the pledge combines two laws that were related in content but which had hitherto been treated separately. On the one hand there was the requirement that all land should be fallow for one year in seven, and that the poor should be allowed to enjoy the benefit of any produce that grew wild upon it; cf. Exod 23:10–11. There is no evidence that this was to be observed simultaneously throughout the country, however, and if it was practiced rather in a rotation, it is not surprising that we have no particular records of it from the pre-exilic period. Later, however, the view developed that one year in seven should be observed simultaneously throughout the land; cf. Lev 25:1–7 and 2 Chr 36:21. Now, there was another, older law that was also tied to a seven-year cycle, that of the release of Israelites who had become slaves; cf. Exod 21:2–6. The most likely cause of slavery was inability to pay one's debts. This practice too became linked in the course of time to a universal seven-year cycle, as Deut 15:1–18 makes clear.

With the development of the seven-year cycle thus affecting both sets of laws, the question must inevitably have arisen how they were to be related to one another. Moreover, the events described in Neh 5 had shown that the Law had not been observed as Nehemiah felt that it should. His reaction on that occasion had of necessity to be immediate, and it did not settle the longer-term question of future practice. Now, however, the point is clearly made that these two laws are to be taken together, the legislation being regarded as cumulative rather than alternative. The fact that we do not have historical records of the practice of these laws until the Maccabean period is no argument whatever against this pledge's being dated to Nehemiah's time or soon after (*contra* Kellermann, *Nehemia*, 40–41).

33–34 (32–33) There is no law in the Pentateuch concerning a tax for the upkeep of the sanctuary. Nevertheless, it became necessary to regulate for a steady income if the cultus was to be maintained. Whether the assistance promised by Darius (Ezra 6:9–10) lapsed after his death we do not know; as seen at 7:21–24, Artaxerxes' support for the temple in Ezra's time was for a limited period only. In addition, the tithes, on which the cultic personnel largely depended, ceased to be given regularly, so that many of the Levites had to leave their duties in order to work the land (13:10). Finally, with the development of a monetary-based economy during the Persian period, the need will have arisen for support in cash as well as kind.

There was thus a strong incentive for those who drafted the pledge to legislate for this deficiency. The rather different manner in which this clause is introduced has suggested to some that they may have been aware that they could not simply appeal to earlier law. Rudolph's objection, based on vv 36–37, probably depends on taking these verses in a closer syntactical relation to vv 33–34 than is necessary. Despite this, however, it would be a mistake to think that they acted without regard to any precedent whatever. Exod 30:11–16 and 38:25–26 tell of the half-shekel tax Moses levied at the time of a census as a form of atonement money. Although Liver, *HTR* 56 (1963) 173–98, is correct in insisting that this is not presented as an annual tax, and that the Exodus account cannot be based on the present passage because the half-shekel offering was not introduced until the Hasmonean period, yet we need not deny all connection between these various texts. Indeed, they appear to be purposely linked first by the phrase "for the service of the house of our God," which closely reflects Exod 30:16 (Liver's explanation of this phrase as referring to the service of the Levites may be exegetically correct but does not mean that the writers were unconscious of the verbal parallel) and by the conclusion of the purpose for the tax, sacrifices "to make atonement for Israel," which is likewise reminiscent of Exod 30:15–16. Thus despite the differences between the passages, and despite even the difference

in the amount of tax to be levied (attempts to harmonize these on the basis
of differing monetary systems are not convincing), we may nevertheless agree
with Haran and others for whom this legislation was "based on a midrashic
interpretation of the half-shekel referred to in" Exodus; cf. M. Haran, "Behind
the Scenes of History: Determining the Date of the Priestly Source," *JBL*
100 (1981) 323, or, as Clines puts it, "creation of a new prescription from
a precedent in Pentateuchal law" (*JSOT* 21 [1981] 111–17). That this was
a generally accepted mode of legal application is suggested by 2 Chr 24:6
and 9.

The money was to be used for a number of the daily and periodic offerings,
all familiar from the priestly portions of the Pentateuch; in addition, the
concluding phrase of v 34 (33) probably refers to the maintenance of the
temple building itself, as at 2 Kgs 12:12, etc.

35 (34) The fifth clause relates to "the wood offering," which again is
not directly mentioned in the Pentateuch. Lev 6:5–6 (12–13), however, speaks
of the requirement that fire should be kept burning continually on the altar
and of the consequent need that "the priest shall burn wood on it every
morning." Obviously, the words "as it is written in the Law" refer to this
requirement ("to burn upon the altar of the Lord our God"). However, if
this was to be accomplished, practical arrangements had to be made. In earlier
times, it had been the responsibility of the Gibeonites to provide the wood
(cf. Josh 9:27), but Nehemiah had evidently found it necessary to adopt a
different approach (13:31). Though he supplies no details, the provision must
have been defective. Here, the community took the responsibility upon itself
by organizing an annual rota through the casting of lots between the various
families (cf. 1 Sam 10:19–21). This, then, was an example of the "creation
of facilitating law" (Clines, *JSOT* 21 [1981] 111–17), legislating to ensure
that a scriptural requirement was carried out.

Rudolph believes that this verse has been misplaced from a point just
before the summarizing clause at the end of v 40. His reason is that in the
present text the infinitives in vv 36–37 are dependent on the lot-casting of
v 35, whereas they should rather depend on the pledge of v 33. His proposal
makes no real difference to the interpretation of the passage; while he may
be right, there is no textual evidence to support his case. It may be wondered
whether the infinitives of vv 36–37 are not rather governed by the whole
context of the pledge. No one clause depends upon the one preceding it;
rather in their different ways each clause depends upon the heading in v
30.

36–40 (35–39) This passage is probably to be regarded as a single clause.
It all deals with questions relating to sacred contributions for the support
of the cultic officials and it seems to have as one of its main aims the gathering
into a single statement of a number of Pentateuchal laws relating to this
subject. There is also careful attention paid to the question where each of
the different types of contribution should be brought. It is, finally, probable
that the passage has undergone some later expansion, so that it appears to
be longer than it originally was.

The Pentateuch contains many statements about different types of offerings
in kind and contributions for the sanctuary, and since the Deuteronomic re-

form at least these will all have been intended for the temple in Jerusalem. We have also seen, however, that this support fell off so badly that it became insufficient to maintain the Levites; cf. 13:10. Mal 3:8–12 has also been considered by some to relate to this situation. Once again, Nehemiah took immediate steps to rectify this abuse (13:11–13, 31), but a full solution to the problem required a thorough study of the law in order to determine how its various relevant items should be related to one another. As we see from the present passage, it was concluded, as in later Halakot, that the laws should be regarded as cumulative rather than as alternatives, a principle of interpretation already noted at v 32b above. The contributions are grouped under the headings of first-fruits (including the law of the first-born; vv 36–37), prime produce (ראשית, v 38a [37a], and tithes (v 38b [37b]).

36–37 (35–36) Regulations regarding first-fruits are found in Exod 23:19 and 34:26. Deut 26:1–11, which is often adduced here, is, strictly speaking, a ראשית, or "prime-fruit" offering. Although these passages speak only of bringing them to the sanctuary, Num 18:12–13 makes clear that they were for the benefit of the priests, and that is explicitly reaffirmed here. The quantity involved is not stated, but it was a token amount of that harvested first each year to acknowledge that the whole was from God and properly belonged to him.

"The first-fruits of every kind of fruit tree" is a new requirement; the law is evidently being understood ever more comprehensively. A pointer in this direction is found already at Num 18:13 ("the first-fruits of all that is in their land").

The offering of the first-born is a parallel to the offering of the first-fruits. Human offspring were "redeemed" (Exod 13:13; 34:20; Num 18:15), and that is doubtless presupposed here. Further details on these offerings are found in Num 18:15–18 and Deut 15:19–23. In the matter of redemption, a distinction was also drawn between clean and unclean animals. As our text stands, it would appear that "our cattle" refers to unclean, and "our herds and flocks" to clean animals; see most recently Brin, *JQR* 68 (1978) 1–15. בהמה "cattle" is used with this sense in the relevant law at Num 18:15 (and cf. Lev 27:27), and this could be the particular force in this context of the added words "as it is written in the Law." Rudolph, however, believes that בהמה was originally used here in a quite general sense, and that it was later glossed by the addition of "the first-born of our herds and flocks . . . etc." It is true that the word order of this second half of the verse is unusual, but in view of Num 18:15–18, it should be retained if possible. It therefore seems that a careful emphasis is being made in the second half on the fact that the first-born of the clean animals were to be brought "to the priests" at the temple. This may have been necessary as a way of showing that the law of Num 18:15–18 (clean firstlings to be eaten by the priests) took precedence over Deut 15:19–20, where the firstling was to be eaten by its owner and his household at the sanctuary.

38 (37)a The ראשית offering is to be distinguished from the first-fruits. It must therefore in such a context have the meaning "choice, best" rather than "first" in a temporal sense (cf. a comparable ambiguity in the English word "prime"). This was also to be brought to the priest, but directly to the storerooms rather than the sanctuary; according to the law of Deut 18:4, it was regarded as the priests' due from the people and not their participation in that which was, strictly speaking, regarded as being offered to God. Wine and oil are repeated from the Deuteronomic law (but for some reason not "the fleece of thy sheep"); the "dough" (translation not fully certain) is mentioned in a comparable context in the law of Num 15:20–21. "The fruit of every kind of tree" does not come in other lists of "prime offerings," but was presumably introduced under a comparable influence with that at v 36 (35).

It is difficult to know quite how to take ותרומתינו "and our sacred contributions." There are several possibilities: (i) In Num 15:20–21 it is emphasized strongly that the Israelites are to set aside a sacred contribution, and that the contribution is to be made from the best (ראשית) of their dough. In our passage, therefore, there may be the intention of underlining that this law was being fulfilled, so that the conjunction *wāw* should be understood epexegetically: "*that is,* our sacred contribution." (ii) On the basis of Ezek 44:30, it has been maintained that only the ראשית of the sacred contribution was to go to the priests, the remainder being for the Levites. This verse is certainly suggestively close to ours (note the continuation, "ye shall also give unto the priest the first of your dough"), but it is not without its difficulties as regards both text and translation. However, it may suggest that ראשית and תרומה were not necessarily identical at all periods (see also Neh 12:44), and that the latter may therefore depend upon the former in the construct state (as translated above; cf. Eissfeldt, *Erstlinge und Zehnten,* 92–94). (iii) In v 40 (39), there is a reference to "the contribution of corn." Since "corn" is not overtly included in the present verse from Deut 18:4, it would be attractive to see a reference to it in this word. None of these three possibilities is free from difficulty, and it is hard to know how to choose among them. In view of the uncertainties, it seems better to adopt one of them, however, than to delete the word altogether with LXX, Meyer, *Entstehung,* 212–13, and Rudolph, or to emend it with Mowinckel, *Studien III,* 150.

38b–40a (37b–39a) It is not possible here to trace the complicated history of the laws relating to tithing; cf. Eissfeldt, *Erstlinge und Zehnten,* and, most recently, H. Jagersma, "The Tithes in the Old Testament," *OTS* 21 (1981) 116–28; particular aspects of the law are also treated by Z. Zevit, "Converging Lines of Evidence Bearing on the Date of P," *ZAW* 94 (1982) 481–511. It is sufficient to observe that, according to Neh 13:10–13, it was by this time understood that tithes were a regular payment for the support of the Levites and that in this pledge the community undertook to meet this responsibility. For the principal legal texts, cf. Num 18:21–24; Deut 14:22–29. Once again the law is interpreted in favor of the cultic personnel against the implication of the Deuteronomic statement.

This passage appears to have been expanded at a later date. Verse 40a (39a) at least must be so regarded: its switch to third person narration is out of place, and it seems to offer a summary of what is to be brought into the storerooms, which is inappropriate in the context of the pledge. It was no doubt added to clarify procedures after these had either been forgotten or neglected.

It is more difficult to decide whether the last clause of v 38 (37)b and v 39 (38) are also additional. In favor of the view that they are, we may observe that "to the Levites" in v 38b (37b) is syntactically parallel with "to the priests at the storerooms of the house of our God" earlier in the verse, from which it might be assumed that the tithes were also to be brought to the temple; in that case, what follows would represent a later revision of this practice. Furthermore, והם הלוים "It is the Levites who . . ." gives the impression of having been added as an afterthought. Finally, there is some tension between the original statements that the people will bring the tithes to the Levites and that the Levites will collect them. On this view, the pledge was not found to work effectively, and so the Levites were obliged to take steps to ensure that they received their dues.

This reconstruction is not certain, however: the presumed addition starts off, at least, in the first person, unlike the clear addition in v 40 (39). Second, we have noted that a good deal of this part of the pledge is indeed concerned with where offerings are to be brought. A statement such as we have here is thus not necessarily out of place. Third, there is no contradiction between the people "bringing" the tithes to the Levites and the Levites "collecting" them. The latter refers to the fact that the Levites established store-centers throughout the province in order to overcome the practical difficulties which the farmers faced; but we may still presume that the farmers had to bring their tithes to the Levites in the first place. Finally, provided that we allow that the final clause of v 38 (37) was added within the pledge itself for clarification of the situation, the syntactical parallel between "to the priests" and "to the Levites" may be allowed to stand without difficulty.

Whichever solution is preferred (and sound method suggests we should retain the text if arguments against it are not compelling), v 39 (38) goes on to insist on priestly supervision of these collecting points outside Jerusalem because, as was stated in Num 18:25–32, one tenth of the tithes was in turn to be given over for the support of the priesthood; see v 38 (37)a above for some parallel procedures.

40 (39)b This final sentence adds nothing material to what has gone before, but serves as a summary statement of intent, nicely answering Nehemiah's rhetorical question in 13:11. Support for the temple and its personnel were not sharply divided.

Explanation

This chapter raises two issues of wider theological interest which have already been dealt with earlier: for a discussion of the issue of separation from "the peoples of the land" we may refer to *Explanation* at Ezra 10, and for some of the questions raised by the hermeneutic displayed in the pledge's interpretation of the canonical Law, see *Explanation* on Neh 8. Here we would dwell rather on two further matters arising out of this description of the commitment into which the people entered following their reception of the Law of God (chap. 8) and extensive confession (chap. 9).

First, there is a major emphasis on the involvement of the whole community. It is true that on the understanding of the composition of the list favored above the means by which this is expressed may seem somewhat artificial to our way of thinking, but the author's intention is clear enough, being confirmed by the gathering together of his favorite titles for the people in v 29 (28). Evidently, he was not content merely to speak of "all the people," but wished to emphasize in the only way he knew how that the individuals who made up the community each gave their personal assent to the pledge. The balance between personal and community responsibility is difficult to maintain in practice, but within the books of Ezra and Nehemiah, as within Scripture as a whole, this chapter has its part to play in illustrating that such a balance is not a compromise but a holding in tension of the twin truths of each extreme.

Second, it is sobering to reflect on the general nature of this pledge: a broad statement of intent in v 30 (29) is followed by a series of stipulations as detailed and specific as could be imagined. Clearly, the latter were determined by the prevailing conditions and, further, by the cultic nature of the Jewish religion at that time, something which for the Christian has been superseded by its fulfillment in the ministry of Jesus. Nevertheless, this effortless conjoining of the general and the particular should serve as a warning that declarations of good will or intent are of limited, if of any, value unless they are translated into specific reforming activity. Neither Old nor New Testament has any place for confessions of faith that leave life-style and practice unaffected.

The Population of Jerusalem, and related matters (Neh 11:1–36)

Bibliography

Albright, W. F. "The Topography of Simeon." *JPOS* 4 (1924) 149–61. **Alt, A.** "Bemerkungen zu einigen judäischen Ortslisten des alten Testaments." *KS* 2, 289–305. **Bartlett, J. R.** "Zadok and His Successors at Jerusalem." *JTS* ns 19 (1968) 1–18. **Har-El, M.** "The Valley of the Craftsmen (Ge' Ḥaharašim)." *PEQ* 109 (1977) 75–86. **Helfmeyer, F. J.** "חנה." *TWAT* III, 4–20. **Johnson, M. D.** *The Purpose of the Biblical Genealogies.* SNTSMS 8. Cambridge: Cambridge University Press (1969) 37–76. **Kellermann, U.** "Die Listen in Nehemia 11 eine Dokumentation aus den letzten Jahren des Reiches Juda?" *ZDPV* 82 (1966) 209–27. ———. *Nehemia,* 41–44, 103–5. **Meyer, E.** *Die Entstehung des Judentums,* 94–102; 105–8; 184–90. **Mowinckel, S.** *Studien I,* 48–49; 145–51. **Rad, G. von.** *Das Geschichtsbild des chronistischen Werkes,* 21–25. **Richter, G.** "Zu den Geschlechtsregistern I Chronik 2–9." *ZAW* 50 (1932) 130–41. **Williamson, H. G. M.** "The Origins of the Twenty-Four Priestly Courses." VTSup 30 (1979) 251–68.

Translation

[1] The leaders of the people settled in Jerusalem. The rest of the people cast lots to bring one out of every ten to settle in Jerusalem, the holy city, while the remaining nine stayed in the (other) towns. [2] And the people blessed all those who volunteered to settle in Jerusalem.

[3] These are the chiefs of the province who settled in Jerusalem; [a] although Israel, the priests, the Levites, the temple servants, and the sons of Solomon's servants settled in the towns of Judah, each in their own property in their towns, [4] yet some of the descendants of Judah and of Benjamin settled in Jerusalem:

Of the descendants of Judah:

Athaiah, son of Uzziah, son of Zechariah, son of Amariah, son of Shephatiah, son of Mehalalel of the family of Perez,

[5] and Maaseiah, son of Baruch, son of Col-hozeh, [a] son of Hazaiah, son of Adaiah, son of Joiarib, son of Zechariah, of the family of Shelah; [b]

[6] The total number of the descendants of Perez who settled in Jerusalem: 468 outstanding men.

[7] These were the descendants of Benjamin:

Sallu, son of Meshullam, son of Joed, son of Pedaiah, son of Kolaiah, son of Maaseiah, son of Ithiel, son of Isaiah, [8] and his kinsmen, men of valor: [a] 928.

[9] Joel, son of Zichri, was their overseer, and Judah, son of Hassenuah, was second in command over the city.

[10] Of the priests: Jedaiah and Joiarib, the sons of [a] [11] Seraiah, son of Hilkiah, son of Meshullam, son of Zadok, son of Meraioth, son of Ahitub, the supervisor of the house of God, [12] and their associates who carried out the work in the temple: 822;

*and Adaiah, son of Jeroham, son of Pelaliah, son of Amzi, son of Zechariah,
son of Pashhur, son of Malkiah,* [13] *and his associates, heads of families: 242;
and Amasai,* [a] *son of Azarel, son of Ahzai, son of Meshillemoth, son of Immer,*
[14] *and his associates,* [a] *men of valor: 128.*

Their overseer was Zabdiel, son of Haggedolim. [b]

[15] *And of the Levites: Shemaiah, son of Hasshub, son of Azrikam, son of Hashabiah,
son of Bunni;*

[16] *—and Shabbethai and Jozabad were those of the chiefs of the Levites who
were in charge of the external business of the house of God—*

[17] *and Mattaniah, son of Micah, son of Zabdi, son of Asaph, the leader of the
praise* [a] *who gave thanks in prayer;*
and Bakbukiah, who held second place among his associates;
and Abda, son of Shammua, son of Galal, son of Jeduthun.

[18] *The total number of Levites in the holy city: 284.*

[19] *And the gatekeepers: Akkub, Talmon, and their associates who guarded the
gates: 172.*

[20] *The rest of the Israelites, the priests, (and) the Levites were in all the towns
of Judah, each in their own property.*

[21] *The temple servants lived on Ophel; Ziha and Gishpa were in charge of them.*

[22] *The overseer of the Levites in Jerusalem was Uzzi, son of Bani, son of Hashabiah,
son of Mattaniah, son of Micah, one of the descendants of Asaph who were the
singers responsible for the service of the house of God;* [23] [a] *for they were under royal
orders which determined their duties on a day-by-day basis.* [a] [24] *Pethahiah, son of
Meshezabel, a member of the family of Zerah, son of Judah, was the king's adviser
on all matters relating to the people.*

[25] *As for* [a] *the villages with their fields: some of the people of Judah lived in Kiriath-
arba and its dependent settlements, in Dibon and its dependent settlements, in Jekabzeel
and its villages,* [26] *in Jeshua, Moladah, and Beth-pelet,* [27] *in Hazar-shual and in
Beer-sheba and its dependent settlements,* [28] *in Ziklag and in Meconah and its dependent
settlements,* [29] *in Enrimmon, Zorah, and Jarmuth,* [30] *Zanoah, Adullam, and their
villages, Lachish and its fields, Azekah and its dependent settlements. Thus they settled
from Beer-sheba as far as the Valley of Hinnom.*

[31] *Some of* [a] *the people of Benjamin (lived) in Geba, Michmas, Aiah, and Bethel and its dependent settlements,* [32] *in Anathoth, Nob, and Ananiah,* [33] *in Hazor,
Ramah, and Gittaim,* [34] *in Hadid, Zeboim, and Neballat,* [35] *in Lod, Ono, and* [a]
the Valley of the Craftsmen. [36] *Some of the Judean Levitical divisions were assigned
to Benjamin.*

Notes

3.a. Some of the Vrs draw ובערי יהודה "and in the towns of Judah" into the first half of
the verse, and Rudolph believes that they are right; the words would clash with בעריהם "in
their towns," if the Masoretic punctuation were retained. He thus thinks that this was a title to
the whole of the chapter, not just vv 4–19, but then has immediately to declare the words
secondary because the latter part of the chapter lists the towns themselves rather than those
who lived in them. Rudolph's principal argument is not compelling: if בעריהם is taken closely
with באחזתו, "in his possession," which immediately precedes it (as though it were a relative
clause without אשר; cf. GKC § 155n), there is no clash. Since, as Rudolph concedes, the repunctu-
ated text does not furnish a satisfactory heading to what follows either, it seems preferable to
attempt to construe the MT. This can be done with a concessive clause, as translated above;

the editor realized that the previous talk had all been of people settling in their own towns; cf. chap. 7. To make sure that the list he is introducing will not be misunderstood, he concedes this point only in order to insist that nevertheless there were some who settled in Jerusalem; note the emphatic word order in the Heb., with ובערי יהודה "and (though) in the towns of Judah," and ובירושלם "and (yet) in Jerusalem," both coming at the start of their respective clauses. The proposal to read וַיֵּשְׁבוּ "and they settled" in place of ישבו "they settled" with some versional support, is then unnecessary. The Vrs were obliged to add the conj once they had reordered the punctuation. These readings are therefore of no additional or independent value.

5.a. Cf. n. 3:15.b.

5.b. MT, "the son of the Shilonite," cannot be right, as Shiloh is in Ephraim, not Judah. Clearly, we must vocalize הַשֵּׁלָנִי "the Shelanite" (cf. Num 26:20) and we should probably emend ב to מן with 1 Chr 9:5.

8.a. MT ואחריו גבי סלי "and after him Gabbai, Sallai," is unlikely to be correct: "after him" makes no sense in the context, there is no conj between the names, and the phrase does not conform to the general pattern of these lists. The most probable emendation has long been recognized: ואחיו גברי חיל "and his kinsmen, men of valor." For the first word, cf. LXX[L]. It looks as though a ר was removed to it from the second word. The corruption of the third word is the least easy to account for; the influence of סלא "Sallu," v 7, is often suggested. However, Brockington helpfully notes a number of doubtful passages where "rhyming" names are set next to each other: "It may be that they are an attempt to put meaning into a corrupt text." The proposed reading may be compared with vv 6, 12, 13, 14, and 19.

10.a. MT has "Jedaiah son of Joiarib; Jakin; Seraiah . . ." This is very disjointed, and quite contrary to the pattern of these lists, which provide long genealogies. The usual solution is to read בן "son of" for יכין "Jakin" (and possibly also יויקים "Joiakim" for יויריב "Joiarib" on the basis of 12:10) so as to make this into a single genealogy stretching back into the high priestly family: "Jedaiah, son of Joiakim, son of Seraiah . . ." It is suggested that the error arose in the period of the Maccabees, since Joiarib was their ancestor (1 Macc 2:1). This is plausible, though it demands a further emendation of ואחיהם "and their brothers" to ואחיו "and his brothers" in Neh 11:12. To avoid this difficulty, we may therefore tentatively offer an alternative suggestion: as Bartlett, *JTS* ns 19 (1968) 4, has noted, the priestly names of Jedaiah and Joiarib occur next to each other in several lists (1 Chr 24:7; Neh 12:6; 12:19), but no relationship is ever expressed. Now, since אחיהם "their brothers" requires a pl antecedent, it is thus attractive to join these two names here again, as in fact happens in the parallel 1 Chr 9:10. The addition of בן־, "son of," in the MT is thus to be regarded as a much later corruption under the influence of the usual composition of these lists. But what of Jakin? Here again, we may develop a suggestion on the basis of Bartlett's observation that Jakin "appears as the fourth son of Simeon (Gen. xlvi.10: cf. Exod. vi.15); in 1 Chron. iv.24 Jarib appears in his place. It seems possible, therefore, that Jachin in 1 Chron. ix.10 and Neh. xi.10 came into the text by way of being an added note on Joiarib." We would suggest that, by a well-attested process of textual corruption, a marginal gl (in this case יכין "Jakin") was later mistakenly thought to be a correction of some orthographically similar, but quite "correct," word in the text (in this case, we propose, בני "sons of") and so came in time to replace it. Our suggested reading, then, would be ידעיה ויויריב בני שריה, to be translated as above. For the sg "supervisor" at the end of v 11 see *Comment* below.

13.a. MT, עמשסי, "Amashsai," represents a combination of עמסי and עמשי, which are merely orthographic variants of the same name.

14.a. Read ואחיו with LXX, as sense demands. MT must have arisen under the influence of אחיהם in v 12 and 1 Chr 9:13.

14.b. This is improbable as a personal name; it means "the great ones." It has been suggested that either (i) it is a corr of some name such as Giddel (Ezra 2:47, 56) or Gedaliah (Ezra 10:18); or (ii) it means "a leading family"; or (iii) the sg הגדול should be read (the ending ־ים having arisen by dittogr from the following ומ), the word (lit., "the great one") being a title of the high priest. It seems impossible to choose between these alternatives.

17.a. MT: "the leader of the beginning." Unless this is a technical term whose significance escapes us, we should make the tiny emendation to תהלה "praise," with LXX[L] and Vg.

23.a-a. Lit., "For there was a command of the king upon them, even (explicative *wāw*) a firm ordinance upon the singers (concerning) the matter of each day."

25.a. The prep אל is not used elsewhere in this sense, but it may be justified on the grounds that ל is and that these two preps are frequently confused. Rudolph maintains that this anomalous usage shows that this phrase was once joined directly to v 20; however, אל would be equally unsuitable in such a context. Nor is it an objection to the present text to observe that what follows is a list of towns rather than villages: the towns are consistently linked with "their villages" or equivalent.

31.a. The *mēm*, which we expect here on the basis of both sense and the parallel with v 25, appears to have been misplaced in the course of transmission to מגבע, "from Geba," where it is clearly intrusive.

35.a. Despite the translation above, the list of places from v 32 on is written in Hebrew without any preposition or conjunction until v 35, where we find "Lod and Ono, the Valley of the Craftsmen." However, since the Valley is not to be identified with Ono (cf. Har-El, *PEQ* 109 [1977] 75–86), it appears that *wāw* has been lost by haplogr.

Form/Structure/Setting

The analysis of the present chapter is complicated by several factors which will need to be borne in mind in the following discussion. First, vv 3–19 have a parallel in 1 Chr 9:2–17; however, even a cursory inspection is sufficient to reveal that there are many differences between the two passages as well; both contain a good deal of material not included by the other, and there are in addition some quite significant differences between them even where they are apparently running parallel. Since by no means all these factors can be attributed to a discernible tendency on the part of either author, the question of dependence or of an independent original is not easily resolved. It also raises the issues of accuracy in the textual transmission of the text and of the possibility of later adaptation. This suspicion is strengthened, second, by the observation that from v 12 on the LXX text is much shorter than the MT, and that not all its omissions can be explained on purely mechanical grounds. It has been suggested that the shorter, LXX text is "probably more original" than the MT; cf. E. Tov, *The Text-Critical Use of the Septuagint in Biblical Research* (Jerusalem: Simor, 1981) 301. Third, although a general pattern can be discerned in the chapter (narrative introduction, vv 1–2; residents of Jerusalem, vv 3–24; list of dwelling places outside Jerusalem, vv 25–36), closer inspection reveals that it does not conform to any strict order or structure. For instance, (i) whereas v 20 looks like a conclusion to follow the list of those who lived in Jerusalem, v 21 immediately reverts to the temple servants' residence there; (ii) the detail about the overseer of the Levites (v 22) seems to be detached from its expected position with vv 15–18; (iii) neither the order nor the contents of the list conform exactly with what is usually thought to be the heading in vv 3–4 (whether or not this has itself been subject to later addition). Aware, therefore, that we are unlikely to find a fully homogeneous text, we turn to analyze it section by section.

It is usually agreed that the narrative heading, vv 1–2, represents the narrative continuation of chap. 7, which was also concerned with the sparseness of the population of Jerusalem. (The only major dissenting voice is that of Kellermann, *Nehemia,* who argues for the continuation of 7:5 in 12:27–43; this view was seen at chap. 7, *Form,* to be unsatisfactory, however.) In addition to the obvious continuity of subject matter, it was also noted at chap. 7 above that there appears to be a conscious use of repetitive resumption at the start of the present chapter in order to draw attention to the connection.

A natural initial conclusion from this consensus would be to suggest that we therefore rejoin the narrative of the NM. Several factors combine, however, to show that this cannot be so: (i) The verses are not couched in Nehemiah's first-person narrative style; indeed, he is not mentioned here at all. As they stand, therefore, they would contribute nothing to the purpose of his first-person account. (ii) The style of writing differs from that of Nehemiah (cf. Mowinckel, *Studien I*, 48–49; Kellermann, *Nehemia*, 43); cf. the use of שאר "rest, remainder," where Nehemiah uses יתר "remainder" (2:16; 4:8, 13; 6:1, 14), the use of שרים "leaders" where Nehemiah generally uses words like סגנים "officials" and חרים "nobles" (2:16; 4:8[14], 13[19]; 5:7, 17; 6:17; 7:5—a reference of particular significance since it is in the same narrative context as our present verses; 12:40; 13:11, 17. שרים "leaders" occurs only at 12:31–32 with a comparable meaning in material possibly to be attributed to Nehemiah, but even there other considerations make it equally likely that it is due to editorial adaptation; elsewhere in his writing it carries a more specific nuance), and the use of עיר הקדש "the holy city" for Jerusalem. (iii) Despite the fact of continuity with chap. 7, these verses do not supply quite what we have been led to expect from Nehemiah's own account. He tells how he gathered the leaders of the people in order to make a genealogical record of them, and that he then found an older genealogical record to help him (7:4–5). We thus expect him to organize the repopulation of Jerusalem with reference to family connections. What we find here instead, however, is that the people (not Nehemiah) make the arrangements on the haphazard basis of lot-casting.

In the light of these points, we must conclude that vv 1–2 neither come from the NM, nor even represent a simple editorial rewriting of something originally found there (*contra* the majority of commentators). What, then, is their origin? A few scholars, principally Meyer, *Entstehung*, 94–102, have suggested that they (together with the following list) represent the direct continuation of the list in chap. 7, and that they originally referred, therefore, to the time of the first return from Babylon. This seems unlikely, however: we know of no concern for the resettlement of Jerusalem at that time, and it might be supposed that it would be more important to encourage those returning first to reestablish the agricultural base to the province's economy. Furthermore, these verses presuppose that the people involved are already settled in their towns to the extent that a move to Jerusalem will be a considerable inconvenience. This could hardly have been the case at the time of the return itself. Finally, it will be seen below that the list in vv 4–19 represents a development from Neh 7 (Ezra 2) with regard to the cultic officials.

It is necessary, therefore, to seek a fresh solution to the question of the original setting of this material. It should hardly need saying that the passage in question is so short that any suggestion can only be tentative. It may be more than coincidence, however, that the only other example of lot-casting in these works comes in the previous chapter, at 10:35 (34), in connection with one of the clauses of the pledge. That, too, is in a context where the people are acting as a community to reorder their lives in the light of their perception of God's will for them. It was noted above, furthermore, that with regard to some of these points Nehemiah may, perhaps, have claimed rather more personal credit for the reforms (cf. chap. 13) than was always strictly the case. We may, therefore, entertain the possibility that something similar has happened here, and that the resettlement of Jerusalem was also recorded twice, once as a united act of the people and once in the NM, where Nehemiah concentrated entirely on his own part in the proceedings.

How this alternative account was preserved is uncertain. The probable chronology of events (i.e., with chap. 10 following chap. 13) makes it unlikely that it was part of the pledge itself (though the "tithing" of the population to go to "the holy city" might be thought to fit well with 10:38–39 [37–38]). Lot-casting was a cultic affair, however; cf. 1 Chr 24:5, 7, 31; 25:8, 9; 26:13, 14, etc., all passages that should, in my view, be attributed to a priestly reviser of the Chronicler's original work, one who was particularly concerned for the disposition of the Jerusalem cult at a date considerably later than Nehemiah; cf VTSup 30 (1979) 251–68. If the present passage describes an activity undertaken with priestly supervision, then its preservation in the temple archives in close proximity, at least, with the copy of the pledge is plausible. It will have been edited by whoever was responsible for combining the Ezra and the Nehemiah material so as to effect the literary join with chap. 7. Why he preferred this account to Nehemiah's own is not certain; he may have thought that it fitted better after chap. 10 in view of the points of similarity in outlook already noted. Also, there may have been a list preserved with this material in the archive that he wished to include in his own account; but this is to anticipate our consideration of the next section of the chapter, to which we must now turn.

The substance of the list in vv 3–20 comprises (a) men of Judah (vv 4b–6); (b) men of Benjamin (7–8); (c) secular leaders (9); (d) priests (10–14); (e) Levites (15–18); and (f) gatekeepers (19). Ignoring the heading in vv 3–4a for the moment, there are internal indications which show that this is a list of those who lived in Jerusalem; cf. vv 6, 9, 11–12, and 18. In addition, v 20 states that the remaining population lived in their towns. All this is exactly what we expect on the basis of the context of vv 1–2, i.e., a list of those who lived in Jerusalem after the city's population had been supplemented. V 20 serves as an admirable conclusion, and nothing more is expected after it. It is noteworthy that the parallel with 1 Chr 9 stops at just this point. We may conclude, therefore, that v 20 marks the end of the original list, and this will be given further support in the consideration of vv 21–36 below.

There should, then, be a strong presumption in favor of the list's authenticity within its present setting, and this is reinforced by the inclusion of specific but unparalleled items of information in the list, by the fact that the names are not drawn from elsewhere in Ezra-Neh (contrast chap. 10 above) and by the precise numbers (though cf. 1 Chr 9); cf. Mowinckel, *Studien I*, 147–48. Of course, it must be remembered that it may have undergone some expansion subsequently in matters of particular detail (cf. LXX), and similarly that other elements we would expect to find included may have dropped out either at the editorial stage or during its subsequent transmission; comparison with 1 Chr 9 points firmly in this direction, as will be noted below. It would therefore be foolish to attempt too much on the basis of this chapter in the way of detailed historical reconstruction. Despite this, one feature in favor of our general conclusion emerges with clarity, even though little has been made of it in discussions of the list. The picture that is presented in the development of the minor cultic officials is just what we should expect at this stage. At the time of the return, none of the singers, gatekeepers, and others were regarded as Levites. Later, they all were; cf. 1 Chr 23–26. In our list, we find that this development has started, but has not yet been completed, since the singers are now clearly accepted as Levites (v 17), but the gatekeepers are not (v 19).

It is in this light that we should examine the arguments which have been directed against the list's authenticity in its present setting. (There are very few nowadays who would argue that it is a complete fabrication.) Mowinckel, *Studien I*, 149–50, argues that it dates from a generation after Nehemiah, because Jedaiah (v 10) was the son of Nehemiah's contemporary Eliashib (cf. 13:28), because Maaseiah (v 5) was a nephew of one of the wall-builders (cf. 3:15), and because the status of the junior cult officials is more advanced than at Ezra 10:24. None of these points is convincing, however: the last depends upon dating Ezra after Nehemiah, which is uncertain. Indeed, as the texts stand they could be used as a small pointer in the opposite direction. The second argument is weak because the difference in age between uncle and nephew is often quite small. The first is also uncertain, both because the names in 11:10 and 13:28 are not the same, so that the passages can be as easily understood as referring to different people, and because the Joiada in 13:28 is in any case himself old enough to have a son of marriageable age.

A far more radical attack on the list's date has come from Kellermann, *ZDPV* 82 (1966) 209–27. Arguing that the list in 1 Chr 9 is derivative from Neh 11, he notes several aspects of our passage that carry military connotations, e.g., גבורי חיל "men of valor" (vv 8 and 14), פקיד "overseer" (vv 9 and 14), the tribal division of the people and the expression ראשים לאבות "heads of families" (v 13) in connection with the tribal clans. All these elements (several of which have been suppressed in 1 Chr 9) have parallels elsewhere in material relating to the muster of the conscript army, on the evidence for which Kellermann follows E. Junge, *Der Wiederaufbau des Heerwesens des Reiches Juda unter Josia* (BWANT iv/23; Stuttgart: Kohlhammer, 1937). He therefore finds an original setting for our list in a record for the arrangements made for the defense of Jerusalem in the closing years of the Judean monarchy.

There can be no doubt that Kellermann has drawn attention to an important feature of the list; the military overtones of the elements he isolates must be accepted; cf. Johnson, *The Purpose of the Biblical Genealogies*, 63–68, where similar points are used to the same end with regard to some of the "genealogies" in 1 Chr 2–9. There may, however, be an explanation for this without dating the list as early as Kellermann does. Against his pre-exilic date may be mentioned (i) the almost certain identification of Col-hozeh, the grandfather of Maaseiah in v 5, with the father of Shallun in 3:15; (ii) the fact that vv 10–11 probably bring us down to a date later than Seraiah, the high priest at the time of the exile; (iii) the inclusion of the singers among the Levites (v 17), which was a post-exilic development (Kellermann has to delete this

as a later gloss); (iv) the expression עִיר הַקֹּדֶשׁ "the holy city" (v 18), for
Jerusalem, an exclusively post-exilic title; and (v) the inclusion of Shabbethai
and Jozabad (v 16), who are probably to be identified with the Levites named
in Ezra 8:33; 10:15, and Neh 8:7, and who were thus contemporaries with
Ezra (and no doubt also with Nehemiah some thirteen years later); cf. Bertholet
and Rudolph. (There are other possible associations of names that would
point in the same direction, but they are less certain because the names are
more common; e.g., should the Uzziah of v 4 be linked with Ezra 10:21?)

If, then, we cannot agree with Kellermann's date for the list, how are we
to account for the phenomena to which he has drawn attention? We would
suggest quite simply that since the movement of people to Jerusalem was
largely for defensive purposes, the associated list was drawn up in terms
reminiscent of the musters of the old conscript army. That these would have
been familiar is clear from the survival of the comparable material in 1 Chr
2-9 and in Num 26. More significantly, Nehemiah had used precisely this
same format for the defense of Jerusalem during the time of the wall-building;
cf. 4:7 (13). The conscious adoption of this old but well-established model
accounts admirably for some of the distinctive elements of the list which
previous commentators have found difficulty in handling.

We must now return briefly to the list's heading in vv 3-4a. It seems not
to have been the list's original, archival heading, but to have been added at
some later stage. This was very probably by the same editor whose hand
we have already detected earlier. The evidence for the heading's being later
than the list is that apparently all the minor cultic officials are regarded as
Levites. The involvement of the editor in the composition is suggested by
the fact that the heading does not so much introduce the list that follows
("the temple servants and the sons of Solomon's servants" do not come in
the list itself) as look back to chap. 7 where the members of all these different
groups are found. There is one important difference, however. Chap. 7 concluded with a note that everyone settled in their own town—and as was seen,
this included Jerusalem (cf. 7:6 and *Comment* on 7:72a [73a]). The editor,
however, failed to appreciate this, and so spelled out with unnecessary care
that some did indeed reside in Jerusalem; see further under *Notes*.

Finally, we should summarize our conclusions of a close study of the comparison of this list with 1 Chr 9. It proves to be difficult to classify the differences as all running in a single direction. For instance, the Chronicler usually
includes more names than Nehemiah, but contrast Neh 11:7-8 and 12. On
the other hand, the Chronicler does not include nearly so much of the detail
regarding the status and function of the people mentioned, but in 1 Chr
9:9 and 13 he includes some material of this sort that is not found in Neh
11. Finally, the summarizing numbers differ significantly, but neither uses
round numbers. In these circumstances, it would be normal to conclude that
both chapters have drawn independently on a common source and adapted
it to the different setting with which each has provided it (1 Chr 9 purports
to deal with the period of the first return from exile); this is, indeed, the
view of many, such as Smend, *Listen*, 7; Bertholet; Noth, *Studien*, 130-31;
and Michaeli. This process of a gradual divergence from a common original
might be exemplified by comparison with the shorter LXX of Neh 11. How-

ever, Rudolph; Mowinckel, *Studien I,* 146–47; and Kellermann, *ZDPV* 82 (1966) 209–27, have argued that 1 Chr 9 must be dependent upon Neh 11 because it includes a parallel with the heading in vv 3–4a, which we have already concluded was composed at the time of the list's inclusion in Nehemiah. (For further arguments, cf. Johnson, *The Purpose of the Biblical Genealogies,* 37–38). Naturally, if this could be established, the argument would be proved. The only reason for hesitation in accepting it without reserve is a comparison of the verses in question. They are not exactly parallel, but include a substantial degree of overlap, including the use of some distinctive vocabulary. Since one presumes that the list must originally have also had its own heading, is it possible that both passages are also free editorial adaptations of this original? In view of what has already been said, this seems on balance slightly less probable than Rudolph's and Kellermann's view, but the case cannot yet be regarded as closed. Either way, it seems likely that some of the differences between the two forms of the list are to be explained by later textual loss. Although this cannot be reconstructed in detail, it is not unreasonable to supply the substance of what is lacking from one to the other.

The bulk of the remaining part of the chapter (vv 21–36) comprises a list of the settlements of Judah and Benjamin apart from Jerusalem. Many commentators regard this as the direct continuation of v 20 and so part and parcel of the list already examined. However, it was pointed out in *Notes* above that there is no grammatical or syntactical connection between vv 20 and 25. Furthermore, the overall context does not lead us to expect such a list; vv 3–20 have told us all that we are led to anticipate, namely a list of those who lived in, or moved to, Jerusalem. There is no good reason, therefore, to regard these verses any differently from 21–24, whose supplementary and secondary nature is universally recognized.

Our reconstruction, then, of what happened is as follows: A reader of the original text (which concluded with v 20) noted that although the temple servants were included in the heading (v 3), they were not mentioned in the list itself. (This was because they all lived in Jerusalem anyway and so would not have been included in an original list of those who moved.) He therefore added v 21. Verse 22 then supplements the list of Levites in vv 15–18 with the kind of information provided for the priests in vv 13–14, and which the sharp-eyed reader noticed was lacking for the Levites. Note that it is shown to be later than the main list by the fact that Uzzi (v 22) is the great grandson of the Mattaniah, son of Micah, an Asaphite, in v 17. V 23 then supplements v 22, and v 24 supplements v 23; there is no way of telling whether the same reader or another added them.

By now, the passage was expanding beyond the strict confines of its original context, and v 20 no longer stood out as so obvious a conclusion. It is thus not surprising that the opportunity should have been taken to continue the process of supplementation with the list of settlements in vv 25–36 (cf. also 12:1–26). The reference to these settlements in vv 1–3 and 20 no doubt furnished the reason.

The list of settlements itself is something of an enigma. On the one hand, many of the places mentioned in chap. 3 are omitted here, while on the other hand several places included here—from the very first name on—were certainly outside the post-exilic province of Judah and, indeed, were not regained by the Jews until 164 B.C. during the Maccabean period. Finally, it is likely that this list is to be associated in some way with others included in the OT. This is suggested not only by the correspondence in names, but by the fact that the list starts with Kiriath-arba, an archaic name for Hebron (Judg 1:10), but one found elsewhere in such lists (cf. Josh 15:13; 21:11). The lists to be principally compared with the present one are those describing the tribal inheritances in the latter part of the book of Joshua, the list of Levitical cities in Josh 21, and the comparable material at various parts of 1 Chr 4–8.

Unfortunately, a full study of these complicated issues would take us far beyond the scope of the present commentary; for summaries of earlier special studies, cf. Myers, and Kellermann, *ZDPV* 82 (1966) 209–27. We must be content to note here the major general options, namely that (i) the list is a pre-exilic relic, reflecting either the settlement pattern of the late Judean monarchy or a list of the same period relating to the defenses of the kingdom (so Kellermann); (ii) the list comes from the time of Nehemiah, but includes not just the towns of the province of Judah but the towns within and beyond the province where Jews were settled (cf. Ezra 7:25), whether by continuous occupation through the exile or by resettlement on return (cf. Albright, *JPOS* 4 [1924] 149–61; Kidner; and Fensham; a variant form of this thesis comes from Alt, *KS* 2, 289–305, who thinks that the list refers to towns occupied by the Levites at this time). This is speculative, however, since as far as we know the far south of the country was completely overrun by the Edomites, and because no explanation is offered for the traditional connections of the list already noted; (iii) the list dates from Maccabean times, and reflects the conditions of that period. Although this is assumed by many, there is considerable difficulty in believing that such a substantial addition could have been made so late. (iv) We are attracted to a generally overlooked suggestion by von Rad, *Geschichtsbild,* 21–25 (see also Vogt, *Studie,* 68). Observing the close dependence of the first part of our list on Josh 15 (a fact that probably accounts for the omission of most of the places mentioned in Neh 3), he argues that "the Chronicler" intended to present post-exilic Israel in an idealized character, and so provided it with a province approximating the extent of Judah in Josiah's day. In taking up this suggestion, we may propose that a later editor has here presented a utopian view of the province's geography, not only, however, with idealizing ambitions derived from the past, but also as an expression of future aspiration. In some respects it thus resembles the list of names in chap. 10, though it is unlikely, on the view of composition adopted here, that it goes back to the same hand.

Comment

Because the bulk of this chapter is made up of lists, the commentator's main interest in them relates to topics dealt with at some length in *Form* above. The following comments are therefore restricted to brief supplementary notes to the points already discussed.

1–2 The people's plan was that both the leaders, secular and lay, and ten percent of the ordinary people should settle in Jerusalem. Lot casting was used because it was believed to reveal the divine will (cf. Num 26:55; Josh 7:14, 16–18; 14:2; 18:6, 8; 1 Sam 10:20–21; 14:41–42; Prov 16:33); this did not mean, however, that the choice was a welcome one. It is therefore probable that those who volunteered were included in the ten percent rather than being added to it, since they reduced the number of those who had to move despite their preference to remain where they were.

3 For the "temple servants and the sons of Solomon's servants," see *Comment* on Ezra 2:43–58.

4b–6 There are good reasons for supposing that this passage is defective: (i) only the clan of Perez is given a summary total (v 6), and (ii) we miss a reference to the clan of Zerah (cf. Gen 46:12; 1 Chr 2:3–6), which is included, as expected, together with a summarizing total, in the parallel 1 Chr 9:6; see also v 24 below. The description אנשי חיל "outstanding men" is doubtless intended with particularly military overtones; cf. *Form.*

7–8 Here again, comparison with 1 Chr 9:7–9 suggests that the original text included a good deal more than one Benjamite clan.

9 The second half of the verse suggests that "overseer" should be understood in terms of urban, not just tribal, authority. משנה, "second in command," is not a usual title, but its meaning in this context is assured by v 17. It is not to be confused with the same word referring to the "second quarter" of Jerusalem (see *Comment* on 3:6).

10–14 Of the four priestly families mentioned in Ezra 2:36–39, that of Harim is missing here. As there is no apparent reason for this, it is probable that we should again reckon with its loss at some stage in the transmission of the text.

Details concerning the first group are also uncertain because of textual difficulties; cf. *Notes.* It is therefore best not to speculate about the identity of Jedaiah (v 10, *contra*, e.g., W. F. Albright, *JPOS* 6 [1926] 96–100). With Seraiah (v 11), however, we join the list of high priests who officiated in Jerusalem until the time of the exile. Despite some slight differences, comparison with other such lists (1 Chr 5:27–41 [6:1–15]; Ezra 7:1–5, etc.) shows that this was relatively well fixed in tradition; cf. Bartlett, *JTS* ns 19 (1968) 1–18. It is not clear, however, why it should have started with Ahitub. "The supervisor of the house of God" means high priest; cf. 2 Chr 31:10 with 13. Since the word נגד "supervisor" is in the singular, it must, on our reconstruction, refer to Ahitub, not those at the start of the list. The description of their associates "who carried out the work in the temple" is to be understood quite generally. (In the later 1 Chr 23:24–32, a similar function is ascribed to the Levites.) Though at first sight it appears to fit uneasily with the descriptions in vv 13 and 14, it may imply that this was their permanent role while the other families could be released for military service in times of emergency.

The description "heads of families" (v 13) has been suspected of being an intrusion from 1 Chr 9:13 because their number, 242, would be too large for heads of houses (Keil), and because it clashes with the specific functions of vv 12 and 14 (Rudolph). However, both objections lose their weight if the term is being used in military, rather than sociological, terms. Though the priests were normally exempt from such duties (this seems to be the implication of Num 1:47–49), exceptional circumstances outweighed this in both earlier (Exod 32:26–28) and later (1 Macc 5:67) times; see also 2 Chr 20:21 and the War Scroll from Qumran.

"Their overseer" refers to all the priestly families just listed. The title is the same as in vv 9 and 22, and so may again refer to military rank. Naturally, in other respects the high priest retained his authority.

15–18 The arrangement of the list of Levites differs from the foregoing in that functions and rank are dispersed through it in a less orderly fashion. Since later additions were made following the list as a whole (vv 21–23) rather than being slotted in at the appropriate points, we must assume that this was so from the first and is not evidence of subsequent reworking.

"The external business of the house of God" is to be contrasted with "the work in the temple" of v 12. It is generally assumed that care of supplies and tithes (cf. 10:38–40 [37–39]) as well as of the temple fabric is involved.

Abda, who heads the third Levitical family, was also numbered among the singers, being a descendant of Jeduthun; cf. 1 Chr 25:1–6. For the place of this information within the development of the guilds of singers in the second temple period in a way that fits a date in Nehemiah's time, cf. H. Gese, "Zur Geschichte der Kultsänger am zweiten Tempel," in *Vom Sinai zum Zion* (BEvT 64; Munich: Chr. Kaiser Verlag, 1974) 147–58, and my refinement of his position in VTSup 30 (1979) 251–68.

19 Two names (cf. 1 Chr 9:17), if not four (cf. Ezra 2:42), appear to have been lost from this list of (heads of families of) the gatekeepers. Since at this point the Chronicler appears to switch to another source giving much fuller details about the gatekeepers' duties, it is not possible to say for certain whether he attests a previously purer form of our text. "Who guarded the gates" adds nothing to what is already included in "the gatekeepers." According to R. Zadok, ZAW 94 (1982) 298, it is an explanatory gloss, though one would hardly have thought that this was necessary.

21 The original list clearly concludes with v 20. A later reader, however, noted the lack of reference to the temple servants (cf. v 3), and so appended this note, thereby opening the way for all the other additions. In fact, however, he knew nothing about them except where they lived (cf. 3:26) and their leaders.

22–24 For the development of these notes, cf. *Form* above. The additional three generations added to the Asaphite family (v 22) would bring us near to the time of the Chronicler, when David's ordering of the Levitical duties— and of the singers in particular—was a matter of especial concern; cf. 1 Chr 25. Neh 12:24 below attests this continuing tradition. This may be reflected in the "royal orders" of v 23, though admittedly, in view of the concern of the Achaemenids for the cults of their subject peoples, a reference to the Persian monarch cannot be entirely ruled out.

At all events, המלך "the king" was evidently taken in the latter sense by whoever added v 24. This note was appended against the confines of the context, however, for the task must have involved residence at the Persian court itself (ליד המלך, lit., "at the king's hand"). Whether this is the office Ezra had formerly held cannot now be determined (see also *Comment* on

Ezra 7:12). Since a good knowledge of affairs in Jerusalem would obviously have been necessary, this verse provides independent, though later, evidence for the residence of the family of Zerah there; see on vv 4b–6.

25–35 For this list of Judean and Benjamite settlements, cf. *Form* above. For the location of the various places mentioned, the reader must, for reasons of space, be referred to the standard historical geographies and Bible dictionaries with their bibliographies to fuller studies.

30 "From Beersheba as far as the Valley of Hinnom" is a perfectly reasonable summary of the traditional inheritance of Judah; cf. Josh 15:8. ויחנו, lit., "and they encamped," is an unusual word to use for the settlement, however. As Kellermann has insisted, it generally refers to military encampments. At the same time, however, it speaks of temporary rather than permanent measures, so that it cannot support his view of this list as one of Judean fortress cities for the defense of the realm either. (The topographical considerations that Kellermann adduces to support his theory are to be explained by the passage's dependence on conventional listings of this nature, and there the definition of borders is a major concern.) Functionally, it stands in parallel with ישבו "(they) settled, lived, dwelt" in v 25, but there is no evidence to suggest that they were simple equivalents, not even on the basis of Isa 29:1, on which see the commentaries and the association with v 3. Nor is the suggestion of Batten very convincing, namely, that this chapter "was originally intended to describe the settlement of a caravan which had recently arrived." Finally, though one might be tempted to think of emendation (e.g., ויניחו "they were at rest, settled"), there is no supporting evidence for any alteration to the text, so that this should only be adopted as a last resort.

Bearing in mind the nature of this list already described in *Form*, we may propose a quite different solution. There is some evidence that in circles close to our author the second temple was not only regarded as standing in direct continuation with the tabernacle but was specifically referred to as such; cf. 1 Chr 9:23 with 19 and 21. This evidently evoked memories of the description of the wilderness period when the people were "camped" in their tribes around the tabernacle (e.g., Num 2), for we find a reference in 1 Chr 9:18 to "the camp of the children of Levi," and to the whole as "the camp of the Lord" (1 Chr 9:19; 2 Chr 31:2). We know too from the Qumran texts that the influence of this ideology continued into later times; cf. Helfmeyer, *TWAT* III, 6. We may suggest, therefore, that this same circle of ideas is reflected here: in what is already something of an idealizing description, the people are in addition portrayed in terms of the prototypical cultic community of the wilderness days.

36 After details about the settlement of the tribes of Judah and Benjamin, a reference to Levi is not surprising.

Explanation

The narrative content of this chapter is sparse, but interesting. In the same spirit as that of the previous chapter, the people respond to the need to repopulate the fortified city of Jerusalem. Since this was primarily for defensive purposes, the list of their leaders was drawn up with an eye on the forms of the musters of the conscript army of pre-exilic times. To this list, other material was added later, especially an idealized description of the province, based on the territorial pattern of the pre-exilic kingdom.

Attention may be briefly drawn to two points emerging from this. First, as in the case of Nehemiah (cf. chap. 7), so the people too recognized that buildings in themselves are lifeless. Once divorced from their purpose of providing a framework within which a community (be it town, Church, or family) may develop, they become nothing more than a liability. There can be little doubt that had the people not acted as they did they would soon have discovered, as the Church has subsequently, all too frequently to its cost, that the refortified city would have become a drain on their energy and resources, putting additional strains on the community's cohesion. It was with a sure instinct that "the people blessed all those who volunteered to settle in Jerusalem" (v 2), and recorded their names with gratitude.

Second, it would be a mistake to dismiss the list of settlements in vv 25–36 just because it is a later addition and historically inaccurate. Its backward glance to former glories, and its conscious imposition upon them of the pattern of life in the wilderness (see *Comment* on v 30) is adequate testimony to the writer's faith that the restrictions which he currently faced could not be God's last word. The writer to the Hebrews, 11:13–16, speaks of earlier heroes of the faith who similarly looked for promises whose physical realization lay still in the future. To all who are thus conscious of a discrepancy between a vision of God's future vouchsafed by revelation and a present frustration at the shortfall in realization, there comes the writer's assurance that "God is not ashamed to be called their God, for he has prepared a city for them."

Notes

4.a. MT גִנְּתוֹי "Ginnethoi" is universally emended to גִנְּתוֹן "Ginnethon" with many MSS, Vg, 10:7 (6) and v 16 below.

8.a. Judah is the name of a Levite in Ezra 10:23 (but not in Ezra 3:9; see *Notes*), but does not occur as a family head. Some, therefore, prefer to emend here to the similar הוֹדִיָּה, "Hodiah" (8:7; 9:5; 10:11 [10] and 14 [13]) or הוֹדַוְיָה "Hodaviah" (Ezra 2:40).

8.b. While there is no doubt about the meaning, הֻיְדוּת is certainly a very odd form in Heb. We should probably read הוֹדוֹת (inf serving as a verbal noun) or הֻדָיוֹת.

9.a. K וְעֻנּוֹ "and Unno"; Q וְעֻנִּי "and Unni." The latter is undoubtedly correct (as many MSS and Vrs agree), since this is both the form found elsewhere (cf. 1 Chr 15:18 and 20) and that which can be most easily explained as a hypocoristicon of Anaiah or Ananiah. Ryle makes the further excellent suggestion that the origin of K was a *wāw* which he restores before אֲחֵיהֶם to give "and their brothers." Without it, the choir would have been extremely unbalanced. There is then no need to follow earlier commentators who read K as a verb and deleted Bakbukiah to give "and their brothers responded (in song) . . ."; cf. Ezra 3:11.

10.a. The meaning will be the same whether or not we restore הוֹלִיד, "beget, be the father of," with several MSS and Vrs.

14.a. K, לְמַלּוּכִי "of Malluchi," results from a dittogr of the following י, and this in turn gave rise to Q, לְמַלִּיכוּ "of Melichu." The restored text, לְמַלּוּךְ "of Malluch," is based on v 2 and supported by LXX.

15.a. לְמָרֵמוֹת "of Meremoth" is restored by many on the basis of v 3, LXX[L] and Syr.

16.a. So Q, Syr., and v 4; K has לַעֲדָיָא, resulting from the common confusion of י and ו.

17.a. This is the full form of the same name Mijamin in v 5.

17.b. A name has clearly been lost from the list in the course of transmission. See also below on v 14. NIV's attempt to avoid this conclusion by translating "of Minjamin's (family) and of Maadiah's, Piltai" is unwarranted, since there is no conj in the Heb.

20.a. An otherwise unattested name. The considerations at n. 11:8.a. apply here too; it is therefore probable that this is a scribal device to fill a gap that had appeared as the result of the loss of a name from the list.

22.a. It is difficult in this verse to separate strictly textual issues from wider considerations. The translation supplied above represents a close translation of MT. At this level, doubt focuses chiefly on the prep עַל, normally "upon." It is here rendered "in" by LXX and Vg, and an attempt to justify this is made by Keil. Others emend to עַד "until," though this is equally conjectural. More boldly, Rudolph draws the passage into line with the following verse by restoring . . . עַד (עַל־) "(in)·the book of records until . . ." This is attractive (though the resulting difference in meaning is not large); however, that a scribe's eye should have jumped from עַל to עַד is perhaps not quite so plausible as Rudolph seems to suppose. Another possible conjecture is that of W. F. Albright, *JBL* 34 (1921) 112–13, who reads מֵעַל "from" for עַל (haplogr); the reference is then to Darius I, called "the Persian" to distinguish him from Darius the Mede (though the latter may be a very late designation). It is less likely, however, that עַל alone means "from," as Myers suggests. In view of the other uncertainties in interpreting this verse, the issue cannot be decisively settled. Moving beyond strictly textual considerations, we should also note here the influential conjecture of Meyer, *Entstehung*, 103, as developed by Rudolph. Observing that v 22a contradicts v 23 and that we do not expect to find Levites here when v 22b reverts to the priests, Rudolph suggests that הַלְוִיִּם "the Levites" was originally a gl on v 23 which displaced the opening of v 22, namely, רָאשֵׁי אֲבוֹת הַכֹּהֲנִים "the heads of the priests' families," a corr form of which now appears later in the verse. His reconstructed text may therefore be translated: "The heads of the priests' families in the time of Eliashib . . . [etc.] are recorded in the Book of Chronicles until the reign of Darius the Persian." This reconstruction is not convincing, however. It fails to explain why v 23 should require to be glossed (בְנֵי לֵוִי "the sons of Levi" is fully intelligible) and why the inclusion of the gl should have involved the transposition of the original subj of v 22; at the most one might have expected the addition of the Levites to the subj. Finally, it is not certain that Rudolph's formulation of the verse's difficulties is the best point from which to approach a solution. See *Comment* below for a different suggestion that avoids radical emendation.

23.a-a. Lit., "The sons of Levi, heads of families." For this formula, see *Form* below.

24.a. MT בֶּן־ "son of." Jeshua is not elsewhere related thus to Kadmiel, nor do we find patronymics in this list. The Vrs suggest slightly different readings, but note especially LXX^L: οἱ υἱοὶ αὐτοῦ, implying בניו "his sons." When linked with the list in v 8, it becomes irresistible to read בנוי "Binnui."

24.b. We should probably add the conj with the Vrs and the use of the phrase in Ezra 3:11; 1 Chr 16:4; 23:30.

24.c. A survey of the concordance suggests that כ "like" and ב "in" are used interchangeably in this phrase.

24.d. As Keil observes, 11:17 shows that the first three names in v 25 are the singers here described.

25.a. This is the same as Shallum, the leading gatekeeper in the comparable lists at 1 Chr 9:17 and Ezra 2:42. Note the variant spellings Shelemiah/Meshelemiah for the same name in 1 Chr 26:1–2 and 14.

25.b. שמרים and שוערים must be inverted. It is not surprising that on occasions words of similar appearance got into the wrong order; for the textual process, cf. my "Word Order in Isaiah xliii.12," *JTS* ns 30 (1979) 499–502.

Form/Structure/Setting

Critical analysis of this passage needs to take account both of internal markers of the structure, and hence possible growth, of the lists and of the points of contact with what we know from other sources of the development of the priestly and Levitical courses in the post-exilic period. Both aspects are highly controversial, and one rarely finds two commentators in agreement. This poses two practical problems. On the one hand, it is not possible within a reasonable compass to deal with all the many theories that have been proposed; on the other hand, in a field of such uncertainty, merely to advance a fresh suggestion with no regard for others would be extremely arrogant. The following remarks therefore represent a conscious compromise, namely, an attempt at a positive statement that is fully aware of alternative views but refers to them only at points where they touch directly on the matters under discussion.

The basic shape of the chapter is straightforward. (1) A list of priests (vv 1–7) and Levites (vv 8–9) relating to the time of the return from exile; (2) a bare chronological list of high priests, stretching from the earliest to the latest named in the chapter (vv 10–11); (3) a list of priests (vv 12–21) and Levites (vv 24–25) from the time of Joiakim, i.e., the generation next after the return; (4) separating the two lists, notes about sources and chronology (vv 22–23); (5) a chronological summary, also referring to the second pair of lists (v 26).

Closer inspection reveals that matters may not be quite so straightforward, however. Taking first the passage beginning with v 12, the words ובימי יויקים "and in the days of Joiakim," which introduce the list of priests (v 12), are exactly paralleled at the start of v 26, where they appear as part of the summary that serves to qualify not only the preceding list of Levites but probably also, as the additional reference to Nehemiah and Ezra suggests, the whole of the second half of the chapter. There is, however, a further, previously overlooked, parallel between the introductory matter relating to these two lists, namely כהנים ראשי האבות, lit., "priests, the heads of families (fathers)," in v 12 and בני לוי ראשי האבות, lit., "the sons of Levi, the heads of families (fathers)," in v 23. This use of apposition is unusual, and certainly stands out within the present context. בני לוי "the sons of Levi" does not occur elsewhere in the passage either (indeed it occurs otherwise in these books only once, at Ezra 8:15), הלוים "the Levites" being the preferred designation. Finally, ראשי האבות comes only in these two verses in precisely this form; compare ראשי הכהנים, "the heads of the priests" (v 7), ראשי אבות "heads of families" (indefinite, v 22), and ראשי הלוים "the heads of the Levites" (v 24). It therefore seems to be a reasonable conclusion that just as v 12 introduces the following list of priests, so v 23 is part of the original introduction to the following list of Levites, and also that these formulations are part of an earlier source. (This latter conclusion receives support from the use of this same list in 10:3–9 [2–8]; having argued that that list was drawn up by the compiler of Ezra-Nehemiah but that the present passage is part of the large later expansion 11:21—12:26, I conclude that 10:3–9 drew its list from a source that underlies the present passage.) There is then no good reason to deny that the remainder of v 23 is the editor's own comment on this self-same source, and that this comment obliged him to add the further recapitulating heading וראשי הלוים "And the heads of the Levites (were):" (his own phraseology), at the start of v 24.

If this is correct, then it must be observed next that the date of the list of Levites in vv 24–25 is given twice: once in v 23 as the time of Johanan, son of Eliashib, and once in v 26 as the time of Joiakim. Our literary analysis has already strongly suggested that the former date is more likely to be historically accurate since it is apparently based on an antecedent source. This is confirmed by the consideration that within the list both singers and gatekeepers are reckoned as Levites, something impossible as early as Joiakim's time on the evidence of lists elsewhere, but not impossible in Johanan's time (end of the fifth century B.C.). In addition, it seems certain (though noted by only few; cf. Smend, *Listen,* 10) that the first two names in the list, Hashabiah and Sherebiah, are the same as the two heads of families listed as having returned with Ezra (Ezra 8:18–19). In that case, they could not have been included in a list from as early as Joiakim's time. (A memory of their slightly different status may be retained in the use of the conjunction before the next group of names, all of which occur in Ezra 2:40 [see *Notes,* Ezra 2:40] as having been among the first to return.) V 26 is thus confirmed as editorial, *contra* Japhet, "Sheshbazzar and Zerubbabel—Against the Background of the Historical and Religious Tendencies of Ezra-Nehemiah," *ZAW* 94 (1982) 81, though of course we agree with her that this author is not to be identified with the author of the rest of the book.

We turn next to the two lists of priests in vv 1–7 and 12–21. As already noted, the first is a simple list for the time of the return, while the second gives the representative for each family a generation or so later. The similarity between these lists (a similarity that was once undoubtedly much closer than it is now on account of textual corruption; see *Comment* below) has convinced nearly all commentators that there must be a literary link between the two passages. There can then be no doubt that vv 1–7 are dependent upon vv 12–21 for several reasons. (i) We have already established the probability that vv 12–21 are drawn from an earlier source. (ii) Comparison of the elaborate list in vv 1–7 with the four priestly families listed for the period of the return in Ezra 2:36–39 points towards the artificial nature of the former. (iii) The names of the added generation in vv 12–21 do not appear to be artificial; they are not paralleled elsewhere, for instance. It is therefore less likely that someone invented all this material than that the names of the family heads were simply transferred back to a previous generation. (iv) In vv 12–21, the names Seraiah, Jeremiah, etc., clearly function as family names; this fits with what we know of their use elsewhere. The effect of their inclusion in vv 1–7 is to make them all into the names of individuals involved in the return who immediately became heads of definitive priestly families. This is improbable, however. We thus conclude that vv 12–21 are the original material from which the editor has written vv 1–7.

Given this conclusion, it seems to me most probable that the editor has followed more or less the same procedure for the Levites in vv 8–9, basing them on vv 24–25. A complicating factor here is the fact that vv 24–25 give only family names, so that these have simply had to be transferred back as they stand to the earlier generation. This proposal has the merit of explaining vv 8b–9 in a simple way. Rudolph has to argue that they are a later addition; we regard them, however, as simply a summary of v 24b. The differences between the two lists of names are not a problem. All come from vv 24–25 except Judah and Unni. Judah, however (see *Notes*), probably derives from Hodaviah in Ezra 2:40, a verse to which our author is likely to have referred in drawing up a list of Levites from the period of the return. Unni stands in the place of Obadiah in the parent list. While no simple solution to this problem presents itself on this or any other theory (cf. Rudolph's bewilderment!), the possibility of one arising by corruption of the other is not unlikely (ע/ע; ד/ן; י/ך; note too that the same name may be represented as עַבְדָא, "Abda," at 11:17). We conclude, therefore, that vv 8–9 derive in an artificial manner from vv 24–25, as vv 1–7 do from vv 12–21. Without this conclusion, the identity of names between the two passages of Levites presents commentators with an all-too-telling embarrassment; cf. Kidner and Fensham.

The next step in our analysis must be the observation of Meyer, *Entstehung*, 173, that the list of priests in both vv 12–21 and in 1–7 has undergone expansion. The evidence for this is the fact that before the last six names in each case there stands the conjunction "and" (used nowhere else in either list) *together with* the observation that precisely these same six names are lacking from the list of priests in 10:3–9 (2–8), a list which, we argued, was dependent upon this one. It is this combination of circumstances that makes the conclusion so compelling; Mowinckel, *Studien I*, 155–56, curiously deals with only one part of it in his unconvincing attempt to bypass this result. It seems clear that the original list was much shorter (fifteen or sixteen names in the present text), and this makes it more reasonable to place it earlier in the post-exilic period. Although only four families of priests are noted at the time of the return (Ezra 2:36–39), it must have been necessary to increase this considerably once the second temple was built, even if, in the first instance, merely by subdivision of the existing families. A more extensive list in the time of Joiakim is thus not unreasonable. At the same time, the rather shorter list should remove any lingering temptation to compare this list with the twenty-four priestly courses known from 1 Chr 24:7–18 and later times; neither names nor numbers are now even remotely similar. The added six names, however, mark a clear step in that direction. They bring the numbers closer to twenty-four; more significantly, the first two names, Joiarib and Jedaiah, are the two that head the twenty-four courses (1 Chr 24:7).

The only verses that remain to be accounted for are 10–11 and 22. V 22 at once strikes us because of its peculiar phrasing. In my view, the first part of the verse is best explained as a somewhat embarrassed note by the editor to explain in advance to the reader why the list of Levites that follows is so close to that already read in vv 8–9; he explains that it is because even in later times they were recorded not as individuals, but as "heads of houses." In that case, we would expect the list of high priests here to come down only as far as the date of the following list of Levites, namely, the period of Johanan. That Jaddua is therefore a tiny, later insertion is made probable by the conjunction before it as well as before Johanan; normally, a conjunction would be used either with every name, or with the last in the list only. The last part of the verse is clearly added; see *Comment* for details.

The period of Jaddua is thus not the perspective of the bulk of this passage, but of a later glossator only. It is therefore probable that vv 10–11 are part of this same late addition. This conclusion is supported by its poor integration into the context. We may assume that it was inserted between the lists of the first and second generations of the return in order to provide a chronological framework for the whole. Its lack of agreement in certain details with vv 22–23 argues for its independent origin; cf. Rudolph.

We are now in a position to summarize our understanding of the literary development of this list. (i) The core of source material is a list of priests from the time of Joiakim (vv 12–18) and a list of Levitical heads of families from the time of Johanan (vv 23a, 24–25); so too Kellermann, *Nehemia*, 109, though for different reasons. (ii) From this the editor responsible for the basic shape of the passage constructed the two lists referring to the first generation of the return (vv 1–9). He added some explanatory material (22a; 23b) to indicate the source for his lists and to deal with the problem of the similarity in his lists of Levites. He also added the summarizing v 26, which links his work with the wider surrounding narrative; cf. *Comment*. (iii) Either he himself, or someone working soon after, added the six names in vv 19–21 and vv 6b–7a, presumably in order to align the lists with the situation in his own day. (iv) Later glossators added vv 10–11 and 22b. Their dates cannot be earlier than the Hellenistic period; cf. *Comment*.

Finally, we must seek to pinpoint the "setting" of this material. Within the Books of Ezra and Nehemiah, there seems little doubt that it continues the later expansion already attested in 11:21–36. It will be suggested later that 12:27 was originally joined directly to 11:20. Since we cannot tell whether 11:21–36 was all added by the same hand or by several, it would be idle to speculate whether the editor of 12:1–26 was this same person or another.

It has emerged, however, that our author's perspective was no earlier than Johanan, and from the way he refers to him in vv 22–23 it is even possible that he worked shortly after that time, i.e., early fourth century B.C. This fits admirably with what we know of the development of the priestly and Levitical families through this period. For fuller details, cf. Williamson, VTSup

30 (1979) 251–68. We may note especially that (i) both singers and gatekeepers
are regarded as Levites, whose work was prescribed by David (vv 24–25).
This is a perspective later than the combining of the Ezra-Nehemiah material,
in which at the latest stage the singers are classed as Levites, but not the
gatekeepers (11:17–19). It is, however, found in the Chronicler's work (e.g.,
1 Chr 15; 23:3–5), to be dated probably in the middle of the fourth century
B.C. (ii) The edited list of priests is approaching, but has not yet reached,
the system of the twenty-four courses, which we have dated to the end of
the Persian period. (Naturally, the shorter source behind this edited list will
be earlier.) The attempts to date this list to much later times, even the Maccabean period, must be rejected. Once the twenty-four courses were established,
we know from an ever-growing body of evidence that they remained unchanged until the fall of the second temple (see VTSup 30 [1979] 251).
The present list, even in its fuller form, must therefore predate this material.

Comment

1–7 The correspondence between this list and vv 12–21 is closer than
appears from MT because originally identical names have sometimes changed
in the course of transmission. Hattush must have been lost accidentally from
v 14; Shecaniah and Shebaniah will have once been the same (ג/ב), as will
Rehum and Harim (transposition of the first two consonants), Meremoth
and Meraioth, Mijamin and Miniamin, and Maadiah and Moadiah. Comparison
with 10:4 (3) has further suggested to some that Pashhur may have been
lost from both lists in this chapter. Though possible, this is less certain. It
was seen that the list in chap. 10 gathers names from a variety of sources,
so that it may include Pashhur directly from Ezra 2:38.

For the heading, see *Comment* on Ezra 2:1–2. Difficulty has been felt with
the summary (v 7b) because it is not immediately apparent to whom "their
associates (brothers)" refers. Rudolph therefore wants to transpose this sentence to follow v 9, where the reference would then be to the Levites. This
is pure conjecture, however, to which we should not resort if it can possibly
be avoided. Mowinckel, *Studien I*, 152–53 (fn.), suggests that the family names
were intended to cover both family heads and their brothers. Others regard
it as a purely mechanical addition, because it usually occurs in such a position
(e.g., 11:12, 14, 19; e.g., Batten and Schneider), while Kellermann, *Nehemia*,
106, suggests that it is the start of the next sentence and so refers to the
Levites. Alternatively, we may propose that the editor intends it to refer to
the six names he has added to the end of the list. He thus shows awareness
that these six were not yet family heads at the time of the return.

8–9 As seen in *Form*, this passage is based on vv 24–25, except that the
editor knew not to include the gatekeepers here. Verse 9b is a reference to
antiphonal singing, for which see also 11:17 and Ezra 3:10–11.

10–11 This list of high priests has been seen to be one of the latest
elements in the chapter. It was apparently inserted in order to show the
connection between Jeshua (vv 1–9) and Joiakim (v 12). It is constructed in
exactly the manner of the high-priestly list in 1 Chr 5:30–40 (6:4–14), and

indeed is its direct continuation. As can be proved for that passage (see my commentary *ad loc.*), "was the father of" may sometimes be used in a wider than literal sense.

Jeshua is, of course, established as high priest at the time of the return and the rebuilding of the second temple, while Eliashib was contemporary with Nehemiah (cf. 3:1) nearly eighty years later. It is possible, but not probable, that Joiakim filled the whole of this gap; cf. Mowinckel, *Studien I*, 158; Cross, *JBL* 94 (1975) 10; Williamson, *JTS* ns 28 (1977) 60–64. It is therefore likely that one or even two names have not been included here for whatever reason. It is important to note this likelihood that the list is not complete.

That Joiada succeeded Eliashib is made probable by 13:28, though some uncertainty surrounds the interpretation of that verse. Jonathan is otherwise unknown. Many commentators identify him with Johanan (vv 22–23). The names are not the same, however, and, according to the explicit statements in the text, their position in the family is not the same either. Jonathan was the grandson of Eliashib, but Johanan was his son (v 23). Since we have already seen that we cannot presume that these lists are complete, it seems wiser not to identify the two or to emend the present passage; whether one is justified then in proceeding to add several more names to the list by appealing to the practice of papponymy, as Cross does, is extremely doubtful; cf. Widengren, "The Persian Period," *History*, 506–9. It seems most probable, therefore, that Jonathan was a nephew of Johanan and that he held office after him.

The last name in this list, Jaddua, is generally identified with the high priest in the time of Alexander the Great's closest contact with Jerusalem, *ca.* 333 B.C. This is based on the evidence of Josephus, *Ant* 11 § 302. Taken at face value, this would again present us with an unusually long tenure. In addition, there is strong evidence, as I have tried to show in *JTS* ns 28 (1977) 49–66, for believing that there was a high priest called Johanan in office late in the Persian period who is clearly not mentioned here. We are thus left with three alternatives; either our present list is incomplete, and Jaddua was as late as Josephus suggests; or Josephus was entirely wrong in dating Jaddua as late as he does; or there was more than one high priest called Jaddua. While all three possibilities can be defended, the first seems most plausible: the third suggestion is a pure guess by Cross, whose views have been shown to be weak (Widengren). Just because papponymy was practiced, we are not justified in postulating it at every point without any supporting evidence. The second possibility may claim in its support the very dubious nature of much of Josephus' treatment of the period of Alexander (cf. Rowley, "Sanballat"; R. J. Coggins, *Samaritans and Jews* [Oxford: Basil Blackwell, 1975], 95–97; and V. Tcherikover, *Hellenistic Civilization and the Jews* [tr. S. Applebaum; New York: Atheneum, 1959], 42–45), but as regards the succession of high priests it is likely that he was more reliably informed; cf. D. R. Schwartz, "κατὰ τοῦτον τὸν καιρὸν: Josephus on Agrippa II," *JQR* 72 (1982) 241–68 (252–54). This point also tells positively in favor of the first possibility, to which may be added the evidence already mentioned that this list is indeed defective at more than one point. We may thus conclude that Jaddua was

probably the high priest at the end of the Persian period, but that, for reasons
noted in *Form* above, this does not mean that the whole of this passage
should be dated as late as this.

12–21 Coming between Jeshua and Eliashib, Joiakim was probably believed by the author to be the high priest during the period of Ezra's activity;
see also v 26. For the list itself see *Comment* on vv 1–7 and *Form* above. Of
the names of the individual priests listed, one has been lost (v 17) and two,
Meraiah and Kallai, are suspicious for the reasons given in n. 20.a. In general,
however, they raise no particular difficulty. If the Zechariah from the family
of Iddo (v 16) is to be identified with the prophet (cf. Zech 1:1), then we
have here a further small indication that the list's chronological setting is
correct and should not be sought later.

22 This is a difficult verse, the interpretation of which can only be tentative. It was seen in *Notes,* however, that attempts at major textual reconstruction could not be justified. We therefore propose that the first half of the
verse be understood as a comment by the editor on the list of Levites which
he is about to introduce. It is intended to explain the otherwise curious fact
that the names are the same as in vv 8–9; throughout this period (i.e., from
Eliashib, the successor of Joiakim, so far as he knew, to Johanan, from whose
time the list he has in his source derives), the Levites were listed, so he
claims, by families rather than as individuals. That this is an artificial device
to cover over the way in which he composed vv 8–9 out of vv 24–25 is shown
by the fact that some of the names with their associated tasks are patently
those of individuals.

"And Jaddua" was seen in *Form* to be a later addition. The original author
stopped at Johanan (see also v 23), whom we must therefore assume to have
been the high priest in his own day or shortly before. All the known information about this Johanan was listed in *Comment* on Ezra 10:6, even though it
was concluded that he is probably not to be identified with the Jehohanan
of that verse. There is therefore no need for further discussion here.

The second half of the verse, introduced simply by והכהנים "and the
priests," is best construed, I would suggest, as the incorporation of a late
gloss into the text. This is shown by its lack of syntactical integration into
the text and by the use of a king as a chronological point of reference, whereas
the passage otherwise always dates the lists by way of the high priests. A
reader who understood v 22a in the way outlined above observed on the
evidence of the lists in the first part of the chapter that the priests presented
a different situation. Whereas the Levites were listed by families throughout
the period concerned, the priests were so listed only for the first generation.
The glossator drew attention to this fact with his reference to Darius, the
king at the time of the building of the second temple when Zerubbabel and
Jeshua are most prominent in the narratives of Ezra 1–6.

The identity of "Darius the Persian" is highly controversial. The use of
the gentilic has suggested to many that it presupposes a date after the fall
of the Persian empire and that, with a reference to Jaddua in the context,
Darius III Codomannus (336–330 b.c.) must be intended. Others, however,
anxious to date these books rather earlier, find a reference to Darius II Nothus
(424–404 b.c.) and seek to find contemporary examples of the use of the

title "the Persian" to show that it does not presuppose the fall of the Persian empire. This is not fully convincing, however; cf. Mowinckel's remarks, *Studien I*, 161, *contra* Rudolph. Mowinckel himself maintains that the debate is to a large extent beside the point; he thinks it is clear that the last Darius is intended, but maintains that later Jewish writers did not distinguish between Darius II and III. In this, he is correct; cf. Williamson, *JTS* ns 28 (1977) 64–65. His mistake, however, is in going on to assert that this "second" Darius was Darius the Persian in distinction to "Darius the Mede" as the first Darius. "Darius the Mede" is a problematic figure known only from the book of Daniel (6:1 [5:31]). What is quite certain, however, is that he is contrasted with, and dated prior to, Cyrus the Persian (Dan 6:29 [28]). Therefore, in whatever form our glossator knew the Daniel material, if he intended a contrast with Darius the Mede, he is much more likely to have been referring to Darius I after the pattern of Cyrus the Persian. And that this is indeed his intention is strongly favored by the fact that these are the only two places in the OT (one in Hebrew, the other in Aramaic) where the gentilic adjective "the Persian" occurs.

To sum up: "Darius the Persian" is a way of referring to Darius I in order to distinguish him from Darius the Mede. The glossator's aim was to show that at that early time the priests were recorded by families, just as the Levites continued to be for several generations. This form of reference is certainly to be dated well into the Hellenistic period, thereby confirming our judgment that v 22b is a late gloss.

23 For most of this verse, see *Form* above. For a defense of the view that Johanan was indeed the son, not the grandson, of Eliashib, see *Comment* on Ezra 10:6. We should not overlook, however, the valuable insight that this verse gives into the preservation of lists of names in an officially recorded manner. There is no reason whatever to doubt the veracity of this evidence, mentioned merely in passing by the author. When it can be shown, as we have tried to do for part of this chapter, that a list goes back to such a source, it should be regarded as firsthand historical material of the highest importance.

24–25 For the names of the Levites with the singers, see *Form* above. Once again there is a reference to antiphonal singing; cf. vv 8–9. The clear statement that the duties of the Levites were ordered by David is also the outlook of the Chronicler, though later this belief seems to have been modified; cf. Williamson, VTSup 30 (1979) 251–68. The title "man of God" is applied to David only rarely (v 36 below and 2 Chr 8:14), always in connection with his ordering of the music for the cult. It would thus seem to be intended less as a prophetic designation (its usual sense) than as a point of comparison with Moses (Deut 33:1; Josh 14:6), the major founder of the Israelite cult.

The gatekeepers are listed in their conventional families (cf. Ezra 2:42), though, as at 11:19, with fewer names than expected.

26 Taking his cue from v 12, the editor summarizes the lists he has recorded as dating from the period of Joiakim. This was strictly accurate for the priests and could be justified for the Levites on the basis of the consideration that they were always recorded by family names, as explained at v 22. More important, however, is the linking of Joiakim with Nehemiah and Ezra.

The author no doubt believed that Joiakim was the high priest when Ezra came to Jerusalem. We might have expected him to know that Eliashib was high priest by Nehemiah's time. Such accuracy was not his concern, however. Rather, he wished to present their work as a united activity in the restoration of Jerusalem, the temple and its worship, something which the interweaving of their accounts in these books already seeks to do, and which our author already had in front of him. It is thus a serious misunderstanding to delete "Nehemiah the governor and" as a later addition (Rudolph). The case is quite different from 8:9; our author is working with a text that has already fused the two reformers' activities. For similar reasons there is no justification for using the order in which they are listed here to support the view that Ezra followed Nehemiah. Rather, the order is determined by reflection on the book of Nehemiah itself, in which Ezra first appears in chap. 8.

Explanation

In this passage we are presented with a list of priests and Levites from the time of the return to Jerusalem and the building of the second temple and another from the next generation, which includes the period of Ezra and Nehemiah. The author is at pains to point out the close family associations between these two periods.

In our understanding of the composition of these books, he already knew of the combination of the material about Ezra and Nehemiah; significantly, however, Ezra 1–6 had not yet been prefaced to this account. It is thus clear that his purpose in adding this material was to draw the lines of continuity between the reestablishment of the Jerusalem cult and its reformation by Ezra and Nehemiah.

Two aspects of the passage may seem particularly strange to modern readers. One is the artificial manner by which the author has justified his injection of later lists into earlier periods. The other is his chronological simplification whereby the restoration and the reform are slotted into two successive generations.

Such schematic presentation in order to present a theological truth was an accepted convention in the author's day, however. He is very close to the world of the Chronicler, the first nine chapters of whose work are replete with examples of such devices. Nor is the NT unfamiliar with such compositions, as Matt 1:1–17 demonstrates. By an apparent oversimplification of historical perspective, the author thus managed to present the complexities of the historical continuum as an orderly progression toward the desired goal of the full restoration of the cult, a progression in which he no doubt detected the overruling direction of God's purposes for his people.

The Dedication of the Wall (Neh 12:27–43)

Bibliography

Burrows, M. "The Topography of Nehemiah 12:31–43." *JBL* 54 (1935) 29–39. **Fuller-ton, K.** "The Procession of Nehemiah." *JBL* 38 (1919) 171–79. **Kellermann, U.** *Nehe-mia,* 44–46, 93–94. **Simons, J.** *Jerusalem in the Old Testament.* Leiden: E. J. Brill (1952) 446–50. **Snaith, N. H.** "Nehemiah xii 36." *VT* 17 (1967) 243. **Williamson, H. G. M.** "Nehemiah's Wall Revisited." *PEQ* 116 (1984) 81–88.

Translation

12:27 *At the time of the dedication of the wall of Jerusalem, the Levites were sought out* [a] *from wherever they lived to be brought to Jerusalem to celebrate the dedication with joy,* [b] *with thanksgiving choirs* [c] *and the accompanying music of cymbals, lutes, and lyres.* [d] 28 *The singers* [a] *were assembled both* [b] *from the district* [c] *round about Jerusalem and from the villages of the Netophathites,* 29 *from Beth-haggilgal and the fields of Geba and Azmavet,* [a] *for the singers had built villages for themselves round about Jerusalem.* 30 *The priests and the Levites first purified themselves; then they purified the people, the gates, and the wall.*

31 *I brought the leaders of Judah up onto* [a] *the wall and organized two large choirs to give thanks. One went* [b] *southward* [c] *along the top of* [a] *the wall to the Dung Gate,* 32 *followed by* [a] *Hoshaiah and half the leaders of Judah,* 33 *and by* [a] *Azariah [Ezra]* [b] *and Meshullam,* 34 *[Judah] and Minjamin* [a] *and Shemaiah and Jeremiah,* 35 *that is, some of the priests* [a] *with trumpets; (also by)* [b] *Zechariah, son of Jonathan, son of Shemaiah, son of Mattaniah, son of Micaiah, son of Zakkur, son of Asaph,* 36 *and his associates Shemaiah and Azarel, Milalai, Gilalai,* [a] *Maai, Nethanel, Hanani, and Judah,* [b] *with the musical instruments of David, the man of God; and Ezra the scribe went in front of them;* 37 *and (they went)* [a] *over the Spring Gate. Then they went straight* [b] *up* [c] *the steps of the City of David, on the ascent to the city wall,* [d] *past the house of David and so finally to the Water Gate on the east.*

38 *The second choir went* [a] *northwards* [b] *(I followed, with [the other] half of the people)* [c] *along the top of the wall past the Tower of the Ovens to the broad wall,* 39 *past the Ephraim Gate, and over the Mishneh Gate,* [a] *the Fish Gate, the Tower of Hananel, the Tower of the Hundred as far as the Sheep Gate and came to a halt at the Gate of the Guard.*

40 *Then the two thanksgiving choirs took up their positions in the house of God, as did I and the half of the officials who were with me;* 41 *likewise the priests, Eliakim, Maaseiah, Miniamin, Micaiah, Elioenai, Zechariah, (and) Hananiah with trumpets,* 42 *and Maaseiah, Shemaiah, Eleazar, Uzzi, Jehohanan, Malchiah, Elam, and Ezer. The singers sang aloud* [a] *under the direction of Izrahiah.* 43 *They offered up great sacrifices that day and they rejoiced, for God had given them very great joy; the women and children also rejoiced. The sound of rejoicing in Jerusalem could be heard from far away.*

Notes

27.a. An impers pl for pass.

27.b. Lit., "to make a dedication and (sc. to make) joy." This latter phrase occurs also at 8:12 ("to celebrate with . . . joy"). The whole expression is best understood as a hendiadys, so that no emendation is necessary (*contra* NEB).

27.c. This is usually understood as "hymns of thanksgiving," in which case the introductory *wāw* has either to be deleted (but the Vrs are not a secure guide in such instances) or taken as epexegetic ("even with . . ."). However, the use of 'וב . . . וב' suggests the possibility that the conjunctions are intended in the sense of "both . . . and" (this construction is found in the following verse too, so that to delete a *wāw* in both verses becomes still less attractive). If that is the case, the two nouns should be semantically parallel. שיר is already taken by many commentators as "music" because of the list of instruments following; cf. 1 Chr 25:6 and v 36 below for parallels. We would then add here the observation that in vv 31, 38, and 40 תודה certainly refers to a choir. It is thus reasonable to suppose that it does here too.

27.d. Delete ב with several MSS and sense as a dittogr of the following כ.

28.a. Lit., "the sons of the singers," but בני may be used to designate membership of a guild or professional class; cf. BDB 121 A, 7a; H. Haag in *TDOT*, 2, 152. It therefore seems unnecessary (though, of course, not impossible) to add לוי with LXX^L, "the Levitical singers."

28.b. Cf. n. 27.c.

28.c. Cf. n. 3:22.a.

29.a. Or Beth-azmavet; cf. Ezra 2:24.b.

31.a. Later on in the passage מעל ל must mean "beside," as at 2 Chr 26:19. While such a meaning may be intended here too, the verb עלה makes more probable the equally possible rendering given above; cf. 2 Chr 13:4 and Burrows, *JBL* 54 (1935) 31.

31.b. MT ותהלכת, a *h.l.* generally thought to mean "processions." However, comparison with v 38 has convinced all commentators that this cannot be right, and that we must make the slight emendation to והאחת הלכת "and the one went." The corr resulting in the present text is easily understood, while the emended text exactly balances (ה)הלכת) והתודה השנית "and the second choir went . . ." of v 38.

31.c. Cf. Williamson, "Nehemiah's Wall."

32.a. Lit., "and there went after them," i.e., the members of the choir.

33.a. Or "namely"; however, this is less likely, because the following seems to be intended as a list of priests.

33.b. Ezra is an alternative form of Azariah (cf. 10:3 [2] and 12:1, 13). While emendation of the latter has been proposed, the textual evidence in support is slight. More likely, a later reader took seriously the statement at the end of v 36 and so added "Ezra" here to point out more clearly the identity of Azariah. (Note the lack of conj, unlike the other names in the list.) The glossator thus understood "in front of them" (v 36) to mean "in front of the priests," since Azariah here heads the list of priests; see further *Form* below.

34.a. It is very probable that בנימן "Benjamin" is a scribal slip for the priestly name מנימין "Minjamin," (as in v 17), even though this name also occurs in v 41. If so, "Judah" may be a later corr of another name by someone who took it to refer to a tribe. It is noteworthy that Judah is the only other name in the list (besides Ezra; see n. 33.b. above) to lack the conj, and is the only name not used elsewhere of a priest. While it is possible that "Judah" was simply added later to the list, the symmetry between the two processions (cf. *Form*) favors the view that it is a corr of some other name. The initial י would then represent the ו "and," which we expect in the context. On the basis of other lists, אביה "Abiah" might be expected here, though there is no great similarity between the consonants. Alternatively, Schneider suggests ידעיה "Jedaiah," while הודויה "Hodaviah," might also be proposed on the basis of the same error at Ezra 3:9. The name is not attested for a priest, however.

35.a. As a descendant of Asaph, Zechariah must be one of the Levites. It is thus clear that the reference to the priests with their trumpets must belong with the previous verse. MT uses the expression "some of the sons of the priests." For this idiom, cf. n. 28.a. It may imply that the priests just listed were "ordinary" priests as opposed to heads of families. If so, the names should not be identified with the priests listed elsewhere in these books.

35.b. Though these words are necessary in Eng., it may not be imperative to add a conj in Heb.

36.a. These two names are questionable, for the reason given at n. 11:8.a. Despite what most commentators say, there are nine musicians listed in 12:42, including their leader, just as there are here with the leader included. It is thus a mistake simply to delete one of these names as a dittogr. Rather, one is likely to be a scribal device to cover over a badly damaged text.

36.b. MT has "and Judah, Hanani." It is simplest to suppose that the two words simply became inverted in the course of transmission; cf. n. 12:25.b. for example.

37.a. It looks as though this verse was once the direct continuation of v 31. The first phrase is therefore still governed by הלכת "went." Strictly speaking, no verb has dropped out, but the insertion of the list in vv 32–36 left the present phrase dangling. Unless we are to put the list in brackets, we must repeat the verb of v 31 in translation.

37.b. For this meaning of נגדם, cf. BDB 617A **i.a.**(b). While the Masoretic accents join it to the first phrase of the verse, it makes better sense with the second. The Masoretes were probably influenced by the abruptness of the opening of the verse in the text as it now stands.

37.c. על might mean "over," but this seems less likely after the verb עלה "to go up."

37.d. As throughout this verse, so here particularly translation is hampered by our lack of knowledge of the topography. The Masoretes take this as an independent phrase, and it may be, therefore, that it describes how the procession rejoined the wall after their detour up the steps. On the other hand, it could equally well be that the steps went up over "(on) the ascent of the wall." The range of meaning of Heb. preps precludes certainty; cf. the brave, but not altogether convincing, attempt by Fullerton to achieve consistency in this regard; *JBL* 38 (1919) 171–79. In the circumstances, major emendation (e.g., Rudolph) is best avoided.

38.a. Delete the art as a dittogr (cf. Vg).

38.b. MT has to be explained as "in the opposite direction." The spelling, however (with א), is exceptional, and the meaning is forced. למול elsewhere means "in front of." Comparison with v 31 suggests that לשמואל "to the north" should be read. In paleo-Heb. script, a ש might well be lost by haplogr with a מ.

38.c. This circumstantial clause is best rendered parenthetically in order to avoid repeating the main verb. It is a mistake to insert שרי "leaders of" before "the people." העם "the people" is here used generally to cover the whole of Nehemiah's procession, both lay and priestly. It is treated more fully in vv 40–42 below, and there the lay element is mentioned separately; so correctly Witton Davies.

39.a. Cf. n. 3:6.a.

42.a. Lit., "caused to hear." We must either understand "their voices" as the object or, as has been suggested, it may be that a reference to musical instruments has been lost from the previous verse (cf. v 36) and that this was originally the intended object here.

Form/Structure/Setting

There is no dispute (apart from Torrey, *Composition*, 43–44, who is tentatively followed, without further reasons, by Burrows, *JBL* 54 [1935] 29–39), that an extract from the NM is included in this paragraph. The first-person narrative is resumed (vv 31, 38, 40) for the first time since 7:5. After so long a gap, it is difficult to attribute this resumption merely to editorial style. The subject matter, too, is something that we expect to find in the Nehemiah material. After all the effort expended on rebuilding the wall, it would have been surprising if there were no ceremony of any kind to mark the achievement.

At the same time, however, scholars are equally unanimous in their opinion that this paragraph as a whole has not been extracted direct from the NM. It is observed that the first four verses include no reference to Nehemiah, that the lists of the names of the priests and musicians both interrupt the narrative flow and are not elsewhere the object of Nehemiah's concern, and that the narrative itself is fragmentary: we are not told, for instance, where the processions started from, what happened to most of the members of the processions as they approached the temple, how the first choir came to the temple, and so on. It is therefore generally agreed that an extract from the NM has here been reworked by the editor more than is usual elsewhere.

As a general statement, this conclusion seems inescapable. Particularly noteworthy is the way in which the list in vv 32–36 cuts right into the narrative which must originally have continued from v 31 to v 37 without any interruption, and the odd placing in the narrative of what must be intended as the description of the second procession (vv 40–42); it would have been more natural in v 38. Using this fact in connection with the symmetry in the description of the two processions (see below) and the criterion of the first-person passages and what is inseparably joined to them, it is possible, in a rough and ready way, to assert that vv 31–32, 37–40, and 43 must contain the nucleus of the material taken from the NM. However, to attempt greater precision than this would be too speculative to be of value.

What, then, is the likely origin of the rest of the material? Most commentators simply ascribe it to "the Chronicler," whom they regard as the editor of these books. It is thereby implied that the material is of little historical value; it merely serves to turn the celebration into a clerically dominated religious ceremony (cf. Kellermann, *Nehemia*, 93–94).

It is by no means certain, however, that this negative judgment is justified. There are several indications that this material may rather be based on an alternative account of the ceremony. (i) Vv 27–30 apparently include some valuable archival material (vv 28–29) and they can be readily understood as the summary of an alternative account of the proceedings. V 30 may well describe the conclusion of (Ackroyd), rather than the introduction to (Rudolph), the ceremony. (ii) These opening verses also imply that the Levites and singers were living away from Jerusalem. As far as our information goes, this was the case at the time the walls were built before the events described in chap. 11 (whose dating is, however, uncertain), and again later (cf. 13:10) until the pledge described in chap. 10 rectified the situation. What seems unlikely, however, is that the editor responsible for the present ordering of these chapters should have invented a description like this at the very point where he has recorded, as one of the community's acts of obedience, the movement of a number of the Levites and singers to Jerusalem. (iii) There is an element of overlap also in the descriptions of the processions. So far as we can judge, the NM was brief on this point, but חצי העם "half the people" (v 38), probably, and חצי הסגנים עמי "the half of the officials who were with me" (v 40), certainly, come from his account. סגנים is one of the words he regularly uses for the leaders of the community (cf. 2:16; 4:8 [14], 13 [19]; 5:7, 17; 7:5; 13:11). In the description of the first procession, however, the lay leaders are designated as שרי יהודה, "the leaders of Judah" (v 32), whereas Nehemiah himself uses שרים for religious and lay leaders together (v 31). It appears, therefore, that two separate descriptions of the processions (of which Nehemiah's may have been quite brief) have been spliced together rather than that the fuller form has evolved directly out of the shorter.

This conclusion, it may be observed, fits in well with what we have already noted in connection with chaps. 10 and 11. It was suggested there that alterna-tive accounts of events were preserved (as, indeed, of the wall-building itself, though that account was already incorporated into the NM at Neh 3). In those two cases, the editor preferred to follow them exclusively (though chap. 13 redresses the balance to some extent); here, by contrast, he has joined the two. He no doubt deemed it appropriate to indicate Nehemiah's personal involvement in this celebration of his major accomplishment.

The structure of the passage is somewhat disjointed, owing to the manner of composition just outlined. For this reason, it is unwise to put too much emphasis on minor internal repetitions (e.g., between verses 27 and 28) as indicators of later additions. It is just as likely that this is the result of amal-gamating two sources or, in the first two verses of the passage, of having an introductory statement (v 27) followed up in greater detail (vv 28–29) in the subsequent narrative.

There is one item, however, that must be pursued more fully here, namely, the balance between the two processions. They appear to have been made up as follows:

(1) Thanksgiving choir (vv 31 and 38)
(2) A prominent layman: Hoshaiah (v 32) and Nehemiah (vv 38, 40)
(3) Half the lay leaders (vv 32 and 40)
(4) Seven priests with trumpets (vv 33–35a and 41)
(5) A director of music: Zechariah (v 35b) and Izrahiah (v 42b)
(6) Eight Levitical musicians (vv 36 and 42)

It can scarcely be supposed that this symmetry is unintentional. As set out, however, there appears to be no place for Ezra the scribe mentioned in connec-tion with the first procession as going "in front of them" (v 36). It is clearly a mistake to treat him as the equivalent of Izrahiah in the second procession (*contra* Bertholet *et al.*). Many have argued, therefore, that the reference to Ezra has been added later by the editor who wished to unite the reforms of Ezra and Nehemiah. Historically, the inclusion of Ezra here would be of no greater value than that of Nehemiah in 8:9.

If the text throughout vv 33–36 is sound, then this conclusion is justified, in my opinion. However, we have seen in n. 33.b. above that this may not be the case. The name "Ezra" there, necessary for the symmetry between the two processions, is most likely a gloss on Azariah before it: both names are the same, and "Ezra" lacks the conjunction which we expect. Now Azariah, it is generally agreed, is not to be identified with Ezra the scribe; he is one of the heads of the priestly families mentioned at 10:3 (2); see also 12:1 and 13 with alternative spelling. Nevertheless, Ezra was of distinguished priestly descent (cf. Ezra 7:1–5), so that if he were present on this occasion, he might well be found among the priests. That, at any rate, is what the glossator of v 33 apparently thought. His mistake, however, was to identify Azariah and Ezra the scribe. Had he inserted Ezra *before* Azariah, he might well have expressed the true situation. At all events, Ezra would be needed in order to maintain the symmetry of the two processions. The position of his name at the end of the list may have a slight parallel at Job 21:33, as observed by Snaith, *VT* 17 (1967) 243. But it is not exact, and is certainly not strong enough in itself to determine the authenticity of the phrase in our passage.

The question of whether Ezra and Nehemiah were ever together in Jerusalem has been one of the major topics of debate in regard to these books. It is thus somewhat curious to have to report that the solution to the problem rests in the end upon the probability of a textual conjecture (i.e., that Ezra in v 33 is a later gloss). However, as it turns out, this may not be altogether inappropriate. We have seen at Neh 8 that all Ezra's significant activity was carried out quite independently of Nehemiah. It is therefore of only slight interest whether he continued to live in Jerusalem as a prominent member of the priesthood. This passage may be held to suggest that he did; but nothing of importance would be changed if he did not.

Finally, we must consider the setting of the passage, and of the events it describes. Historically, we expect the dedication to follow quickly after the building of the walls. In the NM, such an account would fit well after 7:3, or possibly 6:19, but firm evidence is lacking. Clearly, therefore, the editor has moved the account for a particular reason. His treatment of Neh 8 at once suggests itself as an analogy, and this is confirmed by the opening of our passage when it is joined to what in the editor's version immediately preceded it, namely 11:20. (We have seen that 11:21—12:26 has all been added later.) The reference to various groups of the population living in their own towns (11:20) and coming together to Jerusalem for a major ceremony (12:27–28) is exactly the same pattern as that found at the end of chap. 7 and the beginning of chap. 8. And just as there it prefaced an account of the climax of Ezra's ministry, so here it does for Nehemiah's. The editor will not allow us to drive a wedge between religious and secular reform. Rather he has interwoven the accounts and their climaxes in such a way as to suggest that they both arise out of each other and need each other if either is to be brought to a successful conclusion.

Comment

27 The presupposition underlying this verse will have been rather clearer when it was originally joined directly to 11:20. The emphasis falls on the celebration "with joy," a point that will be emphatically resumed at the close of the account (v 43). It was noted as a characteristic of the account of Ezra's reading of the law in chap. 8, and so may well reflect the editor's appreciation of the nature of religion. Music, then as now, was both a stimulus to, and an expression of, joy, so that care was exercised to ensure that the Levites, who are here apparently considered primarily as instrumentalists, should be present in numbers. The last two instruments named (English equivalents are approximate at best) are both stringed instruments played by plucking. In artistic representations the number of strings varies; in addition, instruments both with and without sounding boxes are portrayed. The important point here is that they could obviously be played while being carried. The frequent rendering by "harp" is thus misleading.

28–29 The relationship of the singers to the Levites throughout this passage is ambiguous. Here they appear to be treated separately, and yet it is difficult not to suppose that they are also included among the musicians of the previous verse. A similar ambiguity is found in v 42. It is probable that this reflects the very time when the singers were beginning to be reckoned as Levites.

The beginning and end of the list of the singers' dwellings refer to the same group of settlements, as the repetition of סביבות ירושלם, "round about Jerusalem," shows. ככר in v 28 is therefore best understood generally—"district"—rather than identified with any specific location. "The villages of the Netophathites" means the village of Netophah and its dependent settlements. Netophah is now generally located at Khirbet Bedd Faluh, some 3½ miles to the southeast of Bethlehem; cf. 1 Chr 2:54; Ezra 2:22; A. Alt, *PJB* 28 (1932) 9–12, and K. Kob, "Netopha," *PJB* 28 (1932) 47–54. A nearby spring called ʿAin en-Naṭuf may preserve the ancient name. Beth-haggilgal is presumably the same as the better known Gilgal near Jericho, while Geba and Azmavet were Benjaminite cities a few miles northeast of Jerusalem. These settlements were therefore not concentrated in a specific area but scattered somewhat around the fringes of the province, suggesting that the singers had to gain a foothold on the land as best they could after support from the temple cult failed; cf. 13:10.

30 As the text stands, purification marked the start of the dedication ceremony, just as it did other major religious occasions in ancient Israel; see *Comment* on Ezra 6:20. It may have involved washing of self and of clothes, ritual sprinkling, the sacrifice of a sin-offering, fasting, and abstinence from sexual intercourse; cf. Exod 19:10, 14–15; Lev 16:28; Num 8:5–8; 19. The purification of the wall and gates is an unparalleled idea, but may reflect an increased awareness of the sanctity of Jerusalem, "the holy city" (cf. 11:1), which had so long been defiled by the incursion of the Gentiles and, as Schneider suggests, by the death of so many on the wall itself in the defense of the city. Quite probably the same involved ceremony of sprinkling as was practiced for the cleansing of private houses (Lev 14:49–53) was used on this occasion too (Myers).

31 For the dedication proper, Nehemiah led the leaders of the people up to the top of the wall (cf. n. 31.a.). By "leaders," שרים, he evidently means both lay and religious without distinction. Nehemiah himself thus uses the word in a rather different sense from the alternative account, where it refers to lay leaders only (v 32).

The starting point for the two processions is not stated, but it can be deduced without any doubt as the Valley Gate: (i) though an important landmark, it is not mentioned elsewhere in the itineraries of this passage; (ii) it comes precisely between the first "landfalls" mentioned for each procession, namely, the Dung Gate to the south and the Tower of the Ovens (v 38) to the north; cf. 3:11–14 and Burrows, *JBL* 54 (1935) 33; (iii) it is the gate nearest to a point halfway around the wall from entry into the temple on the east side (v 40). Appropriately enough, it was also the gate from which Nehemiah had set out on his night inspection before the work ever began; cf. 2:13.

Nehemiah divided the people into two processions. The first started off south, and encircled half the city in a counterclockwise direction. It is probably best not to read into the ceremony elaborate ideas of magic circles to ward off evil spirits or the like. It should be noted that neither procession encircled the whole city, and that the section between the Water Gate and the Sheep Gate was not covered by either. The processions were rather a celebration of the completed work and as such a stimulus to thanksgiving and a means of commitment, dedication, of the whole to God. The chanting of such Psalms as 48 (cf. especially vv 13–14 [12–13]) and 147 would have provided an appropriate accompaniment.

For the Dung Gate, cf. 2:13.

32–36 For the composition of the procession, cf. *Form* above. According to Num 10:8; 31:6, only the priests blew trumpets (cf. also 1 Chr 15:24; 16:6). The same rule evidently applied here, while all other aspects of the music were in the hands of the Levites. On "David, the man of God," cf. 12:24.

37 As already indicated in the *Notes*, this verse presents too many uncertainties for detailed explanation. Even the force of the prepositions, let alone some of the topographical information, is unclear. For the Spring Gate and the steps of the City of David, see *Comment* on 2:14 and 3:15. It appears that the procession was obliged to leave the wall at this point, rejoining it further north (cf. Simons, *Jerusalem,* 449, for the contrary view). This may fit with the steepness of the terrain. On the other hand, it was shown in chap. 3 that it was at just this point that Nehemiah's wall began to follow a completely new line, higher up the slope, so that we might have expected that the going would have been made easier. This is one of the chief points in favor of those who believe that the procession went around outside, rather than on top of, the wall. However, since the passage following the reference to the steps is even more obscure, the issue is best left open. A reference to "the house of David" is surprising, though cf. 3:16. Assuming his palace is intended (cf. 2 Sam 5:11), we can hardly suppose that it survived the Babylonian destruction of the city. Its site, however, may still have been known. Again, since it is mentioned in preference to so many other possible landmarks, it may have something to do with the procession's detour. Is there, perhaps, a link with "the tombs of David" (3:16), an area close to the wall that the procession did not wish to traverse?

"The Water Gate on the east" is known from 3:26 and 8:1. The comments on those verses have shown that it lay on the line of the pre-exilic wall of Jerusalem and hence was outside the wall which Nehemiah built. There are then three possible explanations for its presence here: (i) Nehemiah built another Water Gate, higher up the slope from the old one, and this is referred to here. It is strange, however, that it is given exactly the same designation as the old one (cf. 3:26) and curious too that no reference is made to the building of such a gate in chap. 3. (ii) The procession was at this point not on the new city wall, but outside it, and they turned back up the hill at the site of the old Water Gate. The difficulty here is that, so far as we can judge, the procession should now have been either on or inside, but not outside, the city wall. (iii) The description here is to be taken somewhat generally to mean "to a point on the wall opposite the Water Gate." At all events, from this point the procession evidently headed in towards the temple, though curiously we hear no more about it, apart from the choir (v 40).

38–39 The second procession moved northwards from the Valley Gate in a clockwise direction, passing a number of landmarks (in reverse order, of course) that are already familiar from the list in 3:1–11. The Ephraim Gate is not mentioned there, however. It was certainly part of the pre-exilic wall (cf. 2 Kgs 14:13, where it is located 400 cubits from the Corner Gate, itself not certainly identified), and has been universally assumed to have been a gate in Nehemiah's wall too. It then becomes part of the evidence for the fragmentary nature of chap. 3. This may be right. It is striking, however, that a different preposition is used for this gate than for the two following, which certainly were included in Nehemiah's wall (מעל ל as opposed to על). Together with the absence of a reference in chap. 3, this leads us to raise the possibility that the Ephraim Gate was not on the line of Nehemiah's wall. This is just the area where the pre-exilic city began to expand onto the western hill, and the circumvallation of that area need not have been completed all at once; ever-increasing areas may have needed to be enclosed as the size of the city grew. We must therefore reckon with the possibility that there were in this vicinity the ruins of several walls outside that of Nehemiah, and that the Ephraim Gate may have been in one of these. Alternatively, for some reason no longer known to us, Nehemiah's new wall may have simply by-passed the site of the old Ephraim Gate. Interestingly, at 8:16 it is associated with a "broad place" exactly as the Water Gate is in the same verse; yet, as already seen, that Gate too lay outside the line of the wall that Nehemiah was later to build. All these are, however, merely suggestions arising out of attention to the detail of the text as we now have it; it is that very fact, however, which precludes certainty in this matter.

The reference to "the Gate of the Guard" raises some difficulties, especially since it occurs nowhere else. Some identify it with the Muster Gate of 3:31, since this is the next gate on around from the Sheep Gate. However, there is no apparent reason why it should be known under different names; more significantly, comparison of this verse with v 37 suggests that it was at the Sheep Gate that the procession completed its part-circuit of the wall (ועד "and as far as"). Finally, the Gate of the Guard is most naturally associated with the Court of the Guard (cf. 3:25), and is therefore generally located to the south of the temple. If that is correct, then this second procession, entering at the Sheep Gate, must have crossed the temple area before going back into the temple again with the first procession (v 40). It may further be observed that there is no equivalent description of the first choir stopping somewhere. Rudolph therefore proposes to transfer עמדו בשער המטרה (1) "(and) they came to a halt at the Gate of the Guard" to follow v 40; the choirs then enter the temple, while Nehemiah and his fellow laymen stop at the Gate of the Guard. This seems unlikely, however, because (i) the verb should in that case be in the first, not the third, person plural; (ii) there is no reason to deny, and every reason to believe, that the lay leaders would have entered the temple area (though not, of course, the holy place) to take part in the service of praise and thanksgiving; and (iii) there is no evidence for this textual move nor reason for the occurrence of the error. Most likely, therefore, our problems are caused by the fact that, as presented by the editor, the account of the proceedings is defective. We are told the final destination only of the two choirs and of one half of the lay leaders. Nothing is said of the rest of the first procession (including its priests and Levites!), while v 41 is probably a mere description of the second procession rather than a statement of its destination. Probability suggests, therefore, that the first procession moved towards the temple from the Water Gate, and the second from the Sheep Gate. They met up first, however, in the Court of the Guard and there reassembled, the choirs, groups of priests and so on proceeding together thereafter into the temple.

41–42 For the description of the second procession, see *Form* above.

43 The emphasis at this concluding celebration is one of unqualified joy; the word itself, as verb and noun, comes no less than five times in the verse. It thus surpasses even the dedication of the temple itself (Ezra 6:16) and Ezra's presentation of the Law, since the joy at that time (Neh 8:12, 17) had been previously qualified by mourning (v 9). The same point is made by comparison with the other occasion when the sound of a ceremony in Jerusalem "could be heard from far away" (Ezra 3:13), for there too the sound was of joy mixed with weeping. In terms of the reestablishment of Jerusalem as a religious center, this therefore marks a fitting climax to these books, though the closing paragraphs serve as a reminder that it is no easy matter to maintain such heights of experience.

Explanation

The dedication of the newly built wall of Jerusalem is a climax to the books of Ezra and Nehemiah. It marks the last stage in the long process of restoration after the exile, a process which began with the return of the people and the building of the temple, was continued with internal reform on the basis of the Book of the Law and now culminates in a celebration of the rebuilt and repopulated holy city.

The account is unique in its emphasis on unalloyed joy; only the account of the dedication of the temple approaches it in this; cf. Ezra 6:16–22. The processions around the wall must have served as a forceful reminder of the effort which had been invested in the work, and for none more so than for Nehemiah himself, whose earlier excursion through the Valley Gate on his first arrival in Jerusalem (2:12–15) had so impressed him with the enormity of the task in hand. "Every inch of these ramparts had its special memory for one group or another" (Kidner).

There is no need for the commentator to apologize for this display of joy at a task well done. Biblical faith invites us unashamedly to look to future consummation as a tangible reality to work towards and as a motivation to endure hardships in the present. We are reminded in this of the example of Jesus himself, "who for the joy that was set before him endured the cross, despising the shame" (Heb 12:2).

It may be felt by some, however, that this is all too physical; would the editor not have done better to keep this account where it belonged—close to the description of the finishing of the work in chap. 6—and to climax his account with the presentation of the law of God and the people's commitment to it? Is not the physical merely a framework for the spiritual? The biblical author will not entertain such a dichotomy! By his careful splicing of the Ezra and the Nehemiah material he has come as near as he can in narrative terms to an emphatic assertion that the two are but opposite faces of a single reality. If the spiritual be not expressed through the physical, he seems to say, then it is not spiritual at all but mere hypocrisy. But equally, if the physical is not imbued with commitment to and dependence upon God, then it is, quite simply, an arrogant materialism. As if, therefore, to impress this lesson upon his readers, he does not stop, as a mere novelist might have done, with this triumphant and climactic account. Rather, he deliberately presses forward to speak of at first sight comparatively trivial daily arrangements and then of subsequent setbacks, for by these tokens too is true progress to be measured.

The Temple Chambers: Use and Abuse
(Neh 12:44—13:14)

Bibliography

Kellermann, U. *Nehemia,* 47–51. **Mowinckel, S.** *Studien II,* 34–39.

Translation

12:44 *On that day men were appointed to take charge of the rooms for the stores,
the sacred contributions, the prime offerings* [a] *and the tithes, to gather into them,
according to* [b] *the fields of the towns, the portions* [c] *required by the law for the priests
and Levites, for Judah delighted in the priests and Levites who ministered.* [d] 45 *And
they performed the service of their God and the service of purification, as did the
singers and gatekeepers, according to the commandment of David and* [a] *Solomon his
son.* 46 *For long ago, in the days of David and of Asaph, there were* [a] *both heads* [b]
of the guild of singers and directors [c] *of praise and thanksgivings to God.* 47 *In the
days of Zerubbabel and of Nehemiah all Israel gave the portions for the singers and
gatekeepers as each day required.* [a] *They also set aside the portion for the Levites,
and the Levites set aside the portion for the Aaronites.*

13:1 *On that day when they read the book of Moses to the people, they found written
in it that no Ammonite or Moabite should ever enter the assembly of God,* 2 *because
they had not met the Israelites with food and water but he had hired Balaam against
them to curse them, though our God turned the curse into a blessing.* 3 *When the
people heard this law, they separated out from Israel all who were of mixed descent.*

4 *Before this, however, Eliashib the priest, who was appointed to be in charge of
the storerooms* [a] *of the house of our God and who was a relative of Tobiah,* 5 *had
provided* [a] *for his use a large storeroom where there had previously been kept the
grain offering, the incense, and the vessels, together with the tithes of corn, new wine,
and oil as prescribed for* [b] *the Levites, singers, and gate-keepers, and the portion set
aside for the priests.* 6 *Throughout this time I was not in Jerusalem, for in the thirty-
second year of Artaxerxes king of Babylon, I had gone to the king. Then some time
later I had asked permission of the king* 7 *and came back to Jerusalem. That was
when I appreciated the extent of the evil that Eliashib had done to favor Tobiah by
providing him with a room in the courts of the house of God.* 8 *I was very angry
and threw all Tobiah's household belongings out of the room.* 9 *Then I gave orders
that the rooms should be purified, and I restored to them the temple vessels, the grain
offering, and the incense.*

10 *I then found out that the Levites had not been given* [a] *their portions and that
in consequence the Levites and singers who did the work had all fled to their fields.*
11 *I contended with the officials and said, "Why is the house of God neglected?" I
recalled them and reinstated them in their places.* 12 *Then all Judah brought the tithes
of grain, new wine, and oil to the storerooms.* 13 *I put Shelemiah the priest, Zadok
the scribe, and Pedaiah, one of the Levites, in charge* [a] *of the storerooms, with Hanan,
son of Zaccur, son of Mattaniah, as their assistant, for they were considered trustworthy.
Their task was to arrange the distribution to their colleagues.*

¹⁴ *Remember me for this, O my God and do not erase from your memory the good deeds which I have faithfully ᵃ done for the house of my God and its services.*

Notes

44.a. See on 10:38.

44.b. As it stands, this puzzling phrase seems to suggest that the collection was so regulated as to be "checked in" field by field. Some find this incredible and so emend to מִשְּׂדֵי "from the fields of the towns," with LXXᴸ. (Though it is now generally agreed that ל can mean "from," that is unlikely in so late a text as this.) The explanations offered as to how so straightforward a text was corrupted are not completely convincing, however. Is there a possibility that the words are a gl, referring to 10:38b (37b), where it is stated that the Levites are to gather the tithes "in all the towns where we work"? If that phrase is itself a later addition (see the discussion *ad loc.*), this could also have been added to align this passage with that new regulation. It would then mean "to, at the fields of the towns." The reading לשרי, "to the chiefs of the towns," attested by some MSS and Vrs, is undoubtedly secondary.

44.c. Cf. GKC § 95n.

44.d. An ellipsis for עמד לפני יהוה, lit., "stand before the Lord," as at Deut 10:8; Ezek 44:15; 2 Chr 29:11, where specifically priestly duties are in view.

45.a. Restore the conj, lost by haplogr after the ד, with many MSS and Vrs.

46.a. The only possible connection between this verse and the previous one is that, contrary to what a surprised reader might think, the narrator is insistent that as early as David's time the singers were indeed sufficiently organized to be regulated by the king. Emendations that result in such renderings as NEB, "For it was in the days of David that Asaph took the lead . . ." simply produce a *non sequitur.* See also Rudolph, who resorts to even more sweeping alterations to the text. Bertholet's מֻפְקָדִים "were appointed," for מקדם "of old, long ago," is not subject to this problem and is possible; however, מקדם itself is required precisely to effect the connection of thought with the previous verse, so that it would be better to think of a loss by parablepsis; but in fact it is not necessary, and MT is to be preferred.

46.b. We read the pl ראשי with Q, some MSS, and Vg; the sg, ראש, of K and LXX is also possible.

46.c. MT שיר "a song." This is difficult on any understanding of the text. Ehrlich's proposal, *Randglossen* VII, 210, to swap the last two letters around and so to read שָׂרֵי "directors" is most attractive; cf. 1 Chr 15:27 for a parallel.

47.a. Cf. n. 11:23.a.

13:4.a. Repoint to read the pl (לְשָׁכֹת) with most commentators. The sg may have developed under the influence of the references to a particular room in the following narrative.

5.a. For examples of the use of the "impf consec" after a noun used absolutely rather than with the expected ויהי, cf. GKC § 111h.

5.b. An obj gen construction, the whole phrase then being in apposition with the preceding list of tithes. Although מצוה "commandment" is not what might at first be expected in such a context, 10:33 (32) suggests that emendation is not necessary.

10.a. Lit., "the portions of the Levites had not been given." נתנה "been given" is thus governed by the fem pl (const) מניות "portions." We should then normally expect וְנָתְנוּ (pausal form); ה and ו are sometimes confused, and there is a little MS support for such a reading. Precisely because it is easier, however, we must be suspicious of it. More likely, MT represents a rare 3 fem pl form (cf. GKC § 44m, where, however, this solution is rejected, and, for a statement of the problem only, J. Barr, *Comparative Philology and the Text of the Old Testament* [Oxford: Clarendon Press, 1968] 30–31). This form was common in the Aram. of the time, and influence from that quarter is highly probable at this period.

13.a. MT has an unusual (cf. GKC § 53n) hiph denom of אוצר "a storeroom," hence presumably "to set over the storeroom" (GKC § 53g). Many regard the ר as a miswriting of a ו (under the influence of the following line) and so read ואצוה "and I commanded, put in charge," the exact idiom found elsewhere in Nehemiah's writing (cf. 7:2). Either is possible, and there is no difference in meaning.

14.a. "Faithfully" is added in the Eng. in an attempt to capture a little more of the nuance of חסדי, rendered above as "(my) good deeds." On the development of meaning in this word attested by this verse, cf. K. D. Sakenfeld, *The Meaning of Hesed in the Hebrew Bible: a New Inquiry* (HSM 17; Missoula: Scholars Press, 1978) 151–53.

Form/Structure/Setting

Because 12:44—13:3 does not seem to come from the NM, whereas 13:4–14 probably does, commentators nearly always treat 12:44—13:3 as a separate section, and link 13:4–14 with the remainder of chap. 13 under some such general heading as "Nehemiah's second term as governor."

While these observations concerning the origin of the material in 12:44—13:14 are probably correct, it is nevertheless a serious mistake, in my view, to overlook the several indications which the editor has given us that he expects this passage to be read as a unity. First, the chronological notes are clear: ביום ההוא "on that day," in 12:44 and 13:1, links these two paragraphs together (note also the same phrase in 12:43), while ולפני מזה "Before this, however," links 13:4 and what goes with it inseparably with the foregoing. Verses 10–14 are given no separate chronological introduction, while v 15 starts with the rather less precise בימים ההמה "in those days," as does v 23. This is the first of several elements that unite the last two major paragraphs of the chapter together (vv 15–22, 23–30a; see the discussion *ad loc.*) and which in turn then separate them somewhat from the previous verses.

Second, this lack of a break between vv 4–9 and 10–13 is made more apparent by the basic unity of theme in these two sections; both are concerned with the use and abuse of the temple chambers. It is the misuse to which Eliashib has allowed them to be put which is so shocking in vv 4–9: this is where the grain offering, new wine, oil, and so on had previously been stored (v 5), and the result of Nehemiah's cleansing was the restoration of this use (v 9). Verses 10–13 center on the same theme, however, and the result of Nehemiah's action is again that "grain, new wine, and oil" flow into the storerooms (v 12). Verses 4–14 are thus united by similar concerns which again set them off from the latter part of the chapter. Now, it can hardly fail to strike the observant reader that this is precisely the concern of 12:44—13:3. It has generally been assumed that the otherwise isolated fragment of 13:1–3 is included here to prepare the way for Nehemiah's treatment of Tobiah in the following verses; it has equally generally been overlooked, however (though cf. Rudolph), how closely similar are the concerns of 12:44–47 and 13:10–13 (appointment of men to take charge of the storerooms; provision for the support of the temple personnel; ministry of purification—12:45 and 13:9 as a necessary preliminary after 13:4–5 to prepare for 13:10–13). The use of the temple chambers is thus clearly a theme that unites the whole of this passage but which marks it off both from what precedes and from what follows.

Third, the passage is drawn up on the basis of a chiastic structure which further serves to bind it together; thus 12:44–47 is closely linked with 13:10–13, as already observed, while the association of 13:1–3 and 4–9 is equally obvious and is widely accepted.

Finally, the "remember" formula appears at v 14. Not only will it be seen later that it serves as a further pointer towards the separation of this passage from the following, but its structure here gives a further clue to the unity in Nehemiah's thinking of the preceding paragraphs: it is attractive to link his deeds "for the house of my God" with vv 4–9 and "for its services" with vv 10–13.

If, then, we are correct in believing that the editor has forged these paragraphs into a coherent unity, we must naturally inquire next after the origin of the material of which they are comprised. Few doubt that 13:4–14 come in the main from the NM (the question of possible later glosses must be left for *Comment* below). Only Torrey, *Composition*, 44–49, has made a serious attempt to challenge this conclusion, but his analysis on the basis of the use of a few words and phrases is too narrowly based to carry conviction. Moreover, it overlooks some points that are highly characteristic of Nehemiah's style; for instance, compare v 11a (and 17a, 25a) with 5:7, etc. At the same time, it is a probable consequence of our discussion earlier that ולפני מזה "Before this, however" (13:4), is to be attributed to the final editor. It is questionable, therefore, whether it should be taken into account when we come to consider the setting of the passage within the original memoir itself.

The origin of the first two paragraphs of this section cannot be so easily determined. Attempts to link 13:1–3 with the Ezra material must be judged a failure because they overlook the fact that the issue here is not that of mixed marriages but of who may be admitted to "the assembly of God." Nor is there any clue to associate the reading and the decision with any other prominent individual. Many, therefore, attribute these verses, which are in any case heavily dependent upon Deut 23, to the hand of the editor, his aim being to soften the impact of Nehemiah's treatment of the Ammonite Tobiah. This may be correct; the only realistic alternative is to compare the general approach to that found in chaps. 10–11, where we have found evidence for the preservation of an account of a number of decisions in the cultic sphere taken by the people, again without reference to particular individuals. Since, as the editor suggests (13:4), the decision in this case again followed Nehemiah's *ad hoc* action (as did those in chap. 10), an action which may have brought the passage in Deuteronomy more forcibly to the people's attention, the possibility should not be ruled out that we have here a recollection of some such commitment into which the community entered.

There does not appear to be any comparable background available for 12:44–47. The question of tithes and offerings was already dealt with at the close of chap. 10, while the chronological indication in 12:47 suggests that this is a very general reflection on the period as a whole. It is therefore probable that this paragraph was composed by the editor specifically for its present context.

This brings us finally, therefore, to a consideration of setting. That of 12:44–47 and of 13:1–3 has already been discussed as far as the very limited evidence allows. Moreover, the setting of 13:4–14 within the NM is best handled elsewhere (cf. *Introduction*, "The Nehemiah Memoir"). Two points, therefore, remain for discussion: the historical setting of Nehemiah's actions here recorded and the literary setting of the whole passage within the book.

To the first question, 13:6–7 appears to provide a straightforward answer.

After twelve years as governor (445–433 B.C.), Nehemiah returned to the royal court for an unspecified period. Later, however, at least before the death of Artaxerxes in 424 B.C., he returned to Jerusalem (whether as governor or not is not stated) and then took action to rectify a number of abuses which had developed during his absence.

In recent years, however, several scholars, including most notably Mowinckel, *Studien II*, 35–37, and Kellermann, *Nehemia*, 48–51, have challenged the whole idea that Nehemiah served a second term as governor. They claim that the relevant phrases are a later gloss, added to explain how such abuses as those described in chap. 13 could have arisen in the first place. In support of this view, they adduce as evidence the chronological confusion if the "dates" in 12:43, 44 and 13:1, 4 are taken seriously; the title מלך בבל "king of Babylon," where Nehemiah normally refers simply to "the king"; the use of "Babylon," which is thought unlikely in a contemporary writer; and the fact that the whole statement appears to be parenthetical, it being possible to omit it without damage or detriment to the surrounding narrative. On this basis, they argue that the expulsion of Tobiah from the temple was one of the first things Nehemiah did on his original arrival as governor; in his memoir, "before this" (13:4) will have meant before the whole account of the wall-building. The other incidents recorded in chap. 13 are then provided with various historical settings during Nehemiah's twelve-year term as governor (5:14).

However we deal with some of the points of detail raised by Mowinckel and Kellermann (see *Comment* below), the main point of their theory seems to me most improbable on historical grounds. It is agreed that some of these abuses—especially the provision of a temple chamber for Tobiah—cannot have taken place while Nehemiah was present in Jerusalem; yet 13:15–22 presupposes the existence of the walls and gates for the rectification of Sabbath abuse, and must therefore follow their construction. Now, it is true that that is the kind of abuse that might develop gradually, and so have taken place while Nehemiah was in Jerusalem, but this seems less probable than that it arose because his watchful eye was deflected for a period. Also, there is no indication of a setting for vv 15–22 different from that of the remainder of chap. 13.

Second, the suggestion that vv 4–5 describe a situation that Nehemiah discovered on his first arrival in Jerusalem is improbable. Tobiah is mentioned as one of Nehemiah's enemies from the first moment on (2:10), with no suggestion whatever that this incident provoked that enmity. It is hard to see why Nehemiah (or a later editor) should have displaced this account from its original setting had it taken place before Nehemiah commenced work on the wall. Furthermore, our understanding of Tobiah's position before Nehemiah's arrival, for which we are partly dependent on Kellermann (see *Comment* on 2:10), suggests that he would not have needed a toe hold in Jerusalem such as the temple-chamber appears to be; he seems to have had wider contacts, and may well have occupied an official residence. The position described in the present paragraph does not dovetail with that at all; it is more easily understood as a friend's attempt to help him back into a position of influence once Nehemiah was out of the way.

Third, a similar comment may be passed upon Kellermann's proposal (p. 153) that vv 10–13 should also be dated to the very start of Nehemiah's governorship. He is obliged to take this view because this too describes a deteriorating situation (cf. v 10) which we cannot imagine taking place while Nehemiah was present. But to suppose that he made arrangements for the cult officials' support before turning his attention to the building of the wall completely contradicts the priorities that Nehemiah's purpose in coming to Jerusalem in the first place had established for him. Furthermore, we have no evidence that would lead us to suppose that there had been any marked change in this matter in the time shortly before Nehemiah's arrival. Verse 11 especially is suggestive rather of a falling away from a standard which Nehemiah had previously seen maintained.

Finally, both Mowinckel and Kellermann place considerable weight on ולפני זה "before this," at the start of v 4. They find here both a chronological difficulty that raises their initial suspicion and a key to the true setting of these incidents as they see them. We have already seen, however, that this phrase is probably redactional; it should therefore not be used to draw historical conclusions that go beyond the immediate structure of the passage as a whole.

This brings us finally, then, to the setting of this passage within the book. The problem is posed both by the inverted order of the narrative and by the somewhat anticlimactic impression it (together with the remainder of chap. 13) makes after the dedication of the wall in 12:27–43. The latter problem can only be answered by a consideration of the composition of the NM as a whole, on which see the *Introduction*, "The Nehemiah Memoir." Despite the fact that inclusion of this material detracted from the idealized ending that 12:43 might have provided, the editor, who was obviously sympathetic to Nehemiah's work, evidently felt obliged to include these additions to the memoir in order to ensure that Nehemiah's contribution to the cultic reforms was not overlooked; indeed, he gave them a certain prominence by concluding his work with them, and by moving the account of the people's pledge forward to chap. 10, where it no longer stands as a threat to Nehemiah's reputation.

Despite this, to have moved immediately from 12:43 to 13:4 would have been harsh not only chronologically but also, and more significantly, thematically. He solved this problem by introducing the outcome of the reforms first and linking this to the dedication by the completely artificial chronological notation "on that day" in 12:44 and 13:1, linking back to the same phrase in 12:43. That it is artificial is shown both by the longer time span in 12:47 and by the introduction to 13:4. (This latter verse shows, of course, that there was no deliberate attempt at historical deception involved in this device.) To this extent, we may agree with the judgment of S. J. DeVries, *Yesterday, Today and Tomorrow* (Grand Rapids: Eerdmans, 1975), 61, that these phrases function "as an artificial synchronism," though his opinion (pp. 67–68) that these are late supplements, originally quite unconnected with what precedes, has been seen to be unacceptable. The editor thus aimed to show that the outcome of the dedication was support for the cult and maintenance of its purity. This then enabled the reader to accept the remainder of chap. 13 as lapses from the norm (so Rudolph); in a sense, therefore, he regarded the

whole of 13:4–31 as pluperfect, 12:26—13:3 forming the abiding climax of
his work. By this device he not only made his text more smooth to read
but again sought to highlight the contribution of Nehemiah to this final conclusion. We may nevertheless feel that he has not fully succeeded in his aim;
he allowed himself to be dominated too much by the shape of the NM, and
his attempt to avoid its anticlimax is too elaborate to be successfully sustained.
We may respect his motivation and method without having thereby to accept
that they have succeeded in every particular.

Comment

12:44 For the force of "on that day," see *Form* above. The editor was
doubtless aware of those who in his own day were responsible for administering the contributions made to the temple. In tracing their appointment back
to this period he has the support of 13:13 as well as, in a more general
sense, 10:36–40 (35–39). The *Comment* on the latter passage should be con-
sulted for the terminology and practices involved, and n. 44.b. above for
the uncertain expression "according to the fields of the town."

Judah's delight (lit., "joy") in the priests and Levites is an unusual thought,
but one which further associates this verse with the previous one. It strengthens the impression that the climax reached at the dedication was sustained
in general terms, depsite some lapses. The writer does not suggest that only
in such circumstances need the law of tithes and offerings be observed but
that it takes the heaviness out of such observance. There is no doubt an
element of idealism here that he wishes to hold up before his readers.

45 The arrangements it was believed David had made for the new situation
that would develop when the ark was finally housed in a permanent temple
are outlined in 1 Chr 23–26; Solomon is portrayed as faithfully implementing
those arrangements once the temple had actually been built (2 Chr 8:14).
In addition to a general statement, "the service of purification" (cf. 1 Chr
23:28) is singled out for mention, probably in conscious anticipation of 13:9.

It is frequently assumed that the reference to the singers and gatekeepers
has been added secondarily and that the remainder of the paragraph, which
develops from this reference, is therefore likewise secondary. Since we are
already dealing, however, with an editor for whom these groups of officials
were of great interest (see, for instance, *Form* on 12:27–43), and since it is
probable that he is composing freely in these verses, there seems to be no
compelling reason why these words should not have been included by him
in the first place.

46 For the general significance of this explanatory aside, cf. n. 46.a. above.
Although in its definitive form the guild of singers had three leaders (Asaph,
Heman, and either Jeduthun or Ethan), Asaph was at first the only named
leader (cf. Ezra 2:41), and was usually the most prominent of the three.

47 This concluding verse expands the vision of the well-ordered community to include the days of Zerubbabel as well as the whole of the period of
Nehemiah; for the formula involved, cf. G. Brin, "The Formula x‑ימי and
x‑יום: Some Characteristics of Historiographical Writing in Israel," *ZAW* 93
(1981) 183–96. We see here the start of that periodizing of post-exilic history

which is continued in 12:1–26 and which reaches its fullest expression in the books of Ezra and Nehemiah as a whole. Though separated sometimes by many decades, the steps in the process of restoration are gradually isolated from their contexts and merged into a continuous "history of salvation." Periods of regression (cf. Mal 3:7–12; Neh 13:10!) are steadily foreshortened, if not completely forgotten, so that the picture of an ideal emerges which may reflect to the glory of God and act as a stimulus to later generations.

Under such a light, the community is seen fully to support the cult. To "set aside" is literally "to sanctify," i.e., to hand over to the sacral sphere for its exclusive use. For the tithing of the tithe, see *Comment* on 10:38–40 (37–39). The reference to the giving to the singers and gatekeepers makes explicit what is probably implicit there in v 40 (39); see also 13:10–12. We see here no connection with 11:23 (q.v.), *contra* O. Eissfeldt, *Erstlinge und Zehnten im alten Testament* (BWANT 22; Leipzig: J. C. Hinrich, 1917) 100–103, though it is to be agreed that the singers and gatekeepers are not yet fully accepted as Levites.

13:1a No specific setting is provided for this reading from the law and nothing suggests that it was a particular occasion. It is probably intended to reflect a situation that arose in the course of the regular liturgical reading of Scripture.

1b–2 Though "the Book of Moses" refers to the Pentateuch as a whole, the particular law in question is Deut 23:4–7 (3–6). The citation abbreviates to a considerable extent, and of necessity casts the second person of the original law into the third person, but otherwise it follows the wording of Deuteronomy very closely. This even extends to retaining the awkward switch from plural ("they had not met") to singular ("but he had hired"), a switch that is itself dependent upon the fact that in the story to which allusion is made (Num 22–24) it was Balak, king of Moab, who hired Balaam. It is unlikely that any change in the force of the original law was intended by these omissions: together with a number of modern commentators, they probably believed that "to the tenth generation" in Deut 23:4 (3) meant "forever" (Deut 23:4 [3] and v 1 here).

Although the reference to the Ammonites is the more difficult element to account for in the Deuteronomic law (see the commentaries), the community of Nehemiah's day will not have been bothered by such a consideration. For them, this was the most relevant part of all, since Tobiah's Ammonite ancestry was well known (2:10 etc.). Even on the narrowest definition of "the assembly of God" as the people gathered for worship, his presence in the temple (vv 4–5) had flouted the law. It may well be that Nehemiah's action brought home to them in a fresh way the applicability of this law and their need to respond to it. A number of commentators have suggested in addition that the reference to Moabites helps pave the way for Nehemiah's action in v 28. However, it was seen at 2:10 above that there were problems in accepting the Moabite identity of Sanballat on which this theory rests.

3 The extent of the community's response to this law is unclear, though there is nothing to suggest that the break-up of mixed marriages was involved on this particular occasion. The context is suggestive rather of an exclusion from sacral gatherings. Yet converts had always been, and continued to be, admitted to the congregation, and the Book of Ruth assumes this with regard to the Moabites rather than arguing for it. It may therefore be that כל־עֵרֶב "all who were of mixed descent" refers narrowly to the children of a mixed marriage, hence "all who were of mixed descent," before they had become of age to decide which parent's religion they were going to follow for themselves.

4 The identity of Eliashib is uncertain. Many identify him with the high priest of the same name (3:1, 20–21; 12:10, 22; 13:28) but this seems unlikely (see also *Comment* on Ezra 10:6): we would have expected his title "the high priest" as everywhere else if that were the case; the description of his function here is not appropriate for a high priest, but seems to be intended rather to identify him as a distinct personality; and, of course, despite the remarks of a few commentators, the fact that a grandson of Eliashib the high priest was Sanballat's son-in-law is of no relevance to the relationship (undefined) of this Eliashib with Tobiah. We must conclude, therefore, that Eliashib was not the high priest, but one whose function fortuitously enabled him to help forward the ambitions of Tobiah to whom he was related (whether by nature or by politics alone is not stated).

5 There was a considerable number of rooms in the temple used for the collection of the tithes and offerings; cf. 2 Chr 31:11; Neh 10:40 (39), etc. Comparison with what Nehemiah restored in v 9 has suggested that the list in the present verse may have been expanded later; this is not certain, since Nehemiah could equally well be abbreviating in v 9, but if it is the case we need again look no further than the editor himself.

That Eliashib put one of these rooms at Tobiah's disposal rather suggests that he did not expect to see Nehemiah back in Jerusalem, or at the least that the time of his arrival was unexpected. For Tobiah, the room no doubt served as a base from which he could begin to develop again those contacts which he already had (cf. 6:17–19) and so to foster a more "liberal" and "open-minded" policy that would integrate Judah into the wider network of Levantine provinces.

6 Nehemiah now explains how such a situation could have arisen in the first place: he was not present at the time. Because this is of subordinate importance within the context of the concerns that governed his writing, it leaves many questions unanswered about which our historically conditioned minds are inevitably concerned. (A similar position was seen to obtain concerning his first journey to Jerusalem: for instance, we are never told that he was appointed governor; see *Comment* on 5:14.) Was he on a regular leave of absence, or had his term as governor come to an end, so that he did not expect to return? We have already noted Eliashib's action as suggesting the latter, while Arsames' absence from Egypt for some three years (cf. *AD* and *AramP* 30) provides an apt parallel for the former. Again, for how long had Nehemiah been away? Despite various guesses, there is simply no evidence by which to determine the issue. Next, we want to know whether Nehemiah was summoned by the king to answer charges brought against him or whether this was the time originally specified in 2:6. The latter suggestion seems unlikely: 2:6 does not imply a period as long as twelve years; equally, the former suggestion rests on a particular understanding of the NM which is not the most probable in terms of either its form or occasion.

Amidst so many uncertainties, what may we then say? We have already argued in *Form* that Nehemiah was indeed absent from Jerusalem for an unspecified period. Here we would add that Nehemiah's need to "ask permission" to return suggests that such a second visit was not originally contemplated, and this squares well with Eliashib's activity. More than that is guesswork: he may have received news (as at 1:1–3) of developments in Jerusalem that caused his disquiet; it is not necessary to believe that he returned as governor—his own personal authority and following could have allowed him to act as he does in this chapter, but on the whole it is better to respect the silence of our sources on this matter.

The only serious remaining problem that Mowinckel and Kellermann have raised in regard to this verse (see *Form*) is the unusual title of Artaxerxes, "king of Babylon," where elsewhere Nehemiah usually refers simply to "the king." It is possible to acknowledge a problem here without drawing their radical conclusions from it; after all, it remains as much a difficulty to explain the use of "Babylon" in a gloss as in an original source. Comparison with "Cyrus, king of Babylon" in Ezra 5:13 is not especially helpful, because special considerations governed the terminology there, but they do not obtain here. However, it serves at least to remind us that the title could be legitimately used by an Achaemenid king. More likely, therefore, is the suggestion that Artaxerxes was resident in Babylon at the time of Nehemiah's return to him, though Galling's emendation of the text to make this fact clearer is unwarranted.

7–9 The situation was even worse than Nehemiah had been led to expect, so that swift and stern action was required. The aim, however, was positive: to restore the rooms to their former and intended use. The plural of v 9, לשכות "rooms," has puzzled some, as only one room had apparently been occupied by Tobiah (vv 5 and 7). It is a mistake to get around this by emendation or by the gratuitous assumption that several rooms had been knocked into one for Tobiah's benefit. It is far more likely that the whole vicinity of the polluted room was thought to require purification.

10 It is probable that the people's failure to give tithes to the Levites and the fact that Eliashib had a sizable spare room to put at Tobiah's disposal are closely connected. So too will have been Nehemiah's handling of these problems, as the overall structure of the passage, outlined in *Form* above, makes clear. Thus ואדעה "I found out" and ואבינה "and I understood" (v 7, rendered more freely above) are parallel, as is frequently the case in poetic texts; cf. M. Dahood, "Ugaritic-Hebrew Parallel Pairs," in L. R. Fisher (ed.), *Ras Shamra Parallels* I (AnOr 49; Rome: Pontifical Biblical Institute, 1972), 197–98. Unlike the priests, who derived a measure of support from the sacrifices (Deut 18:3; Num 18:8–19) that the people no doubt continued to offer, the Levites were totally dependent on the tithes ("their portions"). When these ceased, they were therefore obliged to seek subsistence elsewhere. Theoretically, they owned no land; cf. Num 18:21–24; Deut 14:29; 18:1. We have already heard, however, of the singers' departure from this ideal (12:28–29), and the settlement of Levites outside Jerusalem (e.g., 7:72 [73]; 11:20) may imply the same thing. No doubt the conditions of those who remained in Judah during the exile had forced such changes, and the Levites were thereafter unwilling to surrender this security. It is unlikely that there is a reference here to the "Levitical cities," for even if these reflect historical reality, the cities in Judah and Benjamin were all, as Schneider observes, for the Aaronites alone (cf. Josh 21).

11–12 Nehemiah reacted in characteristic style, remonstrating with the civic leaders whom he believed had the responsibility to guard against such lapses, and then moving with swift practicality to put right the wrong that had been done. The same pattern (and to some extent the same wording) is found at 5:7 as well as vv 17 and 25 below. It is a measure of his confidence that he speaks of reinstating the Levites even before the contributions have been made. "It was apparently presumed that it was the Levite's obligation to serve, just as it was the layman's to contribute" (Bowman). The parallels with the closing verses of chap. 10 are, of course, apparent; especially striking is the concluding summary there never again to "neglect (עזב, as v 11 here) the house of our God."

13 Again, as in chap. 5 and later on in this chapter, Nehemiah followed up his immediate actions with arrangements designed to ensure that the position would be safeguarded in the longer term also. They are very much the results of his own efforts, while chap. 10 reminds us that such measures could never succeed without the willing consent of the people as a whole.

The men appointed to oversee the storage and equitable distribution of the tithes were carefully chosen. Not only were they men of acknowledged integrity (cf. Acts 6:1–6), but they were representative of the groups who chiefly benefited from the system: a priest and a Levite with a singer (a descendant of Mattaniah; cf. 11:17, 22; 12:8, 25) as their assistant. None can be certainly identified beyond this. With them there worked a professional administrator, "Zadok the scribe" (NEB: "Zadok the accountant"!). Even if he is to be identified with the Zedekiah of 10:2 (1), where he appears to be a close associate of Nehemiah, far-reaching conclusions should not be drawn from this verse about Nehemiah's political purpose in appointing him since it was seen at chap. 10 that his name there could well be directly dependent upon its occurrence here. For some suggestions about this group's successors, cf. S. J. Spiro, "Who Was the Ḥaber? A New Approach to an Ancient Institution," *JSJ* 11 (1980) 186–216.

Finally, this verse has featured in the debate about the date of Ezra, it being argued by some that Nehemiah here establishes a committee which Ezra found in being on his arrival (Ezra 8:33). This is a very uncertain argument, however: (i) The constitution of the committee is quite different—two priests and two Levites in Ezra; a priest, a scribe, a Levite and a layman here in Nehemiah. (ii) The function of the two groups is not identical. Here, it is related to the collection and distribution of the tithes, whereas in Ezra it deals with the temple treasures. (iii) There is nothing in Ezra 8:33 to suggest that we are dealing with a standing committee. It could just as well be an ad hoc representative group of temple officials, as Ezra 8:29 perhaps implies. (iv) It is not certain that Nehemiah is setting up this committee for the first time. It is possible that, with the revival of the practice of tithing he also revived a system for administering it equitably. For any or all of these reasons, the suggestion that this verse favors a date for Nehemiah before Ezra must be rejected.

14 A distinctive element of the formulation of the "remember" formula here is the depiction of God's memory as a slate on which all men's deeds are recorded; Nehemiah prays that his care for the temple (vv 4–9) and its services (vv 10–13) will not be wiped off (מחה: "blot out, wipe away," hence "erase"); cf. K. Galling, "Königliche und nichtköniglicher Stifter beim Tempel von Jerusalem," *ZDPV* 68 (1951) 134–42.

Explanation

In religious experience no less than in many other aspects of life, it is the high points of achievement and triumph that usually impress themselves most forcibly on the memory. However, just as historians today frequently insist that history should not be simply a chronicle of the activities of the great and powerful but should pay more heed to the circumstances and development of the common person, so spiritual growth is generally better gauged by the quality of what passes as normal than by the fleeting moments of particular uplift. One is reminded of the account of the transfiguration of Jesus in Luke 9:28–36 which is immediately followed by a display of "the majesty of God" (v 43, using μεγαλειότης, found elsewhere, strikingly enough, in the account of the transfiguration itself in 2 Pet 1:16), as if to show that what had happened to Jesus on the mountaintop was of a piece with his "normal" work of healing in the valley of doubt and despair below. The paragraphs under consideration show awareness of this truth. Rather than leave the reader in a fairy-tale ending of unsullied celebration in the temple courts, they press on to speak of how that joy could be maintained in the longer term.

The first impression may be of humdrum, because practical, pedantry. We are presented with a statement (which is clearly also intended as an example) of wholehearted material support for the running of the cult. But this is just the point. It is indeed possible to maintain a well-organized cult without its being the expression of any deep-seated reality; conversely, however, our author seems to say that reality is unlikely ever to be sustained if it does not have a properly maintained outward framework through which it can develop and bear fruit. Both are necessary, and both are described here. Not only were tithes and offerings regularly given, but they were rooted in a "delight" for those "who ministered" (v 44), while these officials in turn "performed the service of their God" (v 45) in the spirit of those who, in the ideal period of long ago, had led in "praise and thanksgivings to God" (v 46).

In such a balance, it needs but a small distortion to upset the whole. By the evident close conjunction of the opening paragraphs of chap. 13 the editor makes clear that a decrease in the offerings led to both a cessation of many of the regular temple activities (vv 10–11) and to a foothold for one whose outlook was, to the best of our knowledge, opposed to the preservation of the distinctive purity of the Jewish religion. Without consideration

of this background, Nehemiah's actions seem harsh; might he not have realized, some will ask, that with God even a Gentile curse can be turned into
a blessing (v 2)? In Kidner's memorable aphorism, however, "holiness is
not negotiable." There are some issues where failure to draw a line will
lead to general decline. From a position of strength and security it is possible
to help, forgive, and welcome; in weakness, both parties will sink together.

Concluding Reforms   (Neh 13:15-31)

Bibliography

Kellermann, U. *Nehemia,* 51–55. **Luria, B. Z.** "Men of Tyre also, who lived in the city, brought in fish and all kinds of wares (Nehemiah 13:16)" (Heb.). *BMik* 15 (1970) 363–67. **Mowinckel, S.** *Studien II,* 39–42; 104–18. **Rowley, H. H.** "Sanballat and the Samaritan Temple." *Men of God,* 246–76. **Rüger, H. P.** "Ein Fragment der bisher ältesten datierten hebräischen Bibelhandschrift mit babylonischer Punktation." *VT* 16 (1966) 65–73. **Tigay, J. H.** *"Lifnê haššabbāṭ* and *ʾaḥar haššabbāṭ* = 'on the day before the Sabbath' and 'on the day after the Sabbath' (Nehemiah xiii 19)." *VT* 28 (1978) 362–65. **Ullendorff, E.** "C'est de l'hébreu pour moi!" *JSS* 13 (1968) 125–35.

Translation

¹⁵ *In those days I saw some in Judah* ᵃ *who were treading winepresses on the Sabbath day, collecting heaps of grain and loading it onto donkeys, as well as wine, grapes, figs, in fact* ᵇ *every kind of load, and then* ᶜ *bringing them to Jerusalem on the Sabbath day. I warned (them) on the day when they sold food.* ᵈ ¹⁶ *Moreover, Tyrians who were staying there* ᵃ *were bringing fish and all kinds of merchandise and selling them on the Sabbath to the people of Judah—in Jerusalem itself!* ¹⁷ *So I contended with the Judean nobles and said to them, "What is this evil thing which you are doing—profaning the Sabbath day?* ¹⁸ *Is not this just what your ancestors did, so that our God brought all this evil upon us and upon this city? And now you are bringing more wrath upon Israel by profaning the Sabbath."* ¹⁹ *When it began to grow dark in the gates of Jerusalem* ᵃ *on the day before the Sabbath* ᵇ *I gave orders that the doors should be shut and commanded that they should not be reopened until the day after the Sabbath.* ᵇ *I also stationed some of my own men* ᶜ *at the gates to ensure that no load should come in on the Sabbath day.* ²⁰ *Once or twice the traders and dealers in all kinds of merchandise spent the night outside Jerusalem,* ²¹ *but I warned them and said to them, "Why are you spending the night by the wall? If you do it again, I will lay hands on you." From then on they did not come on the Sabbath.* ²² *Then I commanded the Levites to purify themselves and come and guard* ᵃ *the gates in order to keep the Sabbath day holy. Remember this also to my credit, O my God, and spare me according to your great and merciful love.* ᵇ

²³ *Also in those days I saw some* ᵃ *Jews who* ᵇ *had married* ᶜ *Ashdodite, Ammonite, and Moabite women.* ²⁴ *Half their children spoke the language of Ashdod (or according to the language of the other people mentioned)* ᵃ *and were unable to speak the language of Judah.* ²⁵ *So I contended with them and cursed them, beat some of the men, and pulled out their hair. Then I made them swear by God, saying "You will not give your daughters in marriage to their sons, nor take any of their daughters in marriage for your sons or yourselves.* ²⁶ *Was it not on account of such women that Solomon, king of Israel, sinned? Among the many nations there was no king like him; he was loved by God, and God made him king over all Israel; yet even he was led into sin*

by foreign wives. [27] *In your case, therefore, ought it not be something unheard of* [a] *to do all this great evil, to act unfaithfully towards God by marrying foreign wives?"*

[28] *Now one of the sons of Joiada, son of Eliashib, the high priest, was a son-in-law of Sanballat the Horonite, so I banished him from my presence.*

[29] *Remember them, O my God, because they have defiled the priesthood and the covenant of the priesthood and the Levites.*

[30] *So I purified them of everything foreign and I established rotas of duty for the priests and Levites with specific duties for each person.* [31] *(I also made arrangements) for the wood offering at the appointed times as well as for the first-fruits. Remember this in my favor, O my God.*

Notes

15.a. Since the verse continues with a series of ptcps, it is clear that they are to be regarded as verbs, not nouns. They cannot, therefore, be construed as the object of רָאִיתִי "I saw." This has to be supplied and then in turn understood as the subj of the ptcps. While such a construction is not impossible (cf. GKC § 116t) it is more difficult than the commentators generally allow; compare the parallel in v 23 below. The suggestion of Joüon, *Bib* 12 (1931) 89, that בִּיהוּדָה "in Judah" arose as an abbreviation (ב' יהודה) for בני יהודה "Judeans" (cf. v 16) is thus attractive. On the other hand, Nehemiah is the last writer upon whom one should press conformity to generally accepted style. Fortunately, the difference in meaning is only slight: on Joüon's approach there would be greater emphasis on Nehemiah's concern exclusively with the Jewish element within a mixed population.

15.b. The buildup of products through the verse suggests that this is best construed as an explicative *wāw*.

15.c. MT should not be emended here by deletion of the conj, following LXX^L. To do so makes the previous nouns (. . .) וְאַף יַיִן "as well as wine . . .") into the obj of מְבִיאִים "bringing." This is unlikely, however, both because of the word order and because וְאַף gives the impression of something being added to what precedes; cf. GKC § 153. These nouns are therefore to be construed as further objects of "loading," the whole list then being understood as the object of "bringing."

15.d. This phrase is difficult, and more than one interpretation is possible. Several wish to follow Ehrlich, *Randglossen*, VII, 211, in emending to וָאָעִיד בהם ממכור צִיד(ם) "And I warned them not to sell their food." Naturally, the qualification "on the Sabbath" is to be understood. This is certainly a smoother reading syntactically, as comparison with v 21 shows. However, does it fit the context? The emphasis of the verse seems to be on the transportation of goods on the Sabbath. If those involved were Jews, we can hardly suppose that Nehemiah warned them about selling on the Sabbath but said nothing about the other forms of work involved. If they were not Jews, but nevertheless inhabitants of Judah, the emendation would make better sense, but in that case the start of the verse is irrelevant: it should have been a matter of indifference to Nehemiah that Gentiles were treading the winepresses; it is of significance only if Jews were involved. A similar difficulty faces the view of A. Van Hoonacker, "La succession chronologique Néhémie-Esdras," *RB* 32 (1923) 491–92 (and cf. Kellermann, *Nehemia*, 52), who interprets בַיּוֹם as "au sujet du jour (ou ils vendaient leurs victuailles)." Since, therefore, it appears that Jews are involved (the case of Gentiles being considered in the next verse), and since the emphasis appears to fall on the work referred to in the first part of the verse, we prefer to retain MT (cf. Ryle) as providing the most coherent sense. Nehemiah reprimanded those involved on (presumably) the next day, when they sold their wares in Jerusalem; he preferred not to do so on the Sabbath itself. For another example of הֵעִיד "to warn," used absolutely, cf. Jer 6:10.

16.a. A relative clause without אֲשֶׁר "who, which"; cf. GKC § 155d–n and v 23 below. בה "in it" clearly refers to "Jerusalem" in the previous verse. Rudolph proposes transferring "in Jerusalem" from the end of our verse to the beginning (with minor, consequential alterations), but this is not necessary: as the translation above seeks to show, the words are by no means purposeless in their present position.

19.a. Lit., "When the gates of Jerusalem became shadowy," assuming with most lexicographers that צלל is a verb related to the noun צל "shadow." It would have begun to grow dark in the gates earlier than outside. Others use the same etymology but take "the gates of Jerusalem" as an adverbial accus: "When the shadows began to fall (on) the gates of Jerusalem" (Fensham). Rudolph, however (followed by Myers), paying more attention to the Vrs, repoints צֵלְלוּ, appeals to a Syr. cognate meaning "to clean, purge," and hence arrives at a translation "when the entrances to Jerusalem had been cleared in preparation for the Sabbath" (NEB). In similar vein, Bowman adds the evidence of Akk. *ṣalālu*, among the meanings of which *CAD* lists "to be at rest (of an abandoned city), to remain inactive." This actually fits the versional evidence even better than Rudolph's suggestion but has the disadvantage that Nehemiah is likely to have had a more specific time in mind rather than just waiting until people had returned home.

19.b. For the translation of these phrases, cf. Tigay, *VT* 28 (1978) 362–65.

19.c. See *Comment* on 4:10 (16).

22.a. We regard this as an asyndetic construction. Theoretically, it could also be rendered "come as gatekeepers." This is apparently assumed by R. Zadok, *ZAW* 94 (1982) 298.

22.b. Cf. my "The Sure Mercies of David: Subjective or Objective Genitive?," *JSS* 23 (1978) 37–38.

23.a. For the need sometimes to render the Heb. def art by an indef, cf. GKC § 126q–t.

23.b. Cf. n. 16.a. above.

23.c. See *Comment* on Ezra 10:2b.

24.a. Lit., "and/but according to the language of a people and a people" (i.e., other people). There are three ways of taking this phrase: (i) If it is an integral part of the text, it probably signifies "and so for the language of the other peoples mentioned" (i.e., the Ammonites and the Moabites); cf. Rudolph; Myers; NEB; NIV, etc. The word order tells strongly against this view, however, and the phrase has all the appearance of a gl (it is omitted by LXX). (ii) As a gl, it may have been intended to have a similar meaning to (i). It is possible (see *Comment* below) that Ammonites and Moabites are a later addition in v 23. A later glossator, not fully appreciating the intention of the addition, believed that a reference to these two languages was missing, and thus commented "and so on for the other languages." (iii) Ullendorff, *JSS* 13 (1968) 133–34, believes that the language of Ashdod here signifies "a non-Semitic and totally incomprehensible language" (like "double-Dutch"). The gloss was intended as an explanation of this, i.e., "according to the language of other people." Since I regard "Ammonites and Moabites" as an addition to v 23, I am attracted to the second possibility.

27.a. נשמע may be construed either as 1 pl impf qal, as most translations do (cf. RSV, "shall we now listen to you and do . . ."; NEB, "Are we then to follow your example and . . ."), or as 3 masc sg perf niph, lit., "And as for you, is it heard to do . . ." (so, for instance, Keil, Ryle, and Rudolph). The rendering above is a somewhat free attempt to catch the force of the latter. In its favor is the word order at the start of the verse, which puts most emphasis on the contrast between Solomon and Nehemiah's contemporaries. This is quite lost in the usual rendering.

Form/Structure/Setting

This section falls into two clear paragraphs, some of whose features also serve to mark it off from what has preceded. (i) Each starts with the chronological reference (בימים ההמ(ה) "in those days" (vv 15 and 23). This is rather more general than the singular which was used at 12:43, 44; 13:1 above; it suggests that these paragraphs are grouped on the basis of theme rather than chronology. The additional use of גם "also" at the start of v 23 is a further indication that these two paragraphs are to be taken in conjunction with one another. (ii) Each paragraph continues immediately with ראיתי "I saw." This is the first indication of a parallel in narrative framework. (iii) After a description of the abuses that Nehemiah observed, he then "contends with" (ריב את/עם) those whom he holds responsible (vv 17 and 25). We have seen that this is characteristic of his approach (5:7; 13:11); it is thus not to be denied that the narrative parallels here noted go back in large measure to similarities between actual events. Nevertheless, the wording used allows us also to believe that we are intended to take these parallels seriously at the literary level. (iv) In substantiating his charge, Nehemiah illustrates the seriousness of the situation by means of rhetorical questions that draw on the earlier history of his people (vv 18 and 26). This too marks this material off from the previous section of the book. (v) There then follow supplementary notes dealing with aspects of Nehemiah's treatment of consequential details arising out of the problem in hand. This is clear with regard to vv 19–22. We suggest, however, that vv 28–29 are also to be taken in this light. It is probably out of place chronologically (see below), but has been included here for obvious thematic reasons. What may have started as an expression of personal rivalry is thus subsumed under a matter of wider religious principle. (vi) Finally, each paragraph is rounded off by the "remember" formula (vv 22 and 31; v 29 is different: it is an appeal against Nehemiah's enemies rather than in his favor, and it relates only to the previous verse).

There is thus ample justification for treating this passage as a section on its own with its own coherent structure. This helps to confirm our contention that 12:44—13:14 is also to be taken as a discrete section (see *Form* on that passage). It suggests that there is somewhat greater order in this closing part of the book than would be conceded by those who simply lump 13:4–31 together as an account of Nehemiah's second term as governor.

It is now universally agreed that the passage derives from the NM. The question of whether it can properly be regarded as part of a supplement (so Ackroyd, *The Age of the Chronicler*, 28–29) is best handled elsewhere; we may note, however, that it does not in any way rule out "a quite possible historical basis." Though some earlier commentators detected widespread "glossing" by the final editor (frequently identified with the Chronicler), this is now rightly rejected; cf. Kellermann, *Nehemia*, 51–55; for occasional further comment in this regard, see *Comment* below.

The historical setting cannot be more accurately determined for the most part; in general terms we are bound to presume that these events took place relatively soon after Nehemiah's return to Jerusalem. As we have seen, the chronological indicators give no help in this matter. It is to be presumed, however, that the banishment of Sanballat's son-in-law (vv 28–29a) happened first, perhaps in connection with the expulsion of Tobiah from the temple (vv 4–9); it is hardly likely that Nehemiah would have waited once such a specific situation had come to his notice.

Comment

15 We have already noted some of the issues related to Sabbath observance during this period at 10:32 (31) above. For their integration into the wider problem of the history of the Sabbath, cf. de Vaux, *Ancient Israel*, 475–83, and N.-E. A. Andreasen, *The Old Testament Sabbath. A Tradition-Historical Investigation* (SBLDS 7; Missoula: SBL, 1972).

Because Gentiles appear to be dealt with separately in the next verse, it is probable that "some in Judah" refers to Jews who lived in the province but outside Jerusalem. On some unspecified occasion, Nehemiah had observed that they engaged in various tasks even on the Sabbath day. It is not stated whether he went on a tour of inspection on the day itself (we do not know whether the later regulations about travel were already in force) or whether he simply happened to be staying outside Jerusalem for some other reason.

The harvesting of the produce listed took place at various times of the year: grapes in September–October, grain between April and June, and so on. This need not mean, however, that more than one occasion is involved here: the grapes for treading out in the winepresses were no doubt freshly gathered, but of all the other products the text says only that they were being collected and transported, ready for market. They must therefore have been harvested previously.

This abuse was not new. As early as the eighth century Amos had spoken about those who were impatient with the Sabbath's interruption of their trade (Amos 8:5), while shortly before the fall of Jerusalem, Jeremiah had warned his contemporaries about offenses very similar to those noted here; cf. Jer 17:19–27. The post-exilic period had probably seen some stricter observance, but it was evidently not sustained; if Gentiles living in the province could legitimately trade on that day, many must have felt that the law set them at an unfair commercial disadvantage.

Nehemiah may not have felt at liberty to make an official protest on the day itself; alternatively, he may have preferred not to follow the offenders to Jerusalem until after the Sabbath. For whatever reason, he delivered his formal warning on the occasion when these goods were marketed, presumably the next day.

גתות "winepresses" (to be distinguished from יקבים, "wine vats"), were floors hewn out of the rock in which the juice from the grapes was trodden out. It was then allowed to ferment in settling basins before being decanted and stored (often already in jars) in the wine-vats. The whole process has been well illustrated by the excavation of the "Industrial Area" at Gibeon; cf. J. B. Pritchard, *Gibeon, Where the Sun Stood Still* (Princeton: University Press, 1962), 79–99, and ibid., *Winery, Defenses, and Soundings at Gibeon* (Philadelphia: The University Museum, 1964), 1–27.

16 It is possible that consideration of the disadvantage at which his co-religionists were set by the Sabbath laws led Nehemiah to realize that he could only really settle the issue if Gentile traders were similarly prevented from working. There was evidently a colony of Tyrians who were a particular focus of attention in this regard. They were no doubt Phoenicians, who were famed in the ancient world for their far-flung trading network, with "commercial missions" in many of the centers of population; cf. Ezek 27; S. Moscati, *The World of the Phoenicians* (tr. A. Hamilton; London: Weidenfeld and Nicholson, 1968); D. R. Ap-Thomas, "The Phoenicians," in D. J. Wiseman (ed.), *Peoples of Old Testament Times* (Oxford: Clarendon Press, 1973), 259–86; and Luria, *B Mik* 15 (1970) 363–67. Although the Jewish law might not appear to relate to them, Nehemiah now realized that their trading in Jerusalem on the Sabbath was offensive (in all senses of the word) and would have to be prevented.

17–18 In taking the Jewish nobles to task, Nehemiah shows that he held them responsible for what happened in Jerusalem. It is probable that they had not regarded buying as a profanation of the Sabbath, since only the vendor could properly be regarded as engaging in work. (Such an excuse did not, of course, apply to those mentioned in v 15.) For Nehemiah, however, it was nothing less than an extension of those practices that had led to the destruction of Jerusalem at the hands of the Babylonians; cf. Jer 17:27; Ezek 20:12–24. At all events, buying on the Sabbath—even from a Gentile—was condemned in the pledge that the people probably made soon after this; cf. 10:32 (31).

19 Practical steps followed to ensure that it was not worth the merchants' setting out for Jerusalem before the end of the Sabbath. Although the precise translation of the opening words of this verse is uncertain, the general purport is clear: the gates having been shut and guarded by Nehemiah's personal retainers, no traders would be permitted to enter Jerusalem during the Sabbath. The wall had thus become to some extent a symbol of Jewish separation. The phraseology of the end of the verse suggests that private individuals remained at liberty to come and go, and this, indeed, was the cause of the problem that arose next.

20–21 If the merchants could not bring their wares into the city, they could at least set them up outside the walls in the hope of attracting some of the citizens out. At this flouting of the spirit of what he was attempting to do, Nehemiah had no compunction about threatening to remove them physically. The recent memory of what had happened to Tobiah (vv 4–8) will have encouraged the offenders to take this threat seriously. We may detect a note of dry humor in his conclusion that "from then on they did not come on the Sabbath."

22 The involvement of the Levites in the guarding of the gates has caused the commentators some difficulties, both because this is not their expected role and because of the problem of relating this verse to v 19b. This latter point is probably to be explained, as the order of narration suggests, in terms of temporary and permanent arrangements. Nehemiah at first used his own men because he could deploy them in a hurry and rely on them to carry out his wishes with resolution, even in the face of difficulty. This arrangement could not last indefinitely, however; once the immediate crisis was past and the particular abuse had been stopped, it would be easier for the Levites, more as a token force, to act as a deterrent to a recurrence of the problem.

The use of Levites for this role is intelligible, and there may even have been an early precedent for it; see *Comment* on 7:1–2. Their normal duties related to the temple; now, with an increasing regard for the sanctity of the whole of the city (cf. Isa 52:1; Joel 4:17 [3:17]), and with their new role being associated with the holiness of the Sabbath, this task was probably regarded as only an extension of what they were already doing. The command that they should first "purify themselves" supports this understanding as well as being explained by it.

The paragraph concludes with Nehemiah's renewed prayer that God will "remember" him. The additional request that God should spare him is somewhat stereotyped and so should not be made the basis for particular theories about Nehemiah's purpose in writing. It amounts to little more than a parallel to "remember me"; cf. v 14, with its comparable "remember . . . and do not erase."

23 In again rather obscure circumstances, Nehemiah discovered that some Jews had entered into marriage with foreign women. As will be seen from the *Comment* on 4:1 (7), a reference to Ashdodites is fully intelligible here: Ashdod was the name of a province to the west of Judah, and marriage across a land border is not to be wondered at. The fact, however, that there is no reference to marriages with the people of Samaria to the north (though cf. vv 28–29) or with Edomites and Arabians to the south suggests that Nehemiah's observation was of a particularly localized phenomenon. This conclusion is also supported by the way this incident is introduced, for it tells against something that was general and widespread, and by Nehemiah's treatment of the culprits in the following verses, since it is suggestive of only a small group of people.

Two other nationalities are mentioned besides the Ashdodites, namely, the Ammonites and the Moabites. They raise difficulties, however. Textually, we must observe that they are joined onto the end of the verse without any conjunction (though one has been added in the translation above in order to conform to English usage). This is as curious in Hebrew as it would be in English. Second, these peoples themselves are unexpected here: neither is as obvious as the Ashdodites, for reasons already noted, nor is it likely that there should have been wives from these areas rather than others closer at hand. Ammon, it is true, lay immediately to the east of Judah, though with a natural boundary in between, but Moab had no common border. Third, it is curious that while the language of Ashdod is mentioned by name in the next verse, those of Ammon and Moab are not, though a glossator's addition seems to attempt to remedy this defect. For these reasons, "Ammonite and Moabite" is best regarded as a later addition to Nehemiah's text (see also Mowinckel, *Studien II*, 41, and Kellermann, *Nehemia*, 53, who cites a number of earlier commentators). The reason for its inclusion is obvious: Ashdodites were not specifically included in the lists of nations with whom intermarriage was forbidden; see *Comment* on Ezra 9:1–2. A glossator therefore explained Nehemiah's action against them in the light of the law cited in vv 1–2 above: Ashdodites were to be regarded as Ammonites and Moabites from the point of view of the law.

24 Nehemiah was not only shocked by the marriages as such, but by the language which the children spoke and by their complete inability to converse in Hebrew, "the language of Judah" (cf. 2 Kgs 18:26, 28, and parallels). For a religion in which Scripture plays a central part, grasp of language is vital; one might compare the importance of Arabic for Islam. When religion and national culture are also integrally related, as they were for Judaism at this time, a knowledge of the community's language was indispensable; indeed, it was one of the major factors that distinguished and sustained the community itself. It was probably an appreciation of this that caused Nehemiah to react so strongly.

The record that "half their children spoke the language of Ashdod" is curious; were some fathers more conscientious about teaching their children their own language than others for whom the children's education was consid-

ered an entirely maternal concern? Or was it a question of age, a knowledge
of Hebrew coming only as the children began to mix outside the immediate
confines of the home? Even without this last possibility, this verse still poses
a difficulty to the view of Rudolph that Ezra came to Jerusalem during Nehemiah's absence from Jerusalem. He calculates that Nehemiah was away for some
two to three years. Ezra's work, however, lasted for one full year, and we
can hardly suppose that these marriages were contracted until after that;
this hardly leaves time for the children to be born and be able to speak.
On either the traditional date for Ezra, or on a late date (i.e., 398 B.C.),
our verse creates no difficulty.

We do not know precisely what is meant by "the language of Ashdod."
A number of scholars believe that it was a non-Semitic language, being a
relic of the language of the Philistines. In favor of this is the fact that a
somewhat larger gap appears to be intended between this language and Hebrew than the differences between, say, the closely related languages of Hebrew, Moabite, and Ammonite, so far as our limited knowledge of the latter
two goes. It is just this fact, however, which, as we saw in *Notes* above, has
led Ullendorff (*JSS* 13 [1968] 125–35) to believe that "Ashdodite" is not
the name of a language as such at all, but merely a label for any unintelligible
language. Fortunately, our understanding of the passage is not greatly affected
by this.

25a Nehemiah's violent outburst may have been a spontaneous reaction
to his discovery; if so, it again suggests that only a small number of marriages
were involved. It is not clear how far we should press the language: that he
harangued the culprits in no uncertain terms is not in doubt, but the fact
that he beat but "some of the men" is not suggestive of any kind of judicial
procedure. Similarly, that he "pulled out their hair" was an indication of
the disgrace into which he thought they had sunk (cf. 2 Sam 10:4); again, it
need not have involved very much or have been formally administered.

This incident has been interpreted by a number of scholars as evidence
that Ezra had not yet undertaken his reforms in Judah; cf. for instance, Rowley,
"Chronological Order," *Essays,* 162–64. Brockington, 19, goes so far as to
call it "the strongest argument" for dating Ezra after Nehemiah. Nehemiah's
action does not attempt to implement, or even refer to, Ezra's earlier reform
in this regard. It is thought to be easier to understand as an isolated, rough-
and-ready response to a problem that was not fully dealt with until later.

Several factors suggest, however, that this is to read more into the situation
than is justified. First it should be noted that, whenever we date Ezra, his
approach to the issue of mixed marriages did not settle the problem permanently. So far as we can tell from Josephus, whose evidence in this regard
there is no reason to doubt (cf. Williamson, *Israel,* 138), the problem persisted
throughout the Persian period. From this angle, therefore, it makes no difference whether we date Ezra before or after Nehemiah. Second, the understanding of this whole episode which we have advanced above leaves us with no
sense of surprise that Nehemiah made no direct reference to Ezra's reform.
The incident was, we believe, quite localized and restricted; there was no
question of a major problem that was in danger of getting out of hand. In
addition, Nehemiah was provoked by the children's language into a sudden

and violent outburst; this was a matter of personality, which ties in with what we know of the man. Finally, he may have judged that, since the question as a whole was largely under control, there was no need to go to the length of forcing these men to divorce their wives. (In any case, did he have the authority to do so?) It was sufficient that the problem be contained at this low level, and the oath that he next made them swear was, he judged, sufficient for this purpose. For the implications of this interpretation for the question of the chronological order of the two reformers, see *Introduction*, "The Chronological Order of Ezra and Nehemiah."

25b By making the people swear not to be party to any further marriages of this sort, Nehemiah presumably hoped to contain the problem. No doubt the use of quasi-scriptural language (cf. Deut 7:3, and note Ezra 9:2 and 12) was intended to make it easier for the people to consent to what was demanded.

26–27 The example of Solomon is cited to support the argument that if a person so advantaged both materially and spiritually could be led into sin by his foreign wives, how much more were these ordinary folk not put at risk by their marriages. The verse refers principally to 1 Kgs 11. It is significant that this is omitted by the Chronicler in his parallel account of Solomon's reign. It is evident that Nehemiah (and probably the editor who incorporated his work into the present books) was more at home with the Deuteronomic version of his people's history; cf. Williamson, *Israel*, 60–61. For מעל "to act unfaithfully," see *Comment* on Ezra 9:2.

28 When Nehemiah first came to Jerusalem, Eliashib was high priest (3:1). This verse does not make clear whether now, more than twelve years later, he was still in office or whether he had been succeeded by Joiada (12:10, 22); grammatically, "the high priest" could qualify either name. At all events, one of Eliashib's grandsons, not otherwise identified, had married a daughter of Sanballat. Such a blatant disregard for the law as then understood (cf. Ezra 9:2) within the high priestly family was intolerable, and Nehemiah had no hesitation in banishing the culprit altogether (an action that goes even farther than Ezra's divorce procedures). We may guess that the couple returned to the bride's home in Samaria.

Many details about this episode are obscure, so that again we must beware of building too much upon it. Nehemiah evidently regarded the marriage as indicative of the laxity of the leading priestly family as a whole (and this is linked by some—wrongly, we believe—with the events in 13:4–9). The fact that no action was taken against anyone other than the couple immediately involved should warn us not to read too much in the way of politics into the marriage. We are, however, left with a picture of much closer contact between Judah and Samaria than Nehemiah might have wished; and that this was not isolated is confirmed both by biblical (e.g., 6:18) and by slightly later extrabiblical (e.g., *AramP* 30; 32) sources.

The incident is not dated, and there is no reason to link it chronologically with the other events recorded in this paragraph. It was more probably another of Nehemiah's initial "statements of intent" on his first arrival back in Jerusalem; cf. *Form* above.

We must note finally that this story has been linked by many scholars to the more detailed account of a similar incident related in Josephus, *Ant.* 11 §§ 306–312. According to this version, Manasseh, a brother of the high priest Jaddua, was married to Nikaso, a daughter of Sanballat. When "the elders of Jerusalem" obliged Manasseh to leave Jerusalem rather than divorce his wife, he found consolation in that his father-in-law had a temple built for him on Mount Gerizim. All this took place at the time of the demise of Darius before the advance of Alexander the Great.

There are four main ways of approaching this account, all of which have been adopted at some point in the history of scholarship: (i) Josephus' story is completely accurate, and any overlap with our verse in Nehemiah is the result of historical coincidence. (ii) Josephus' story is complete fabrication, being spun out of our verse in Nehemiah and combined with a good deal of legendary material. (iii) The story is the same as that recounted in Nehemiah, but Josephus dated it a century too late. (iv) The stories are the same, and the date in Josephus is correct; Nehemiah lived at the end of the Persian period.

The last possibility is the least probable of the four. We have already examined it at Neh 1, *Form.* See further Rowley, "Sanballat." There is therefore no need to pursue it further here.

The first possibility, though it has attracted some support in recent years, is also difficult to accept without qualification. The fact that the Samaria Papyri show that there was a Sanballat II as governor of Samaria makes plausible the suggestion that there was also a Sanballat III at the end of the Persian period. Though this may appear to remove a major objection to Josephus' account, many other problems remain. Josephus himself clearly made the impossible identification of the Sanballat of his account with the enemy of Nehemiah. We also know (cf. my "The Historical Value of Josephus' *Jewish Antiquities* xi. 297–301," *JTS* ns 28 [1977] 49–66) that Josephus reduced the length of the Persian period by two full generations; it is therefore likely that he regarded his account as an alternative version of our verse, and this is reinforced by the fact that he omitted a parallel reference at the point where this story should appear in his retelling of the career of Nehemiah (cf. *Ant.* 11 § 182). Finally, there are many internal incoherences in Josephus' story taken as a whole. These have been frequently rehearsed (e.g., by Rowley, "Sanballat," and Mowinckel, *Studien II,* 104–18), and the recent discoveries and discussions have done nothing to remove them. It is clear that the narrative of Josephus at this point cannot simply be accepted at face value.

Equally, however, it is difficult simply to transfer it without modification into the time of Nehemiah (the third possibility noted above). As it stands, it cannot be neatly extricated (e.g., by a source analysis) from contact with personalities who certainly lived later, and it is also virtually impossible to believe, on either literary or archeological grounds, that the Samaritan temple was built before the Hellenistic period; cf. G. E. Wright, *Shechem. The Biography of a Biblical City* (London: Duckworth, 1965), chap. 10; R. J. Bull, "The Excavation of Tell er-Ras on Mt. Gerizim," *BA* 31 (1968) 58–72; R. J. Bull and G. E. Wright, "Newly Discovered Temples on Mt. Gerizim in Jordan," *HTR* 58 (1965) 234–37; H. G. Kippenberg, *Garizim und Synagoge* (RVV 30; Berlin: de Gruyter, 1971) 50–57; R. J. Coggins, *Samaritans and Jews* (Oxford: Blackwell,

1975) 93–99; F. Dexinger, "Limits of Tolerance in Judaism: The Samaritan Example," in *Jewish and Christian Self-Definition*, II, ed. E. P. Sanders (Philadelphia: Fortress, 1981) 88–114, together with the literature cited earlier in this discussion.

Everything, therefore, points to the conclusion that the story in Josephus is a garbled variant of that found in our verse of Nehemiah. One possible piece of additional information that he may supply is the names of the couple involved. However, since there is no shred of evidence to support this either (e.g., no Manasseh occurs in Samaritan lists of high priests), we should be cautious about accepting even this much from Josephus. The other element of interest to us is his ascription of the expulsion of Manasseh to "the elders of Jerusalem." This is reminiscent of the account of the reforms we have found in several places in Neh 10–13, which seems to parallel the work of Nehemiah in many details but ascribes them more generally to the community as a whole. It is tempting, therefore, to speculate that Josephus has here preserved a further element of this account and that Nehemiah's version is again his response to it. But in view of all the difficulties already noted, it would be hazardous to put any weight on this suggestion.

29 The negative use of the "remember" formula is found elsewhere only at 6:14. Here, it serves to extend the previous verse alone, and so should not be understood as a conclusion to the paragraph as a whole. The plural "they" refers to all those mentioned in v 28; Nehemiah clearly held them jointly responsible for the marriage. It "defiled the priesthood" because of the requirement of Lev 21:13–15 that a high priest should not marry a Gentile: "A virgin of his own people shall he take to wife. And he shall not profane his seed among his people."

The "covenant of the priesthood and the Levites," though not referred to directly in the Pentateuch, is mentioned also at Mal 2:4–8. It included reverence for God, righteousness in life and speech, and a knowledge of God which the priest is then responsible for teaching to the people. This should have brought "life and peace" to the nation. Malachi accused the priests of turning aside from this ideal, in particular because of bribery (2:9); Nehemiah may have had in mind that a priest who had married a Gentile would be in no position to give teaching in this area which was clearly so sensitive an issue at that time.

30–31 Nehemiah briefly summarizes other aspects of his reforms before concluding the paragraph and therewith his memoir as a whole. Verse 30a summarizes vv 23–29 as a whole. The details of the regulation of the priestly and Levitical duties are not supplied. There is no justification for seeing here the institution of the twenty-four priestly courses; rather, these were measures consequential upon the restoration of support for the Levites (vv 10–13); they were now in a position to resume their full commitment to the service of the cult.

For the wood offering and the first-fruits, cf. 10:35 (34), 36 (35).

The "remember" formula in this verse is unique in that it is not followed by any additional or parallel comment. It is possible that this is to be taken as an indication that this was in fact the close of Nehemiah's account as a whole; cf. Kellermann, *Nehemia*, 74.

Explanation

After the climax in chap. 12, the Book of Nehemiah seems to peter out in a series of reforms in areas that have all been the subject of attention earlier and none of which are applicable, as they stand, to the life of the Christian. As we have seen, by putting these paragraphs after the positive portrayal of chap. 10 and 12:44—13:3, the editor intended to show that these issues were but isolated lapses from a normally high standard. But the device does not fully succeed, and it is difficult to come away without a sense of anticlimax, a sense that is only strengthened when we remember that several of these abuses were to recur time and again in later years. Clearly, external measures were inadequate, in the last resort, to control the perversities of the human heart. The book thus points to its own failure in some respects, and indicates by its narrative shape that need which is expressed more clearly elsewhere (cf. Jer 31:31–34) for a radically new approach, an approach which was inaugurated by the events recorded in the NT (e.g., Heb 8 and 10).

We should pause, however, before we adopt a critical attitude towards the rigor of Nehemiah's actions when understood within their own historical context. The major topics dealt with in this section—Sabbath observance, preservation of a strong cultural, and hence religious, solidarity, and exemplary leadership of the community's religious life—were all at the heart of Judaism's distinctive identity at its best; without this, its witness to the world would have been lost, and there would simply have been no context within which the work and teaching of Jesus could have had any meaning.

Finally, a passage such as the present one serves as a powerful reminder of the dilemma that constantly confronts the Christian Church over the point at which precisely it too should draw its lines of demarcation. It is never easy to be sure on what issues a Christian dare not compromise, and we may well feel that in general a positive witness is to be preferred to a negative attitude. Yet ultimately both are necessary, as the role of the disciples as both light and salt makes plain (Matt 5:13–16). Should the Church ever become completely indistinguishable from the world, she would no longer be able to function as its servant.

Index of Authors Cited

Index of Principal Subjects

Index of Biblical Texts

A. The Old Testament

B. The Apocrypha

C. The New Testament